McDougal, Littell
English

To the Student,

When was the last time you had a textbook that you felt was written just for you, with your interests and experiences in mind? When was the last time you felt challenged to stretch your own talents, solve difficult problems, or seek out new ideas?

McDougal, Littell English encourages you to do all of these things and more. Even while teaching you the skills necessary for effective thinking, writing, and speaking, the book takes learning one step further. It invites you to explore the world around you as well as the potential of your own mind.

Briefly skim through the book. Images dealing with our history, our culture, and even our sense of humor appear throughout each lesson. Each one is designed to intrigue, challenge, or amuse you, to broaden your range of experiences and provide you with starting points for writing and discussion.

We hope you will enjoy exploring the images and ideas in this book. We also hope you will enjoy a similar sense of discovery as you develop your own unique talents and abilities.

The Editors

"We leave traces of ourselves wherever we go, on whatever we touch."

Lewis Thomas

McDougal, Littell
English

Orange Level

ℳ𝐿

McDougal, Littell & Company

Evanston, Illinois
New York   Dallas   Sacramento   Raleigh

Senior Consultants

Linda Flower, Professor of Rhetoric at Carnegie-Mellon University and Co-director, Center for the Study of Writing, the University of California at Berkeley and Carnegie-Mellon University.

Barbara Sitko, Researcher, Center for the Study of Writing, the University of California at Berkeley and Carnegie-Mellon University

Consultants

Nancy McDuffie Cox, English Teacher, Northampton County High School-East, Northampton County Schools, Conway, North Carolina

Mary Helen Black Ellis, English Teacher/Coordinator, Pampa Middle School, Pampa Independent School District, Pampa, Texas

Cheri L. Hannon, Language Arts Instructional Specialist, Mohawk Instructional Center, Shawnee Mission Public Schools, Shawnee Mission, Kansas

Ann H. Herlong, Language Arts Consultant, Charleston County School District, Charleston, South Carolina

Rosemary Leibold, English Department Coordinator, Barry Goldwater High School, Deer Valley Unified School District, Phoenix, Arizona

Patricia Soule Ludwig, English Teacher, Manual High School, Denver Public Schools, Denver, Colorado

Patricia J. Martin, Language Arts Curriculum Coordinator, Andover High School, Bloomfield Hills, Michigan

Millicent S. Rinehart, Secondary Language Arts Supervisor, Cumberland Valley Schools, Cumberland Valley School District, Mechanicsburg, Pennsylvania

Dr. Frances M. Russell, Director of English and Reading K-12, Winchester Public Schools, Winchester, Massachusetts

Sally J. Tupponce, English Chairperson, Hackensack High School, Hackensack School District, Hackensack, New Jersey.

Acknowledgments: Sources of Quoted Materials **6:** Harcourt Brace Jovanovich, Inc.: For "To Look at Any Thing," from *The Living Seed* by John Moffitt; copyright © 1961 by John Moffitt. **8:** Charles Scribner's Sons, an Imprint of Macmillan Publishing Co.: For an excerpt from *From (continued on page 813)*

ISBN: 0-8123-5161-4

1 2 3 4 5 6 7 8 9 10 / 92 91 90 89 88

Composition

Developing Writing Skills

For a list of literature selections and special features, see the last section of this table of contents.

Writing for Different Purposes

Resources and Skills

Grammar, Usage, and Mechanics

Special Features

Other Featured Writers

Bud Abbott

Sherwood Anderson

Maya Angelou

Sharon Balter

Polly Bannister

Dave Barry

Nathaniel Benchley

Carl Bernstein

Robert Bly

Kay Boyle

Ken Boyle

Ray Bradbury

Dee Brown

James Burke

Lewis Carroll

Raymond Chandler

J. Chiles

Eugenia Collier

Douglas Colligan

Richard Connell

Adele Conover

Bill Cosby

Lou Costello

Lynne Cox

Will Cuppy

Richard C. Davids

Annie Dillard

Tom D. Dillehay

Thomas A. Dooley

Daphne Du Maurier

Bob Elliott

Barbara Emberly

Willard R. Espy

Bernard Evslin

Barbara and D.X. Fenten

Robert Francis

Lewis Burke Frumkes

Bob Greene

Emily Greenspan

Ray Goulding

James Haskins

James Herriot

Georgia I. Hesse

Dwight Holing

Jane Howard

Langston Hughes

Franz Kafka

Helen Keller

Michael Kimball

Galway Kinnell

Doris Lessing

Jack London

Joseph Lovece

Jean McCord

R.C. McManus

Peter J. McQuaid

Ralph McTell

Durango Mendoza

Steve Millhauser

John Moffitt

Charles Osgood

Francis Parkman

Robert Remini

Conrad Richter

Andrew Rooney

Russ Rymer

Mari Sandoz

William Saroyan

Toni Schlesinger

John Steinbeck

Jessamyn West

E.B. White

Merry White

Bob Woodward

On the Lightside

Writing Inside Out

Cover Photography: Joel Meyerowitz, © 1983

Cover Quote: Copyright © Lewis Thomas, 1974. All rights reserved.
From an essay that originally appeared in the
New England Journal of Medicine, Copyright ©
Massachusetts Medical Society, 1971, 1972, 1973.

Title Page Photography: James Carmichael, Image Bank
Joel Meyerowitz, © 1983

Unit Opener Photography: Pages 2 and 3   R. P. Kingston, Stock Boston
Pages 326 and 327   Robert Llewellyn
Pages 426 and 427   Andras Dancs, After Image

Composition

1

Using the Senses in Writing

Yellow Cactus Flowers, Georgia O'Keeffe, 1927.

*I*magine competing in a spaghetti-eating contest. How would you describe the smells and tastes, the feel of pushing your face into the steaming pasta and sauce?

Artists and writers must closely examine their experiences in order to share them with others. For example, when Georgia O'Keeffe painted these yellow cactus flowers, she took the time to really see the flowers up close, to know how they felt and smelled, and to study their construction.

Writers focus intently on their subjects to capture sensory details. They know it is the sensory details they use to convey experiences that enable readers to more fully and intimately share in them.

In this chapter you will learn to use sensory details to convey your experiences as vividly as possible.

Part 1
Improving Your Awareness

How can you sharpen your awareness of your world? What techniques can you use to improve your powers of observation? Perhaps the most important requirement is simply to let yourself be "wrapped up" in what you are experiencing. Such keen involvement is the quality that the following poem describes.

Literary Model

To look at any thing,
If you would know that thing,
You must look at it long:
To look at this green and say
"I have seen spring in these
Woods," will not do—you must
Be the thing you see:
You must be the dark snakes of
Stems and ferny plumes of leaves,
You must enter in
To the small silences between
The leaves,
You must take your time
And touch the very peace
They issue from.

From "To Look at Any Thing" by John Moffitt

Tips for Improving Your Awareness

John Moffitt's poem provides a good starting point for improving your awareness. The following suggestions are helpful as well.

1. **When you focus on something, "look at it long."** Study its features. Look for the following characteristics:

size	age	parts	taste	feel	function
shape	color	sound	weight	smell	condition

2. **Develop a healthy curiosity.** The next time you start to walk by something, observe its details. Then wonder a little about what you

see. Look, for example, at the front of your home. How would you describe the style of architecture? Why was that style chosen? How is it similar to and different from other nearby homes?

3. **Gather many details.** Like a newspaper or magazine reporter, you should be prepared to collect two to three times the amount of information you'll need for your writing. In this way, you'll be able to choose the best, most relevant details.

4. **Don't overlook the things right in front of you.** You don't have to travel around the world to find interesting things to observe or write about. The nineteenth-century poet Emily Dickinson rarely left her home, yet the images in her poetry are considered among the best in American literature.

5. **Look at something from a different perspective.** How would it look from an ant's perspective? a bird's view? How would it look turned upside down?

6. **Start by focusing on things you enjoy.** Writing is likely to seem more enjoyable if you begin with a focus that interests you. This is a tip that even experienced writers follow.

The Writer as Observer

All good writers are, first of all, good observers. In the following Starting from Literature selection, writer Thomas Wolfe demonstrates the importance of using one's powers of observation to the fullest as a preliminary to writing about a subject.

Writing Activities Improving Awareness

A Read the awareness directions and questions that follow. Answer in as much detail as possible.

1. Describe the sign that names your school.
2. Describe what the teacher of your last class was wearing.
3. What was the saltiest thing you tasted yesterday?
4. Was the moon out last night? If so, what shape was it?
5. What, if anything, hangs on the refrigerator in your kitchen?
6. How would you describe your best friend to a stranger?

B Visit your community's main street or a construction site where you can observe many different activities. On a sheet of paper, record everything you are aware of with your five senses.

Starting from Literature

The Circus at Dawn

Thomas Wolfe

The writer Thomas Wolfe was especially good at using sensory details, bringing out the magic of the world in which we all live. The following passage is taken from Wolfe's book From Death to Morning. *In this autobiographical account, Wolfe describes his boyhood experience of watching a circus train arrive in his town at dawn.*

*T*here were times in early autumn . . . when the greater circuses would come to town—the Ringling Brothers, Robinson's, and Barnum and Bailey shows . . . I would rush madly through my [paper] route in the cool and thrilling darkness that comes just before break of day, and then I would go back home and get my brother out of bed.

Sense of touch introduced

. . . My brother and I would "catch" the first street car of the day bound for the "depot" where the circus was. . . .

Then, having reached the dingy, grimy, and rickety depot section, we would get out, and walk rapidly across the tracks of the station yard, where we could see great flares and steamings from the engines, and hear the crash and bump of shifting freight cars, the swift sporadic thunders of a shifting engine, the tolling of bells, the sounds of great trains on the rails.

Sense of sight introduced

Sense of hearing introduced

And to all these familiar sounds, . . . to all the sharp and thrilling odors of the trains—the smell of cinders, acrid smoke, of musty, rusty freight cars, the clean pine-board of crated produce, and the smells of fresh stored food . . . there would be added now, with an unforgettable magic and familiarity, all the strange sounds and smells of the coming circus.

Sense of smell introduced

The gay yellow sumptuous-looking cars in which the star performers lived and slept, still dark and silent, heavily and powerfully still, would be drawn up in long strings

upon the tracks. And all around them the sounds of the unloading circus would go on furiously in the darkness. The . . . departing night would be filled with the savage roar of the lions, the murderously sudden snarling of great jungle cats, the trumpeting of the elephants, the stamp of the horses, and with the musty, pungent, unfamiliar odor of the jungle animals: the tawny camel smells, and the smells of panthers, zebras, tigers, elephants, and bears.

*T*hen, along the tracks, beside the circus trains, there would be the sharp cries and oaths of the circus men, the magical swinging dance of lanterns in the darkness, the sudden heavy rumble of the loaded vans. . . .

The great iron-gray horses, four and six to a team, would be plodding along . . . to a rattling of chains and traces and the harsh cries of their drivers. The men would drive the animals to the river which flowed by beyond the tracks, and water them; and as first light came one could see the elephants wallowing in the familiar river and the big horses going slowly and carefully down to drink.

Trying Out Your Powers of Observation Choose a place that you like to be: in a neighborhood park, at a shopping mall, at lunch with friends. Now, using your powers of observation, list every detail you notice.

Next, close your eyes and listen to the sounds around you. Record what you hear. Do the same exercise using your sense of touch and your sense of smell.

Part 2

Using Your Senses

So far in this chapter you have practiced ways of becoming more aware of the world around you. Now you will work on sharpening each of the five senses that are part of your awareness—sight, sound, touch, taste, and smell. You will also study words that make these sensations come alive for your readers. The words are presented in separate charts, according to the sense they describe.

The Sense of Sight

Writers combine a talent for seeing with the ability to communicate what they have seen. In the following paragraph the writer leads you through an old-time corner store. Steven Millhauser probably visited such a store in the days of his childhood. Which details help you to see this scene clearly?

Literary Model

On the corner of a small shady side-street, across from the tall wire fence that borders the playground . . . , stands Rapolski's. . . . [In this store] lies a low glass case covered with brown wood and containing pencil cases, erasers, colored pads, yellow pencils, brass fasteners, and bottles of blue-black ink. Beside it lies a taller glass counter with a sloping face, filled with black licorice pipes, red licorice shoestrings, . . . packages of white pumpkin seeds, packages of black Indian seeds, chocolate babies, rootbeer barrels. . . . The tall, sloping counter stretches past the window . . . and continues in front of a wall that is hung to the ceiling with rubber daggers, plastic water pistols, whistles with white balls inside, strips of tattoos, false noses, one-way silver eyeglasses, handlebar mustaches, black masks, silver masks, rubber cameras, blue harmonicas. On top of the glass counter sit bright orange-and-green yo-yo's, small blue boxes of red caps. . . . Old Rapolski stands behind the counter, smiling with broken teeth, and watching with small dark suspicious eyes. . . .

From *Edwin Mullhouse* by Steven Millhauser

Training in Seeing

Eighty percent of what we know about the world comes to us through our sense of sight. You are already an expert at observing the world with your eyes. For example, you notice shades of differences in the colors of clothes when you pick out a shirt and subtle changes in expression on people's faces when you speak to them.

You can train your sight to be even sharper. Begin a writer's journal in which you record your work for this chapter. Your first entries will be responses to the following exercises for training your sight.

1. Select a small object near you—something on your desk, on the floor, or on the wall. Study it carefully for a short time. Then move so that you can no longer see it and write a detailed description without naming the object. Include specific information about size, color, shape, texture, and unusual characteristics. Try comparing it to other objects. Read your description to someone. Can this person recognize what you are describing?
2. Visit a familiar place where you can observe many varied activities. Imagine you are a video camera, turning slowly in a full circle. Write down everything you see. First, notice all the things you usually see in this spot; then concentrate on finding something unexpected. Describe it as specifically as you can.
3. Choose a three-dimensional object, like the Giacometti sculpture pictured on this page, and examine it from all angles. How does its appearance change with your perspective?

Nose, Alberto Giacometti, 1947.

The following list of "sight" words shows only a few of the thousands of words you may choose to describe sights. As you read the words, picture an object that fits that description. Look up words that are unfamiliar to you; then, think of others you could add to the list.

Sight Words

Colors

Red	rose	cardinal	crimson	vermilion
Green	lime	kelly	emerald	pistachio
Blue	azure	turquoise	aquamarine	cobalt
Brown	cinnamon	hazel	bronze	mahogany
Yellow	straw	citron	canary	sulfur
Black	jet	ebony	licorice	raven
White	milky	ivory	pearl	bleached

Movements

Fast	careen	zoom	fly	swat
	bolt	hurl	whisk	plummet
	scamper	scramble	dart	gallop
Slow	creep	slouch	tiptoe	amble
	plod	lumber	slink	lope
	saunter	loiter	waddle	droop
Shapes	oval	portly	tufted	scalloped
	wavy	flared	shapely	irregular
	domed	tapered	jutting	triangular
	rotund	swollen	angular	proportioned

Appearance

arid	supple	sturdy	freckled
frail	glossy	serene	muscular
stout	shabby	fragile	shimmering
rigid	bruised	slender	ramshackle
opaque	flushed	blotched	flamboyant

The Sense of Hearing

Have you ever temporarily lost your sense of hearing after swimming or from a cold? At such times you become aware of how much you depend on this particular sense as you move through your day, from hearing the alarm clock on waking up, to the sounds of traffic as you cross the street, to the greetings of friends at school.

Notice the sounds recorded by the writer of the following passage. What are some of the words that appeal to the sense of hearing?

Literary Model

   . . . Then he began to hear sounds. Peculiar sounds. Like animals under the earth. Hissings and groanings and muffled cries that a dying creature might make dislodging the stones of his underground cave. There was no doubt of it now. The noises came from underneath. . . . It was then the crashing began. First a sharp crackling, like a monstrous snapping of twigs; then a roar like the fall of a whole forest of trees; then an explosion that tore earth and sky. . . .

From "The Dog of Pompeii" by Louis Untermeyer

Training in Listening

So many noises wash over us during the day that small sounds often get lost—a robin's chirp, a child's laugh. To increase your sensitivity to sounds, close your eyes and concentrate on listening without the distraction of seeing. Careful listening adds a rich dimension to your life and to your writing. Here are some suggestions for training yourself to hear even more.

1. In the evening, get yourself settled comfortably in a dark, quiet room. For several minutes listen carefully to every sound you hear. Try to stretch your senses beyond hearing the clocks tick or the walls creak. After several minutes turn on a light and write down all the sounds you heard.
2. List five sounds that you like to hear. Then list five sounds that you do not enjoy hearing.
3. Listen to three conversations: one at school, one at a store, and one on TV. Listen to the speakers' tone of voice. How does it affect the meaning of what is said? Re-create one of the dialogues, using parentheses to indicate tone of voice as shown below.

Customer (loudly and angrily): That item is marked a dollar and nine cents!
Cashier (bewildered): Isn't that what I charged you? It's right here on the sales slip.

Hearing Words

Loud	thud	yowl	blare	screech
	boom	rasp	shriek	piercing
	roar	grate	raucous	caterwaul
	bray	whine	whistle	deafening
Soft	hum	mute	faint	mutter
	sigh	murmur	chime	tinkle
	hiss	rustle	clink	silent
	buzz	patter	gurgle	inaudible
Speech	yell	drawl	giggle	stutter
	sing	snort	bellow	chatter
	growl	laugh	scream	whimper
	blurt	stammer	guffaw	whisper

Writing Activities Using Sight and Hearing

A Write a sentence describing how each of these items looks. Use the list of sight words to help you.

1. the inside of a car
2. someone's hair
3. a dog or cat
4. the inside of a locker
5. a street scene

B Stretch your senses of sight and hearing by careful observation as you walk a familiar route, such as to a friend's house. Find ten things that you never noticed before. Write this list of new sights and sounds in your journal.

C Write a sentence about each of the following sounds. Use the list of hearing words to help you describe each sound vividly.

1. a fire
2. a sigh
3. sawing a board
4. a door closing
5. a garbage truck
6. a police car siren

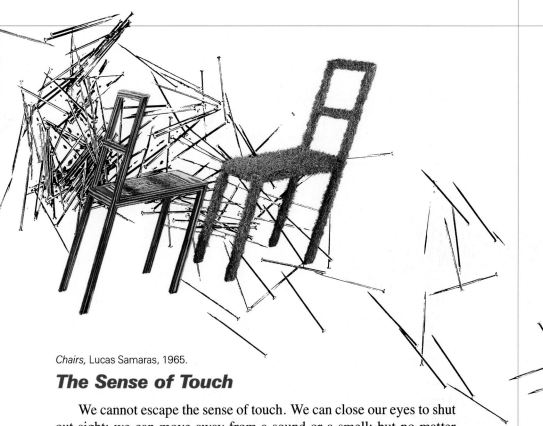

Chairs, Lucas Samaras, 1965.

The Sense of Touch

We cannot escape the sense of touch. We can close our eyes to shut out sight; we can move away from a sound or a smell; but no matter what we do, we will still be touching something. This fact is dramatized in the following paragraph describing the sensations of a person caught in a forest rainstorm. Which words help to describe how the rain and the vegetation feel to the person?

Literary Model

There were things that crawled on his skin. Things grew upon him in layers. Drops fell and touched other drops and they became streams that trickled over his body, and while these moved down his flesh, the small growths of the forest took root in his clothing. He felt the ivy cling and make a second garment over him; he felt the small flowers bud and open and petal away, and still the rain pattered on his body and on his head. . . . The rain hit his face. He covered his face with his hands. The rain hit his neck. He turned over on his stomach in the mud, on the rubbery plants, and the rain hit his back and hit his legs.

From ''The Long Rain'' by Ray Bradbury

Training in Touching

The following activities will help you gain a greater appreciation of your sense of touch.

1. Describe your physical sensations now. Are you cold, warm, comfortable? How do you know?
2. Think about some things that are rough to the touch. Then list and describe them.
3. List and describe some things you feel with parts of your body other than your hands.

Touch Words

icy	waxy	fuzzy	mushy	gritty	rubbery
cool	damp	satiny	sandy	sticky	fragile
oily	silky	spongy	velvety	steamy	slippery

The Sense of Taste

Unlike your other senses, the sense of taste does not operate well alone. Much of what you experience as taste is a reaction to the way foods look and smell or to the way they feel against your mouth and tongue. Therefore, when tastes are described, references to other senses are usually included. Which words in the following paragraph appeal to the sense of taste? Which appeal to other senses?

▬ Literary Model ▬

On Sunday mornings Momma served a breakfast that was geared to hold us quiet. . . . She fried thick pink slabs of home-cured ham and poured the grease over sliced red tomatoes. Eggs over easy, fried potatoes and onions, yellow hominy and crisp perch fried so hard we would pop them in our mouths and chew bones, fins and all. Her cathead biscuits were at least three inches in diameter and two inches thick. The trick to eating catheads was to get the butter on them before they got cold. . . . When, unluckily, they were allowed to get cold, they tended to a gooeyness, not unlike a wad of tired gum.

From *I Know Why the Caged Bird Sings* by Maya Angelou

Training in Tasting

Increase your awareness of your sense of taste. Record the following in your journal.

1. At your next meal, sort out the flavor of each thing you eat. After the meal make a list of the foods you had, and beside each food write a short phrase that describes the flavor.
2. List five foods you like and describe in detail their taste.
3. Make a list of five unusual things you have tasted and describe how they taste. Example: frog legs—chickeny and chewy

Here is a list of "taste" words. As you read each word, think about the taste it names and something that tastes that way.

Taste Words

sour	tart	sweet	lemony	salty	fruity
oily	spicy	tangy	mellow	sugary	buttery
ripe	burnt	fishy	bitter	gingery	bittersweet

The Sense of Smell

Humans do not have the highly developed sense of smell that many other animals do. Nonetheless, we are influenced by many of the smells around us—they evoke strong memories, emotions, and moods. What moods are evoked by the sense of smell in this passage?

▬ Literary Model ▬

. . .There were all the smells of salt and seaweed, of fish and water and wind. There were all the human smells too of the hundreds of people who filled the boardwalk: ladies in print dresses smelling like passing gardens; swimmers with their scents of suntan oils and skin lotions; there were the smells of the eating places: of mustard and onions, of hamburgers frying; and the sudden sharp smell of stacks of dill pickles, as brisk in the nose as a sudden unintended inhalation of sea water. There was the smell of frying fish from the many fish grottos. . . .

From *Cress Delahanty* by Jessamyn West

Training in Smelling

The following activities will help you increase your awareness of your sense of smell.

1. Think about things you can smell. List your favorite smells; then list the smells you dislike.
2. Think about the various seasons of the year. Then list the smells associated with one season.
3. Think of two homes that you've visited. Describe the particular smells of each.
4. Find a place having a variety of strong smells, such as an outdoor market. Describe three of the smells. Describe how these smells change through the course of the day.
5. Think of one of your favorite holidays. Describe the smells associated with this holiday.
6. Think of an early memory from your childhood that has a particular smell connected with it. List what you can remember about the place, such as the time of day, what happened, and the smells you remember.

Following is a list of words related to smell. As you study these words, try to recall experiences with each smell. Can you think of additions to the list?

Smell Words

briny	gaseous	spoiled	acidic
sweet	minty	acrid	rancid
fragrant	scented	fresh	flowery
aromatic	spicy	stench	reeking
earthy	piney	odorous	gamey
sharp	musty	dank	stale

Writing Activities Touch, Taste, and Smell

A Write a sentence describing how each of these things feels.

1. walking barefoot along a beach
2. walking into a cobweb
3. a sunburn
4. a spring shower
5. the bark of a tree
6. putting on a sweatshirt

B Following are some things you may have tasted. Choose five of the items. Then, write a sentence for each one, using exact words to describe how each tastes to you.

1. crunchy peanut butter
2. a piece of raisin toast
3. an orange
4. sour milk
5. cough medicine
6. a blade of grass
7. the eraser on a pencil
8. a chocolate-chip cookie
9. the glue on the back of a postage stamp

C Write a sentence or two describing the smell of each of the things listed below.

1. burning leaves
2. chicken roasting
3. toothpaste
4. a rose
5. perfume
6. chalk
7. popcorn
8. a skunk

D Look at the picture on this page. What kinds of sensory images does it evoke? List as many details as you can, drawing from all five of your senses.

Part 3
All of the Senses Together

You have practiced using the five senses by sharpening one at a time. Most good writing, however, uses a combination of the senses to create a complete scene. The following piece, a student writer's description of a public swimming pool in summer, draws on a variety of sensory details to create a memorable impression. Note the use of precise, descriptive words.

Student Model

The locker room itself was deserted, its benches scarred with graffiti from long-ago romances. The darkened walkway to the pool seemed faintly slimy in spite of the strong odor of industrial-strength chlorine bleach. Outside, the sunlight danced rainbowlike off the pool's crisp, rippling surface. At one end, a toddler crouched and shrieked while his mother crooned from the water: "Don't be afraid, darling! Jump to Mommy!" In deeper waters, nine- and ten-year-old boys in brightly colored trunks snickered and shouted as they cannonballed into the sparkling blue, each trying for the biggest splash. Their game disturbed three teenaged girls sunning nearby. "Little monsters!" muttered one of them, as an unexpected wave soaked her glossy, suntan-oiled legs. And at the snack bar, an off-duty lifeguard occupied himself by munching a plateful of nachos and melted cheese and checking out the sleek-haired trio of girls working on their tans.

Writing Activity All of the Senses

Reread John Moffitt's poem "To Look at Any Thing" on page 6. Then write a paragraph in which you are something other than yourself. Put all your senses to work in describing your particular world. *Be the thing.* Read the items listed below. Choose one of them or create one of your own.

1. a motorcycle	3. a bee	5. a bird	7. a tooth
2. a snake	4. a pillow	6. a rug	8. a seed

Folk Etymology

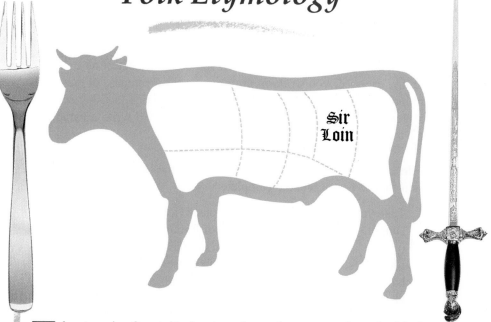

Sir Loin

T he story is often told about a prince who was so pleased with the roast he was eating that he tapped it with his sword and dubbed it Sir Loin. If only it were true! The real story behind the word *sirloin* is much less dramatic. The *sir* comes from the French *sur,* meaning "above," so the sirloin is merely the piece of meat above the loin.

The tale of the prince is an example of folk etymology. Many times, the origin of a word is obscure or difficult to understand, so people come up with a simpler explanation. For example, it might seem obvious that a greyhound is a dog with grey coloring. Yet the *grey* in its name comes from an early Scandinavian word meaning "dog."

Sometimes, words themselves change over the centuries to reflect folk explanations. For instance, the *hang* in *hangnail* began as *ange,* an Old English word meaning "painful." Since the word refers to a piece of skin hanging from a fingernail, however, people gradually added the *h. Muskrat* comes from the Algonquian word *musquash;* it has nothing to do with either musk or rats.

Other times, folk explanations simply seem right. The popular salad made of shredded cabbage may get its name—*coleslaw*—from the Dutch words for *cabbage* and *salad,* but many people think that this cool, refreshing side dish tastes better as *cold slaw.*

Folk tales about the meaning of words often appear to be more logical—and certainly more romantic—than the real thing.

Chapter 1
Application and Review

The following exercises will help you become a better observer. In the first exercise, you work on improving your awareness of the world around you. The second exercise gives you practice in using sensory images in writing. Finally, in Exercise C, you will write a paragraph on a topic of your own choosing.

A Improving Your Awareness Read the following exercises. Then choose one of them to complete.

1. Take your journal to some public place (for example, a park, a shopping mall, an airport, an exercise room in your local YMCA, or a bus station), and sit for fifteen minutes. Observe your surroundings, making use of all of your senses. Write about what you have observed. Use as many sensory details as possible.
2. Gather together a half-dozen potatoes. Pick out one potato and write a detailed description of it, noting all the features that make that potato unique and different from the other potatoes. Then pass your description and the six potatoes to a classmate. See if your classmate can pick out the potato you described by reading your description.

B Using Your Senses Choose one of the following exercises.

1. Look at the photo on page 23. Make a list of the sights, sounds, touches, smells, and tastes that one might associate with this scene.
2. Choose an ordinary sound such as sneezing and write a paragraph that is a wild exaggeration of the sound.
3. Write about a time when you tasted something new and unusual, such as squid or a persimmon. Include as many sensory words as possible.
4. Think about a particular smell that triggers a powerful memory for you, either pleasant or unpleasant. Recall as much as you can about the memory. Then, describe it in a paragraph.
5. Choose two widely different forms of transportation, such as a horse and a school bus. Think about the kind of ride you might get on each one. Then, write a paragraph describing and comparing those two kinds of rides.

c *Starting Points for Writing* We are constantly remembering people, places, and events. Sensory details usually trigger these memories. For example, think about the sensory details evoked by the images and quotes below. What memories do these call to mind? Write about one of these memories in your journal.

Boys are playing basketball around a telephone pole with a backboard bolted to it. Legs, shouts. The scrape and snap of Keds on loose alley pebbles seems to catapult their voices high into the moist March air blue above the wires.

John Updike

He had small, hungry, heavy-lidded eyes, as restless as fleas.

Raymond Chandler

2
Thinking Skills
for Writing

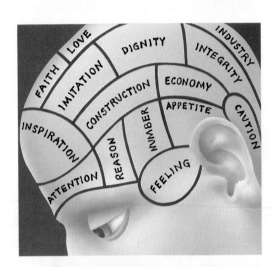

To develop new ideas your mind recombines old ideas, memories, thoughts, and information. Some unusual combinations may arise during this process. In fact if you could paint a picture of the images in your mind as you were thinking, the picture might look very much like the painting on the right by Joan Miró or the one above. However, if you know how to explore, evaluate, and improve upon your ideas, even a seemingly absurd combination can be the inspiration for a brilliant discovery, a marvelous work of art, or inspired writing.

In this chapter you will learn to take charge of your thinking processes to generate ideas, explore these ideas, and organize and evaluate them. As you develop these thinking skills, you will be improving your writing as well.

Detail, *Carnival of Harlequin,* Joan Miró, 1924–25.

Part 1

Thinking About Thinking

Are you aware of *how* you think or *when* you think? Certainly you know that your mind is at work when you're doing homework or solving a puzzle. But what about when you're running? having supper with your family? playing the trumpet?

In fact, your mind is continuously working, sending out dozens of thoughts and images and taking in others. During this process ideas may be changed and rearranged and new ideas often emerge, sometimes unexpectedly.

The world around—and inside—you is so rich with ideas that much of this thinking occurs naturally and automatically, without your having to work at it. What would happen, then, if you actively worked at thinking? You would probably astound yourself with your ability and creativity.

Writing is one way of expressing your thoughts, and good writing stems from clear thinking. Thus, when you master some thinking skills, you will become a better writer.

Types of Thinking

As you begin to focus on thinking, bear in mind that you are in control. Although our minds sometimes race with thoughts, remember that you have the ability to focus and guide the direction your thoughts take.

Avoid becoming locked into one way of thinking. A myriad of ideas stand ready to be tapped and stretched and rearranged by the constant workings of your mind. Becoming aware of how you make use of those ideas—in short, how you think—will help you generate better ideas, both in your daily life and in your writing.

This chapter will discuss two of the most important kinds of thinking that you do—creative thinking and critical thinking.

Creative Thinking The word *create* means "to make something that has not been made before." When you think creatively, you produce ideas or combinations of ideas that have not been produced before—at least not by you.

Creativity often involves the ability to rearrange ideas in new and different ways, to look at things with fresh eyes. For example, in 1830 an Englishman named Sir Goldworthy Gurney thought of powering a stagecoach with a steam engine, which led to the invention of the bus.

Athletic coaches showed creative thinking when they came up with the idea of using videotape to review the performance of their own team and that of the competition. Here's how a student used his creative thinking skills to come up with a great idea.

Jerome was walking home after visiting his grandmother, a woman in her eighties who lived in a senior-citizen home. A former vaudeville entertainer and voice teacher, Jerome's Grandma Lucille had led an interesting life and was full of stories. In addition, she was a good listener and often came up with ideas that helped Jerome solve his problems. Many of the home's residents had no family nearby. Lonely for young company, they often gathered around when Jerome visited.

As Jerome walked on, he thought about people at the residence and all the stories they could tell. He also thought about school friends who had no grandparents nearby. What if there were some way to bring the two groups together? What if young people could ''adopt'' grandparents? What if . . .?

Jerome went home and worked on a plan. The next day, he presented his idea to the director of the residence and the school principal. Three months later, the ''Adopt-a-Grandparent'' program was launched.

Everyone is capable of creative thought, including you. It doesn't demand great bursts of imagination, just a bit of effort and attention to your task.

Critical Thinking It is not enough to come up with new ideas, however; you also need to examine them and decide whether they have any merit. This is where critical thinking comes in.

Critical thinking is a process with many tasks, among them judgment, evaluation, analysis, classification, and synthesis of ideas. This chapter will concentrate on the two most important of those tasks: judgment and evaluation.

Successful scientists, artists, writers, and business people are all aware of the importance of critical thinking. They know that in the course of developing anything they must examine, test, rearrange, and sometimes discard ideas.

For a scientist this might mean modifying—or even abandoning—what had at first seemed like an important finding. For a writer it might involve changing words, composing new sentences, or throwing out paragraphs that had taken hours to write. People who are successful at what they do have first had to learn to think critically about their own ideas.

Gloria enjoyed playing the cello and wanted to go to a world-famous summer music camp. To achieve her goal, however, she would need financial aid.

Gloria worked hard on the scholarship application. Here are her thoughts as she looked over her first draft.

> Let's see, have I stated clearly what it is I'm asking for? Yes, I have.
>
> Is my list of qualifications specific? It is. I even mention that my brother's a professional musician. Hmm, maybe that's not relevant. I'll take it out.
>
> Now, why do I deserve the scholarship? Well, I give good, clear reasons for wanting to go to the camp, and I show that I don't have enough money.
>
> That's convincing, but is it enough? A lot of other kids are probably applying for a scholarship. How do I make myself stand out?
>
> I could say that I've earned some money playing at parties for my parents' friends and I could use it to pay a small part of the camp tuition. That will show how serious I am. Good. I'll add that.

Now, what about my language? I don't want it to sound as if I'm writing to a friend. Uh-oh, I wrote *don't*. I guess I'd better change it to *do not*.

Writing Activities *Thinking About Thinking*

A What ideas have you come up with lately? Below are some questions to jog your memory. In your journal, write some of the good ideas you have had recently on these and other subjects.

1. Did you create a piece of music or art?
2. Did you think of a new use for an old item?
3. Did you come up with a great idea for a story? report? essay? article? poem?
4. Did you find a good solution to a problem?
5. Did you give a friend some good advice?
6. Did you state an argument that left the other person speechless?
7. Did you find a way to help someone?
8. Did you put some clothing together in an original, attractive way?
9. Did you think of an on-the-spot joke that left everyone laughing?
10. Did you think of a winning strategy for a game or sport?

B Think about the ideas you listed in Exercise A. How did each idea occur to you? Write these thoughts in your journal.

Part 2

Generating Ideas

The ancient Roman poet Lucretius once said, "Nothing can be created out of nothing." If this applies to ideas, too, where do they come from? They come from information, events, and ideas already in your mind as well as from the world around you.

Have you ever stared at an empty sheet of paper and wondered what to write? Even that blank sheet is "filled" with ideas. By concentrating on the paper, you can reach out to those ideas and allow them to lead you to other ideas. Your thoughts might go like this.

> This page is made of paper. It's white and rectangular. If I were the paper, how would I describe myself?
> Newspapers are paper too. I wonder how they're printed.
> The school paper had an article about soccer injuries. Are school sports dangerous? I wonder how soccer was invented. I remember the time I kicked the soccer ball. . . .

If you can generate so many ideas from a blank sheet of paper, imagine what you can think of by concentrating on the ocean or a book or a stadium full of people—or yourself. To help in your search for ideas, use the skills of remembering, observing, and associating. Use the skills not only as they're presented here, but also in any combination that works for you.

Remembering

One day in prehistoric times, a man on the move came to a stream. As he stared at the rushing water, he recalled having once seen a deer bound over a tree trunk that had fallen across a similar stream. Off he went to find a log of the right size. He placed it over the stream and walked happily across; he had created the first bridge.

Perhaps the invention of the bridge did not happen exactly that way, but it could have. New ideas can come from old thoughts that you rearrange or combine with new information. Your mind is a gold mine of ideas waiting to be uncovered. One way to tap its wealth is by freewriting.

Freewriting The key to freewriting is the word *free*. You want to unearth your thoughts and let them go free. The steps listed on the following page will help you to begin.

1. Start with any idea you want to explore. You can use a picture, an experience, or even just a word to get your thoughts going.
2. Write whatever comes into your mind.
3. Keep your pen moving. Try to let it "think" for you. Do not worry about spelling, grammar, or punctuation; just keep writing.
4. Time yourself. Write nonstop for three to five minutes.

Eva sat on a bus, watching the snow. Then she recalled her teacher's suggestion to jot down daydreaming thoughts. She might use them later in a story or essay. Eva took out her journal and began to write.

> It's snowing again. Snow seems terrific at first but by February I'm sick of it—just dirty and slushy. Boots—sweaters, coats, scarves, gloves, always losing them. Wish I lived someplace warmer. Florida, Arizona. Aunt Fay in Arizona. Visited her once—sure is different there. So hot. Not much green. Huge cactuses—weird looking—needles, odd shapes, no leaves. Wonder why they're so different from other plants. Report topic!

Observing

As you learned in Chapter 1, observing is not the same as seeing. When you see something, you simply notice that it's there. When you observe something, however, you become aware of its characteristics, the particular features that make it what it is.

Here are some characteristics to look for.

size	age	sound
shape	smell	depth
color	value	taste
weight	width	feel
height	condition	duration
quantity	function	importance

When you truly observe a person, place, thing, or situation, it becomes more interesting because it reveals itself to you. You become more interesting as well because you enlarge your store of ideas. Observing techniques include listing and gleaning/researching.

Listing When you observe something, list its features or characteristics. How large is it? How old? How valuable? Zero in on the most prominent features, and be precise. If an object is blue, is it azure? turquoise? navy?

Here is part of Mark's list for a paragraph about the beach.

endless white sand	cry of seagulls
baby-blue sky	deserted
clear, warm water	sparkle of sun on sand
hermit crab scooting by	burning sun
curve of larger waves	wet sand khaki-colored
hiss of foam on sand	disappearing footprints
cloudless	bleached driftwood
salt on skin	tiny silver fishes darting
crash of waves	dazzling brightness
slight breeze	shells washed up on shore

Gleaning/Researching The word *glean* means ''to gather, bit by bit.'' When you glean, you gather interesting sights, sounds, words, and ideas the way a naturalist gathers interesting specimens. From time to time, examine what you've gleaned. Which ideas are worth thinking about? Which are worth writing about?

If an idea strikes you, keep it in mind as you go through your day. Then, when you have time, add it to your journal. Look for related ideas around you; always be open to the ''writable'' idea.

In researching, you will probably spend time in the library, looking for answers to your questions. Another way to research is to talk to others about your subject. Make a list of questions and use them to interview someone.

On her way home from school, Marianne passed a construction site. Usually the site was shut down for the day, but this time it was bursting with activity. Here's what Marianne observed.

> There's a woman wearing a suit and a hardhat, talking to the supervisor. She's pointing to something on the blueprint. I never realized that architects visit the building site; that would be fun! Wonder what else they do?
>
> Now the architect is pointing at the cement mixer. The glop coming down the chute is lumpy and steam is rising from it. I never noticed steam coming from concrete! And shouldn't it be smooth?
>
> Now the supervisor picks up a bullhorn and shouts loudly, "Stop pouring!"
>
> What's going on? Something must be wrong with the concrete, but what? This would make a pretty funny story: a truck carrying oats is hijacked and the missing cargo is later discovered in a cement mixer!

The box on this page summarizes the observing techniques.

Using the Observing Techniques

Listing
1. Be aware of the features that make things what they are.
2. List details about the appropriate features.
3. Zero in on the most important details, making them more and more specific.

Gleaning/Researching
1. Keep your mind and senses open for interesting ideas.
2. Record "writable" ideas in a journal or notebook.
3. If necessary, research an idea in the library.
4. Prepare questions and interview people about an idea.
5. Be on the lookout for related things to read.

Associating

You have recalled old ideas by remembering, and you have collected new ones by observing. You can generate still more ideas by associating—combining, in new and different ways, what you have already absorbed.

When you look into a kaleidoscope, you see a certain pattern of colors. Rotate the kaleidoscope and the colorful fragments rearrange themselves into different patterns.

Using associating techniques is like rotating a kaleidoscope. Think of your mind as a kaleidoscope of ideas: make your ideas regroup into different patterns. Associating techniques include creative questioning, clustering, and brainstorming.

Creative Questioning To help you make new associations and see things in new ways, learn to ask creative questions. Use your imagination to think of unusual, even silly ''what if'' questions. Even in forming these questions you will be thinking creatively, and their answers may lead you to some original results.

Here are some sample ''what if'' questions.

1. **What if I combined two objects that are normally separate?** (Someone thought to house an alarm clock and a radio together in a boxlike case, thus creating the clock radio.)
2. **What if I used this object in a new or unusual way?** (Fashion designers are constantly finding different ways to use scarves.)
3. **What if this person, place, object, event, or idea had never happened?** (Imagine the world without cars.)
4. **What if I changed just one part of this thing or situation?** (Someone thought of putting wheels on skis so that skiers could stay in shape year-round.)
5. **What if I changed this object's composition or shape in some way?** (The invention of plastic revolutionized the manufacture of literally hundreds of thousands of items.)
6. **What if the relationships were different?** (What if you changed the people, places, objects, or events? Suppose you changed places with a teenager of the 1950's?)
7. **What if I put these opposing ideas together?** (What would happen if the people of a desert culture were moved to the North Pole?)
8. **What if I changed the location of something?** (What would happen if a skyscraper were built in the middle of a jungle?)
9. **What if people changed their actions in some way?** (What would happen if people slept all day and stayed awake all night?)

Clustering A cluster is a number of similar things that are grouped or ''grown'' together. The process begins with a central idea or focus that leads you to related ideas. When you use clustering, you enable these related ideas to ''grow'' from other ideas. Follow these steps:

1. Write a focus or central idea in the center of a paper. Circle it.
2. Think about your focus. Outside the circle write any related ideas that you think of. Circle these and draw lines to connect them to the central idea.
3. Think about each related idea. Write new ideas that occur to you. Circle these and draw lines to connect them to the related ideas.

Carlos needed a report topic. All he knew was that he wanted to write about something having to do with music. To find a topic he used the technique of clustering.

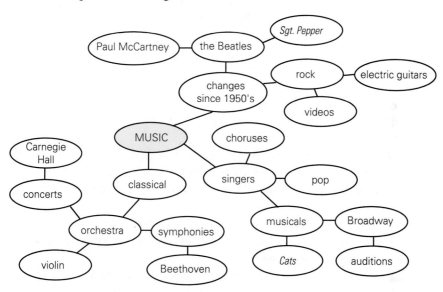

Brainstorming Brainstorming is quite similar to the techniques of freewriting and clustering in that you let your thoughts run free. In freewriting, however, you begin with a focus and write continuously on whatever comes to mind. In clustering, you build a diagram that connects thoughts about an idea. In brainstorming, you jot down every idea that hits you, whether it is related or not. One of the rules of brainstorming is that no idea is considered inappropriate or too off-base to be suggested.

You do freewriting and clustering on your own. Although you can brainstorm alone too, it is even more productive when done in a group. Here's how an entire class used the technique.

A new student, Han Ho, would soon join Mr. Solomon's English class. Han had recently arrived from a refugee camp in Southeast Asia, where he and his family lived while waiting to enter the United States. As the class brainstormed about situations and things that might be new and difficult for Han, Mr. Solomon wrote their comments on the board.

supermarkets	language	sports
cold weather	department stores	transportation
snow	electric stove	needs help!
heavy clothing	washing machine	language tutors
shopping	new foods	school

By the end of the brainstorming session, the class had created such an extensive list that Mr. Solomon decided to present it at the faculty meeting scheduled for that afternoon.

The box on this page summarizes the associating techniques and outlines how to use them.

Using the Associating Techniques

Creative Questioning
1. Ask yourself questions that begin "What if?"
2. Use your imagination. Don't let yourself be limited by conventional ways of thinking about your world.

Clustering
1. Write the central idea in the middle of a page. Draw a circle around it.
2. Outside the circle, write related ideas. Circle each one and draw a line connecting it to the central idea.
3. Think about each related idea. Write additional ideas, circling them and connecting them to the related idea.

Brainstorming
1. By yourself or in a group, list every thought that comes to mind about a subject.
2. Do not organize or order the ideas. Do not "censor" any idea as too inappropriate or unrelated to be useful.

Writing Activities Generating Ideas

A Following is a list of familiar objects. Choose one and examine it closely, if you can; if not, close your eyes and try to picture it. In your journal, list details about the appropriate features. Remember to be as specific as possible. See if you can find something new to say about the object.

a classroom window	a sports event
a swing	day-old pizza
your shoe	a princess
a gorilla	yourself five years ago
a school assembly	a peaceful place
a famous person	an apple or other fruit

B Choosing a subject from the list below, freewrite in your journal to generate writing ideas. Next, form a small group with some classmates who chose the same subject. Brainstorm with them to generate more ideas on the subject. Afterward, compare the results of your freewriting and brainstorming.

photographs	plastic
marathons	red
success	steam

C Study the list below. Using any number of the subjects on the list, combined in any way you like, write five "what if" questions and their answers in your journal. See how creative you can be. Can you come up with an invention? a story idea? an idea for a party? a new solution to an old problem?

lamp	zebra
mail carrier	Alaska
green	mask
February	ancient Rome
paper	highway
onion	rock musician
summertime	tangerine
eraser	tree
saxophone	truck driver

D Choose a subject from the following list. Use clustering to record your thoughts about it in your journal.

jewelry	frozen food	bears
flying	feet	Wednesdays
insects	water	popularity
Canada	hockey	reunion
cities	tape recorder	war

Part 3
Exploring Ideas

Knowing how to generate ideas is important, but it is not enough. You also need to know what to do with them.

It was 1956, and Vic Mills was a happy man: he had just become a grandfather. But after taking care of the baby for a weekend, Mills learned something: he hated changing the baby's cloth diapers! As director of research for a consumer-products company, Mills was used to analyzing problems and focusing on solutions. After he thought about the task, he concluded that it wasn't the changing process that was so bad—it was more the rinsing and holding of used diapers, and then washing and drying them. This led him to wonder, "What if a diaper didn't need to be laundered?"

"Professional thinkers" like Vic Mills have tools and methods that help them do their work. For example, Mills and his staff created numerous "test diapers" and gauged their performance on thousands of babies before marketing what we know of as disposable diapers.

You too have techniques at your disposal, for examining an idea in detail and for seeing where it can lead. Some of these techniques fall under the categories of describing, analyzing, and associating.

Describing

You already know that observing is an important way of generating ideas. For example, Vic Mills began thinking about diapers only after the experience of diapering his grandchild. Observing is also a way of exploring ideas. When you observe something carefully, you get to know it better. You are able to recognize and name the details that make it what it is.

Careful observation helps you describe things. It helps you find the details that would allow you to re-create your subject for someone else, the way television breaks an image into tiny dots and reassembles them on the screen. The technique of charting can help you describe what you observe.

Charting When you used the listing technique earlier, you simply wrote down everything you observed. In charting, you arrange those features and characteristics in a certain order.

To use a chart to help you describe something, first decide what the most important parts or features are. Use these features to head up your columns.

Stephanie had an idea for a story that takes place during a tornado. Realizing how important the setting was, she used the charting technique to explore its possibilities. Following is a portion of her chart.

Tornado Setting

Time and Place	Sights	Sounds
1980's	sky has yellowish	whoosh of wind
July	cast	bangs, crashes
afternoon	dark funnel-like	child whimpering
central Iowa	cloud	roaring of sirens
small farm town	trees bending over	car motor droning
two-lane county	in the wind	car passengers
road	dust swirling	shouting

Analyzing

Analyzing, one of the most important thinking skills, is a great aid in exploring and carrying through on ideas. To analyze an idea, you divide it into its basic parts and examine each part.

Suppose, after reading about a local shelter for the homeless, you wanted to organize a canned-food drive for the shelter. Is the idea practical? How do you carry it out? How do you even begin? To analyze the task, divide it first into its main parts. In order to organize such an effort, you would have to (1) inform people about the collection, (2) coordinate the collection of the food, and (3) arrange for its delivery to the shelter. Your idea is already closer to becoming a plan.

Next, you must examine each task in detail. You can use a chart—like the one you studied on page 39—to analyze an idea by having each column stand for a main part. In addition, you can use an idea tree and questioning.

Idea Trees Just as a diagram of a ship helps you to visualize its parts and how they are related, a diagram of an idea enables you to see how its parts fit together. An idea tree is one such diagram. It is called a "tree" because of its general shape.

The idea tree on this page features the idea of holding the canned-food drive. The subject appears at the base of the tree. The three main work areas of the drive are represented by the three "limbs" of the tree. Each branch, in turn, stands for the details of the effort.

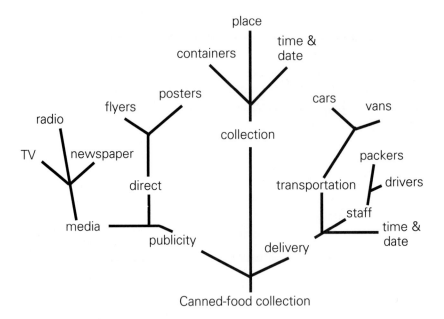

Questioning A simple but effective way to analyze an idea is to ask questions about it. As reporters know, the most important questions begin with the five *W's*—*who, what, where, when,* and *why*—and the word *how.*

To analyze the idea for a canned-food collection, you might ask—and answer—questions like these.

- *Why* should the collection be undertaken?
- *Who* will benefit?
- *What* are the main jobs that need to be done?
- *What* publicity is required?
- *Who* will handle publicity? collection? delivery?
- *Where* is a good collection spot?
- *When* is a good time for the collection? for the delivery?
- *How* can funds be raised to pay for publicity and other needs?

Associating

Associating, as you already know, means setting your ideas on new paths, arranging them in new patterns as one thought takes you to another. Associating not only helps you discover ideas, it can also help you explore them. The familiar techniques of questioning, clustering, and brainstorming can lead you through the paths of an idea. Another associating technique is mapping.

Mapping Mapping can be a useful way to explore an idea. It helps reveal to you the characteristics and details of your idea and the ways in which they are related. A spider map is one kind of map.

Joy had volunteered to handle publicity for the collection of canned foods for the local shelter. To help herself think about and plan the task, she constructed this spider map.

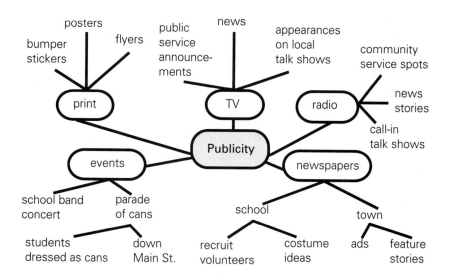

Writing Activities *Exploring Ideas*

A Choose one of the following subjects. Construct a chart to help you describe it.

> running in the early morning
> the rules of a game show
> objects in outer space
> the inside of a human lung
> a movie about a sports event
> an aisle in the supermarket
> a real or imaginary plant, flower, or tree

B Choose a subject from the following list. Analyze it by drawing an idea tree.

> the life of a student   a school newspaper
> a Spanish Club program   budgeting money
> my family tree   water sports
> kinds of TV programs   an imaginary government

C Choose a subject from the list below and write at least six questions about it. Next, answer the questions.

> a car that needs no gas
> a worthwhile TV program about political parties
> doing yard work in your community as a way to earn money
> space-saving furniture that conforms to the shape of the room
> a football strategy devised by a ten-year-old
> the first shopping mall in the United States
> organizing a concert tour for your high-school marching band
> a medical discovery that may cure the common cold

D Choose one of the following topics. Using the example on page 41, construct a spider map of it.

> how humans use animals
> things I fear
> life in the city (or the country)
> planning a party
> information in a newspaper
> the truth about sharks
> contents of a book on photography
> setting up the school art show

Part 4

Organizing Ideas

You have just learned to explore the world of your ideas. When explorers travel through new territory, they map their discoveries. Maps are a way of ''organizing'' the territory so that it can be recorded and understood more easily. As you explore your ideas, organize your discoveries so you and others can follow your thoughts more easily. To organize ideas, classify them into groups or arrange them in sequence.

Classifying

Classifying means grouping things on the basis of what they have in common. Classification not only makes things easier to find, but also easier to understand, evaluate, and use. Nearly everything in your world is subject to classification of some kind. The Yellow Pages classifies businesses according to what they sell or the service they offer. In biology class, you learn to identify plants and animals according to a highly organized system known as scientific classification. Anything is classifiable—from sweaters to sports to short-story ideas—as long as you can identify some basis on which to group them.

Here is how Leslie used classification to help start a club.

> One day at work, Leslie and her friends began talking about the idea of forming a photography club for employees of their company. Leslie tried to jot down everyone's suggestions, but the list quickly became unmanageable. Then she realized that some ideas applied to organization, others to programs, others to fund raising, and so on, so she tried arranging them under those headings. When people offered to head up the various areas of responsibility, the photography club was on its way.

Steps for Classifying

1. **List the items or ideas to be classified.**
   rent videos, have speakers, elect officers, charge dues, . . .
2. **Look for features that only some things have.**
   relate to organization, develop programs, get funds, . . .
3. **Divide your list into groups under headings.**
   Organizations, Programs, Finances, . . .

Similarity/Difference Do you want to compare election candidates or school courses or computers or short stories? One way to go about it is to list the features that are important to you, then evaluate them in terms of the items you are comparing. The Hirsch family used this technique to decide on a vacation spot.

After years of entering contests and sweepstakes, Mrs. Hirsch had finally won first prize: four airplane tickets to the U.S. city of her choice. She narrowed her list to Honolulu and Denver first; then she asked her husband and children to help her decide.

In coming to a decision, the Hirsch family listed items that were important to them. Then, they made these comparisons:

Feature	Honolulu	Denver
Beaches	many, beautiful	none
Snow Sports	none	various kinds
Sightseeing	a great deal	not as much
Weather	warm year-round	four seasons
Souvenir Shopping	a great deal	not as much
Natural Beauty	yes	yes
Foreign Restaurants	many	fewer

The Hirsches deliberated: should they take a ski vacation in Denver or bask on the beaches of Honolulu? In the end, they decided on Honolulu because of the year-round summerlike temperatures there.

Main Idea/Supporting Details The quality of a piece of writing depends not only on how the words are put together but also on how the ideas are put together. To organize written ideas, classify them into main ideas and supporting details. What are the principal messages you want to convey? What message does a group of ideas communicate? Such questions point out the main ideas. What details help to explain, describe, or back up the main ideas? These are the supporting details.

Suppose you have brainstormed ideas for a paragraph on hockey. Since you are a player, many of your notes are about improving your skills. Here you have a main idea for your paragraph. You cross out notes on uniforms, rules, and other ideas not related to hockey skills, then you circle notes that deal with playing better hockey. You have now classified your ideas into a main idea and supporting details.

Ordering

Suppose you took a recipe for macaroni and cheese, cut it into several pieces, and mixed up the pieces. Would you still be able to make macaroni and cheese? Ordering is needed to make sense of a recipe. Ordering can help you make sense of other kinds of ideas too.

When you order your ideas, you arrange them in a certain sequence, on the basis of time or importance or other considerations. The arrangement itself provides a logical organization that can help you and others comprehend your ideas. By placing one idea after another, you are saying, "This step comes after that one," "This was caused by that," or "This idea is more important than that one."

There are different ways to order your ideas in a logical sequence. Three of the most useful arrangements are chronological order, causal order, and cumulative order.

Chronological Order Chronological order refers to time order, the order in which things occur. Chronological order is probably the most straightforward way to arrange things. It is most useful when you are dealing with actions or events, such as building a bookcase or explaining how a traffic jam occurred. A time line is a graphic way to order things chronologically.

Corey created the following time line to trace the major steps in the development of the bicycle.

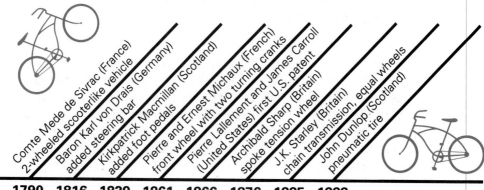

Causal Ordering Ordering can also be used to show cause and effect. When you hear a good joke, you laugh. When ice forms on a road, cars skid. The first event (the cause) brings about the second (the effect). Sometimes a chain of causes and effects is produced. By ordering appropriate ideas in such a chain, you can clearly demonstrate how they are connected.

After Joe read a humorous story about a Rube Goldberg "invention," he decided to create one of his own: a device that would let him shower in the morning without waking up first.

1. Sunshine streaming through window is collected by solar cell
2. Solar cell creates electricity
3. Electricity powers miniature food vat
4. Vat releases hamster food into chute
5. Food slides down chute and into cup in hamster cage
6. Hamster eats food and feels full
7. Feeling of fullness leads hamster to climb onto wheel
8. Spinning of hamster wheel powers turbine
9. Turbine pushes water through hose and shower head positioned over Joe's bed
10. Shower sprays on Joe

Cumulative Ordering Ideas can also be ordered on the basis of degree. For example, some ideas are more important, or more familiar, than others. By considering their degree of importance or familiarity, you can comprehend your ideas better. By presenting them in their order of importance or familiarity, you can explain them better.

Suppose you believe that your community should create bicycle lanes on the main streets leading to your school. These might be some of the reasons you feel that way.

1. Lots of students bike to school.
2. There are/have been many near-collisions.
3. Other towns have bicycle lanes.
4. There is a likelihood of a serious accident.
5. Drivers are not on the lookout for bicycles.
6. Automobile traffic on these streets is heavy.

While these are all good reasons, they do not make a strong case, for they are scattered. To create more impact, try arranging the reasons from least to most important: begin with reason number 3 and end with number 4. Such a sequence clarifies the relationships between the reasons and builds to a strong ending. Can you see the difference?

Writing Activities Organizing Ideas

A Find two ways to classify the following book titles.

Biking in Britain
Teach Yourself French
Run for Your Heart
American Slang
Restaurants of Italy
Speak Portuguese!
First-Aid Handbook

Eating for Good Health
Play Better Tennis
White-Water Canoeing
Soccer Statistics
A Better Thesaurus
Eating in India
Baseball Facts

B Arrange these facts about Mexico in chronological order. Also look for and label one example of a cause-effect relationship.

1. A new constitution provided for social reform in the twentieth century.
2. After three centuries of Spanish rule, the people rebelled.
3. The dictator Porfirio Díaz ruled as president for about twenty years around the end of the nineteenth century.
4. The Spanish conqueror Hernán Cortés and his soldiers destroyed the Aztec Empire.
5. Mexico lost land to the United States after the war of 1846–48.
6. Indian civilizations flourished before the Spanish arrived.
7. A republic was declared in 1823.

Part 5

Evaluating Ideas

After you have collected, explored, and organized ideas, it is time to put them to use and see whether they really work.

Think of a softball pitcher trying out a new pitch or a hiker consulting a map to check a new route. When the umpire signals a strike, the pitcher knows that her idea—the pitch—worked. The hiker, however, finds that his route leads him to the edge of a cliff. He has some rethinking to do. Perhaps he can modify the route, or perhaps he must change direction entirely.

Both the pitcher and the hiker tested an idea in order to evaluate it. Here is how another individual used the evaluation process.

Veronica Chen was working on a new commercial for Smirk toothpaste. First she researched her client's product, competitors' products, and consumers' likes and dislikes. Then, she began gathering material for the commercial. To do this, Veronica "planted" an actress in a supermarket. Whenever a shopper reached for a tube of Smirk, the actress criticized the shopper's choice. A hidden camera recorded the conversations that

ensued. Veronica reviewed the tapes to find the best customer response, and used it in her commercial.

When the commercial aired, however, Veronica discovered a big problem: research showed that viewers didn't recall the commercial, and sales of Smirk remained low. In questioning viewers, Veronica learned that she had not chosen the right customer for the commercial after all; the shopper had defended Smirk so smoothly that viewers incorrectly assumed he was an actor. Veronica reviewed the supermarket conversations again. This time, she produced the commercial using the responses of a customer who mumbled and looked irritated. Viewers adored the new commercial and Smirk sales soared.

Veronica Chen evaluated her idea—the TV commercial—by judging its effectiveness. When she found that the commercial had scored low on viewer recall, she attempted to learn why by questioning some viewers. In doing this, Veronica was able to pinpoint where she'd made her mistake, and corrected it. You can—and should—use the same techniques for evaluating your own ideas.

Judging an Idea's Effectiveness

When you evaluate something, you judge it in terms of what it is supposed to do. In the scenario about the commercial, for example, the first customer proved to be a good speaker but an inappropriate choice for the commercial. Therefore, as Veronica Chen found, the commercial did not "work." To judge the effectiveness of something, you must first establish appropriate criteria.

Establishing Criteria How you evaluate something depends on what you are evaluating—on its function and its purpose. For example, you do not evaluate a joke using the same criteria that you would in buying a birthday card for your mother.

In judging the effectiveness of the Smirk commercial, Veronica asked herself these questions: Do viewers remember the commercial? Do product sales increase when the commercial is shown?

To judge a TV drama, you would ask other questions: Is the plot believable? Is the acting convincing? Does the photography enhance the program? Does the viewer want to keep watching?

Such questions represent the criteria you use to evaluate something. From your answers, you draw a conclusion about its effectiveness. Evaluating, then, involves setting appropriate standards or criteria for something and then determining how well it meets those standards. In this way you break down a single big judgment into a series of smaller, more manageable judgments.

Solving Problems

You have just seen how to evaluate your ideas so that you can detect problems. Now you will learn how to solve those problems. If all ideas worked perfectly the first time, you would not have to concern yourself with this step. In reality, however, most ideas—even good ones—must be worked and reworked to some degree before they are ready to be implemented.

Problem solving is a part of daily life, involving everything from putting together an appropriate outfit to composing an effective composition. If the shirt you planned on wearing doesn't go with your pants, you try a different shirt. If that doesn't work, you might try still another or choose different pants.

While you may do it automatically, this type of problem solving is no different in principle than the process of writing. Writing *is* problem solving, from defining the task to experimenting with the results.

To help you solve any problem, follow the steps outlined in the box on page 51.

The maze at Longleat House, Wiltshire, England.

1. Define the problem. State the problem as clearly as you can. The more specific you are, the more likely you are to find a solution.
2. Explore the problem. Describe it, analyze it, ask questions. Think about possible causes and possible effects.
3. List possible solutions. Don't confine yourself to the obvious. Consider possibilities that are unusual and untried.
4. Explore each possible solution. Consider how to carry it out and what its effects might be. Compare different solutions.
5. Decide on one solution. Choose the one that seems most likely to solve the problem in the best way.
6. Examine the results. If the solution works, fine. If it fails or if it works only in part, go through these steps once again.

Writing Activities Evaluating Ideas

A For each situation below, write a list of appropriate criteria on which it could be evaluated.

1. Unhappy about the strategy of the standard mousetrap, you have figured out how to build a better one.
2. As the mediator of a strike at a sewing-machine factory, you have come up with what you think is a workable settlement proposal.
3. You have written an adventure story for children, and you want to publish it.
4. Dissatisfied with the unreliable bus service in town, you write a letter of complaint to the editor of the newspaper.
5. As a famous Hollywood producer, you have just released your latest film—an original musical.
6. You have reviewed a new horror movie for the local newspaper.

B Select a book you have read recently or a movie or video that you have viewed. Establish appropriate criteria on which the work could be evaluated. Use those criteria to write a brief review of the work.

C Think about a problem that you have encountered. Write a paragraph or two in which you briefly identify the problem and the solution. Explain the process you used in reaching the solution.

Chapter 2
Application and Review

Now that you have learned several thinking skills, use them to complete the following activities.

A Thinking About Thinking What ideas have impressed you lately? Use the list of questions on page 29 to help you make a list of good ideas you have come across. Then choose an idea and write about how it occurred to you.

B Generating Ideas Using one of the subjects below, see how many ideas you can generate from it by using the associating techniques discussed in this chapter. After reviewing everything you have done, present your best idea for a work of art, a solution to a world problem, a new game show, a useful tool, or something else.

leaves	time	tears
cotton	glue	sunlight
exercise	eyeglasses	exhaustion

C Exploring Ideas Imagine that some of your friends are thinking about publishing a weekly neighborhood newspaper. They have canvassed the area and discovered considerable interest in the idea. To help analyze the issues to be considered, they have started the idea tree below and have shown it to you. On a separate sheet of paper, continue the tree.

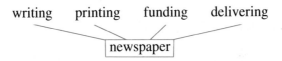

D Organizing Ideas Choose one of the following pairs and compare the items by classifying their relevant features into similarities and differences. You may have to do some research.

1. birds and dinosaurs
2. movies and plays
3. pens and pencils
4. Alaska and Hawaii
5. lyricists and composers
6. yourself last year and now
7. applauding and cheering
8. youth and old age

E *Starting Points for Writing* Brainstorm or freewrite about the images and the quote below to generate a list of writing ideas. Then use some of the creative questions given as Springboards to think of even more ideas.

I hear . . . music . . .
I see this young woman
at her aerobics class. She's the
only one working out
in dangling earrings
and clanking bracelets.

Jane Wagner

Springboards

- What if this came alive?
- What if there were no such thing as gravity operating in this scene?
- What might someone from a previous century make of this?

Chair, Timothy P. Curtis, 1987.

Focus On

A WRITER'S JOURNAL

A journal can be the repository of your thoughts, feelings, and dreams, as well as a "warehouse" for ideas you can write about in the future.

A journal is a place of your own, where you can write what you want—when you want—and not worry about crossing every *t* and dotting every *i*.

A journal is helpful for several reasons. You can keep a journal for enjoyment, for clearing your mind, and for freeing your imagination. You can use a journal to collect ideas and save items of interest.

A journal can be a place where you practice and experiment with different writing styles. Many writers, including the professionals, keep a journal so that they can remember their observations, reactions, and feelings and later use them in their writing.

What Goes into a Journal?

Anything that you can think of is appropriate for a writer's journal. You can make sourcebook entries, collecting such items as quotes, observations, song lyrics, and photos to use as sources for writing ideas. You can include diary entries, recording personal experiences and your thoughts and feelings about those experiences. Finally, in a journal you can write imaginative entries—science-fiction stories, humorous essays, poems, or other works.

How to Keep a Journal

There are no rules for journal-keeping; it is a highly individualized process. However, the tips that follow will help you to get started.

1. Find a format that works for you. Whether you write in a spiral-bound notebook, a black artbook, a composition book with a drawing on the cover, or a file folder of loose-leaf paper, your journal should feel comfortable and inviting. Your journal should be like a room of your own, with your favorite posters on the walls and your own kind of music playing.

2. Carry your journal with you or keep it in an easily accessible place. Write in it whenever and wherever inspiration strikes. Give yourself frequent opportunities to write.

3. Date your journal entries. Dates provide a simple way of organizing your material. They also serve as useful, interesting landmarks when you read and think about past entries.

4. Some writers find it helpful to divide their journal into three parts: a sourcebook section, another section for diary entries, and a third section for imaginative entries, such as original poems.

Write Sourcebook Entries

A sourcebook entry can be any piece of the world that catches your interest. You could quote a passage from a book, a lyric from a song, or a line from a movie. You might include a newspaper clipping or an advertisement, observations of people on the street, or a list of story ideas. You might even tape a photograph, a ticket stub from a concert, or a four-leaf clover in your journal. Each of these items should be accompanied by some important writing that explains what the object means to you and your reasons for saving it.

You can use your journal to react to things you experience. One student wrote in her journal after reading a powerful book. Notice how the following passage triggered some interesting writing.

I am tired of fighting. Our chiefs are killed. . . . The old men are all dead. . . . The little children are freezing to death. My people, some of them, have run away to the hills, and have no blankets, no food; no one knows where they are—perhaps freezing to death. I want to have time to look for my children and see how many of them I can find. Maybe I shall find them among the dead. Hear me, my chiefs! I am tired; my heart is sick and sad. From where the sun now stands I will fight no more forever.

Chief Joseph

November 14
This passage from *Bury My Heart at Wounded Knee* is the surrender speech of Chief Joseph of the Nez Percé nation. When I read it, I got tears in my eyes. What happened to the Indians makes me sick. Fighting is so stupid—so much of a waste. Joseph's speech brings out this point. He sounds so defeated. But his words are courageous too. His words are so simple and honest and basic. It was a very sad speech, but noble at the same time.

Using a Sourcebook

This student's sourcebook entry gives her an outlet for her feelings about what she has read. Sourcebook entries can also provide an important practical benefit: they can supply good ideas for assigned writing. For example, this student's interest in Chief Joseph could be a starting point for a future social studies-report. A source-book keeps you primed for discovering good writing ideas.

Write Diary Entries

In a diary entry, you write about things that happen to you, and your thoughts and feelings about those happenings. When keeping a journal for a class, however, include only the thoughts and feelings that you wouldn't mind sharing. You may wish to keep another, more private diary.

One benefit of diary writing is that it gives you a chance to do some good mental "housecleaning." Also, like sourcebook entries, diary entries can provide good ideas for assigned writing. Most important, perhaps, is what happens in the future when you read your past diary entries. The entries give you a way to remember how it felt to be *you*.

When writer Bob Greene was in high school, a journalism teacher recommended keeping a journal as a way to improve one's writing. Greene took the teacher's advice and kept a diary through the year 1964. As you read these excerpts from Greene's diary, think about the thoughts, concerns, and events that *you* might relate in your own diary.

January 15

We took a quiz in Algebra class today and for once I knew what I was doing. I got a 100. Not that it will count for much, but it put me in a good mood. Those quizzes that we hand across the desk to someone else and grade right away in class are sort of like Polaroid pictures; you find out how you did immediately, but there's no suspense.

My good mood only lasted for one period. Our chemistry test came back and I got a 40 on it. I've flunked them before, but 40 is really pretty bad. . . .

February 1

I was in my room playing my guitar tonight when Dad tried to walk in. I had the door locked. He started shaking the door, and when I opened it he said, "Why do you always lock this? What are you trying to hide?"

I don't know why I do it. It seems to be the only privacy I have in the world—Timmy's room is right across the hall from me, and Debby's is right next door, and Mom and Dad's is right across from hers. It's like we're right on top of each other all the time, and the only way I can have a place that's mine is to lock the door.

I don't think that's such an irrational idea. I guess if I had tried to explain it that way to Dad, he might have understood. But I just said, "I'm not trying to hide anything."

He looked around the room and shook his head. Then he walked out; he left the door open a few inches. . . .

February 10
Right before the bell to start homeroom, I went into the boys' locker room. About twelve guys were standing in front of the big mirror, trying to comb the front of their hair down on their foreheads.

The only thing people are talking about is the Beatles. All during the last month there have been some of us who have liked their music, but the *Ed Sullivan* appearance changed everything. Now virtually everyone in the school is Beatles-crazy. It was funny to see guys with crew cuts and flattops standing in front of that mirror, trying to make their hair look like Paul McCartney's.

From *Be True to Your School*
by Bob Greene

Write Imaginative Entries

It is not necessary to limit your diary writing to things that have actually happened. Your journal can also include imaginative entries such as poems, short stories, jokes, character sketches, fantasies, and writing experiments. Your journal can be a laboratory for your expanding imagination.

In the following journal sample, a student imagined shooting the winning basket in the state high-school basketball tournament. Drawing on this fantasy, he wrote a short poem.

Seven thousand fans
Stood staring, frozen
*   in time*
As my shot sailed home.

Journal Topics

Begin a journal. If you need some writing ideas to get you started, here are a few suggestions.

1. Copy the lyrics of your favorite song in your journal. Then write about the thoughts and feelings these lyrics first triggered in you.

2. Find an interesting newspaper or magazine article, clip it out, and put it in your journal. Write a paragraph or two telling why the story interests you.

3. As the day begins, record your hopes, plans, and expectations for that day. As the day progresses or when it's nearly over, describe what happened to each hope, plan, and expectation. Include specific details.

4. Imagine that you are a world-famous explorer-adventurer. Write a diary entry for one day of a recent adventure you had in the Australian outback.

5. Imagine yourself at the age of thirty. Describe yourself, where you live, the kind of work you do, what kind of music you listen to, and a few of your friends.

6. Imagine that you are the Incredible Shrinking Human Being. Now that you are only two inches tall, explore your room or some other familiar place. Describe it from your new perspective.

3

The Writing Process: Prewriting and Drafting

*B*efore a ship sets sail, its navigator plots a course that will bring the ship safely to its intended destination. To do this the navigator gathers information from maps and weather bureaus and employs various specialized skills to check instruments and make mathematical calculations.

Before writers actually sit down to write a first draft, they also plot the course of their draft. They, too, gather information and engage in various and specialized prewriting activities.

In this chapter you will study these prewriting activities until you are able to plot the course of your drafts as skillfully and as easily as any navigator can chart the course of a ship.

Part 1

What Is Writing?

Writing is a process through which we discover what we think about ourselves and the world around us. Joan Didion, who has written novels, screenplays, and articles, says, "I write entirely to find out what I'm thinking, what I'm looking at, what I see, and what it means." In this chapter, you will study the relationship between thinking and writing and you will gain practice in using thinking skills.

A Series of Stages

The writing process is different for every writer, but most writers complete the following four stages: **prewriting, drafting, revising** (or **editing**), **publishing and presenting**.

Prewriting During prewriting, you decide what to write about. You think about your topic in order to establish your purpose, analyze your audience, and choose a form for your writing. You review what you already know about the topic, and you gather further information as needed. You also organize your ideas and plan how to present them.

Drafting In this stage you experiment freely to find the best way to communicate your ideas, without worrying about spelling or punctuation. As you draft, you might go back to prewriting and alter your writing plan, or go ahead to revising sentences or paragraphs.

Revising, or Editing In revising, or editing, you take a fresh look at what you have written. You look for trouble spots, and make any changes that will improve your work. Finally, you proofread to correct errors in spelling, grammar, usage, and mechanics.

Publishing and Presenting You can find an audience for your writing in a variety of ways. For example, you could submit your story to the school newspaper for possible publication or you could read your poem aloud to a group of classmates.

The writing process is flexible. At any point, you might go back to an earlier stage or work on two stages at once. After you become familiar with the basic process, you will see ways of adapting it to fit a particular writing project or your own individual writing style.

A Process of Thinking

The writing process is a thinking process. The problem solving method referred to in the last chapter can help you analyze a writing task and determine the best way to accomplish it. Here are the steps.

The Steps in Problem Solving

1. Identify the task or problem.
2. Examine alternatives.
3. Choose an approach.
4. Try out the approach.
5. Evaluate the results.

The first part of prewriting is to **identify the task,** or determine the goal of your writing. You should state the goal in your own words. For example, you could say: I want to write an interesting and informative report on ancient Egypt. Then ask yourself these questions: What do I already know about this topic? What else do I need to find out?

Another part of prewriting is to **examine alternatives.** For example, consider a range of topics, such as Cleopatra, the pyramids, mummies. Consider different forms, such as a factual report, a news story, a diary entry. Consider a variety of audiences, such as classmates, members of the history club, or readers of the school paper.

To complete your prewriting, you **choose an approach;** that is, you make choices among the alternatives you have examined. For example, you are most interested in mummies, so you decide to write on the burial customs of ancient Egypt. You choose a lively, up-to-date form, a script for a TV news story about the funeral of an Egyptian king. Your audience will be the members of your world history class, since they share your interest in ancient Egypt.

The next step in problem solving is to **try out the approach.** In writing, you do this in the drafting stage by experimenting with different ways of expressing your ideas. You might also share an unfinished draft of your story with a friend, asking for comments.

The last step in problem solving is to **evaluate results.** In the writing process, evaluation is part of revising. You check to see whether your paper accomplishes the purpose you stated during prewriting. If not, you can revise to improve it. You can always circle back to prewriting and begin the process again.

Clear Thinking

Good writing requires clear thinking. The thinking techniques you learned in Chapter 2 are essential for developing and organizing ideas for writing. **Brainstorming** and **freewriting,** for example, are strategies you can use to find topics or discover new ways to present your ideas. **Inquiring** is a good technique for developing details about a topic. You can use graphics, such as **charts** and **time lines,** to visualize the connections between ideas and to communicate them clearly. The thinking skill of **determining relationships** comes in handy as you consider and answer questions like these.

1. How can I best present my ideas?
2. What connections do I see among my ideas?
3. How can I show these connections?

Writing: A Flexible Process

Writing, since it involves thinking, is a flexible process. Prewriting, drafting, revising, presenting—these are not separate steps that you complete one at a time. In fact, you may return at any time to any previous stage. For example, Jen was revising her report when she decided to focus on one small part of her topic, making it the subject of her whole paper. She went back to the prewriting stage to rethink her purpose, find more information, and organize her ideas.

Another example is Peter, who chose a topic, gathered information, and arranged his ideas in a certain order. But he waited until the drafting stage to arrange the details within each paragraph. He organized his ideas during two stages, prewriting and drafting.

The diagram below illustrates the flexible nature of the writing process.

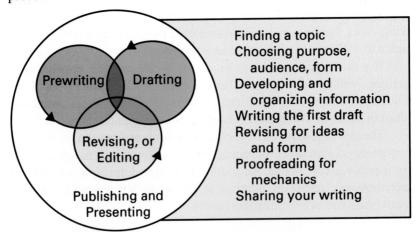

Prewriting / Drafting

Revising, or Editing

Publishing and Presenting

Finding a topic
Choosing purpose, audience, form
Developing and organizing information
Writing the first draft
Revising for ideas and form
Proofreading for mechanics
Sharing your writing

Writing Activity Thinking and Writing

Answer the following questions to help you understand how you use thinking skills while writing.

1. How do you usually get ideas for writing? Have you ever tried brainstorming or freewriting?
2. What kind of planning or prewriting do you generally do?
3. How do you usually develop details about a topic?
4. Do you usually organize your ideas before writing? How do you go about organizing? Have you ever used a chart, a time line, or another graphic?
5. Do you ever revise as you draft?
6. Have you ever shared an unfinished draft?
7. Did you ever start over on a writing project? Why?
8. Who have been your audiences?

Part 2
Prewriting: Focusing

Focusing is thinking clearly about a piece of writing before you start to write. You focus by answering four main questions to determine your topic, purpose, audience, and form: What will I write about? Why am I writing about this topic? Who am I writing for? How can I present my ideas most effectively?

Finding a Topic

Writing is most enjoyable when you choose a topic that interests you or that you want to learn more about. One useful technique is to observe people, places, and things carefully and note your impressions in a journal. You can also practice freewriting or creative questioning. In your journal you can jot down things you want to reflect on, such as a passage from something you've read or the words to a song you like. Reading through your journal can jog your memory and stimulate your imagination to think of writing topics. For more about using your journal, turn to "Focus on the Writer's Journal" on page 54.

When you are writing to fulfill an assignment, brainstorming can often turn up new angles. Gleaning ideas by glancing through books and magazines can also lead to new and interesting ways of thinking about your subject.

No two writers use the writing process in exactly the same way. For example, a ninth-grade history class had studied the early history of flying. As a final activity, the teacher asked the students to write about flying and its meaning for them personally. The rest of this chapter will follow two students, Dan and Sara, as they prepare their papers, using the writing process in two entirely different ways.

Dan used his journal to get an idea. In it, he found this entry.

Dan   There was a story in the newspaper today about a ten-year-old boy who flew a small plane across the United States. His flight instructor went with him. What a great adventure that must have been! I wonder what flying lessons are like. Someday I'll find out!

Reading this entry reminded Dan of how excited he'd been about learning to fly. He decided to write about flying lessons.

Once you've decided on a topic, you usually need to set limits. You narrow your focus to an aspect of the topic that you can cover thoroughly. One way to do this is by inquiring—listing questions on a topic and deciding which ones to answer.

Writing **Inside Out**
Kevin Appleton, Training Specialist

Computers can help businesses do their work faster and more efficiently. Before this can happen, however, people need to know all about the software they use. For this reason most companies that develop and manufacture software also offer training programs to users. Kevin Appleton develops these programs for one such company, Cyborg Systems, Incorporated.

Mr. Appleton says his work as a training specialist is a little like writing a school textbook and the teacher's guide that accompanies it. But he uses a whole different form, full of short summary outlines instead of well-developed paragraphs. "This is a good way to explain very technical material. But it takes strong writing skills to do it well," he says.

Here are the questions Dan listed.

Dan   Who can take flying lessons?
What happens during a flying lesson?
Where are the lessons given—ground or air?
When can you get a pilot's license?
Why do I want to learn to fly?

As he thought about these questions, Dan realized that he wanted to write a paper describing a flying lesson.

Sara used another approach to selecting and narrowing her topic. First, she and some friends brainstormed about possible topics and came up with these: *the Concorde, women pilots, stunt flying, the Wright brothers,* and *hot air balloons.* Sara then chose the topic of women pilots.

To narrow her focus, Sara used gleaning and research. She found a book in the library about women flyers. A photograph in the book interested her. It showed a jet plane diving toward the desert. The caption read, "The fastest woman in the world, Jackie Cochran, breaks another record—the sound barrier." Sara decided to find out more about Jackie Cochran and write a paper about her accomplishments.

How does Mr. Appleton create good training materials? Prewriting is important. Mr. Appleton spends a lot of time just thinking about the clearest ways to present the information. He decides what the goals of the class will be. He divides the material into chapters and breaks each chapter into important topics. He creates a page design that will catch the reader's eye and make for quick and easy reading.

When he actually starts writing a training program for users, his motto is "the simpler the better." He avoids "fancy words" and keeps his sentences short. "The simpler the writing the more understandable it is."

How did Mr. Appleton get into this field? One reason was necessity. In college he majored in English and planned to be a high-school English teacher. He was living in Detroit, and there were no teaching jobs at the time. Then an investment firm hired him and gave him the job of creating investment training materials.

"I liked the field a lot," he says. "It's a real challenge to take something so complicated and make it simple. I like creating things and trying to figure out what the students will need to know. Our instructors will tell me what the students think of my programs, and I always try to improve them based on what students want."

Establishing a Purpose

There are four main purposes for writing: **to express yourself, to entertain, to inform,** and **to persuade.** Sometimes a piece of writing has one purpose. For example, the primary purpose of a humorous narrative about an eccentric inventor and his incredible flying machine would be to entertain.

However, some writing has more than one purpose. A letter to your state representative about your opposition to the expansion of a nearby airport might have two main purposes. The first might be to inform your representative of your views. The second might be to persuade the representative to vote against funds to expand the airport.

To determine the purpose of a piece of writing, reflect on your thoughts and feelings about your subject. Ask these questions.

1. What do I want to accomplish in this piece of writing?
2. What effect do I want my writing to have on my audience?
3. How can I best accomplish this?

Let's see how Sara and Dan determined the purposes of their reports. Here are Sara's answers to the questions above.

> **Sara** Many people don't think about women being jet pilots. So first of all, I want to inform them that there have been women pilots like Jackie Cochran. Next, I want people to understand what she accomplished. Breaking the sound barrier was pretty special at that time, and I want to tell how she did it. She set other records too. I want my readers to admire her for what she did, so I should make my report as exciting as possible.

Notice how Dan's answers led him in a different direction.

> **Dan** I am excited about learning to fly. I want to express this excitement and cause my readers to share it. Flying lessons would be fun, so my paper should be entertaining too. How can I do this? Probably the first time up in a plane with a flight instructor is the most thrilling. That's it! I'll describe the first flying lesson. That will make my paper entertaining and will express how I feel about flying.

Identifying Your Audience

Sometimes your audience is chosen for you. For example, if you are writing a talk about the job of an air traffic controller to give at a Career Day assembly, your audience is the students and teachers who will attend the assembly. Other times, you can choose your audience. You might write for an audience with a special interest, such as the members of the Model Aircraft Club. Once you know who your readers will be, you should analyze them by asking yourself questions like these.

1. What part of my subject will my readers find most interesting?
2. What information do my readers need? What do they know now?
3. What kind of language will be most appropriate?

Here is how Dan answered the questions above to identify and analyze his audience.

> **Dan**   I've noticed that <u>Pilot</u> magazine sometimes prints stories and articles about flying lessons. I will send my paper to the magazine for possible publication. Since readers of the magazine would be familiar with aircraft terms like <u>cockpit</u>, <u>wing flaps</u>, and <u>altimeter</u>, I can concentrate on describing what a flying lesson feels like without stopping to define every term.

Sara chose a less-specialized audience.

> **Sara**   I see that our local newspaper is sponsoring an essay contest on the theme of "Achievers." The editors will judge the entries, and the winning essay will be printed in the paper. I'll enter the contest. The editors and readers of the paper will be my audience. Because my readers may not have heard of Jackie Cochran, I'll include background information about her. I'll focus on her achievements.

Choosing a Form

The **form** is the type of writing in which your ideas are expressed. The form may be a story, play, poem, letter, article, essay, or report. You choose a form by thinking about your topic, your purpose, and your audience.

Sometimes one of the prewriting decisions you have made determines the form. For example, since Sara decided to enter her writing in an essay contest, its form will be an article or essay.

Dan, on the other hand, was free to choose a form. He could interview pilots and flight instructors and write an article about what usually happens during the first lesson. Or he could make up a story about a young student pilot's first flight. Dan decided that a fictional narrative told from a young pilot's viewpoint would be most exciting.

Writing Activities Focusing

A Below are several general writing topics. Alone or in a small group, use brainstorming to list several related but limited topics.

1. outdoor adventures
2. the insect world
3. space exploration

4. America the melting pot
5. humor on television
6. sports heroes

B *Writing in Process* Choose one of the limited topics you listed in Activity A. If you prefer, use a topic suggested by the picture above, by an entry in your journal, or by a thinking technique such as freewriting or clustering. Be sure you have narrowed your focus to an aspect of your topic that you can cover thoroughly. Establish your purpose, identify and analyze your audience, and choose a form. Make a special writing folder and save your notes in it.

Part 3

Prewriting: Developing and Organizing Information

After you have planned your writing, you gather information about your topic. Then you organize the information so that the relationship between ideas is clear.

Gathering and Developing Information

There are several ways in which you can gather and develop information. Depending on your topic, you may use a single method or a combination of methods.

Analyzing and Inquiring When you **analyze** a topic, you divide it into parts. Thinking about the parts helps you decide what kinds of information you will need. Here is how Dan analyzed his topic.

> **Dan** Topic: a pilot's first flying lesson
> Parts:
>   1. the aircraft and controls
>   2. the takeoff
>   3. the feeling of flying
>   4. the landing

Once you have analyzed your topic, you can use another thinking technique called **inquiring** to develop questions about each part of the topic. Here are the questions Sara asked herself.

> **Sara** Topic: Jackie Cochran and her achievements
> Parts and Questions:
> Part 1: Background information
>   1. What was Jackie Cochran's family history?
>   2. How did Jackie Cochran become a pilot?
> Part 2: Achievements as a pilot
>   1. What records did Jackie Cochran set?
>   2. How did Jackie Cochran break the sound barrier?
>   3. What did Jackie Cochran do that helped other women pilots?

Gleaning Probably the most useful technique for gathering information is **gleaning.** Notice that Sara started gleaning information for her report when she studied the photograph of Jackie Cochran's jet breaking the sound barrier. Next, Sara went to her school library and found some books about the history of aviation that mentioned Jackie Cochran. She also found a book by Jackie Cochran about her own life. Gleaning information from both sources helped Sara understand her subject better.

You can also glean information from non-print sources, such as films, filmstrips, or videocassettes. You can interview someone who knows about your topic. Dan used a combination of these methods. At his local library he watched a video about piloting. Then he listed some questions and used them to interview a flight instructor at the county airport. Here are some of Dan's questions and some notes he took during his interview.

> ***Dan*** Question: What happens during a flying lesson?
> Answer: The flight instructor demonstrates a
>   maneuver--such as a turn, climb, or glide--then
>   talks the student through the same maneuver.
> Question: Are flying lessons dangerous?
> Answer: An experienced instructor knows when to
>   let a student go on and when to take over the
>   controls. There are few accidents.
> Question: What skill is hardest to learn?
> Answer: Landings are hardest to master. Some new
>   pilots come in too high and glide over the field
>   without landing. Others come in too low and have
>   to add power to clear the trees.

Creative Questioning When you do **creative questioning,** you play with ideas and use your imagination. You ask yourself ''What if?'' questions and record the answers. This technique is useful for developing a narrative. Here is how Dan used this method.

> ***Dan*** What if something happens to the flight in-
>   structor and the student pilot has to land the
>   plane? The instructor may still be able to talk--
>   to tell the student what to do. The student might
>   make mistakes, but the plane would land safely.
>   That could make an exciting ending for my paper.

Organizing Information

There are several ways to organize the ideas you have gathered for a piece of writing. To find the best way, you will need to use the thinking skill of **determining relationships.** Depending on the information, you might use one or a combination of several of the following methods.

Chronological Order Sometimes ideas are related by time. If so, they can be arranged in **chronological order,** or the order in which events happen. The events in a narrative or the steps in a process are often organized this way. A good technique for arranging details chronologically is to place them on a **time line,** beginning with the one that happens first. For example, here is a time line that Dan made to organize the steps a pilot completes during the takeoff.

Dan

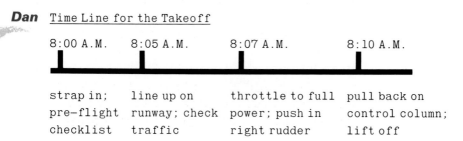

Time Line for the Takeoff

8:00 A.M.	8:05 A.M.	8:07 A.M.	8:10 A.M.
strap in; pre-flight checklist	line up on runway; check traffic	throttle to full power; push in right rudder	pull back on control column; lift off

Chronological order is used for organizing biographical or historical events. Here are Sara's notes about Jackie Cochran's background. The numbers on the left show how Sara arranged the events in chronological order.

Sara

(3) In Miami, Jackie Cochran met her future husband, Floyd Odlum, who said she would "almost need wings" to succeed in the cosmetic business.

(1) As a child, Jackie Cochran was very poor. Her dresses were made of old flour sacks.

(4) After meeting Odlum, she took flying lessons and earned her pilot's license in three weeks.

(2) As a young woman, she worked as a beauty operator in New York and Miami and sold cosmetics.

Spatial Order Sometimes the details you have gathered are related to one another by position. If so, you can arrange them in **spatial order.** In Dan's story the flight instructor explained the main components of the airplane. Dan arranged the details in spatial order, from the front of the plane to the back. The instructor described the engine and propeller first; then the wings, with their flaps and aileron controls; then the fuselage or body of the aircraft; finally the parts of the tail assembly.

Order of Importance or Familiarity Sometimes you can arrange your details in **order of importance or familiarity.** You can start with the least important or familiar idea and end with the most important or familiar. Here are the details Sara gathered about Jackie Cochran's achievements as a pilot. The numbers on the left show how she arranged them in order of importance, ending with the detail she considered most important.

Sara

(2) The first woman to fly a jet across the Atlantic Ocean.

(4) The first woman to fly faster than the speed of sound.

(3) Helped establish the WASPs, the Women Airforce Service Pilots, during World War II.

(1) The first woman airplane pilot to win the Bendix Transcontinental Air Race, flying from Los Angeles to Cleveland.

Sara might organize other details in order of familiarity. For instance, if comparing Jackie Cochran to other record-breaking aviators, she might start with a less famous flyer like Harriet Quimby, who was the first U.S. woman pilot, and end with the very famous Charles Lindbergh, who first flew the Atlantic solo.

Combining Methods of Organization Some types of details are better suited to one method of organization than to another. Because of this, you might use more than one method of organization to arrange details of different types within a longer piece of writing. Both Dan and Sara did this. Dan used chronological order for the steps of the takeoff and spatial order for details about the airplane. Sara used chronological order for Jackie Cochran's background and order of importance for her accomplishments as a pilot.

Sometimes none of these methods of organization will work. As you examine your details closely, you may find that the relationship between them is cause and effect, or problem and solution, or something else. In general, you should choose a method of organization that is appropriate for the details in each part of your composition.

Writing Activities Developing and Organizing

A Study the following details that Lindsey gathered for a science report she was writing about insect colonies. Decide whether they should be arranged in chronological order, spatial order, order of importance, or order of familiarity. Number the details in the order you have chosen.

1. Compass termites of Australia build castles of mud which always point north and south.
2. Leaf-cutting ants of South America build enormous underground nests.
3. Honeybees live in hives built by worker bees for a colony of several thousand bees and a single queen.
4. Tree ants in Southeast Asia construct nests by sewing plant leaves together.

B *Writing in Process* Take out your notes from Activity B on page 68. Gather details about your topic by using one or a combination of these methods: analyzing and inquiring, gleaning from books and non-print sources, and creative questioning. Decide what method of organization is best for each part of your composition and arrange your details in that order. Keep your notes in your writing folder.

Part 4
Drafting

Drafting means writing your ideas down in sentences and paragraphs. It is an experimental stage of the writing process. In the drafting stage you are free to try a variety of different ways of expressing your ideas. You are also free to cross out, add, and reorganize details. You do not have to worry about correcting mistakes in grammar, usage, and mechanics at this point. That will come later, as the last part of the revising stage. If you get stalled, you can even go back to the prewriting stage and look for another way of thinking about your topic.

As you prepare to begin drafting your paper, read over the notes you took during prewriting. Ask yourself whether you are satisfied with your planning of the topic, the purpose, the audience, and the form. Also think about whether you have gathered enough information to develop your topic fully, and whether you have chosen a logical plan of organization.

Next, choose a method of drafting. You should experiment with the methods that are described in this section to find the method that is best suited to your personal style of writing and to your particular writing project.

Loosely Structured Draft When you write a **loosely structured draft,** you work from prewriting notes that are rough and somewhat incomplete. As you write, you experiment with ideas and organization. This kind of draft works well when you are not sure what you want to say or how you want to say it.

One technique for writing a loosely structured draft is **bridge building.** You begin with three or four main ideas, and you build "bridges," or logical connections between them. You ask yourself questions like these: What details will get me from this idea to that one? How can I shape the writing so that I will be able to connect these two ideas? This method is useful for personal writing, in which you discover ideas as you go along.

Dan used bridge building to draft his story. During the prewriting stage, he had decided that his story would have four main ideas (see his notes on page 69). As he was drafting, he asked himself how the four ideas were related, and then he worked to connect them into a smooth and exciting narrative.

Highly Structured Draft When you write a **highly structured draft,** you work from prewriting notes that are complete and detailed. You follow your writing plan carefully, changing little in the content or the organization. This method works well when you already have a clear idea about what you wish to write or when you have a lot of detailed information to present.

Sara, for instance, wrote a highly structured draft of her report on Jackie Cochran. She chose this method because she had planned the organization of her report thoroughly during prewriting (see her notes on page 69) and because she included a lot of detailed information about Jackie Cochran and her achievements.

Quick Draft or Slow Draft Whichever drafting method you choose, you can prepare a quick draft or a slow draft. When you write a **quick draft,** you can use your prewriting notes if you wish, but your goal is to get your ideas down quickly. Writing a quick draft is a good idea if frequent stops cause you to lose track of your ideas. When you write a **slow draft,** on the other hand, you write one sentence or paragraph at a time, and you revise as you go along. This method is best when you want to include detailed information or when you are uncomfortable with leaving an idea unfinished.

Writing Activities Drafting

A Think about each writing project below in terms of the drafting method you would use. Discuss the following questions with your classmates: Which projects suggest a loosely structured draft? A highly structured draft? Which projects suggest a quick draft? A slow draft? When might you use bridge building?

1. a research paper on monarch butterflies for science class
2. a short story based on a personal experience
3. an explanation of the process of developing film
4. a letter to a friend who has moved away
5. a letter to the editor of the local newspaper

B *Writing in Process* Take out the writing folder that you began for Activity B on page 68. Read over your prewriting notes to see whether you are satisfied with your planning. Think about whether your notes suggest a loosely structured draft or a highly structured draft. Think about whether your writing style and topic are suited to a quick draft or a slow draft. Write a first draft about your topic. Keep your draft in your writing folder.

Chapter 3
Application and Review

In this chapter you discovered what a writer does in the first two stages of the writing process—prewriting and drafting. Use what you have learned to complete one or more of the following activities. Activity A leads you step by step, Activity B leaves many choices up to you, and Activity C simply provides starting points, allowing you to adapt the process to your own interests and writing style. Save your drafts for use in the editing activities at the end of Chapter 4.

A Writing About a Competition What race or contest have you entered? A swim meet? A music contest? A livestock show at the state fair? What race or contest would you like to enter someday? The Iditarod dog-sledding race? The Boston Marathon? Plan and write a composition about a race or contest. You can use personal experiences, outside information, or both. Follow these guidelines.

Prewriting With a partner, brainstorm about races and contests. Choose one and freewrite about it for five minutes. Read your freewriting for ideas and list several reasons why this competition interests you. If necessary, find more information. Choose a suitable method of organization, such as chronological order or order of importance.

Drafting Decide whether you will prepare a loosely structured draft or a highly structured one, a quick draft or a slow one. Then, using your notes, write a first draft of your composition.

B Writing About a Person Use these guidelines to plan and write a narrative about a person who has demonstrated courage.

Prewriting Brainstorm with other students about courageous people. You might list figures from history, like Joan of Arc; people in the news, like teacher-astronaut Christa McAuliffe; local heroes, like a child who rescued a drowning friend; characters in books and movies, like Luke Skywalker; people you know, even family members. Use a thinking technique such as creative questioning to develop ideas to use in a story about the person. The story can be based on reality, or it can be fictional.

Drafting Decide on a method of drafting. Using your notes, write a first draft of your story.

c *Starting Points for Writing* Each of the images and the quote below focus on someone's idea of a good time. What do you think is fun? Use the images and the quote as starting points for developing a list of twenty-five possible sources of fun you might use as writing topics.

My idea of having a good time was to lie on my back in my greasy overalls under a car's belly . . . working on some old bolt or screw, with the smell of oil about me, and someone starting up an engine, and the other chaps around clattering their tools and whistling.

Daphne Du Maurier

4

The Writing Process: Revising and Presenting

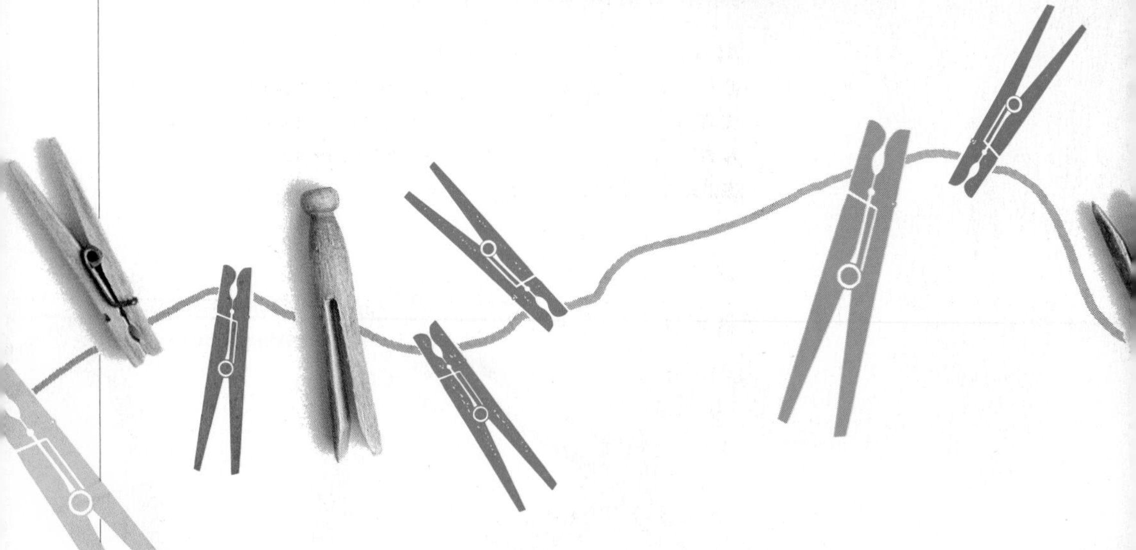

*B*efore Claes Oldenburg completed the giant clothespin sculpture, he studied many objects like those pictured above, making preliminary sketches and revising his ideas.

Writers, like artists, are constantly revising their work. However, in writing, preliminary drafts take the place of preliminary sketches. Writers produce, evaluate, and refine drafts of a piece of writing the way artists produce, evaluate, and refine preliminary sketches.

In this chapter you will learn the techniques writers use to revise their work so that by evaluating and refining your preliminary drafts you will be able to develop masterpieces of writing.

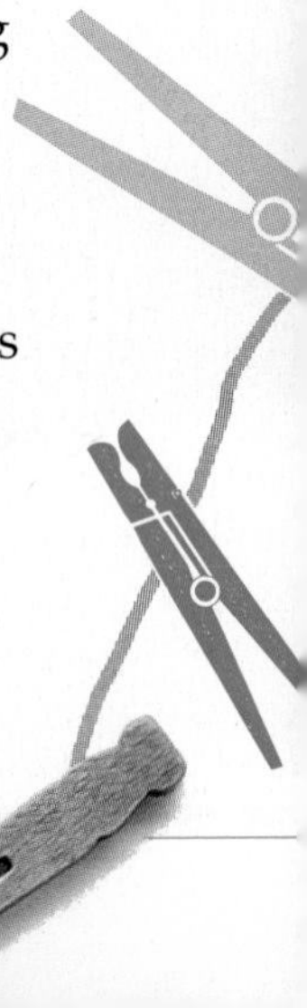

Clothespin, Claes Oldenburg, 1976.

Revising, or Editing

Revising, also called **editing,** is the evaluation stage of the writing process. During revising, you judge your own writing and seek input from others. Then you rework what you have written to solve problems in three areas: ideas, form, and mechanics.

After you have finished a draft, put it aside for a few hours, even a day or two, and use this time for **reflecting.** Decide whether you are satisfied with the choices you made during prewriting. Don't worry about how to fix specific problems. Instead, think about the paper as a whole to identify its strengths and weaknesses. This period of reflection helps you gain distance and objectivity.

Revising for Ideas

Revising for ideas is a writer's most important job. If the ideas are not well thought out or clearly expressed, your writing may need major changes. You may even need to rethink your topic or start over.

When you revise for ideas, first decide whether your focus is clear. You will waste time reorganizing an article that lacks a clear main idea or adding details to a story that doesn't seem to go anywhere. You also need to read your draft with your purpose in mind. Ask yourself whether you have accomplished what you set out to do. If you are not satisfied, think about whether you need to add ideas or rework the way ideas are presented.

You should also make sure you have kept the needs of your audience in mind. For instance, you may have bored your readers by including ideas that they already know, or you may have confused them by omitting ideas that they need.

When you revise for ideas, think about the following questions.

Revising for Ideas Checklist

1. Does my draft have a clear focus or main idea?
2. Do I need to add ideas to accomplish my purpose?
3. Do I need to rework the way I present ideas?
4. Have I deleted any unnecessary ideas?
5. Have I omitted any ideas my readers need?

Revising for Form

When you revise for form, you make sure your draft is unified. You also work to correct problems with the way your ideas are organized and connected. You might be reluctant to revise a draft that contains interesting ideas. However, good ideas that are not arranged logically or connected smoothly may not be communicated successfully to your reader.

First, read your draft with your focus or main idea in mind. Check to see that each detail relates directly to this focus. Irrelevant details may be confusing to your reader. Therefore, you should revise sentences or paragraphs to remove details that do not fit into a unified draft.

Next, think about how your ideas are arranged. Ask yourself whether you have organized your material in the best and most logical manner. If necessary, move sentences and paragraphs around to improve the organization. Finally, read your draft out loud and listen to the flow of ideas. If sentences or paragraphs are not smoothly and clearly connected, consider adding transition words and phrases to make the relationship between ideas clear.

When you revise for form, think about the following questions.

Revising for Form Checklist

1. Do my details relate directly to my focus or main idea?
2. Is my material organized in the best and most logical way?
3. Do my sentences and paragraphs flow smoothly and clearly?
4. Do I need to add transition words and phrases to make the relationship between ideas clear?

Proofreading

Proofreading is the final step of the revising process. At this time, you read your draft closely to find and correct errors in mechanics—punctuation, capitalization, spelling, grammar, and usage. These changes help you prepare a final copy of your paper to present to your audience.

When you are proofreading, think about the following questions. (Additional information on these concepts can be found on the indicated pages in your textbook and in the "Writer's Handbook," which begins on page 767.)

1. Have I ended each sentence with the proper punctuation mark? (See pages 697–699.)
2. Have I used commas, semicolons, apostrophes, hyphens, and quotation marks correctly? (See pages 700–730.)
3. Have I capitalized where necessary, especially sentence beginnings and proper nouns and adjectives? (See pages 677–679.)
4. Have I used a dictionary to check the spelling of all unfamiliar words? (See pages 362–367.)
5. Have I spelled all plural and possessive forms correctly? (See pages 738–741.)
6. Have I corrected all run-ons and fragments? (See pages 457–461.)
7. Have I made all verbs agree with their subjects? (See pages 631–640.)
8. Have I used correct pronoun forms? (See pages 502–510.)
9. Have I used all adjectives and adverbs correctly? (See pages 566–572.)

Using Proofreading Marks

When you make corrections, you should use a set of standard symbols to indicate changes you want. These symbols, called **proofreading marks,** are a kind of code that makes it easy for you and anyone who reads your draft to understand how you want it corrected.

Study the proofreading marks in the following chart.

Proofreading Marks

∧	Add letters or words.	⌒	Close up.
⊙	Add a period.	¶	Begin a new paragraph.
≡	Capitalize a letter.	∧	Add a comma.
/	Make a capital letter lower-case.	∼	Trade the position of letters or words.

—— *or* ✗ Take out letters or words.

Improving Spelling and Vocabulary

Revision provides many opportunities to sharpen your vocabulary and spelling skills. It's a good idea to set apart a section of your journal for a Personal Vocabulary List. Record the new words and definitions that you come across in researching your paper. You might set aside another section for a Personal Spelling List. Include new words and the common but often-missed "spelling demons."

Writing Activities Revising

A Rewrite the paragraph below, using the checklist on page 81. Remove any irrelevant details. Rearrange sentences to improve organization. Add transition words and phrases for smoothness and clarity.

> Louis Braille was born in France in 1809. In school he read by using a system of raised letters called "embossing." The system was slow and awkward. Louis became blind at the age of three. His father owned a saddle and harness shop. Louis invented the Braille system, which made it possible for blind people to read easily. A retired army captain came to Louis's school with a code he had invented. The system, which consisted of raised dots and dashes, was too confusing. Louis worked hard to improve it, inventing a system of raised dots.

B Study the proofreading marks in the following paragraph, referring to the chart on page 82. Then rewrite the paragraph as a final draft.

A high light of our trip to Georgia was the boat

ride we took in the Okefenokee swamp. The name of

the swamp comes from an Indian word that means

"trembling earth," and we understood the origin

of the name as we rowed through the trembling
water
plants that float on the lakes. We saw cypress

trees, Spanish moss, and lilies. We saw also sev-

eral alligators--luckily from a distance.

Part 2
Self-Editing

To be a good writer, you need to develop the ability to look at your own work critically. It is often easier to recognize the strengths and weaknesses in another writer's work. You should, therefore, try to read a draft you are self-editing as if it had been written by someone else. It sometimes helps to read your draft out loud. You might hear problems with the flow of ideas that you would otherwise miss.

A good way to self-edit your draft is to check it over several times. First, use the Revising for Ideas Checklist on page 80 to make sure your draft fulfills your writing goals and is well suited to your audience. Then use the Revising for Form Checklist on page 81 to make sure that your ideas are linked logically and smoothly. Complete your check by using the Proofreading Checklist on page 82 to help you find and correct mechanical errors.

Sara used this self-editing process to revise the first draft of her article about Jackie Cochran. Below is a paragraph that Sara wrote telling how Jackie Cochran became a pilot. The revisions show how Sara edited for ideas and form. Sara's thoughts are shown in the margin.

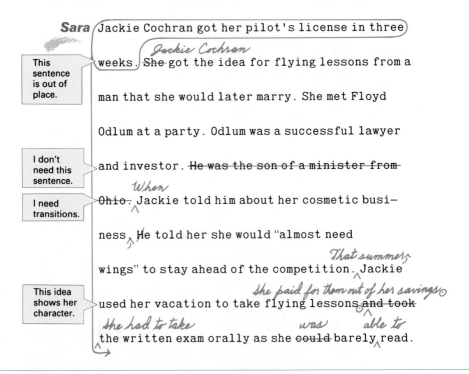

Next, Sara used the Proofreading Checklist to find mechanical errors. Notice the changes that Sara made in this paragraph.

Sara Jackie Cochran is credited with several important "firsts" in aviation. In 1937, she both broke the national and the world women's speed record. In the same year, she ~~breaks~~ broke the transcontinental record by flying from New York to Miami in four hours and twelve minutes. In 1938 she was the first woman to win the bendix air race from Los Angeles to Cleveland. Her plane was an untested model. Jackie tested it while winning the race. In May 1953, flying a canadian Sabre Jet, Jackie became the first woman to fly faster than sound. Jackie flew the Sabre thirteen times, breaking three mens records and tying for a fourth.

Jackie Cochran.

Writing Activities *Revising*

A Study a paragraph that a student has revised for ideas and form. Analyze each revision to see why the student made it, and write each reason on your paper. Rewrite the paragraph to include the revisions.

> *Its*
> ⌄Ancient Indian and Hispanic cultures co-exist
>
> ~~in Albuquerque~~ with modern technology. Old Town
> *selling turquoise jewelry and colorful piñatas,*
> Albuquerque, with its adobe shops⌄ represents
>
> Albuquerque's past. Downtown has glass office
> *This*
> buildings, fountains, and modern sculpture. ~~A~~
> *mix of old and new makes Albuquerque an*
> ~~good place to see the city is from nearby Sandia~~
> *exciting place to visit* ⊙
> ~~Peak~~. (Albuquerque is a city of contrasts)

B Use the checklists on pages 80 and 81 to revise the following paragraph. Then rewrite it to include all your changes.

The National Air and Space Museum is part of the Smithsonian Institution. We saw the plane *Flyer,* which the Wright brothers flew at Kitty Hawk. We touched a moon rock and walked through a Skylab space station. I would like to visit Washington, D.C., again. The museum was the highlight of our trip.

C Use the proofreading chart on page 82 to help you identify the mechanical errors marked below. Rewrite the paragraph correctly.

> ¶The American ⌄Alligator ~~are~~ *is* no longer
>
> endanger/ed. Twenty years ago many were killed
>
> for their skin. A new law cracking down on poach-
>
> ers has let alligators recover⊙ there may now be
>
> sev⌄ral million alligators in the Gulf states.

Part 3
Peer Editing

Peer editing is sharing a draft of something you have written with another student or group of students. Your readers' questions and comments give you valuable information about your draft. For instance, a peer editor can tell you whether your main idea is clear, whether your organization makes sense, and whether your details are interesting. A peer editor can also point out those parts of a draft that are written especially well. Positive feedback is often as useful to a writer as negative criticism.

Peer editing is most helpful when you are revising a draft for ideas and for form. Remember that you want your peer editors to react primarily to your ideas and how you present them, not simply to point out mechanical errors.

Methods of Peer Editing

There are two basic methods of peer editing. In the first method, you work with a partner. You and your partner read each other's draft and comment or ask questions about any issues on the Revising for Ideas and Revising for Form Checklists. Both partners benefit. As a writer, you gain an objective audience. As a reader, you help another writer, and at the same time, you sharpen your own evaluation skills.

In the second method of peer editing, you work with a small group. Each student thinks about a different aspect of the draft under consideration. For instance, one student might check to see whether the topic is thoroughly developed, while another examines the organization of ideas.

Dan used the second method of peer editing to get feedback on his story. He asked one reader in his peer-editing group to comment on the ideas in his story. Following is one of the comments that he received from this reader.

> I wish I knew more about the instructor, Mr. Huff. Could you tell about his background and appearance?

Dan asked another student in the group to think about the form of his story. Here is one of that reader's comments.

> It's hard to see how the description of the parts of a plane fits into your story. Could it be left out?

Types of Responses

There are several ways a peer editor can respond to a piece of writing. In an **oral response,** a peer editor asks the writer oral questions about a draft and talks about its good and bad points. For example, Dan's peer editor asked, "What is a pre-flight checklist?" and said, "The beginning of your story really got me interested." Another type of response is **notes and queries** written in the margin of a draft. For example, Dan's peer editor could have written, "I can't picture how Carl landed the plane. Could you explain this more?"

A peer editor might also respond to a draft by filling out an **evaluation form.** A sample evaluation form filled out about Dan's story appears on page 90. In a **written response,** a peer editor writes answers to questions posed by the writer. For example, Dan might ask a peer editor, "How can I make my ending more exciting?"

A peer editor will help a writer most by coming to a piece of writing with specific ideas about how to evaluate a paper. The following checklist can help you be an effective evaluator. Think about these questions when you read a draft. Feel free to add others.

Checklist for Peer Editing

1. What is the focus or main idea of the draft?
2. What supporting details do I find most interesting?
3. What do I want to know more about?
4. Does the draft have a clear plan of organization?
5. Is there anything I find confusing?
6. Does the draft read smoothly? Are there any awkward or unclear sentences or paragraphs?
7. What does the draft make me think or feel? Is this effect what the writer intended?
8. What do I like best about the draft?

Being a Good Evaluator

Here are things to keep in mind when you evaluate someone's draft.

- Be sensitive to the writer's feelings and needs. Be courteous.
- Point out strengths as well as weaknesses.
- Supply constructive criticism. Offer suggestions for improvement.
- Avoid proofreading. Focus instead on ideas and form.

Below is part of Dan's draft, along with a peer editor's comments.

Dan "I can do it," Carl thought nervously. "I've done the routine in the simulator twenty times."

Carl saw the airport, a green square with two runways, crossing at an angle.

> I like to know Carl's thoughts. It shows his tension.

"Cut the throttle and set the flaps," Mr. Huff was saying. "Keep airspeed steady at 80 knots."

> I can really tell the plane is landing.

The big numbers painted on the end of the runway grew steadily larger. The center line was almost under the plane now. Carl worked the rudder controls to keep the wind from pushing them off course.

"Keep back pressure on the control column," Mr. Huff said. "Let the plane settle easily."

> Landing seems too easy here. Show the problems.

There it was—the squeak of tire on concrete. The nose-wheel came down with a hard thump, not like the smooth landing Carl had practiced in the simulator. But it didn't matter. They were safe.

Using an Evaluation Form

Another way to comment on a draft you are peer editing is to fill out an evaluation form. Here's an evaluation form about Dan's story.

Evaluation Form	
Questions About Ideas	**Comments**
Is there a clear focus or main idea?	The focus is a flying lesson that turned into an adventure.
Are there enough supporting details?	The landing needs more details. It seems too easy.
Are the supporting details interesting?	I like the details about the view from the air.
Questions About Form	
Is the information arranged clearly and logically?	The organization is clear.
Are the details relevant to the focus or main idea?	The description of the plane isn't needed.
Are ideas linked smoothly and clearly?	The first part is choppy, but the end is smooth.

Using a Reader's Comments

Comments from peer editors can tell you how others react to your writing, but you do not have to use every suggestion. Think about whether each suggestion would help you fulfill your purpose and make your paper better. Then act on those that seem valuable.

Writing Activities Revising

A Take out the draft you wrote for Exercise B on page 76. Use both self-editing and peer editing to gather comments about your work. Begin with peer editing. Work with a partner or in an editing group, and use the checklist on page 88. Then self-edit your draft, using the checklists on pages 80 and 81.

B *Writing in Process* Study the comments you have gathered and use them to revise your draft. As a final step, use the checklist on page 82 to find and correct mechanical errors.

Part 4
Publishing and Presenting

The last stage in the writing process is sharing your writing. Usually you will publish your writing in some way, but you may also choose some other form of presentation. Notice the options shown below.

Writing Exchange Groups Your class could circulate writing within an exchange group or between your group and one at another school.

Booklets Your class could publish a booklet about a particular topic. The booklet might feature one kind of writing—poetry, for example.

Newspapers and Magazines You could submit your writing to your school or local newspaper or send it to a magazine that accepts student writing.

Performances You could adapt a story or poem to the form of a play and act it out for your drama club.

Writing Activity Publishing and Presenting

Writing in Process Brainstorm alone or with your classmates about how you will present the final draft of your paper. Choose the best way to share your writing with others.

Chapter 4
Application and Review

A Revising a Composition Imagine that a classmate wrote the following composition, and you are serving as a peer editor. Revise the composition for ideas using the checklist on page 80. Revise it for form, using the checklist on page 81. Make notes on your paper about the changes you think would improve the composition.

Will Pandas Survive?

Pandas are an endangered species. There are now only about seven hundred pandas roaming the mountains of central China. Some pandas live in zoos but not enough to ensure their survival. The future looks bleak for pandas.

The biggest problem faced by pandas today is people. Over the years farmers have cut down many of the stands of bamboo that were once their main food supply. As a result, pandas have been forced to move to higher ground. Another problem is that pandas are solitary animals by nature. They reproduce with great difficulty. Their main food, bamboo, is not very nutritious.

Pandas must eat as much as forty pounds of bamboo a day. At least 138 pandas died in China in the mid-1970's, when there was a bamboo famine.

The Chinese government and conservation groups have set aside twelve reserves for pandas in rural China with different varieties of bamboo to feed them. But the reserves should be made larger, and they should be connected so that pandas can move from one to another.

There are panda breeding programs in several zoos. In 1986 a cub was born in the Tokyo Zoo. Ling Ling, a female panda that lives in the Washington Zoo, has had several cubs. None have survived.

Everyone who sees these animals agrees that everything possible should be done to save them. There is something special about pandas.

B Rewriting a Paragraph The paragraph below has been revised for ideas and form. Rewrite it, responding to the comments. Prepare a final draft using the Proofreading Checklist on page 82.

> Transitions needed: *later, then, finally.*

> This idea doesn't fit.

> Begin with this idea.

∧ The first ice skates were animal bones tied to boots with leather. There were wooden skates with iron blades and all-metal skates with steel blades. In the 1870's Jackson Haines made the first modern skates, with the boot and blade a single unit. ~~Our local ice rink is open all year.~~ Haines added dance steps and did spins, jumps, and glides. He did much to change ice skating into the exciting sport it is today. For hundreds of years, ice skating was mainly a way of getting from place to place.

C Proofreading a Paragraph Proofreading symbols indicate the mechanical errors in the following paragraph. Use the chart on page 82 to identify the errors, and rewrite the paragraph correctly.

¶ ∧ Every generation has it's share of styles that now seem silly. One such style was the zoot suit worn by men in the 1930s and 1940s. The zoot suit was dark with light thin stripes it had baggy pants that came up to the chest and a *baggy* ∧ jacket that went down to the knees. For accessories, a man wore suspenders a floppy hat and a long chain. the zoot suit was once familiar to every one, though worn by few.

D Preparing Your Final Draft Take out the draft or drafts you wrote for the Application and Review on page 76. Revise each draft, using the appropriate checklists. First, peer edit each other's drafts. Then self-edit your own drafts, proofreading as a final step.

Focus On

WORD PROCESSING

Find out how a high-tech innovation—the word processor—can help you to become a better, more effective writer.

In this age of "electronic miracles," we've become accustomed to having computers help us out. Computers can help us drive our automobiles and cook our food. Thanks to computer technology, we can phone the next-door neighbor or a friend on another continent. Now the same technology can make the task of writing easier, faster, and more effective.

What Is a Word Processor?

A computer becomes a word processor when a word-processing software program is loaded into it. Programs for word-processing are contained on a storage device,

such as a floppy disk. The computer works in combination with a printer, which on command will print on paper any text that has been composed. Although computers vary and individual word-processing programs may differ in the features they offer, all word processing offers certain benefits to assist writers.

Type Without Knowing How

Perhaps the simplest and most elementary benefit of word processing is that it allows non-typers to produce printed words on a page. It's true that the computer's keyboard is like a typewriter and that to word process you must key in the words. However, because the word processor makes it so easy to correct errors and automatically takes care of many of the spacing and formatting decisions, it is not necessary to possess extensive typing skills.

Face the Blank Page Bravely

Even during the beginning stages of writing, when you're still thinking about a writing topic, word processing can help make your job easier. The screen light on many computers is adjustable and can be dimmed. Try free-writing with the screen dimmed, typing any ideas that come to mind. Not being able to see what you're typing frees you from concerns about form and correctness. It also keeps you from trying to re-write prematurely. After you've exhausted your supply of ideas, turn up the monitor screen and review what you've written. Then, you can tell the computer to store your ideas, print them out, or both.

If a great idea hits you during the drafting stage, simply call up your idea file briefly. . . .

Extend Your Memory

A computer can store, or "remember," a great deal of material. You can use this fact to your advantage both while you're organizing your ideas and while you're composing. In a computer, a body of information is called a *file*. Word processors store written material as files. For example, if you have a list of questions that help you explore writing ideas, you can create a file to store it. If you'd like to keep an ongoing list of ideas, you can give it a file of its own, calling it up and adding to it as needed.

Some word processors let you work on more than one file at a time. This allows you to move back and forth between drafting and prewriting while the computer stores the other file for you. For example, suppose a great idea hits you during the drafting stage.

Like other important things, ideas can be stored.

Simply call up your idea file, store the inspiration, and return to your drafting. Later, you can refer to your idea file, pull out the idea, and insert it in the appropriate place in your text.

Handle Words with Confidence

Word processing simplifies adding or deleting material and moving words or passages around on the page. "Cut-and-paste" commands allow you to arrange and rearrange items in a writing plan or outline. You can also develop the points in your outline in order, or skip around as you fill in material. You can update and correct information quickly and without mess.

Throughout the planning and drafting stages, you have the option of working on-screen or making a paper copy (called a *hard copy*) of your text.

Find Your Own Drafting Style

The cut-and-paste feature is extremely useful during the drafting stage as well because it allows the word processor to accommodate alternative writing styles.

If you work best by first organizing and then writing, you could review your idea file on-screen or print out your ideas on paper to form prewriting notes. Then, use the cut-and-paste command to form a plan. Finally, expand your plan into sentences.

A word processor produces a hard copy that is free from deletions, inserts, carets, smudges, and other marks.

An alternative drafting method is to write and organize as you go. Produce text quickly and experiment on the spot with several ways of expressing an idea, or with several plans for developing it. Later, you can delete unneeded text or reorganize your draft.

The word processor also gives you the flexibility to use different approaches in your writing. For example, you may want to follow the

David Jacobson.

outline as you write, or you may want to write parts of the composition out of order—say, the conclusion first or the middle sections interspersed with the introduction and the conclusion.

Be Two People at Once

Competent writers are constantly aware of—and concerned with—the impact of their words on the reader. Word processing enables you to become author and audience at the same time. In fact, some word-processing programs have a "split-screen" feature that permits you to view onscreen more than one file at a time. The split screen is divided into separate sections called *windows,* and each window displays a portion of a file. You can move back and forth between windows and make changes, creating two versions of text simultaneously. You can experiment by moving words and even entire passages around. You can try a variety of locations for the same paragraph. The split screen allows you to test the merits of several versions and choose the one you consider to be the most effective.

Choose the Best Word

Word-processing programs have a "search-and-replace" function that indicates the number of times a given word is used in the text. If in revising your writing you suspect that you've overused a word, use this function to learn how many times it's mentioned in your text. (Some programs even display the location in the text of each occurrence.) Then, you can decide in each case whether to keep the word or to replace it with another.

Some word-processing programs have a built-in thesaurus to help you find a synonym. If yours does not, use your own thesaurus or a dictionary.

Produce a Perfect Paper

One of the best features of the word processor is its ability, at the stroke of a key, to produce a hard copy that is free of deletions, inserts, carets, smudges, and other marks. You can edit your writing onscreen or the "old-fashioned" way—with pencil on paper.

If you prefer, the word processor can print a copy with wide spacing and/or wide margins so that you can easily pencil in corrections. In this case, after careful proofreading you would add each of your corrections onto the

Producing perfect paper in the 18th century.

screen and then print out a clean final version.

Spell Perfectly

Another feature of many processors, the *spelling checker*, automatically scans the text for misspelled or unfamiliar words. Spelling checkers call up each questionably spelled word so that you can check it against a built-in dictionary or one of your own.

Become a More Effective Writer

Without doubt, word processors make composing and revising easier. They enable you to concentrate your efforts on the most important aspect of writing: saying what you have to say in the best possible way.

5
Understanding the Paragraph

*D*ance is a carefully choreographed art in which each dancer plays a role in developing the theme of the dance. All of the dancers must work together to make the performance a success.

Writing paragraphs involves its own form of choreography. Each sentence of a paragraph plays a role in supporting or developing the main idea of that paragraph. As in a dance, all of the sentences must work together to create a unified and coherent whole.

In this chapter you will study the roles that each sentence of a paragraph must play so that you can produce well-choreographed paragraphs that clearly and effectively express your ideas.

What Is a Paragraph?

A **paragraph** is a group of sentences that work together to develop a single main idea. In most paragraphs, the main idea is expressed in one sentence. All the other sentences in that paragraph add to, explain, or clarify the main idea.

Read the following paragraph and find the main idea.

▬ *Literary Model* ▬

The town was dead. Its beds were empty and cold. The only sound was the power hum of electric lines and dynamos, still alive, all by themselves. Water ran in forgotten bathtubs, poured out into living rooms, onto porches, and down through little garden plots to feed neglected flowers. In dark theaters, gum under the many seats began to harden with tooth impressions still in it.

From *The Martian Chronicles* by Ray Bradbury

This selection is an example of a well-organized, well-written paragraph. Note that the main idea of the paragraph is stated in the first sentence: "The town was dead." All the other sentences in that paragraph support the main idea by giving details that "prove" that the town is dead: beds were empty, bathtubs forgotten, flowers neglected, the theater dark.

Although from time to time you will need to write a single paragraph that "stands alone"—when answering questions on forms and on essay tests, for example—more often than not the paragraphs you write will belong to a larger piece of writing. In Chapter 6 you will learn to write a composition, several related paragraphs that develop a single topic.

Types of Paragraphs

There are many kinds of paragraphs, each serving a special purpose. The paragraph about the deserted town is called a **descriptive paragraph** because it uses words and details that "paint a picture" of a subject. Other paragraphs accomplish other goals. **Narrative paragraphs** use a sequence of events that tell a narrative, or story.

Persuasive paragraphs use logical arguments to persuade readers to accept the writer's opinion. **Expository paragraphs** use facts to explain how something works or is done.

Not all paragraphs can be so conveniently labeled, however. One paragraph may use a combination of description and narration to describe a setting or a character as well as tell a story. Another paragraph may blend description and explanation in an effort to persuade the reader to adopt a certain viewpoint. There are as many combinations as there are purposes for writing.

You will learn more about narrative, descriptive, persuasive, and expository writing in later chapters of this book.

Writing Activities What Is a Paragraph?

A Read each of the following paragraphs and identify its main idea. Each paragraph contains one sentence that does not develop the main idea. Identify this sentence and write it on another sheet of paper. Be ready to defend your answer.

1. Ants are highly developed social insects. They live in colonies with thousands, or even millions, of other ants. Each ant colony has at least one queen whose primary job is to lay eggs. Most of the ants in the colony, like the queen, are female. They are the workers. The workers build the nest, find food and carry it back to the colony, take care of the young, and fight enemies. Ants can inflict painful bites on unwary humans. Male ants live in the colony only at certain times. The only purpose of the male ant is to mate with the young queens.

2. The mountain at dawn was spectacular. The sun rose directly behind it, gradually painting the outer edges of its base with a soft rose glow. Slowly the glow moved upward, silhouetting the massive black bulk of the mountain against the brightening sky. At last the sun gained the summit, rimming the peak like a sparkling, ruby crown, too bright for mortal eyes. While the others slept, I took a series of pictures of the entire process. Now I could distinguish a few objects on the dark slopes. Here, a pine tree stood out against the sky; there, a granite boulder materialized.

3. Do not judge television too harshly. Its commercials may be too numerous and many of its programs stale and uninspired, but over the years it has accomplished much—and promises even more. Educational programs teach the young how to read and write. My nephew, who is only two years old, loves cartoons. Live coverage of important national events keeps adults aware of the world they

live in. Public service announcements and documentaries on a variety of subjects give much-needed advice and information to people of all ages. Popular programming, which is improving each year, will make even greater strides as viewers demand more than mindless entertainment from television producers.

4.   It's surprisingly fun and easy to make pizza. All you need are a packaged pizza mix, the toppings of your choice, shredded mozzarella cheese, and your imagination. Follow the package directions to make the dough. Then, with your hands, pat the dough into a greased pan. (Don't get discouraged if the dough looks a little uneven.) Spread pizza sauce over the dough, and then add the toppings. My favorite topping has always been anchovy, although none of my friends likes it. Last, sprinkle on the mozzarella—the more the merrier. Bake the pizza in a hot oven.

B Look at the following picture of an armadillo race. Use it or a similar humorous experience as a focus for writing a paragraph. Make sure your paragraph has a main idea and that all of the sentences in the paragraph relate to that idea.

Part 2

Prewriting:
Beginning a Paragraph

The first step in writing effective paragraphs of your own is to choose a topic. Remember that you yourself are a good source for interesting topics. Page through your journal; survey your own interests, abilities, and concerns. Use the thinking skills described in Chapter 2 to help you explore or find new aspects of the topics you come up with. After thinking about and exploring your ideas, choose a subject that appeals to you, and limit it to a size suitable for a single paragraph. A little background reading or observation might help you in this task. Determining your audience and purpose will also provide some helpful direction.

By devoting careful attention to this part of the writing process, you can come up with many interesting and varied topic possibilities. For example, you could find several different ways to write about rock music. You could describe the recent concert performance of a new group from Australia to someone who didn't attend. You might attempt to convince a jazz fan that rock is a more enduring form of music. Or, you could compare the music of one contemporary group with the music of the Beatles.

All of these paragraph ideas are valid ones. Yet each paragraph would include very different material based on considerations of purpose and audience.

Establishing a Main Idea

Once you have chosen a topic, you must establish the main idea. The **main idea** controls or drives the entire paragraph. Consider the following paragraph:

> Why do scientists think that so many ships and planes have vanished in the Bermuda Triangle? More than fifty have gone down since the 1850's. These losses have resulted in great expense for some cruise lines and airlines. This forces commercial carriers to raise their fares, which are already high. Imagine how long the average tourist must save in order to take a Caribbean cruise—and then to have the vacation spoiled by a violent and unexpected storm. On the other hand, maybe it's not a storm at all: maybe the Loch Ness Monster's to blame!

This paragraph suffers from a lack of direction. It wanders and does not advance the main idea: that more than fifty ships and planes have disappeared in the Bermuda Triangle since the 1850's. By concentrating on the main idea and providing details to support it, the writer will be able to improve the paragraph significantly, as you can see by reading the following.

▬ *Student Model*

Since the 1850's, more than fifty ships and airplanes have mysteriously vanished in the Bermuda Triangle. Why is this 440,000-square-mile section of the Atlantic Ocean the scene of so many unsolved disappearances? Scientists are unsure. Some speculate that violent and unexpected storms cause the accidents. Then, the wreckage is swept away by powerful ocean currents. This would help explain why search parties rarely find wreckage in the area.

Choosing Supporting Details

After you have formulated the main idea, you can begin to gather the details to support it. Supporting details include sensory details, specific examples, and facts or statistics.

Sensory Details Words that appeal to the five senses provide sensory details. They help develop the main idea of a paragraph by telling how things look, sound, smell, taste, or feel. By selecting exact, vivid sensory words, you can help readers experience the scene or process you are writing about. Read the paragraph that follows, noting the highlighted details that help bring the scene to life. What other details appeal to the senses?

▬ *Literary Model*

Sensory details

Early morning is a time of magic in Cannery Row. In the gray time after the light has come and before the sun has risen, the Row seems to hang suspended out of time in a silvery light. The street lights go out, and the weeds are a brilliant green. The corrugated iron of the canneries glows with the pearly lucence of platinum or old pewter. No automobiles are running then. The street is silent of progress and business. And the rush and drag of the waves can be

heard as they splash in among the piles of the canneries. It is a time of great peace, a deserted time, a little era of rest.

From *Cannery Row* by John Steinbeck

Specific Examples Sometimes the main idea can be supported with one or more examples. How many can you find in the following paragraph?

Literary Model

. . . Life was hard for Stevie. No matter how developed his sense of touch became, there were some things he could never understand through touch. He could never touch the sun, or the horizon. He could never touch a mountain. Some things were too fragile, like snowflakes or live butterflies. It would be too dangerous to try to understand burning or boiling through touch. No matter how developed his ability to measure "sound shadows" became, he would only be able to measure the width and bulk of a large building, not its height. He could learn that the sky is blue and the grass green, but he would never *see* blue or green. . . .

From *The Story of Stevie Wonder* by James Haskins

Sometimes an example consists of an entire incident or anecdote. In that case, use narrative details—the events of the story—to develop the paragraph.

Facts or Statistics These kinds of details also can support main ideas. Facts are statements that can be proven through observation, experience, or reference: "The earth is round"; "George Washington was the first president of the United States." Statistics are facts that involve numbers: "The population of Atlanta is over 525,000"; "The building is 620 feet high." Note the examples of facts and statistics in the following paragraph.

Professional Model

Fact

> Fibrillation of the heart, a rapid quivering of muscle fibers rather than the contractions needed to pump blood, is one of the leading causes of sudden death by heart attack. A study . . . compared cardiac arrest victims treated by emergency medical technicians [EMTs] to those treated by paramedics. The eventual survival rate among those patients treated by EMTs was only six percent. This rate rose dramatically, to twenty-seven percent, for patients treated by paramedics.

Statistics

From "State of the Art Emergency Care" by Sharon Balter

Writing Activities Supporting Details

A Choose two of the following main ideas. Use the technique provided in the suggestion to list three or four details that support or develop the main idea.

1. Autumn was advancing, and the sky was full of luminous clouds.
   Suggestion: Use clustering along with observation or memory to gather **sensory details.** (See pages 10–18.)
2. Weather often affects the way people think and act.
   Suggestion: Brainstorm with others to recall **specific examples** of human behavior you have observed during periods of intense heat, cold, rain, or snow. (See page 105.)
3. The engine of the car coughed and sputtered, fouling the air with smoke.
   Suggestion: Observe cars in a parking lot or on the highway to gather **sensory details.** (See pages 10–18.)

4. It was one of the largest and busiest airports in the country.
   Suggestion: Develop questions and use them to research in reference books for **statistics** about the airport and its employees, passengers, and planes. (See page 106.)
5. People often lavish much affection on their pets.
   Suggestion: Interview a veterinarian or a pet store owner to gather **facts** or **specific examples** about the attention and care some owners give their pets. (See pages 40–41.)
6. The California gold rush began in 1848.
   Suggestion: Use gleaning and research techniques to gather **facts** and **statistics** about the topic and develop a time line of events. (See page 32.)

B *Writing in Process* Choose a topic, limit it, and write a topic sentence. Next, using the thinking and gathering techniques of your choice, locate several supporting details for your topic sentence. Save your work for the next activity.

Part 3
Drafting a Paragraph

After you chose a topic for your paragraph and began to develop the supporting details, you may have found your purpose shifting. Now is the time to ''firm up'' the ideas in your paragraph and write a first draft. You will want to begin by writing a topic sentence.

The Topic Sentence

A **topic sentence** states the main idea of the paragraph. A good topic sentence also engages readers and keeps them reading. Consider the following topic sentences.

> The cave was full of bats.
> Flapping and screeching, hundreds of bats swooped down on us as we explored the cave.

While both sentences ''promise'' to describe bats, the first topic sentence is boring. It will be hard to engage readers with the first sentence. The second sentence, on the other hand, claims readers' attention by using a vivid sensory image: ''Flapping and screeching, hundreds of bats swooped. . . .''

Position of Topic Sentence In most of the paragraphs you have studied so far, the topic sentence is the first sentence. In that position, it immediately lets the reader know what to expect in the rest of the paragraph. However, the topic sentence can also appear at or near the end of the paragraph. In that position, it makes a point or sums up what precedes it.

Student Model

He was born Ehrich Weiss in 1874. As a young child, he taught himself to make small items appear and disappear. Because Ehrich's family was quite poor, he went to work for a locksmith at the early age of 12. Before long, he knew how to pick almost any lock in existence. Thus began the career of Harry Houdini—one of the most remarkable magicians of all time.

Sometimes the topic sentence is implied rather than stated directly. In the next paragraph, we know without being told that the man in the black suit is running late and is worried about missing a plane.

Student Model

The man in the black suit threw the last of the items into the leather suitcase and yanked at the zipper. He glanced at the clock on the mantle and saw that it was 2:17. Forty-three minutes, he calculated quickly. Was it enough time to get to the airport? Perspiration beaded his upper lip as he snatched his tickets off the dresser. Grabbing his suitcase, he strode purposefully out of the room. What if he couldn't catch a cab? He would have to, he thought.

Organizing Supporting Details

Once you have written a topic sentence, you will need to decide on a good order for presenting your ideas. An orderly and logical presentation is helpful to your readers. It enables them to understand how your ideas are related to each other.

In selecting a method of organization, consider both the purpose and type of development you have decided on for your paragraph. Then ask yourself questions like those on the top of the next page.

1. How does each detail relate to the others?
2. Does one piece of information logically precede another in degree of importance?
3. Is one idea more familiar to my readers than another?

When you make decisions about paragraph development based on the answers to these questions, you are taking the first steps toward achieving coherent writing.

There are a number of logical organizations you could use to develop a paragraph. However, most types of organization fall into one of the six following categories:

1. Chronological, or time sequence
2. Spatial order
3. Order or degree of importance
4. Order of familiarity
5. Comparison and contrast
6. Cause and effect

Chronological Order When you organize your paragraph in chronological order, or time sequence, you arrange your details in the order in which they happened. This method of organization is particularly useful for paragraphs developed by anecdote or incident, as in the next example.

▬ *Literary Model* ▬

Words that signal time order

Soon the biggest of the boys poised himself, shot down into the water, and did not come up. The others stood about, watching. . . . After a long time, the boy came up on the other side of a big dark rock, letting the air out of his lungs in a sputtering gasp and a shout of triumph. Immediately the rest of them dived in. One moment, the morning seemed full of chattering boys; the next, the air and the surface of the water were empty. But through the heavy blue, dark shapes could be seen. . .

From "Through the Tunnel" by Doris Lessing

This writer describes what happens when a group of boys go swimming. First, while the group watches, the biggest boy dives in. After some time, he surfaces. Next, the others dive in. The paragraph describes the action in the order in which it occurred.

Spatial Order Detail sentences also can be arranged in spatial order, or the order in which the subjects are related in space. For example, you might describe the details of a scene from top to bottom, from near to far, or from left to right. The following paragraph is arranged in spatial order.

▬ *Literary Model* ▬

Words that signal spatial order

On one side, beginning at the very lip of the pool, was a tiny meadow, a cool, resilient surface of green that extended to the base of the frowning wall. Beyond the pool a gentle slope of earth ran up and up to meet the opposing wall. Fine grass covered the slope—grass that was spangled with flowers, with here and there patches of color, orange and purple and golden. Below, the canyon was shut in. . . . The walls leaned together abruptly and the canyon ended in a chaos of rocks, moss-covered and hidden by a green screen of vines. . . .

From "All Gold Canyon" by Jack London

Order or Degree of Importance This method of organization is appropriate for organizing facts or examples. Evaluate your supporting details according to the impact you think they will have on readers. Then when you write your paragraph, organize them, beginning with the least important statement and ending with the strongest, or most important, one.

▬ *Student Model* ▬

Space has sometimes been called "the last frontier," and we continue trying to tame it. Yet, unlike the frontier of the Old West, space is one unknown that we can never hope to explore or understand completely. Once an explorer could start a private land or sea expedition with little more than several thousand dollars and a crew of volunteers. Now governments spend billions of dollars developing state-of-the-art equipment and training technical personnel to administer a massive space program. Despite these numbers, each mission results in only a tiny increase in our knowledge of the universe. No matter how often we explore space, an infinite amount will still remain unknown.

Order of Familiarity In this method of paragraph organization, you move from ideas that are familiar to your readers to those that are probably not familiar. In this way, you prepare readers for new concepts by providing familiar background information first. This method is particularly effective when you are organizing facts and statistics or specific examples.

Here's how one student used this organizational method in a report on compact disk players.

Student Model

> A revolution's going on in the audio industry. With periodic improvements in quality, the needle-and-groove technology of Thomas Edison's phonograph has been able to maintain the standard for more than a hundred years. However, a product developed in the late 1970's—the compact disk player, or CD player—promises to eventually turn record albums and the turntable into quaint antiques. Music for this stereo sound system is represented by a digital code embedded under the surface of a 4.5-inch disk. When a compact disk is played, the information is "read" by a low-power laser beam that erases background noise and the hiss found on conventional records.

Comparison and Contrast Your details may lend themselves to arrangement by comparison (showing the similarities) and contrast (showing the difference).

The following paragraph illustrates how one writer used the comparison-and-contrast method in his writing, noting the similarities and differences between his subjects.

Literary Model

> Henry Chatillon and Tête Rouge were of the same age, that is, about thirty. Henry was twice as large, and about six times as strong as Tête Rouge. . . . Henry talked of Indians and buffalo; Tête Rouge of theaters and oyster cellars. Henry had led a life of hardship and privation; Tête Rouge never had a whim which he would not gratify at the first moment he was able.

From *The Oregon Trail* by Francis Parkman

Cause and Effect Some details lend themselves to a cause-and-effect order of organization. Paragraphs with this method of organization often have a topic sentence that states a cause; supporting details provide the effects. Or, the topic sentence can state an effect, with supporting sentences indicating what led to that effect.

Study for Aspects of Negro Life: Slavery to Reconstruction, Aaron Douglas, 1934.

▬ *Literary Model* ▬

Cause
Effect

In the 1930's disaster struck the United States. A great depression swept across the country, bringing massive unemployment in its wake. The people of Harlem suffered even more than the rest of the country, and the black art movement might have floundered completely but for the Federal Works Project. The government provided financial aid to both black and white artists. Com-

Cause

missions to paint murals—pictures which are painted directly on a wall or ceiling—were given to black artists.

Effect

Colorful murals began appearing on the walls of government buildings, schools, hospitals, and libraries all over America.

From *Exploring Black America* by Marcella Thum

Writing Activities Drafting a Paragraph

A Read each group of details and identify the method that should be used to organize them in paragraph form.

1. United States flag: red, white, blue
   flag of Luxembourg: red, white, blue
   Luxembourg flag: three stripes
   United States flag: thirteen stripes
2. red asphalt-shingle roof   white clapboard sides
   cement block foundation   two stories
3. cellars fill with water   heavy rain falls
   streets covered with water   rivers overflow
4. write paragraph   get facts from reference books
   write topic sentence   choose and limit topic

B *Writing in Process* Examine the details you gathered for the topic you chose during Activity B on page 107. What kind of relationship do they suggest? Write a paragraph using the most appropriate method of organization.

Part 4
Revising: Unity and Coherence

A good paragraph is unified and coherent. In a paragraph with **unity,** all of the sentences support the main idea. In a paragraph that exhibits **coherence,** all of the sentences relate clearly and logically to each other.

Unity

Writers can achieve paragraph unity in a variety of ways. In most paragraphs, a good topic sentence plays a key role in establishing unity. In paragraphs without a topic sentence, unity is achieved in other ways. For example, all of the sentences may develop the implied main idea, or they may follow a logical progression, as in narrative writing.

Topic Sentence A good topic sentence serves an important function in paragraph unity. In effect, it tells the reader, ''I have an idea to explain to you.'' In a unified paragraph, the rest of the sentences are related to the topic sentence, and they proceed to explain the idea ''promised'' in the topic sentence.

In the paragraph that follows, the writer's first sentence establishes the main idea: her father enjoyed collecting puzzles and other devices that pique the curiosity. Note how the other sentences in the paragraph support the idea stated in this topic sentence, fulfilling the ''promise'' it makes.

▬ *Literary Model* ▬

Main idea

My father loved all instruments that would instruct and fascinate. His place to keep things was the drawer in the ''library table'' where lying on top of his folded maps was a telescope with brass extensions. . . . In the back of the

Supporting details

drawer you could find a magnifying glass, a kaleidoscope, and a gyroscope kept in a black buckram box, which he would set dancing for us on a string pulled tight. He had

Supporting details

also supplied himself with an assortment of puzzles composed of metal rings and intersecting links and keys chained together, impossible for the rest of us, however patiently shown, to take apart; he had an almost childlike love of the ingenious.

From *One Writer's Beginnings* by Eudora Welty

Implied Main Idea Although the writer of the next paragraph does not say so, he is torn between logic and emotion. The paragraph has unity because all sentences communicate the writer's dilemma and struggle.

▬ *Literary Model* ▬

I thought, ''Now, Dooley, you've got a job, and it doesn't necessarily mean that you must stay in this village. You must go where you can do the greatest good.'' But deeper inside me a voice said, ''Stay in your village, stay wrapped in the love of being needed. Here Asians need you and you need that need.'' I remembered the words of a Chinese philosopher who said that life was like a tightrope. On this tightrope man walks, balanced between what he must do and what he wishes to do. If these two remain in perfect balance, he can walk forward on the rope with ease. If they do not remain in balance, he falls down on one side or the other. I must keep walking, I must walk straight forward. I must.

From *The Night They Burned the Mountain*
by Thomas A. Dooley, M.D.

Logical Progression In the next paragraph, the main idea is neither stated nor implied. Unity is achieved through the logical progression of details in the paragraph.

Literary Model

Paul was cutting trees one morning up in Minnesota. He had to get them to the sawmill which was in New Orleans and he decided the best way to do it would be by river—but there was no river. So Paul had a light lunch of: 19 pounds of sausage, 6 hams, 8 loaves of bread, and 231 flapjacks, and each flapjack was slathered with a pound of butter and a quart of maple syrup. It was a skimpy lunch for Paul. . . . Paul dug his river that afternoon and he called it the Mississippi, which as far as I know, is what it is called to this day.

From *The Story of Paul Bunyan* by Barbara Emberley

As you revise the paragraph you wrote for Activity B on page 113, work at achieving unity. If the paragraph has a topic sentence, do the other sentences support it? If your paragraph's main idea is implied rather than directly stated, does each sentence work toward forwarding this idea? If you are writing a narrative paragraph in which the main idea is neither stated nor implied, make sure that each sentence contributes to a logical progression of thought.

Coherence

A paragraph is said to be coherent when all its sentences are logically related to one another. Each sentence of the paragraph should be linked, either by word or by thought, to the sentences that come before and after it.

In the following student paragraph, all of the sentences seem to be about the killing of whales, but the ideas are difficult to follow. In order to analyze the paragraph and suggest revisions, a peer reader first numbered each sentence.

     1. A whale, one of the largest animals in the
world, is killed by Soviet and Japanese whale
hunters every seventeen minutes. 2. This makes
many people very angry. 3. Whales might be like
the dinosaur and disappear forever. 4. People are
showing their anger in many ways. 5. One Japanese
businessman says, ''Many Japanese could not live
without whale meat.'' 6. Some people are writing
letters to the Japanese Prime Minister, and others are asking people not to buy Japanese products. 7. Perhaps the Japanese government may stop
the whale hunting.

    The peer editor noted that sentences 1 and 3 both dealt with the kill-
ing of the whales. Sentences 2, 4, and 6 were concerned with people's
attitudes toward the killing. The peer editor also pointed out that the
sentence about the Japanese businessman (sentence 5) did not support
the main idea implied in the paragraph.

    The writer reviewed these comments. She also realized that sen-
tences 2 and 4 repeated some of the same ideas, so she combined them.
Finally, she added some transitional words to the paragraph to help
hold the ideas together. After the writer made all these changes, the paragraph read as follows:

    A whale, one of the largest animals in the
world, is killed by Soviet and Japanese whale

Transition   hunters every seventeen minutes. Someday, if
this killing continues, whales might be like the

Combined   dinosaur and disappear forever. People are
sentences   angry, and they are showing their anger in several ways. Some people are writing letters to the
Japanese Prime Minister, and others are asking

Transition   people not to buy Japanese products. If this
hurts Japanese business enough, the Japanese
government may stop the whale hunting.

    The preceding paragraph has several transitions in it. These words
and phrases create logical links between sentences. Transitions can
show time *(finally)*, place *(above, below)*, order of importance *(first,*

next, last), or cause and effect *(therefore)*. You will learn more about transitions in Chapter 6.

Grammar Note Adverbs and prepositional phrases used as adverbs are good transitional devices (see pages 556 and 584). Some adverbs and prepositional phrases help readers follow a spatial order: *at the base of the mountain, on the trail, higher, below the cliff, at the summit*. Others help readers follow time sequence: *at first, afterwards, then, after a long pause*.

Writing Activities *Unity and Coherence*

A Rewrite each of the following paragraphs, improving its unity and coherence. Delete any details that do not support the main idea of the paragraph. Arrange details in the best order. Add transition words where needed.

1. In 1848, gold was discovered at Sutter's mill in California. California is heavily populated. People staked out claims and panned for gold. A few of them became rich. News of the discovery spread throughout the world. The first organized group of American settlers came to California in 1841. Most of the prospectors found little or no gold.

2. Birds and reptiles share similarities but display just as many differences. Both birds and reptiles, having a backbone, are called vertebrates. Birds are warm-blooded; their body temperature remains about the same regardless of the temperature of their surroundings. Humans are warm-blooded also. The body of a bird is covered with feathers. The body of a reptile is covered with dry, scaly skin. Reptiles are cold-blooded; that is, their body temperature changes with that of their surroundings.

3. We could see the effects of the ocean tides in the river. Each day, as the tide rose in the ocean, water flowed up the river. Where we had stood in water no more than six inches deep at low tide, the water was over our heads at high tide. We could see the river from our house. As the tide in the ocean fell, water in the river flowed back toward its mouth. The tall grass, high and dry on the marsh at low tide, was almost completely submerged at high tide. At full tide the water paused.

B *Writing in Process* Revise the paragraph you wrote in Activity B on page 113. Make sure it has unity and coherence; use transition words where appropriate. Share your writing with a classmate.

Chapter 5
Application and Review

The following exercises will help you write paragraphs. The first exercise makes a specific writing assignment: to describe a person you admire. The second exercise gives guidelines about planning and writing a persuasive paragraph on a topic of your choice. The third exercise allows you to use your imagination and creativity.

A Describing a Person Who was the most impressive person you ever knew or read about? Was that person known only to family and friends, well-known in this country, or world-famous? Use brainstorming to think of a person, dead or alive, whose contributions you admire. Write a paragraph about him or her.

Prewriting Use inquiring; list questions your audience would like answered about the person selected. Research, if necessary, to find information. Look for a relationship among the details that will help you select a method of organizing the paragraph.

Drafting Write the paragraph, referring to your prewriting notes. Begin with a good topic sentence. Support the main idea with detail sentences in the order you have chosen.

Revising Check your paragraph for unity and coherence. Use the Proofreading Checklist and the Proofreading Symbols on page 82. Copy your revised paragraph.

B Persuading Others Use the following guidelines to plan and write a persuasive paragraph. In that paragraph you will try to persuade adults to do something that will improve life for everyone.

Prewriting Use clustering to determine which changes in your school or community would improve the quality of life. For example, should the school day be extended? Are other courses needed? Should work experience be integrated with classes? Does your community need more laws dealing with housing, pets, use of local resources? Select and limit a topic. Use a thinking technique to gather information. Organize the details.

Drafting and Revising Write a first draft, stating the main idea in the topic sentence. Revise with an eye toward unity and coherence. Proofread your revision and make a copy of it.

c *Starting Points for Writing* The best subjects for an expository paragraph are those things that you know a lot about or that you know how to do well. List the various elements in the images below about which you think you could explain or teach something. As you examine these images, ask yourself one or two of the questions given as Springboards. This may help you discover more items you could tell about.

Springboards

- Do I collect this or anything like it?
- Can I explain what these people are doing?
- Do I know how to use this?
- What do I know about this building or the place where it stands?

6

Writing Effective
Compositions

Blue Terrace, David Hockney, 1982.

D avid Hockney created both the
self-portrait at the right and the
photo collage above. Although the artist uses two different techniques, each results in a pleasing composition,
combining elements such as color, shape, and point-of-
view.

The elements that writers work with are different
types of paragraphs. In this chapter you will learn a variety of ways in which you can combine paragraphs to
build an interesting and effective composition.

Self Portrait, David Hockney, 1976.

Part 1
What Is a Composition?

In Chapter 5 you learned how to develop a paragraph. Since a paragraph focuses on a single idea, however, it may limit your ability to explore ideas fully. Most paragraphs are part of a larger piece of writing called a **composition**. Like a paragraph, a composition needs an introduction and supporting details. Unlike a paragraph, which often ends with a link to the next paragraph, a composition needs a conclusion to restate, summarize, or comment on the information presented. The box below compares a paragraph and a composition. Notice the similarities and differences.

Paragraphs and Compositions

A paragraph needs	A composition needs
a topic sentence	an introductory paragraph
sentences with supporting details	one or more body paragraphs
	a concluding paragraph

As the box shows, a composition has three types of paragraphs. Each type serves a specific function. The **introductory paragraph,** which opens the composition, tells the reader what the composition will address. Like the topic sentence of a paragraph, the introductory paragraph states the main idea.

After the introductory paragraph has presented the main idea, the **body paragraphs** develop this idea. For example, in a composition about a trip to the Canadian Rocky Mountains, the writer might tell of the area's scenic beauty in the first body paragraph. A second paragraph might tell of the many things to do there, and a third might tell of the convenient campgrounds.

Following the body paragraphs is the **concluding paragraph,** which lets the reader know that the composition is ending. The writer may use the conclusion to restate the main idea, to summarize the supporting information, or to provide a general concluding comment.

In later chapters, you will learn how the relationship between the paragraphs of a composition may vary according to the type of writing you have chosen.

Read the following example of a well-developed composition.

━ Student Model ━

Have you ever considered challenging yourself to climb mountains that touch the sky, or white-water raft down a raging river, or sail a stormy ocean in record time? If this type of adventure appeals to you, then you might want to give Outward Bound survival programs a try. Outward Bound programs offer a variety of challenges and some exceptional benefits.

Introductory paragraph

In Outward Bound, learning about yourself is the main objective. By being faced with the physical challenge, for example, of hiking across the desert for a stretch of eighteen hours, you can discover new strengths and abilities. You might learn that you can navigate well or simply that you can hike for an extended period of time.

Topic sentence

Body paragraph 1

Besides learning about yourself, you are also learning how to work within a group. In Outward Bound, you might be roped to a group of students trying to scale the face of a steep mountain, everyone working together to accomplish the climb. Working within a team is a vital skill you will have to master in Outward Bound.

Topic sentence

In the Outward Bound programs not only do you learn about group spirit, but you learn to appreciate nature as well. While mastering the climb, hike, or sail, you are in constant contact with nature. Therefore, you gain a greater appreciation of its forces.

Topic sentence

Outward Bound programs are not vacations. They are a chance to challenge your abilities with students who share the same goals in the beautiful, yet dangerous wilderness.

Concluding paragraph

Notice how the paragraphs in this section work together to convey the writer's main idea. In the introductory paragraph, the writer presents the idea that Outward Bound programs offer a variety of challenges and benefits. In the body paragraphs, the writer provides examples of the types of challenges and benefits you would expect on such an adventure. In the concluding paragraph, the writer mentions that Outward Bound is not a vacation. The conclusion also echoes the introduction, outlining the experiences an Outward Bound participant would encounter in the wilderness.

Writing Activity Prewriting

Writing in Process Look at the images above and use them as starting points for possible topics for a composition. Also, use your thinking skills to develop three or four lists of possible topics. The lists might contain interesting experiences you've had, places you've been, things you can explain to others, or opinions you would like to express. A good topic is narrow enough to cover thoroughly and interesting enough for you to enjoy. Decide on a topic and write it down.

Part 2
Writing an Introduction

How many times have you seen a coming attraction for a new film and thought, "I have to see that movie!"? Just as the coming attraction piques the viewer's curiosity, the introductory paragraph in a composition must catch the reader's attention. In addition, the introduction sets the tone of the composition. It lets the reader know whether the composition will be serious or humorous, casual or formal.

The introduction must also introduce the composition's main idea, or **thesis statement**. This statement reveals your topic and controlling purpose and limits your topic to a workable size.

Catching the Reader's Interest

If you want to catch the reader's attention, avoid dull opening sentences like the four listed below. All four of these opening sentences lack specific details.

> The flute is a popular instrument among high school musicians.
> Most people in the United States are not physically fit.
> It is sometimes difficult to get along with your neighbors.
> In this paper I am going to describe someone who died.

Listed below are some ways in which you can start introductory paragraphs. Compare the dull introductory sentences you just read with these interesting introductions.

1. A **quotation** is simply a repetition of someone else's exact words.

> "A flute," wrote an early nineteenth-century British critic, "is a musical weed which springs up everywhere." Nancy Toff

2. **Startling or interesting facts** suprise your readers or make them curious.

> Alarming evidence about the state of fitness—or lack of it—in the United States continues to mount. A Center for Disease Control survey of more that 25,000 adults revealed that 55 percent *do not* exercise three times a week for 20 minutes at a time, the minimum amount needed to provide health benefits.
> Runner's World

3. An **anecdote** is an interesting or amusing incident, usually about an individual.

> A man in Cambridge, Mass. took his neighbor to court because the neighbor hadn't cut his grass in fourteen years. . . . There are something like sixty million single family homes in the United States and I'll bet ninety percent of the people living in those houses are having some kind of trouble with their neighbors. Andrew A. Rooney

4. A **vivid description** of a person or of a place strikes the reader's imagination.

> Charley Lockjaw died last summer on the reservation. He was very old—a hundred years he had claimed. He still wore his hair in braids as only the older men do in his tribe, and the braids were thin and white. Dorothy Johnson

Introductions vary, depending on the kind of writing you are doing. In Chapters 8 to 12, you will learn to adapt your introductions to different kinds of writing.

Techniques for Developing Paragraphs

No matter what technique you use to spark your reader's interest in the introduction, you will find that you can often use one of the following **paragraph shapes.**

One of the techniques for developing introductions is to begin with a single detail or example and broaden to a general statement.

Student Model

Specific example

> During his summers in high school, Eric ran his own lawn-care service. After five years, his business has become a lucrative corporation, designing landscapes for industrial parks and shopping malls. Like Eric, many young people with initiative and determination have become successful entrepreneurs in the business community. Becoming an entrepreneur involves hard work, planning, and determination.

General statement

Writing Inside Out

Ginna Domm, Director of Marketing

Ginna Domm is not a writer by profession, but if she couldn't write well, she would not be able to do her job. As a marketing director for the Bennigan's Restaurants, Ginna makes decisions about how the company's 212 restaurants can increase their business. From company headquarters in Dallas, she communicates her ideas to others, sometimes orally, but often through written memos and compositions in the form of reports.

"For instance, when we need a new series of radio ads, I write directions to writers who work at our advertising agency in New York," she explains. "I tell them exactly what points the ads should cover, and their order of importance. I also tell them what kind of mood we want.

In the previous example, a young person's specific work experience led into a general statement about successful entrepreneurs. Also, a paragraph may begin with a general statement that is then supported by details that lead into the body of the composition. This is the opposite of a specific-to-general paragraph "shape."

Professional Model

General statement

As the hawk sees it, northeast Minnesota's Superior National Forest is a rolling green carpet patterned with hundreds upon hundreds of shimmering lakes and laced with the silver threads of rivers. The forest serves as a spectacular laboratory for wildlife biologists. It was here

Specific example

that one of them, Dr. Lynn Rogers, learned to ride black bears, an activity he does not recommend to others. Based at a U.S. Forest Service research station a few miles outside the town of Ely, Rogers and other researchers have studied Superior's bears, timber wolves, white-tailed deer and beavers.

From "Getting to Know Black Bears—Right on Their Own Home Ground" by Adele Conover

"The directions are usually only a page long, but they have to be very detailed and very clear," Ginna continues.

Recently Ginna helped Bennigan's write new menus. "Customers told us our menu was too long so we decided to make it shorter." The menu went through many rewrites by many writers.

"We wrote new descriptions for each food item," she says. "The descriptions had to be informative, telling how each dish is made and what is in it. They also had to be somewhat romantic. If the dish doesn't sound appealing people won't buy it."

When Bennigan's puts something new on the menu, Ginna writes a report, using a composition format. She comments on how the new item is doing and whether she thinks the company should continue to sell it. She also helps write an annual plan in which the company sets its goals for the coming year.

Ginna likes marketing because in this field she can "make things happen." While she was still in school, she realized that she would need strong writing skills to succeed in her chosen occupation. She has found that people who don't have good grammar skills or who cannot organize their thoughts on paper have great difficulty moving ahead in the competitive area of marketing.

In addition, a paragraph may begin with a specific idea, then switch to the opposite and expand upon it.

▬ *Professional Model* ▬▬▬▬▬▬▬▬

Specific idea — They're saying that families are dying, and soon. They're saying it loud, but we'll see that they're wrong.

Opposite — Families aren't dying. The trouble we take to arrange ourselves in some semblance or other of families is one of the most imperishable habits of the human race. What families are doing, in flamboyant and dumfounding ways, is changing their size and their shape and their purpose.

From *Families* by Jane Howard

Writing Activities *Writing an Introduction*

A Read the following introductory paragraphs. Using what you have learned in this part, rewrite each introductory paragraph to make it more interesting.

1. Minor league baseball can be quite exciting. Last week some friends and I went to the local stadium to see the Albuquerque Dukes play the Calgary Cannons. It was a good one.

2. For the past year, Carlos has been building model airplanes. These models are made of wood, and they can fly by twisting rubber bands that turn the propeller as they untwist. This is preparing him for his next goal, which is to build a radio-controlled model. He has always wanted to build such a model.

3. Volcanoes spew forth various materials. Sometimes, a volcano will send out billowy clouds. Lava may flow down the mountainside. Volcanoes have caused horrible disasters. However, volcanoes also provide benefits.

B *Writing in Process* Use the topic you generated in Part 1 to develop a main idea, or thesis statement. You will have to narrow your topic to a specific idea that covers less information than the topic itself. For example, your topic could be the role of television in setting trends and your main idea could be that the more popular the television program, the greater will be its impact on fashion trends. Now that you have a main idea, write an introduction based on this thesis statement. Remember to catch the reader's attention and to use an effective paragraph shape.

Writing the Body

In Chapter 5 you learned about the importance of unity and coherence in the writing of paragraphs. Unity and coherence are important not only to your individual paragraphs but also to the composition as a whole.

Unity and Coherence

As you write your composition, try to keep the ideas unified. Make sure that each body paragraph relates directly to the thesis statement in the introductory paragraph. Then, check to see if the supporting details in each body paragraph relate to the topic sentence of that paragraph. By using these techniques, you will write a unified composition. In addition to being unified, a good composition must be coherent. The reader should see clear connections among paragraphs. To write a coherent composition, first develop an organization that works logically. Then use transitions and paragraph links to help your paragraphs flow together.

Logical Organization In order to write a coherent composition, you need to organize your information in an order that makes sense to the reader. To choose a logical method of organization, look for relationships among the ideas and details. Remember, you can use different organizations in the same composition. For more information about types of paragraph organizations, see Chapter 4, pages 78–93.

You can use **chronological order** for any part of your composition that is made up of events in a specific time sequence. For example, chronological order is used in this introduction to an expository article.

▬ *Professional Model* ▬

Time reference
Just before eight o'clock on the evening of August 15, 1907, a girl was fixing her hair in the servants' quarters of the Hotel Emerson in Old Orchard Beach, the grandest summer resort in Maine. She tipped over her oil lamp. The fire spread so quickly through the huge hotel that

Time reference
within seventeen minutes the building was totally engulfed . . .

From "Old Orchard Beach, Maine" by Michael Kimball

Another form of organization is **cause and effect.** This type of organization is common in expository writing.

Effect:
the gathering
of eagles

Cause:
the run of
salmon

"You won't find this kind of gathering of eagles anywhere else in the world," says Erwin Boeker, a biologist who spent four years studying the Chilkat phenomenon for the National Audubon Society. "There are times in November when you can stand in one place with a pair of binoculars and see 2,000 of them. It's just amazing."

What brings the birds to this isolated spot, fifty miles north of Juneau in Alaska's southeastern panhandle? They come to take advantage of another animal invasion: the annual spawning run of chum and silver salmon up the forty-five-mile-long Chilkat.

From "Making a Spectacle" by Russ Rymer

Sometimes, the details in your composition differ from one another in degree of importance. You can then organize your writing according to **order of importance** by starting with the least important idea and ending with the most important. Descriptive and explanatory writings often use this form of organization.

Less
important

More
important

A [steam]boat pilot must have a memory: but there are two much higher qualities which he must also have. He must have good, quick judgment and decision, and a cool, calm courage that no peril can shake. Give a man the merest trifle of pluck to start with, and by the time he has become a pilot he cannot be unmanned by any danger a steamboat can get into; but one cannot quite say the same for judgment. Judgment is a matter of brains, and a man must *start* with a good stock of that article or he will never succeed as a pilot.

From *Life on the Mississippi* by Mark Twain

Transitional Words and Phrases Transitional words provide another method of achieving coherence in your writing. Such words or phrases connect the main idea of one paragraph to the main idea of the next paragraph. They also connect ideas or details within paragraphs. The following chart provides some examples of transitions you can use when writing your composition.

Transitions	
Time	always, before, finally, first, meanwhile
Place	above, around, beneath, down, here, there
Order of importance	first, second, mainly, more important, most important
Cause and effect	as a result, because, therefore, so, for, consequently
Contrast	on the other hand, yet, but, however, unlike, by contrast
Comparison	as, than, in the same way, similarly, likewise

Now read the selection on the next page. Notice each of the methods the writer uses to achieve coherence and to indicate organization. Transitional words and phrases and clues to organization are noted on the left.

Professional Model

There's no point in getting mad at machines, I suppose. Machines are dumb, inanimate objects, after all. Yet who among us has not, from time to time, worked up a case of frustration, resentment, and hatred over a car, a typewriter, or a soft drink machine. People have been known to yell at machines, to hit and kick and even shoot at them. The advantage of getting mad at a machine and beating up on it is that machines (unlike people) don't harbor grudges.

Example of transition: contrast

At least they haven't until now. . . .

Here is Robert Wenger of Monroe, Wisconsin, trying to withdraw some money from his bank account. . . . All he wants is ten dollars, and he knows there's enough money in his account because he deposited forty dollars just the day before.

Chronological order

But the automatic bank teller refuses to listen to reason. Wenger then does what people often do when they get mad at machines. He hits it right in the face with his fist. Had the teller been a real human being, Wenger would probably not have punched him (or her) in the nose. But this wasn't a him or a her. It was an it and it was now broken, requiring $298 worth of repairs, as the bank people discovered when they reopened for business the next day.

Example of transition: time

By that time, of course, Wenger was long gone. But the machine turned him in. It remembered who had punched it in the nose. Wenger. Wenger, eh? Wenger, Robert L.

The computer memory said to itself, "I'm gonna get that guy if he comes in here again. In fact, even if he doesn't. Here's his name. Here's his address." It was an open-and-shut case, and Wenger was the assailant, all right.

He's been convicted of criminal damage.

So, if you get mad at a machine, remember this. Machines are not as dumb as they used to be. Make sure, before you kick it, that it doesn't know where you live.

From *There's Nothing That I Wouldn't Do*
If You Would Be My POSSLQ
by Charles Osgood

Paragraph Links There are a variety of "links" that can help you hook your paragraphs together. You may want to repeat an important word from an earlier sentence or paragraph. This can help your reader see the connections among your ideas.

In the following selection, notice how Polly Bannister repeats the word *flower*.

Professional Model

Carol Duke has built her life around flowers. Even when she is not in the garden at . . . her hilltop home in Williamsburg, Massachusetts, she is immersed in

Repeated word

flowers—teaching, lecturing, designing, and arranging. She has created arrangements for clients as diverse as the New York City Ballet, the Chase Manhattan Bank. . . .

Repeated word

For Carol, a visual artist by training, arranging flowers is an ideal blend of her interests in art and gardening. . . .

From "The Next-To-Last Word in Flower Arranging"
by Polly Bannister

Another way to link your paragraphs is by rephrasing a word or term that was mentioned earlier in the selection. Notice how the expression *exercise just for sheer pleasure* has been rephrased in the following model.

Professional Model

"A runner's biggest bugaboo is the stopwatch," says Jim Couts, a sports psychology consultant in Long Beach, California. "Many runners feel compelled to keep track of how long it takes to go from here to there, and as Type A personalities, they're uptight and under too

Phrase

much stress. They definitely need to learn to exercise just for sheer pleasure."

Rephrasing

The perfect place to experience such a refreshing change is the swimming pool. A cool, clear pool becomes the perfect think tank—a refuge where you can improve your mental training without overworking your body. The water insulates and protects you from outside stimuli, allowing you to think without interruption.

From "Into the Think Tank" by Lynne Cox

You can also achieve coherence by using a series of closely related words or ideas. For example, in the following passage, the term *strange power* is used as a link for the terms *mystical ability, magic suggestiveness,* and *secret spring*.

Music, the great English novelist Joseph Conrad once wrote, has a "magic suggestiveness" that reaches "the secret spring of responsive emotions." Because it makes its way into the mind so forcefully through our senses, he implied, it has an almost mystical ability to transform us.

Relates to magic, secret, and mystical

You've undoubtedly experienced this strange power. Standing on a street corner, staring dejectedly at the ground, you heard a rock song on a passing car radio and had a fresh jolt of energy. . . .

From "Mind Bending Music" by Mark Teich

Grammar Note Using pronouns in place of nouns can be a way of improving coherence. However, they must be used cautiously. In the following sentences, notice that it is not clear which antecedent goes with which pronoun. The reader is not sure who supported a tax cut or who was finally elected.

Candidate O'Connor said the major issue in his race with Mr. Rivera was his position on taxes. He supported a tax cut while his opponent said additional tax revenue was needed. When the election returns were counted, it was clear that the voters favored his position, because he was elected.

Writing Activities Achieving Coherence

A Read the paragraphs below and on the next page. Use transitional devices to make a stronger link between the paragraphs.

It is a hot, humid day for the annual boat race at Montauk Bay. Spectators line the shore, eagerly awaiting the beginning of the race. Brightly colored sailboats jam the harbor. The captains and crews board their boats. They carefully survey their equipment. Sails are tightened, ropes are retied, knots are checked, and navigation equipment is logged in.

Boating accidents are often a result of not checking things on board or ignoring foul weather. It is important that rules are followed to ensure a safe race. Both the captain and crew should survey the equipment on board the ship in order to cover any possible problems.

B *Writing in Process* Write the body of the composition that you began in Part 1 of this chapter. Use the methods you have learned for achieving unity and coherence.

Part 4
Writing the Conclusion

In the conclusion, you tell the reader that the composition is coming to an end. You tie everything together clearly and present the last idea the reader will take away from the composition. The following sections describe three methods for writing conclusions.

Restate the Main Idea You can sometimes conclude by simply restating your composition's main idea, as in the following example.

Student Model

As you have seen, there has been a soccer "explosion" among youth in the United States over the past twenty years. Much of that explosion has been sparked by the efforts of the American Youth Soccer Organization.

Summarize the Ideas of the Body Paragraphs Similarly, you can summarize the information you used to support your main idea.

These hurricane safety rules can save your life. So remember, board up all windows and remove objects from the front and back yards. Stock up the house with canned foods, bottled water, a first-aid kit, a portable radio, a flashlight, batteries, and candles. Most important, stay inside. Do not go out at the first sign of calm: the hurricane might not be over. Listen to your radio to know when it's safe to venture outdoors.

Comment on the Information Given Sometimes, you may want to comment on the information you have presented. Be careful when you comment not to introduce unrelated ideas. In the following conclusion, the writer comments on the threat to polar bears.

Cooperation between the five circumpolar nations—the United States, Canada, Denmark (because of Greenland), Norway and the Soviet Union—has restored a fading population to a robust 20,000 to 40,000 bears. . . . The bear's future lies in an environment that can be thrown into severe imbalance. A slight warming resulting in a decrease of the ice cover would be catastrophic to the seals and bears. A more immediate threat might be an increase in energy exploration and development in the

Commentary   untapped Arctic. The ecosystem is fragile. So is the future of its lordly world citizen without continuing human aid.

From "Masters of the Ice" by Richard C. Davids

Revising

When you have written your conclusion, you can begin the final revisions of your composition. Usually, however, it is best to set the composition aside for awhile—to get some ''distance'' from it.

This break will give you a chance to reflect on what you have written, to consider your thoughts anew.

1. Have I included everything I wanted to? Have I taken out all the unnecessary or unrelated details?
2. Have I written an effective introduction, body, and conclusion?
3. Have I expressed each of my main ideas clearly and thoroughly?
4. Have I chosen an order that shows how my ideas are related?
5. Have I used transitions to link my ideas and paragraphs?

There are a number of ways to revise. You may use **self-editing, peer editing,** or **teacher conferences.** For more information about revising, see Chapter 4, pages 78–93.

Writing Activities *Writing a Conclusion*

A Decide which of the two following paragraphs is the weak conclusion and which is the strong conclusion. Explain your answer and rewrite the weak conclusion, explaining your changes.

1.   It is clear, then, that discontinuing our school newspaper would be a serious mistake, since the paper provides major benefits for both the school and the students. For the school, it provides a popular extracurricular activity to keep students constructively occupied. For the students, it provides valuable instruction in a variety of fields, including writing, photography, and typesetting. And perhaps most important, it gives students the satisfaction of seeing an excellent final product that they themselves created.

2.   Often, you do notice someone playing a radio on the bus. They might be playing rock music or classical. No matter what the type of music, many feel that playing a radio on the bus is inconsiderate.

B *Writing in Process* Write a conclusion to the composition you began in Part 1 of this chapter. Then, use the checklist on page 80 to revise the entire composition. After you have revised, proofread your composition using the checklist on this page. Finally, share your composition with classmates and get feedback on your writing.

Chapter 6
Application and Review

Here are three ways to practice your composition skills. The first activity is structured, the second activity lets you choose the topic, and the third activity uses quotations and photos to help you select a topic. Read the exercises and select one or more to work on.

A Writing Coherently Amusing incidents, such as Robert Wenger's dispute with a machine on page 132, often provide a wealth of material for compositions. Plan and write a composition that relates an amusing incident. Your **purpose** is to inform and entertain. Your **audience** is an auditorium of students.

Prewriting With a partner, brainstorm to create a list of amusing incidents. You may want to skim some magazines and newspapers or listen to the evening news. Choose one incident and freewrite about it for five minutes. Next, determine the details you will present and the best form of organization. Then, write an outline.

Drafting Using your outline, write a first draft. As you write be aware of leading your reader from one point to another in a logical manner. Use paragraph links and transitions to connect ideas.

Revising Use the checklist on page 137 to help you revise. When you revise, consider these questions: Will my introduction catch the reader's interest? Does it state the main idea and develop it? Will my form of organization make sense? Have I chosen the right conclusion? Then, proofread using the checklist on page 82.

B Using Order of Importance for Coherence Use the following guidelines to write an order-of-importance composition.

Prewriting Brainstorm for topics that might make interesting order-of-importance compositions. For example, you might choose why you are looking forward to learning to drive. Then use a thinking technique such as charting, analyzing, or classifying to determine the relative importance of the different details you are going to present.

Drafting and Revising Write your first draft and share it with another student. Ask the student to use the checklist on page 137 to peer edit your draft. Use the student's comments as you revise.

c *Starting Points for Writing* What do the pictures and Springboards below make you wonder about? Focus on one picture. What in that picture grabs your attention? What else in it is of interest to you? Brainstorm or freewrite about your answers to these questions to develop a list of topics for writing.

New Shoes for H,
Don Eddy, 1973–74.

*"They were learning to draw,"
the Dormouse went on, yawning
and rubbing its eyes, for it was
getting very sleepy, "and they
drew all manner of things—everything that begins with an M—"*

*"Why with an M?" said
Alice.*

*"Why not?" said the March
Hare.*

Lewis Carroll

Springboards

- a disturbing event I witnessed
- something I did at the last minute
- the last television program I watched

7

Developing Sentence Style

*I*f you're like most people, you probably mix and match the clothes you wear instead of always wearing them in the same combinations. In this way you create a variety of outfits that suit your different moods and purposes.

Writers engage in a similar activity for much the same reasons. They mix and match sentence parts to lend variety to their writing, to create certain moods, and to achieve specific purposes.

In this chapter you will learn how to combine related sentences, adding or eliminating words and phrases, to become a more effective writer.

Part 1
Combining Sentences and Sentence Parts

The sentences you write in a first draft may be short ones, each containing a single idea. Although some short sentences are effective, too many may result in dull, choppy writing. When you revise, one way to add interest and variety to your writing is by combining related sentences and sentence parts. Combined sentences will sound smoother, and show your reader the relationship between ideas.

Combining Sentences

Two sentences of equal importance may express similar ideas, contrasting ideas, or a choice between ideas. These sentences may be combined by using different conjunctions. A **conjunction** is a word that connects words or groups of words.

For similar ideas, use a comma and the conjunction *and*.

> Jupiter is the largest planet.
> Pluto is the smallest planet.
> Jupiter is the largest planet, **and** Pluto is the smallest.

Sentences with similar ideas can also be joined by a semicolon.

> The storm will pass today.
> Tonight will be calm.
> The storm will pass today; tonight will be calm.

For contrasting ideas, use a comma and the conjunction *but*.

> Sue can play many instruments.
> Tom plays only the guitar.
> Sue can play many instruments, **but** Tom plays only the guitar.

For a choice between ideas, use a comma and the conjunction *or*.

> We could take the train to the park.
> Instead, my mom could drive.
> We could take the train to the park, **or** my mom could drive.

Grammar Note When sentences of equal importance are combined into a single statement, they form a **compound sentence**. For more information about compound sentences, see page 662.

Combining Sentence Parts

Two sentences may express such closely related ideas that words are repeated in the sentences. Often, you can combine these sentences into one sentence by eliminating the repeated words.

For similar ideas, use *and* (italicized words are eliminated).

> Geologists study the structure of the earth. *They also study the* composition *of the earth*.
> Geologists study the structure **and** composition of the earth.

For contrasting ideas, use *but*.

> Golf requires skill. *Golf also* involves luck.
> Golf requires skill **but** involves luck.

For a choice between ideas, use *or*.

> Pilots manually control an airplane. *They also* use an automatic pilot.
> Pilots manually control an airplane **or** use an automatic pilot.

By eliminating the repeated words, the sentence parts can be combined with a conjunction. No comma is necessary.

In the following examples, notice the differences between combining sentences and combining sentence parts.

Combining Sentences   They could rent a good movie, or they could sunbathe at the beach.

Combining Parts   They could rent a good movie or sunbathe at the beach.

Writing Activities Combining Ideas

A Combine each pair of sentences. Use the word given in parentheses and eliminate the words in italics.

1. Daniel Boone explored the Kentucky wilderness. *Daniel Boone* searched for Indian trails. (*and*)
2. Reptiles are numerous in the tropics. Many *reptiles* live in colder climates. (*but*)
3. Tonight's concert has been cancelled. Refunds will be available tomorrow. (;)
4. Mammals may lay eggs. *Some mammals* bear live young. (*or*)
5. Texas had been claimed for Spain in the early 1500's. It remained unoccupied by Spaniards for almost two centuries. (*but*)

B Rewrite the following passage, using the combining techniques in the lesson. Eliminate the words in italics and combine the sentences that are enclosed in parentheses.

(Hot-air balloons are used for sport ballooning. Gas balloons *are also used for sport ballooning*.) (Balloonists participate in races. *They participate in* rallies. *They also* drift over the countryside.)

(Sport balloons are considered easy to operate. Balloonists must pay attention to weather conditions, *however*.) (Balloonists should ascend in the early morning. *It is also good to balloon in the* late afternoon.)

Part 2
Adding Words to Sentences

Sometimes two sentences contain related ideas that are not equally important. When you revise, you discover that a single word in one of the sentences could add significant meaning to the main idea in the other sentence. By adding that one word, you will create a more effective and concise sentence.

Inserting Words Without Change

You may be able to add words to another sentence without changing the form of the words. Place the words close to the person, thing, or action they describe.

The girls saw a boat on the lake. *It was* gliding *on the lake*.
The girls saw a boat **gliding** on the lake.

He was in an exuberant *mood*. His mood was contagious.
His **exuberant** mood was contagious.

Sarah paddled the canoe to the other shore. *She paddled the canoe* quickly.
Sarah **quickly** paddled the canoe to the other shore.

You may be able to combine more than two sentences when one sentence carries the main idea and each of the other sentences adds only one important detail. Sometimes when you add more than one word to a sentence, you will have to use a comma or the word *and*.

The critics enjoyed the film. *The critics are* hard-to-please. *It was a* foreign *film*.
The **hard-to-please** critics enjoyed the **foreign** film.

The skis were strapped to the top of the car. *The skis were* long. *The car was* compact.
The **long** skis were strapped to the top of the **compact** car.

The dog had black fur. *His* teeth *were* sharp and pointy.
The dog had black fur and **sharp, pointy** teeth.

Inserting Words with Change

Occasionally, a word must be changed before you can add it to another sentence. The most common change is adding an ending such as *-y*, *-ed*, *-ing*, or *-ly*. Words ending in *-ly* can be placed in various positions in sentences.

Her hair was covered by a scarf. *She had* brown curls.
Her brown **curly** hair was covered by a scarf.

Pour the cake batter into the pan. Butter *the pan*.
Pour the cake batter into the **buttered** pan.

We walked under the willow trees. *The willow trees* swayed.
We walked under the **swaying** willow trees.

He painted the house with a wide brush. *He was* careful.
He **carefully** painted the house with a wide brush.
He painted the house **carefully** with a wide brush.

Writing Activities Adding Words

A Combine each group of sentences. In sentences *1–5*, use the directions in parentheses and eliminate the words in italics. In sentences *6–10*, decide on your own how to join the sentences. Remember, you may need to change the form of a word.

1. The ruby sparkled in the light. *The ruby* glistened. (Use *-ing*.)
2. "Thank you," Margaret said, smiling. *Margaret's smile was* bright. (Use *-ly*.)
3. Al walked across the porch. *The porch* creaked. (Use *-y*.)
4. The ancient map was etched in stone. *The ancient map had many* details. (Use *-ed*.)
5. The animal looked hungry. *The animal was* large. *She was in a* playful *mood*. (Use a *comma*.)
6. The sculptor molds the clay. The clay is soft. The sculptor is old.

7. A police officer caught the thief running from the scene of the crime. The officer wore a uniform.
8. The musicians practiced in the recording studio. They were famous. They practiced all day.
9. I can run on any track. I can run swiftly. I can run easily.
10. The shopkeeper surveyed her store. Her expression was proud.

B Rewrite the following passage, eliminating the words in italics and combining the sentences in parentheses. Only use connecting words or add an ending: -y, -ed, -ing, or -ly.

(Music takes many forms. *It also* reflects various ways of life.) (At first, music existed only as voice sounds. *These sounds were* simple and natural.)

(Eventually, people made music with objects. *There were* many different *objects*.) (The ancient Egyptians clapped sticks together. *They clapped in a* rhythmical *pattern. They also* jingled metal rods.) (The early Chinese played an instrument called the zither. *This instrument was* interesting.) (It had forty strings stretched across a board. *The strings were stretched* tight.)

(*The ancient Greeks* used the alphabet for musical tones. *They were* creative.) (The Romans copied Greek music. *They also* invented an instrument called the tuba.) (The musicians in India used formulas called ragas. *The formulas were* complex.)

Inserting Word Groups

Sometimes when making revisions, you recognize that a group of words from one sentence can be added to another. By combining these sentences, you will be able to create stronger, more accurate sentences.

Inserting Groups of Words Without Changes

Sometimes you can add a group of words to another sentence without changing their form. Place the words near the person, thing, or action they describe. When the words add information to the entire main idea, place them at either the beginning or end of the sentence.

> The clowns were amusing. *The clowns were* in the miniature car.
> The clowns **in the miniature car** were amusing.

> The board members hold a meeting. *This happens* every Friday.
> **Every Friday**, the board members hold a meeting.

You can add a word group from one sentence that simply renames one or more words in another sentence. A group of words that renames a noun is called an **appositive phrase.**

> The Rocky Mountains form the Continental Divide. *The Rocky Mountains are* the largest mountain system in North America.
> The Rocky Mountains, **the largest mountain system in North America**, form the Continental Divide.

> Franklin D. Roosevelt established a program called the New Deal. *He was* the only President elected four times.
> Franklin D. Roosevelt, **the only President elected four times**, established a program called the New Deal.

> The Civil War took many American lives. *The Civil War is* often called the War Between the States.
> The Civil War, **often called the War Between the States**, took many American lives.

Punctuation Note Set off appositive phrases with a comma or a set of commas. For more information about **appositives** and how to punctuate them, see pages 622–624.

Inserting Groups of Words with -ing or -ed

When you add a group of words to a sentence, you may have to change the form of one of the words by adding *-ing* or *-ed*. Sometimes, more than one group of words can be added to a sentence.

The face of the cliff scared the climber. *The cliff's face* sloped dangerously.
The **dangerously sloping** face of the cliff scared the climber.

The swim meet is at Meadowbrook Pool. *The meet is* next on the schedule.
The **next scheduled** swim meet is at Meadowbrook Pool.

Several oak trees remain. *They* surround the home's perimeter.
Several oak trees remain **surrounding the home's perimeter.**

A cloud of dust blew over the valley. *It* arrived at dawn. *The dust* covered the area.
A cloud of dust blew over the valley **at dawn, covering** the area.

Writing Activities Adding Word Groups

A Combine the following sentences. In sentences *1–5*, eliminate the words in italics. Additional clues are provided in parentheses. In sentences *6–10*, decide on your own how to combine the sentences.

1. The detour signs are posted every twenty-five miles. *The signs are posted* along Route 91.
2. The construction crew worked steadily. *They* stopped only for a quick break. (Use *-ing*.)
3. The artifacts were kept in glass displays. *The displays were* tightly secure. (Use *-ed*.)
4. Alexander the Great was king of Macedonia. *He was* one of the greatest generals in history. (Use commas.)
5. Rescue workers combed through the piles of debris. *They* looked for survivors. (Use *-ing* and commas.)
6. An architect designed the new capitol building. The building is on Jefferson Avenue. He designed it in memory of Senator Deaver.
7. The author has written several historical novels. The author is often called the literary genius of her decade.
8. The telegram was from Anita Sanchez. She is a defense attorney.
9. The store contains antique furniture and glass. The furniture and glass date back to the nineteenth century.
10. At the end of the hall is a metal door. It leads to a secret chamber.

B Rewrite the following passage, eliminating the words in italics and combining the sentences in parentheses. You will have to separate some groups of words with commas, or you may have to add *-ing* or *-ed* to a word in the group.

(Baseball has an interesting history. *Baseball is* one of the most popular sports in the United States.) (Some people claim that baseball evolved from another game. *This game was* called rounders.)

(The British played rounders. *They played it* as early as the 1600's.) (American colonists played it. *They played* in New England. *They played* in the 1700's.)

(Rounders was different from baseball. *Rounders was* a game of hitting a ball with a bat and advancing around the bases.) (Soaking took the place of tagging the runner. *Soaking was* the technique of throwing the ball at the runner.) (Americans changed this practice. *They changed this* into tagging the runner.)

Part 4
Combining with Who, Which, *and* That

When you revise, you may find that you have repeated ideas needlessly. You may have presented an idea in one sentence and given details about that person, place, or thing in the following sentence. You can avoid unnecessary repetition by combining these two sentences into one longer sentence.

Inserting Word Groups with Who

Use the word *who* to add information about a person or group of persons.

The student received a grant. *She wanted to study genetics.*
The student **who** wanted to study genetics received a grant.

Marie Curie won the Nobel Prize for chemistry. *She* founded the Radium Institute in Paris.
Marie Curie, **who** founded the Radium Institute in Paris, won the Nobel Prize for chemistry.

In the first example, the added words tell which student received a research grant. Because the added words are essential to the meaning of the sentence, no comma is needed. In the second example, the added words supply additional information that is unnecessary to the meaning. Therefore, the added words are set off with commas.

Inserting Word Groups with That or Which

That or *which* can also be used to add word groups.

Here is a machine. *The machine* helps patients breathe.
Here is a machine **that** helps patients breathe.

Political campaigns need volunteers. Political campaigns are
    very exciting.
Political campaigns, **which** are very exciting, need volunteers.

In the first example, the added words are necessary to the main idea of the sentence; therefore, *that* is used. In the second example, the information is not necessary to the sentence; therefore, *which* is used and commas set off the word group.

Writing Activities Combining with Who, Which, *and* That

A Combine each pair of sentences. In sentences *1–5*, eliminate the words in italics and follow the clues in parentheses. In sentences *6–10*, decide on your own whether to use *who, which,* or *that.*

1. This computer uses floppy disks. *This computer* is used for word processing. (Use *which* and commas.)
2. Nancy suggested the theme for the homecoming float. *Nancy* was the president of the student council. (Use *who* and commas.)
3. This is the puppy. I told you about *him* yesterday. (Use *that.*)
4. The awards program originated in Los Angeles. *The program* aired in over 2 million households. (Use *which* and commas.)
5. The comedian made the audience laugh hysterically. *She* was on several television specials. (Use *who* and commas.)
6. I need the key for my safety deposit box. The key is in my purse.
7. The jewels were sold at the auction. They were Mrs. Wang's.
8. Senators supported the bill. Senators represented my state.
9. The plane landed safely. The plane had encountered turbulence.
10. The manager retired the pitcher in the seventh inning. The manager had coached the team for twenty years.

Shots from *Raiders of the Lost Ark.*

B Rewrite the following passage. Eliminate the words in italics and combine the sentences in parentheses. Use *who, that,* or *which,* with or without commas.

(Film uses an immense vocabulary of images. *It is* a form of communication.) (Film communication starts with the shot. *The shot* is film's basic unit.)

(Directors talk to their audience through the use of shots. *The directors* are in charge of all aspects of production.) (V. I. Pudovkin wanted directors to observe things, then show them. He was an early Russian film director.)

(Directors can spend hours preparing for a shot. *This shot* may only be seen for a few seconds.) (Yet, a series of shots can make a scene memorable. *These shots* are carefully planned.)

(A director must select an angle. *This angle* has a particular perspective.) (The long shot is one perspective. *A long shot* includes the entire area of action.) (The long shot can present an overview to the viewer. *The long shot* was the only shot in the early days of film.) (The medium shot is another alternative. The director often chooses *this alternative*.) (The usual distance for a shot is the medium shot. *It* can be described as an intermediate shot between the long shot and the close-up.) (The close-up shot is an effective tool. Directors often use *this tool* to display emotion.)

Part 5
Combining with When, Because, *and* Although

You may discover, as you revise, that the ideas in two sentences are related in a specific way. One sentence may provide more important information than the other sentence. You can combine these sentences by subordinating the less important information in one sentence to the information in the other sentence. The combining word you choose will show the relationship that exists between the ideas.

Showing Relationships

When you combine two sentences, you can employ the word *when* to show time, the word *because* to show why something happened, and the word *although* to explain under what conditions something occurred. In the following examples, notice how the combining word that was chosen shows the connection between the two ideas.

> The soldiers stood at attention. The flag was raised high above the army base.
> The soldiers stood at attention **when** the flag was raised high above the army base.

> The farmers quickly harvested their orange crops. The frost had come early this year.
> The farmers quickly harvested their orange crops **because** the frost had come early this year.

> Jerry enjoyed the New York Philharmonic's performance. He usually attends rock concerts.
> Jerry enjoyed the New York Philharmonic's performance **although** he usually attends rock concerts.

There are often times when the subordinate idea may be placed at the beginning of the sentence, followed by a comma.

> **Although** Jerry usually attends rock concerts, he enjoyed the New York Philharmonic's performance.

Grammar Note The word groups subordinated to explain when, why, and under what conditions are called **subordinate clauses.** For more information about subordinate clauses, see pages 647–670.

Here are some other words that can express relationships of time, cause, and condition.

Words to Introduce Subordinate Clauses		
When	**Why**	**Conditions**
after	as	considering (that)
until	for	whether (or not)
while	since	unless

Writing Activities *Subordinating Ideas*

A Combine the following sentences. In sentences *1–5*, follow the directions enclosed in parentheses. In sentences *6–10*, decide on your own whether to use *when, because,* or *although.*

1. Barbara walked home. Her brother offered to drive her. (Use *although.*)
2. The play was postponed. The star broke his leg. (Use *because.*)
3. Alonzo ignored Tanya's comments. She teased him. (Use *when.*)
4. The students listened quietly. Juan told the class about his three-week trip to Europe. (Use *when.*)
5. Children are receptive to computers. They learn about them at an early age. (Use *because.*)
6. Jim is a good athlete. He isn't as good as a professional.
7. The crowd at the stadium was enormous. The football game was the first of the season.
8. I enjoyed tutoring chemistry. It took a great deal of my time.
9. The police officer called for back-up help. She heard a gunshot.
10. Everyone wants tickets. The show comes to town only once a year.

B Rewrite the following passage. Combine the sentences enclosed in parentheses. Use *when, because,* and *although.*

(Photography offers a wide variety of career opportunities. Many events and people need to be visually documented.) (Commercial photography is one of the most popular fields for the prospective photographer. Many other fields present career opportunities.) (Commercial photographers take pictures for advertisements. They work with varied subject matter.) (Commercial photographers must be skilled and imaginative. They are creating memorable images.) (Portrait photographers pose their subjects. People often feel awkward about posing.) (Photojournalists may work for only one newspaper or magazine. Some work for and sell their photographs to various publications.) (Scientific photographers must be specialists in their particular field. They work with highly complex subject matter.)

C Revise the following passage, using what you have learned about combining sentences in Parts 1 through 5.

The Maya developed an extraordinary civilization in Central America. The Maya were an American Indian people. The Maya civilization reached its peak about A.D. 300. It continued to flourish for almost 600 years. The Maya made advances in astronomy. The advances were outstanding. They also developed an accurate calendar.

Entire Maya families lived together in one domicile. This included parents, children, and grandparents. The Maya did not have schools. The children learned by observing and helping adults.

Maya farmers raised beans, corn, and squash. Maya farmers lived in rural homes or small villages. The farmers cleared their fields during the harvest. They used stone axes.

Part 6
Avoiding Empty Sentences

Sentence combining is only one way to improve the quality and variety of your sentences. You may find that some sentences in your draft merely repeat an idea already presented. Other sentences might make a statement but fail to support it by a fact, a reason, or an example. These sentences are called **empty sentences.** In this part, you will discover several ways of revising empty sentences.

Repeating an Idea

When revising your writing, eliminate repetitive ideas by combining or omitting sentences. Notice the repetition in these examples:

Faulty   The unemployment rate was high in the city, and many people were out of work. (Because the ideas of *unemployment* and *out of work* are similar, only one is necessary. Omit the second clause.)

Revised   The unemployment rate was high in the city.

Faulty   The sun's rays beat down on the people at the beach. They were hot under the sun's rays. (Omit the second sentence. It simply repeats the idea.)

Revised   The sun's rays beat down on the people at the beach.

Faulty   On Tuesday our class is going on a field trip. Our class is going to the art museum. We can go on the field trip only if the bus is working. There are fifteen students in our class. (Combine sentences and related ideas.)

Revised   If the bus is working on Tuesday, our class of fifteen students is going on a field trip to the art museum.

Making Unsupported Statements

When statements are not supported by reasons, facts, or examples, empty sentences may result. Can you find the unsupported statement in this paragraph? Look for the statement that makes you wonder *why*.

New York City is the largest city in the United States and the sixth largest in the world. It is one of the most important centers of business, trade, and culture. New York has many serious problems.

There is a great deal to know about New York City, but you might not share the writer's opinion about New York having problems. The writer should add one or more examples to justify the opinion.

When you revise, look for unsupported statements that can be strengthened by adding reasons, facts, or examples. Including the following examples, for instance, helps support the writer's opinion.

> I think New York City has many serious problems, such as air pollution, crime, and unemployment.

Writing Activities *Revising Empty Sentences*

A Revise the following sentences. Eliminate the repeated ideas or combine them in new sentences. There is no single "correct" answer.

1. Many bicyclists are interested in the *Tour de France* because it is an interesting race.
2. The pit bull knew I was afraid of him. He could sense my fear.
3. Diane was unjustifiably rude to her friends. She was rude for no reason. She thought she was superior.
4. If you have ever been to Yellowstone Park, you know what a wonderful time you can have there. This park is a place to visit often. At Yellowstone Park, there is always something enjoyable.
5. Have you ever been to a crowded concert? If you haven't been to a crowded concert, you don't know what it is like to see a concert with 10,000 people.
6. You can't watch a movie without eating popcorn. It is impossible to watch a movie without eating popcorn.
7. On Saturday, we are going hiking. I am sure it will be a good hike if the park is not crowded. There are five of us going hiking and everyone wants a good climb.
8. In our school, you have to wait in a long line to get your books. In the line you might pick up a math or an English book. To get any of your books, you have to stand in line in the science wing.
9. I was curious to know if she had received a phone call. I asked her if she had heard from Helen.
10. The cast laughed at my fear. They laughed because the idea of being afraid to perform was funny to them.

B Revise the following statements by adding necessary reasons, facts, or examples. You may need to do some research.

1. Newspapers inform the public on current national and local events. Newspapers have advantages over television newscasts.

2. The ocean is a great body of water that covers 70 percent of the earth's surface. The ocean is a dangerous force.
3. Opera is a drama in which the characters sing instead of speaking their lines. Opera is a complex art form.
4. Neptune is one of the two planets that cannot be seen without a telescope. Scientists do not know much about its surface.
5. I want to buy a car this year. It would cost as much money as I have in my savings account although I am still working at my part-time job. My parents do not approve of the idea.
6. The Environmental Protection Agency regulates the air pollution produced by factories. This is a good procedure.
7. Many city dwellers may object to a thunderstorm or rainshower, but rain is a necessity for all life. Too much rain, however, is not good for the environment.
8. The Red Cross is an organization that works to relieve human suffering. Its services are widespread.
9. According to federal law, you have to be eighteen years old before you can vote. This law is unfair and should be changed.
10. The Renaissance was a time period of human achievements and growth. It was the most important time period in history.

Part 7
Avoiding Overloaded Sentences

When you revise, look for overloaded sentences. An overloaded sentence contains a number of main ideas connected loosely by the word *and*. The reader has to sort out these ideas and may have difficulty seeing how they are related. Break up these ideas into separate thoughts. The use of transition words or other combining techniques will help show the relationship between ideas.

Lengthy   Juan walked up the steps of the deserted house, and then he turned the knob on the front door, and he heard voices.

Revised   Juan walked up the steps of the deserted house. When he turned the knob on the front door, he heard voices.

Lengthy   I saw a lightning bolt in the sky, and the sky was grey, and then I heard a clap of thunder and it frightened me.

Revised   I saw a lightning bolt in the grey sky. Then, I heard a frightening clap of thunder.

Lengthy	The hot-air balloons glided over the town, and their bright colors filled the sky, and people came out of their homes to watch the balloons as they passed overhead.
Revised	The hot-air balloons glided over the town, filling the sky with bright colors. As the balloons passed overhead, people came out of their homes to watch.

Writing Activities *Overloaded Sentences*

A Revise the following sentences. Remember these points:

• Separate each sentence into two or more shorter sentences.
• Reduce the number of *and*'s.
• Try to show a logical connection between ideas. Use words such as *when, then, as, but, with,* and *because.*

1. The tourists went to the Louvre Museum, and they saw the *Mona Lisa,* and later they saw the Eiffel Tower, and they took several photographs of the structure.
2. I went to the annual art fair, and I purchased some paintings, and the paintings were oils, and then I bought some sculptures.
3. Ana auditioned for the play, and she read a monologue from *Romeo and Juliet,* and then she sang a song from *West Side Story*.
4. The turtles crawled down the bank to the pond, and they waded into the water, and they stuck their heads in their shells.
5. I went to the game at Busch Stadium, and I sat behind home plate, and the Cardinals beat the Mets, and the score was 9 to 0.
6. The house looked very old, and it needed a paint job, and the shutters needed to be replaced, and I wondered how the house looked before it needed so much repair.
7. For the costume party, Carlos dressed as Count Dracula, Susie dressed as Queen Elizabeth, and Matthew came as an astronaut, but everyone liked Bill's Charlie Chaplin outfit the best.
8. Andy got a part-time job, and he works at the stadium, and he sells souvenirs, and he's saving for a new ten-speed bicycle.
9. Mom lost her car keys, and we searched the entire house for them, and they finally showed up in her coat pocket, and she was very grateful we had found them.
10. The karate instructor demonstrated the basic maneuvers, and the maneuvers were very precise and difficult to execute, and then she showed her students how to block their opponents' moves.
11. The music department offers orchestra classes, and next year there will be a jazz-band class, and many students are interested.

12. The camp was nestled in the Pocono Mountains, and it offered the campers water-skiing, and they could also go on canoe trips.
13. Randi bowled the highest game, and she had six strikes and no gutter balls, and she did well and she used her own bowling ball.
14. Pedro learned how to windsurf, and he felt he needed a wet suit, and then he could surf in cold water, and he could surf for hours.
15. The Congress has the power to legislate, and it has the power to make laws, and the Congress works on a committee system, and the committees prepare most of the legislation.

B Revise the following passage by separating overloaded sentences. Use transition words and combining techniques to show the relationship between ideas.

Archaeology is the study of ancient buildings and objects, and archaeology is also a way of discovering the past. Archaeologists are like detectives solving a mystery, and they find an object, and they treat it as a clue, and the clue helps them discover information about the ancient civilization. Archaeologists rely on scientific aids, and the aids are often aerial photographs, and the photographs may show traces of buried structures. After a site has been found, archaeologists might pass an electric current through the ground, and then they can measure the ground's moisture, and this measurement will help determine if ancient buildings remain.

Left: Gold coin, late 7th century B.C.
Right: Sphinx, Giza, Egypt.

Part 8
Avoiding Padded Sentences

A **padded sentence** contains unnecessary words or phrases. Although a padded sentence may be grammatically correct, its wordiness keeps the reader from following the ideas in the sentence. One type of sentence padding consists of extra words that simply repeat an idea such as *the fact that* and *the point is*. Another type of padding consists of whole groups of words that could be reduced to shorter phrases without influencing the ideas involved. As you revise your writing, remove the padding and shorten wordy expressions.

Taking Out Extra Words

The following expressions contain extra words that merely repeat ideas. Next to each example is a simpler way of saying the same thing.

"Fact" Expressions	Reduced
because of the fact that	because, since
on account of the fact that	because, since
in spite of the fact that	although

"What" Expressions	Reduced
what I want is	I want
what I mean is	(Just say it!)
what I want to say is	(Just say it!)

Other Expressions to Avoid

the point is	the thing is	it happens that
the reason is	being that	it would seem that

Sentences are clearer and less wordy when you avoid the types of sentence padding shown in the following examples:

Padded   Pat hasn't been to school because *of the fact that* she has a bad cold.

Revised   Pat hasn't been to school because she has a bad cold.

Padded   *The thing is* Yuki wants to go to the ballpark instead of the beach.

Revised   Yuki wants to go to the ballpark instead of the beach.

Padded   *What I mean is* that I have time to finish the project.

Revised   I have time to finish the project.

Reducing Clauses to Phrases

Frequently, clauses beginning with *who is, that is,* or *which is* can be simplified to phrases. Review the following examples.

Lengthy   Skydiving, *which is often considered a dangerous sport,* requires specific training and equipment.

Revised   Skydiving, often considered a dangerous sport, requires specific training and equipment.

Lengthy   The statue *that is in the plaza* towers over the capitol building.

Revised   The statue in the plaza towers over the capitol building.

Lengthy   Phil Collins, *who is the lead singer in the band Genesis,* also performs and produces solo material.

Revised   Phil Collins, the lead singer in the band Genesis, also performs and produces solo material.

Writing Activities Padded Sentences

A Revise each sentence. Omit extra words that do not contribute to the meaning of the sentence. Look for *who, that,* and *which* word groups that can be simplified.

1. It just so happens that the football game at Central High has been cancelled for tonight and rescheduled for tomorrow.
2. What I want to do is finish this article and submit it to *Life* magazine for the September issue.
3. Congresswoman Connor, who is a member of the National Security Committee, submitted a report on defense spending.
4. Dion left the reception early on account of the fact that she had another party to attend.
5. Being that the trial was held in Washington, D.C., the press coverage was unusually heavy.
6. The Guggenheim Museum, which is located in New York City, houses an impressive collection of paintings and sculptures.
7. Due to the fact that the rain was heavy, we had to pull the car to the side of the road.
8. The state track meet, which was the most important sporting event of the year, attracted talent scouts from universities.
9. What I think is that if you don't believe in your own abilities, no one will.
10. Her latest book, which is about rising to the top of the literary world, is included in this semester's curriculum.

B Revise the following passage. Omit extra words that repeat ideas and look for *who, that,* or *which* word groups that can be simplified.

This year, what I decided to do was travel around the United States. First, I went to St. Louis, which is the "Gateway to the West," to start my trip. From there, I went to Memphis because of the fact that I have some cousins living there. My first cousin, who is an avid traveler, had many suggestions for my trip. He said I had to see the Grand Canyon being that it was one of the world's most awesome sights.

C Revise the following passage. Use what you have learned about combining and improving sentences in Parts 1 through 8.

The Statue of Liberty has always been a symbol of American freedom. It was dedicated by France in 1884.

The statue depicts a woman in a loose robe. She is a proud woman. Her right arm holds a torch. Her left arm grasps a tablet. This tablet bears the date of the Declaration of Independence.

The statue is the most important example of repoussé work. Repoussé work is a process of hammering metal over a mold. Alexandre Gustave Eiffel built the supporting framework. He designed the Eiffel Tower. The statue was shipped from France, and it was placed in 214 cases. It was shipped in pieces on account of the fact that it was so large.

Restoration of the Statue of Liberty, 1986.
© 1985 Peter B. Kaplan

LANGUAGE LORE
Place Names

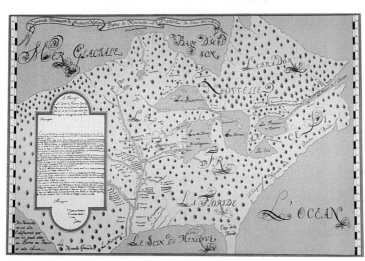

Joliet's map of New France, 1674.

The explorers of the New World learned many place names from the Native Americans. However, the paths those names have followed in becoming a part of the language have sometimes been as twisted as the trails followed by the explorers.

The seventeenth-century French explorers Jacques Marquette and Louis Joliet traveled up and down the Mississippi River to places we now call *Wisconsin, Des Moines, Peoria, Missouri, Omaha, Wabash,* and *Kansas*. However, some of these names bear little resemblance to the names Marquette and Joliet first heard. *Wisconsin,* for example, comes from a Native American word of uncertain meaning, *Mesconsing*. To the Frenchmen, it sounded like "Ouisconsing," and that is how they wrote it down. The English changed it to its present form, since the French word sounded like "Wisconsin" to them.

Des Moines followed an even more twisted path. Marquette and Joliet found a tribe called the Moingouena living on a river in what we now know as Iowa. The Frenchmen named the river after the tribe, Riviere des Moingouenas, and later shortened it to Riviere des Moings. *Moings,* however, is similar to the French word *moines,* which means "monks." Over time, their discovery came to be called *des Moines,* which means "of the monks." The names of the city and river Des Moines have nothing to do with monks. The name is simply the result of the jumbled influences of the past.

Chapter 7
Application and Review

A Combining Sentences Combine the following sentences, using the combining techniques you learned in Parts 1 through 5.

1. The project deadline cannot be extended another day. You can use more students to help you with the research.
2. The babies enjoyed crawling around the backyard. The babies were playful. The backyard was enclosed.
3. Dan quickly ran to the store. He realized he was out of food.
4. The basketball player dribbled the ball down the court. He dribbled the ball aggressively down the court.
5. Firefighters combed through the rubble. They tried to find the cause of the blaze.
6. Barbra Streisand sings beautiful ballads. She is considered one of the most talented vocalists.
7. Taking the train to work is tiresome. It is better than driving.
8. This is the painting from the students' art gallery. I told you about it yesterday.
9. The Lake of the Ozarks has a long shoreline. The lake is always teeming with summer vacationers.
10. The heat wave will subside this weekend. The heat wave has lasted a full week. A cold front will bring cooler temperatures.

B Improving Sentences Revise the following sentences which are empty, overloaded, or padded.

1. Manuel cannot attend the play on account of the fact that he has to baby-sit his younger sister.
2. The World's Fair was filled with exhibits, and the exhibits were fascinating, and visitors toured the exhibits, and the visitors were from all over the world.
3. The gusty winds blew the shingles off the roof. The winds damaged the house, and everyone had to be evacuated.
4. The animals that are housed in the neighborhood shelter need medical care and special attention, and then they need someone who will adopt them and take them home.
5. In spite of the fact that Glenda had every right to move out of the apartment, she was still responsible for the lease, and she had to move her furniture out, and she had to clean.

C Revise the following passages, using these techniques:

- Combine sentences and parts of sentences.
- Add words and groups of words to sentences.
- Use *who, which,* and *that* to combine sentences.
- Combine or condense empty sentences.
- Separate overloaded sentences.
- Remove the stuffing from padded sentences.

1. Scuba diving is a popular way to explore beneath the surface of the ocean. Scuba diving is the act of diving with the aid of air tanks. Recreational divers take underwater photographs. They also collect tropical fish. Professional divers perform important tasks under water. They repair ships, recover objects, and build structures. Divers use equipment to perform their tasks, and the equipment is extensive, and the divers must be skilled and trained in how to use their equipment properly.

2. William Shakespeare understood human nature better than any other artist. He is considered the greatest dramatist in history. He could create unforgettable characters. These characters had universal qualities. Shakespeare wrote numerous plays. He wrote at least thirty-seven dramas. He had a great influence on culture on account of the fact that he helped the development of the English language. Shakespeare invented words such as *assassination* and *lonely.* These words are common.

3. Sculpture is the most interesting form of art. A sculpture can be small enough to stand on a table. It can be as large as the Statue of Liberty. Sculpture often has a monumental quality. It frequently expresses noble ideas. Sculptures were created 30,000 years ago. These were the oldest known sculptures. Prehistoric humans carved small amulets, and the amulets were called charms, and they also carved idols from bone. Modeled objects are called sculpture in spite of the fact that they are not actually cut from materials.

4. The modern Olympics were organized to encourage peace. They were also organized to promote friendship among all nations of the world. The Olympic symbol represents this desire for global cooperation. The symbol consists of five interlocking rings. In the past, there has been a great deal of controversy and criticism of the games. Many countries have boycotted the Olympics. They boycotted to express political protest. The United States led a boycott of the 1980 Summer Olympics in Moscow on account of the fact that the Soviet Union invaded Afghanistan in late 1979.

8

Using Description in Writing

I am driving; it is dusk; Minnesota.
The stubble field catches the last growth of sun.
The soybeans are breathing on all sides.
Old men are sitting before their houses on carseats
In the small towns. I am happy,
The moon rising above the turkey sheds.

Robert Bly

*T*he poet Robert Bly and the photographer Tom Nelson have each conveyed their own personal vision of rural Minnesota. To do this each captured significant details that convey a sense of the place and its people.

In this chapter you will learn to recognize and use significant details to communicate your impressions of places and people vividly and effectively.

Part 1

Using Descriptive Writing

The difference between poor descriptive writing and good descriptive writing is like the difference between a wall and a window. When you read poor descriptive writing, the page becomes a wall of flat and meaningless words. No matter how hard you try, you can't see through the wall, and you can't climb over it. When you read good descriptive writing, the page turns into a window that allows you to see all the things the writer describes. If the descriptive writing is particularly good, you can open the window and walk into a world on the other side of the page.

Here are two models of effective descriptive writing. One is by a student, and one is by an experienced writer for a travel magazine. Notice how descriptive writing makes each of the models come alive.

▬ *Student Model*

To my surprise, the family reunion I thought would be so dull took on the atmosphere of a carnival. Old Uncle Al, usually so stern and pale, stood beaming with his arm around his tall, lively brother. The silly, old-fashioned strains of a folk song blasted from someone's radio, and a few people broke into a jig that they made up as they went along. Laughter bubbled out of small groups and mixed with the greetings of long-lost cousins and sisters and friends of the family. I nearly got the air squished out of me by an exuberant aunt who was glad to see me. Almost immediately after I arrived, the air was soaked with the sweet smell of roasting corn and potatoes.

Discussing the Model Now talk about these questions with your classmates.

1. What is the first thing you learn about the scene?
2. What words and phrases in the paragraph above help you imagine the scene as a carnival?
3. Which senses does the writing appeal to? Which sense is appealed to most often?
4. Which words and phrases help you understand how the writer feels?

It is early morning. A friend and I, bundled against the spring chill, stand near the bow of our great ship as it slides across the mirror of waters in southeast Alaska's Glacier Bay. The vessel is stately and slow as a limousine, easing among blocks of ice, engines slowed to a throaty rumble. Suddenly, we catch sight of a pod of seals sleeping peacefully on a gently bobbing iceberg. Moments later they hear, or sense, our approach, and unhurried and unafraid, they roll off the ice and splash into the water, snuffling and snorting in the morning sun.

From "Passage to Alaska" by Georgia I. Hesse

Discussing the Model Now discuss answers to these questions with your classmates.

1. What is your impression of Glacier Bay, after reading the paragraph? What words and phrases help create that impression?
2. Which senses does this writer appeal to? What words and phrases leave the most lasting impression? Why?
3. Where do you imagine the writer of the model is standing as she describes the scene?
4. What do you think was the author's intention in writing this paragraph? In what instances do you think she achieved her goal?

Understanding Descriptive Writing

The authors of both of the models above used descriptive writing to make a scene come alive. Both writers used the same techniques. They figured out their purpose in writing and decided upon a mood they wanted to create. Then they gathered precise details and organized them to support their purpose and mood. Finally, both writers appealed to the senses. They added colorful figurative language to enliven the scenes they described. Their descriptions helped involve you in the scene you read about.

Description in Literature The following story of events on a distant planet includes a number of striking descriptions. As you read the selection, notice the mood the writer creates and the way in which the description is organized. Look for the imaginative words and phrases that surprise you and help to make the descriptions memorable.

Description in Literature

from *Dragondrums*
Anne McCaffrey

The inhabitants of the planet Pern periodically combat a destructive rain of "threads" that fall from deep space. They combat the rains while mounted on dragons. Riders and dragons have a mystical, telepathic relationship that begins the day a dragon hatches and chooses its human companion. As you read this passage, notice how McCaffrey makes an unreal world seem real through precise and vivid description.

Strong impression noted

A blur of white, seen from the corner of his eye, drew Piemur's attention to the Hatching Ground entrance. The candidates were approaching the eggs, their white tunics fluttering in the light morning breeze. Piemur suppressed his amusement as the boys, stepping further on

Sense of touch introduced

the hot sands, began to pick up their feet smartly. When they had reached the clutch, they ranged themselves in a loose semicircle about the gently rocking eggs. . . .

A startled murmur ran through the audience as one of the eggs rocked more violently. The sudden snapping of the shell seemed to resound through the high-ceilinged

Sense of hearing introduced

cavern, and the dragons on the upper ledges hummed more loudly than ever with encouragement. The actual Hatching had begun. Piemur didn't know where to look because the audience was as fascinating as the Hatching: dragonriders' faces with soft glows as they relived the magic moment when they had Impressed the hatchling dragon who became their life's companion, minds indissolubly linked. . . .

Figurative language

Abruptly an egg split open, and a moist little brown dragon was spilled to his feet on the hot sands. Dragging his fragile-looking damp wings on the ground, he began to lunge this way and that, calling piteously, while the adult dragons crooned encouragement, . . .

Specific detail

*T*he boys nearest the dragonet tried to anticipate his direction, hoping to Impress him, but he lurched out of their immediate circle, staggering across the sands, his call plaintive, desperate until the next group of boys turned. One, prompted by some instinct, took a step forward. The little brown's cries turned joyous, he tried to extend his wet wings to bridge the distance between them, but the boy rushed to the dragon's side, caressing head and shoulders, patting the damp wings while the little hatchling crooned with triumph, his jeweled eyes glowing the blue and purple of love and devotion. The day's first Impression had been made! . . .

Figurative language

The excitement was over too soon, Piemur thought, just moments later. He wished that all the eggs hadn't hatched at once, so this dizzy happiness could be extended. . . . Not that there wasn't some disappointment and sadness, too, because far more candidates were presented to the eggs than could Impress. Only one little green had not Impressed, and she was mewling unhappily, butting one boy out of her way, lurching to another and peering up into his face, obviously searching for just the right lad. She had worked her way toward the tiers, despite the efforts of the remaining candidates to attract her attention and keep her well out into the Ground. . . .

Details supporting description

"**S**he's going to hurt herself," said Mirrim in an agitated mutter and pushed past the three people seated between her and the stairs. "She'll bruise her wings on the walls."

The little green did hurt herself, slipping off the first step and banging her muzzle so sharply on the stone that she let out a cry of pain, . . .

"Now, listen here, you silly thing, the boys you want are out there on the Ground. Turn yourself around and go back to them," Mirrim was saying as she made her way down the steps to the little green. Her fire lizards, calling out in wildly ecstatic buglings, halted her. She stared for a long moment at the antics of her friends, and then, her expression incredulous, she looked down at the green hatchling determinedly attacking the obstacle of steps. "I can't!" Mirrim cried, so panic-stricken that she slipped on the steps herself and slid down three before her flailing hands found support. "I can't!" Mirrim glanced about her for confirmation. "I'm not supposed to Impress. I'm not a candidate. She can't want me!" Awe washed over the consternation on her face and in her voice.

"If it's you she wants, Mirrim, get down there before she hurts herself!" said F'lar, . . .

With one final startled look at her Weyrleaders, Mirrim half-slid the remaining steps, cushioning the little green's chin from yet another harsh contact with the stone of the step.

"Oh, you silly darling! Whatever made you choose me?" Mirrim said in a loving voice as she gathered the green into her arms and began to soothe the hatchling's distressed cries. "She says her name is Path!"

Trying Out Descriptive Writing Now that you have read some examples of descriptive writing, try writing some descriptions of your own in your journal. Look at the things that surround you every day. How can you describe them so that others can imagine them? What sense words can you use?

After writing, think about which descriptions were the most lively and interesting. Why did they work well? What was most memorable? What would you do differently if you were to revise your descriptions? The rest of the chapter will teach you more techniques for writing lively, effective descriptions.

Part 2

Planning a Description

No matter what kind of writing you plan to do, description will play an important role. In order to be effective, descriptions must be carefully planned. This process involves three major steps: choosing a focus, discovering details, and organizing the description.

Choosing a Focus

When you focus on something, you bring it into clear view. A description can cover a vast scene, such as a view from a mountaintop, or it can concentrate on a single object, such as a strand of hair or a dalmation's spots. By focusing your thoughts on subject, purpose, and mood, you can make your descriptions clear no matter how vast or limited their scope.

To begin with, decide what subject you want to describe. Then define your purpose in describing that subject. Finally, figure out what sort of mood you want your description to create. For example, if you plan to explain how to build a model of an atom, your purpose is to communicate instructions. Your mood will be businesslike, and your descriptions will probably be factual to suit your purpose. On the other hand, if you are writing about the wonderful surprise party your best friend planned for you, your purpose might be to entertain or impress your reader. You will probably choose a lighter mood and include more sensory details and figurative language.

Discovering Details

To make your descriptions effective, show your readers how things look, sound, smell, taste, or feel. (See Chapter 1 for a discussion of sensory images.) How you collect and combine the details depends on the kind of description you plan to write.

Observation If you plan to describe something that you can observe, then you need to study it closely and discover its details.

Memory If you plan to describe something you observed in the past, you can collect the details from memory. First construct a mental image of your subject. Then study the mental image just as if it were something real.

Imagination Use a similar technique when describing something that exists only in your imagination. Create a strong mental image and study it closely. Add as many details as you want.

Here is a model of a fully imagined and wonderfully described imaginary world. As you read the passage, notice how the many different details contribute to your impression of the creature.

Literary Model

Modifiers making the creature specific

Deep down here by the dark water lived old Gollum, a small slimy creature. I don't know where he came from, nor who or what he was. He was Gollum—as dark as darkness, except for two big round pale eyes in his thin face. He had a little boat, and he rowed about quite quietly on the lake; for lake it was, wide and deep and deadly cold. He paddled it with large feet dangling over the side, but never a ripple did he make. Not he. He was looking out of his pale lamp-like eyes for blind fish, which he grabbed with his long fingers as quick as thinking. He liked meat too. Goblin he thought good, when he could get it; but he took care they never found him out. He just throttled them from behind, if they ever came down alone anywhere near the edge of the water, while he was prowling about. They very seldom did, for they had a feeling that something unpleasant was lurking down there, down at the very roots of the mountain.

Sensory words making the image clear

From *The Hobbit* by J.R.R. Tolkien

No matter how you observe details, you will need to record them in some way. You can list the details as you become aware of them, or you can create categories—sight, sound, and smell, for example—and classify the details accordingly. Whichever method you choose, list as many details as you can. Later, you can always combine or discard some of the things you recorded.

Organizing a Description

After you have collected sensory details through observation or memory, you will need to organize them so that you can create a clear, well-ordered impression instead of a jumbled one. The method of organization you choose should depend on the subject, purpose, and mood of your essay or story.

Spatial Order If your purpose is to present objective facts, you would want your description to convey a neutral and scientific mood. One way to organize an objective description is to arrange the details in spatial order. If you wanted to describe the front of a house, for example, you could stand on a spot in front of the house and describe what you see as your eyes move up from the basement to the roof. Such a description would be in bottom-to-top order. If your purpose is to describe a dog for an objective report, your description might move from front to back, beginning with the dog's face, moving to its body, and ending with its tail. Other orders might include left-to-right, inside-to-outside, and near-to-far. Of course, each of these orders can be reversed.

Read the model below to find out how one writer used spatial order to create a clear picture of the Mississippi River. Notice how the order affects your impression of the scene.

▬ *Literary Model* ▬

Far-to-near order

I still kept in mind a wonderful sunset which I witnessed when steamboating was new to me. A broad expanse of the river was turned to blood; in the middle distance the red hue brightened into gold, through which a solitary log came floating, black and conspicuous; in one place a long, slanting mark lay sparkling upon the water; in another the surface was broken by boiling, tumbling rings, that were as many-tinted as an opal.

From *Life on the Mississippi* by Mark Twain

In writing a spatial order description, it is important to remember that you, the observer, are viewing the subject from a particular point in space—the spot in front of the house, for example. The point in space you choose to start from is called your point of view. The simplest spatial-order descriptions are written from a single point of view. You can, of course, change your point of view during the description— by moving to the back of the house, for example—but you must make sure that your reader is aware of the change. Whatever your point of view, choose a logical starting point and make it clear to your reader.

Order of Impression Another way to organize a description is to show your changing impressions of the subject—your order of impression. In describing a football player, for example, you might start with the details that first grab your attention, such as a loud voice or bulging muscles, and then move on to the details that you notice later, such as his eyes or his helmet. A description organized by order of impression often conveys a strong feeling, rather than a sense of neutrality.

The following model was organized by order of impression, beginning with the mood that the writer felt. What do you think was Rachel Carson's purpose in using order of impression? How do you think the writer's choice of order affected the mood of the paragraph? Did the mood of the writer change, or did all the details included support a single impression?

Literary Model

Mood established first

The flats took on a mysterious quality as dusk approached and the last evening light was reflected from the scattered pools and creeks. Then birds became only dark shadows, with no color discernible. Sanderlings scurried along the beach like little ghosts, and here and there the darker forms of willets stood out. Often I could come very close to them before they would start up in alarm— the sanderlings running, the willets flying up, crying.

Details adding to the sense of mystery

Black skimmers flew along the ocean's edge silhouetted against the dull, metallic gleam, or they went flitting above the sand like large, dimly seen moths. Sometimes they "skimmed" the winding creeks of tidal water, where little spreading surface ripples marked the presence of small fish.

From *The Edge of the Sea* by Rachel Carson

Order of Importance Yet another method of organization is to arrange the details by their order of importance. If you were writing to describe a difficult situation, for example, you might begin by describing the biggest, most demanding obstacles.

The model below shows how one writer used order of importance to put the reader in the place of one of his characters. Notice how the writer presents the most significant fact first and then goes on to less important details.

Literary Model

Most important fact first

As Gregor Samsa awoke one morning from uneasy dreams he found himself transformed in his bed into a gigantic insect. He was lying on his hard, as it were armor-plated, back and when he lifted his head a little he could see his dome-like brown belly divided into stiff arched segments on top of which the bed quilt could hardly keep in position and was about to slide off completely. His numerous legs, which were pitifully thin compared to the rest of his bulk, waved helplessly before his eyes.

From *The Metamorphosis* by Franz Kafka

The Employee Cloak, Melissa Grimes, 1984.

In general, spatial-order descriptions are the most objective descriptions. Order-of-impression and order-of-importance descriptions are more often used to create subjective moods or to support an opinion. You can use these methods of organizing details to support the purpose you choose for your writing and to help create a mood.

Grammar Note Modifiers such as adjectives or prepositional phrases are important to any descriptive paragraph. Unclear modifiers, however, can result in confusing, strange, or even humorous statements. Careful placement of modifiers can help create vivid impressions and ensure clear writing. For more information about misplaced modifiers see pages 620–621.

Misplaced Modifier	The man spoke loudly with the red hat.
Improved Placement	The man with the red hat spoke loudly.
Misplaced Modifier	Donna watched her playful kitten finishing her homework.
Improved Placement	Having finished her homework, Donna watched her playful kitten.

Writing Activities *Planning a Description*

A Tell whether you would use spatial order, order of impression, or order of importance to write the following descriptions. Explain your answers.

1. You want to write an ad that describes a new sports car you hope to buy.
2. You are writing a story and want to describe a puzzling character.
3. You want to recover your wallet from a lost-and-found.
4. You have just visited a palace in France, and you want to write a letter home that describes the place.
5. You are a newspaper reporter and need to describe a forest fire.
6. You want to describe to a repair clerk the kinds of problems that you are having with your cassette player.

B *Writing in Process* Find or imagine a place or event that you would like to describe. Focus on your purpose for writing the description and determine the mood you want to create. Then collect sensory details by carefully observing the place or creating a strong mental image. Finally, choose a method for organizing your description and write an outline of the description. Save the outline you create for a later activity.

Part 3

Drafting a Description

In planning a description, you have chosen a focus, discovered details, and selected a method of organization. These steps will lead to the unity, coherence, and emphasis of your final description.

A description has **unity** if it creates a single, unified impression. Well-defined moods and carefully chosen details can lead to unity. A description has **coherence** if its parts fit together logically to create a clear picture. Finally, a description has **emphasis** if it centers on a particular point of interest.

Any time you describe a subject, you are confronted with a mass of sensory details. In order to make your subject come alive, use only the details that create a single, unified impression.

Choosing Details to Achieve Unity

In describing a classic car, for example, you might brainstorm to develop a list of details about the car. Then you would eliminate the details that don't fit the impression you want to create.

Observable Details About the Car

glistening red hood	old-style steering wheel
rusty tailpipe	chrome-plated hood ornament
reflective chrome	worn upholstery
gleaming, clean hubcaps	precise pinstriping

Descriptive Language

The power and unity of your description come not only from the details that you include but also from the words that you use to describe those details.

Which of the following descriptions conveys a matter-of-fact mood? Which is more poetic?

> The sleek, gleaming, classic car glowed as red as an apple just ripe for picking.
>
> The long, low car from the 1960's was deep red and very shiny.

Literal Language Literal language is straightforward and matter-of-fact: the words mean what they say. "His hair was red" is an example of literal language, because the words mean exactly what they say. Most descriptions include some literal language, and literal words and phrases are especially useful in factual, objective reports.

One of the problems with literal language is that there are only a limited number of descriptive words. You can describe a taste, for example, as sweet, sour, bitter, spicy, or salty, but then you start running out of words. In contrast, figurative language allows you to make an infinite number of comparisons.

Figurative Language Words that are poetic and imaginative are figurative words. They carry meanings beyond their literal definition. "Her hair was like coal" is an example of figurative language: the sentence implies that her hair resembles coal in some way, perhaps because both are black. Using figurative language, you can compare a tough steak to an old raincoat, a glass of water to a cloud, or a full moon to a silver coin.

At the top of the next page is part of a story written by a student. Read the model and think about which literal and descriptive words helped you to imagine the scene more clearly.

Writing **Inside Out**

Sandra Cisneros, Writer and Teacher

Sandra Cisneros is a writer and a teacher whose first book of fiction, *The House on Mango Street* (Arte Publico Press), won the 1985 American Book Award. It is based on her life growing up in Chicago's Mexican community. Ms. Cisneros, who has also published two books of poetry, now lives in Chico, California. We talked to her about her work.

Q Why is it important for you to write?
A I write to explore and discover things about myself. For me writing is also a form of surviving, of conquering life. No matter what happens, even something very sad, I can write about it and create something positive. Even when I'm in the middle of an argument I think, this is wonderful. I could use this in a story!

The river looked inviting at the place where it met the shore. It was cool and fresh, and the water tasted almost sweet. The currents made gurgling sounds as the water jumped and skipped like a cat over the rocks. When Joe began wading, however, his opinion changed. The currents had incredible strength. They tossed Joe to his knees. He held on to a nearby boulder while his hat tumbled downstream.

Types of Figurative Language

Among the most common types of figurative language are similes, metaphors, and personifications.

Similes make a comparison and use the words *like* or *as*. "His hands are like leather" and "Her voice was as irritating as a fingernail scratched across a chalkboard" are examples of similes.

Metaphors make a comparison without using the words *like* or *as*. Sometimes they imply comparisons without stating them directly. "Her eyes were beacons" and "He weaseled out of the job" are both metaphors.

Q How do you write a story?
A My stories often start with a person or thing that haunts me from my past. Good gossip also gives me ideas, or even a title I see floating on the side of a truck. I will wonder about the idea for a while and then start writing. Once I put the first line down and get the rhythm, I know what should come next.

Q Do you rewrite?
A Oh, yes. The first time I just accept anything that comes to mind. That's the most fun part, just dumping everything out of your brain and seeing what comes out. It isn't even a draft. It's very raw. After that I polish.

Q Your writing has a wonderful sound to it. How do you do this?
A I'm always conscious of listening to what I write. Poetry has been good training for this. I love words. I hover over language. I listen to the way people say things, the way they arrange words.

Q Your writing is so descriptive. How are you able to accomplish that?
A I try to use all the senses when I write. I like to compare things to something else. I open a jar of vanilla or smell a magnolia and think, what does this scent remind me of? I'm always transforming anything that's happening in my life into language.

Personifications are metaphors that give human qualities to non-human objects. "The tree shivered in the wind" and "The engine groaned" are both personifications. The first example compares a shaking tree to a shivering person; the second compares an engine noise to a human groan.

Some examples of figurative language are used so frequently that they become worn-out phrases called **clichés.** "He eats like a bird" and "She's busy as a bee" are clichés. It's best to avoid using clichés because they no longer bring sharp images to a reader's mind. Therefore, they make your writing sound trite and dull.

You can use both literal and figurative language in most descriptions. If you are writing an objective, spatial-order description, you will probably want to use mostly literal language. If you are writing a subjective, order-of-impression description, you might want to use mostly figurative language.

Writing Activities *Drafting a Description*

A Make a list of eight details about the picture shown below. For each of the eight details you have noted, write a simile, metaphor, or personification.

B *Writing in Process* Draft a description based on the outline you wrote for Activity B on page 178. Strive for a description that has unity, coherence, and emphasis. Choose your details carefully and use precise words. Try to use figurative language. Save your description for a later activity.

Part 4
Revising and Proofreading a Description

Once you complete your first draft, you will need to make a careful revision. One part of the revision process is to go back over the steps that led to your description and see how well you performed each step. For example, have you included the important details and decided on a coherent method of organization?

Another part of the process is to make your description more specific. Replace vague words with specific ones, as shown in the sentence that follows.

The ~~beautiful bird~~ *spectacular parrot* was ~~covered~~ *decorated* with ~~colored~~ *bright red, green, and yellow* feathers.

A peer evaluator can also play an important role in the revision process by serving as your first audience. Find someone who is willing to read your description and offer suggestions. Both of you might want to consult the following revision checklist.

Revision Checklist for Descriptive Writing

Purpose
1. Is the purpose of the description clear?
2. Does the description create a single mood or impression?
3. Is the subject of the description clear?

Organization
1. Is the description clearly organized?
2. Does the description have a consistent point of view?
3. Does each detail contribute to the mood?

Language
1. Does the description use precise words?
2. Is the figurative language appropriate and imaginative?
3. Does the description lack clichés and tired phrases?
4. Are modifiers next to the words or phrases they modify?

A student revised the following description of her little sister with the help of a peer evaluator.

If you smile at her, she smiles too, *happily* showing
you her *toothless* gums. She'll even make soft *gurgling* noises and
~~move~~ *flail* her arms *up and down like a scarecrow*. But just when you think you have
~~appealed to her~~ *won her heart*, she repeats the show for her
stuffed ~~animal~~ *dinosaur* inside of her playpen.

The last step in the revision process is to proofread your revised draft. Use the Proofreading Checklist on page 82. Then make a clean copy, and share it with an audience.

Writing Activities Peer Evaluation

A For this activity, you will act as the peer evaluator for a fellow student. Exchange first drafts with a classmate. Then use the following guidelines to evaluate your fellow student's description.

Guidelines for Peer Evaluators

- Use the Revision Checklist on page 183 to evaluate the description in terms of its purpose, organization, and language.
- Determine what you like best about the description. Does it create a strong impression? What do you find appealing?
- Note your specific suggested changes on the page. Add general comments in the margins or on another sheet of paper.
- Remember, your job is to make positive suggestions. If you think part of the description is weak, suggest an improvement.

B *Writing in Process* Revise your description based on your peer evaluator's comments and the Revision Checklist on page 183. Proofread your draft using the Proofreading Checklist in Chapter 4 before making a final copy on a clean sheet of paper.

Part 5
Other Uses of Descriptive Writing

Virtually all types of writing make use of description at some point. Some types of writing include entire paragraphs of description, while other types use only occasional descriptive words, phrases, and sentences.

As you have learned, your use of description depends on your overall purpose for writing. If you are writing a report on woodland animals, for example, you will probably want to include carefully detailed descriptions of the animals. If you are writing a recipe for pancakes, on the other hand, you probably won't need to include any lengthy descriptions, because your readers will be interested mainly in clear, specific instructions.

The following chart lists some of the uses of descriptive writing. The chart shows the type of writing and a possible purpose for the writing. The last column gives an example of how that type of writing might use description.

Uses of Descriptive Writing

Type	Purpose	Example
Fiction	To create vivid characters	Imaginative description of a story character
Report	To show what subject looks like	Straightforward description of the set for *The Wiz*
Ad	To attract buyers	Glowing description of a new car
Editorial	To affect opinion	Compelling description of an endangered bird
Manual	To give useful instructions	Illustrated description of panel on tape recorder
Textbook	To teach facts	Evocative, factual description of clothing in other countries

The following models describe the same animal—a porcupine. The first example is from an encyclopedia; the second is a poem. Read the examples carefully and compare their descriptive language. (By the way, the poem contains two words you may not know. *Bast* is a material on the stems of plants and *phloem* is plant tissue.)

▬ *Professional Model*

One of the larger rodents, the porcupine is 2 to 3 feet long and weighs from 7 to 40 pounds. Its name is derived from the French for "spiny pig." The large, chunky body has a high-arching back and the legs are short. The body is covered with long hairs in the front, and sharp quills are on the rump and tail.

From *The Encyclopedia of North American Wildlife*

▬ *Literary Model*

Fatted
on herbs, swollen on crabapples
puffed up on bast and phloem, ballooned
on willow flowers, poplar catkins, first
leafs of aspen and larch,
the porcupine
drags and bounces his last meal through ice,
mud, roses and goldenrod, into the stubbly high
fields.

From "The Porcupine" by Galway Kinnell

The encyclopedia gives an objective picture of the porcupine; the poem emphasizes the porcupine's exotic diet and its comical motion. In each case, the description is suited to the writer's purpose.

Writing Activities *Uses of Descriptive Writing*

A Find examples of descriptions from two different types of writing, such as advertisements, textbooks, short stories, or technical manuals.

B Review the types of descriptive writing listed on the preceding page. Pick at least two types of descriptive writing and write a description for each type, following the procedures in this chapter.

Guidelines: *Descriptive Writing*

Planning
- Focus on your subject, purpose, and mood. Figure out what you want to describe and why. Then determine the mood or impression you want to create. (*See pages 173–176.*)
- Discover details. Use observation, memory, or imagination to determine your subject's sensory details. Record the details in a list or a chart. (*See page 174.*)
- Organize the description. Decide which method is best suited to your purpose—spatial order, order of impression, or order of importance. Then arrange the details accordingly. (*See pages 175–178.*)

Drafting
- Concentrate on those details that create a unified mood or impression. (*See pages 179–180.*)
- Use words that are precise and meaningful. (*See pages 179–181.*)
- Try to maintain a consistent point of view. (*See page 179.*)
- Use literal or figurative language according to your purpose. If you use figurative language, avoid clichés and try to make imaginative use of similes and metaphors. (*See pages 180–181.*)

Revising
- Go back over each step and look for better ways to support your purpose and mood. (*See pages 183–184.*)
- Replace vague words with specific ones. (*See pages 183–184.*)
- Use the Revision Checklist on page 183 to evaluate the purpose, organization, and language of your description.
- Have a peer evaluator read your description and offer comments. Then make changes based on your peer evaluator's comments. (*See pages 183–184.*)

Proofreading
- Use the Proofreading Checklist on page 82 to check your grammar and spelling.
- Make a final copy of the description on a clean sheet of paper.

Chapter 8
Application and Review

Now you can use your knowledge about descriptive writing in a variety of creative assignments. Read the instructions below. Then choose one or more assignments and use your imagination and knowledge to write lively, interesting descriptions.

A Describing from the Imagination Pretend that you are a traveler who has discovered an unmapped island in the Pacific Ocean. Apparently, no one has ever recorded any information about this island and its inhabitants. Your purpose is to provide an accurate description of the island's inhabitants. Use the following guidelines as you write about your discovery.

Prewriting Imagine the people who live on the island. How do they look? What language do they speak? What do they eat? Add details to create a clear image of these people. Then organize the details and outline the description.

Drafting Using your outline, write a first draft. Try to use exact words. Use figurative language where appropriate. Remember that your draft should have unity, coherence, and emphasis.

Revising Use the Revision Checklist on page 183 to help you revise your first draft. Exchange your description with a peer evaluator, and consider his or her comments as you revise. After revising, proofread (using the Proofreading Checklist on page 82) and prepare a final copy for your newspaper.

B Describing an Object Use the guidelines below to plan and write a description of an object.

Prewriting Carefully observe the objects that you encounter during a particular day and select one that interests you, such as a car, a tree, a building, or a work of art. Note the object's sensory details—its look, smell, taste, sound, and feel—and the mood you want to create. Organize a description of the object.

Drafting and Revising Use your notes to write a first draft. Try to use precise words and figurative language. Then revise your draft and share it with someone.

c *Starting Points for Writing* Look at the pictures below. Focus on the details in them. Imagine something or someone suggested by one of the Springboards below, or picture the person described in the song lyrics, also noting details. Then think about the larger scene in which each subject is set. Finally, freewrite to describe one of these subjects and its setting.

In the all night cafe at a quarter past eleven, same old man sitting there on his own, looking at the world over the rim of his teacup, each tea lasts an hour, and he wanders home alone.

Ralph McTell

Springboards
- something you wish you could do
- someone who gave you bad advice
- your least favorite place

9

Writing a Personal Narrative

What stories are suggested to you by the photos on these pages? Have you ever done anything as challenging or exciting as climbing a mountain? If so, you have probably told many wonderful stories about the dangers and triumphs of your adventure. Certainly you have stories to tell about more everyday challenges—obstacles you overcame, deadlines you almost missed because of crazy circumstances, or difficult things you learned to do.

Narrative writing is writing that tells a story. In this chapter you will learn how to use your writing skills to create your own personal narratives.

Part 1
Analyzing Narrative Writing

Writing that tells a story is called **narrative writing.** Narrative is used in history books and in biographies, in short stories and in novels. Newspaper reporters use narrative to tell what happened at the town meeting or to review the ninth inning of last night's baseball game. Narrative writing answers the question, What happened?

Here are two examples of narrative writing. The first is a personal narrative written by a student named Julio. The second is part of a magazine article about wildlife conservation. Notice that both narratives describe an event.

Student Model

One day after school, Dad stopped me with a question. "Late again, Julio? Not in trouble, are you?"

"Uh . . . no, Dad, nothing like that."

I wasn't sure why I didn't tell him about the judo classes. My sister asked me about it later. "I don't know, Laurie. Maybe it's because of Mike. Dad's so proud of his football-star son."

"Well, sure he is. Remember, football was Dad's big thing in school, and it still is. Even so, I think you ought to tell him what you're doing."

But I didn't. I certainly didn't tell him Saturday would be our annual judo demonstration day. But when Saturday came, and it was my turn to go out on the mat, there was Dad in the front row. I almost tripped on the mat.

My routine went well, though, and afterwards Dad was waiting at the locker room door. "So that's what you've been up to," he said, grinning. I could tell he was pleased. "That was great! But why the big secret, Julio?"

"You know what, Dad?" I said. "I have no idea."

Discussing the Model Think about Julio's story and discuss these questions with your classmates.

1. Who is this narrative about? Who is telling the story?
2. What is the problem, or conflict, in the narrative?
3. How is the problem solved?

As dawn arrives in California, Thomas O'Farrell is racing the sunrise to check the live animal traps he set the night before. The wildlife biologist must work fast. Daytime temperatures can soar over 100 degrees during the summer on the bone-dry uplands of the Elk Hills Naval Petroleum Reserve southwest of Bakersfield, and he can't afford the risk of his prey—the San Joaquin kit fox—getting heatstroke. The endangered animal already has enough problems as it is.

The biologist parks his truck near a gigantic mechanical grasshopper—an oil pump. . . . Since O'Farrell began work here seven years ago as part of an ambitious effort to save the kit fox, he has made important new discoveries about the unusual animal that are helping to protect it.

Grabbing an armful of equipment, O'Farrell trots into the saltbush where a small, wire-mesh trap sits draped in canvas. He kneels beside it and slowly lifts the corner of the tarp. As he looks inside, a tiny vixen no bigger than a house cat peers back.

From "Desert Fox" by Dwight Holing

Discussing the Model Now think about the narrative you just read, and discuss these questions with your classmates.

1. Who is the narrative about? Who is telling the story?
2. Where and when does the narrative take place?
3. What happens in the narrative?
4. How is this narrative like the first one? How is it different?

Understanding Narrative Writing

The narratives you read were written for different purposes, but they each have three elements common to all narratives. They relate a sequence of events, the **plot**. The events involve people, the **characters**. The events happen in a certain time and place, the **setting**.

Narration in Literature A **personal narrative** like Julio's tells about something that happens to the writer. In the following personal narrative we come to know the writer through his actions. After you read it, you will learn how to plan and write a personal narrative.

Narration in Literature

from "Three Poems and an Essay"
Pablo Neruda

There is an ancient belief about swans that has given us the expression "swan song." In this story by a Chilean poet, the narrator discovers something about swans and about that ancient belief.

Beginning of plot

I'll tell you a story about birds. On Lake Budi some years ago, they were hunting down the swans without mercy. The procedure was to approach them stealthily in little boats and then rapidly—very rapidly—row into their midst. Swans like albatrosses have difficulty in flying; they must skim the surface of the water at a run. In the first phase of their flight they raise their big wings with great effort. It is then that they can be seized; a few blows with a bludgeon finish them off.

Someone made me a present of a swan: more dead than alive. It was of a marvelous species I have never seen since anywhere else in the world: a black-throated swan—a snow boat with a neck packed, as it were, into a tight stocking of black silk. Orange-beaked, red-eyed.

Setting

This happened near the sea, in Puerto Saavedra . . .

They brought it to me half dead. I bathed its wounds and pressed little pellets of bread and fish into its throat; but nothing stayed down. Nevertheless the wounds slowly healed, and the swan came to regard me as a friend. At the same time, it was apparent to me that the bird was wasting away with nostalgia. So, cradling the heavy burden in my arms through the streets, I carried it down to the river. It paddled a few strokes, very close to me. I had hoped it might learn how to fish for itself, and pointed to some pebbles far below, where they flashed in the sand like the silvery fish of the South. The swan looked at them remotely, sad-eyed.

For the next twenty days or more, day after day, I carried the bird to the river and toiled back with it to my house. It was almost as large as I was. One afternoon it seemed more abstracted than usual, swimming very close and ignoring the lure of the insects with which I tried vainly to tempt it to fish again. It became very quiet; so I lifted it into my arms to carry it home again. It was breast-high, when I suddenly felt a great ribbon unfurl, like a black arm encircling my face: it was the big coil of the neck,

dropping down.

It was then that I learned swans do not sing at their death, if they die of grief.

Trying Out Narrative Writing Now that you have read some examples of narrative writing, use your journal to try some narrative writing of your own. Where will you find a writing idea? What kinds of details will you use to develop your idea? How will you organize your narrative?

After writing, think about what parts of the process worked well, what parts gave you trouble, and what you could do differently the next time. The rest of this chapter will teach you some additional techniques for writing more narratives of your own.

Part 2

Elements of Narrative Writing

Before you begin your own narrative, you must understand what a narrative is and how it can be used. Sometimes a piece of writing is wholly narrative —a short story, a novel, a fable. Narratives may also appear in other kinds of writing. An article about computers might begin with a story about how a new computer solved an old problem. A study of Canada geese might include a story about how some geese were tagged and followed.

Characteristics of a Narrative

In Part 1 you learned that a narrative contains characters, setting, and plot. How these are used depends on the writer's purpose. In a biography the emphasis may be on character; in a mystery story, plot.

The writer's purpose also determines the point of view, the "angle" from which the story is told. In **third-person point of view** the narrator—the voice telling the story—seems to know everything, including what the characters think and feel.

■ *Literary Model* ▬▬▬

They and *he* signal third person.

They were big boys—men, to Jerry. He dived, and they watched him; and when he swam around to take his place, they made way for him. He felt he was accepted and he dived again, carefully, proud of himself.

From "Through the Tunnel" by Doris Lessing

In **first-person point of view** the narrator is involved in the events.

■ *Literary Model* ▬▬▬

I signals first person.

One day I happened to spill water on my apron, and I spread it out to dry before the fire which was flickering on the sitting-room hearth. The apron did not dry quickly enough to suit me, so I drew nearer and threw it right over the hot ashes. The fire leaped into life, the flames encircled me so that in a moment my clothes were blazing.

From *The Story of My Life* by Helen Keller

Personal Narrative

A personal narrative tells about something that happened to the writer. It is written from the first-person point of view, and the narrator is often the main character. Because of the narrator's involvement in the story, a personal narrative does more than just describe the events. The narrator explains what the events mean. In the following personal narrative, James Herriot describes himself caught in a snowstorm on an English moor.

▬ *Literary Model*

I was convinced I had gone too far to the left and after a few gasping breaths, struck off to the right. It wasn't long before I knew I had gone in the wrong direction again. I began to fall into deep holes, up to the arm-pits in the snow reminding me that the ground was not really flat on these high moors but pitted by countless peat haggs [ground broken from digging] . . .

The numbing cold seemed to erase all sense of time. Soon I had no idea of how long I had been falling into the holes and crawling out. I did know that each time it was getting harder work dragging myself out. And it was becoming more and more tempting to sit down and rest, even sleep; there was something hypnotic in the way the big, soft flakes brushed noiselessly across my skin and mounted thickly on my closed eyes.

From *All Creatures Great and Small* by James Herriot

Herriot does more than describe the situation. By letting readers follow his thinking, he shows the danger of his circumstances—the effect of the cold on his strength and on his mind. He shows how the events lead to disbelief and to a feeling of panic. Readers share in his experience.

Writing Activity Finding Narratives

Find three examples of narrative writing. One of your examples should be a personal narrative. Articles in newspapers or news magazines, biographies, history books, and fiction of all sorts are good possibilities. You should be able to point out the elements that make each piece of writing a narrative. Share the examples you find with your classmates.

Part 3
Prewriting and Drafting

Writing a personal narrative is a chance for you to reflect on something that happened to you—something you think is important. Parts 3 and 4 will guide you in planning and writing a personal narrative.

Choosing a Topic

Look through your journal for an event that had meaning for you. Make a list of people who have been important to you, events that affected you deeply, times when you made tough decisions, situations that made you laugh, like the one shown in the picture below. These lists will suggest topics for a personal narrative.

The topic you choose should be clear enough in your memory that you can write about it in detail. It should be a story; that is, it should involve a sequence of events with a beginning, middle, and end. Most important of all, it should have meaning for you.

Purpose and Audience

Ask yourself who your readers will be. Your family? Your class? Why should others read your story? What can you say so that they can share in your experience? Will your tone be serious? Humorous?

Exploring the Topic

With a topic, a purpose, and an audience in mind, you can fill out the topic in depth. You need to think about the details you will include. The thinking and prewriting techniques in Chapters 2 and 3 will help you—especially clustering and freewriting. Here is how a student named Margo used freewriting to think about her topic.

One Student's Process

I learned a lot by entering the photo contest in the school paper—try to show "school spirit" in a photo. Tried posing cheerleaders. Took photo at auto graveyard. Some people didn't want me taking their picture. Finally, the picture I didn't plan to take.

Freewriting can help you get details on paper, but you still need to organize those details. Since most narratives follow a time sequence, you'll want to arrange your details in chronological order, or the order in which the events happen.

A personal narrative does more than just list events. It interprets them. That is, it shows what they mean to the narrator. Margo used her freewriting notes to make a Personal Narrative Worksheet. On it she listed the events and told how they made her feel. She ended with a controlling idea about the meaning of the whole experience.

One Student's Process

Personal Narrative Worksheet

Details	Responses
1. Read about contest.	Eager to enter.
2. Posed cheerleaders.	They goofed around.
3. Took "arty" picture at auto graveyard.	Felt like big-name photographer.
4. Took unposed photos around school.	People acted like I was a snoop.
5. Danny took picture.	I felt annoyed.
6. Developed the photos.	Danny's was best.

Controlling Idea: I learned two things: how to take a picture and what school spirit really is.

Writing a First Draft

The next step is to expand the items in the chart into a first draft. You may wonder how much you need to add. The answer is enough to *show* what happens. Use sense details to help your readers see, hear, smell, taste, and feel. Use dialogue to bring your characters to life. Use lively verbs to help your readers picture the action.

As you write, you will need to divide your narrative into paragraphs. The following chart shows how to do this.

When to Start a New Paragraph

1. A major change in the place
2. A major change in the time
3. A major shift in the action
4. A change of speaker in dialogue

Margo can see by looking at her Personal Narrative Worksheet that each numbered item marks a change of scene and action. Her narrative will, therefore, have at least six paragraphs.

While you are drafting, you will constantly move from describing events to explaining their meaning for you. As you conclude, you should state your overall impression of the experience and its meaning. The controlling purpose on your worksheet will help you write your concluding paragraph. Here is Margo's concluding paragraph.

One Student's Process

The only picture that was any good was the one Danny had taken. I'd been careful to set the camera right for him, focus the shot, and get the sun behind him. Danny had found an interesting scene. I learned two things from all this—one about photography and one about school spirit. To get a good picture, I can't just point a camera and push a button. I have to think about what I'm doing. And school spirit has less to do with pompons and cheerleading than with how people treat each other. I guess that's why when I won the prize in the photo contest, I gave it to Danny. After all, he took the winning picture.

Writing Activities Prewriting and Drafting

A Read the beginning of a personal narrative by a student named Mike. It should have three paragraphs, but it has only one. Be ready to explain where Mike should start two new paragraphs and why.

> It was 7:00 A.M. I had promised Jodie I'd pick her up at 7:30 and we'd go biking on the Prairie Path. The idea had sounded great the night before, but now I wasn't sure. I was still half asleep, but Jodie would be waiting, so I rolled out of bed. Ten minutes later I was downstairs searching the refrigerator for a slice of cold pizza. My brother Nate spotted me and asked, "Hey, what's going on? It's Saturday, and you're up before noon." "See you later," I mumbled, and escaped out the back door.

B *Writing in Process* Look at the photo above. Has anything funny ever happened to you? It might be something that didn't seem funny at the time—just embarrassing—but it seems funny now, from a distance.

Use freewriting to help you think of an event—funny, not so funny, maybe even sad—that you could write about in your own personal narrative. Consider your purpose and audience. Organize the events chronologically on a worksheet like the one on page 199, including your reactions and your controlling idea.

Use the completed worksheet as a guide in drafting a personal narrative. Describe each event fully. Don't just *tell* your story; *show* it. Use sense details, dialogue, and action to make your story live.

Save your work. You will be using it later.

Part 4
Revising and Proofreading

How well does your first draft say what you wanted to say? Look at what you have written from the point of view of your readers. You should provide enough information so that your readers can follow the story. For instance, if you do not explain how characters are related, your readers may not understand why they act as they do. Your writing needs to be clear to readers who do not know the story as you do.

It's possible, on the other hand, to include too much. If you said too much about a minor character, readers could be uncertain about the real purpose of your narrative. Part of revising is deciding what to cut out to make your story simple, direct, and understandable.

The checklist below will help you or a peer editor evaluate your first draft and will guide you in revising it. And the example on page 203 may help you see how you can go about revising your first draft.

Revision Checklist for Personal Narratives

Purpose
1. Do you make clear your purpose in writing the narrative?
2. Do you have your audience in mind throughout, so that your tone and vocabulary are consistent and appropriate?

Organization
1. Have you kept the narrative clear by dealing only with the events directly related to the main topic?
2. Do you tell your story chronologically? Do you use appropriate transition words and phrases?
3. Do you start a new paragraph for each major shift in time, place, and action, and for each new speaker?
4. Do you conclude by telling what meaning the events had for you?

Development
1. Do you describe the events fully, showing and not just telling?
2. Do you get into the action without a long introduction?
3. Does the tone of your writing fit the events?
4. Do you go beyond the events, explaining their meaning and their significance to you?

Many writers see their first draft as just a good beginning. The real work of writing, they say, is revision. Look at part of Margo's first draft and her revisions. Her thoughts, in the margins, show how she used some of her peer editor's suggestions.

One Student's Process

I've been interested in photography for a long time. ~~My uncle has about a dozen different cameras and a big darkroom.~~ So when I read about the photo contest in the school paper, I was excited. The contest was a good excuse to take some pictures, and the idea of the contest sounded interesting_submit a picture that shows real school spirit._

> Doesn't add anything.

> My peer editor said to explain contest idea.

The first thing I thought of was an action shot of the cheerleaders. I went to a practice session and asked them to pose. *It was frustrating.* They kept jumping around while I was shooting. I didn't have time to ~~get it~~ *focus the camera or check the light level or frame the shots.* ~~right~~.

The next day I decided I wanted to try taking something different, and I thought of using an auto graveyard as a background, *because* ~~I thought~~ it would be very artistic and suggest something deep. I took a few props with me *—a textbook, a school jacket, a pad of note paper, and some dark sunglasses.* I spent almost all day setting up shots.

> Include my response.

> My peer editor suggested more detail here.

> Use time transition.

> Show rather than tell.

Proofreading

The last step in revision is to proofread your work. Refer to the Proofreading Checklist on page 210 to remind yourself of the kinds of things to look for. In addition to these general guidelines, check to make sure you maintain a consistent point of view. Do not shift from first person to third person. Also, be sure to check verb tenses. If you start in the past, do not shift to the present.

Grammar Note Adverbs of time serve as transitions, connecting one part of the narrative to another and to the whole story. Notice how the writer has used adverbs of time to connect the ideas in the following excerpt.

> **Literary Model**
>
> When the two boys tired of fishing, they gathered shag bark and pine knots. *Then* they waited for a night when their uncle, the Moon, lay abed. *First* they set a clump of freshly picked branches in the dugout's bow . . .
>
> From *The Light in the Forest* by Conrad Richter

Writing Activities Peer Evaluation

A A peer editor made these comments about the following paragraph: "Use sense details" and "Include responses." Rewrite the paragraph, responding to the suggestions.

> When Elna got up that morning, it had been raining for several hours. The water filled the street and came up the driveways. Soon, children were outside splashing in the water. Some were riding their bikes in it. Some were floating down the street on a rubber raft. Parents stood in doorways, staring out. The water was still rising.

B *Writing in Process* Find an editing partner and exchange first drafts of your personal narrative. Evaluate your partner's paper as your partner evaluates your paper. Use the following guidelines to help you make your evaluation.

• Use the Revision Checklist on page 202 to guide you in thinking about your partner's narrative in terms of its purpose, organization, and development. Write your reactions neatly in the margins of the paper.

- In a sentence or two, write what you like best about your partner's narrative.
- Write one or two brief, general suggestions for how the writer might improve the narrative.

Guided by the Revision Checklist and by the comments of your editing partner, revise your first draft. Make a neat final copy and proofread it carefully. Afterwards, share your personal narrative with your classmates.

Part 5
Other Uses of Narrative Writing

Narrative writing serves many purposes in many different settings. The following chart shows some of the places in which narrative writing is used within another kind of writing, such as expository or persuasive writing.

Using Narrative Writing

Type	Purpose	Example
Magazine article on Civil War	To introduce article and catch reader's interest	Story about Lincoln and General Grant
Nonfiction book on deafness	To illustrate teaching of deaf	Episode about Helen Keller recognizing word *water*
Friendly letter	To keep in touch with a friend during vacation	Story about raccoon in food supply
TV evening news	To inform about the day's events	Summary: mayor's news conference
Textbook on American history	To bring history to life	Story: struggle of Nez Percé Indians
Editorial opposing discrimination	To sum up argument	Specific example of discrimination

The story that follows is an example of narrative writing that is used within another kind of writing. This narrative was used to introduce a scientific magazine article about some research balloons that were sent up by NASA.

Professional Model

On a hot bright morning in May, three cars and a truck are rolling down an oily dirt road in the Piney Woods of southeast Texas. Suddenly, two-way radios crackle and a twin-engine plane flashes overhead just above the trees. The convoy halts, doors slam, and men start gathering by the roadside. "Over that way," one of the men calls out, "maybe a quarter of a mile." He points to the east, into a thicket of saplings, low bushes, and spikey tendrils that the local people call "whoa vines." It's an odd combination of men that starts into the brush: three riggers, five astrophysicists, and an unemployed steel-worker familiar with these woods who's stopped to lend a hand after seeing activity on the road. They're on a scientific search-and-rescue mission.

Writing Inside Out
Len Strazewski, Comic-book Author

The wonderful thing about writing comic books is that you can take all of your daydreams and fantasies and turn them into exciting stories. So says Len Strazewski, author of a number of popular "Speed Racer" and "Dai Kamikaze!" issues published by Now Comics. How the characters in his comics behave is based on real feelings and emotions, Len adds.

Len and a friend first tried to write comics when they were both twelve years old. Now, after studying writing and art in college, they are still partners. They like to do prewriting together to develop good characters and narrative. "You have to create a world for your characters," says Len. "Then you use your imagination to learn all you can about them."

"There's snakes in there, you know," says the steel-worker's wife as I follow the group. "Deadly ones."

Five hundred yards and no snakes later, we find what we are looking for: a large white box nestled up against an oak tree (above) and attached by steel cables to a big parachute. It's a one-ton cosmic gamma-ray telescope, landed by parachute after a short flight into the stratosphere via balloon.

From "NASA's Giant Research Balloons" by James Chiles

Chances are that many people would not begin reading an article if all they knew about it was that it concerned space research. However, most people would find the beginning of this article intriguing. The author starts with a story, a narrative about a group of men who are searching for something. The narrative is the story of that search.

Generally, when people hear the beginning of a story, they want to find out what happens next. It is this natural human desire for stories about other people that causes writers to begin serious, factual articles with narratives. You may be able to use narrative in the same way in your own writing.

One time, in order to find out more about a character, Len wrote a speech in which the man turned down the Nobel prize. "That speech will never be printed. It happened ten years before the story starts. But it helped me understand the character better," he says with satisfaction.

A good comic book also needs a strong plot with a lot of action. Again, Len plans ahead. "I write the beginning and the end first, then work on the middle. I *know* what changes the characters will go through. I *know* what problems they will have to solve. I *don't* know the steps they will take along the way. I work those out as I go along."

Because the narrative moves along mostly through dialogue, writing a comic book is a lot like writing a movie script. Len has to think visually, and he must be able to suggest pictures for the artist to draw.

Most comic book readers are boys between ages eleven and nineteen. Len gears his stories to this particular audience. "I write about real problems that teenagers have trying to make it in an adult world. I raise real issues that make people think."

Like his own favorite hero, newspaperman Clark Kent, Len is also a journalist. But he has a special love for the very creative world of comic-book making.

The following incident from a biography of Andrew Jackson helps to describe Jackson's character and to explain some of his attitudes in later life.

▬ Literary Model ▬▬▬▬▬▬▬▬▬▬▬▬▬▬▬▬▬▬▬

Later in the day Andrew found his brother, who had escaped unhurt, and the two boys took refuge in a thicket where they passed a hungry and anxious night.

In the morning they looked for food. The nearest house belonged to Lieutenant Crawford [Andrew's cousin]. Leaving their muskets and horses in the thicket, the boys crept toward the house and reached it without being observed. Meanwhile a Tory neighbor discovered the muskets and horses and notified the dragoons. A search immediately began. Soon the Crawford house was investigated. Before the family knew what was happening the place was surrounded, the doors secured, and the boys taken prisoner.

Then mayhem broke out. The soldiers started wrecking the house—breaking glasses, smashing furniture, and tearing clothes to shreds. While this destruction was in progress, the officer in command of the dragoons ordered Andrew to clean his boots—a rather curious command in view of what was happening. Curious or not, that was what the Officer wanted, . . .

Andrew struggled to control himself. In a calm voice he replied, "Sir, I am a prisoner of war, and claim to be treated as such." Incensed by this retort, the officer lifted his sword and aimed it straight at Andrew's head. Instinctively the boy ducked, throwing up his left hand in time to break the full force of the blow. He received a deep gash on his head and fingers, the marks of which he took through life as a constant reminder of British affection.

From *Andrew Jackson* by Robert V. Remini

This excerpt takes an incident from Jackson's life and turns it into a story. What happens in the story is simple and easily told. Andrew and his brother attempt to hide from the British. They are found and ill-treated, and Andrew is finally wounded. These are the events that take place in the narrative.

However, the biographer has a purpose that goes beyond telling the details of the story. Notice how the narrator reports not only on the events but also on what people are thinking about the events. The narrator knows that Andrew struggles to control himself and that the officer is incensed by Andrew's words.

This intimacy—this getting inside the characters—is appropriate here. The writer's purpose is to highlight the sort of boy young Jackson was as well as to set the stage for some of Jackson's later attitudes toward the British. Getting inside the characters' minds helps to fulfill that purpose and makes the narrative richer. The biography becomes more than just a list of dates and events; it takes on the fullness and personality of a real life.

Writing Activities Using Narrative Writing

A Tell which of the following might contain narrative writing. Explain what purpose the writer might have in using narrative in each of the items.

1. a letter of application
2. a magazine article about a trip to a foreign country
3. a health textbook
4. a cookbook
5. a diary entry

B Are there any well-known people who stir your imagination? Jesse Owens at the 1936 Olympics in Germany? Anwar Sadat working and dying for peace in the Middle East? Mother Theresa receiving the Nobel Peace Prize? Use what you have learned to write a biographical narrative about an incident in one of their lives.

Prewriting and Drafting With two or three classmates, brainstorm a list of incidents from the lives of the people named above and others that interest you. Choose an incident you know something about. If necessary, do some simple research to fill out your knowledge. Then, drawing on what you have learned in this chapter, draft a short narrative describing the incident. Try to bring out your reasons for thinking the incident is worth writing about. Explain the meaning of the events as well as describing them.

Peer Evaluation and Revision When your draft is complete, give it to a peer editor to read. Then revise your narrative, keeping your peer editor's responses in mind and referring to the Revision Checklist on page 202.

Guidelines: Narrative Writing

Prewriting
- Use a prewriting technique to list incidents from your life that contain the elements of a story. *(See page 198.)*
- Choose an incident that had meaning for you and would make an interesting narrative. *(See page 198.)*
- Decide what your purpose is in writing the narrative and what audience you are writing for. *(See page 198.)*
- List the events involved in the incident. *(See page 199.)*
- Arrange the events chronologically. Add your responses and your controlling idea, the meaning of the event for you. *(See page 199.)*

Drafting
- Use sense details, dialogue, and action to *show* your story rather than to *tell* it. *(See page 200.)*
- Expand on your notes, composing a paragraph for each change of scene, action, and speaker. *(See page 200.)*
- Include your responses to the events along with your description of them. *(See page 200.)*
- In your conclusion, briefly explain the significance the episode had for you. *(See page 200.)*

Revising
- Do you give enough information to readers so that they can easily follow the story? *(See page 202.)*
- Do you use transitional words and phrases to make the sequence of events clear? *(See page 202.)*
- Do you stick to the main story line? *(See page 202.)*
- Is the point of the story clearly expressed? *(See page 202.)*

Proofreading
- Do you maintain a consistent point of view? *(See page 202.)*
- Are you consistent about verb tenses? *(See page 202.)*
- Have you punctuated quotations correctly? *(See page 723–726.)*
- Is your story free from errors in grammar, usage, capitalization, and spelling?

The Scotch-Irish

The roots of American country music are generally traced to the hills of Appalachia, but they actually go one step farther into the past. Listen to a country song, and you may actually be hearing music passed down from the ballads of the Scottish Lowlands in the sixteenth and seventeenth centuries.

The Scotch-Irish settlers came to America in great numbers in the 1700's. They moved through the Cumberland Gap and settled in the frontier land of the Appalachian Mountains. They brought with them a rich oral culture that survives today in the speech and music of Appalachia. Phrases such as *bonny-clabber* for curdled sour milk and *flannel-cake* for wheat cake come from the Scotch-Irish. So do pronunciations such as ''tharr'' for *there* and ''barr'' for *bear*.

The settlers also brought with them the Scotch-Irish storytelling tradition. Their stories and ballads, told with attention to the colorful turn of phrase, have had a strong influence on American country music. As Robert McCrum, William Cran, and Robert MacNeil note in *The Story of English,* ''Today, the ballads of the Scots-Irish that traveled here during the eighteenth century are imitated and reproduced from Arkansas to Alberta, by singers like Dolly Parton and Kenny Rogers who have internationalized a style that was once confined to the hills.''

Chapter 9
Application and Review

In the activities below, you will practice your skills in narrative writing. Activity A leads you in planning and writing a personal narrative. Activities B and C leave more of the decisions up to you, allowing you to adapt the writing process to your own personal style. Choose one or more of these activities.

A Writing a Personal Narrative Like most people, you probably enjoy reliving memories—especially the times when you felt good about yourself. Think back to some of those times. When were you at your best? Winning a prize in a band contest? Helping a friend in trouble? Taking your first dive off the high board? Finishing a job no one thought you could do? Plan and write a narrative describing a time when you were at your best. Use these guidelines.

Prewriting List as many incidents as you can in which you were at your best. Choose one of them. Consider your purpose and audience; then make a chart listing the events and your responses to them. Conclude with a statement about the meaning the events had for you.

Drafting Use your chart as a guide in drafting your narrative. Expand the items in your chart by developing a paragraph for each change of scene, action, and speaker. Use sense details, dialogue, and action to bring the events in your narrative to life.

Revising Referring to the Revision Checklist on page 202, try to see your first draft as it might be seen by someone who does not know the story as you do. Is there enough information? Will anything be confusing? After revising, make a final copy. Proofread it carefully before sharing it. (Use the checklist on page 210.)

B Writing a Biographical Narrative Use the following guidelines to plan and write a narrative about a famous invention or discovery.

Prewriting With two or three other students, brainstorm a list of inventions and discoveries, such as the invention of the lightbulb by Edison or the discovery of radium by Marie Curie. Choose one, and do some simple research on it. Make a list of the main events.

Drafting and Revising Draft your narrative, using chronological order. Use the Revision Checklist as you evaluate and revise your draft.

c *Starting Points for Writing* What stories do you tell over and over again? What events have happened recently that you enjoy relating to friends or family? Make a list of these stories. Add to this list stories you relive in your mind that you may never have told anyone. Brainstorm about the pictures below to see what other familiar stories they call to mind and include these on your list. Or expand your list of stories by using one of the springboards below as an aid to recalling special events you might want to tell about. Finally, write a personal narrative based on one of the stories from your list.

Springboards
- an object with special significance to me
- an upsetting event
- something I recently did for the first time
- my greatest disappointment

10
Exploring Expository Writing

*H*ow is planting a field of corn like building a housing development such as Levittown? How is it different? Explain in writing the similarities and differences between these two activities, and you are writing exposition.

Exposition is writing that informs or explains. In this chapter you will learn three different techniques of expository writing and how to use each technique to explain processes, examine cause-and-effect relationships, and compare-and-contrast subjects.

Part 1

Analyzing Expository Writing

Expository writing, or exposition, is writing that informs or explains. This chapter will discuss three types of development used in exposition. One type explains a **process,** such as how to make a skateboard or how to perform magic tricks. A second type describes **causes and effects,** such as an explanation of what causes a solar eclipse. A third technique uses **comparison and contrast,** for example, explaining the differences or similarities between tornadoes and hurricanes.

Here are three models of expository writing, each using a different development technique. The first model uses the process technique.

Student Model

Have you ever wondered how to build an airplane? You might think it's a specialized job, but some high-school students proved that you don't have to be a mechanic to build an aircraft. Starting from detailed blueprints, the students cut, fit, and shaped wood and metal for the plane's body and wings. Then the wood was covered with fiberglass. To pass inspection, all materials had to be cut to a perfect fit. Next, the students wired the plane's electrical system. The process took over five years to complete.

The following model uses the cause-and-effect technique.

Professional Model

Caves and rock shelters with confined habitation space, hunting grounds where prey was killed, quarries from which stone for tools was extracted—these are the kinds of sites that have told us most of what we know about how New World people lived when the last Ice Age drew to a close, between 12,000 and 10,000 years ago. . . . Often preservation is poor, so that only stone tools and perhaps some bones and plants remain. As a result, more is known of hunting and butchering technology than of domestic life for these times. . . .

From "By the Banks of the Chinchihuapi" by Tom D. Dillehay

The following model uses the comparison and contrast technique to describe the two reporters who uncovered details of the Watergate scandal in 1972.

Literary Model

Bob Woodward was a prima donna who played heavily at office politics. Yale. A veteran of the Navy officer corps. Lawns, greensward, staterooms, and grass tennis courts . . . but probably not enough pavement for him to be good at investigative reporting. . . .

Bernstein was a college dropout. He had started as a copy boy at the *Washington Star* when he was 16, become a full-time reporter at 19, and had worked at the *Post* since 1966. He occasionally did investigative series, had covered the courts and city hall, and liked to do long, discursive pieces. . . . Bernstein looked like one of those counterculture journalists that Woodward despised. Bernstein thought that Woodward's rapid rise at the *Post* had less to do with his ability than his Establishment credentials.

From *All the President's Men*
by Bob Woodward and Carl Bernstein

Discussing the Models Read these questions. Then discuss your answers with the class.

1. What process is explained in the student model?
2. What causes and effects are explained in the second model?
3. In the third model, explain Woodward and Bernstein's similarities and differences.

Understanding Expository Writing

Different types of development—process, cause and effect, and comparison and contrast—can help you explain something clearly. This chapter will help you understand and choose the most effective technique for what you want to explain.

Exposition in Literature As you read Russell Baker's instructions on how to carve a turkey on the following pages, notice how the process technique sustains the humor in the piece.

Exposition in Literature

Slice of Life

Russell Baker

Russell Baker's popular columns appear in newspapers around the country. In the following essay he uses the process technique to capture the humor in an ordinary situation.

*H*ow to carve a turkey:
Assemble the following tools—carving knife, stone for sharpening carving knife, hot water, soap, wash cloth, two bath towels, barbells, meat cleaver. If the house lacks a meat cleaver, an ax may be substituted. If it is, add bandages, sutures and iodine to above list.

Begin by moving the turkey from roasting pan to a suitable carving area. This is done by inserting the carving knife into the posterior stuffed area of the turkey and the knife-sharpening stone into the stuffed area under the neck.

Thus skewered, the turkey may be lifted out of the hot grease with relative safety. Should the turkey drop to the floor, however, remove the knife and stone, roll the turkey gingerly in the two bath towels, wrap them several times around it and lift the encased fowl to the carving place.

You are now ready to begin carving. Sharpen the knife on the stone and insert it where the thigh joins the torso. If you do this correctly, which is improbable, the knife will almost immediately encounter a barrier of bone and gristle. This may very well be the joint. It could, however, be your thumb. If not, execute a vigorous sawing motion until satisfied that the knife has been defeated. Withdraw the knife and ask someone nearby, in as testy a manner as possible, why the knives at your house are not kept in better carving condition.

Exercise the biceps and forearms by lifting barbells until they are strong enough for you to tackle the leg joint with bare hands. Wrapping one hand firmly around the thigh, seize the turkey's torso in the other hand and scream. Run cold water over hands to relieve pain of burns.

Transition to another step

*N*ow, take a bath towel in each hand and repeat the above maneuver. The entire leg should snap away from the chassis with a distant crack, and the rest of the turkey, obedient to Newton's law about equal and opposite reactions, should roll in the opposite direction, which means that if you are carving at the table the turkey will probably come to rest in someone's lap.

Get the turkey out of the lap with as little fuss as possible, and concentrate on the leg. Use the meat cleaver to sever the sinewy leather which binds the thigh to the drumstick.

Alternative step

If using the alternate, ax method, this operation should be performed on a cement walk outside the house in order to preserve the table.

Repeat the above operation on the turkey's uncarved side. You now have two thighs and two drumsticks. Using

the wash cloth, soap and hot water, bathe thoroughly and, if possible, go to a movie. Otherwise, look each person in the eye and say, "I don't suppose anyone wants white meat."

If compelled to carve the breast anyhow, sharpen the knife on the stone again with sufficient awkwardness to tip over the gravy bowl on the person who started the stampede for white meat.

While everyone is rushing about to mop the gravy off her slacks, hack at the turkey breast until it starts crumbling off the carcass in ugly chunks.

The alternative method for carving white meat is to visit around the neighborhood until you find someone who has a good carving knife and borrow it, if you find one, which is unlikely.

This method enables you to watch the football game on neighbors' television sets and also creates the possibility that somebody back at your table will grow tired of waiting and do the carving herself.

Conclusion   In this case, upon returning home, cast a pained stare upon the mound of chopped white meat that has been hacked out by the family carving knife and refuse to do any more carving that day. No one who cares about the artistry of carving can be expected to work upon the mutilations of amateurs, and it would be a betrayal of the carver's art to do so.

Trying Out Expository Writing Now that you have read Russell Baker's humorous process for carving the turkey, try some expository writing on your own. Think of a process you are very familiar with, such as starting an aquarium, or swimming the butterfly stroke, and write about it in your journal. Or you might like to compare two friends or contrast Mikhail Baryshnikov and Walter Payton. You could also discuss the effects of air pollution on the environment or the causes of prison overcrowding. Think about how you will choose a topic for your writing. What technique will you use for developing the writing? How will you organize your ideas? How will you make the writing flow well?

After writing, think about which parts of the process gave you the most trouble. Which parts worked for you? Did you enjoy the writing? Write down your thoughts in your journal.

Part 2

Explaining a Process

How was the Great Wall of China built? How do you perform cardiopulmonary resuscitation, or CPR? How are bridges built over large bodies of water? When you explain how something happened, how something works, or how to do something, you are using expository writing to explain a process. You will have one of two purposes when you use this type of writing: to share knowledge or to teach a skill. For example, you might want to explain what makes videocassette recorders work. In that case your purpose would be to share knowledge. If you wanted to tell someone how to use a VCR to record a program, however, your purpose would be to teach a skill.

In the following example, a professional writer explains how a radar gun measures the speed of a baseball. Think about the writer's purpose in explaining this process, and notice the order in which the steps are given.

Professional Model

A radar gun emits microwave beams of a known frequency. These beams have a conical shape and a width of 16 degrees. A baseball moving within this radar field toward the gun reflects the waves back toward the gun. The difference in frequency between the reflected waves and the original waves is then calculated and the information is translated into miles per hour.

From *How Do They Do That* by Caroline Sutton

Discussing the Model Think about these questions and discuss your answers in class.

1. What is this writer's purpose: to share knowledge or to teach a skill?
2. How would you describe the order in which the steps are presented? Is the order logical?
3. What is the process being explained?

The authors of the following example explain the process of growing bean sprouts. As you read, think about the authors' purpose in explaining this process and the way in which the steps are organized.

Giant plant in
Little Shop of Horrors.

▬ *Professional Model* ▬

Here's a quick and easy way to grow bean sprouts. Put about two tablespoons of bean seeds into a wide-mouthed jar and cover with at least three-quarters of a cup of warm water. Let the seeds soak overnight. In the morning, drain the water off the swollen seeds and rinse them with warm water. Drain well and return to the jar. Cover the jar with two layers of cheesecloth held in place with a rubber band. Keep the jar in a dark place. Rinse the seeds with warm water morning and night. The sprouts will be about one inch long in two to three days. When they are one to two inches long, place them in the refrigerator to stop growth. You can eat the entire sprout—root, seed, and if there are some, the tiny leaves.

Barbara and D.X. Fenten

Discussing the Model Think about these questions and discuss your answers in class.

1. What is the writers' purpose?
2. How have the writers organized the steps in the process?
3. What transitions do the writers use in explaining the process?

Prewriting: Explaining a Process

During the prewriting stage, there are several steps you must take in order to write a well-organized and interesting process explanation.

Choosing a Topic When you choose a topic for a process explanation, think of topics that you know well or that are interesting to research so you can write with confidence. Also consider your audience so that you choose a topic that will appeal to your readers. Look back at Chapter 2 on thinking skills, and Chapter 3 on prewriting, for more ideas on how to get started.

Understanding Your Audience The information you provide and the way you present it will vary depending upon who your audience is. Before you can prepare an explanation of how to set up a darkroom, for example, you need to determine whether your audience consists of experienced photographers or beginners. To analyze your readers and tailor your explanation to their needs, consider the following questions: How much do your readers already know about your topic? What types of information will be most interesting and helpful to them? What are the most important pieces of information they should know about your topic?

Analyzing Your Topic Once you have chosen a topic and defined your audience, you are ready to begin gathering and analyzing information. The following chart explains the steps in preparing a process explanation.

Planning a Process Explanation

1. Gather information by making lists of what you know, by reading about your topic, and by observing the process if possible.
2. Create a statement of purpose telling why the process is important, useful, or worth understanding.
3. Divide the process into steps; consider what details are needed to explain each step.
4. Arrange the steps in chronological order.
5. Define unfamiliar terms and procedures; for a process that teaches a skill, tell what supplies or equipment are needed.
6. Explain the results of the process.

Drafting: Explaining a Process

The first task in drafting is to decide on your tone. Will your writing be formal? informal? serious? humorous? Even though your goal is to explain a process, you need to do more than simply give a list of directions. Try not to sound like a computer spewing out information. Think about ways to make your explanation lively and interesting for your audience. Remember: all writing is communication between people, so try to be as interesting and informative as possible.

Writing an Introduction Your introduction should be in the form of a thesis statement that lets readers know what you are writing about. Also, the introduction should explain how readers will benefit from your exposition. In addition, it should capture their interest.

Below, comedian Bill Cosby begins an essay on how to read faster. Notice how he organized his introduction and how he caught the reader's attention.

Professional Model

When I was a kid in Philadelphia, I must have read every comic book ever published. . . . As I got older, though, my eyeballs must have slowed down. I mean, comic books started to pile up faster than my brother Russell and I could read them. It wasn't until much later, when I was getting my doctorate, that I realized it wasn't my eyeballs that were to blame. The problem is that there is too much to read these days, and too little time to read every word of it. That's when I started to look around for common-sense, practical ways to help me read faster. I found three that are especially good. And if I can learn them, so can you—and you can put them to use immediately.

From "How to Read Faster" by Bill Cosby

Including Specific Details As you write, think about what your readers need to know to understand your topic. Since you are familiar with your topic, you could take for granted information that readers might not understand. Try to anticipate questions your readers will ask, and select details that will answer their questions.

On the following page, notice how Bill Cosby used carefully selected details to explain the process of reading faster.

Selected
details

Transitions

The first way is previewing. It is especially useful for getting a general idea of heavy reading like long magazine or newspaper articles and nonfiction books. To preview, read the entire first two paragraphs of whatever you've chosen. Next read only the first sentence of each successive paragraph. Then read the entire last two paragraphs. This will give you a quick, overall view of the long, unfamiliar material. It will keep you from spending time on things you don't really want—or need—to read. The second way to read faster is skimming . . .

Using Transitions Transition words can be valuable tools in guiding your readers as they follow your explanation. They help readers understand how the steps in the process are related and what the time sequence is. Transitions such as *first, meanwhile, after,* and *finally* tell time or sequence. *Also, in addition,* and *furthermore* indicate added information. *As a result, consequently,* and *therefore* show results. In longer pieces of writing, a new paragraph generally starts each major step, especially if the step is supported and explained with details.

In the example above, Bill Cosby used the transitions *first, next, then,* and *second.*

Writing a Conclusion Once you have completed your process explanation, the next step is writing the conclusion. An effective conclusion reports the end result of your process or summarizes your explanation, restating the benefits to your reader. It also gives you an opportunity to leave a strong impression with the reader. Here is how Bill Cosby ended his essay.

Professional Model

Summary

End result

So now you have three ways to help you read faster: previewing to cut down on unnecessary heavy reading; skimming to get a quick, general idea of light reading; and clustering to increase your speed and comprehension. With enough practice, you'll be able to handle more reading at school and at home in less time. You should even have enough time to read your favorite comic books!

From "How to Read Faster" by Bill Cosby

Revising: Explaining a Process

You might want to look back at Chapter 4 for strategies that can help as you make revisions. Peer editing in particular may be helpful in order to see if a reader can understand the process being explained. In addition, consider the questions in the following checklist.

Revision Checklist for a Process Composition

Purpose
1. Do you clearly state the purpose of your explanation?
2. Do you consider who your audience is and what information your audience needs to know?

Organization
1. Do you clearly explain each step in the process?
2. Do you use transitions to help the reader understand how the steps are related?
3. Do you include specific details that explain the process?

Development
1. Do you introduce your topic in an interesting way?
2. Do you include necessary definitions and background?
3. Does your conclusion report the result of the process or summarize your explanation?

Writing Activities Explaining a Process

A What do you know how to do well? Is there a certain skill you can explain thoroughly? Use brainstorming to develop a list of topics, or consult the Writer's Handbook. Think of skills that you are familiar with so that you will be able to write with authority. Also consider skills that will be interesting to a specific audience and that lend themselves to a specific purpose for writing.

B *Writing in Process* Select one of the topics you generated in Exercise A. Then plan, write, revise, and share a composition that explains a process, using the strategies you have learned.

Prewriting and Drafting Begin by using brainstorming to write down what you know about your topic. Follow the steps outlined in this section to gather information, identify your audience, analyze your topic, and organize your explanation. As you write, be sure to use specific details and transitions in the body of your composition and to create an interesting introduction and conclusion.

Peer Evaluation and Revising When you have completed your draft, have a peer editor read it, using the following guidelines.

Guidelines for Peer Editors

1. Using the Revision Checklist on page 226, respond to the purpose, organization, and development of the expository composition. Write your comments in the margin of the paper you are reading.
2. Write a statement telling what you liked best about the exposition.
3. Write one or two general suggestions for ways the writer could improve this expository composition.

Review the responses of your peer editor and refer to the Revision Checklist as you revise your expository composition. Although the suggestions of peer editors can be very helpful, you do not have to accept all of them. Use your own judgment as you prepare a final copy, making sure to proofread your composition.

Part 3
Explaining Causes and Effects

What caused the energy crisis in the 1970's? What are the effects of weightlessness on astronauts? When you explain why something happened or exists, or when you examine the result of an action or condition, you are using cause and effect. Your purpose is to help your reader understand the connection between an event and its causes or between an event and its effects. Sometimes you focus on the causes, and other times you focus on the effects.

Cause-and-effect writing involves more than simply explaining events that occur one after another. You must make sure that one event *causes* another to happen. For example, a newspaper report that examines the damage caused by a hurricane is an example of cause-and-effect writing. A newspaper report that traces the path a hurricane followed, however, merely shows a sequence.

Notice the cause-and-effect relationship in the following paragraph by television journalist James Burke.

Professional Model

Cause

When Enrico Fermi, an Italian immigrant to the United States, and his colleagues triggered the world's first atomic pile in Chicago in 1941, science opened Pandora's box. Out of it came new ways of healing, new tools with

Effects

which to study the structure of the universe, the potential for virtually free electric power—and the atomic bomb. Of all the developments of atomic physics, two possibilities affect our future more than any others: electricity produced by the fusion process and annihilation by nuclear strike.

From *Connections* by James Burke

Discussing the Model Read and discuss the following questions with your classmates.

1. Identify the cause-and-effect aspects in Burke's paragraph.
2. Does Burke concentrate on explaining causes or effects?
3. What does Burke identify as the most significant effects?

Prewriting: Cause and Effect

When identifying an idea to develop through cause-and-effect technique, you will need to ask yourself: What caused an action or event? What effect has the action or event had? If these questions apply to your subject, then it is suitable for a cause-and-effect development.

Analyzing Your Information Once you have identified your topic, you need to determine whether you will concentrate on explaining causes, or effects, or both. Use brainstorming to generate lists of causes and effects. Your prewriting notes might take the form of a flow chart, showing how one cause or effect led to others. Charlene's assignment for biology was to write an essay on one theory of why dinosaurs became extinct. She made the following notes.

Cause: Earth's geography began to change 65
          million years ago.

Effects: Changes in climate brought changes in
         the geography.

         Dinosaurs had difficulty adapting to
         harsher climate.

         Harsher climate had adverse effects on
         reproduction.

         Mammals adapted to climate changes and
         challenged dinosaurs.

         Dinosaurs couldn't adapt to climate
         changes, so they died out.

Dinosaurs gave way to mammals, some as tiny as the shrew.

Organizing Your Information There are two basic patterns for organizing cause-and-effect writing. In the **cause-to-effect pattern,** you begin by stating the cause or causes, and then proceed to the effect or effects. In the **effect-to-cause pattern,** you begin by showing the effect or effects, and then examine what caused them.

Cause-to-Effect Patterns		Effect-to-Cause Patterns	
A	**B**	**A**	**B**
Introduction	Introduction	Introduction	Introduction
Cause	Cause 1	Effect	Effect 1
Effect 1	Cause 2	Cause 1	Effect 2
Effect 2	Cause 3, 4	Cause 2	Effect 3, 4
Effect 3, 4	Effect	Cause 3, 4	Cause
Conclusion	Conclusion	Conclusion	Conclusion

With either pattern, there are three methods for organizing your details. You can use **chronological order,** listing the causes or effects in the order in which they occurred. In **order-of-importance** organization, start with the most important or least important cause or effect. With **familiar-to-unfamiliar order,** start with the most well-known cause or effect; then proceed to less familiar causes and effects.

In some essays, especially those involving historical events, you may find several causes and effects. Using the patterns discussed here will help you keep these relationships clear.

Writing a Clear Thesis Statement Even though you have chosen a topic, you need to take one more step to focus your writing—you need to develop a thesis statement. The thesis statement tells the central point of your writing.

Often, the thesis statement will become clear to you during prewriting as you analyze and organize your information. One piece of information may stand out as the key point you wish to make, or one fact may seem to you the most important piece of information you want your audience to understand. Writing a thesis statement helps you narrow your topic and focus on the most important details to include. The thesis statement generally should be included in your introduction.

When Charlene was analyzing the information for her composition on dinosaurs, she decided that the key reason why they became extinct was the change in climate. So she wrote the following thesis statement.

Most scientists agree that the age of the dinosaurs ended be-cause dinosaurs could not adapt to changes in climate.

Charlene's thesis establishes that she will focus on the effects of cli-mate rather than on other issues, such as other theories about extinction or the threat to dinosaurs by mammals.

Drafting: Cause and Effect

As you learned in Part 2, you need to decide on your tone as you begin drafting. If, for example, you want your writing to be humorous, decide this before you start writing, and it will be easier to write in a hu-morous way. You also must think of an interesting introduction, a way to let your reader know what you will be writing about. Next, decide on the appropriate pattern for arranging your details, and develop a con-clusion that clearly summarizes the cause-and-effect relationship.

Showing Logical Connections Transitions such as the ones in the chart can be effective in showing cause-and-effect relationships.

Transitions Showing Causes and Effects

as a result	for this reason	consequently
because	therefore	thus
if . . . then	due to	owing to
since	so	although

Writing a Conclusion Like the conclusion for a process explana-tion, the conclusion of a cause-and-effect composition restates the main idea and summarizes the information presented. You also may want to draw conclusions or make predictions based on the information you have presented. Here is how Charlene concluded her composition.

One Student's Process

Dinosaurs had ruled the earth for 150 million years, but 65 million years ago the reign ended. Although there are still some questions about what caused their death, it seems clear that changes in climate played a leading role. The failure of the dinosaurs to adapt to the new cli-mate brought the age of dinosaurs to a close.

Revising: Cause and Effect

Consider the following questions as you revise your cause-and-effect composition.

Revision Checklist for a Cause-and-Effect Composition

Purpose
1. Does the topic of your composition have a true cause-and-effect relationship?
2. Do you have a clear thesis statement?

Organization
1. Do you organize causes and effects logically?
2. Do you use transitions to show cause-effect connections?

Development
1. Do you have an effective introduction and conclusion?
2. Do you use specific details to explain causes and effects?

Charlene made the following revisions as she worked on paragraphs about the dinosaur's food supply. Notice her thoughts as she worked. They are shown in the margin.

One Student's Process

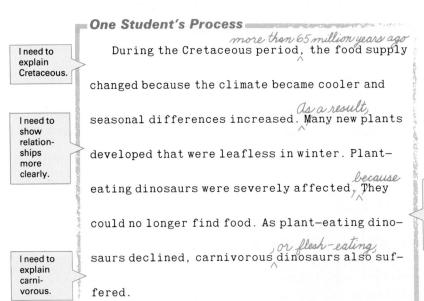

I need to explain Cretaceous.

During the Cretaceous period, the food supply ^more than 65 million years ago

changed because the climate became cooler and

I need to show relationships more clearly.

seasonal differences increased. ^As a result, Many new plants

developed that were leafless in winter. Plant—

eating dinosaurs were severely affected, ^because They

I should combine sentences to make my writing smoother.

could no longer find food. As plant—eating dino—

I need to explain carnivorous.

saurs declined, carnivorous ^, or flesh—eating, dinosaurs also suf—

fered.

Writing Activities *Causes and Effects*

A Study the photographs at the top of this page. Then ask yourself the following questions: What caused _____? What effect has _____ had?

B *Writing in Process* After you have answered the questions in Exercise A, plan, write, and revise a cause-and-effect composition. Follow the suggestions below.

Prewriting and Drafting Use brainstorming to develop a list of causes and effects, and analyze how they are related. Then write a thesis statement to help you focus your writing. As you write, include specific details and use transitions to show connections between these causes and effects. In your conclusion, summarize the information and try to make predictions.

Peer Evaluation and Revising Now you are ready to have a peer editor respond to your completed draft, using the Guidelines for Peer Editors on page 227. Then refer to the Revision Checklist on page 232 as you revise.

Part 4
Explaining Through Comparison and Contrast

How are karate and judo similar? What are the differences between the rock music of today and twenty years ago? An effective way to examine two or more related items is to compare and contrast them.

When you **compare** items, you examine how they are similar; when you **contrast** items, you point out their differences.

Comparison and contrast techniques are often used to analyze literature. For example, you might study the similarities between two poems or two stories, or you might look at the differences between two characters or two writers. There are many other uses as well, such as comparing scientific theories, products, sports teams, political candidates, or proposals.

The following comparison from a magazine article examines two figure skaters who come from very different "worlds."

Professional Model

One is the world of Katarina Witt, the beautiful skating star of East Germany. Her life is dominated by discipline and total commitment to skating. A heroine in her hometown of Karl-Marx-Stadt, Katarina exemplifies the excellence that can be attained through state-sponsored athletics.

The other world is that of Debi Thomas, last year's premiere U.S. skater and the reigning world champion. Bold and brash, Thomas answers to no one but herself. She has grown up full of grit, determined to make her mark on the world. For her, that mark comprises success in skating, success in academics, and a career devoted to helping others.

From "Fire on Ice" by Emily Greenspan

Discussing the Model Read and discuss the following questions.

1. What is the main idea of the comparison?
2. How are Katarina Witt and Debi Thomas similar and different?
3. Does the writer concentrate on similarities or differences?

Prewriting: Comparison and Contrast

Although it is possible to compare almost any two items, you must be selective in choosing a topic for a comparison and contrast composition. When choosing a topic, keep these guidelines in mind.

Guidelines for Choosing a Topic

1. Do the two items have enough common traits to make a comparison reasonable and interesting?
2. Will the comparison interest your audience?

A comparison of soccer and golf, for example, would not be effective because the two sports have little in common. Soccer and rugby, however, have common traits that could be compared and contrasted.

Once you choose a topic, you should decide on your purpose for making a comparison. You may wish to prove that the items you are comparing are either similar or different. You may simply wish to analyze the similarities and differences and draw conclusions.

Analyzing the Relevant Features In order to structure your comparison, you need to determine what the significant points of comparison are. Using a chart may be helpful in deciding which features are most relevant to the purpose of your composition.

Terry was writing a composition comparing compact discs and record albums. He made a chart to analyze the relevant features.

One Student's Process

Comparison and Contrast Worksheet

Features	Compact Discs	Record Albums
Sound quality	excellent	not as clear
Durability	almost inde- structible	scratches
Cost	more expensive	less expensive
Titles available	limited, but improving	great variety
Material	plastic, aluminum	vinyl
Maximum length	74 minutes	48 minutes

Organizing the Comparison There are two basic patterns for organizing comparisons. One is the **subject-by-subject** pattern, in which you discuss all the features about one subject and then discuss all the features about the other. The second pattern is **feature-by-feature** comparison. In this pattern you use the features to organize the comparison, not the subjects.

Organizing Comparison and Contrast

Subject-by-Subject Organization	Feature-by-Feature Organization
Introduction	Introduction
Subject 1	Feature 1
Feature 1	Subject 1
Feature 2	Subject 2
Feature 3	Feature 2
Feature 4	Subject 1
Subject 2	Subject 2
Feature 1	Feature 3
Feature 2	Subject 1
Feature 3	Subject 2
Conclusion	Conclusion

The following excerpt from a magazine article about film critics Gene Siskel and Roger Ebert uses the feature-by-feature pattern. Notice how the comparison is organized by features, not the subjects of Siskel and Ebert.

▬ Professional Model ▬▬▬▬▬▬▬▬▬▬▬▬▬▬▬▬

Ebert was an only child; his father was an electrician and his mother was a bookkeeper in Urbana, Illinois. Siskel had three brothers and two sisters and they lived in a big colonial house in Glencoe. Ebert went to the University of Illinois and majored in journalism. Siskel went to Yale and studied philosophy . . . .

Example of a feature: education

Ebert is a workaholic. Siskel admits he's lazy. . . .

Ebert is short. Siskel is tall. Ebert is the pear. Siskel is the banana.

From "Best Enemies" by Toni Schlesinger

Drafting: Comparison and Contrast

The skills you learned in Parts 2 and 3 will help you get started with drafting the parts of a comparison and contrast composition.

Writing the Introduction In addition to letting the readers know what your topic is, your introduction must present the subjects that you will compare and state the purpose of your comparison. Will it analyze the similarities and differences of your subjects? Will it prove your subjects are similar? Will it prove they are different?

Terry began his comparison of compact discs and record albums like this.

One Student's Process

When you go to a record store these days, chances are the first thing you see will not be stacks of long-playing record albums. In their place you probably will see racks of compact discs. Compact discs, or CDs, are revolutionizing the music scene. When compared with albums, CDs have many advantages and few drawbacks.

Thesis statement

Using Transitions Transition words are particularly important in comparisons because they signal to the reader whether you are discussing similarities or differences. Transitions that show similarities include *also, likewise, similarly, in the same way,* and *too.* Differences can be indicated by *but, although, on the other hand, in contrast, despite,* and *yet.* Notice the transitions in the following paragraph Terry wrote.

One Student's Process

Transitions

Both record albums and CDs store sound on circular discs. However, that is where the similarities end. Conventional albums store sound in the form of waves cut into vinyl grooves. In contrast, CDs store sound as microscopic pits etched into an aluminum disc. Albums are played by a diamond or sapphire stylus that touches the grooves, while CDs are played by a laser that "reads" the sounds stored on the disc without actually touching it.

Writing the Conclusion The conclusion should clearly restate the main idea. You also should draw a conclusion about your comparison. Terry wrote the following conclusion.

Restates the
main idea

Conclusion
drawn

> A comparison of compact discs and record albums shows why many people are turning to CDs. Just as the 33 r.p.m. record albums replaced 45 and 78 r.p.m. records, it appears compact discs are on their way toward replacing albums. Who knows what will replace CDs in the decades to follow?

Grammar Note Use the comparative form to compare two items. Use the superlative form to compare more than two items:

Comparative Mainframe computers are *larger* than desktop computers.

Superlative The *smallest* computers can be held in the palm of your hand.

For more information on the comparative and superlative forms of modifiers, see pages 562–567.

Revising: Comparison and Contrast

Refer to the following checklist as you revise your comparison.

> ## Revision Checklist for
> ## a Comparison-and-Contrast Composition
>
> **Purpose**
> 1. Do your subjects have enough traits in common?
> 2. Do you clearly state the purpose of your comparison?
>
> **Organization**
> 1. Do you use subject-by-subject or feature-by-feature order?
> 2. Do transitions signal similarities and differences?
>
> **Development**
> 1. Does your introduction state what you are comparing?
> 2. Did you choose relevant features to compare?
> 3. Do you draw a specific conclusion about your comparison?

Terry shared his composition with a peer editor, who suggested that Terry improve the organization and add transitions. Here is how Terry revised three paragraphs. Notice his thoughts in the margin.

One Student's Process

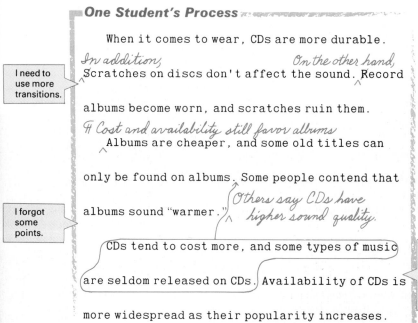

When it comes to wear, CDs are more durable.

In addition, *On the other hand,*

Scratches on discs don't affect the sound. Record

[*I need to use more transitions.*]

albums become worn, and scratches ruin them.

¶ Cost and availability still favor albums

Albums are cheaper, and some old titles can

only be found on albums. Some people contend that

albums sound "warmer." *Others say CDs have higher sound quality.*

[*I forgot some points.*]

CDs tend to cost more, and some types of music

are seldom released on CDs. Availability of CDs is

[*I need to improve the feature-by-feature organization.*]

more widespread as their popularity increases.

Writing Activities *Comparison and Contrast*

A Develop a list of topics for a comparison using some of the thinking skills you studied in Chapter 2. As you think of items to compare, chart their traits to see if they have enough traits in common to make a comparison worthwhile. Count the points of comparison. The topic with the most interesting points of comparison will make the best comparison-and-contrast composition.

B *Writing in Process* Choose one of the topics from Exercise A and then plan, write, and revise a composition that explains through comparison and contrast.

Prewriting and Drafting Think about your purpose for making the comparison. Do you wish to prove the items are either similar or different? Do you wish to analyze the similarities and differences and draw conclusions? Make a comparison-and-contrast chart to analyze the relevant features. Decide whether to use the subject-by-subject or feature-by-feature organization. As you write, make sure that you compare each relevant feature and use transitions. Write a conclusion that restates the main idea and makes a comment about the comparison.

Peer Evaluation and Revising Ask a peer to respond to your draft of a comparison exposition. Use the Guidelines for Peer Editors on page 227. Then review the editor's responses and refer to the Revision Checklist on page 239 as you revise and proofread your composition.

Part 5
Other Uses of Expository Writing

You encounter expository writing daily, in everything from newspaper reports to cookbook recipes to novels. Often, the different techniques for expository writing—process, cause and effect, and compare and contrast—are used together to make an explanation clearer and more effective. Exposition is also frequently combined with other types of writing, such as narration, description, or persuasion. The following chart lists some of the ways expository writing can be used.

Using Expository Writing

Purpose	Example
To inform a general audience	Newspaper report that tells the effects of a tax increase on the economy
To provide facts on specific topics	Encyclopedia article explaining how the process of photo-synthesis works
To teach skills and provide information	History text discussion of the background of the War in Vietnam
To enhance a story	Excerpt from an autobiography telling how the author narrow-ly escaped from a sinking boat
To examine issues of public concern	Television editorial comparing the benefits and disadvan-tages of nuclear and solar energy
To show significance	Passage in a historical novel explaining the effects of the Civil War
To persuade	Campaign flyer comparing the qualifications of two can-didates running for governor of a state

Exposition is often used in narrative writing. Notice how Jack London uses the techniques of process and cause and effect in his short story about survival in the Yukon.

▬ *Literary Model* ▬

At half-past twelve, to the minute, he arrived at the forks of the creek. . . . He unbuttoned his jacket and shirt and drew forth his lunch. The action consumed no more than a quarter of a minute, yet in that brief moment the numbness laid hold of the exposed fingers. He did not put the mitten on, but instead struck the fingers a dozen

One Effect

Process　　sharp smashes against his leg. . . . He struck the fingers repeatedly and returned them to the mitten, baring the other hand for the purpose of eating. He tried to take a

Cause　　mouthful, but the ice muzzle prevented. He had forgotten to build a fire and thaw out.

From *To Build a Fire* by Jack London

Writing Activities *Using Expository Writing*

Writing in Process Choose one of the ways of using expository writing on page 241. You may write a newspaper article, for example. Then plan, write, revise, and share an expository composition.

Prewriting and Drafting Decide whether you will explain a process, explain cause and effect, or explain through comparison and contrast. Then follow the steps you have studied in this chapter to find a topic, gather information, identify your audience, analyze your topic, organize your explanation, and develop a thesis statement. As you write, be sure to use specific details and transitions.

Peer Evaluation and Revising When you have completed your draft of expository writing, have a peer editor read and respond to it, using the Guidelines for Peer Editors on page 227. Then refer to the appropriate Revision Checklist as you revise your work.

Guidelines: *Expository Writing*

Prewriting
- Use thinking skills such as brainstorming to develop a list of topics and choose a topic. *(See Chapter 2.)*
- Think about who your audience is so that you can tailor your explanation to your readers' needs. *(See page 223.)*
- Is your purpose to explain a process, to examine causes and effects, to compare and contrast, or a combination of all of these? *(See pages 221, 228, and 235.)*
- Choose a logical pattern to organize your explanation. *(See pages 230, 235, and 236.)*

Drafting
- Write a thesis statement that clearly states the central point of your composition. *(See pages 230 and 231.)*
- Write an introduction that captures the interest of your readers and tells them the purpose of your composition. *(See pages 224 and 237.)*
- Include specific details. *(See page 224.)*
- Use transitions to show connections in cause-and-effect relationships. *(See pages 225, 231, and 237.)*
- Write a conclusion that summarizes the information or draws a conclusion. *(See pages 225, 232, and 238.)*

Revising
- Ask a peer editor to review your draft. *(See page 227.)*
- Use the appropriate Revision Checklist for the type of explanation you have chosen. *(See pages 226, 232, and 239.)*
- Keep your peer editor's comments as well as your own ideas in mind as you revise your work. *(See pages 87–88.)*

Proofreading
- Check for errors in grammar and usage.
- Check for errors in spelling and punctuation.

Sharing
- Prepare a final copy of your explanation.
- Share your work with your audience. *(See page 91.)*

Chapter 10
Application and Review

Here are three exercises to help you write expository compositions. The first activity takes you through the process for writing on a specific topic. The second activity includes more choices, and the third activity uses photos and quotes. Select one or more to work on.

A Writing a News Report Imagine that unusual atmospheric conditions interfered with TV broadcasting, forcing all stations off the air. Consequently, no one could watch TV. Plan and write an expository article explaining the effects of this bizarre occurrence. Your audience is the readership of a national newsmagazine.

Prewriting Freewrite for five minutes about how life would be different if no one could watch television. Make a chart showing how the causes and effects are related.

Drafting Using your chart, write a first draft. Develop a thesis statement to help you focus your writing. As you write, be aware of leading your readers from one effect to another in a logical manner. Be sure to use specific details and transitions to guide your readers.

Revising Ask a peer editor to review your first draft, using the Revision Checklist on page 232. After using your editor's comments to revise, proofread and prepare a final copy for the newsmagazine.

B Writing Directions Use the following guidelines to plan and write an expository composition that explains a process.

Prewriting Using brainstorming, develop a list of processes that are interesting and familiar. You might explain how to use origami to make paper objects or how to photograph sports events, for example. Once you have chosen a topic, create a statement that tells your purpose. Then divide your process into steps arranged in chronological order.

Drafting and Revising As you write, be sure to use specific details and transitions. Make sure your introduction and conclusion state the main idea of your explanation and capture the reader's interest. Share your draft with a peer editor. Ask him or her to use the Revision Checklist on page 227 to review your draft. Consider your editor's comments as you revise your work.

c *Starting Points for Writing* Magazines, almanacs, and books that are compilations of odd facts can provide you with starting points for writing. For example, brainstorm about one of the quotes or about one of the images below to come up with writing ideas. As you think about these items, you may want to ask yourself some of the questions provided as springboards.

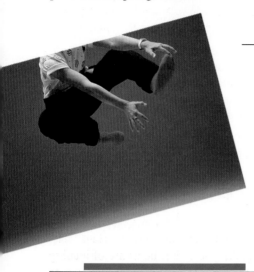

In 1982, a whimsically optimistic Californian named Larry Walters took to the skies in a lawn chair suspended from 42 helium-filled weather balloons.

Outside Magazine

When a cat died in ancient Egypt, it was mandatory for its owner to shave off his eyebrows to register grief.

David Wallechinsky and Irving Wallace

Springboards

- Is this similar to anything that I know about?
- How does this differ from what most people do these days?
- Why might someone have done something like this?

World's Greatest Comics, Ben Shahn, 1946.

Focus On

ESSAY TESTS

Your fear of essay tests can change to confidence as you discover another way to use the writing process.

Do your hands start sweating when you hear the words "essay test"? Do you wish you could acquire an exotic illness, just for one day, to avoid taking the test? The following pages will not make essay tests go away, but they will help you develop test-taking skills that will boost your confidence and performance.

Preview the Test

Before you start answering any questions, look over the entire test carefully. This preview will help you work more effectively.

Read the test carefully. Read all the questions and directions. Be sure to get an overview of what you are supposed to do.

Budget your time. Be sure to plan ahead and spend your time wisely. For example, if one question is worth twenty-five points and the next question is worth seventy-five points, divide your time accordingly. In a sixty-minute exam, you might budget fifteen minutes for the first question and forty-five minutes for the second.

Analyze the Questions

Before you start to write, read each test question carefully. Circle the key words to determine exactly what the question is asking you to do. Verbs such as those listed in the chart on the opposite page are cues that will help you to know how you should organize your answers.

I LIKE THESE ESSAY QUESTIONS...

THEY GIVE ME A CHANCE TO PERFECT A VITAL LANGUAGE SKILL...

SOMETHING I CAN USE THE REST OF MY LIFE:

THE ABILITY TO DISGUISE TOTAL IGNORANCE WITH GOOD WRITING.

Key Words in Essay Exams

Analyze Break something down into its component parts; explain the function of each part and show how each part relates to the whole.

Compare Show how things are alike and how they are different; support the similarities and differences you point out with details and examples.

Contrast Show how two or more things are different; support and emphasize differences you point out with details and examples.

Describe Provide word pictures; use precise details that show you clearly understand the main or the distinctive characteristics of the process or historical period you are describing.

Discuss Provide general statements supported with facts and details that show how well you understand key points or relationships.

Explain Make a problem, a relationship, or a process clear and understandable; include examples, reasons, or facts to show how a process or reaction happens, why a specific relationship occurs, or what has caused a particular problem.

Identify/Define Provide specific facts or details to establish or explain the unique identity of a significant historical or literary character or event.

Interpret Explain in your own words the meaning or importance of something. You can do this by supplying examples, facts, or reasons as support for your main idea.

Summarize Give a condensed version of a process, an event, or a sequence, briefly covering the most important points and omitting the less important facts and details.

Writing the Essay

Prewriting Remember that an essay test answer is an essay, so you can make use of the writing skills you have learned. During an essay test, follow these steps to organize each answer.

1. **Analyze the question,** underlining key terms. Read the following example: "Explain four improvements in technology that made the European Age of Exploration possible."
2. **Jot down notes** to refresh your memory about the main points of the subject. Sample notes:
- development of the triangular lanteen sail
- increased use of a few navigation aids—astrolabe, compass, maps
- development of three-masted ships
- the introduction of steering with single rudder
3. **Develop your thesis statement,** or main idea, by restating the question. Example: Improvements in steering, sails, masts, and navigation made the European Age of Exploration possible.

4. Outline your answer. Use the informal outline form. (See page 385 for details.)

I. Steering
- single rudder increased dependability
- replaced steering oars

II. Sails
- triangular lanteen sail could use headwinds
- replaced square sails that could use only tailwinds

III. Masts
- three-masted ships sturdier, more powerful
- advantage over one-masted ships

IV. Navigation
- magnetic compass made available
- astrolabe to determine location more precisely
- more accurate maps

Writing The following guidelines can help you write more effectively and efficiently.

1. Meet the answer head-on. Express your thesis in your first sentence if possible. Your opening sentence should show that you understand the question. It should also give your reader a sense of the direction that you will be taking in your argument.

2. Use your outline to help you write quickly but not frantically. You should depart from your outline only when you find something wrong or unworkable. Use transition words to introduce each new point that you are including in your answer.

3. Support your thesis with sufficient examples and relevant

Three-masted ship, c. 1650.

details. Referring to your outline often as you write will help you stay on track. A good essay test answer is not padded with information that is either unnecessary or irrelevant.

When you answer an essay question, try to use a simple, direct style. Make sure your answer is complete but not wordy.

4. Conclude with a strong sentence that restates your thesis in light of the evidence you have presented.

Revising and Proofreading You will have to work quickly to revise your essay, and you will not have time to make major revisions. Use the following guidelines to help you make the best use of your limited time.

1. Read each question. Make sure that each of your answers responds directly to the question.

2. Check your outline. Make sure that your answer covers all the necessary points. Look for places where you need to add more facts or details.

3. Correct problems in content and organization first. Then go back and correct any errors in grammar or mechanics.

4. Use proofreading symbols. Neatly mark any changes that you want to make. Consult the list of proofreading symbols that appears on page 82.

Sample Student Essay Read the following student essay. Compare it with the essay question, notes, thesis statement, and outline on pages 247 and 248.

Student Essay

Technological improvements in steering, sails, masts, and navigational aids made the European Age of Exploration possible. In the late thirteenth century, Muslims introduced the Europeans to the single rudder that made steering more dependable. The rudder replaced steering oars on both sides of the ship, a less efficient means of steering.

Another improvement in the structure of the ships themselves was the development of lanteen sails that could help the ships travel even in headwinds by tacking, or zigzagging, across the wind. The triangular lanteen sails replaced the square sails that could move ships only in tailwinds.

A third improvement, also in the structure of the ships, was the use of three masts instead of one. The additional masts made ships sturdier, faster, and more powerful than they had been.

Finally, the Chinese and Muslims developed navigational aids that helped sailors to determine their location and to set more accurate courses. These navigational aids included two instruments: the compass and the astrolabe (later replaced by the sextant). Another aid was improved maps.

Because of these developments in steering, sails, masts, and navigation aids, European explorers were able to sail to all parts of the world.

11

Using Persuasion in Writing

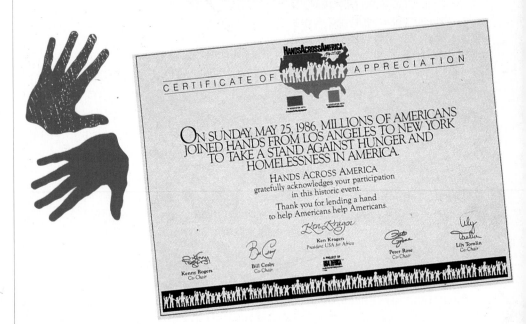

On Sunday, May 25, 1986, millions of Americans joined hands from Los Angeles to New York to take a stand against hunger and homelessness in America.

HANDS ACROSS AMERICA
gratefully acknowledges your participation
in this historic event.

Thank you for lending a hand
to help Americans help Americans.

Ken Kragen
President USA for Africa

Kenny Rogers
Co-Chair

Bill Cosby
Co-Chair

Peter Rose
Co-Chair

Lily Tomlin
Co-Chair

*O*rganizations committed to abolishing world hunger mount new campaigns each year to convince people to give them money and assistance that will help them progress toward their goal. The amount of aid raised by these campaigns depends to a great extent upon the quality of the persuasive writing in campaign speeches, newsletters, and leaflets.

The techniques of persuasive writing can enhance the effectiveness of all sorts of writing, from letters to science fiction stories. In this chapter you will learn the elements of persuasive writing and how to incorporate them in your writing.

Part 1
Analyzing Persuasive Writing

Persuasive writing attempts to influence the opinions of others or to convince people to take a specific action. It can be presented to a meeting of the student council or published in a local newspaper. It can urge a representative to act, or convince a friend to visit. To be effective, persuasive writing must show that you have thought clearly about your thesis and developed solid supporting arguments. Strong persuasive writing can help you reach and affect a wide audience.

The following models show two common uses for persuasive writing. One is by a student, and the other is by a professional writer. As you read, think about the ways in which the writers persuade you.

Student Model

Dear Congresswoman:

A television news report yesterday said that the government might cut funds that support public libraries. Please vote against this idea.

My classmates and I often use the town library for projects or recreational reading. Many other people in the community also use the library. My neighbor found a book in the library that helped her repair her plumbing. Once I saw the mayor there, checking out books on urban studies. In fact, libraries are used by 42 percent of the people in most towns.

Our library needs more money, not less. Many of the books need repairs. If funds are cut the library will be open fewer hours. Please help by voting no to these cuts.

Sincerely,
Paul Stewart

Discussing the Model   Now discuss the following questions.

1. What is Paul's position in this letter? How does he make his position clear at the beginning?
2. Give some of the arguments Paul uses to support his position. Are all of them equally effective?
3. What leads you to think that Paul understands the nature of his audience? Has he written to the right person?

Many people buy "all-terrain bikes" (ATB's) because they've discovered that bikes built for the rigors of off-road trips are well suited to life among the potholes and railroad tracks of the less-than-forgiving urban jungle. For bicycle commuting and around-town use, ATB's are generally more durable, more comfortable, and more stable than the familiar dropped-handlebar ten-speed.

An all-terrain bike's upright handlebars provide a comfortable riding position and as many as 18 gears help riders up the steepest streets while loaded down with groceries; wide tires offer more stability than road-racing tires; a strong frame and components withstand urban abuses; and heavy-duty brakes are right at home when needed to avoid unwanted contact with errant motorists.

Top-of-the-line mountain bikes are equipped to withstand more punishment than even the most brazen city biker will encounter (or want to encounter) on paved streets.

From "Two-Wheeling in the Urban Jungle" by R. McManus

Discussing the Model Now discuss these questions with your classmates.

1. What is the writer persuading readers to think or do?
2. What does the writer say in support of ATB's? Which supporting argument did you find most convincing? Why?
3. What other arguments or facts might you include?

Understanding Persuasive Writing

Effective persuasive writing always has a sense of audience and a clear purpose. Both of the models you just read also included a clearly stated position, which the writers defended with logical arguments. The student writer stated his position at the end of the introductory paragraph and supported it in the body of his letter. The professional writer stated his position with his first mention of ATB's.

Persuasion in Literature An effective persuasive essay begins with a clear purpose and is supported by careful, logical, and well-organized arguments. Look for those features in the following essay.

Persuasion in Literature

A Fable for Tomorrow

Rachel Carson

In the following essay from Silent Spring, *Rachel Carson presents an evocative fable in order to introduce her topic. The fable she presents appeals to the reader's emotions, but it is based in scientific fact. (For many years the author worked for the U.S. Fish and Wildlife Service.) Carson follows the fable with strong, direct arguments in favor of conservation. She presents her arguments in a general way and then with specific, detailed facts. As you read the essay, ask yourself which of her arguments are most effective and why. What do you think her next arguments might be?*

Appeal to emotion based in supportable fact

There was once a town in the heart of America where all life seemed to live in harmony with its surroundings. The town lay in the midst of a checkerboard of prosperous farms, with fields of grain and hillsides of orchards where, in spring, white clouds of bloom drifted above the green fields. In autumn, oak and maple and birch set up a blaze of color that flamed and flickered across a backdrop of pines. The foxes barked in the hills and deer silently crossed the fields, half hidden in the mists of the fall mornings.

Details support the point

Along the roads, laurel, viburnum and alder, great ferns and wildflowers delighted the traveler's eye through much of the year. Even in winter the roadsides were places of beauty, where countless birds came to feed on the berries and on the seed heads of the dried weeds rising above the snow. The countryside was, in fact, famous for the abundance and variety of its bird life, and when the flood of migrants was pouring through in spring and fall people traveled from great distances to observe them. Others came to fish the streams, which flowed clear and cold out on the hills and contained shady pools where trout lay. So it had been from the days many years ago when the first settlers raised their houses, and their wells, and built their barns.

The Trapper, Rockwell Kent, 1921.

Change in
setting based
on author's
position

*T*hen a strange blight crept over the area and everything began to change. Some evil spell had settled on
the community: mysterious maladies swept the flocks of
chickens; the cattle and sheep sickened and died. Everywhere was a shadow of death. The farmers spoke of much
illness among their families. In the town the doctors had
become more and more puzzled by new kinds of sickness
appearing among their patients. There had been several
sudden and unexplained deaths, not only among adults
but even among children, who would be stricken suddenly
while at play and die within a few hours.

There was a strange stillness. The birds, for example—
where had they gone? Many people spoke of them, puzzled and disturbed. The feeding stations in the backyards
were deserted. The few birds seen anywhere were mori-
bund; they trembled violently and could not fly. It was a
spring without voices. On the mornings that had once
throbbed with the dawn chorus of robins, catbirds, doves,
jays, wrens, and scores of other bird voices there was
now no sound; only silence lay over the fields and woods
and marsh.

On the farms the hens brooded, but no chicks hatched. The farmers complained that they were unable to raise any pigs—the litters were small and the young survived only a few days. The apple trees were coming into bloom but no bees droned among the blossoms, so there was no pollination and there would be no fruit.

The roadsides, once so attractive, were now lined with browned and withered vegetation as though swept by fire. These, too, were silent, deserted by all living things. Even the streams were now lifeless. Anglers no longer visited them, for all the fish had died.

In the gutters under the eaves and between the shingles of the roofs, a white granular powder still showed a few patches; some weeks before it had fallen like snow upon the roofs and lawns, the fields and streams.

No witchcraft, no enemy action had silenced the rebirth of new life in this stricken world. The people had done it themselves.

*T*his town does not actually exist, but it might easily have a thousand counterparts in America or elsewhere in the world. I know of no community that has experienced all the misfortunes I describe. Yet every one of the disasters has actually happened somewhere, and many real communities have already suffered a substantial number of them. A grim specter has crept up on us almost unnoticed, and this imagined tragedy may easily become a stark reality we all shall know.

What has already silenced the voices of spring in countless towns in America?

*T*he history of life on earth has been a history of interaction between living things and their surroundings. To a large extent, the physical form and the habits of the earth's vegetation and its animal life have been molded by the environment. Considering the whole span of earthly time, the opposite effect, in which life actually modifies its surroundings, has been relatively slight. Only within the moment of time represented by the present century has one species—man—acquired significant power to alter the nature of his world.

During the past quarter century this power has not

only increased to one of disturbing magnitude but it has changed in character. The most alarming of all man's assaults upon the environment is the contamination of air, earth, rivers, and sea with dangerous and even lethal materials. This pollution is for the most part irrecoverable; the chain of evil it initiates not only in the world that must support life but in living tissues is for the most part irreversible. In this now universal contamination of the environment, chemicals are the sinister and little-recognized partners of radiation in changing the very nature of the world—the very nature of its life. Strontium 90, released through nuclear explosions into the air, comes to earth in rain or drifts down as fallout, lodges in soil, enters into the grass or corn or wheat grown there, and in time takes up its abode in the bones of a human being, there to remain until his death. Similarly, chemicals sprayed on croplands or forests or gardens lie long in soil, entering into living organisms, passing from one to another in a chain of poisoning and death. Or they pass mysteriously by underground streams until they emerge and, through the alchemy of air and sunlight, combine into new forms that kill vegetation, sicken cattle, and work unknown harm on those who drink from once-pure wells. As Albert Schweitzer has said, "Man can hardly even recognize the devils of his own creation."

Specific example

Authoritative opinion

Trying Out Persuasive Writing Now that you have read some examples of persuasive writing, give some thought to some of the issues you feel strongly about. List these issues in your journal. For each of the issues, state your position and list several reasons why you feel the way you do. Decide which of your logical arguments best support your opinion about the issue you listed. Which are your strongest arguments? Which of your arguments are inappropriate for an essay? What details can you use to make your arguments convincing? Whom do you need to convince?

Then choose two or three of the issues and try writing some persuasive essays of your own. Organize your arguments as effectively as possible.

After writing, decide which of your arguments were most convincing. Ask yourself the following questions. What makes the arguments strong? How do they appeal to the audience you have in mind? The rest of the chapter will teach you more techniques for effective persuasion.

Part 2
Prewriting

We all use persuasion in everyday life. You may have used persuasive techniques to support your position on a school policy or to convince a friend to go to a party. To influence the opinions of others effectively, you must first explore your ideas about an issue and define the position you want to support.

Selecting an Issue

The issue you choose to write about should be debatable—something about which people disagree. It helps if you feel strongly enough about the issue to defend it with research and specific details. Also make sure your issue is not simply a matter of personal taste.

If a suitable issue does not come to mind, you can brainstorm by talking with friends or family members about topics of concern within your neighborhood, school, or community. You can also think about issues discussed on television, in newspapers, and in magazines. Check your thinking by asking yourself the following questions.

Guidelines for Selecting an Issue

1. Is the issue debatable?
2. Is the issue interesting and important to you?
3. Can you gather evidence to support your position?
4. Can you separate the issue from matters of personal preference?

Defining Your Position

The position you take on an issue will become your thesis statement. It must be debatable, important, and more than a matter of personal taste. A fact such as "Dolphins are mammals, not fish" is not a suitable thesis statement. Neither is a statement that merely expresses personal preference, such as "Dolphins are cute." "Captive dolphins should be set free" is, however, a suitable thesis statement. It is neither a fact nor a statement of personal taste. In addition, it is debatable. Zoo managers and some scientists might not agree.

Gathering Evidence

Once you have defined your position on the chosen topic, you can continue the prewriting process by gathering evidence. Facts, examples, anecdotes, observations, and authoritative opinions are among the kinds of evidence you can use.

Facts are statements of information. They are not debatable, though they can be proven to be accurate or inaccurate.

Examples are single instances that illustrate a concept or rule. An example is usually representative of a type or group.

Anecdotes are brief stories illustrating a fact or situation. Most anecdotes have emotional appeal. Unless an anecdote also supports a fact, however, it is weak evidence.

Observations are statements describing events or situations a person has actually seen. An anecdote becomes an observation when related in factual terms by a witness to the event.

Authoritative opinions are statements of opinion expressed by experts. They are educated, professional opinions. A doctor who specializes in sports medicine, for example, could give an authoritative opinion about the seriousness of a football injury.

If you evaluate your evidence as you gather it, you can judge the strength of your position as it develops. Althea used the following evidence to support her argument that dolphins should be set free.

One Student's Process

Persuasive Writing Worksheet

Kind of Evidence	Supporting Material
Fact	Dolphins have larger brains than humans.
Observation	Dolphins live a normal life in the ocean: they hunt for food and raise their young.
Authoritative Opinion	Dr. John C. Lilly says we should treat dolphins as equals
Anecdote	Dolphins have saved sailors who have fallen overboard
Example	A dolphin will purposely make its sounds audible to humans.

Determining and Analyzing Your Audience

In persuasive writing, it is especially important to understand the nature of your audience. You can more effectively appeal to your readers if you know something about their ages, interests, and points of view. The topic you choose, the way you word your thesis statement, the kind of evidence you gather, and the style in which you write will all depend how you judge the target audience.

Suppose you have decided to write in favor of protecting the wild horses of the American West. A member of your family might agree with you with little or no persuasion. An uncle whose cattle have been panicked by wild horses might not be convinced by any evidence. However, a letter published in a major newspaper would probably be read by a mixed audience. You could expect some readers to agree at once, some to be strongly opposed, and some to have no knowledge on which to base an opinion. When your target audience is likely to be mixed, you will need to do more than present strong evidence to support your position. You will also have to give enough background information to attract the attention of a wide range of readers.

Organizing Prewriting Notes

At this point it is a good idea to look back over the work you have done. Evaluate your topic and the evidence you have gathered, and discover what arguments your audience might have against your position and how you would respond to them.

Guidelines for Persuasive Writing

1. **Topic:** Is the topic I have chosen debatable? Does the topic really interest me? Will it interest others?
2. **Issue:** Have I defined my position on the issue in a clearly worded thesis statement?
3. **Evidence:** Have I gathered enough strong evidence to support my position? What kinds of evidence do I have? Which items of evidence are the strongest?
4. **Audience:** Who is my audience? Are they likely to have a single point of view or is it likely to be mixed? Are they likely to agree or disagree with me about the issue?
5. **Appeal:** How can I best present my topic to the audience? What kind of evidence will appeal to them? How can I present it in a convincing way?
6. **Background:** If the audience is mixed or mostly unknowledgeable about my issue, how much background information do they need? Shall I include background in the arguments, or provide it at the outset?
7. **Organization:** How can I organize my writing effectively to influence the opinions of my audience?

Writing Activities Prewriting

A While watching television news and documentaries, or reading newspapers and magazines, you have probably noticed that some general topics appear over and over again. These topics include the environment, endangered species, product safety, nuclear energy, human rights, government spending, and health care. Think of an issue related to each of these broad topics. Then write a thesis statement for each of the topics you have developed.

B *Writing in Process* Choose one of the thesis statements you wrote in Activity A, or choose another issue that interests you. Then develop a thesis statement telling your position on that issue. After you have written a thesis statement, write a paragraph defining the position you have stated. Gather different kinds of evidence that will convincingly support your position. You may need to do some research on the topic involved. Finally, check your work by using the Guidelines for Persuasive Writing.

Part 3

The Language and Logic of Persuasion

You have made a judgment about the nature of your audience. You have evaluated your topic, defined your position, and gathered supporting evidence. Now you can focus on the language and logic you will use to express your ideas and develop your arguments.

Grammar Note Using the active voice can make your persuasive statements more direct and powerful (see pages 523–524). You make a stronger statement when you claim that "we can end world hunger," for example, rather than claiming that "world hunger can be ended."

Approaches to Persuasion

A writer can persuade by appealing to emotion or reason. Generally it is more effective to appeal to reason, using logic and solid evidence. Logical arguments can withstand careful scrutiny.

Writing Inside Out
Clarence Page, Columnist

"Everyone has opinions, but it is not easy to write about them," says Clarence Page, whose opinions appear regularly in the *Chicago Tribune* and many other newspapers around the country. You have to create a voice, he says, a way of saying things that reflects your personality.

Mr. Page writes a syndicated column that expresses his views on a variety of important issues. He also writes some of the editorials that express the views of the entire newspaper. When he is expressing the newspaper's views he uses a different, more formal voice than the one in his own column.

How does he decide what to write about? Every day he meets with a group of other editorial writers that decides which news

Faulty Thinking

Language is the pattern of words through which we express our ideas and feelings. Logic is the study of correct reasoning. Both the language and logic of your persuasive writing can suffer if they are based on faulty thinking. Look at the explanations below. Be careful to avoid these illogical arguments and unfair uses of language in your persuasive writing.

Loaded Language The dictionary definition of a word is its **denotative** meaning. The additional emotional meanings associated with a word form its **connotative** meaning. The denotative meaning of *mutt*, for example, stirs up few feelings. But the connotative meaning, which suggests ''an inferior dog of little value,'' would offend many people. **Loaded language** is an emotional appeal that takes advantage of connotative meanings. Take care not to overuse loaded language or use it unfairly.

Circular Reasoning A writer who states, ''We should protect endangered animals because it is important to help threatened wildlife survive,'' is using **circular reasoning**. The writer is attempting to prove a statement simply by repeating the statement in different words.

events the paper will take a stand on. These writers also meet with top business and political leaders to get information to use in forming their opinions.

To find topics for his own column, Mr. Page reads many newspapers and magazines and looks for things he feels strongly about. Because he is black and cares about the welfare of other black people, he often writes about the national and local events that will affect blacks. He usually forms a strong opinion about an issue right away.

''Something just hits me and I know how I feel,'' he says. ''I'll do some research to find out what the other side thinks, but once I make up my mind I don't change it.'' Mr. Page adds that he also tries to express his views in a believable and interesting manner.

How did Mr. Page get to be a columnist? Being a newspaper columnist is something he has wanted ever since he wrote for his high school paper in Middletown, Ohio. He thinks it helped that he set his career goal very early and stuck to it.

During his career Mr. Page has also been a newspaper and television reporter, hosted local television talk shows, and written for many magazines. Although he has done all of these things, he still thinks nothing beats having a column.

Cause-and-Effect Fallacy When one event follows another, you might assume incorrectly that the first event caused the second. For example, if you found that the crime rate had risen in the past week, and then noticed the full moon, you might want to urge people to stay home when the moon is full. Yet the two events are not related in a provable way.

Either/Or Fallacy A writer who argues that there are only two alternatives, when actually there are many, is using the **either/or fallacy.** The statement "Either we raise taxes or we close the parks" is an example. It leaves out other, creative options.

Over-Generalization Generalizations are statements that apply to a number of persons, places, or things. When a generalization becomes too broad to be proven, it is called an **over-generalization.** The statement "Everyone who likes sports likes hockey" is an example.

Bandwagon/Snob Appeal When someone argues that you should believe or do something in order to follow the crowd, that person is using the old-time campaign fallacy of **bandwagon appeal.** The statement "Millions prefer Sudsy detergent" is an example of bandwagon appeal. **Snob appeal** is a form of bandwagon appeal. Someone using snob appeal implies that a belief or action will make you part of an elite group. "Own a Golden Arrow—a special car for special people" is an example.

Name-Calling An argument that uses name-calling is directed at who a person is, not at what a person knows and thinks. "Smyth can't possibly understand what democracy is all about; he is not even an American" is an example of the name-calling fallacy because it does not discuss the issue at hand.

Writing Activities *Identifying Fallacies*

A Examine the following ten statements. What kind of fallacy is illustrated in each statement? Which of the statements contain loaded words? Rewrite each statement, correcting the fallacy and substituting less suggestive words for loaded words. Add logical statements where necessary.

1. Nowadays if you are not a straight A student you won't get into college.
2. Mr. Gutierrez is a sour man with a silly attachment to the past; of course his exhibit will be irrelevant.
3. Friday's game ended in embarrassing defeat for the team and the entire student body. We propose, therefore, that games never be scheduled for Friday the 13th.
4. You basically have two choices in life, a career as a Scrooge in business or a career as a martyr in the arts.
5. Team sports are more interesting than individual sports, because working with a team is more interesting than working alone.
6. Regular guys go out for sports. Only saps work on the school newspaper.
7. All of us want to be rich and famous some day, whether or not we admit it.
8. Why would you follow a bum like that, when everybody who is anybody supports the mayor?
9. This school deserves praise for social awareness. One of our students is on the local conservation task force.
10. The present committee has always planned picnics on rainy days; we think a new committee should be formed.

B Look through the advertisements in a magazine or newspaper or watch several commercial messages on television in order to study persuasive techniques. Find an advertisement that uses one or more of the fallacies you have studied in this chapter. Write several paragraphs discussing the fallacies you found and the ways in which they were employed. Which fallacies were used? Which were most effective? Which were least effective? Why?

Part 4
Drafting

You have reached the end of the prewriting stage when you are satisfied with your answers to the questions in Guidelines for Persuasive Writing. Now you can begin writing your first draft. By keeping the guidelines in mind as you write, you can evaluate your progress step by step, and gain assurance as you go along. If you discover weaknesses in your thesis statement or supporting arguments, you can alter your position or gather more evidence. In any case, you will want to review your notes from time to time as you write.

Style The style of your writing may be formal or informal, but avoid the use of loaded words and keep appeals to emotion at a minimum.

Introduction The sentences in which you introduce your topic and define your position must capture the interest of your audience. If your audience is uninformed, follow the opening paragraph with a paragraph of background information that explains and reinforces the importance of the topic.

Body The body of your composition should be a well-organized presentation of your evidence. It may include a statement of the opposing point of view and the reasons why it is unsound. Make the transitions between arguments as smooth as possible.

Conclusion An effective concluding paragraph summarizes your arguments and restates your thesis. State clearly how you would like the audience to think and feel about the issue. You might also suggest an action for them to take.

Methods of Organizing Persuasive Writing

In an earlier section of this chapter, you learned the skill of identifying errors of reasoning in arguments. The skill of organizing sound arguments in a composition is equally important. Just as your audience may become impatient with faulty arguments and appeals to emotion, they may lose interest even in good arguments that are presented without apparent order. If your audience cannot follow your reasoning, your best efforts will not persuade them. The following chart shows five principal methods of organizing arguments.

Type of Audience	Method of Organization
Neutral	Weakest to strongest
Friendly or agreeable	Weakest to strongest
Point of view unknown	Strong to weak, then restate strong
Point of view well-known	Argument easy to agree with, step-by-step to arguments more difficult to agree with
Hostile or disagreeable	Attack weaknesses of opposing views, then present weakest to strongest arguments *or* Strongest arguments, then weakness of opposing views, then remaining arguments, then restate strong arguments

Writing Activities Drafting

A Suppose that you have chosen nuclear energy as a topic. The issue is: Should we develop nuclear power as our main source of energy? Your thesis statement is: *The development of nuclear energy diverts us from the development of clean, renewable energy sources.* Your arguments are listed below. Decide what kind of audience you are addressing. Then rearrange the arguments according to one of the methods of organization shown in the chart above.

1. There is still enough oil in reserve to give us time to develop alternatives to nuclear energy.
2. Nuclear energy is extremely expensive.
3. The waste products of nuclear energy remain dangerous for centuries. There is no safe place to store them.
4. Opponents may argue that nuclear reactions are a source of unlimited energy.
5. Opponents may argue that current non-renewable energy sources seriously damage the environment.

B *Writing in Process* Review the paragraphs stating your position that you wrote for Exercise B on page 261. Then write a first draft of your arguments, using the evidence you have gathered.

Part 5
Revising and Proofreading

When you have finished the first draft of your composition, you will probably want to take a break. Go ahead; often, it is wise to put your draft aside for a while, so that when you come back to it you have gained a fresh perspective on what you have written. After you have taken a short break, you should be ready to begin the revision of your first draft.

Read the draft to yourself at least three times—once for purpose, once for organization, and once for development—focusing on clarity and style. Make improvements as you read, because even minor errors can diminish your influence on an audience. It might be helpful to show your draft to a classmate who can act as a peer evaluator. The comments of a peer evaluator can help you judge the effectiveness of your work. Make sure you ask your peer evaluator to comment on the logic of your arguments and supporting statements.

Use the following checklist to focus your attention while you are revising your composition.

Revision Checklist for Persuasive Writing

Purpose
1. What is your purpose in writing the composition? Does your persuasive writing accomplish this purpose?
2. Does your thesis statement define your position clearly?
3. Are your facts accurate? Are your arguments logical?

Organization
1. Do you have enough strong, logical arguments to persuade your audience?
2. Have you organized your arguments according to the nature of your audience?
3. Is your reasoning clear?

Development
1. Is your style appropriate? Are your transitions smooth?
2. Have you chosen strong, convincing language, without using faulty logic or loaded words?
3. Is your language clear and grammatically correct?

Note how a student used the comments of a peer evaluator, along with her own ideas, in revising the first draft.

Free the Dolphins

From ancient times, dolphins have helped peo-

rarely, if ever

ple survive at sea. They have ~~never~~ hurt humans.

Yet, people imprison dolphins to experiment on

them, teach them military tasks, and make them do

of imprisoning dolphins

tricks. Instead, we should be attempting to com-

them

municate with ~~the dolphins~~ and learn from them.

People say that dolphins are very smart to

such as John C. Lilly, who worked with dolphins,

learn the tricks they perform. Scientists agree.

Dolphins have a great range of communications

skills. Though they communicate beyond our range

when

of hearing, they often change frequencies ~~so that~~

are nearby

humans ~~can hear them~~.

Margin comments:

- Over-generalizing!
- My transition should be more specific.
- I need an authoritative opinion.
- Cause/effect fallacy!

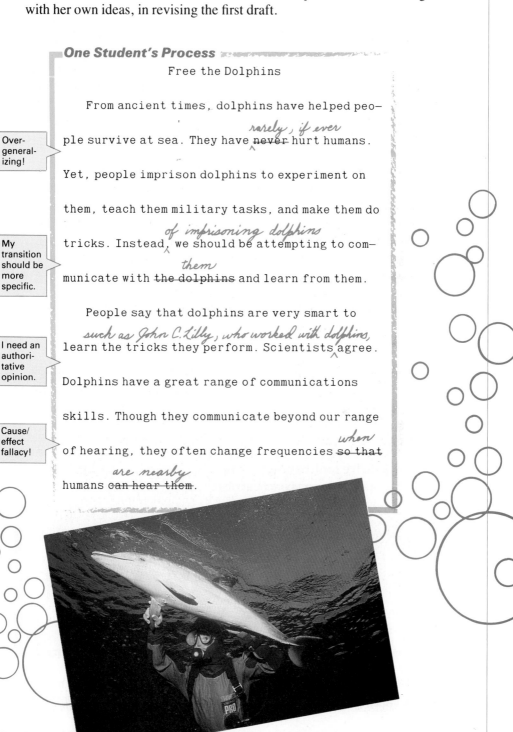

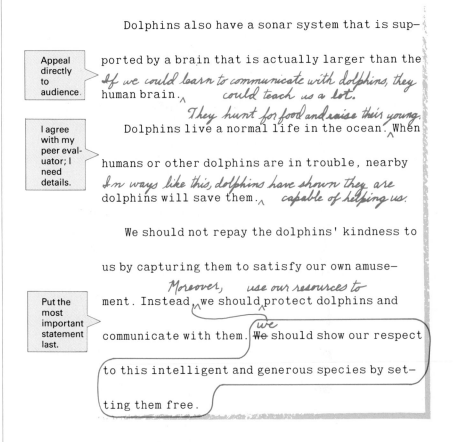

Dolphins also have a sonar system that is sup-

Appeal directly to audience.

ported by a brain that is actually larger than the human brain. *If we could learn to communicate with dolphins, they could teach us a lot.*

I agree with my peer evaluator; I need details.

They hunt for food and raise their young. Dolphins live a normal life in the ocean. When humans or other dolphins are in trouble, nearby dolphins will save them. *In ways like this, dolphins have shown they are capable of helping us.*

We should not repay the dolphins' kindness to us by capturing them to satisfy our own amuse-

Put the most important statement last.

ment. Instead, *Moreover,* we should *use our resources to* protect dolphins and communicate with them. ~~We~~ *we* should show our respect to this intelligent and generous species by set-ting them free.

Writing Activity Revising

Writing in Process Exchange with another student the first draft that you wrote for Exercise B on page 267. Use the Guidelines for Peer Evaluators to help you comment on the paper you are reading.

Guidelines for Peer Evaluators

- Use the Revision Checklist for Persuasive Writing on page 268 to evaluate your purpose, organization, and development.
- Describe what you like best about the ideas, organization, and language of the draft.
- Suggest improvements for the paper.

Now revise your own draft. Use your peer evaluator's comments and the Revision and Proofreading Checklists in Chapter 4.

Part 6

Other Uses of Persuasive Writing

People use persuasive techniques whenever they discuss important issues. Persuasion also is a part of many other written forms, including description and narration. In fact, for almost any form of writing, writers use persuasive techniques in order to get their readers to agree with their ideas.

Persuasive essays can help you make your point in critical papers, letters to the editor, or essay tests. They also have many other applications, some of which you may read every day. Now that you have learned the fundamentals of persuasive writing and have applied them in writing a composition, you can begin to use these skills in many areas of your life.

The chart below shows some of the most common forms of persuasive writing.

Uses of Persuasive Writing

Type	Purpose	Example
Editorials	To express views of news media management	Local TV station editorial after broadcast
Advertisements	To persuade audience to buy product or service	Newspaper ad for computer sale
Speeches	To influence the political views of voters or change their votes	Political campaign speech
Letters	To persuade the reader of your ability or potential	Letter applying for a summer job
Articles	To influence opinions and encourage action	Movie review: "See this film!"

Two models of persuasive writing are given below. The first is an advertisement, and the second is an editorial that might appear in a school newspaper. Read the models and note the kinds of arguments and the organization each writer used.

▬ *Professional Model* ▬▬▬▬▬▬▬▬▬▬▬

Wings of Fire is having the greatest pre-school sale ever on running shoes. All sizes are available at half price! We only stock shoes that have been endorsed by former Olympic Gold Medal Winners! Every style comes in several colors, with extra shock-absorbing heel cushions at no extra cost. This will be the only sale of its kind at Wings of Fire this year. Be sure that you don't miss this Gold Medal opportunity!

▬ *Professional Model* ▬▬▬▬▬▬▬▬▬▬▬

It seemed so glamorous when you started. . . . But now you can't run the way you used to; you get a lot of colds; your boyfriend says your hair stinks and your breath is bad.

Cigarette smoking is related to 320,000 (about the same number of people who live in Tucson, Arizona) deaths annually from cancer of the lung, mouth, pharynx, larynx, esophagus, pancreas, or bladder. And we found out [you don't] have to smoke for forty years to get these things.

From "Word Up," edited by Peter J. McQuaid

Writing Activities Uses of Persuasive Writing

A Review the categories and examples in the chart on page 271. Try to think of additional categories of persuasive writing and find examples for them. The examples should demonstrate a variety of uses for persuasive writing.

B *Writing in Process* Apply the skills you have learned to a persuasive writing project of your choice. Choose one of the categories from the chart on page 271. Next, brainstorm for a topic, using the techniques you learned in this chapter. Then decide upon a debatable issue, gather and organize your evidence, and write your composition.

Guidelines: *Persuasive Writing*

Prewriting
- Develop a list of possible topics based on conversations with others, gleaning from television news, newspapers, or magazines, and your own thoughts concerning current events. *(See pages 258-261.)*
- Choose a serious topic that interests you, one that contains an issue about which people are likely to have varying opinions. *(See pages 258-261.)*
- Define your position on the issue, expressed in a clearly worded thesis statement. *(See pages 258-261.)*
- Gather evidence to support your position in the form of facts, examples, anecdotes, observations, and authoritative opinion. Organize your evidence in an outline. *(See pages 259-261.)*
- Make a judgment about the nature of your audience: age, interests, point of view. *(See pages 260-261.)*
- Organize your arguments effectively, keeping the nature of your audience in mind. *(See pages 260-261.)*

Drafting
- Write a strong opening paragraph containing your thesis statement. *(See pages 266-267.)*
- Use your organized arguments to write the body of the composition, making sure that transitions are smooth and that your reasoning can easily be followed. *(See pages 266-267.)*
- Write a concluding paragraph that summarizes your position on the issue. Be sure to express clearly how you wish your audience to feel about the issue, and what action (if any) you would like them to take. *(See pages 266-267.)*
- Develop your arguments on the basis of the evidence, and check them for fallacies, excessive appeals to emotion, and loaded words. *(See pages 263-265.)*

Revising and Proofreading
- Give your composition three readings, once for purpose, once for organization, and once for development. When possible, show your composition to another person for comment. Revise and proofread accordingly. *(See pages 268-270.)*

Chapter 11
Application and Review

In this chapter you have learned how to compose a debatable thesis statement. You have also learned how to plan and write a variety of persuasive essays. Now use your skills to complete one or more of the following exercises.

A Writing a Proposal Imagine that you are part of a recreation task force to recommend park improvements to the mayor or town council. The mayor wants to make sweeping reforms, but many members of the council do not want to spend city funds on recreation.

Prewriting List your reasons for suggesting park improvements. What does your community need? What would be the benefits of the improvements you suggest? What are the drawbacks to consider? Once you have listed your arguments, organize them to appeal to both the mayor and the town council.

Drafting Using your outline, write a first draft of your persuasive essay. Try to use strong arguments and specific examples. Take care to avoid using unfair language.

Revising Use the Revision Checklist on page 268 to help you revise your first draft. Exchange your essay with a peer evaluator and consider his or her comments. After revising, proofread (using the Proofreading Checklist in Chapter 4) and prepare a final copy for the mayor and the council.

B Writing a Review Use the guidelines below to plan and write a review of a restaurant.

Prewriting Go to a popular fast-food restaurant in your town. Note in detail the things you liked and disliked about the atmosphere, food, and price. Then note why you think your readers should or should not patronize the restaurant. Use the knowledge you have gained in this chapter to analyze the audience you will probably be addressing. Organize your notes to help you appeal to a specific audience.

Drafting and Revising Use your notes to write a first draft. Try to tailor your arguments to your audience. Then revise your draft and share it with someone.

c *Starting Points for Writing* What are your reactions to the images and quotes below? These reactions are good starting points for writing. Use a thinking skill such as brainstorming or freewriting to explore your responses.

You can tell the ideals of a nation by its advertisements.

Norman Douglas

Effect of acid rain.

. . . laws are felt only when the individual comes into conflict with them.

Suzanne LaFollette

12
Writing About Literature: Fiction

Detail, *Peasant Life*.

When an art student wants to learn how Marc Chagall created the mood in the painting shown at the right, the student analyzes various elements of that painting. For example, the student might examine the composition, setting, color, and brushwork Chagall used to learn how each contributes to the mood of the artwork.

When a student of literature wants to understand how an author created a particular mood in a story, the student engages in a similar process. This student examines various elements of the story—composition, setting, word choice, sentence style—to understand how these help create the mood.

In this chapter you will learn to recognize and analyze these various elements of fiction as you learn to write about literature.

Peasant Life, Marc Chagall, 1925.

A Short Story to Analyze

When you write a composition analyzing a piece of fiction, such as a short story or a novel, it is called a literary analysis. In this chapter you will learn how to analyze a short story, how to organize your ideas, and how to draft a literary analysis. The model of a literary analysis that is developed in the chapter is based on the following short story, "Lather and Nothing Else." As you read the story, try to answer these questions: Where does the story take place? When? What happens? Who is involved? What is the conflict?

Lather and Nothing Else

Hernando Téllez

*H*e came in without a word. I was stropping my best razor. And when I recognized him, I started to shake. But he did not notice. To cover my nervousness, I went on honing the razor. I tried the edge with the tip of my thumb and took another look at it against the light.

Meanwhile, he was taking off his cartridge-studded belt with the pistol holster suspended from it. He put it on a hook in the wardrobe and hung his cap above it. Then he turned full around toward me, and loosening his tie, remarked, "It's hot as the devil. I want a shave." With that he took his seat.

I estimated he had a four-days' growth of beard, the four days he had been gone on the last foray after our men. His face looked burnt, tanned by the sun.

I started to work carefully on the shaving soap. I scraped some slices from the cake, dropped them into the mug, then added a little lukewarm water, and stirred with the brush. The lather soon began to rise.

"The fellows in the troop must have just about as much beard as I." I went on stirring up lather.

"But we did very well, you know. We caught the leaders. Some of them we brought back dead; others are still alive. But they'll all be dead soon." . . .

He leaned back in the chair when he saw the brush in

my hand, full of lather. I had not yet put the sheet on him. I was certainly flustered. Taking a sheet from the drawer, I tied it around my customer's neck.

He went on talking. He evidently took it for granted that I was on the side of the existing regime.

"The people must have gotten a scare with what happened the other day," he said.

"Yes," I replied, as I finished tying the knot against his nape, which smelled of sweat.

"Good show, wasn't it?"

"Very good," I answered, turning my attention now to the brush. The man closed his eyes wearily and awaited the cool caress of the lather.

I had never had him so close before. The day he ordered the people to file through the schoolyard to look upon the four rebels hanging there, my path had crossed his briefly. But the sight of those mutilated bodies kept me from paying attention to the face of the man who had been directing it all and whom I now had in my hands.

It was not a disagreeable face, certainly. And the beard, which aged him a bit, was not unbecoming. His name was Torres. Captain Torres.

I started to lay on the first coat of lather. He kept his eyes closed.

"I would love to catch a nap," he said, "but there's a lot to be done this evening."

I lifted the brush and asked, with pretended indifference: "A firing party?"

"Something of the sort," he replied, "but slower." . . .

I went on lathering his face. My hands began to tremble again. The man could not be aware of this, which was lucky for me. But I wished he had not come in.

I would have to shave his beard just like any other, carefully, neatly, just as though he were a good customer, taking heed that not a single pore should emit a drop of blood. Seeing to it that the blade did not slip in the small whorls. Taking care that the skin was left clean, soft, shining, so that when I passed the back of my hand over it not a single hair should be felt. Yes. I was secretly a revolutionary, but at the same time, I was a conscientious barber, proud of the way I did my job. And that four-day beard presented a challenge.

I took up the razor, opened the handle wide, releasing the blade, and started to work, downward from one sideburn. The blade responded to perfection. The hair was tough and hard; not very long, but thick. Little by little, the skin began to show through . . . I paused to wipe [the razor] clean, and taking up the strop once more went about improving its edge, for I am a painstaking barber.

The man, who had kept his eyes closed, now opened them, put a hand out from under the sheet, felt the part of his face that was emerging from the lather and said to me, "Come at six o'clock this evening to the school."

"Will it be like the other day?" I asked, stiff with horror.

"It may be even better," he replied. . . .

Once more he leaned back and shut his eyes. I came closer, the razor on high.

"Are you going to punish all of them?" I timidly ventured.

"Yes, all of them."

*T*he lather was drying on his face. I must hurry. . . . The razor kept descending. Now from the other sideburn downward. It was a blue beard, a thick one. He should let it grow like some poets, or some priests. It would suit him well. Many people would not recognize him. And that would be a good thing for him, I thought, as I went gently over all the throat line. At this point you really had to handle your blade skillfully, because the hair, while scantier, tended to fall into small whorls. It was a curly beard. The pores might open, minutely, in this area and let out a tiny drop of blood. A good barber like myself stakes his reputation on not permitting that to happen to any of his customers.

And this was indeed a special customer. How many of ours had he sent to their death? How many had he multilated? It was best not to think about it. Torres did not know I was his enemy. Neither he nor the others knew it. It was a secret shared by very few, just because that made it possible for me to inform the revolutionaries about Torres's activities in the town and what he planned to do every time he went on one of his raids to hunt down rebels. So it was going to be very difficult to explain how it was that I had him in my hands and then let him go in peace, alive, clean-shaven.

His beard had now almost entirely disappeared. He looked younger, several years younger than when he had come in. I suppose that happens to men who enter and leave barbershops. Under the strokes of my razor, Torres was rejuvenated; yes, because I am a good barber, the best in this town, and I say this in all modesty.

A little more lather here under the chin, on the Adam's apple, right near the great vein. How hot it is! Torres must be sweating just as I am. But he is not afraid. He is a tranquil man, who is not even giving thought to what he will do to his prisoners this evening. I, on the other hand, polishing his skin with this razor but avoiding the drawing of blood, careful with every stroke—I cannot keep my thoughts in order.

*C*onfound the hour he entered my shop! I am a revolutionary but not a murderer. And it would be so easy to kill him. He deserves it. Or does he? No! No one deserves the sacrifices others make in becoming assassins. What is to be gained by it? Nothing. Others and still others keep coming, and the first kill the second, and then these kill the next, and so on until everything becomes a sea of blood. I could cut his throat, so, swish, swish!

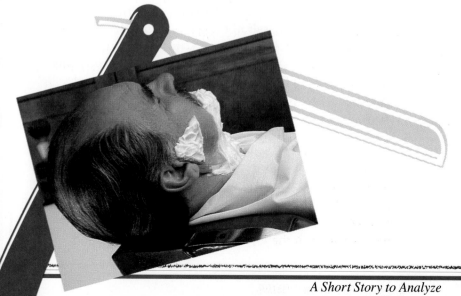

He would not even have time to moan, and with his eyes shut, he would not even see the shine of the razor or the gleam in my eye.

But I'm shaking like a regular murderer. . . .

I'm sure that with a good strong blow, a deep cut, he would feel no pain. He would not suffer at all. And what would I do then with the body? Where would I hide it? I would have to flee, leave all this behind, take shelter far away, very far away. But they would follow until they caught up with me. "The murderer of Captain Torres. He slit his throat while he was shaving him. What a cowardly thing to do."

And others would say, "The avenger of our people. A name to remember"—my name here. "He was the town barber. No one knew he was fighting for our cause."

*A*nd so, which will it be? Murderer or hero? My fate hangs on the edge of this razor blade. I can turn my wrist slightly, put a bit more pressure on the blade, let it sink in. The skin will yield like silk, like rubber, like the strop. There is nothing more tender than a man's skin, and the blood is always there, ready to burst forth. A razor like this cannot fail.

But I don't want to be a murderer. No, sir. You came in to be shaved. And I do my work honorably. I don't want to stain my hands with blood. Just with lather, and nothing else. You are an executioner; I am only a barber. Each one to his job. That's it. Each one to his job.

The chin was now clean, polished, soft. The man got up and looked at himself in the glass. He ran his hands over the skin and felt its freshness, its newness.

"Thanks," he said. He walked to the wardrobe for his belt, his pistol, and his cap. I must have been very pale, and I felt my shirt soaked with sweat. Torres finished adjusting his belt buckle, straightened his gun in its holster, and smoothing his hair mechanically, put on his cap. From his trousers pocket, he took some coins to pay for the shave. And he started toward the door. On the threshold he stopped for a moment, and turning to me he said, "They told me you would kill me. I came to find out if it was true. But it's not easy to kill. I know what I'm talking about."

The Elements of Fiction

All the elements of fiction—plot, characters, setting, theme, mood, and point of view—make up a short story. It is important to understand each element separately, on its own, before you can relate these elements to one another in a literary analysis. As you review each of these elements, try to think about the role they play in the short story "Lather and Nothing Else."

Plot The **plot** is the series of events that happen in the story. Two key aspects of plot are the conflict and the climax. The **conflict** or problem is the major struggle of the main character. In "Lather and Nothing Else," on pages 278–282, the conflict is the internal struggle of the barber. As he shaves the beard of his enemy, he considers using his razor to cut the Captain's throat. The **climax** is the turning point or high point of the story. Events in the story build excitement and interest to a crucial peak where the outcome of the plot often becomes clear. The climax of "Lather and Nothing Else" is the point at which the barber comes to the end of his task—his last chance to take advantage of the situation—and he decides that he is not a murderer. It is at this point that the reader knows he will let the Captain leave the shop unharmed.

Characters The **characters** are the individuals in a story. The revolutionary barber is a main character and Captain Torres, the military leader of the existing government, is another character. We learn about characters by their behavior, their words, and the things others say about them. The barber sweats, showing his nervousness. His anguish over the decision to murder Captain Torres demonstrates that he is a person who will not act impulsively for his cause.

Setting The **setting** is the time and place in which the action of a story occurs. "Lather and Nothing Else" takes place in a barber shop, usually a peaceful location. However, due to the rebellious time of the story—the shop is like a battleground, the revolutionary barber facing his deadly enemy, the Captain.

Theme The **theme** is the meaning of a story—the main point the author is trying to make. In conveying the theme, the author uses the elements of fiction to express the most important idea. Hernando Téllez, in ''Lather and Nothing Else,'' focuses on the theme of self-understanding. The main character struggles to resolve a conflict between his responsibilities as a revolutionary and his sense of honor. His rejection of the role of a treacherous executioner reveals that his honor was more important to him.

Mood The **mood** of a story is the feeling that the author creates and that you, as reader, sense through the words, style, and action of the narrative. ''Lather and Nothing Else'' is filled with a feeling of tension and conflict. The inner turmoil the barber experiences builds the tension and conflict of the story until the barber makes his decision not to murder the Captain.

Point of View The relationship between the narrator (storyteller) and the narrative (story) is the **point of view.** The author has three basic points of view from which to choose.

1. In **first-person** point of view the narrator, who may be a major or minor character, is also in the story. The reader is able to see inside this character's mind and to feel what the character feels. A first person narrative uses the pronouns *I, me, my, we,* and *our.* ''Lather and Nothing Else'' is an example.
2. In **limited third-person** point of view, the narrator tells the story from the perspective of one character. The narrator is not a character, but an outsider who views the action from the vantage point of a single character.

Outdoor sculpture, Nancy Holt, Saginaw, Michigan.

3. In **omniscient third-person** point of view, the narrator is also an outsider, but one who is able to describe everything that is going on—including the actions and thoughts of all the characters. This is sometimes referred to as the all-knowing point of view.

In analyzing a short story, you will choose one or more of these elements of fiction as the focus of your paper.

Writing Activities *Selecting a Short Story*

A Get together in classroom groups of four or five and list three or four short stories with which everyone in your group is familiar. Discuss the elements of fiction you have just studied as they relate to these stories and work together to identify plot, characters, setting, theme, mood, and point of view in each of them.

B *Writing in Process* At this point, you should review the stories you discussed in Activity A and select one to be the subject of your analysis.

Part 2
Prewriting: Analyzing Literature

A literary analysis is similar to a book report in that it is a discussion of an author's work. However, since the book report is usually written for an audience that is not familiar with the work, it generally contains an overview of the book and ends with a recommendation of whether or not to read it. The literary analysis treats a work of literature with which the audience is usually familiar. Thus, it concentrates chiefly on an interpretation and analysis of the work rather than an overview and recommendation.

Three Main Parts of Literary Analysis

The literary analysis paper has three main parts. The **introduction** presents basic information: title and author of the work in question, type of work (also called genre), the main idea of the paper, and—if it is significant to the analysis—an indication of the author's purpose in writing the work.

The **body** of the paper contains points supporting the main idea arranged in a logical order. These points support the focus of the paper with examples and details from the work. Any relevant information that explains and supports your main idea should be clearly presented in the body of the paper.

Finally, in the **conclusion** of the literary analysis paper you restate the main point, relate it to the story as a whole, and neatly tie up all the strings of your analysis.

Exploring the Short Story

Try to select a story that you think you will enjoy and find interesting. Read the story first just for the pleasure of the experience and to get a general impression. Then reread or review the story and take notes on the elements of fiction: character, plot, setting, theme, mood, and point of view, as they apply to your selection.

Throughout this chapter we will follow Raoul through the process of writing a literary analysis. Here is a sampling of questions that Raoul used to explore ''Lather and Nothing Else'':

One Student's Process

Character
- How does the main character change in the course of the story? The barber grows more upset as he struggles with the dilemma of whether or not to kill his enemy, until he makes up his mind and is more at peace with himself.

Plot
- Where does the action take place? Is it physical or mental action? Explain. The action is mostly mental action—the barber internally struggling with the pros and cons of murdering the Captain and deciding that his loyalty lies with his sense of honor as a barber.
- How does the story make use of the element of surprise? Because the story is told only through the barber's eyes, the Captain's statement as he exits the shop completely surprises the reader.

Setting
- How does the setting affect the plot? Because the

---

setting is the barber shop, where the barber earns his livelihood, he feels a very strong tie for his sense of honor as a barber and decides not to kill the Captain.

Theme

- How would you paraphrase the theme of this story? There are several related themes—the struggle for self-understanding, the conflict between responsibility or duty and honor, and the complexity of moral action.

Mood

- How does the author establish the mood? The author's use of the first-person point of view gives the reader a unique view inside the barber's mind. Thus all the barber's thoughts and anxieties can be felt by the reader. Also, the author's use of appropriate language, such as "stiff with horror" and "mutilated bodies," helps to reinforce the tension and foreboding in the air.

Point of View

- Would the story have been very different if another point of view had been chosen by the author? Why? Yes. Limited third-person would not have had as intimate a feeling. We would not have felt as closely involved in the barber's inner struggle. Omniscient third-person would have revealed the thoughts of Captain Torres but would have also distracted us from the barber's conflict. Also, it may have given away the Captain's secret.

After you formulate and respond to questions about your story, review your answers and use them to zero in on a focus for your literary analysis.

Finding a Focus

To determine a focus for your literary analysis, you should identify a key point that interests you and is important to the work. Asking yourself about the elements of the story may help you to zero in on your main idea. Express your focus in the form of a thesis statement that will identify the main idea of your analysis.

For example, a thesis statement like the following one Raoul wrote can be designed for "Lather and Nothing Else": *The author's choice of first-person point of view is vital to the development of the plot.*

Formulating an Argument

Having determined what your focus and thesis statement will be, it is time to design an argument in support of your main point. The first step in formulating this argument is to collect important details, quotes, and passages from the story that support your thesis. Some of these—if not all—will ultimately work their way into your paper.

Here is Raoul's list of some of the details from "Lather and Nothing Else" that he used to support his thesis statement.

One Student's Process

- In "Lather and Nothing Else," the story is told exclusively by the barber.
- Much of the initial suspense is created by the intimate revelations of the barber. He tells us about his "nervousness" and says he "started to shake" when Captain Torres entered the shop.
- We only know what the barber knows, so we believe him when he says that Torres "did not notice" his uneasiness. Later the barber assumes that the Captain "evidently took it for granted that I was on the side of the existing regime."
- The barber is in a state of inner conflict, trying to decide whether or not to kill the Captain. If he were to kill him, the barber wonders, would he be called "the avenger of our people" or a man who had done a "cowardly thing"? The barber's reasoning is key to the plot development. The deliberate shaving of the man quietly continues on as his mind rages. "I . . . polishing his skin with this razor but avoiding the drawing of blood, careful with every stroke—I cannot keep my thoughts in order."
- The barber thinks that the Captain "is a tranquil man, who is not even giving thought to what he will do to his prisoners this evening." We have no way of knowing Torres except through the barber's eyes.

- The climax is in the form of a silent resolution that only we hear: "I don't want to be a murderer. No, sir. You came in to be shaved. And I do my work honorably. I don't want to stain my hands with blood. Just with lather, and nothing else."
- Because the story is from the barber's point of view, the final revelation is as much a shock and surprise to us as it is to the barber. Captain Torres says, "They told me you would kill me. I came to find out if it was true. But it's not easy to kill. I know what I'm talking about." The Captain has been aware of the barber as his enemy all along and has sensed the barber's turmoil.

Writing Activity Prewriting

Writing in Process   Look at the general questions that were posed earlier about the elements of fiction. Answer these questions as they relate to the story you chose in Part 1. Then use these answers to create notes from the story to support the points you think are important. Finally, formulate a single focus for your analysis of the story. Express this main idea in a thesis statement.

Part 3
Prewriting: Organizing Your Ideas

Once you have decided on the focus of your literary analysis paper, you will need to organize the details you have collected. You will want to design a logical sequence of information in support of your main idea. If you are concerned with plot, the order might be chronological. If you are discussing character or setting, the order might progress from least important detail to most important detail. To organize ideas logically, you will need to work within a structure.

Providing a Structure

It is helpful to design a visual device to organize your ideas. A chart like the one on the next page compares two characters in a story. Notice how the chart helps you observe the characters' differences.

	Barber	**Captain Torres**
Position	Barber and member of resistance	Executioner for repressive regime
Manner	Nervous, professional, wary	Cool, matter-of-fact, confident
Motivation	Desires to be hero and do job correctly	Determined to catch and punish rebels
Changes in Story?	Yes, his decision made, he is more at peace.	No, he goes out as confident as ever.

A formal or informal outline is another way to organize the material you have collected. Remember the three main parts of a literary analysis—the introduction, the body, and the conclusion—and distribute your information according to this format. You may have to go back to the story for more information and/or discard some details you have already assembled if they seem inappropriate or unnecessarily repetitive. Here is Raoul's informal outline for his literary analysis.

I. Introduction
   A. Title, author—"Lather and Nothing Else" by Hernando Téllez
   B. Type of work—short story
   C. Elements to examine—point of view, plot
   D. Thesis statement—The author's point of view is vital to the plot development.

II. Body
   A. The plot occurs in the barber's mind.
      1. He describes the Captain's entrance.
      2. He sets up the antagonism.
      3. His mind races but he acts calm.
   B. The conflict and climax are experienced internally by the barber.
      1. The barber conveys his nervousness.
      2. The barber shares his inner struggle.
      3. The resolution is internal.
   C. The conclusion is a complete surprise.
      1. Torres is seen through the barber's eyes.
      2. Torres seems calm and oblivious.
      3. Torres's final statement is a shock.

III. Conclusion
   Restatement of thesis from introduction

Writing Activity *Organizing*

Writing in Process Organize your notes from Part 2. Decide on a logical order. Then make an informal outline of your analysis.

Part 4
Drafting and Revising

When you write a literary analysis, be sure that the information you use accurately reflects what happens in the story. Make certain the quotations you include are accurate. Here are some other key points.

1. Make sure you understand the purpose of your paper.

2. Tailor your presentation to suit your audience.
3. Review your supporting details. Be certain they are valid.
4. Follow your outline or other organizational device.

Here is Raoul's literary analysis of "Lather and Nothing Else."

One Student's Process

Through a Barber's Eyes

Title introduces point of view

"Lather and Nothing Else" is a powerful short story by Hernando Téllez. The action takes place in a quiet, simple barber shop, but a storm of re-

Setting Mood

bellion swirls around the town. An oppressive military regime is being challenged by a band of rebels. The main character of the story is a bar-

Point of view

ber who is also a secret rebel. It is the barber who narrates the events when an enemy leader be-

Thesis statement

comes his customer. Because much of the story depends on the barber's thoughts and reactions, the author's chosen first-person point of view is vital to the development of the plot.

Rising action of plot

In the beginning, the story heats up when Captain Torres walks into the barber shop. Outwardly, this is the arrival of just another customer in need of a shave. But the reader sees—and feels—the importance of this arrival

Incorporation of quotation

through the barber's eyes: "When I recognized him, I started to shake." Thus the rising action of the plot occurs mostly in the barber's mind.

The barber's recollections of his conversation with the Captain supply vital bits of information about the barber. He asks about his endangered comrades "with pretended indiffer-

Contrast drawn

ence," but is "stiff with horror" when he is invited to witness their execution. While he works methodically, his mind races wildly.

Both the conflict and climax of the plot are experienced internally by the barber, and the reader has an intimate, personal view of these important events. As he works on the Captain's

Inner conflict

beard, the barber shares his confused thinking with the reader. The razor is in his hands and he is "sure that with a good strong blow, a deep cut, [the Captain] would feel no pain." But what would be the result of this act? The barber would have to flee, pursued by the avengers who would call him a coward for slitting the Captain's throat. On the other hand, others would call him "the avenger of our people." The barber is tortured by indecision: "Which will it be? Murderer or hero? My fate hangs on the edge of this razor blade."

Climax
expressed
internally

As most of the plot occurs in the barber's mind, the reader is front row center for the climax. The barber reveals his silent resolution: "I don't want to be a murderer. No, sir. You came in to be shaved. And I do my work honorably. I don't want to stain my hands with blood. Just with lather, and nothing else."

Uses point of
view to
withhold
evidence

While the reader is closely involved with the internal action of the barber's struggles and solution, the author shields the reader from information about the Captain and therefore sets up a surprise ending. The reader's view of Torres is strictly through the barber's eyes. When they begin to talk, the barber assumes that the Captain "took it for granted that I was on the side of the existing regime." When his hands tremble, he says, "the man could not be aware of this, which was lucky for me." The reader is told that Torres is oblivious, and his casualness, as he closes his eyes in the chair, for example, seems to reinforce the barber's observation.

Surprise
ending

So Torres's final statement is a shock to the barber and, therefore, to the reader as well. "They told me you would kill me. I came to find out if it was true. But it's not easy to kill. I know what I'm talking about."

Restatement
of thesis

Thus the author cleverly uses the first-person point of view to convey intimate details about conflict and climax—basic elements of plot development—even as he sets up the reader for a dramatic ending. The reader knows enough to follow the plot along closely and feverishly yet is kept from knowing just enough and thus experiences a powerful and surprising conclusion.

Revising

Your job is not finished after you have drafted your literary analysis paper. Sometimes when you have been very much involved in a subject and related details, you start to think that you know them by heart. This may be true, but the post-writing phase is a vital time to check the accuracy of all the information you have used. Here are guidelines to help you revise your literary analysis.

Guidelines for Revising Literary Analysis

1. Be certain all your quotes are presented word-for-word, and they are integrated smoothly into your copy.
2. Review your arguments and conclusions, making sure the supporting material bolsters your thesis statement.
3. Check that you have accurately paraphrased information.
4. Make sure your ideas are presented logically, and are relevant to the main idea. If you have chosen a specific order of organization, make sure it is consistent.
5. Address your audience properly.
6. Be sure that your tone is appropriate and consistent.
7. Make sure to follow these proofreading guidelines.
   The first letter of every important word in a title should be capitalized.
   The title of a short story should be within quotation marks.
   Quotation marks should enclose direct quotes from the story.
   Quotations of four or more lines should be indented and set off.
   Missing words in a quotation should be indicated with an ellipsis.
   Place all words added to a quotation within brackets ([]).

Writing Activity Drafting and Revising

Writing in Process It is time to write, revise, and proofread the literary analysis you have been planning. Remember to create a clear thesis statement as a starting point using one or more literary elements as a focus. Design an argument by collecting support material from the story. Organize your material. Write a draft of your paper. Finally, revise and proofread your work carefully.

Chapter 12
Application and Review

Here are two activities to help you practice literary analysis. The first activity suggests a particular author you could analyze. The second one simply suggests a type of story to study. Select one or both of these activities for practice.

A Analyzing Mood Edgar Allan Poe, an American poet and short story writer who lived from 1809 to 1849, was a master at creating a powerful atmosphere in his stories. Select one of Poe's stories or find a short story by another author that seems to use mood as an essential element.

Prewriting Brainstorm with other students to create a list of the ways that mood may interact with other elements of fiction. For instance, a sinister character with shifty eyes may enhance a mood of evil or dread. Next, read your story, taking notes on the author's use of mood in the story. Form a thesis statement and prepare a list of supporting quotes and details from the story. Create an informal outline.

Drafting and Revising After deciding on a thesis statement and creating an outline for your paper, write a first draft. Share the draft with partners to get their impressions. Use these opinions as well as your own critical analysis to revise your work. Be sure to proofread.

B Analyzing Character Select a short story that concentrates on at least two characters as the chief element in the story.

Prewriting Create a chart that compares two main characters in your chosen story. How are they alike and different? How do they change over the course of the story? What do they say or do that reveals details about their personality? Next, read your story several times, taking notes about your characters and filling in the chart. Form a thesis statement and prepare a list of supporting quotes and details.

Drafting and Revising Using your thesis statement, documentation, and character chart, prepare a first draft. When the draft is complete, check that you've clearly expressed your main idea and defended it. Finally, check your draft for punctuation errors and revise your paper as necessary.

Focus On

READING SKILLS

Some writing is easy to read; other writing, next to impossible.
How do you "crack the code" on reading assignments?

The printed word is alive and well and waiting to be read. Although computer technology has changed communication, reading remains one of the best ways for you to get information.

Your assignment notebook probably bears proof that reading skills are vital to success in school. In addition to that, however, reading can be a pleasurable way to spend your leisure time.

It's Not Always Easy

Have you ever wondered why, at times, you can zip through something you're reading with almost perfect recall while at other times you just stare at the same paragraph over and over? For instance, a column on the sports page makes easy reading, but the beginning of a novel may seem to go on forever.

One very simple reason that your reading speed varies is that some materials, such as classic novels or computer manuals, are more difficult to read than others. Therefore, you have to learn different techniques to read different materials.

By mastering certain strategies, you can get the most from what you read while spending the least amount of time.

Previewing: Staying Tuned In

One of the first things to do when you are reading, especially if the material is long or difficult, is to preview the piece to get an idea of the overall meaning.

To preview a magazine article, for example, read the first two paragraphs of the material. Then read the first sentence of each successive paragraph.

You will remember from your experience with writing compositions that the first sentence in a paragraph is often the topic sentence and states the main idea of that paragraph. By selecting these sentences to preview, you will be able to concentrate primarily on the main ideas in the selection.

Finally, read the last two paragraphs. From these you will learn what conclusions the writer has drawn, if any.

After using the previewing strategy, you can reread the selection in its entirety, noticing how details support and enhance main ideas.

Solving the Puzzle: Identifying Relationships

The words, sentences, and ideas in a selection are like the pieces of a jigsaw puzzle: if you see each fragment separately, you can't appreciate the whole picture. When you read, it's important to identify relationships between the ideas being presented. Three important relationships to look for are relationships between main ideas and supporting details, sequence relationships, and relationships based on cause-and-effect.

Recognizing relationships between main ideas and supporting details helps you to see which

ideas the writer feels are primary, or have priority, and which ideas are subordinate. As you've seen, main ideas often can be identified by their position. That is, they frequently come first in a chapter or section, and they are followed by supporting ideas.

Sequence relationships establish the time order of events. A reader who can follow sequence won't become confused by fictional selections that use such literary techniques as flashback.

Understanding that one event occurred before another may also signal a possible cause-and-effect relationship. Causes precede and have an impact on effects. You can improve your comprehension of historical selections, if you know which events are causes and which are results.

Using clues . . . to predict an outcome is both fun and beneficial since it helps readers understand what's happening. . . .

Reading Between the Lines: Making Inferences

Sometimes writers make you dig to get the message. You must read between the lines, or make inferences about what the author means.

To infer meaning, you combine your knowledge with what the writer has revealed in order to figure out what is happening. For example, a story could begin with a direct statement: "Deborah woke early one morning." That same story might instead open, "The sky changed from deep purple to pale pink as Deborah sleepily opened her eyes."

In the second case, you can infer that it is morning because you know that the sky becomes lighter at dawn and because you read that Deborah sleepily opens her eyes.

Whodunit: Predicting

When you guess who the murderer is while reading a mystery, you are predicting an outcome. Good readers find that using clues, or guessing, is both fun and beneficial since it helps them understand what is happening. Predicting is a useful skill in non-

> *The classics of literature—those select books that have stood the test of time—are the gems of reading. . . .*

fiction as well. As you read, try to anticipate the writer's next point or conclusion. In this way, you are actively following the writer's thoughts and thus can spot any fallacies in the writer's reasoning. As you anticipate the writer, check to make sure that the writer provides

sufficient evidence to support his or her conclusions.

Taking on the Heavyweights: How to Enjoy the Classics

The classics of literature—those select books that have stood the test of time—are the gems of reading. Yet, great books don't seem great when you can't understand what you're reading. Some special strategies will help you enjoy and write effectively about the classics you read.

Before you begin, discover as much as you can about what you'll be reading. Learn about the author, the time in which the book was written, and the society in which the writer lived. Preview portions of the book to get an idea of what to expect.

What does it say? Your understanding of a work begins with literal comprehension—understanding the words at their face value. Don't just skip over unfamiliar words. Use context clues, word

© 1977 United Feature Syndicate, Inc.

clues, or a dictionary to define them.

Literary works written in an earlier time may contain dated language and long sentences that by today's standards seem extremely complicated. Context clues will often serve to solve the mystery of any dated language. Tackling troublesome sentences slowly, phrase by phrase, will help you to unravel their meaning.

Classics sometimes contain numerous characters. Keeping track of all of them may seem confusing at first, but stick with it until you feel as if you know them as friends.

It's also important to stay on top of the plot. Occasionally pause to recall what has happened in the story so far and to predict what may happen next.

What does it mean? To interpret a literary work, use all of the previously discussed skills: previewing, seeing relationships, making inferences, and predicting outcomes. Probe beneath the surface to understand the main character and the author's purpose. Analyze figurative language and look for possible symbols.

What does it matter? Evaluate what you read, measuring what the book offers against your own experience. Does anything in it help you to understand more about your life? your world? your relationships with others?

How well was it done? Analyze the technique of the writer. For example, if a selection is intended to be humorous, determine what devices the writer has used to create the humor. Did they work? Examine the word choices and sentence structure. These are elements of style that may cause you to return again and again to the works of a particular writer.

Read on. All of the classics bear rereading. If you read a classic novel a few years ago, read it again. Even though you already know the plot and the characters, the book may have so many new things to "say" to you that you will find it hard to think of it as the same book. Don't forget, reading is enjoyed most by those who do it well.

Check Your Comprehension
How much do you remember when you read? Complete the following exercises.

1. Preview a magazine article that you must read for current events or as part of your research for a report. Then write a statement that captures the main idea presented in the article.

2. Which three relationships should you look for when you read?

3. What is involved in making inferences?

4. What is the value of predicting outcomes as you read?

5. As your teacher directs, choose a classic work of literature to read. To read more effectively, apply the techniques discussed in this chapter.

13
Writing Reports

*F*or centuries, people in many cultures have been interested in earth
art. What form of earth art are the people pictured
above doing? Who created the earth sculpture of the
horse shown on the opposite page? When was it done?
To find answers to these questions, you need to be a
good investigator.

In this chapter you will learn the research skills you
need to investigate topics that interest or concern you.
You will also learn how to plan, organize, and write reports so that you can effectively share with others what
you have discovered.

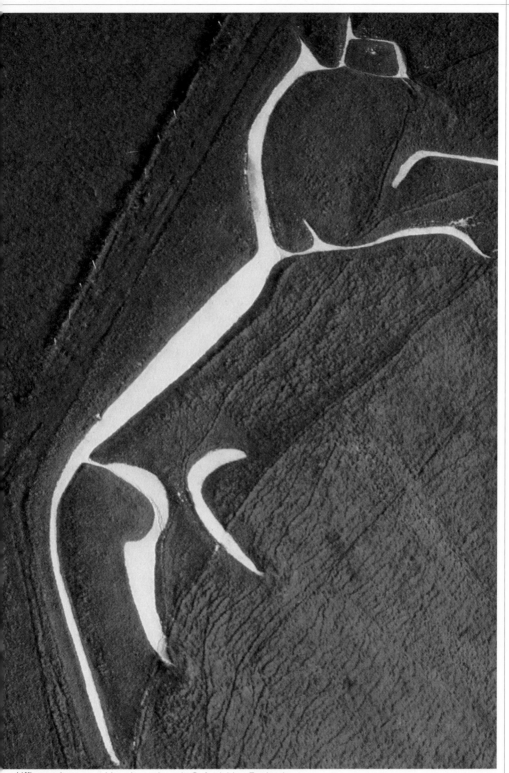

Uffington horse, prehistoric earthwork, Oxfordshire, England.

Planning Your Report

In art class, your teacher asks you to write a paper on the paintings of Vincent van Gogh. Your biology teacher asks you to report on the migration patterns of monarch butterflies. In economics class, you must report on the major products of one country, and you choose Jamaica. What do these three assignments have in common? In each, while you may know something about the subject, you do not know enough to write a fully developed composition.

Getting Started

A **report** is a composition based upon material from outside research rather than your own knowledge and experience. When you prepare a report, your main goals are to gather material from a variety of sources and then to present your information clearly and accurately. As you write a report, you go through the same stages you would with any other composition—prewriting, drafting, and revising. These stages help you organize and present the facts and ideas you have collected.

Keep in mind, however, that a report is more than simply a recounting of facts and ideas. You must select the facts and ideas that are most important. You must also decide on the best way to organize your information. Sometimes a review of your information will present new insights and new ways of thinking about the subject. A good report includes new ideas formed during this review.

Even in the planning stages, you shape your report by a number of judgments you make. As you plan your report, you choose a subject, limit your topic, prepare research questions, determine your purpose, and identify your audience.

Choosing Your Subject

You may have to write a report for any class—science, social studies, English, art, music, or physical education. Sometimes the subject may be assigned. Many times, however, you will have some choice. In a social studies lesson on the history of Mexico, for example, you may choose to report on something that particularly catches your interest, such as the beautiful Aztec city of Tenochtitlán.

To choose a subject, begin by making a list of possible subjects that interest you and that you feel would interest your readers. Be sure that these subjects require outside research. Remember that in a report, the subject should not involve you personally and you should not be the main source of information. For example, appropriate report subjects would be "The Problem of Acid Rain," "The Origins of Rock Music," or "Rainbows and Mirages."

Once you have listed about ten possible subjects, use the guidelines below to choose one for your report.

Guidelines for Choosing a Subject for a Report

1. The subject should interest both you and your audience.
2. The subject should be one on which there is enough information available.
3. The subject should be narrow enough to be developed in a short report.

Determining Your Purpose

Any subject can be approached in a variety of ways. Determining the purpose of your report will help you decide on the best approach for your particular subject. It will also help focus your thinking and research. The next section is broken down into different ways to approach your particular subject.

Informing Your Audience For most reports, your purpose will simply be to inform your readers about a subject. For such reports, you need to present facts and details that will help your readers understand the subject. The following reports inform the audience.

Hawaii's Volcanoes
Making Coins at the United States Mint
Zone Ball: A New Sport

Comparing and Contrasting Items In some reports, you compare and contrast two or more items. To do this, you can begin by reading about each item separately. Then you can decide how the items are similar and how they are different. For more information on comparison and contrast, see Chapter 10, pages 234–239. Listed below are some reports that compare and contrast.

Nuclear Energy vs. Solar Power
Athens and Sparta: Contrasting Greek Cultures

Discussing Cause and Effect Another purpose of a report is to discuss causes and effects. Such a report helps your readers understand the connection between an event and its causes or between an event and its effects. For more information on cause and effect, see Chapter 10, pages 228–233. The following reports discuss causes and effects:

> The French Influence on New Orleans
> Aerobics and Blood Pressure

Analyzing Still another purpose of a report could be to analyze. In such a report, you break the topic into smaller parts and examine their parts. The information you provide should help your reader draw conclusions about the topic, based on an understanding of the relationships between its parts. The following are reports that analyze their topics:

> Should School Officials Be Allowed to Search Students?
> Does Too Much TV Make Us Passive?

Limiting Your Topic

Another essential step in focusing your report is limiting your topic. You may find that a subject interests you and presents limitless research possibilities but is too broad for a short report. Which of these subjects could make a good two-page or three-page report?

1. Ice Hockey
2. Space Flight
3. Ocean Life
4. Robots: Early Development and Future Uses

The fourth topic is the correct choice. It limits the topic of robots to their early development and future uses. Therefore, it is detailed enough to be treated in a brief report. The first three subjects are too broad and would need to be narrowed. The following guidelines can help you narrow such topics.

Guidelines for Limiting a Report Topic

1. Consider how much information is available on the topic.
2. Consider how long your report must be.
3. Do some preliminary reading to find out some possible ways to limit the topic.

How could you narrow the three broad subjects presented on the previous page? For "Ice Hockey," you could focus on a specific playing position and report on "Expert Advice on How to Play Goalie." For "Space Flight," you might do some historical research and report on "The Apollo 11 Moon Landing." "Ocean Life" can be narrowed to one species, such as "The Humpback Whale."

Once you have limited your topic, you can clarify it by writing a statement of purpose, or **thesis statement.** For example, a thesis statement for a report on robots might be the following:

> Robots of today, and those planned for the future, have little in common with the popular science fiction images of robots.

A thesis statement is a valuable aid in writing your report. You may want to use it in the introduction of your report. As you plan and write, you can refer back to your thesis statement to be sure you are not straying from the purpose of your report.

Preparing Your Research Questions

Once you have narrowed your topic, you can attain even more focus for your report by preparing research questions to be answered in the report. For the report on robots, for example, you might ask the following questions:

1. What images do people have of robots?
2. What *is* a robot?
3. How were today's robots developed?
4. What can modern robots do for us?
5. What might robots be able to do in the future?

Determining Your Audience

Another step in focusing your report is to determine your audience. Who will be reading your report? How much will they know about your topic? How interested will they be in your topic?

Your audience's level of expertise will help you decide how much background information you need to provide and how technical your language can be. Sometimes your audience will be made up of "experts." For example, you may be reporting on an endangered animal—such as the brown bear of the western United States—to an ecology class whose members are quite familiar with the idea of endangered species. Thus, you will be able to limit your background information and discuss technical information more extensively.

Often, however, your audience will be made up of non-experts. In such cases, you will need to provide a clear overview of your subject, sufficient background information, and understandable language.

Level of audience interest also affects how you will write your report. If you suspect that your audience may not be interested in your topic, you will need to develop a strategy to catch their attention. For example, you may present the report in an unusual manner or from an unexpected viewpoint. You may want to use quotes, anecdotes, or interesting facts to catch your audience's interest. For more information about how to catch the interest of an audience, see page 25.

Writing Activities Prewriting

A Read the following list of topics. Decide which topics are too broad to be covered in a short report. Narrow each broad topic so that it is suitable for a two-page or three-page report.

1. Snakes
2. Photography
3. Why Dinosaurs Disappeared
4. Why We See Mirages
5. Tennis
6. Three Top-Performance Cars

B Choose three narrowed topics from the list above. Identify a possible audience for each topic. Tell whether each audience is expert or non-expert and assess its level of interest. Next, write five research questions for each topic you have chosen.

C *Writing in Process* Choose a topic for a report of your own. Begin with a broad topic and limit the topic to make it suitable for a four-page report. Develop your thesis statement. Then, prepare a list of five to ten research questions.

Part 2
Researching Your Topic

With your topic narrowed and your research questions written, you are ready for a trip to the library. There, you will find most of the information you need to prepare your report. Keep in mind, however, that *people* can also be excellent sources of information, so interviews provide another method of gathering information.

The library contains a wealth of information. Tracking down the information you need for your report can be stimulating, challenging, and fun, like putting together a jigsaw puzzle or finding the clues in a detective story. Library research is a complex process that requires a methodical, step-by-step approach before the entire effort begins to make sense.

Locating Your Materials

The first step in your research is to locate your sources of information. The library arranges books according to broad subjects. For example, science books will be shelved together, as will books on sports. Each subject will be divided further into subsections. Under science, you will find subsections covering fields such as astronomy, biology, chemistry, earth science, and physics. Each book has a number based upon its location. By referring to these numbers, your library's card catalog can lead you to any book or general subject area.

A good report also includes information obtained from reference materials and periodicals (magazines, journals, or newspapers). Your library has a section devoted to reference materials. In this section, you can find encyclopedias, handbooks, atlases, biographical dictionaries, and indexes—all potential sources of information for your report. One essential index you will find is called the *Readers' Guide to Periodical Literature,* which can direct you to specific articles in the library's periodicals section.

You can see that the library offers a great many sources of information. When researching your own topic, you will not have time to sift through all these sources. You will need a plan—a method of doing your research efficiently. Try starting by reading an encyclopedia article on your topic. Then check the card catalog and the *Readers' Guide* to find relevant books and articles. In addition, look for reference books that might relate to your subject. For more guidance in using the library, see Chapter 16.

Using Reference Works

When researching your report, the library's reference works can help you in a variety of ways. The chart below lists some of the resources you will find.

Library Reference Materials		
Reference	**Contents**	**Examples**
Dictionaries	spelling, pronunciations, and meanings of words	*Webster's New World Dictionary*
Encyclopedias	detailed articles on nearly all subjects	*Encyclopaedia Britannica, World Book Encyclopedia, Encyclopedia of Computer Science, Dictionary of American History, Harper Encyclopedia of Science*
Almanacs and Yearbooks	up-to-date facts, statistics, and unusual information	*Facts on File, Information Please Almanac*
Atlases	detailed maps and geographical information	*Hammond World Atlas, Times Atlas of the World*
Biographical References	detailed information about the lives of well-known people	*Dictionary of American Biography, Webster's Biographical Dictionary, Dictionary of American Authors*
Vertical File	pamphlets, booklets, catalogs, handbooks, and clippings filed by subject	
Indexes	listings of articles that have appeared in periodicals	*Readers' Guide to Periodical Literature, Social Sciences Index, General Science Index, Art Index*

Creating Your Working Bibliography

Once you have located your source materials, your next step is to begin a **working bibliography,** a record of the sources you have found.

Skim the source. If the source seems helpful, use the following guidelines to record it as a bibliography card on a 3″ × 5″ index card.

Guidelines for Bibliography Cards

1. **Books** Give the author (or editor), last name first; the title of the book; the name and location of the publisher; and the year of publication. Put the library call number in the upper left-hand corner of your card.
2. **Magazines** Give the author, last name first (unless the article is unsigned); the title of the article; the name of the magazine; the magazine's date; and the page numbers.
3. **Encyclopedias** Give the title of the entry; the name of the encyclopedia set; and the year of the edition.

Lisa, whose report we will follow throughout this chapter, had the following cards in her working bibliography. Notice the numbers in the upper right-hand corner. These numbers will help you later as you take notes, write footnotes, and prepare a final bibliography. Notice also that Lisa made a comment about the reference on the last card.

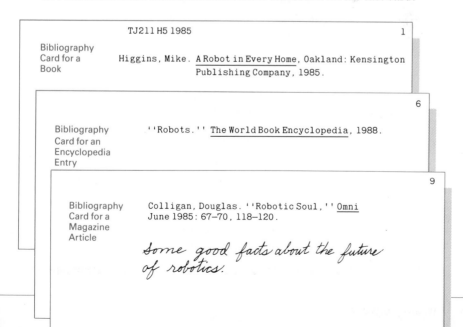

TJ211 H5 1985   1

Bibliography
Card for a   Higgins, Mike. A Robot in Every Home, Oakland: Kensington
Book   Publishing Company, 1985.

6

Bibliography   ''Robots.'' The World Book Encyclopedia, 1988.
Card for an
Encyclopedia
Entry

9

Bibliography   Colligan, Douglas. ''Robotic Soul,'' Omni
Card for a   June 1985: 67–70, 118–120.
Magazine
Article

Some good facts about the future of robotics.

Taking Notes

Now you can begin reading your sources in search of the facts that will make up your report. Record the facts you plan to use on 3" × 5" index cards. These cards allow you to consider each fact individually and to shuffle your information into various forms of organization.

As you take notes, write only one piece of information on each card. Notice that note cards, like bibliography cards, can be annotated. Notice also that note cards have a number and a letter in the upper right-hand corner. The number refers to the bibliography card, telling you the source of the note. The first note from that source is labeled *A*, the second *B*, and so on. Note how Lisa organized her note card.

> 3a
>
> Human-like robots were the villains in a number of movies, including *Zombies of the Stratosphere* (1935), *Target Earth* (1944), and the *Phantom Empire* (1952). Might be good introductory information.

Paraphrasing Most of your notes should be *paraphrased*, or written in your own words, not in the words of your source. Thus you will avoid the problem of *plagiarism*—the uncredited use of another person's material. Lisa read the following fact about robots.

> The wall-walking spider is being custom-designed for rescue work . . . a spidery robot crawls up the side of a burning skyscraper. It's carrying a lifeline to a group of anxious people peering through a broken window.
>
> From "Robotic Soul" by Douglas Colligan

Lisa paraphrased the facts she just read by writing, "Robotics experts are developing a wall-walking robot to rescue fire victims."

Direct Quotations If a quotation is useful and can improve your report, copy it accurately onto a note card and put quotation marks around it.

Writing Activities *Researching Your Topic*

A Paraphrase each of these quotations as you would on a note card.

> The space around our planet is polluted. . . . The North American Air Defense System (NORAD) currently tracks 6,194 radar-trackable objects—baseball sized and larger—in terrestrial and interplanetary orbit . . . The debris includes expended rocket stages, rocket panels, fragments from exploded satellites, . . . even hand tools that have slipped from the gloves of space-walking astronauts.
>
> From "The Impending Crisis of Space Debris"
> by Joseph A. Lovece

Gravity experiment.

> By the time a (Japanese) child is in high school, he or she spends several hours a day on homework. In sum, 65 percent of Japanese students spend more than five hours per week on homework; the figure is 24 percent for American seniors.
>
> From *The Japanese Educational Challenge*
> by Merry White

B *Writing in Process* Research the report topic you decided on in Part 1 of this chapter. On 3" × 5" index cards, create a working bibliography of five to ten sources. Try to use books, magazines, and reference sources. Next, write your note cards, using all of your sources. Use at least one quote in your note cards.

Part 3
Drafting Your Outline

Once you have a complete set of note cards, you can begin to organize your information. You will probably notice that most of your notes fall under one key idea or another. A good organizational technique is to divide your notes into groups based on these key ideas.

Here are some facts from Lisa's note cards on robots.

One Student's Process

1. A robot is a mechanical device that operates by following a program, or set of instructions, that specifies its task.
2. In a 1922 play by Czech writer Karel Capek, human—like robots, built to do the world's work, rebel and overthrow their human masters.
3. The majority of today's robots are stationary structures with a single arm.
4. In Japan, experts are developing a wall—walking spider robot to rescue fire victims.
5. Sinister, human—like robots have threatened the world in a number of movies, including <u>Zombies of the Stratosphere</u> (1935), <u>Target Earth</u> (1944), and <u>The Phantom Empire</u> (1952).
6. The factory of the future may be filled with computerized robots.

Lisa found she could sort her note cards into the following groups.

One Student's Process

I. Popular Images of Robots
II. Definition
III. Origins
IV. Robots of Today
V. Robots of the Future

Order of Information Sorting your facts into groups helps you arrange them into a logical order. For more information about logical order, see Chapter 6, pages 129–132.

Writing Your Outline

Your outline lays a framework for your report, showing how your facts should be arranged. Any one of the methods you learned about in Chapter 3 can help you organize your notes into a working plan for your report.

In your outline, each group of note cards becomes a main heading, labeled with a Roman numeral. Beneath each main heading are subheadings that summarize the individual note cards of that group. These subheadings are labeled with capital letters. They may be followed by more specific subheadings, labeled with numbers. Notice how Lisa uses an outline to structure her work.

One Student's Process

Robot: From Science Fiction to Reality

   I. Popular Images of Robots
      A. Play by Karel Capek
      B. Movies about robots
        1. Sinister robots
        2. Friendly robots

  II. Definition
      A. What a robot is
      B. How it works

 III. Origins
      A. Advances in electronics
      B. Devol's invention

  IV. Robots Today
      A. ''First generation''
        1. Computer and arm
        2. Work in factories
      B. ''Second generation''
        1. Sensing and interacting abilities
        2. Examples

   V. The Future of Robotics
      A. ''Third generation''
        1. Improved sensing and intelligence
        2. Existing ''third-generation'' robots
      B. Plans for the future
        1. Examples
        2. Factories of the future

You may find that your outline needs more facts under a certain heading. If so, return to the library and search for new sources.

Writing Activities *Drafting Your Outline*

A Read the following facts about the Amazon rain forest. Group these facts and arrange them in logical order. Then write an outline.

1. Tropical rain forests are rapidly being destroyed—faster than any other ecological community, in fact.
2. A tropical rain forest is an equatorial forest of tall trees with heavy rainfall and year-round warmth.
3. The Amazon rain forest covers 2.4 million square miles, including most of Brazil and parts of Peru, Venezuela, and Colombia.
4. Cattle-ranching is a great source of deforestation in the Amazon.
5. Many prescription drugs have ingredients from the rain forest.
6. The logging industry is responsible for much of the deforestation in the Amazon rain forest.
7. The Amazon rain forest has the world's greatest array of plants and animals. Scientists found 3,000 species in one square mile.
8. Of 24 hundred million acres of rain forest in the world, 14 million are permanently destroyed each year.
9. Agricultural settlements cut down many trees of the rain forest.
10. At the present rate of destruction, there may be no accessible tropical rain forests by the year 2000.

B *Writing in Process* Group the note cards for the report you began in Part 1 of this chapter. Put the facts into a logical order and then write an outline for your report.

Part 4

Drafting Your Report

With the outline and note cards before you, you are ready to begin the first draft of your report. Be sure that your note cards are arranged in the sequence of headings on the outline. Then begin writing from your outline, using information from note cards to fill in the needed details. Each time you use information from a note card, write the number of that card near the fact. These numbers will help you prepare documentation for your report.

Each section of your draft should make a specific, coherent point, and all of your sections should fit together logically. Remember to use transitional words and phrases where needed to help give your report unity and coherence.

The Introduction

A report, like other compositions, has three main parts—an introduction, a body, and a conclusion. Your introduction may use the facts from the first part of your outline. However, you may use another type of introduction, such as a question, an unusual fact, an amusing anecdote, or a quotation.

Whatever its form, your introduction should capture the reader's attention. It should also state the report's topic or main idea clearly in a thesis statement. Read these two possible introductions.

1. This report will be about robots. Robotics is quite an interesting field of technology. Robots themselves are interesting because of the many amazing things they can do.
2. Human-like robots, built to do the world's work, rebel and overthrow their human masters. "A new world has risen," announces the robot leader, "the rule of the robot." This scenario is from a 1922 play by Czech writer Karel Ĉapek. Sinister robots resembling humans also threatened the world in a number of movies, such as *Zombies of the Stratosphere* in 1935 and *The Phantom Empire* in 1952. In 1977 the popular movie *Star Wars* introduced the friendly robots C3PO and R2D2. Evil or friendly, human-like or machine-like, all these science-fiction robots are quite fascinating; but they have little in common with the actual robots that exist today and with those that are planned for the future.

The first introduction is dull and lifeless. The second, however, introduces the topic and treats the factual material with a fresh approach. With her details from science fiction images of robots and her thesis statement, Lisa captures the reader's interest in the topic of robots.

The Body

Be sure that your introduction, like the one above, leads the reader smoothly to the body of your report. Then draft a series of body paragraphs that follow the writing plan presented in your outline. Each main division in the outline should become one or more paragraphs in your report. Remember that each paragraph must have a topic sentence and information to support that topic sentence.

Documenting Your Sources

Before you begin writing the body paragraphs, you must remember to document your sources. In this chapter you have learned to either paraphrase or directly quote information from your sources. When you are incorporating the information you borrowed from sources into the body paragraphs of your composition, you must document this information.

Common sense should help you decide which information must be documented. Of course, familiar proverbs (''A watched pot never boils''), or well-known quotations (''To be or not to be''), or common knowledge (''Christopher Columbus discovered the New World'') don't need to be documented. However, information that may be mistaken as your own needs to be credited to the appropriate source.

You can document your sources in a number of ways. You can have notes that follow the report or notes that are inserted in the paper. Notes incorporated in the paper are often the most practical.

Parenthetical Documentation Often, the best way to document your sources is to insert brief **parenthetical notes** (footnotes in parentheses) in your paper whenever you use someone else's words, facts, or ideas. Most often the author's last name and a page reference are adequate to identify the source. The following example contains information taken from a source that is identified with a parenthetical footnote at the end of the sentence.

> The best jazz musicians in the world consider New York their final testing ground and their fellow musicians the most important critics (Hentoff 46).

The parenthetical reference indicates that this information comes from page 46 of a book by Hentoff.

To determine what information you need to document your sources, keep the following guidelines in mind.

Guidelines for Documentation

1. **Works with one author.** Give the author's last name in parentheses at the end of a sentence, followed by the page numbers (Jones 58).
2. **Works with more than one author.** List all the last names in parentheses, or give one last name followed by *et al.* (Smith, Jones, and Wilcox 87) or (Smith *et al.* 87).
3. **Works with no author listed.** When citing an article that does not identify the author, use the title of the work or a shortened version of it (''Robotics'' 398).
4. **Two works by the same author.** If you use more than one work by the same author, give the title, or a shortened version, after the author's last name (Jones, *Robots* 398).
5. **Two works cited at the same place.** If you use more than one source to support a point, use a semicolon to separate the entries (Jones 398; Smith 87).

In the report on robots, the introduction covered Part I of the outline. The body paragraphs will cover the information listed under Parts II–V.

Now read the final version of Lisa's report on robots. Notice the use of **parenthetical documentation.**

One Student's Process

Robots: From Science Fiction to Reality

Interesting introduction

Human-like robots, built to do the world's work, rebel and overthrow their human masters. "A new world has risen," announces the robot leader, "the rule of the robot." This scenario is from a 1922 play by Czech writer Karel Capek. Sinister robots resembling humans also threatened the world in movies such as Zombies of the Stratosphere in 1935 and The Phantom Empire in 1952. In

Thesis
statement

1977 the popular movie <u>Star Wars</u> introduced the
friendly robots C3PO and R2D2 (Marsh 26–27). Evil
or friendly, these science-fiction robots have
little in common with the actual robots that
exist today.

Defines
the
subject

A robot is a mechanical device that operates
by following a program, or set of instructions,
that specifies its task ("Robots" 348). These instructions are stored in a computer. By changing
the program, a person can alter the robot's behavior. Thus, according to one expert, a robot is
"a computer to which limbs, organs, tools, and
other equipment have been attached" (Barrett
37).

Cause:
advances
in
electronics

Effect:
first
practical
robot

The rapid advances in electronics during and
after World War II and the development of the tiny
computer microchip in the late 1950's provided
the technology necessary to help inventor George
J. Devol, Jr., create the first practical robot.
Hardly resembling its science-fiction ancestors, this robot was a computerized arm that
could perform routine operations with precision
(Asimov 865).

Paren-
thetical
note
Transition

Like Devol's early models, the majority of today's robots are stationary structures made up of
a single arm. The arm can lift objects and use
simple tools (Asimov, <u>Guide</u> 35), making it ideal
for repetitive assembly line tasks in factories.
Most industrial robots perform their tasks in the
automobile industry, where they do such jobs as
welding, spray painting, cutting, drilling, and
polishing (Asimov and Frenkel 46–68).

Transition

Use of
comparison
as
paragraph
link

Already, however, scientists have progressed
beyond these "first-generation" robots that simply perform repetitive tasks (Barrett 39).
"Second-generation" robots, while still stationary, have basic sensing abilities. Some can "see"
with the aid of a television camera, or "feel" with
sensors attached to their hands (Marsh 20–21).
Second-generation robots can even interact with
their surroundings. For example, if an object is
not there to be picked up, the robot will perform

some other programmed behavior ("Robotics" 10).
One of these more intelligent robots harvests oranges in Florida, choosing only the ripe ones to
pick (Barrett 38–39).

Transition

Even today, though, scientists are developing
"third–generation" robots, giving us a glimpse of
what the future holds. One of these third–generation robots is the "personal robot," which can be
programmed to serve food, clean house, or act as a
watchdog (Asimov and Frenkel 95–107).

Concluding
paragraph

In a sense, then, the future of robotics is
here, and scientists need only to continue in the
directions they are going. They are already planning robots that can diagnose illness, mine for
precious metals, and even rescue fire victims
(Barrett 39; Colligan 67–69). The factory of the
future may be filled with computer–controlled
robots. Some of these factories may even be in
space or on the moon and may involve robots producing other robots (Marsh 24–25, 30–31).

Refer back to page 313 to see how these body paragraphs follow
the outline. Do not feel "trapped" by your outline, however. You may
always add, delete, or reorganize information to improve your report.

The Conclusion

No matter how effective your body paragraphs may be, your report should end with an interesting conclusion. The conclusion ties the report together and tells the reader that the report is coming to an end. It may also summarize the report's main points, evaluate the topic and its effects, or provide a general statement that points to future research or future ideas. Lisa ended her report on robots with this conclusion.

One Student's Process

Quotation to add interest

> The future of robotics is speculation, however. As it unfolds we need to ask Karel Capek's question of 1922: Are robots a threat to us? As one writer puts it, "No one knows how the real-life super-robot story will end. But it seems likely that, one day in the distant future, we will find out" (Higgins 894).

Writing Activities Drafting Your Report

A Read the following information, which was included in a report about summer jobs. Write a conclusion based on the information. It can either restate, summarize, or make a comment on the information provided.

1. The availability of summer jobs for high-school students depends on the state of the economy.
2. If businesses are expanding and making a profit, their use of summer employees increases.
3. There are many different types of summer jobs suitable for high-school students, such as working for a department store or an amusement park.
4. Some students work for themselves, creating their own small businesses during the summer months.
5. A student could start a lawn service, baby-sitting service, or odd-job service.
6. It takes time, energy, and determination to find the perfect summer job or initiate a small business.

B *Writing in Process* Using the outline you prepared, draft the introduction, body, and conclusion for the report you planned in Part 1 of this chapter. Use transitions to link paragraphs.

Part 5
Revising and Proofreading Your Report

Once you have finished drafting your report, be sure to reread it carefully. Use the guidelines on page 80 to revise your report.

Checking Your Facts For reports in particular, however, there is one additional revision guideline: *check your facts*. Double check to be sure you have stated your facts correctly. If one fact seems unusual, you may even want to check its accuracy in a second source.

Writing Your Bibliography Be sure to acknowledge all sources in your footnotes and in a bibliography at the end of your report. List only the sources from which you have actually taken information. List them alphabetically according to authors' last names (or the name of the article if no author is given). Here is the bibliography for Lisa's report.

One Student's Process

Bibliography

Asimov, Isaac. <u>Asimov's New Guide to Science</u>. New York: Basic Books, 1984.

Asimov, Isaac and Frenkel, Karen A. <u>Robots</u>. New York: Harmony Books, 1985.

Barrett, F.D. "The Robot Revolution." <u>The Futur-ist</u> Oct. 1985: 37–40.

Colligan, Douglas. "Robotic Soul." <u>Omni</u> June 1985: 67–70, 118–120.

Higgins, Mike. <u>A Robot in Every Home</u>. Oakland: Kensington Publishing Company, 1985.

Marsh, Peter. <u>Robots</u>. New York: Warwick Press, 1983.

"Robot." <u>The World Book Encyclopedia</u>. 1988 ed.

"Robotics: What Does the Future Hold?" <u>USA Today Magazine</u> June 1984: 9–10.

When you have finished revising your report and writing your bibliography, make a clean final copy. Proofread your final copy, using the proofreading guidelines on page 82 for help.

The Admiral Speaks COBOL

O ne of the foremost language experts of the past fifty years has worked with languages that are never spoken and are not even intended for communication between people. Instead, these languages are the languages of computers.

The expert is Navy Admiral Grace M. Hopper, a pioneer in developing computer systems and computer languages. During her 43-year military career, which ended in 1986, she was in the forefront of the computer revolution. When she began, each computer had its own unique language, so communication between machines was difficult, and new programs had to be written for each machine. Hopper created the computer language COBOL (Common Business-Oriented Language), which was the first language that could be used by computers made by different manufacturers. She also worked to bring computer users together by standardizing computer languages.

Along the way, Hopper had an impact on English as well. In 1945, she and her colleagues coined some terms that are familiar to all computer users. The computer they were using at the time stopped working one day, and when they took it apart they found that a moth had become caught in one of the circuits. *Debugging,* the now-popular term for checking a system or program for errors, had a very literal meaning when Hopper and her colleagues removed the dead moth from their computer. Ever since, computer glitches have been known as *bugs*.

Guidelines: *Writing a Report*

Planning Your Report
- Make a list of interesting topics and select a subject from this list. (*See pages 302–303.*)
- Determine your purpose by picking an approach such as informing your audience, comparing and contrasting items, discussing cause and effect, and analyzing your information. (*See pages 303–304.*)
- Limit and narrow your topic for a short report. (*See pages 304–305.*)
- Prepare your research questions. (*See page 305.*)
- Determine your audience so you know the amount of background information you will have to include. (*See page 306.*)

Research Your Topic
- Locate your reference works in the library. (*See page 307.*)
- Use reference works to gather information. (*See page 308.*)
- Create a working bibliography for all your sources. (*See page 309.*)
- Take notes from your sources, making sure to paraphrase the information you use or directly quote the material. (*See page 310.*)

Drafting Your Outline
- Sort your facts into groups so you can arrange them in a logical order and then pick a type of organization. (*See page 312.*)
- Write an outline showing how your facts are arranged. (*See page 313.*)

Drafting Your Report
- Write an introduction using the first part of your outline or using a question, fact, anecdote, or quotation. (*See pages 315–316.*)
- Write your body paragraphs, following your outline. (*See page 316.*)
- Use parenthetical footnotes to document the information you borrowed. (*See pages 316–317.*)
- Write an interesting conclusion that ties your report together and tells the reader the report is coming to an end. (*See page 320.*)

Revising and Proofreading Your Report
- Check that your facts are accurate and documented. (*See page 321.*)
- Create a bibliography, alphabetically listing only the sources from which you have taken information. (*See page 321.*)
- Proofread your final copy. (*See page 321.*)

Chapter 13
Application and Review

Here are three activities for writing reports. Activity A guides you through the steps of writing a report. The second activity includes more choices, and the third activity uses photos and quotes to help you generate writing ideas. Select one or more for your next report.

A Writing a Science Report What new forms of technology do you find most interesting? Lasers? Super computers? Plan and write a science report whose purpose is to explain a technological advance. Try to discuss popular misconceptions about the technology. These misconceptions may come from movies, television, and books.

Prewriting With a group of students, brainstorm to create a list of modern technological innovations. Try to think of kinds of technology that people may misunderstand or have misconceptions about. Choose one of the technologies for your own report. Narrow the subject for a three-page to four-page report and develop a thesis statement.

Research your topic at the library. Use at least one science book, one reference book, and one periodical. Create a working bibliography and a set of note cards. Then create an outline.

Drafting Using your outline, write a first draft. Be sure that you are leading your reader in a logical manner. Consider using ''paragraph links'' and transitional words and phrases to connect your ideas.

Revising Use the checklist on page 80 to help you revise. Ask yourself: Will my introduction capture the reader's interest? Does it state my thesis? Have I followed my outline? Have I written an interesting conclusion? After revising, prepare a bibliography. Then proofread your report using the checklist on page 82.

B Writing a Social Studies Report Use these guidelines to plan, research, and write a three-page to four-page social studies report.

Prewriting Skim your social studies textbook, making a list of topics that intrigue you. You may choose any topic related to social studies. Narrow your topic, research it, and write an outline.

Drafting and Revising Write a first draft from your outline. Ask your teacher to edit your draft. Use your teacher's comments to guide your revision.

C *Starting Points for Writing* What would you like to know? Asking yourself this question is a good way to begin thinking up topics for a report. Ask it about something in particular. For example, what in the images might you like to know more about? What do the quotations make you curious to know? Answer these questions as you freewrite about the images and quotes. Your answers are good starting points for writing.

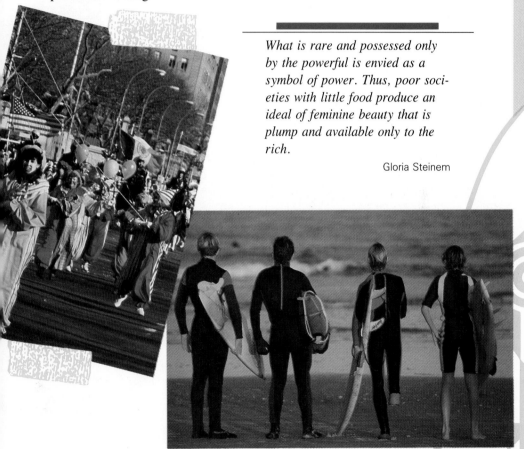

What is rare and possessed only by the powerful is envied as a symbol of power. Thus, poor societies with little food produce an ideal of feminine beauty that is plump and available only to the rich.

Gloria Steinem

They [the porpoise massacres] came to light because tuna boats would arrive in San Francisco and San Diego with the corpses of porpoises still aboard.

Ted Crail

Resources and Skills

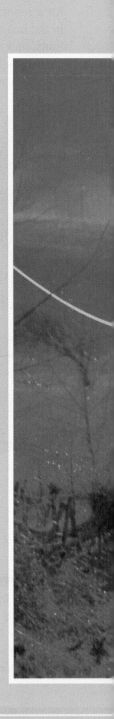

14

Building Your Vocabulary

The City, Fernand Leger, 1919.

*B*uilding a powerful vocabulary is an even more complex task than constructing a skyscraper.

In this chapter you will learn how to increase your vocabulary. You will discover how to determine the meanings of unfamiliar words by using context clues and analyzing word parts. An extensive vocabulary can be an effective tool for communicating complex ideas in today's information-oriented society.

Part 1
Inferring Word Meanings from Context

Like a detective searching for clues at the scene of a crime, you can often learn the meaning of an unfamiliar word by examining the "scene," or context, in which the word is used. The **context** of a word is the sentence or group of sentences in which the word appears. You may find the meaning of a word in an obvious clue in the same sentence, or you may have to look for clues in surrounding sentences and **infer,** or make an educated guess about, the meaning.

The most common types of context clues are these: definition and restatement, example, comparison and contrast, and cause and effect.

Definition and Restatement

In a definition or restatement clue, a writer reveals the meaning of a word by defining it or restating it in different words. Definition and restatement clues are often signaled by certain key words or phrases.

Key Words for Definition and Restatement		
in other words	this means	that is
to put it another way	which is to say	or

The clues can also be signaled by punctuation, such as the dash in the following example.

> The long climb up the steep cliff was a *grueling* experience— one that left us utterly exhausted.

Grueling means "very tiring, exhausting." Notice that the phrase following the dash is nearly the same as the dictionary definition.

A common type of restatement clue is the **appositive,** often set off by commas, as shown in the following example:

> The directors of the Bay City Zoo have announced the purchase of a pair of *quetzals,* crested birds native to Central America.

The appositive phrase "crested birds native to Central America" helps you to understand the meaning of *quetzals.*

Using Examples

Context can also help unlock the meaning of a word by providing one or more examples. When examples are cited, you can often guess the meaning of the word. Certain key words introduce examples.

Key Words for Examples

like	for instance	this
such as	especially	these
for example	other	to illustrate

Note the use of examples and key words in this sentence.

A small Georgia museum contains some excellent Civil War *memorabilia,* such as flags, cannonballs, maps, guns, photographs, and Union and Confederate uniforms.

The key words *such as* and the examples suggest the meaning of *memorabilia*—''a collection of things worth remembering.''

Sometimes the unfamiliar word is itself one of the examples of a familiar word, as in the following example.

A few small mammals, such as the Australian *wombat,* are in danger of becoming extinct.

You can understand the general meaning of the example *wombat* because the classification ''small mammals'' has already been given.

Comparison

Comparison is another category of context clues. With a comparison clue, the writer compares the unfamiliar word with other, more familiar words. By noting these comparisons, you can unlock the meanings of many unfamiliar words. Certain key words often signal comparison clues.

Key Words for Comparison

like	in the same way
as	similar to

In the following example, note how the key word and the comparison help you understand the word *ocotillo*.

> The *ocotillo,* like many other desert plants, has stiff, thorny stems and branches that protect against grazing animals.

The comparison clue shows you that the *ocotillo* is a desert plant.

A **simile** is a comparison between two different things; it uses the word *like* or *as* to make the comparison. A simile such as the following can give you a helpful clue to the meaning of an unfamiliar word.

> The letter from home had a *salutary* influence on Ginger. Like a swim on a hot day, it helped her regain her energy.

The *salutary* influence is compared with "a swim on a hot day." From this you can infer that *salutary* means "beneficial."

Contrast

In a contrast clue, the writer contrasts an unfamiliar word with something familiar. Here again, certain key words will help you to determine the meaning of the unknown word.

Key Words for Contrast	
but	on the other hand
although	unlike
on the contrary	in contrast to

In the following example, note how the key word and the contrast help you determine the meaning of *hirsute.*

> He noticed the goalie's *hirsute* look, which contrasted with the short-haired, clean-shaven appearance of the other players.

By paying attention to the contrast clue, you can infer that the goalie was long-haired and unshaven. *Hirsute* means "hairy."

Cause and Effect

Understanding the relationships between ideas in a passage is what finding context clues is all about. One very common relationship between ideas is cause and effect. Certain key words may signal cause and effect. They are listed on the following page.

The cause-effect relationship in this sentence, the fumes causing illness, leads you to infer that *noxious* means "harmful to health."

We knew the fumes were *noxious* when everyone became ill.

Inference from General Context

Context clues to the meaning of an unfamiliar word often do not come in the same sentence. The clues may not be obvious, and you will have to look carefully to infer the meaning of the unfamiliar word. In the following paragraph, a series of descriptive details add up to help you infer the meaning of *impromptu*.

> It was an intensely hot summer Sunday. Most of the neighbors were indoors with air conditioners and color TV's going full blast. Suddenly, there was a power failure. After about a half hour, most houses had lost their pleasing coolness, and people began to drift outdoors in search of a gentle breeze. Before long, food began to appear, someone fetched picnic tables, and an *impromptu* block party developed. All around me, people were getting acquainted.

The descriptive details in this scene create a context for *impromptu*—"done without previous preparation." In the cartoon below, however, context doesn't seem to matter much to the first speaker.

In the following paragraph, the term *obsolescence* is followed by an explanation and examples of the term.

> Much of the American economy is based on the principle of planned *obsolescence*. Consumer groups have criticized manufacturers for turning out products that are designed to wear out in a short time, although the technology exists to make longer-lasting products.

From the explanation in these sentences, especially wording such as "products . . . designed to wear out in a short time," you can infer that *obsolescence* means "uselessness" and "outdatedness."

When you look at the entire paragraph to infer the meaning of a word, you will often be helped by the same context clues discussed earlier. In the following example, an entire paragraph of contrasts helps you to infer the meaning of the word *transformation*.

> Sophia took a hard look at him; an astounding *transformation* had taken place. No longer did he appear lackluster or even middle-aged. His expression sparkled, his clean-shaven face was flooded with color; he had shifted his shoulders about until his coat fitted him the way the tailor had meant it to; he bristled with a youthful zest and energy.
>
> From *The Greek Treasure* by Irving Stone

The paragraph lists the differences that Sophia is seeing in the man. By considering the differences, you can easily determine the meaning of *transformation*—"change."

Here is a cause-effect context clue occurring in a paragraph from a history textbook.

> Not long after the new political party came to power, the voting districts in the state were *gerrymandered*. As a result, districts where the opposing party had been strong were now split up. Several very strangely shaped districts were created. The new party considerably strengthened its hold on the state.

Although *gerrymandered* is never actually defined, the effects of it are explained; therefore, you can infer that the word means "to divide a voting area in such a way that one political party gains an unfair advantage."

Exercises

A The sentences below contain words that may be unfamiliar. Using context clues, select the best meaning for each italicized word. Write down the letter that you think represents the correct response.

1. Several *lustrous* objects brightened the room: a chrome sculpture, a crystal chandelier, and sparkling silver doorknobs.
   a. stolen
   b. expensive
   c. shining
   d. handmade
2. I like a *succinct* sports announcement, not one that rambles.
   a. brief; clear
   b. witty; joking
   c. wise; well-informed
   d. wordy; repetitious
3. Some nations have unwisely *exploited* their colonies, taking as much wealth out of them as they could.
   a. taken advantage of
   b. enslaved
   c. destroyed
   d. bought and sold
4. Sonia's personality is an *amalgam* of the most desirable traits of the other members of her family. She has her father's cheerfulness, her mother's sense of humor, and her grandfather's calm.
   a. cause
   b. contrast
   c. mixture
   d. abundance
5. Because she complained of difficulty reading the blackboard at school, her parents suspected she was *myopic*.
   a. fatigued
   b. lazy
   c. malnourished
   d. near-sighted

B Read each of these passages. Write the letter that represents the best definition of the italicized word.

1. Many politicians are masters at the art of *circumlocution*. This fact is often illustrated in press conferences. In response to a controversial question posed by a reporter, some politicians can talk for several minutes without ever really answering the question.
   a. talking around a subject
   b. traveling from place to place
   c. pleasing people
   d. lying
2. Most Americans would find it difficult to adapt to the *ascetic* lifestyle of a monk. Garage door openers, dishwashers, garbage disposals, stereos, and color televisions—the luxuries that many Americans consider necessities—are missing from a monk's life.
   a. religious
   b. extravagant
   c. vigorous
   d. self-denying

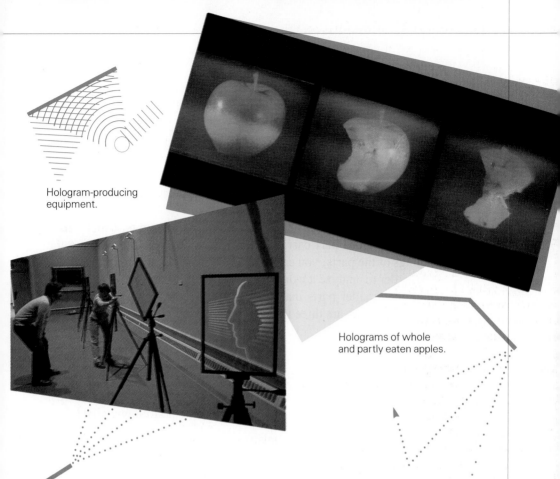

Hologram-producing equipment.

Holograms of whole and partly eaten apples.

3. One young scientist used a laser to create a *hologram* of an apple for her exhibit. Viewers would be able to see all sides of the apple.
   a. three-dimensional image of a scene or object
   b. moving picture
   c. scene painted on a large wall
   d. life-sized scene

4. Since her injury, Eileen Gardner was able to do little more than watch television and carry out light chores around the house. Though she had been a capable athlete, her muscles were beginning to *atrophy*. Then she decided to rebuild them.
   a. waste away
   b. develop
   c. strengthen
   d. elongate

5. A true *gastronome* like Julia Child is probably unimpressed by the billions of hamburgers sold by fast-food restaurants. Better known as "The French Chef," Mrs. Child is the author of a number of books on French cooking. For her, the measure of cooking rests more in the quality than in the quantity of the final product.
   a. a world traveler
   b. an expert on fine foods
   c. a fast-food lover
   d. a busy person

Part 2

Analyzing Word Parts to Determine Meaning

In Part 1, you learned to determine the meaning of a word by examining the sentence or sentences in which it appears. Sometimes, however, the word itself contains the clues.

Many English words are composed of smaller units, called **word parts**. Each word part carries its own meaning. If you combine the meanings of the parts, you can infer the meaning of the entire word.

In order to analyze a word in this way, you must first be able to recognize the smaller parts that can make up a word. Base words, prefixes, and suffixes are three types of word parts.

Base Words

Base words are short English words that lie at the heart of longer words. Other word parts may be added to a base to create new words. What base word was used to make the words in the following list?

> distrust   trustful   mistrust   distrustful

The base word is *trust*. The beginnings *dis-* and *mis-* and the ending *-ful* were added to it. The new words still have the idea of *trust* in their meanings. If you know the meaning of the base word, you can begin to understand the longer word. You can complete the process if you know the meanings of the other word parts, prefixes and suffixes.

Prefixes

A **prefix** is one or more syllables placed at the beginning of a base word to change the meaning of the base word. You can make many new words simply by adding a prefix to a base word. (Note that the spelling of a word never changes when a prefix is added.)

Prefix	+	Base Word	=	New Word
in-	+	correct	=	incorrect
extra-	+	ordinary	=	extraordinary
mis-	+	manage	=	mismanage

Every prefix has one or more meanings. If you can identify the prefix and the base word and if you know the meanings of both these parts, you can often determine the meaning of the longer word.

The prefixes in the following chart mean "not" or "the opposite of." For example, *appropriate* means "suitable." *Inappropriate* means "not suitable."

Prefixes That Reverse Meaning

Prefix	Meaning	Examples
dis-	the opposite of	displace
in-	not	inconsiderate
		intolerable
ir-	not	irregular
		irresponsible
im-	not	immobile
		immaterial
il-	not	illegible
		illiterate
non-	not	nonpoisonous
		nonessential
un-	the opposite of	untie
		unbutton

The following prefixes show relationships in time or space. For example, *submerge* means "place under water."

Prefixes That Show Relationships

Prefix	Meaning	Examples
sub-	beneath, lower	subcommittee
pre-	before	prepaid
ante-	before	antecedent
post-	after	postdated
super-	over, above, beyond	superstructure
circum-	around	circumscribe
re-	back, again	reappear
extra-	outside, beyond	extralegal

The following prefixes show judgment. For example, *malpractice* means "improper practice."

Prefixes That Show Judgment

Prefix	Meaning	Examples
pro-	in favor of	probusiness
contra-	against, opposed to	contravene
anti-	against	antislavery
mis-	wrong	misplace
mal-	bad or badly, wrong	malnourished

When you analyze words, be careful not to confuse words that have prefixes with words that contain letters that only resemble prefixes. For example, *prepaid* is a base word with a prefix. *Pressure* is simply a word that begins with the letters *p, r,* and *e.*

Suffixes

A **suffix** is one or more syllables placed at the end of a base word to form a new word. Each suffix has its own meaning or meanings. You can use suffixes to determine the meanings of longer words. In the following chart, see how suffixes have been added to base words to form new words.

New Words Made with Suffixes

Base Word	+	Suffix	=	New Word
compose	+	-er	=	composer
friend	+	-ship	=	friendship
guard	+	-ian	=	guardian
fury	+	-ous	=	furious
believe	+	-able	=	believable
percent	+	-age	=	percentage
truth	+	-ful	=	truthful
care	+	-less	=	careless
excite	+	-ment	=	excitement
material	+	-ism	=	materialism
dark	+	-ness	=	darkness

The spelling of a base word may change when a suffix is added. In the previous examples, the final *y* in *fury* was changed to *i* when *-ous* was added. For information about spelling rules for adding suffixes, see pages 740–741. Also, when a suffix is added to a base word, it often forms a new part of speech. For example, the noun *fury* becomes the adjective *furious*; the noun *harmony* becomes the verb *harmonize*.

Noun Suffixes

Syllables that make nouns out of the base words to which they are added are called **noun suffixes.** The suffixes in the following chart all mean "one who does something" or "that which does something."

Noun Suffixes That Refer to Action

Suffix	Meaning	Examples
-arian	one who	librarian
		humanitarian
		octogenarian
-eer	one who	volunteer
		puppeteer
		musketeer
-er	that which	computer
		amplifier
		copier
-ist	one who	botanist
		physicist
		dentist
-ian	one who	electrician
		mathematician
		beautician
-or	one who	conductor
		actor
		director

The words in the chart on the next page are all abstract words; that is, they describe a state of being or a quality. For example, *boredom* is the state of being bored, *cleverness* is the quality a clever person has, and *amazement* is the state of being amazed or surprised. Remember that the spelling of a base word may change when a suffix is added to it.

Noun Suffixes That Make Abstract Words

Suffix	Examples
-dom	boredom, wisdom
-hood	statehood, womanhood
-ism	patriotism, realism
-ment	amazement, encouragement
-ness	cleverness, kindness
-ship	leadership, friendship
-ity	sanity, rapidity

Adjective Suffixes

Suffixes that change base words to adjectives—words that modify other words—are called **adjective suffixes.** For example, the suffix *-able* changes the word *believe,* a verb, into the adjective *believable.* Study the chart below to learn about types of adjective suffixes.

Adjective Suffixes

Suffix	Meaning	Examples
-ous	full of	glorious
-ose	full of	verbose
-ful	full of	graceful
		bountiful
-al	relating to	regional
		fanatical
-ic	pertaining to	scientific
		symbolic
-ical	pertaining to	historical
		economical
-ish	relating to	stylish
		smallish
-ive	pertaining to	active
		manipulative
-able	capable of being	imaginable
-less	without	blameless
-like	like	childlike

Verb Suffixes

Verb suffixes change base words to verbs. For example, the suffix *-en* changes the base word *short,* an adjective, into the verb *shorten.* The following chart gives four common verb suffixes.

Verb Suffixes That Mean "to Become"

Suffix	Meaning	Examples
-ate	become	illuminate
-en	become	strengthen
-fy	become	liquefy
-ize	become	memorize

Exercises

A For each of the following words, draw lines to separate the word into its three parts—prefix, base, and suffix. Determine the meaning of the prefix and suffix. Then, by adding the meanings of the prefix and suffix to the base word, write the meaning of each complete word. Use a dictionary to check your answers.

> *Example*   un|avoid|able = not able to be avoided

1. inexcusable
2. immortality
3. nonconformism
4. mismanagement
5. prearrangement
6. irregularity
7. disadvantageous
8. precolonial
9. malodorous
10. inhumanity

B In each of the following sentences, there is a blank followed by a base word in parentheses. Add a suffix to the base to form the word's correct part of speech to fit the sentence.

> *Example*   At the village water station, engineers added chemicals to _____ (pure) the water. *purify*

1. The leaders of the two nations decided to meet annually for talks, and this _____ (agree) lasted for thirty years.
2. With _____ (cat) movements the burglar circled the house quickly and silently.
3. The _____ (auction) was well known throughout the county for her sense of humor.

4. Those blinking neon signs will _____ (bright) the street, turn- ing it colorful and exciting.

5. Nina tried to think of a _____ (tact) way of telling her boyfriend that he had egg on his shirt.

6. Sir Gawain, taking his _____ (knight) very seriously, spent most of his adult life defending King Arthur.

7. May Shin shouted with joy after hearing she was now a _____ (violin) with the Springfield Symphony Orchestra.

8. Alonso dived into the icy waters to save a drowning person and for this _____ (courage) act was given the Citizen's Award.

9. When the team started to lose, the fans started to _____ (critic) the coach.

10. Unlike traditional warfare, a nuclear war could easily result in _____ (globe) devastation.

Part 3
Applying Your Skills

You now have two useful tools for unlocking the meanings of words—using context clues and analyzing word parts. The following exercises will allow you to practice using these tools. The exercises are much like those you will encounter in the vocabulary sections of stand-ardized tests. Use the skills you have learned in this chapter to deter-mine the meanings of the words.

Section 1: Word Meanings from Context Clues Select the best meaning for the italicized word in each passage. Write the letter that represents the best answer.

1. A rainbow is an *evanescent* thing; it gradually disappears, leaving only a memory.
   a. temporary   c. even; balanced
   b. shaped like an arch d. beautiful

2. Like any other beginner, a *novice* in the kitchen is likely to make mistakes.
   a. cook   c. helper
   b. young person   d. someone new to an activity

3. Of course this narrative is *fictitious;* it has no basis in fact.
   a. colorful   c. important
   b. changeable   d. imaginary

4. The child was *precocious*. She could read before she started nursery school.
   a. hard to manage
   b. ahead in development
   c. likely to brag
   d. very young
5. A guinea pig is *vulnerable*. It can't fight well, it can't run fast, and it has no tough hide or bad scent to protect it.
   a. hopeless
   b. lovable
   c. popular as a pet
   d. easily hurt
6. Tell me the *gist* of the movie. I don't have time for a long description right now.
   a. rating
   b. characters
   c. complete explanation
   d. main idea
7. The story is too *somber*. I prefer something with a more cheerful ending.
   a. sleepy
   b. sad
   c. lengthy
   d. noisy
8. A feeling of *anxiety* about the future replaced her peace of mind.
   a. quiet
   b. uneasiness
   c. understanding
   d. interest

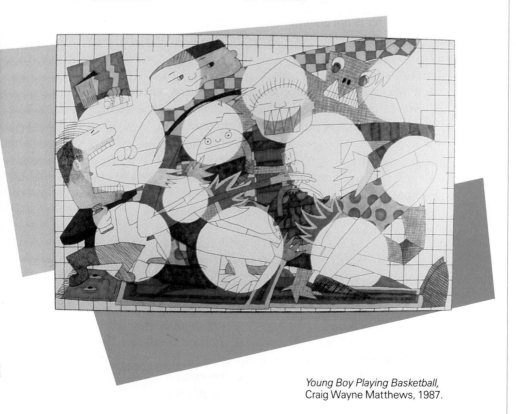

Young Boy Playing Basketball,
Craig Wayne Matthews, 1987.

Section 2: Word Meanings from General Context Read each paragraph. Write the letter that represents the best definition of the italicized word.

1. The Battle of Antietam was the bloodiest twelve hours of the Civil War; 22,719 soldiers were killed or wounded. Yet Clara Barton did not turn back in horror from the *carnage* of the battlefield. She had taken upon herself the duty of nursing the injured. She did not flinch from stepping across corpses to the mangled survivors.
   a. combat
   b. enemy
   c. filth
   d. mass killing

2. When news broke that a tanker had spilled tons of oil off shore, students from the local high school rushed to the beach. There they cleaned oil from the feathers of helpless seabirds. The students had *mitigated* at least some of the damage caused by the spill.
   a. made worse
   b. made milder or less serious
   c. caused
   d. ignored

3. The damage caused by the testing of the new insecticide has angered local residents. In an attempt to *mollify* its outraged neighbors, the Kental Corporation has offered to pay for any damage. The offer is not enough. Residents say that money cannot make up for the fear, worry, or loss of crops resulting from the tests.
   a. make fun of
   b. soothe
   c. accuse
   d. mislead

4. Friday was the *antithesis* of the rest of that whole, miserable week. The sun shone for the first time, the air was warm, and the pools of water began slowly to evaporate.
   a. cause
   b. opposite
   c. last day
   d. best

5. In his old age Frank led a *sedentary* life. Most days he read his books and tended to his carrier pigeons.
   a. settled
   b. vigorous
   c. sad
   d. angry

Section 3: Word Meanings from Word Parts Write the letter that represents the best definition for each italicized word.

1. *antislavery*
   a. after slavery
   b. before slavery
   c. opposed to, or against, slavery
   d. in favor of, or for, slavery

2. *postmeridian*
   a. come back again
   b. before noon
   c. around evening
   d. after noon

3. *disquiet*
   a. a quiet mood
   b. the lack of mental peace
   c. anger; disgust
   d. suddenness
4. *illimitable*
   a. not legal
   b. one who places limits
   c. able to be confined
   d. without limit; infinite
5. *impractical*
   a. difficult to practice
   b. perfectly possible
   c. involved in preparation
   d. a condition of not being practical
6. *inglorious*
   a. full of glory
   b. dishonorable
   c. beautiful; magnificent
   d. victorious
7. *mischance*
   a. luck; fortune
   b. misconduct
   c. another chance; second try
   d. bad luck; unlucky incident
8. *pro-American*
   a. not an American
   b. a professional athlete
   c. opposed to America
   d. in favor of America
9. *nonmetallic*
   a. not made of metal
   b. like metal
   c. an unknown metal
   d. a metalworker
10. *supernatural*
   a. frightening
   b. fiction
   c. beyond the natural world
   d. less than natural
11. *statistician*
   a. one who studies oceans
   b. a photographic machine
   c. one who works with numbers
   d. full of static
12. *untactful*
   a. nonviolent
   b. lacking skill in dealing with people
   c. polite, diplomatic
   d. adhesive
13. *imprecise*
   a. not fast
   b. proper
   c. well-proportioned
   d. not exact
14. *incurable*
   a. unable to be remedied
   b. long-lasting
   c. not caring
   d. able to be corrected
15. *antifreeze*
   a. favoring cold
   b. a children's game
   c. against heat
   d. a substance that prevents water from freezing

The Cherokee Language

F or centuries Native American lore was passed down through the generations mainly by word of mouth. At the beginning of the nineteenth century, however, a Cherokee named Sequoyah gave his people the ability to keep a written record of their culture.

Cherokee Indian.

The Sequoya Alphabet of the Cherokee Indians

As a child, Sequoyah had been fascinated by the "talking leaf" used by white settlers. He had seen these people write messages on paper and then read them; he wondered why his own people did not know the secret of the talking leaf. The question continued to haunt Sequoyah as he grew up. Although he became an accomplished silversmith, painter, and warrior, he—like the rest of his people—was illiterate. Then, a hunting accident left him partially crippled. With time on his hands, he began to investigate the mystery of the talking leaf. For twelve years he studied the way the Cherokee people spoke, and he developed a way to break down Cherokee words into individual sounds. Adapting letters from English, Greek, and Hebrew, he developed an alphabet of eighty-six symbols, each corresponding to a syllable of spoken Cherokee language. At last, the Cherokee people had a system for reading and writing their own language.

The alphabet Sequoyah invented earned him the respect of his own people and of the nation. Developing an entirely new alphabet had been a giant undertaking. For Sequoyah's efforts, the giant California redwood trees—the sequoias—were named after him.

Chapter 14
Application and Review

A Inferring Word Meanings from Context Read the following passage very carefully. Copy the underlined words onto a separate sheet of paper. After each word, write the meaning that you inferred from its context using the techniques presented in the chapter. Check your answer with a dictionary.

(1) Shortly after the *Golden Clipper* left Pago Pago, several crew members became ill with <u>enterocolitis</u>. (2) Since everyone who suffered from this intestinal disorder had eaten at the same cafe, the ship's doctor <u>surmised</u> that the crew members had contracted this disease by eating tainted fish.

(3) The <u>authorities</u> in the Philippines, however, feared an epidemic, and refused to let the ship dock in Manila Bay. (4) Instead, the entire crew was transferred to a <u>lazaretto</u> floating three miles off shore. (5) A staff of doctors and nurses cared for the ill and carefully observed the other crew members for any signs of the <u>malady</u>. (6) When no new cases developed after three days, the Philippine doctors ruled out any possibility of a <u>contagion</u>. (7) The ailing crew members were then conveyed to a hospital in Manila, and the others were permitted to return to the *Golden Clipper* and to dock in Manila Bay.

B Analyzing Word Parts to Determine Meaning For each of the following words, draw lines to separate the word into its three parts—prefix, base, and suffix. Determine the meanings of the prefix and suffix. Then, by adding the meanings of the prefix and suffix to the base word, write the meaning of each complete word.

1. unemotional
2. subtropical
3. illegality
4. reappointment
5. nonrenewable
6. preelection
7. inhumanity
8. disenchantment
9. replacement
10. unapproachable

15
Learning About Our Language

R odeo, saxophone, cab—each of these words has entered the English language from a different source. The word *rodeo* was borrowed from Spanish; *saxophone* was named for its inventor Adolph Sax; and *cab* is the shortened form of *cabriolet*, a two-wheeled carriage.

In this chapter you will learn about some of the ways in which the English language grows and develops. You will also learn the appropriate uses of the various levels of English.

Part 1

How Words Enter Our Language

Since its beginnings over 1,500 years ago, English has grown to be the largest language in the world, containing over 790,000 words. Our language continues to grow as new words are borrowed and created.

Borrowed Words

When another language has a word for which we have no term of our own, we may borrow the word. The borrowed word may enter English unchanged, or it may change somewhat in spelling or pronunciation. For example, cowboys of the Old West, handling angry herds of cattle, changed the Spanish word *estampida* to *stampede*.

The chart below lists some borrowed words that have enriched our language. Can you think of others?

Words Borrowed from Other Languages

African	canary	tote	jazz	okra
Chinese	yen	typhoon	silk	catsup
French	machine	liberty	chic	blouse
German	zinc	hoodlum	snorkel	pretzel
Italian	volcano	carnival	studio	trombone
Japanese	soybean	karate	kimono	haiku
Native American	pecan	skunk	chipmunk	powwow
Scandinavian	ski	skirt	sauna	geyser
Spanish	canyon	comrade	vanilla	renegade

People and Place Names

Some words in English have been taken from the proper names of people and places. The term *mesmerize,* for example, comes from the name of Dr. F. A. Mesmer, an Austrian physician who was known for his work with hypnotism. The list on the following page shows other words derived from proper names.

Compounds, Blends, Clipped Words, and Acronyms

New concepts and inventions are continually being developed. To communicate these ideas, new words are often created. There are several ways in which new words enter our language.

Compound Words A **compound word** is made by combining two existing words to form a new word. People develop compound words to describe new ideas or things while still using familiar terms. For example, the relatively new word *spacewalk* is a combination of two older, more familiar words: *space* and *walk.*

Blends If two words are combined, but some of the letters are dropped, the resulting word is called a **blend.** For example, the television term *sitcom* is formed from the words *situation comedy.*

Clipped Words Sometimes one or more parts of a word are dropped, and the remaining part is used alone as a word. Such words are called **clipped words.** The word *gym,* coming from *gymnasium,* is an example. Clipped words are used in less formal situations.

Acronyms A new word created from the first letters of a group of words is called an **acronym.** *Scuba,* for instance, is an acronym for "self-contained underwater breathing apparatus." Here are other examples of compounds, blends, clipped words, and acronyms.

Ways to Form New Words

Compounds

loud + speaker	= loudspeaker	skate + board	= skateboard
knee + cap	= kneecap	red + wood	= redwood

Blends

motorcycle + cross-country	= motocross
splash + surge	= splurge
telescope + photograph	= telephoto

Clipped Words

teen-agers = teens	examination = exam
cabriolet = cab	pianoforte = piano

Acronyms

radar = *ra*dio *d*etection *a*nd *r*anging
COBOL = *Co*mmon *B*usiness *O*riented *L*anguage

Exercises

A Using a dictionary, find the origin of each of the words below. If the word is borrowed, write the name of the language from which it originally came. If the word comes from a name or place, write the name or place from which it comes.

1. ensemble	6. tangerine	11. turquoise
2. boycott	7. khaki	12. Braille
3. calico	8. mosquito	13. veldt
4. tea	9. Wednesday	14. diesel
5. jaguar	10. cardigan	15. gusto

B In a dictionary, the words from which acronyms and blends are made are often shown in brackets before the word's definition. Using a dictionary, identify each of the following words as a *Compound*, *Blend*, *Clipped Word*, or *Acronym*. Then write the word or words from which each one is made.

1. paratroops	5. brunch	9. sonar	13. wristwatch
2. fence	6. dorm	10. bookkeeper	14. flu
3. typewriter	7. chortle	11. smog	15. airport
4. laser	8. gasohol	12. telex	

Levels of Language

English has grown and changed as words have been added in various ways. Some words enter English and become part of the main body of commonly used words. Other words, although also considered part of English, may be used only by particular groups of people or only in informal situations.

No speaker or writer of English uses the language in the same way all the time. For example, you probably speak one way when you are talking with your friends, another way when you are speaking in class, and perhaps a third way when you are giving a formal speech or oral report. The same language variation occurs in written material.

The types of language that are used for different situations are called the **levels of language.** The careful user of English can effectively vary the way he or she speaks or writes to suit the particular audience addressed.

Standard English

Standard English follows accepted grammatical rules and guidelines. It is the language of most professional writing in magazines, books, and newspapers, and of most professional speaking on television and radio. The rules and guidelines of standard English enable all speakers and writers to communicate clearly. This textbook presents the rules and guidelines for using standard English.

Formal and Informal English Standard English can be divided into two levels of language, formal and informal. **Formal English** is found primarily in writing but is appropriate in any situation that is serious, dignified, or ceremonial. **Informal English,** also known as conversational or **colloquial English,** is appropriate in everyday situations. It is used in magazines, newspapers, casual letters, and in conversation.

Dialects, differences in English due to geographical location, may also be considered part of informal usage. Note the differences in these examples of formal and informal English.

Formal   No written law has ever been more binding than unwritten custom supported by popular opinion.

Informal   Traditions and habits are both hard to break.

The chart on this page lists the different characteristics of formal and informal English.

Characteristics of Formal and Informal English

	Formal	**Informal**
Tone	Serious, reserved, academic, ceremonial	Personal, friendly, casual, conversational
	Sometimes uses longer or more complicated words	
Vocabulary and Mechanics	Avoids contractions, clipped words, and slang	Uses simpler words
		Often uses contractions and clipped words
	Uses correct grammar, spelling, and punctuation	Uses correct grammar, spelling, and punctuation
Organization	Longer, carefully constructed sentences	Similar to conversational English
		Sentences of greater variety of lengths

Often, you must choose between formal and informal English so that your language is appropriate to your purpose and audience.

The terms **formal** and **informal** do not name two separate categories. Picture formal and informal English as two ends of a spectrum.

What Is Your Audience and Purpose?

Informal ◄━━━━━━━━━━━━━━━━━► **Formal**

Informal		Formal
Conversation	Writing for	Formal speeches
Letters between	magazines and	Professional
friends	newspapers	documents
	Speaking for radio	Reports for
	and television	serious occasions

One characteristic of informal English is the presence of certain kinds of conversational expressions, such as idioms and slang.

Certain words and phrases called **idioms** have a meaning different from the exact meanings that the words suggest. In the idioms that are underscored below, what would each phrase mean if you defined each word exactly?

> Hold your tongue.
> I am tickled pink about the news.
> We won that contest hands down.

Idioms are present in every language and help make a language colorful and unique.

Slang consists of expressions coined by members of a group and often serves as a sign of belonging to that group. Some slang words lead brief but colorful lives and then drop out of common usage. For example, *groovy* and *far out,* words popular with young people in the 1960's, sound dated today. Occasionally, however, a slang word will remain in use and gain acceptance as part of informal English. *Hassle*, a verb meaning "to annoy," is an example of such a word.

Slang is appropriate only in very informal situations. It can help enliven conversation with friends or dialogue in a short story, but it is inappropriate in a classroom discussion or a business letter.

Many dictionaries indicate whether a word or phrase is considered a colloquialism, an idiom, or a slang expression. Check the guide at the front of your dictionary to see how these labels are indicated. Such labels help you to match your audience and purpose with your level of language.

Nonstandard English

Nonstandard English describes language that does not follow the grammatical rules and forms presented in this textbook. A sentence demonstrating nonstandard English might use *ain't* or double negatives such as *He ain't right* or *I don't need no help*. In standard English these would be changed to *He isn't right* and *I don't need any help*. Written English that contains errors in punctuation, spelling, capitalization, and manuscript form is also considered nonstandard.

Exercises

A The paragraphs on the facing page are part of a formal report. The paragraphs contain several levels of language. Rewrite the report to eliminate all nonstandard English.

(1) Gerbils belong to the scientific family *Cricetidae*. (2) There are approximately one hundred different species of these furry, ratlike rodents, but the one most folks know is the Mongolian gerbil. (3) As a matter of fact, all pet gerbils in the United States are descendants of twenty-two Mongolian gerbils sent to America by a Japanese laboratory in 1954. (4) Gerbils make really neat pets because of all the interesting stuff they do.

(5) Pet gerbils should be fed commercial gerbil pellets or a mixture of fruits, small seeds, and raw vegetables. (6) Watching them eat is a real blast, because they stuff a lot of food in the pouches of their cheeks. (7) Water should be made available in their cages, though they sure don't drink much. (8) Gerbils get water mostly through moisture in the food they eat. (9) If properly cared for, a pet gerbil should live up to four years, give or take a little.

B One acceptable purpose for the use of slang is the writing of realistic dialogue. The following slang expressions were popular during the 1920's. Using these expressions, write a conversation between two young people of 1925.

1. *lam*—to leave quickly
2. *dive*—a cheap restaurant or public place
3. *scrim*—a large dance party
4. *on the shelf*—out of circulation
5. *the bee's knees*—any excellent or popular thing

Street scene in the 1920's.

Part 3
Regional Dialects

If there are certain "rules" for the use of English, why do people across the country speak so differently? Because people in a certain area speak more frequently to one another than to people outside their community, they develop habits of speech unfamiliar to outsiders. Language that is spoken in a particular region or by a particular social group is called **dialect.**

Dialects can differ in vocabulary, pronunciation, and in grammar. For example, a person from New York may say *pail* for metal container, while someone from Missouri may say *bucket.* A person in southern Illinois may pronounce the word *greasy* as *greezy*, while one from northern Illinois may pronounce it *greecey.* Further, a person from Wisconsin may say *dove* for the past tense of the verb *dive,* while someone from Kentucky may say *dived.*

Everyone speaks a particular dialect, and there is no one "correct" dialect. Dialect is appropriate in certain situations. In fact, it adds to the uniqueness of each person's language. However, it is also important to be able to adapt your language to more formal situations when dialect may not be appropriate.

The chart below illustrates some items that have four or five different names, depending on the area of the country in which they are used.

Vocabulary Differences in Regional Dialect

insect that glows at night:
firefly, glowworm, lightning bug, candle bug
large sandwich meant to be a meal in itself:
hero, submarine, hoagy, grinder, poor-boy
vehicle for small baby:
baby buggy, baby cab, baby carriage, baby coach
become ill with a cold:
catch cold, get a cold, take cold, come down with a cold
grass strip between sidewalk and street:
berm, boulevard, parkway, sidewalk plot, tree lawn
amusement park ride (on tracks):
coaster, roller coaster, rolly-coaster, shoot-the-chutes

Exercise

Write the word that you use from each of the five groups below. Then compare your choice with someone from a different region of the United States. List the words used by the person and note the difference in your dialects.

1. **Carbonated drink:** pop, soda, soda pop, tonic, soft drink
2. **Sink fixture:** faucet, hydrant, spicket, spigot, tap
3. **Food eaten between meals:** a bite, lunch, piece meal, a snack
4. **Ways to hit water when diving:** belly-flop, belly-bust
5. **Public drinking-water fixture:** water fountain, bubbler

Part 4
Multiple Meanings of Words

Effective use of English involves not only using levels of language comfortably but also being sensitive to the multiple meanings of many words. For example, here are three uses of the word *court*.

1. Helen and Alice went to the tennis *court* for a game.
2. The strolling players performed in the inner *court* of the castle.
3. The judge presided over night *court*.

Now look at this excerpt from *Webster's New World Dictionary, Students Edition*. Which definition suits each usage in the sample sentences above?

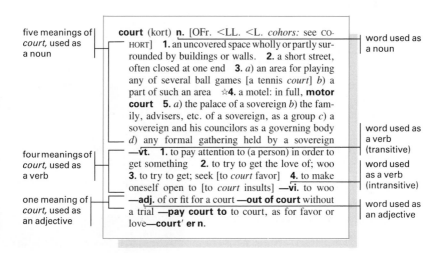

five meanings of *court*, used as a noun

court (kort) **n.** [OFr. <LL. <L. *cohors:* see CO-HORT] **1.** an uncovered space wholly or partly surrounded by buildings or walls. **2.** a short street, often closed at one end **3.** *a)* an area for playing any of several ball games [a tennis *court*] *b)* a part of such an area ☆**4.** a motel: in full, **motor court 5.** *a)* the palace of a sovereign *b)* the family, advisers, etc. of a sovereign, as a group *c)* a sovereign and his councilors as a governing body *d)* any formal gathering held by a sovereign

word used as a noun

four meanings of *court*, used as a verb

—**vt. 1.** to pay attention to (a person) in order to get something **2.** to try to get the love of; woo **3.** to try to get; seek [to *court* favor] **4.** to make oneself open to [to *court* insults] —**vi.** to woo

word used as a verb (transitive)

word used as a verb (intransitive)

one meaning of *court*, used as an adjective

—**adj.** of or fit for a court —**out of court** without a trial —**pay court to** to court, as for favor or love—**court′ er n.**

word used as an adjective

Denotation and Connotation

The dictionary definition of a word is the word's **denotation.** A word may also have a **connotation,** the emotional meaning attached to the word because of the thoughts or feelings it creates. Consider the word *home,* for instance. The denotation of *home* is "a place where a person lives." However, for many people the connotation of *home* involves positive feelings of family and security.

It is important in writing and speaking to consider not only the denotative meaning of a word, but also its connotation. Persuasive writing is especially dependent upon the connotations of words. A writer of an ad, for example, may describe a shirt as being economical. Why is *economical* a better word choice here than *cheap*?

Exercises

A Use a dictionary to find the multiple meanings for the words below. Write at least three sentences for each word. Each sentence should illustrate a different meaning for the word.

bark	key	part	rook
case	light	pat	round
counter	note	pound	sharp
grounds	pan	ring	turn

B Show the difference in the connotations of the pairs of words below. Write a sentence using the first word, and then write a sentence using the second word.

> *Example*   defeat, trounce
> The Bulldogs narrowly *defeated* the Jets, winning by one point in the final quarter.
> Last year our team *trounced* the Jets 39-0.

1. unique, odd
2. old, antique
3. bashful, reserved
4. clumsy, uncoordinated
5. clever, sneaky
6. skinny, thin
7. perspiration, sweat
8. friend, buddy
9. forceful, bossy
10. thrifty, stingy

Part 5
The Thesaurus

A **thesaurus** is invaluable as a storehouse of synonyms and antonyms. If you need a synonym for a word, a thesaurus offers a quick way to see all the possibilities. Precision in writing depends on accurate word choice, and a thesaurus can help you find the exact word you need. If the thesaurus you are using does not arrange entries in alphabetical order, consult the index to learn how to locate words.

Read this entry from *Roget's Thesaurus*. How many synonyms are given for the noun *danger*? What other words are formed from the base word *danger*?

> **DANGER.**—I. *Nouns*. **danger,** chance, hazard, insecurity, jeopardy, peril, unsafety, risk, pitfall, endangerment; storm brewing, clouds gathering, clouds on the horizon; crisis.
> **dangerousness,** riskiness, touch and go, unsafety, treachery; venturousness, etc. (see *Adjectives*). [*dangerous person*] **menace,** threat, serpent, viper; dangerous woman, *femme fatale* (*F*.).
> II. *Verbs*. **endanger,** expose to danger, hazard, jeopardize, peril, imperil, risk, speculate with, venture, compromise.
> [*accept danger*] **risk,** hazard, venture, adventure. dare, stake, set at hazard, speculate.
> III. *Adjectives*. **dangerous,** chancy, risky, ticklish, touch-and-go, venturous, venturesome, adventurous, adventuresome, speculative; hazardous, perilous, parlous, precarious, insecure, jeopardous, critical, queasy, unsafe, ugly, treacherous, serpentine, viperous.
> See also CHANCE, FEAR, THREAT, WARNING.
> *Antonyms*—See PROTECTION.

Remember, there are shades of differences in meaning among these synonyms. If you use a synonym from the thesaurus, check its precise meaning in a dictionary to be sure it fits the use you intend.

Exercise

Use a thesaurus to find two synonyms for each of the words below. Use each synonym in a sentence that clearly shows its precise meaning.

     fear   scoff   spite   observe   error

Biography of a Word

Tawdry lace is often seen at Renaissance fairs.

T ime has a way of changing words. Some words undergo a change in reputation by moving up or down the social ladder. For example, *marshal,* which now refers to an esteemed occupation, once meant one who held horses. On the other hand, *villain* meant "farmer."

Sometimes, little remains of the first spelling and meaning of a word. Take, for example, the adjective *tawdry,* which now means "cheap and gaudy, or showy." This word owes its existence to Ethelreda, the pious daughter of a seventh-century Saxon king.

Ethelreda was known and honored for her religious devotion and good works. However, she always regretted her youthful love of beautiful necklaces. She died of a throat disease, and she blamed the sickness on her early fondness for rich jewelry.

Ethelreda was named the patron saint of the island village where she had established a monastery, but already the forces of change were at work. She was remembered not as Saint Ethelreda, but as Saint Audrey, a shortening of Ethelreda. The townspeople honored her memory by selling necklaces of fine silk—Saint Audrey's laces—on her feast day. As time passed, these beautiful laces gave way to gaudy, poorly made scarves. By the 1700's, even the name had been cheapened. In common speech, "Saint Audrey" was pronounced " 't Audrey." Soon the laces became Tawdry laces. Today *tawdry* is used to refer to anything cheap and showy. None of Ethelreda's spirit has survived in the word, and all that remains of her sainthood is the *t.*

Chapter 15
Application and Review

A Understanding Word Origins Identify the origin of each of the underlined words in the passage below.

> The WATS lines stayed busy as volunteers at the telethon hurriedly answered phones. Although the volunteers could not be seen on camera, their silhouettes were visible behind a screen. A cameraman followed the movements of two ballet dancers as they drifted off stage. The audience anxiously waited for the new total for contributions to be announced.

B Levels of Language and Multiple Meanings of Words Use a dictionary to become familiar with the multiple meanings of each of the following words. Then write a paragraph that might be part of a formal talk to a bird watcher's club. Include all of the words that are listed below.

> case   rook   tail   nut   sharp

C Application in Literature Many writers capture the richness of dialects in the speech of their literary characters. Read the quotations below from several literary figures. Imagine that each of the characters has been asked to speak in a formal situation. Rewrite each quotation making it suitable for formal usage.

1. Mr. Kaplan's response was instantaneous. ''I'm so glad you eskink me dis! . . . I'm usink 'Keplen' . . . because I don't want the reader should tink I am prajudiced . . . '' Leo Rosten
2. ''Ain't they no Shepherdsons around?''
   ''They said no, 'twas a false alarm.''
   ''Well,'' he says, ''if they'd a' ben some, I reckon I'd a got one.'' Mark Twain
3. ''Well, he can make somebody's will so air tight can't anybody meddle with it.'' Harper Lee
4. ''Dat widder woman bring her daughters up very nice. Polly got lots of spunk, an' she got some style, too. Da's nice for young folks to have some style.'' Willa Cather
5. ''It's aw rawt: e's a gentleman: look at 'es boots. She just thought you was a copper's nark, sir.'' George Bernard Shaw

Focus On

THE DICTIONARY

Get acquainted with this versatile reference work. Knowing how to make full use of a dictionary is a valuable skill.

What Does It Mean?
How Is It Spelled?

You probably use the dictionary most often to answer those two questions. However, dictionaries offer much more than definitions and spellings. For example, they provide information on word origins, pronunciation, and usage. In addition, most dictionaries contain a number of very helpful resource sections.

From A to Z:
Types of Dictionaries

The number of words, or entries, in a dictionary depends on the kind of dictionary it is. The largest and most complete, an unabridged dictionary, is invaluable for serious research. For example, *The Oxford English Dictionary,* also called the *OED,* lists most words of the English language, dating back to the year A.D. 1000. Another unabridged dictionary, *Webster's Third New International,* contains over half a million words.

As impressive as these two books appear, however, no dictionary is ever complete. Because the English language is constantly growing and changing, dictionaries cannot keep up with it. This is one reason that

dictionary publishers publish revised editions.

The dictionary that most people use is an abridged dictionary. Even though these "desk," or "collegiate," editions are shorter, they offer extensive listings and are quite satisfactory for everyday use. For example, *Webster's New World Dictionary Student Edition* contains over 160,000 entries.

A pocket dictionary is handy for checking spelling, but it has fewer words and the information within the entries is limited. A pocket

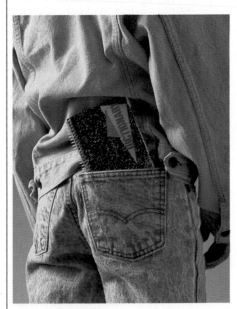

The right place for a pocket dictionary.

dictionary is not a good choice for high-school or college use.

What's So Special?

A specialized dictionary focuses on a particular field of knowledge or part of the language. Such dictionaries have been published in dozens of diverse fields, such as architecture, ballet, botany, computer science, foreign languages, medicine, and paleontology.

Specialized dictionaries are particularly useful when you're researching a particular area of information. These dictionaries are commonly available in the reference sections of most large metropolitan libraries.

Even graffiti artists need dictionaries.

> *"The trouble with the dictionary is that you have to know how a word is spelled before you can look it up to see how it is spelled."*
>
> Will Cuppy

Finding a Ptarmigan: Using Guide Words

Although some dictionary features vary, certain elements are standard. For example, all dictionaries list words in alphabetical order and most provide guide words. This pair of words at the top of each page indicates the first and last words on that page. For example, you would find the word *ptarmigan* on the dictionary page that displays the guide words *psychosis* and *public.*

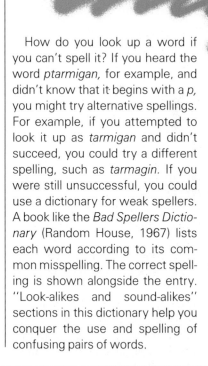

How do you look up a word if you can't spell it? If you heard the word *ptarmigan,* for example, and didn't know that it begins with a *p,* you might try alternative spellings. For example, if you attempted to look it up as *tarmigan* and didn't succeed, you could try a different spelling, such as *tarmagin.* If you were still unsuccessful, you could use a dictionary for weak spellers. A book like the *Bad Spellers Dictionary* (Random House, 1967) lists each word according to its common misspelling. The correct spelling is shown alongside the entry. "Look-alikes and sound-alikes" sections in this dictionary help you conquer the use and spelling of confusing pairs of words.

The Main Event: The Entry Word

In a dictionary, the entry word is printed in boldface type. To show proper word division, the dictionary separates the entry word into syllables.

Occasionally, what appears to be the same entry word is printed twice on a page. Each word is distinguished by a small raised number. Such words are called homographs—that is, words that have the same spelling but different meanings. The entries for *pale*[1] and *pale*[2] on the sample dictionary page (shown on page 365) are examples of homographs. Can you find others?

Pronunciation An entry word is immediately followed by its pronunciation. If a word can be pronounced more than one way, the various pronunciations will be included. The first pronunciation, however, is the preferred one.

Since some letters have more than one sound, a dictionary uses symbols to represent sounds and to show how the words are pronounced. Those symbols are explained in a pronunciation key, often placed at the bottom of the right-hand page. A pronunciation key is shown on the sample dictionary page.

Part of Speech Each entry word is labeled according to the part of speech it is: noun, adjective, and so forth. This label normally follows the pronunciation.

Words in the English language can be used as more than one part of speech. In such cases, the definition often changes with the different uses.

Look once again at the entry word *pale*[1] on the sample dictionary page on page 365. The notation *adj.* after the pronunciation indicates that the meanings that follow are for *pale* when used as an adjective. Later in the entry, *pale* is labeled (and defined) as a transitive verb.

Inflectional Endings An inflection is a change in the form of a word. For example, *bigger* and *biggest* are inflected forms of the adjective *big*. Forms of verbs and plural forms of nouns are also inflections. Inflectional endings are shown in bold-

By permission of Johny Hart and North America Syndicate, Inc.

pal·ate (pal'it) n. [L. palatum] 1. the roof of the mouth, consisting of a hard, bony forward part (the hard palate) and a soft, fleshy back part (the soft palate) 2. taste [the food was delicious to his palate] 3. liking

pa·la·tial (pə lā'shəl) adj. [see PALACE] 1. of, suitable for, or like a palace 2. large and splendid; grand; magnificent —pa·la'tial·ly adv.

pa·lat·i·nate (pə lat''n āt', -it) n. the territory ruled by a palatine

pal·a·tine (pal'ə tīn, -tin) adj. [< OFr. < L. < palatium, palace] 1. of a palace 2. having royal powers in his own territory [a count palatine] 3. of or belonging to a palatine or palatinate —n. a medieval vassal lord having the rights of royalty in his own territory, or palatinate —[P-] one of the SEVEN HILLS OF ROME

pa·lav·er (pə lav'ər) n. [Port. palavra, a word, speech < LL. parabola, PARABLE] 1. a conference, as orig. between African natives and European explorers or traders 2. talk; esp., idle chatter 3. flattery; cajolery —vi. 1. to talk; esp. idly or flatteringly 2. to confer —vt. to flatter or wheedle

Pa·la·wan (pä lä'wän) island in the W Philippines, southwest of Mindoro: 4,550 sq. mi.

pale[1] (pāl) adj. pal'er, pal'est [OFr. < L. < pallere, to be pale] 1. having little color in the face [pale after a sunless winter; pale with fright] 2. lacking intensity or brilliance; dim; faint: said of color, light, etc. 3. feeble; weak [a pale imitation] —vi., pal'ing 1. to become pale; lose color [her face paled at the news] 2. to seem weaker or less important [my work paled beside his] —vt. to make pale — pale'ly adv. —pale'ness n.

SYN.—pale is the most general of the words describing an unnatural whiteness or lack of color, often temporary, of the complexion; pallid suggests a ...ess resulting from exhaustion, faintness, emotional strain, etc.; wan ...sts the paleness resulting from a serious illness; ashen implies the ...n, as of one in great rage or fear —ANT. ruddy, rosy

...pāl) n. [< MFr. < L. palus, a stake: for IE. base see PEACE] ...arrow, pointed stake used in fences; picket 2. a fence; ...ure; boundary: now chiefly figurative [outside the pale of ...] 3. a district enclosed within bounds

...face (pāl'fās') n. a white person: a term said to be first ... N. American Indians

...bang (pä'lem bäŋ') seaport in SE Sumatra, Indonesia: ...3,000

...[< Gr. palaios, ancient] a combining form meaning an...rehistoric, primitive, etc. [Paleozoic, paleolithic]: also, ...vowel, pa·le-

...cene (pā'lē ə sēn', pal'ē-) adj. [< PALEO- + Gr. ...ecent] designating or of the first epoch of the Tertiary ...the Cenozoic Era —the Paleocene the Paleocene ...its rocks: see GEOLOGIC TIME CHART

...ra·phy (pā'lē äg'rə fē, pal'ē-) n. 1. ancient writ...ms of writing 2. the science of identifying or translat...t writings —pa·le·og'ra·pher n. —pa·le·o·graph'i·cal adj. —pa·le·o·graph'ic

...th·ic (pā'lē ə lith'ik, pal'ē-) adj. [PALEO- + -LITHIC] ...g or of the middle part of the early Stone Age, during ...e and bone tools were used

...ol·o·gy (-än täl'ə jē) n. [< Fr.: see PALE(O)- & ...OGY] the branch of geology that deals with prehis...rough the study of fossils —pa·le·on·to·log'i·cal ...l), pa·le·on·to·log'ic adj. —pa·le·on·tol·o·gist n. ...ic (-ə zō'ik) adj. [PALEO- + ZO- + -IC] designat...e era between the Precambrian and the Mesozoic ...zoic the Paleozoic Era or its rocks: see GEOLOGIC

...lər'mō; It. pä ler'mō) seaport on the N coast of ...59,000

...(pal'əs tin') 1. region on the E coast of the ...n, the country of the Jews in Biblical times 2. ...is region, west of the Jordan River, held by the ...andate from 1923 until the establishment of the ...in 1948 —Pal'es·tin'i·an (-tin'ē ən) adj., n.

Pal·es·tri·na (pä'les trē'nä; E. pal'ə strē'nə), Gio·van·ni (Pierluigi) da (jô vän'nē dä) 1525?-94; It. composer

pal·ette (pal'it) n. [Fr. < L. pala, a shovel] 1. a thin board with a hole for the thumb at one end, on which an artist arranges and mixes his paints 2. the colors used, as by a particular artist

palette knife a flexible steel blade on a handle, used by artists for mixing, scraping, and applying paints

pal·frey (pôl'frē) n., pl. -freys [< OFr. < ML., ult. < Gr. para, beside + L. veredus, post horse] [Archaic] a saddle horse, esp. a gentle one for a woman

PALETTE

Pa·li (pä'lē) n. the Old Indic dialect which has become the religious language of Buddhism

pal·imp·sest (pal'imp sest') n. [< L. < Gr. < palin, again + psēn, to rub smooth] a parchment, tablet, etc. that has been written upon several times, with previous, erased texts still partly visible

pal·in·drome (pal'in drōm') n. [< Gr. < palin, again + dramein, to run] a word, phrase, or sentence that reads the same backward or forward, as the word madam

pal·ing (pāl'iŋ) n. 1. a fence made of pales 2. the action of making such a fence 3. a pale, or a number of pales

pal·i·sade (pal'ə sād', pal'ə sād') n. [< Fr. < Pr. < L. palus, a stake, PALE[2]] 1. any of a row of large pointed stakes set in the ground to form a fence as for fortification 2. such a fence ☆3. [pl.] a line of steep cliffs, usually along a river —vt. -sad'ed, -sad'ing to fortify or defend with a palisade

pall[1] (pôl) vi. palled, pall'ing [ME. pallen, short for appallen, APPALL] 1. to become tiresome, boring, dull, etc. [his jokes are beginning to pall on me] 2. to become tired or surfeited [his interest in stamps soon palled] —vt. to bore after a time

pall[2] (pôl) n. [< OE. < L. pallium, a cover] 1. a piece of velvet, etc. used to cover a coffin, hearse, or tomb 2. a dark or gloomy covering [a pall of smoke] 3. a cloth, or cardboard covered with cloth, used to cover the chalice in some Christian churches —vt. palled, pall'ing to cover as with a pall

Pal·la·dio (päl lä'dyô), An·dre·a (än dre'ä) (born Andrea di Pietro) 1518-80; It. architect —Pal·la·di·an (pə lā'dē ən, -lä'-) adj.

Pal·la·di·um (pə lā'dē əm) n., pl. -di·a (-ə) 1. the legendary statue of Pallas Athena in Troy on which the safety of the city was supposed to depend 2. [p-] anything supposed to ensure the safety of something; safeguard

pal·la·di·um (pə lā'dē əm) n. [ModL., ult. < Gr. Pallas, the goddess] a rare, silvery-white, metallic chemical element: it is used as a catalyst, or in alloys with gold, silver, etc.: symbol, Pd; at. wt., 106.4; at. no., 46

Pal·las (pal'əs) Gr. Myth. Athena, goddess of wisdom: also Pallas Athena —Pal·la·di·an (pə lā'dē ən) adj.

pall·bear·er (pôl'ber'ər) n. [PALL[2] + BEARER] one of the persons who bear the coffin at a funeral

pal·let[1] (pal'it) n. [< MFr.: see PALETTE] 1. a wooden tool consisting of a flat blade with a handle; esp., such a tool for smoothing pottery 2. same as PALETTE (sense 1) 3. a low, portable platform for storing goods in warehouses, etc. 4. any of the clicks or pawls in the escapement of a clock, etc. which engage the teeth of a ratchet wheel to regulate the speed: see illustration at PAWL

pal·let[2] (pal'it) n. [< MFr. < OFr. paille, straw < L. palea, chaff] a small, crude bed or a mattress filled as with straw and used on the floor

pal·li·ate (pal'ē āt') vt. -at'ed, -at'ing [< LL. pp. of palliare, to conceal < pallium, a cloak] 1. to lessen the pain or severity of without curing; alleviate [aspirin palliates a fever] 2. to make appear less serious or offensive; excuse [to palliate an error] —pal'li·a'tion n. —pal'li·a'tor n.

pal·li·a·tive (-āt'iv, -ə tiv) adj. that palliates, eases, or excuses —n. something that palliates, as a drug

pal·lid (pal'id) adj. [L. pallidus, PALE[1]] lacking in normal or natural color or brightness [a pallid face] —see SYN. at PALE[1] — pal'lid·ly adv. —pal'lid·ness n.

face type and appear after the part-of-speech label.

Definition The word's definition, or meaning, is the part of the entry you probably use most.

Since some entry words have more than one meaning, it is wise to read all the meanings for a word, even if you think that you've found the one you want.

Why is this so important? In doing this, you may discover another meaning of the word that is more specific, or more suitable to the context in which you intend to use the word.

Etymology Some words are quite new; others date back to ancient times. However, all words have a history. The etymology traces the origins of a word. It is customarily bracketed within the entry. The symbols and abbreviations used in etymologies—as well as those used in other parts of the dictionary—are usually explained in a key in the front or back of the dictionary.

On the sample dictionary page, the etymology for *palladium* indicates that the word comes from the name of the Greek goddess Pallas. The word then became part of Latin and finally, it entered English. (To learn who Pallas was, see the next entry on the sample dictionary page.)

Synonymy All crossword-puzzle fans will agree: English is a language rich in synonyms. Knowing the shades of difference between synonyms can help you select pre-cisely the word you need. A synonymy lists words that are similar in meaning to a given entry word and draws distinctions between the words. It generally appears as a separate paragraph at the end of an entry. The abbreviation *SYN.* marks the beginning of a synonymy. The abbreviation *ANT.* at the end of some synonymies introduces antonyms, words with the opposite meaning. Can you find a synonymy on the sample dictionary page?

All in the Family: Other Entry Notes

Dictionary entries may also tell about related words, unusual word usages, and other places to find information about a word.

Etymology is the signpost that tells the direction a word has traveled.

Americanisms are word forms that originated in the United States. Many of them are quite old and are said to date back to Indian days. . . .

Derived Words Many English words belong to word families that have grown from a common root word. A derived word is a form of an entry word made by the addition of a suffix.

Like the entry word, a derived word is set in boldface type and is divided into syllables. Derived words appear at the end of the entry. The entry for *pallid* on page 365 includes the derived words *pallidly* and *pallidness.*

Americanisms An Americanism is a usage that originated in the United States. Some dictionaries mark Americanisms with a star. For example, in the entry for *pale*[2], the word *paleface,* an Americanism, is designated by a star.

Cross-References Occasionally, a dictionary provides a cross-reference—a notation that directs you to another entry or part of the dictionary for more information.

On the sample dictionary page, a cross-reference appears at the end of the *Paleozoic* entry. It directs you to the Geologic Time Chart located near the entry for *geology.* Can you find other instances of cross-references on the sample page?

From Cover to Cover: Front and Back Matter

The front matter and back matter of a dictionary contain a great deal of useful information. In addition to a table of contents, the front matter provides specific directions on the use of the dictionary. The front matter may also include notes on usage and an account of the history of the English language.

The back matter in some dictionaries features lists of commonly used foreign words and phrases; tables of useful knowledge, such as metric conversions and lists of weights and measures; alphabetical lists of universities and colleges in the United States and Canada; and biographical and geographical names.

Try Your Skill

Use the sample dictionary page on page 365 to answer the following questions. Some answers are found in the pronunciation key.

1. What is the etymology of the word *palliate?*

2. Which synonym for *pale* suggests paleness resulting from an illness?

3. Would you expect a person whose hobby is paleography to be interested in ancient Egyptian hieroglyphics?

4. What cross-reference is given in the entry for *pallet*[1]?

5. Which definition of *palisade* is an Americanism?

6. Two entry words on the sample page have a different meaning when they are capitalized. Name the words.

16
Using the Library

*T*oday's libraries house more than books. They offer a rich variety of resources including magazines, newspapers, pamphlets, records, tapes, films—even computers. To find the materials and information you want, you need to know how to use the card catalog and reference works. In this chapter you will learn how to use the library's resources, whether you are doing research for a report on the Amazon River or looking for a copy of a popular magazine or novel.

Part 1

Arrangement of the Library

To locate resources efficiently, you must be familiar with the arrangement of the library. Review the sections listed below.

Sections of the Library

Your public and school library will have similar sections.

Stacks Fiction and nonfiction books are stored in the stacks.

Catalogs These include the card catalog and computer catalog. Information about all library books and their location is filed here.

Reference Reference materials include dictionaries, encyclopedias, almanacs, and atlases. They are often kept in a separate room.

Periodicals Newspapers, magazines, and the *Readers' Guide to Periodical Literature* are found in this section. This area may be housed separately or may be part of the reference section.

Young Adult and Children's Section Books for younger readers are often stored together in their own section.

The Librarian

Today's librarian is a skilled professional who is eager to help you. When asking for help, tell the librarian what steps you have already taken so he or she will know how to help you.

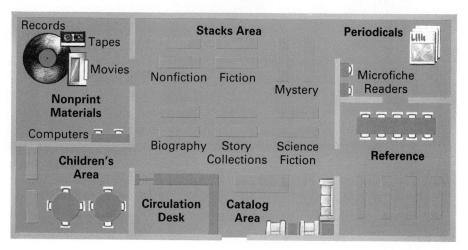

How Books Are Classified and Arranged

All libraries, no matter what their size or purpose, arrange their materials systematically.

The Classification of Books

In the library, books are separated into two types—fiction and nonfiction.

Fiction Novels and short-story collections are usually arranged on the shelves in alphabetical order by author. For example, if you want to read *The Pearl,* by John Steinbeck, you would first look for the section in the library marked FICTION. Then you would find the book among those by authors whose last names begin with *S*.

Nonfiction Most libraries classify nonfiction books according to the **Dewey Decimal System.** This system, which is named for librarian Melvil Dewey, classifies all books by number in ten major categories:

Dewey Decimal System

000–099	General Works	(encyclopedias, handbooks)
100–199	Philosophy	(psychology, ethics)
200–299	Religion	(the Bible, theology, mythology)
300–399	Social Science	(government, education, law)
400–499	Language	(languages, grammars, dictionaries)
500–599	Science	(mathematics, chemistry, biology)
600–699	Technology	(medicine, cooking, inventions)
700–799	Fine Arts	(music, painting, theater, sports)
800–899	Literature	(poetry, plays, essays)—not fiction
900–999	History	(biography, travel, geography)

In the Dewey Decimal System, each field has a classification number. For example, all science books have a number between 500 and 599, and all history books have a number between 900 and 999. Each of these major groups is also subdivided. The 800's section, for instance, is further divided into 810 for American Literature, 820 for English Literature, and so on. To help define an exact subject, a subcategory such as American Literature can be further broken down into 811 Poetry, 812 Drama, with the divisions continuing up to 820.

The **Library of Congress Classification,** or LC, is another way that libraries classify books. The LC system uses twenty-one broad categories designated by letters of the alphabet. A second letter is added for a subdivision within a category. For example, *Q* identifies science, and *QB* designates astronomy.

The list below shows the twenty-one LC categories.

Library of Congress Classification

A General Works	**M** Music
B Philosophy, Psychology, Religion	**N** Fine Arts
	P Language and Literature
C–F History	**Q** Science
D General History	**R** Medicine
E–F American History	**S** Agriculture
G Geography, Anthropology, Recreation	**T** Technology
	U Military Science
H Social Sciences	**V** Naval Science
J Political Science	**Z** Bibliography and Library Science
K Law	
L Education	

Arrangement of Books on the Shelves

Most school and public libraries use the Dewey Decimal System. Shelves are marked with numbers that show which books can be found in each particular section. Books are arranged on the shelves numerically in order of classification. Within each classification, except biography, books are arranged alphabetically by authors' last names.

Biography and Autobiography Libraries often place biographies and autobiographies in a separate section. Books in this section are labeled with a *B* and are arranged in alphabetical order by the last name of the person the book is about. A book containing the biographies of two or more persons is called a **collective biography.** The Dewey Decimal classification for biographies is 920.

Reference Books Reference books are also shelved together, often with the letter *R* above the classification number. You will learn more about reference books in Part 4 of this chapter.

Exercise

In which major division of the Dewey Decimal System and LC classification would the following information be located?

1. Plays for high school productions
2. *The Life of Abe Lincoln*
3. A comparison of Greek and Roman gods
4. "Killer bees"
5. Motocross racing
6. Woodworking as a hobby
7. Rules for playing lacrosse
8. How to say "no" in any country
9. Financial recessions and depressions in the United States
10. Reproductions of paintings by Leonardo da Vinci

Part 3
Using the Card Catalog

You can easily locate a book you need by using the card catalog. The card catalog is a cabinet of small drawers or file trays containing alphabetically arranged cards. Each card has the title of a book that the library has on its shelves. For nonfiction books the card also carries the classification number, often referred to as the **call number,** in the upper left-hand corner.(See illustration on page 374.) The call number directs you to the shelf in the library where a particular book is located. The same call number you found on the catalog card will be on the spine of the book.

There are usually three cards for the same book in the card catalog: the *author card*, the *title card*, and the *subject card*. The three different kinds of cards contain essentially the same information, but the arrangement of the information varies according to the type of card. Study the sample author, subject, and title cards on page 374.

The Author Card An author card can help you locate a book if you do not know the title. The author's name, with the last name first, forms the **heading,** or information on the top line of an author card.

The call number of nonfiction books appears in the upper left-hand corner of the card. Author cards for all books by the same author will be filed together alphabetically according to title.

The Title Card If you know the title of a book, but not the author, look for the title card. The title of a book forms the heading for a title card with the author's name directly under the title. For nonfiction books, the call number appears in the upper left-hand corner. For fiction books, an *F* appears in that corner. Title cards are filed alphabetically by the first major word in the title.

The Subject Card Subject cards help you locate a book on a topic of interest when you do not know an author or title of a book on the subject. Subject headings are printed in capital letters at the top of a subject card. Below the heading, you will find the author's name and the book's title. The card may indicate whether a book has chapters on a single aspect of the topic you are interested in. The publication date on the card will help you find the most up-to-date book on your subject.

Cross-Reference and Guide Cards

Cards that read *See* or *See also* are called **cross-reference cards.** They refer you to another subject heading in the catalog that will give you the information you want. For example, you might look under the subject heading TELEVISION COMMERCIALS and find a card that reads ''See Television Advertising.'' This card means that all books on television commercials are under TELEVISION ADVERTISING.

The *See also* card refers you to other subjects closely related to the one you are interested in. For example, under the subject heading ''Biology,'' you might find ''*See also* Natural History, Physiology, Psychobiology, and Zoology.''

Guide cards are blank cards with a guide word printed on a tab that projects above the other cards. Guide cards, like guide words in a dictionary, aid you in finding other catalog cards quickly.

Computerized Catalogs

Many public libraries offer a computerized catalog system that is more compact and often easier to use than the card catalog. If you know the author, title, or subject of a book, the computer will tell you if the library has that book. If you need a listing of the books the library has on a certain subject, type in the subject and the computer will provide a list of titles and call numbers of books available.

Author, Title, and Subject Cards

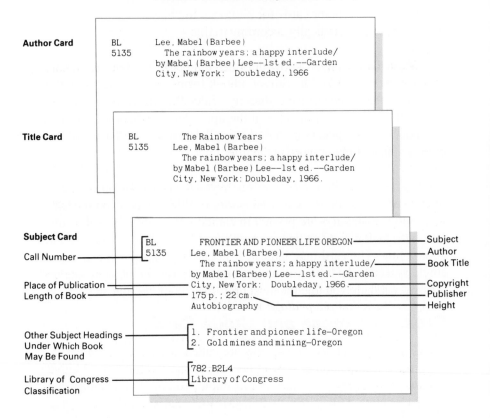

Author Card

BL
5135
Lee, Mabel (Barbee)
   The rainbow years; a happy interlude/
by Mabel (Barbee) Lee--1st ed.--Garden
City, New York: Doubleday, 1966

Title Card

BL
5135
   The Rainbow Years
Lee, Mabel (Barbee)
   The rainbow years; a happy interlude/
by Mabel (Barbee) Lee--1st ed.--Garden
City, New York: Doubleday, 1966.

Subject Card

Call Number ⎡ BL
         5135

Place of Publication
Length of Book

Other Subject Headings
Under Which Book
May Be Found

Library of Congress
Classification

FRONTIER AND PIONEER LIFE OREGON —— Subject
Lee, Mabel (Barbee). —————————————— Author
   The rainbow years; a happy interlude/—— Book Title
by Mabel (Barbee) Lee--1st ed.--Garden
City, New York: Doubleday, 1966. —————— Copyright
175 p.; 22 cm. —————————————————— Publisher
Autobiography   Height

1. Frontier and pioneer life–Oregon
2. Gold mines and mining–Oregon

782.B2L4
Library of Congress

Exercises

A Use the card catalog in your library to find and write the title, author, call number, and publication date of the following books.

1. A book about Harry S Truman; a book by Harry S Truman
2. A book on Renaissance art
3. A book with statistics on immigration to the United States
4. A book with plays by Eugene O'Neill and Tennessee Williams
5. A book about cross-country skiing

B What subject cards will direct you to books on the following topics?

1. "Peanuts" cartoons
2. Repairing minibikes
3. Developing photographs
4. Stamp collecting
5. Popular music

6. The origin of the Olympics
7. The first astronauts
8. How films are made
9. Fashions of today's youth
10. The first television program

Part 4
Other Resources

Most libraries have a wealth of reference works. Resources, such as those explained below, can help you in your search for information you might need for such assignments as reports and speeches.

Encyclopedias These are collections of articles, alphabetically arranged, on a wide variety of subjects. Guide letters on the spine of each volume and guide words at the top of the pages aid you in finding your subject. It is best however, to check the general index when first looking for information. For up-to-date information on a topic, check the yearbook that many encyclopedias issue. Four frequently used encyclopedias are *Collier's Encyclopedia, Encyclopaedia Britannica, Encyclopedia Americana,* and *The World Book Encyclopedia.*

The library also has many special-purpose encyclopedias such as *The Baseball Encyclopedia, The Concise Encyclopedia of Archaeology,* and *The Encyclopedia of World Art.*

Almanacs and Yearbooks Published annually, almanacs and yearbooks are useful sources for facts and statistics on current events, government, economics, population, sports, and other fields. Some almanacs are shelved in the 000–099 category of the Dewey Decimal System, others in 300–399. Frequently used almanacs and yearbooks include the *Guinness Book of World Records; Information Please Almanac, Atlas, and Yearbook;* the *World Almanac and Book of Facts;* and the *Statesman's Yearbook.*

Biographical References Brief biographical notations about contemporary and historical figures from all over the world may be found in *Webster's Biographical Dictionary.* Longer biographical articles may be found in encyclopedias. The librarian can direct you to additional biographical references that offer detailed information on noteworthy persons both living and deceased. The *Biography Index* gives the reference book in which information on a person is listed.

Literary Reference Books Some reference books are especially helpful for literary research. Well-known quotations and proverbs are arranged by author, topic, and key word in *Bartlett's Familiar Quotations. Granger's Index to Poetry* is another tool that is useful in locating a specific poem.

Vertical File Many libraries have current information in the form of pamphlets, handbooks, booklets, and clippings on subjects such as vocations, travel, and census data. All of these are kept in a set of file cabinets called the **vertical file**. Collections of college catalogs may also be kept in the vertical file.

Atlases Besides maps, an **atlas** also contains interesting data on a number of subjects. The *National Geographic Atlas of the World*, for example, lists some of the following topics in its table of contents: ''Great Moments in Geography,'' and ''Global Statistics,'' as well as sections on population, temperatures, oceans, and place names.

Periodicals and Newspapers When you are researching a current topic, periodicals—which include magazines and journals and newspapers—are important resources. They often contain the latest available information on a subject. Recent issues of newspapers, magazines, and journals are usually kept on open racks for easy reference. Back issues of magazines and journals are stored in bound volumes or on microforms.

Microforms To save space, magazine and newspaper articles are often stored on microforms. **Microforms** are very small photographs of printed pages. The microforms are stored on filmstrips, called **microfilm,** and film cards, called **microfiche.** Microforms are viewed on a special machine that is simple to operate and that the librarian can demonstrate for you.

The Readers' Guide to Periodical Literature The *Readers' Guide* is an invaluable aid for finding magazine articles covering the latest information on a subject. This index lists the titles, authors, and subjects of articles, stories, and poems published in over 150 magazines. Bound volumes are published once a year, and paperback issues are printed throughout the year. Articles are listed alphabetically under subject, author, and title. A list of all the magazines covered in the *Readers' Guide* is in the front of the volume. See Chapter 13 for a list of other periodical indexes.

In the following excerpt from the *Readers' Guide*, important parts have been labeled. These parts include the following items:

Entry Listing Like the card catalog, the *Readers' Guide* lists an article by the author, the title, and the subject. Notice that only the first word in the title is capitalized.

Subheading Sometimes a subject entry can be divided into subcategories. Each subcategory has a subheading in bold print and is centered in the column.

Source Information Each listing gives the periodical name, date, and page where the article can be found. Additional information such as volume numbers and illustrations may also be included. Much of the source information, including the month of publication, is abbreviated. An explanation of the abbreviations appears in the front pages of each volume of the *Readers' Guide*.

Cross-Reference *See* and *See also* listings suggest additional headings under which information may be listed.

Excerpt from the *Readers' Guide*

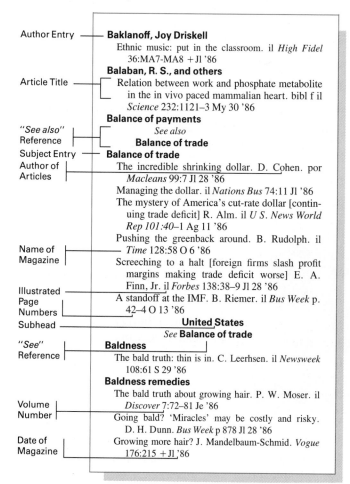

Author Entry — **Baklanoff, Joy Driskell**
Ethnic music: put in the classroom. il *High Fidel* 36:MA7-MA8 + Jl '86
Balaban, R. S., and others

Article Title — Relation between work and phosphate metabolite in the in vivo paced mammalian heart. bibl f il *Science* 232:1121–3 My 30 '86
Balance of payments

"See also" Reference — *See also*
Balance of trade

Subject Entry — **Balance of trade**
Author of Articles — The incredible shrinking dollar. D. Cohen. por *Macleans* 99:7 Jl 28 '86
Managing the dollar. il *Nations Bus* 74:11 Jl '86
The mystery of America's cut-rate dollar [continuing trade deficit] R. Alm. il *U S. News World Rep* 101:40–1 Ag 11 '86
Pushing the greenback around. B. Rudolph. il

Name of Magazine — *Time* 128:58 O 6 '86
Screeching to a halt [foreign firms slash profit margins making trade deficit worse] E. A. Finn, Jr. il *Forbes* 138:38–9 Jl 28 '86

Illustrated — A standoff at the IMF. B. Riemer. il *Bus Week* p.
Page Numbers — 42–4 O 13 '86

Subhead — **United States**
See **Balance of trade**

"See" Reference — **Baldness**
The bald truth: thin is in. C. Leerhsen. il *Newsweek* 108:61 S 29 '86
Baldness remedies
The bald truth about growing hair. P. W. Moser. il

Volume — *Discover* 7:72–81 Je '86
Number — Going bald? 'Miracles' may be costly and risky. D. H. Dunn. *Bus Week* p 878 Jl 28 '86

Date of — Growing more hair? J. Mandelbaum-Schmid. *Vogue*
Magazine — 176:215 + Jl '86

Audio-Visual Materials Many libraries contain filmstrips, tape recordings, records, and videocassettes. Ask the librarian about how these materials are cataloged and the circulation policy.

Exercises

A Using the encyclopedias, atlases, almanacs, and biographical and literary reference works in your school or public library, answer the following questions. Name the reference work you used to locate each answer.

1. Who wrote the following lines, and from what poem are they taken: ''You are better than all the ballads/That were ever sung or said,''?
2. How many billions of dollars did the U.S. government collect in income taxes last year?
3. Where are the following national parks: Everglades, Mammoth Cave?
4. Which American magazine has the largest circulation?
5. List one audio-visual source available in your library.
6. Who said, ''I regret that I have but one life to lose for my country.''?
7. For what is Louis Sullivan well known?

Alfred Hitchcock, director of suspense films.

8. Name two kinds of wild edible mushrooms.
9. List one source in your library that is stored on a microform.
10. What was the most expensive film ever budgeted?

B Use the excerpt from the *Readers' Guide* on page 377 to answer the questions below.

1. Who is the author of the article, ''Growing More Hair?''?
2. What is the title of the article from *Newsweek* magazine?
3. What subhead appears on the page?
4. In the excerpt, what is ''Baldness'' an example of?
5. How many author entries are given?

Chapter 16
Application and Review

A Using Reference Materials Write the type of reference book you would consult to find the following information.

1. General information on writing systems of Japan
2. The location and length of the Volga River
3. The author of the poem that begins "The tide rises, the tide falls,"
4. The birthdate and birthplace of John Steinbeck
5. The name of the team that won the Stanley Cup in hockey last year

B Using Library Resources for Research Suppose that you are preparing a report on ventriloquism. Briefly describe the process you would use to find five sources of information on your subject in the library.

C Using the _Readers' Guide_ Use the _Readers' Guide to Periodical Literature_ to answer the following items.

1. Turn to the "Key Abbreviations" in the _Readers' Guide_ and write the meaning of the following symbols:

1. bibliog	5. Je	9. pub	13. Jl
2. O	6. rev	10. bi-m	14. Ja
3. v	7. Mr	11. abr	15. por
4. il	8. no	12. ed	16. My

2. List the titles of three articles on each of three subjects of current international importance. (Use the correct bibliographic form you learned on page 309 to write your answers.)
3. Study the entry from the _Readers' Guide to Periodical Literature_ given below. Copy the entry on your paper. Label the following parts: _Title, Author, Magazine, Volume, Pages,_ and _Date._ Is the article illustrated? How can you tell? Does the listing appear under a subheading? If so, what is it?

Entry from _Readers' Guide_

> **California**
> National Video Festival: fast-forward. M. Brody
> il. _Film Comment_ 22:73–4 Ja/F '86

17
Developing Study Skills

L earning to juggle takes practice. In fact, practice is the key to learning many skills—from flipping a pizza to reading a road map.

Success in school often depends on your ability to juggle many assignments, such as writing a history report, studying for a French test, and solving a set of math problems. To handle all your homework, you need to develop and practice good study skills. In this chapter you will learn the SQ3R study method, and you will discover techniques for improving your skills in reading, taking notes, memorizing, and understanding graphic aids.

Part 1
Adjusting Reading for Purpose

Studying for your various classes requires different kinds of reading. Frequently, you will have to adjust your reading speed to suit your purpose and the type of material you are reading.

Fast Reading

There are two kinds of fast reading, each with its own method and purpose. These are skimming and scanning.

Skimming involves moving your eyes quickly over a whole page or selection. As you skim, note titles, topic sentences, chapter headings, and highlighted words or phrases. Also examine the table of contents, the index, and pictures or other graphic aids. Skim to get a general idea of a book's content. For example, skim to decide whether a book might be a useful reference source. Skimming is also an excellent tool to use when studying for a test and reviewing material you have already read.

Scanning is helpful when you need to find a specific fact or definition. You scan when you look for a name and number in a phone book. Scanning involves moving your eyes quickly across a line or down a page to locate the particular information. To train yourself to scan, choose a textbook that you use in one of your classes, place a folded paper or a card over the first line, and move the paper quickly down the page. Look for key words and phrases that indicate you are close to the information you need. When you locate such a clue, stop scanning and read slowly.

In-Depth Reading

Skimming and scanning provide only a general understanding of material. Much of your reading, however, requires you to understand specific information. To absorb thoroughly the material in a book, read it slowly and carefully. To understand and remember what you read, first look for main ideas. You will often find main ideas in titles and subheadings and in the first sentences of paragraphs. Key words and phrases such as *first* and *most important* often identify main ideas. Also, look for important terms that are defined in boldface. After noting the main ideas, locate supporting details—names, dates, statistics, and reasons.

Exercise

Follow these directions, one at a time. Do not read through all of the directions first.

1. Skim the following article. Note the topic sentence and the italicized words. Write one sentence summarizing the main idea of the passage.
2. Scan the article to identify examples of carnivorous animals that have canine teeth. Write your answer.
3. Skim the selection. Then make a list of questions to answer after doing an in-depth reading.

Carnivorous mammals. Some mammals are *carnivorous*. They eat animal flesh. Many of them are speedy animals that catch, hold, and stab their prey with long, pointed *canine teeth*. Such mammals, which include leopards, lions, and wolves, do not thoroughly chew their food. They swallow chunks of it whole. Dolphins, seals, and other fish-eating mammals also use their teeth to grasp prey, which they swallow whole. Some carnivorous mammals commonly feed on the remains of dead animals, instead of hunting and killing fresh prey. Hyenas are especially adapted to such a diet and have extremely powerful jaws that can crush even large bones.

The World Book Encyclopedia

The SQ3R Study Method

Have you ever read a chapter in a textbook, closed the book, and then forgotten most of what you had just read? If so, you need a more effective approach to studying written material.

One way to get the most from what you read is to use the **SQ3R** study method. This method consists of five steps: **S**urvey, **Q**uestion, **R**ead, **R**ecord, and **R**eview.

Using SQ3R

Survey **the material.** First skim the selection to find the main idea. Look for titles, headings, topic sentences, and highlighted words or phrases. Also note charts, maps, and other graphic aids. Read the introduction and, if there is one, the summary.

Question. Decide what questions you should be able to answer at the end of your in-depth reading and make a list of these questions in the notebook you keep for your class. Use any study questions presented in the book or provided by your teacher. You can also make up your own questions by turning the titles, headings, or highlighted words into questions. Pictures, maps, or charts can also be used to make up questions.

Read **the selection carefully.** Look for the answers to the questions as you read. Also identify the central thoughts in each section.

Record, **in your own words, the answers to your questions.** Make sure that you understand other important points in the selection, and record those as well.

Review **the selection.** Quickly read over your notes and look over main points to impress them on your memory. Look up the answers to any questions that are still unclear.

Exercise

Apply the SQ3R method to Part 3 of this chapter, "Taking Notes." Be sure to complete all five steps.

Part 3

Taking Notes

Few people can remember all that they read and hear. Taking notes is one method of remedying this problem. Notes are useful as memory aids and as references or study guides for review.

When to Take Notes

Take notes on all important information that you encounter as a student. In class, take notes on material presented by your teacher, on useful comments or presentations made by other students, on lab work, and on in-class reading.

When you are listening to a lecture or explanation, listen for clues that indicate which points are emphasized. Such clues include key words and phrases such as *most important, for these reasons, first, for example,* and *to review.* A speaker's vocal signals, such as slowing down, repeating, or pausing for emphasis, can also be clues. Finally, the speaker's use of a chalkboard or transparency almost always signals important information.

For all classes, take notes on any special projects and readings. Also take notes as you conduct research. Before taking notes on written material, skim the selection to discover which points are the most important. Then take notes on those points. Also, record the answers to any questions that you wrote while using the SQ3R study method.

How to Take Notes

Use a separate notebook for each class or a single, large notebook divided into class sections. Make sure that the subject and the date appear on each page.

Do not try to record every word that you hear or read. Instead, record only essential information. Note important details such as dates, definitions, events, and names of people, places, and events. After class, go back over your notes, asking yourself why certain subjects were emphasized, how topics were grouped together, and what some of the main points of the lecture were. Write down your thoughts on these points and attach these notes to your class notes. When reviewing for an exam, this reflection technique helps you understand the larger picture or main thrust of the lecture instead of simply focusing on the small details.

A modified outline form is useful for taking notes. (For information regarding the formal outline, see Chapter 12, pages 290–291.) Below are notes from a history lesson. How has the formal outline format been modified?

Notes in Modified Outline Form

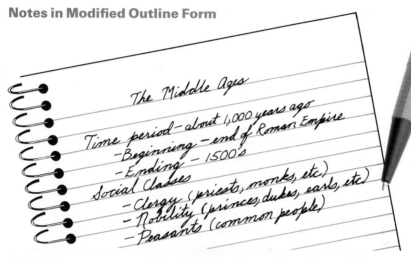

The Middle Ages

Time period — about 4,000 years ago
- Beginning — end of Roman Empire
- Ending — 1500's
Social Classes
- Clergy (priests, monks, etc.)
- Nobility (princes, dukes, earls, etc.)
- Peasants (common people)

Notice that main ideas are placed to the left. Related details are introduced by dashes and indented beneath the main ideas to which they refer. As with all the notes, writing in phrases instead of complete sentences allows you to follow the lecture more closely.

If your notes are to be complete, you must be able to record information quickly. Develop your own set of abbreviations and symbols and you will notice you can save time and take notes more effectively. Omitting the period after an abbreviation will also save time. The following chart suggests abbreviations to use.

Some Abbreviations and Symbols for Note-Taking

w/o	without	def	definition
&, +	and	*	important
#	number	re	regarding
>	more than	<	less than
e/	not	=	equals
y	why	∴	therefore

You can get the most out of your notes if you review them immediately after your class or study session. At that point you can also examine any questions, ideas, conjectures, or feelings you have about the lesson. Writing answers to questions such as those in the chart below can help you clarify and remember what you have learned.

Questions About What I Am Learning

1. What have I learned?
2. What is another way of saying this?
3. What can I apply this to?
4. What is a related idea?
5. What don't I understand?
6. Where can I go with this idea?
7. I wonder why . . . ?
8. What would happen if . . . ?
9. What can I do to learn more about this?
10. One interesting part of this idea is . . .

Exercises

A Take notes on Part 1 of this chapter using a modified outline. Also use abbreviations where possible.

B Interview a friend or family member concerning some event or experience, for example, an encounter with a bear during a camping trip. During the interview take notes using a modified outline form.

C Choose a class period when your teacher is presenting a new lesson. You might choose a social studies or a science class. During this class take notes using a modified outline form and abbreviations.

D In a textbook for one of your classes, find a paragraph that explains a concept. Choose a paragraph that you found difficult to understand. Rewrite the paragraph in your own words.

E For your next assigned composition, keep notes on your writing process. At each stage in the project record any thoughts, problems, and feelings you have concerning the writing. This technique can tell you quite a bit about your learning and thinking styles.

Part 4
Memorizing

You need to know some facts without consulting a book or your notes. You must memorize such information as your phone number, locker combination, and your character's lines in a play. Of course, you will also have to memorize facts in your courses.

Memorizing requires effort. Here are some techniques that you might try for memorizing new information. Experiment to find the ones that work for you.

Memorization Strategies

1. **Read and repeat the information out loud.** Hearing it may help you remember. Frequent repetition will help you fix the information in your mind.
2. **Write down the information.** Seeing it on paper helps you see it in your mind later. Close your eyes and visualize what you want to remember.
3. **Make connections between facts.** For instance, to memorize indefinite pronouns, you might first learn those with *one: anyone, everyone, no one,* and *someone*.
4. **Employ memory games.** One game is to turn the fact into a rhyme: *In 1492 Columbus sailed the ocean blue* helps you recall an important historical date. Another memory aid is to think of a word that helps you remember information. For example, the word *rice* can help you recall how to treat a sprained ankle—rest, ice, compression, and elevation.

Exercise

The following items are some of the key structures of a cell. Try to memorize them by making up a sentence using words that start with the same first letters as these structures. If this method doesn't work, try one of the others in the chart.

cell membrane	endoplasmic	mitochondria
nucleus	reticulum	chloroplasts
cytoplasm	Golgi bodies	vacuoles

Part 5
Using Graphic Aids

Graphic aids present data in the form of charts, tables, diagrams, maps, and graphs. Here are some guidelines for studying them.

Common Graphic Aids

Type	Purpose	Study Tips
Pictures, Sketches, Diagrams	To illustrate text, to show the parts or functions of the subject	Read caption or title; relate image to text; note labels of parts.
Maps	To display geographical areas or distribution	Read caption or title; find **legend** or **key.**
Tables and Charts	To list information, to compare information	Read caption or title; check key to determine organization.
Graphs	To show relationships between groups, to show development in time	Read caption or title; determine what relationship is shown.

Reading Tables

Tables present large amounts of information simply and clearly. **Statistical tables** present information in numerical form. Study the table shown below. What information does it provide?

Average Hours of TV Usage Per Day in America

(6:28 means six hours and twenty-eight minutes of viewing.)

	1971	1976	1984	1985	1986	1987
February	6:53	6:49	7:38	7:49	7:48	7:35
July	5:08	5:33	6:26	6:34	6:37	6:32
Year's Average	6:01	6:11	7:08	7:07	7:10	7:10

Source: A. C. Nielsen estimates, 1987

Every table presents information about one or more subjects which are called **variables** because the numbers associated with them vary. The table on page 388 indicates the average hours of TV watching per day in American households. Variables in vertical columns include the number of hours and minutes of watching in February and in July as well as the average number of hours for the year. Variables in horizontal rows indicate the amounts of watching in six different years.

When you read a table, make sure that you identify the variables shown and determine what information is given about each.

Reading Graphs

Graphs are used to show relationships between sets of variables. To understand a graph, read the title and the key to symbols and abbreviations. Then determine what variables are presented by the graph and how these are related. One of the most common types of graphs is the circle graph.

The circle graph below shows how the money from an $8.98 record album is distributed.

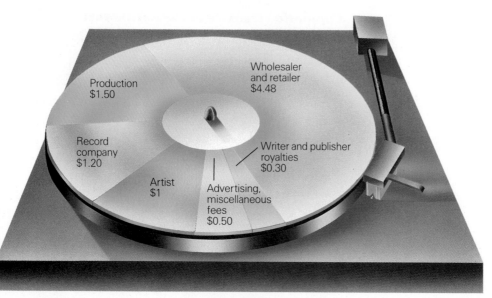

Note: Numbers are approximated.

The circle represents 100 percent, or the whole, of something. The sections within the circle graph represent parts of the whole. In the circle graph above, what do the six parts of the whole represent?

Exercises

A Answer the following questions referring to the statistical table on page 388.

1. How many hours a day did American households watch television in February during 1985? in July during 1985? What conclusion can you draw from this information?
2. How many hours a day did American households watch television on an average day in 1976? in 1987? What conclusion can you draw from this information?

B **Bar graphs** usually show one variable expressed in numbers and the other variable expressed in words. A bar extends from the variable expressed in words. To determine the amount of the variable expressed in words, draw an imaginary line from the end of the bar to the numerical variable. Study the bar graph given below, and answer the questions.

1. Which continent has the lowest population density?
2. Which continent has the greatest population density?

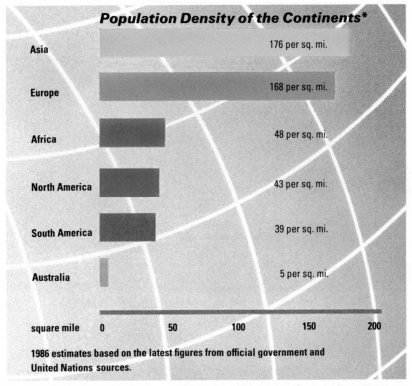

Population Density of the Continents*

Asia	176 per sq. mi.
Europe	168 per sq. mi.
Africa	48 per sq. mi.
North America	43 per sq. mi.
South America	39 per sq. mi.
Australia	5 per sq. mi.

square mile   0   50   100   150   200

1986 estimates based on the latest figures from official government and United Nations sources.

*Antarctica has no permanent population.

Chapter 17
Application and Review

A Adjusting Your Reading Speed Skim the paragraph below to find the topic. Write the topic. Then scan to find the answers to the following questions. Write your answers.

1. In Roman mythology, what activities did Mars control?
2. Who were Romulus and Remus?
3. How are Mars and the month of March connected?
4. Who was the Greek god of war?
5. What is the meaning of the word *martial*?

> **The Roman God Mars.** Mars was the god of war in Roman mythology. The ancient Romans gave Mars special importance because they considered him the father of Romulus and Remus, the legendary founders of Rome.
>
> **Origin.** Originally, Mars was a god of farmland and fertility. The month of March, the beginning of the Roman growing season, was named for him. Since ancient times, the area enclosed by a bend in the Tiber River in Rome has been called the field of Mars. Romans dedicated this section of land to Mars because of its fertility.
>
> **Mars, God of War.** Mars became the god of war after the Romans came into contact with Greek culture. They gave him many characteristics of the Greek god of war, **Ares.** In time, the Romans associated Mars principally with war. . . . The word *martial,* which means ''warlike,'' is based on his name. The planet Mars is named for him.
>
> The World Book Encyclopedia

B Using Graphic Aids Construct a bar graph. Use the information given below.

> Of the eight major religions of the world, Christianity is the largest, with approximately 1,061,711,600 members. Islam has approximately 554,700,200 adherents, followed closely by Hinduism, with 463,815,200. In addition, the following religions all have members numbering in the millions: Buddhism (247,587,500), Confucianism (150,984,000), Shinto (32,048,000), Taoism (20,056,000), and Judaism (16,932,000).
>
> Encyclopaedia Britannica Book of the Year 1986

18
Taking Tests

*W*inning a chess game requires successful strategies and careful concentration. Good chess players often plan their moves far in advance, anticipating their opponents' moves as they do so.

Test taking too requires advance planning and effective strategies. Whether you are taking a classroom test in biology or a standardized achievement test, your final score reflects not only your knowledge of the subject material but also your skills in test taking. This chapter will help you develop successful test-taking skills and strategies for answering various types of questions.

Part 1
Preparing for Tests

In school, you take two kinds of tests. **Classroom tests** measure your knowledge of the specific topics covered in your courses and textbooks. **Standardized tests** measure your general knowledge. These guidelines will help you study for a classroom test.

How to Study for Classroom Tests

1. Know what kind of test it will be and what it will cover.
2. Allow sufficient study time; avoid cramming.
3. Review your notes. Underline or highlight key points.
4. Skim any reading covered by the test.
5. Answer any study questions provided by your teacher.
6. Make separate lists of important facts and formulas.
7. If the test requires memorization, practice with flash cards, or use memory tricks (See page 387).

Exercise

On a separate paper, write short answers to these questions.

1. How do classroom tests differ from standardized tests?
2. What can you do that will help you review your notes?
3. What strategies will help you memorize material?

Part 2
Objective Test Questions

An objective test question has a single correct answer. When taking an objective test, mark difficult questions and return to them later. Then, if you cannot determine the correct answer, guess. Try to eliminate some answers to increase your chances of guessing correctly.

Four kinds of objective items are seen on classroom tests. The chart on the next page describes these types of questions. Study each description and the strategies for answering each type.

Objective Test Strategies

True/False
You are given a statement and asked to tell whether the statement is true or false.

1. If any part of a statement is false, the whole statement will be false.
2. Words like *all, always, only,* and *never* often appear in false statements.
3. Words like *generally, probably, some, usually, often,* and *most* often appear in true statements.

Matching
You are asked to match items in one column with corresponding items in a second column.

1. Check the directions to see whether each item is used only once and whether some are not used.
2. Read all items in both columns.
3. Match those items you know first.
4. Cross out items as you match them, unless items are used more than once.

Multiple Choice
You are asked to choose the best answer from a group of answers provided on the test.

1. Read all choices before answering.
2. Eliminate incorrect answers.
3. Choose the answer that is most complete or accurate.
4. Note all choices given, including *none of the above* or *all of the above*.

Completion
You are asked to fill in a blank or several blanks in a statement on the exam.

1. Make sure your answer fits grammatically into the space that is provided.
2. If several words are needed to make sense in the statement, write in all of them.
3. Write legibly, using proper spelling, grammar, punctuation, and capitalization.

Sample Test Questions

True/False

false   Amphibians are cold-blooded animals that live only in water.

true   Newts are amphibians.

true   If a newt loses a leg, often the leg will grow back.

false   Amphibians never develop lungs.

Matching

b   1. simile

c   2. personification

e   3. metaphor

a   4. paradox

d   5. hyperbole

a. I'm so happy about my sister's promotion I could cry.

b. The room was as gloomy as a November day.

c. The sun smiled down on us that day.

d. I told you a million times.

e. The road was a ribbon of moonlight.

Multiple Choice

Mark Twain was born

a. on the banks of the Mississippi

b. in Hannibal, Missouri

c. in Florida, Missouri

d. none of the above

Mark Twain wrote

a. *The Adventures of Tom Sawyer*

b. "The Mysterious Stranger"

c. *Life on the Mississippi*

d. all of the above

Completion

In the feudal system a piece of land given in return for services was called *a fief*.

In feudal times a person bound to the lord's land and transferred with the land to a new owner was called *a serf*.

A person who held land in feudal times and who did homage to a lord was called *a vassal*.

Exercise

On a separate paper, write answers to the following questions.

1. Answer the statements below by writing *True* or *False*.
   a. Standardized tests cover the material in the courses you are currently taking.
   b. You should complete difficult questions first, and save easier ones for when you may be rushed for time.
   c. In matching questions, the same answer item may be used more than once and some items may not be used at all.
   d. Completion questions always require one- or two-word answers.

2. Match the following types of objective tests with their corresponding strategies.

   1. True/False
   2. Multiple Choice
   3. Completion
   4. Matching

   a. Make sure your answer fits grammatically into the space provided.
   b. Read all items in both columns before starting.
   c. Remember that, if any part of a statement is not true, the entire statement is not true.
   d. Choose the most complete or accurate of the answers provided.

3. Choose the best answer of the four choices given. Which one of the following types of objective test question does not present a choice of answers?
   a. matching
   b. true/false
   c. multiple choice
   d. completion

4. Supply the words or phrases that best complete the sentence. In a true/false question, words such as _____, _____, _____, and _____ often appear in false statements.

Calvin and Hobbes
by Bill Watterson

396   *Taking Tests*

Part 3

Short-Answer and Essay Questions

Short-answer questions require you to write an answer, usually one or two sentences in length. **Essay questions** require a longer written answer, often one paragraph, sometimes several paragraphs.

Short-Answer Questions

Always respond to short-answer questions in complete sentences. Answer completely, but be brief and to the point. Write legibly, paying close attention to grammar, spelling, punctuation, and capitalization. In the following example, note how the answer is given in a complete sentence and how it provides the three facts requested.

When, where, and by whom was paper invented?

Paper was invented in China by Ts'ai Lun in A.D. 105.

Essay Questions

Essay questions require a lengthier, more detailed explanation than short-answer questions. On a social studies test, for example, you might find the following question: ''Describe three of the earliest river-valley civilizations.'' Such a question would probably require three paragraphs, one for each civilization.

An essay question requires you to develop your answer by discussing the relevant facts. Be sure to follow the steps of the writing process as you would when writing a composition. However, shorten each stage, especially the revising, because you have a limited time period. For complete instruction about writing answers to essay questions, see pages 246–249, ''Focus on Essay Tests.''

Exercise

Write a one-paragraph essay explaining the need for providing wheelchair ramps for the physically disabled in all municipal buildings. Be sure to use your own words, giving reasons or examples to support your topic sentence and following the strategies outlined in this section. You should allow yourself no more than fifteen minutes to write this paragraph.

Part 4
Standardized Tests

Standardized tests are given to groups of students nationwide under similar conditions. These tests can measure a student's academic skills, help in decisions about entrance to other courses and schools, and help a school evaluate its own performance.

The amount of specific study that you can do for standardized tests is limited. However, for some tests, such as the college board exams, preparation is possible and advisable. Books that will help you prepare for the tests are available from both bookstores and testing services.

One good way to be ready for these tests is to understand the kinds of questions they include.

Reading Comprehension Questions

A reading comprehension item requires you to read a passage and then answer several questions about it. The questions may ask you to pick out the central idea, recall a fact, identify the mood, draw a conclusion, or define a word. Preview the questions before reading the passage so that you will know what details to look for. Then read the passage quickly but carefully, looking for these details. As you read the passage, also note the main idea and pay attention to words that show relationships. Read all the answer choices first, and then choose the one that best answers the question. Watch for answers that are only partially correct.

Vocabulary Questions

Several kinds of questions measure vocabulary.

Synonym Questions In this common type of vocabulary question, you identify the word or phrase closest in meaning to the given word. Study the following sample.

Interrogate: a. imprison   c. punish   e. question
                 b. torture   d. curse

Remember, no two words are identical in meaning, although many have close associations. People who are *interrogated* may be imprisoned, tortured, or punished; but *interrogate* actually means "question." Be patient enough to read all the options before choosing.

The short
and long of it.

Antonym Questions These questions require you to choose the word or phrase that is most nearly opposite the given word.

> Depress: a. force c. clarify e. loosen
>   b. allow d. elate

Remember no two words are exact opposites, and many words have more than one meaning. *Depress* means both "to push down" and "to sadden." No antonym of "to push down" (such as *raise*) is given. However, *elate* is the opposite of *sadden* and is therefore the best choice.

Sentence Completion In these questions, select the word or words that best fit the meaning of the sentence. Your completed sentence must make sense and be grammatically correct.

> Marcia was _____ by the team's refusal to accept her, yet she _____ her training program.
>
> a. encouraged . . . joined   c. frustrated . . . continued
> b. annoyed . . . quit   d. discouraged . . . discontinued

Try all of the options before you choose. While this question might appear difficult at first, in fact only choice *c* is logical.

Analogy Questions An analogy question is a special kind of vocabulary question. You are given a related pair of words and asked to select a second pair of words that expresses a similar relationship. Following is a typical analogy question.

Colt : Horse   a. dachshund : dog   c. robin : bird

                b. herd : buffalo   d. fawn : deer

The colon between the words means ''is to.'' Think of analogy questions as a type of sentence completion problem.

A colt is to a horse as a _____ is to a _____.

First, establish the relationship between *colt* and *horse* by devising a sentence that relates the pair.

A colt *is a young* horse.

Then try each of the paired answers in your sentence.

A *dachshund* is a young *dog*?   A *robin* is a young *bird*?

A *herd* is a young *buffalo*?   A *fawn* is a young *deer*?

Only the last sentence expresses the correct relationship.

Grammar, Usage, and Mechanics Questions

This type of test question measures writing skills. You are given a sentence with certain parts underlined and are asked to tell whether there is an error in grammar, usage, punctuation, or capitalization—or no error at all. If you see an error, mark the corresponding letter on your answer sheet. If there is no error, mark ''No error.''

Here is an example of a grammar/usage question.

<u>Although</u> both Jennifer and Heather <u>are</u> talented, each <u>have</u>

  a   b   c

very distinct kinds of ability. <u>No error.</u>

                                          d

Each is singular and requires the singular verb *has*. Therefore, *c* is the error in this sentence. You would mark *c* on your answer sheet.

Here is an example of a punctuation/capitalization question.

Mark <u>T</u>wain wrote <u>''</u>The Celebrated Jumping Frog of

        a   b

Calaveras County'' before he wrote *The <u>a</u>dventures of*

                                            c

Huckleberry Finn. <u>No error.</u>

                            d

All major words in the titles of books are capitalized; therefore, *c* marks the error in this sentence.

Exercises

A Choose the word that is most nearly opposite the given word.

Malevolent: a. sickly   c. malicious

                  b. kind   d. fast

B Complete this analogy.

Bird : Flock   a. caterpillar : butterfly   c. colt : horse

                    b. robin : sparrow   d. wolf : pack

C Write the letter that corresponds to any error.

On the first day of her vacation Jill <u>laid</u> in the sun at Clearwater

                                         a

<u>B</u>each for over <u>two</u> hours. <u>No error.</u>

b   c   d

Part 5

Taking the Test

Use the following techniques on classroom and standardized tests.

Strategies for Taking Tests

1. **First, survey the test.**
2. **Next, plan your time.** Read all the directions, decide in which order to answer the questions, and allow time for review.
3. **Read each test item carefully.**
4. **Begin by answering the questions that you know.**
5. **Be careful when using answer sheets.** Fill in the answer circle darkly and completely so the mark will register in the scoring machine. Make thorough erasures because stray marks may be counted as incorrect answers. Make sure that the number of the test item corresponds with the number on the answer sheet.
6. **For essay tests, read all directions and questions before beginning so that you do not repeat yourself.**

Teen-ager

It may come as something of a surprise, but until the 1940's teen-agers did not exist. If you look in an old dictionary, the closest you will find is *teenage,* a seldom-used term for the brushwood that is gathered to make fences and hedges. *Teen* is listed as an obsolete word for injury or misery.

There were no teen-agers primarily because there was little need for the word. The group of young people between the ages of thirteen and nineteen did not have much in common. Many people in their mid- and late teens were already earning a living or raising a family, so they had little to do with their younger brothers and sisters just entering the teen years. All of that changed with the advent of universal public education in the twentieth century. When school became the common ground for young people throughout their teen years, teen-agers emerged as a large and easily identifiable bloc. By the mid-1940's the word *teen-ager* had become a commonly used description.

Now, teen-agers are perhaps the single most identifiable age group in society. Music, clothes, consumer goods, movies, television, and language all bear the stamp of teen-agers and teen culture. Although the word *teen-ager* didn't even exist fifty years ago, today advertisers and merchants would be lost without it!

Hair styled in distinctive disarray

Portable music to ward off boredom

Jeans with a lived-in look

High-top gym shoes for style and comfort

Chapter 18
Application and Review

A Matching Questions On a separate sheet of paper, write answers to the following matching questions.

1. Reading Comprehension
2. Synonym
3. Analogy
4. Grammar, Usage

5. Sentence Completion

a. Establish the relationship between a pair of words.
b. Read for accuracy and speed.
c. Find the error in the sentence.
d. Find the combination that best fits the meaning and the grammar of the sentence.
e. Choose the word closest in meaning to the given word.

B Other Types of Test Questions On a sheet of paper, write answers to the following standardized test questions.

1. Identify the word closest in meaning to the word at the left.

   Forestalled: a. forced   c. prevented   e. discharged
   b. excluded   d. moved

2. Select the pair of words that expresses a similar relationship to the first pair.

   Knife : Incision   a. engine : automobile   c. shout : cry
   b. bulldozer : excavation   d. hot : cold

3. Select the word pair that best fits the meaning of the sentence.

   The bear was able to return to _____ den _____ the paw injury.

   a. some . . . although   c. it's . . . before
   b. a . . . during   d. its . . . after

4. If there is an error, write that letter on your paper. If there is no error, mark *d*. Look for errors in both usage and mechanics.

   <u>Although</u> every square is a rectangle<u>;</u> not every
   a   b

   rectangle is a square<u>.</u> <u>No error.</u>
                                    c   d

19

Business Letters and Forms

2525 Pineberry Lane
Sanford, Florida 3͏
September 5, 19--

Oberlin's Trick Shop
7534 West Oldham Road
Madison, New Jersey 13224

Dear Sir:

The trick escape set I ordered from your catalog arrived two days ago. Everything seemed to be in order, so I threw the box away.

After trying out the handcuffs for my Houdini escape trick, I discovered that the key to the cuffs was missing. I am typing this letter with one finger since I cannot get the handcuffs off.

Although I appreciate the sturdiness of the merchandise, my movements will be definitely curtailed until I can get the cuffs off. Please rush a key to me immediately.

Sincerely yours,

Ralph S. Aleck

Ralph S. Aleck

O ut of every ten thousand letters that the United States Postal Service processes, only one is a personal letter. The rest are business letters written for a variety of purposes. Think about the business letters you have sent. Did they achieve the purposes for which they were written?

Whether you are requesting information or ordering merchandise, the business letters you write should be brief, clear, and to the point. You also need to follow guidelines in filling out forms, such as catalog order forms. In this chapter you will learn how to write effective business letters and correctly fill out business forms.

Part 1

Preparing the Business Letter

Business letters have six parts: the **heading,** the **inside address,** the **salutation,** the **body,** the **closing,** and the **signature.** These six parts can be arranged in either **block form** or **modified block form.**

Block Form and Modified Block Form

For all business letters, use plain white $8\frac{1}{2}''\times 11''$ paper, whether you handwrite or type them. In **block form,** all parts begin at the left margin. Use this form only when you type the letter. In **modified block form,** the heading, closing, and signature are aligned near the right margin, and the other parts are at the left margin.

Block Form

Heading	1246 Prairie Avenue Minneapolis, Minnesota 55435 April 4, 19—
Inside Address	U.S. Cycling Federation 1750 East Boulder Street Colorado Springs, Colorado 80409
Salutation	Dear Sir or Madam:
Body	I am interested in joining a cycling club and in participating in bike races that your organization sponsors. Please send me information about clubs in my area and instructions for entering federation races. Thank you for your assistance.
Closing	Yours truly,
Signature	*José Martinez* José Martinez

Modified Block Form

631 Inca Lane
St. Louis, Missouri 63101
April 3, 19—

Edgar Drexler, Manager
Sutton's Department Store
432 Oak Street
St. Louis, Missouri 63142

Dear Mr. Drexler:

In March I purchased a pair of All World basketball shoes in your sporting goods department for
$39.95. Enclosed is a copy of the sales receipt.

I wore these shoes for less than one week before
the sole came loose on the left shoe. When I took
them back to the store, the sales clerk said they
could not be returned. I feel this is unfair because the shoes I bought were obviously defec-
tive. I am requesting a full refund or an exchange
for another brand.

Your prompt attention to this problem would be
appreciated.

Very truly yours,

Benjamin Erickson

Benjamin Erickson

Heading The heading is written at the top of the page. The first line contains your street address; the second line contains your town or city, state, and ZIP code. Separate the city and state with a comma and write out the name of the state. The third line gives the date of the letter. Place the heading at the left or the right margin, depending on whether you use the block form or the modified block form.

Inside Address The inside address tells to whom the letter is being sent. Place the inside address at the left margin at least four lines below the heading. On the first line you should place the name of the receiver. If there is room, place the person's title on the same line, separated from the name by a comma. Otherwise, place the title on the next line. If you do not know the name of the person who will receive your letter, use the person's title or the name of the department. On the succeeding lines, place the company name and address, including the city, state, and ZIP code.

The inside address is important because occasionally a letter is opened by someone other than the addressee, and the envelope is discarded. If this happens, the name and address of the receiver can still be found in the inside address. Following are two typical inside addresses. Refer to the sample letters on pages 405 and 406 for placement of the inside address.

> Ms. Janet McPherson, Personnel Director
> Lakeland Craft Cooperative
> 3701 Bloom Street
> Rochester, New York 14619

> Recreation Department
> City of New Orleans
> 121 Canal Street
> New Orleans, Louisiana 70130

Salutation Position the salutation two lines below the inside address. Begin with the word *Dear*, follow it by the name of the person to whom you are writing, and end with a colon. Use only the person's last name, preceded by a title such as *Mr., Mrs., Ms., Dr.,* or *Professor.* If you do not know the person's name, use a general salutation such as *Ladies and Gentlemen:* Another alternative is to write to a department or to a position within a company. The following forms are acceptable:

> Dear Mr. Allen: Dear Sir or Madam:
> Dear Ms. Kreutzer: Dear Customer Service Department:
> Dear Mrs. Jackson: Dear Editor:

Body The body, the main part of the letter in which you write your message, begins two spaces below the salutation. The body may contain a single paragraph or several paragraphs. Leave a space between each paragraph.

Closing The closing is placed two lines below the body, in line with the heading. Closings commonly used for business letters include *Sincerely, Sincerely yours,* and *Very truly yours.* Note that only the first word is capitalized and that the closing ends with a comma.

Signature Type or print your name four spaces below the closing, and sign your name in the space between.

Exercise

The following letter has errors in business letter form. On your paper, rewrite the letter correctly using modified block form. Correct any errors in spacing, location, capitalization, and punctuation. Then label each of the parts of the letter.

March 23, 19—
Huber Heights Ohio 45424
5230 Peters Drive

Coordinator
Whitewater rafting trips, Inc.
105 main street
Evergreen, Co, 80439

    Dear Coordinator,

My family and I would like to take a Whitewater
Rafting Trip this summer. Please send me information about dates, fees, and registration. I also
would appreciate any information about campsites
and motels in the area.
I look forward to taking part in one of your
trips. Thank you for your help.

Sincerely Yours

Bill Barnhart

Bill Barnhart

Knowing Where and to Whom to Write

You can spend a great deal of time writing the ''perfect'' letter, but unless you address it correctly, your efforts may be wasted. If you do not know the address of the company to which you are writing, check the library for directories that list business names and addresses. If you are writing about a product, the company's name can usually be found on the label or obtained from the place of purchase.

Take time to address your letter to the proper person or department. Companies have many departments to handle orders, service calls, complaints, and other responsibilities. If you address your letter simply to the company, it may never find its way to the person who is qualified to respond. When in doubt, address your letter to the company's customer service department.

Once you have found the proper address, be sure to include city, state, and ZIP code information. Your post office and library have complete ZIP code listings for every community in the United States.

Addressing the Envelope

Use block form for addressing an envelope. Write the address on the lower half of the envelope. Write or type the address clearly and make sure it is identical to the inside address of your letter. The United States Postal Service recommends that you use their two-letter abbreviations for state names. When using these abbreviations, you do not need to separate the city and state with a comma, for example, Underwood MN 56586. Write your return address in the upper left corner of the envelope. Before mailing your letter, make a copy so that you will have a record of it.

Exercise

On your paper, draw two rectangles in the shape of envelopes. Use the corrected form of the items below to address each envelope.

1. Return address: your name and address
   Send to ms. yolanda diaz, public relations director, fun world, 10 river drive, memphis tn 38101
2. Return address: jay gold, box 40, wykoff mn 55990
   Send to sales department, music videos ltd., 77 sunrise boulevard, hollywood ca 90028

Different Types of Business Letters

To write effective letters, keep several guidelines in mind. Business letters are more formal than personal letters, so you should avoid informal language, slang, contractions, and abbreviations in your writing. State your purpose as clearly and concisely as possible, and include only the details that are necessary to accomplish your purpose. The tone of a business letter should be courteous and businesslike, never rude or demanding. Most business letters fall into one of these categories: **letters of request, order letters,** and **letters of complaint, adjustment,** or **appreciation.**

Letters of Request

Perhaps you have been thinking about buying fishing equipment. You could write a letter to a fishing equipment manufacturer requesting information about its products. Make your request letter as specific as possible. Include all details the person or company needs in order to respond. Make sure that your request is reasonable. Consider the time and effort required for someone to answer your request. Leave enough time to receive a reply before you need the information.

The business letter on page 405 is an example of a direct, concise, and specific letter of request.

Exercise

Choose one of the following situations and write a letter requesting appropriate information. Use the modified block form, and make up any names and addresses you need to complete the letter. When you have finished the letter, address an envelope.

1. You are researching your family history, and you are trying to get information about your great-great-grandmother. Write to the city clerk in her city of birth. Ask if the clerk can provide any records about her and other members of her family.
2. In groups of three to five, plan a dream vacation to an exotic place. Write a letter requesting information about possible tours. If there is time, exchange your letters with your classmates and answer one another's letters.

Order Letters

When you want to buy a product through the mail and the company does not supply an order form, you can write an order letter. Be sure to include all necessary details, such as size, color, model number, quantity, and price, so that your order can be processed without delays or mistakes. Give complete and accurate information about where the product should be sent. Indicate your method of payment, and be sure to include any costs for tax, handling, shipping, or insuring.

The following order letter shows the kinds of information that should be included. Notice that it is in block form.

Order Letter

```
1942 Griffin Road
Indianapolis, Indiana 46227
June 14, 19—


Sales Department
Johnson's Sporting Goods, Inc.
637 Front Street
San Luis Obispo, California 93401

Dear Sales Department:

Please send me the following items listed on page
235 of your summer catalog:
    Items:  two terry cloth wrist sweatbands
    Size:  women's (medium)
    Colors:  one blue, one green
I have enclosed a money order for $7.50 to cover
the cost of $3.75 per sweatband. As stated in your
catalog, I understand that my prepayment will
cover all shipping, handling, and insurance
costs.

Yours truly,

Sandra Anderson

Sandra Anderson
```

Exercise

Write a letter for one situation below. Check the letter carefully to make sure all necessary information is included. When you have finished the letter, address a corresponding envelope.

1. Friendly Photos, 7601 South Magnolia Avenue, Cincinnati, Ohio 45229

   24 $2\frac{1}{3} \times 3\frac{1}{2}$ wallet photos 2.50
   2 5×7 enlargements 1.75
   Add 1.25 for handling and postage

2. Walter Drake & Sons, 4085 Drake Building, Colorado Springs, Colorado 80940—Advertisement in August issue of *Better Homes and Gardens*

   No. S717—two sets of 1,000 name labels @ $ 1.00 per set
   No. S854—one set of personalized pencils @ $.89 per set
   Postage and handling—$.40

3. Sea Horses, Box 342096, Coral Gables, Florida 33—Advertisement in July issue of *Boy's Life*

   3 live sea horse kits @ $ 2.98
   2 custom aquariums @ $ 5.98
   1 deluxe aquarium @$10.95
   Air mail postage paid by advertiser—live delivery guaranteed

Letters of Complaint or Appreciation

A letter of complaint or adjustment should be written when you receive the wrong merchandise, when it is damaged, or when for some other reason you are dissatisfied with a product or service. However, a letter of complaint is not a "gripe" letter. Avoid an angry, sarcastic, or vulgar tone. Instead, simply give the reasons you are dissatisfied, and state how you would like the company to resolve your complaint.

Most companies are interested in hearing from you. If you are not happy with a purchase, you probably will not buy that brand again. This is of great concern to the seller. After all, he or she wants you to keep buying that particular product or coming to the store. Do not merely tell friends how upset you are; let the proper people know you are unhappy. You may be surprised by the response you receive.

When a product pleases you or a person does good work, a letter of appreciation can be equally effective. Such a letter gives the person or company receiving it valuable information about the product or service provided. For an example of a letter of adjustment, see page 406.

Exercise

Choose one of the numbered situations. Write a complaint or appreciation letter. Use one of the block forms, and make up any names and addresses you need.

1. Four weeks ago you ordered $28.50 in supplies for a science project. You have not received them, and it is now too late to complete your project. Write to the hobby shop where you ordered the supplies and ask for a refund.
2. The record albums you ordered from your club were warped when they were delivered. Write to the record club, stating that you are returning the albums and would like replacement albums.
3. A radio or television station recently has added a program that you especially like. Write a letter telling the station manager that you like the program and hope it will be continued.
4. Your family celebrated your grandmother's birthday at the Copper Kettle Restaurant. The service and the meal were both excellent, and your family especially enjoyed the way the entire dining staff gathered to sing "Happy Birthday" to your grandmother. She said the evening was one of the nicest she has ever had. Write to the manager and express your appreciation for a wonderful evening.

Part 3
Completing Forms

Forms fulfill many needs and perform many different functions. Their primary purpose is to obtain specific information in a particular order. An employer needs an application form to determine your qualifications. A bank uses a deposit form to keep a record of your money.

The following guidelines may be helpful to you as you complete various types of forms:

Completing Forms

1. Read all directions carefully and skim the entire form before making any marks on it. Notice any special requirements. Then gather all information you need, such as your social security number, parents' birthdates, telephone numbers, references' names and addresses.
2. Assemble your writing tools. Use a good pen or typewriter. Do not use pencil unless directed to do so.
3. Begin filling out the form line by line, rereading all directions. Directions for procedures as simple as filling in your name vary from form to form.
4. When you are finished filling out the form, check it for accuracy, spelling, and completeness. Proofread carefully.
5. If references are required, remember to obtain permission from the people whose names you plan to use. Use their complete addresses, including ZIP codes. Also provide their daytime telephone numbers.

Keep in mind that you will usually have only one copy of a form. Take time to complete this copy correctly.

Exercise

You are organizing a newspaper staff. Design a form for students who want to apply for a position on the newspaper. The form should provide specific information such as the student's year in school, the position the applicant is interested in, previous experience, grade point average, and how the student can be contacted.

Chapter 19
Application and Review

1. What are the six parts of a business letter?
2. Which part of a business letter includes the name, title, and address of the person to whom the letter is being sent?
3. Why is it important to address a letter to a specific person or department?
4. You are gathering information about summer jobs in your area. Write to a local company for information on summer employment. Include your age, qualifications, and previous experience.
5. You have been saving money to buy a good tape recorder. The sales people at the first store you visited were particularly helpful, so after checking other stores you returned to the first store to buy your recorder. Write a letter to the store manager telling why you decided to buy from that store .
6. Below is a sample order form from a catalog house. Examine it carefully. Then tell whether each of the following statements is true or false.
   a. Information may be printed or cursive.
   b. Charge cards are not acceptable for payment.
   c. Sporting goods should be listed on the same form as other items being purchased.

WHEN WILL MY ORDER GET HERE?

1679116

InstaBuy Warehouse
TO PURCHASE MERCHANDISE FROM SHOWROOM OR CATALOG, COMPLETE THIS FORM AND PRESENT IT TO THE INFORMATION DESK. *PLEASE PRINT.*

FOR PROMPT SERVICE ON SPECIALTY ITEMS
JEWELRY PHOTOGRAPHY SPORTING GOODS
PLACE YOUR ORDER ON A SEPARATE ORDER BLANK AND
PRESENT IT IN CASH TO THE CASHIER IN THAT DEPARTMENT

CUSTOMER ORDER BLANK

NAME

ADDRESS   STATE   ZIP

CITY   ☐ CASH ☐ CHECK ☐ BANKCARD

PHONE   WHSE USE   QTY

COMPLETE CATALOG NUMBER
FROM CATALOG OR SAMPLE TAGS

ITEM DESCRIPTION
SPECIFY COLOR, SIZE

YOUR

ALL RETURNS MUST BE ACCOMPANIED BY SALES RECEIPT AND IN THEIR ORIGINAL

20

Group Discussion and Informal Speaking

W hether you are reviewing a social-studies assignment with a group of friends or leading a discussion in history class, you need effective speaking skills. In both situations you need to be well organized and have a specific purpose in mind to communicate clearly with your audience.

School activities often involve such informal oral presentations. Think about the presentations you've given in school so far this year. In this chapter you will learn how to participate effectively in group discussions and how to improve your informal speaking skills.

Part 1
Group Organization and Purpose

Group discussions are most effective when they are well organized and have a specific purpose. Groups often include a **chairperson** who leads the discussion and maintains order, a **secretary** who takes notes during the discussion, and **participants.** Under the guidance of the chairperson, participants address themselves to the discussion topic. Effective discussions usually develop in four stages:

1. **Statement of subject and purpose** Usually the chairperson explains what the discussion is to be about and why the discussion is being held. Common purposes for holding discussions include sharing information on topics of mutual interest, solving common problems, and planning courses of action for group projects. For a discussion to be effective and efficient, it is essential that everyone be in agreement on the purpose.

2. **Definition of key terms and narrowing of topic** Group members should agree upon definitions for the words that will be central to their discussion. In a discussion on energy sources, for example, a group might agree to define an energy source as ''that which can be used to produce mechanical or electrical power.'' Defining such key terms helps to clarify the topic for discussion. If members of a group are using a key word or phrase in different ways, arguments and misunderstandings may result.

    At this point, the group might also decide to limit the range of its discussion by narrowing the topic. For example, instead of dealing with all energy sources, a group might decide to deal only with natural sources of energy, such as the sun and wind.

3. **Analysis** In this stage, the group discusses the topic in detail. The goal is to arrive at a plan of action or to reach an agreement, or consensus, about how a problem can be solved. What happens in the analysis stage will vary according to the nature of the topic and the purpose of the group.

4. **Summary** In this stage, a group member, either the chairperson or the group secretary, summarizes the major points made during the discussion by the various members of the group. A summary makes the group aware of its progress and can also serve to point to unresolved matters that need further investigation or action.

Part 2
The Duties of Group Leaders and Participants

Both the chairperson of a group and its members have distinct duties. The success of any group discussion depends largely on how effectively these duties are carried out. Study the following guidelines.

Guidelines for Discussion

Duties of the Chairperson

1. **Prepare for the discussion.** Become familiar with the subject. Read or think about the topic.
2. **To begin, introduce the topic and state the aim of the discussion.** Briefly mention the important points to be considered.
3. **Encourage everyone to contribute.** Direct specific questions to those who are not actively participating.
4. **Keep the discussion orderly.** Politely but firmly insist that only one person speaks at a time.
5. **Keep the discussion moving forward.** Ask stimulating questions if the discussion lags. Avoid getting sidetracked.
6. **End the discussion by briefly summarizing key points and decisions.** Take notes during the discussion to use in making the summary.

Duties of a Participant

1. **Take part in the discussion.** An effective discussion needs the viewpoints and contributions of each participant.
2. **Speak only when the chairperson recognizes you.** Do not interrupt others.
3. **Support your statements and opinions.** Provide relevant facts, examples, or authoritative opinions.
4. **Listen attentively.** Maintain good eye contact with each speaker. Take notes on key points.
5. **Be courteous and tactful.** A successful discussion requires a courteous give-and-take. Try to see the other person's point of view. Ask questions for clarification of opinions you don't agree with.

Part 3
Strategies for Achieving Agreement

A group discussion is successful only when an agreement, or consensus, is reached. The variety of viewpoints is what makes group discussion a good way to solve a problem. However, different opinions also make it difficult to reach an agreement. Study the strategies below to learn how a group can arrive at consensus:

1. **Each side gives in a little.** Usually, no one person or side wins in a group discussion. Instead, one side sacrifices a little in order to gain the support of the other group members. The other side also compromises. In this way a course of action is reached that meets everyone's approval.
2. **The group redefines the issue.** Sometimes, key terms have not been adequately defined and group members misunderstand each others' positions. Stating the issue in different terms may allow all members to see the issue in a way that they can agree with.
3. **The group finds a new alternative.** Sometimes group members get too involved in defending their own individual positions. Each side can see only its own point of view. It may be wise to explore alternatives to find a solution that is satisfactory to everyone.
4. **The group postpones a decision.** If more information on the subject is needed or if group members have become too emotional during discussion, it may be wise to postpone action.

Exercises

A Read the following portion of a discussion held after a class had a report of shoplifting from the school-supply store. The issue under discussion is: What can students do that will help to solve the problem of shoplifting by teen-agers? Then, answer the questions that follow.

> **Chairperson (Kim):** Shoplifting is the crime of stealing merchandise from a store while pretending to be a customer. Unfortunately, this problem has been occurring in our own school-supply store. In addition, our athletic department has been reporting missing equipment. The question, then, is this: What can we as students do to help solve the problem of shoplifting in our school?

Jay: Kim?

Chairperson: Yes, Jay.

Jay: I think there's a problem about getting involved at all. It seems like you're wrong no matter what! Sometimes, I go to the school-supply store with my friend. This friend thinks that it is sort of a game, like taking a dare, to see if he can take something without getting caught. I still want to be friends with this guy, but—

Todd: But what? Are you trying to say that you'd squeal on a friend? Some kind of friend you are. Remind me never to go to the shopping mall with you!

Chairperson: I'm sure that everyone has an opinion on how to handle this difficult situation. Let Jay finish what he was saying, and then, Todd, you can say what you think.

Jay: I didn't say that I'd tell anyone. It's just that my buddy doesn't listen to me when I tell him that what he is doing can get him into a lot of trouble if he's caught.

Todd: Kim, can I say something now?

Chairperson: Todd. (As the discussion continues, the chairperson recognizes each speaker in turn and by doing so gives him or her the right to speak.)

Todd: I know plenty of kids who take a pencil or a book from the school store. The store probably never misses the stuff.

Chairperson: Rachel, what do you think? You look angry.

Rachel: I don't agree that the store never misses the stuff. What happens when athletic equipment or art supplies run out? We suffer. I think kids need to know that the store charges higher prices to cover the cost of its losses.

Jessica: Rachel's right, and so is Jay about his friend getting in trouble. I read that people who are caught shoplifting can get a police record that can prevent them from entering college or getting a job!

Adam: But who should Jay go to for advice? How can he help his friend?

Jay: I guess you do have to get involved to help. Maybe we can find some way to get kids to help other kids—to talk to each other about the problems shoplifting can cause.

Chairperson: Rachel, Jay, and Adam are close to two possible ways of handling the problem: educate students and maybe provide some kind of student hot line. Does anyone else have other ideas that the group should consider?

Benjamin: My dad owns a hardware store in town. He's had to go to a lot of expense hiring extra security personnel and installing a closed-circuit television for surveillance. I know that he'd appreciate it if other customers would say something to him if they saw anyone stealing.

Jessica: Some of the clothing stores that I have shopped at have been using sensitized tags on their merchandise that set off an alarm if you leave the store with unpaid-for clothing. Is there a way the school store could do something like that?

Chairperson: I think that some good points have been raised. Before we try to come to a conclusion, maybe we should invite some adults—parents, police officers, merchants—to talk to us about this issue. What do you think?

1. How well did the chairperson introduce the subject? Were the topic and purpose of the discussion made clear?
2. How would you rate each student's contribution? Were all comments related to the topic under discussion? Give specific reasons for your answers.
3. Did the chairperson effectively carry out all of her duties during the discussion? Give specific reasons for your answer.
4. Did the group reach a consensus? What further action were they asked to consider?

B Read the following comments by three participants in the preceding discussion. Assume the role of the chairperson, and write a response or rephrase the comments the chairperson might have made.

1. **Todd:** [Interrupting the comments of Jessica] You think that you know everything! Shoplifting is not such a big deal!
2. **Beth:** I agree with Rachel. Shoplifters should be punished so that the school store doesn't have to keep raising the prices.
3. **Ted:** I have always been loyal to my friends. I belonged to a club once, and our motto was "All for one and one for all."

Read the following comments and respond as if you were a group participant.

4. **Jay:** I'd be risking my friendship with the person who is shoplifting if I tell his mom or report him to a faculty adviser.
5. **Ann:** Students need to learn that everybody pays for shoplifting.
6. **Lee:** It's not fair when shop owners charge more because of theft.

Part 4
Types of Informal Speaking

In addition to the informal speaking that is part of group discussion, you often make other informal oral presentations. For example, you might introduce a speaker at a school assembly or demonstrate a skill for an athletic team. In this part of the chapter, you will learn what elements such informal talks should contain.

Announcements

Announcements, such as those made to students over your school's public address system, are examples of the simplest kind of informal talk. Such announcements should include answers to these important questions:

> *What* is happening?
> *Where* is it happening?
> *When* is it happening?

Keep announcements short and simple. However, since *where* and *when* are so important, it is wise to repeat this key information at the end of the announcement.

Introducing a Speaker

An effective introduction requires more than "This is Anita Rivera, president of the ninth grade." An audience wants to know something about the person. Gather some background information on the person. Use that information to explain who she is. Be sure also to mention what she has done and why she is here. If possible, try to include an interesting anecdote to lighten the introduction. Take care, however, that the anecdote does not make anyone feel awkward or embarrassed.

Demonstration Talks

Some activities, such as explaining a physical exercise, make you realize that there are instances when it is absolutely necessary to demonstrate what you mean. In a demonstration talk you tell how something is done, while demonstrating the action at the same time.

Because you will be speaking and showing at the same time, a demonstration talk must be extremely well organized. Begin by gathering all the materials that you will need for your demonstration. Write careful notes for your talk; make certain that you cover every part of the procedure and that you explain each step precisely and thoroughly. Carefully coordinate the physical aspects of the demonstration with your speech, and practice using your props as you speak. When you deliver the speech, stop occasionally to see if your listeners have understood you up to that point. Remember, what seems easy to you can be very frustrating for a listener.

Guidelines for Informal Speaking

Informal talks require less thought, time, and preparation than many other forms of speaking and writing. The process, however, still includes preparation, delivery, and evaluation.

Guidelines for Informal Speaking

Preparation

1. Informal speaking, like all effective communication, requires some background work. You should know what you will say and be sure your information is accurate.
2. Take notes to help you remember content; practice to assure a smooth delivery.

Delivery

1. Maintain good eye contact with the audience, and keep gestures natural and relaxed.
2. When possible, suit your remarks to the interests and experiences of the audience.
3. Remember to speak clearly and distinctly. Force yourself to speak more slowly than you usually do.

Follow-up

Informal talks are effective if they give needed information. Audience comprehension and response are indicators of your success. Ask questions to confirm understanding.

Exercises

A Choose a character from a book, movie, or television series and introduce him or her to the class.

B Make a mock announcement to your class about the organization of a new club. Include the name, functions, and meeting time. The next day, check to see how many details your classmates remember.

C Prepare a two- to four-minute demonstration talk for your class on one of the following skills, or choose a topic of your own.

Editing a videotape	Chording a guitar
Drawing cartoon characters	Swinging a golf club
Handling a rod and reel	Running a computer program

Chapter 20
Application and Review

A Having a Group Discussion Look through current periodicals to discover a topic for discussion. Form a group and discuss a solution to a problem that everyone is concerned about. Following are some problems you might discuss:

1. conservation of energy resources
2. air pollution
3. homeless people
4. physical fitness in teen-agers

B Making Introductions Choose a well-known historical figure, perhaps someone you have studied this year. Use the library to discover some interesting information about the person. Introduce this person to your class. Decide on the occasion and circumstances for the introduction. Be sure to check the accuracy of any important historical facts you include.

C Making Announcements Make an announcement to the class regarding one of the events below or something else that is happening at school.

> an athletic event
> a field trip
> a pep rally
> a parent-teacher meeting
> an awards assembly
> college-representative visits
> a jazz concert
> a car wash

D Giving a Demonstration Observe a television or videotape demonstration, such as a cooking lesson, a car-repair demonstration, or a home-improvement program. List the steps in the process being demonstrated. Take notes on the props and charts used in the demonstration. After the program, see if you can explain the process clearly enough for another person to follow. Write a short evaluation of the effectiveness of the demonstration. Comment on the speaker's demonstration organization and use of equipment.

Grammar, Usage, and Mechanics

Grammar and Writing

When you opened your first language arts textbook in elementary school, you began a study of English grammar, usage, and mechanics that has continued throughout your school career. From time to time, though, you may have wondered, ''Why am I studying this? What good does it do me?''

Teachers and students ask themselves these questions every year. *McDougal, Littell English* was written to help you find answers to these questions. In the chapters that follow, you will see that the study of language involves more than rules and exercises. The study of language encompasses writing, thinking, speaking, understanding literature—even humor.

Grammar Does Help

The study of grammar, usage, and mechanics can have some useful benefits, depending on how you approach it.

Improved Skills in Usage The way you use language can affect many things, from a grade on a paper to the result of a job interview. The details of language—subject–verb agreement, pronoun usage, verb tense—directly affect the clarity of what you say or write. The rules of language, therefore, can make a tremendous difference in the impression you make on others through your schoolwork, in any written correspondence, in interviews, and eventually in your career.

Improved Thinking Skills The study of grammar involves a number of thinking skills, especially the skills of analysis, classification, and application. As you dissect a sentence, classify a word, or apply a concept to a piece of writing, you are stretching your ability to think clearly and effectively.

A Vocabulary for Writing It would be difficult to learn to drive a car if you had to talk about ''the round thing in front of the dashboard'' instead of a *steering wheel*. Similarly, it would be difficult to discuss ways to improve your writing without the proper vocabulary. For example, you can add variety and interest to your writing through the appropriate use of participial phrases. Conjunctions and clauses can help you combine short, choppy sentences into longer, more graceful ones. Yet without using these terms, a teacher or peer editor would have a hard time communicating suggestions to you, and you would have an even harder time trying to implement those suggestions.

More Effective Writing The artist Picasso understood the rules of color, shape, and perspective. Yet, when it suited his purpose, he bent those rules to create a certain effect or make a unique statement. Professional writers do the same thing. How often have you pointed out to a teacher that an author has used sentence fragments in dialogue or unusual capitalization and punctuation in poetry? These writers, however, bend the rules only after understanding how language works. The resulting sentences are still clear and effective. The more you understand the rules, the better you too will be able to use language as a powerful means of expressing ideas.

Appreciation of Literature A sport like football is much more enjoyable if you know something about the strategies that are used during the game. Similarly, you can appreciate a work of literature much more if you are sensitive to the techniques and strategies that the author is using. For example, you might notice how a writer uses certain modifiers and verbal phrases to create an atmosphere of suspense. In another piece of writing, you might recognize how a writer uses punctuation to introduce rhythm and movement. Through an awareness of language, you can savor each sentence of a story or poem.

Applications in This Book

In *McDougal, Littell English,* you will find lessons and activities designed to help you achieve all the benefits that language study can bring.

Meaningful Explanations When you learn about a concept, you will be shown how it can affect your writing. You will also be told when everyday language departs from the rules.

Writing Opportunities Throughout the chapters, you will be given opportunities to apply what you have learned in creative writing activities that will stretch your imagination.

Literature-Based Activities Some exercises will give you the opportunity to work with the writing of famous authors, to see how they use the rules—and sometimes why they break them.

On the Lightside Language can be fun. The light essays included in these chapters will show you that words can have a sense of humor, too.

21

The Sentence and Its Parts

Untitled mobile, Alexander Calder, 1976.

*T*he multicolored pieces in this mobile by American sculptor Alexander Calder hang in delicate balance. Some pieces are large, others are small. Yet each piece is important to the overall composition.

How does the structure of Calder's mobile reflect the structure of a sentence? In this chapter you will learn about the major parts of a sentence and how they work together to express a complete thought.

Part 1
The Complete Sentence

Sometimes in conversation we use only parts of sentences.

Not now.   That one.   Yes.   Over that hill.

In standard written English, however, complete sentences are important. With them, we can express our ideas more clearly.

A sentence is a group of words that expresses a complete thought.

The following groups of words are sentences:

Tom agreed to the plan.
That red car is blocking the alley.
The alarm at the bank sounded late last night.

When part of an idea is missing from a sentence, the group of words is a sentence fragment.

A sentence fragment is a group of words that does not express a complete thought.

Agreed to the plan. (Who agreed?)
That red car. (What about the red car?)
Late last night. (What happened?)

You will learn more about sentence fragments in Chapter 22.

Exercises

A On your paper, write *S* for each group of words that is a sentence. For each sentence fragment, write *F*.

1. A jigsaw puzzle of the American flag
2. Chandra grew up in New Delhi
3. One of the most amusing characters in the novel
4. Heat rises
5. Actually videotaped all the episodes of *The Honeymooners*
6. No one was awake for the end of the movie
7. Some musicians filed into the studio
8. On most Friday afternoons after school
9. The African violet in the kitchen seemed to wither overnight
10. Collecting all the albums ever made by Whitney Houston

B On your paper, revise the following paragraph to eliminate sentence fragments. Correct each fragment by adding information to it or by joining it to a nearby sentence.

> Charlotte Brontë's novel *Jane Eyre* depicts the life of a courageous and independent young woman. As a poor orphan child, Jane is treated badly. By her cruel aunt. At the age of ten, Jane is sent to Lowood. A boarding school for homeless girls. After eight years, she leaves the school as a teacher. Accepts a position as governess at Thornfield. There she meets Mr. Rochester, her wealthy employer. Eventually falls in love with him. Secrets from Mr. Rochester's past complicate their relationship. Nevertheless, finds happiness through her moral strength and courage.

c *Write Now* The following notes are from a reporter's interview with the members of a rock group. The notes are all sentence fragments. Write an account of the interview. Include the notes in your account, making the fragments into complete sentences.

> are just starting a three-month tour of the States
> five new songs especially for this tour
> now experimenting with new elements in their music
> favorable initial response of audiences to the new works
> plans for recording a live album during the tour

Part 2
Kinds of Sentences

Sentences can be grouped into four basic categories, depending on the purpose of the writer or speaker.

1. **A declarative sentence makes a statement. It always ends with a period (.).**

   An opera house overlooks the harbor of Sydney, Australia.

2. **An interrogative sentence asks a question. It ends with a question mark (?).**

   When did the United States buy Alaska?

3. **An imperative sentence gives a command. It usually ends with a period.** An imperative sentence may sometimes end with an exclamation mark (!) when the writer wants to make a strong command.

   Do ten more push-ups. Hurry up!

4. **An exclamatory sentence expresses strong emotion. It ends with an exclamation point (!).**

   I passed the test! What a day this has been!

Exercises

A On your paper, write *Declarative, Interrogative, Imperative,* or *Exclamatory* to identify each of the following sentences. Then indicate the appropriate end punctuation by writing *Period, Question Mark,* or *Exclamation Mark.*

1. When did rock-and-roll originate
2. Close all the mouse cages before you leave the lab
3. My superstitious friend dislikes the thirteenth floor
4. Mrs. Henry didn't cover any new material in algebra class
5. How hot this summer is
6. Show us the pictures from the birthday party
7. Do the elevators in your building ever get stuck
8. Jefferson submitted a design for the President's mansion
9. What a waste of money that computer game was
10. Did Mary Lou Retton win Olympic medals in gymnastics

B For each sentence, write *Declarative, Interrogative, Imperative,* or *Exclamatory.* Then indicate the appropriate end punctuation by writing *Period, Question Mark,* or *Exclamation Mark.*

(1) Do you sometimes have trouble remembering facts for your schoolwork (2) Has your mind ever gone blank during a history test (3) What a frightening feeling that can be (4) Fortunately, there are ways you can improve your memory and your ability to recall facts (5) For example, what can you do when you have a list of words to learn for a class (6) People who study memory have a suggestion for you to try (7) First, write down the beginning letters of the words (8) Then create a sentence, with each word in the sentence starting with one of the words in your list (9) For example, I learned the sentence "My very eager monkey just slid under Nan's poinsettia" so I would remember the names of the planets—Mercury, Venus, Earth, Mars, Jupiter, Saturn, Uranus, Neptune, Pluto (10) Wow! What a way to study

Checkpoint *Parts 1 and 2*

On your paper, identify each *Fragment.* Then develop the fragment into a sentence. Identify each sentence as *Declarative, Interrogative, Imperative,* or *Exclamatory.* Add the correct end marks.

1. Show us the pictures from the party
2. A jigsaw puzzle with hundreds of pieces
3. Who won the tennis tournament
4. Musicians entered the studio
5. Whistling in the dark
6. How close that race was
7. Doesn't she have any sense of humor
8. Does anyone know where the telephone book is
9. Be sure to lock the door when you leave
10. Cared for the wounded fox
11. You won't believe who just called
12. Everyone came to the party, but no one wanted to clean up
13. There's fire coming from the second-floor window
14. Sarah looks good in bright pink, but I can't wear that color
15. Please don't open my mail

Part 3

Complete Subjects and Predicates

A sentence has two parts: the subject and the predicate. The subject tells whom or what the sentence is about. The predicate tells what the subject is, what the subject did, or what happened to the subject.

Subject	Predicate
The volcano	erupted again.
A reporter from the paper	relayed the news.
My cousin	became a graphic artist.

The complete subject includes all the words that identify the person, place, thing, or idea that the sentence is about. The complete predicate includes all the words that make a statement about the subject.

A complete subject or predicate may consist of one word or a number of words.

Complete Subject	Complete Predicate
Continents	drift.
The plants in the classroom	need more sunlight.
Basketball and astronomy	are two of my interests.

Exercises

A On your paper, write the complete subject of each of these sentences.

1. Lady Jane Grey was queen of England for only nine days.
2. Elizabeth, one of my cousins, can write three languages.
3. The huge trawler fished in the rough, stormy waters.
4. One of the curious things about the platypus is its unusual, broad duck-like bill.
5. The large apartment building on the corner was sold.
6. Three of my friends have tried out for this part.
7. Honesty pays.
8. My favorite dish at the Chinese restaurant is duck.
9. One of the visiting journalists spoke of her experiences in South America.
10. Two stars in the Big Dipper point to the North Star.

B On your paper, write the complete predicate of each of the sentences in the following paragraph.

(1) The great Cambodian city of Angkor was the capital of the Khmer kingdom from 800 until 1431. (2) This amazing metropolis covered forty square miles. (3) Its elaborate temples, roads, irrigation canals, reservoirs, and hospitals were the wonder of the ancient world. (4) Angkor was captured by Thai troops in 1431. (5) The Khmers abandoned their capital in great haste. (6) The nearby jungle covered Angkor very quickly with a thick green blanket. (7) The sleeping city was not rediscovered until the nineteenth century. (8) A French journalist stumbled accidentally into the overgrown ruins of the once majestic Angkor. (9) The Frenchman, Henri Mouhat, had only been looking for rare butterflies. (10) He found one of the world's most remarkable "lost" cities instead.

Ruins of Angkor, Cambodia.

c *Write Now* Choose one of the following subjects. Add a predicate to it. Then use the sentence in a paragraph.

much of the best music today
the elephant with the broken tusk
my most comfortable outfit
the hit movie of the year

Part 4
Simple Subjects and Predicates

The simple subject is the key word or words in the complete subject.

The simple subject names the person, place, thing, or idea the sentence is about. Modifying words are not part of the simple subject. In proper nouns the simple subject may include more than one word. In the following sentences the simple subjects are in boldface type.

Complete Subject	Complete Predicate
John Lennon	wrote many songs.
One of my friends	plays the trumpet.
Star Wars	is a good movie.

The simple predicate, also called the verb, is the main word or words within the complete predicate.

The simple predicate, or **verb,** tells what the subject of the sentence is or does. Other words that add to the meaning of the predicate are not part of the verb. In the following sentences the verbs are bold-faced.

Complete Subject	Complete Predicate
All the lines in this picture	**converge.**
I	**returned** home.
The radio	**was** once a novelty.

Finding the Verb and the Subject

In any sentence, the verb and the simple subject, referred to in this textbook as the **subject,** are the most important words.

To find the key words in a sentence, first find the verb. It will express some kind of action or state of being. Then place the words *who* or *what* in front of the verb. The answer will tell you the subject.

An attendant at the station checked the oil.
Verb checked
Who checked? attendant
Subject of verb attendant

Sentence Diagraming For information on diagraming the subject and verb of a sentence, see page 754.

Exercise

Make two columns on your paper. Label them *Subject* and *Verb*. For each sentence write these parts in their proper columns.

1. The lights attracted swarms of pesky insects.
2. Jonathan reads to children at the hospital every Saturday.
3. Abraham Lincoln declared the slaves free.
4. The green <u>taxicab</u> idled at the curb.
5. Six ingredients topped the gooey pizza.
6. *Moby Dick* is Melville's masterpiece.
7. The network officials canceled the situation comedy.
8. Rachel is allergic to cats and dust.
9. After school my brother met me downtown.
10. In her long career, Agatha Christie wrote more than ninety books.

The Verb Phrase

A verb may consist of one or more words. It may consist of a **main verb** and one or more **helping verbs,** also called **auxiliary verbs.**

A verb phrase consists of a main verb and one or more helping verbs.

Helping Verb	+	Main Verb	=	Phrase
was		sinking		was sinking
must have		caused		must have caused

Venice *is sinking* one fifth of an inch each year.
The storm *must have caused* the damage to the house.

Common Helping Verbs

be (*and its forms*: am, are, is, was, were, being, been)
have (*and its forms*: has, had)
do (*and its forms*: does, did)

can	may	will	shall	must
could	might	would	should	ought

Some of these words can also be used as main verbs.

The ostrich *has* a life span of fifty years. (main verb)
It *has disappeared* from much of Africa. (helping verb)

Exercises

A Write each of these sentences on your paper. Draw a vertical line between the complete subject and the complete predicate. Then draw one line under the simple subject and two lines under the verb or verb phrase.

1. The kookaburra is a bird with a laughlike call.
2. My friend Charlene is recruiting sponsors for the walkathon.
3. *Orthodontics* comes from the Greek words for ''straight'' and ''tooth.''
4. Sherlock Holmes solved the crime.
5. Thoreau lived at Walden Pond for twenty-seven cents a week.
6. The counselor at school should have given you job information.
7. I will need a pair of snowshoes for my trip north.
8. A stamp with an error has more value than a perfect one.
9. The polka had originated as a European folk dance.
10. All the concert tickets must have been sold already.

B Write each of the following sentences on your paper. Draw a vertical line between the complete subject and the complete predicate. Then draw one line under the simple subject and two lines under the verb or verb phrase.

1. A famous place in London is Madame Tussaud's Exhibition.
2. This museum contains lifelike wax figures of famous people.
3. Nearly three million people visit the museum yearly.
4. The realism of the exhibits astounds visitors.
5. Marie Tussaud first exhibited wax figures in 1802.
6. She had modeled the figures of many famous people of her time.
7. Descendants of Madame Tussaud still maintain the museum.
8. The exhibits in the museum change every year.
9. Celebrities have donated clothes for their wax figures.
10. Visitors to the museum can see figures ranging from Henry VIII's wives to Princess Diana.

C *Write Now* Every business or profession uses specialized vocabulary. Baseball players talk about bunts and sliders. Theater people discuss scrims and flies. Choose a sport, job, hobby, or school subject that interests you. List three or four specialized words from the area you have chosen. Use those words as simple subjects of sentences in which you define the words. Then incorporate them into a paragraph that has as its topic the specialized language of an area.

Part 5
Subjects in Unusual Positions

In most sentences the subject comes before the verb or verb phrase. Sometimes, however, this order is changed for variety.

Sentences with Inverted Order

A sentence is in inverted order when the verb or any part of the verb phrase comes before the subject.

In the following examples, each subject is underlined once, and each verb is underlined twice.

> Along the drive to the house were tall trees.
> Next to the ocean liner chugged the tugboat.

To find the subject, first locate the verb or verb phrase. Then place the words *who* or *what* before the verb or verb phrase. The word that answers the question is the subject.

> Out of the magician's hat squirmed ten white rabbits.
> *Verb*: squirmed
> *Who or what squirmed?* rabbits
> *Subject*: rabbits

Sentences Beginning with **Here** or **There**

In some sentences beginning with *Here* or *There*, the subject comes after the verb. *Here* and *there* are never used as subjects.

> Here is the photo for my identification card.

Sentence Diagraming For information on diagraming sentences in inverted order or sentences beginning with *Here* or *There*, see pages 754–755.

Interrogative Sentences

In interrogative sentences the subject typically comes either after the verb or between parts of the verb.

> Is the new gym ready for use?
> Have the students written in their journals today?

To find the subject of an interrogative sentence, change the sentence to a declarative one. Then find the verb and ask *who?* or *what?*

> Is Appomattox in Virginia?
> *Declarative*: Appomattox is in Virginia.
> *Verb*: is
> *What is?* Appomatox
> *Subject*: Appomattox

In interrogative sentences beginning with *Who, What, Where, When, Why,* and *How,* the subject often comes between the parts of the verb phrase.

> When <u>will</u> the <u>World Series</u> <u>end</u>?

Sometimes a word such as *who* or *what* is the subject. Then the subject comes before the verb.

> <u>What</u> <u>was</u> the verdict?   <u>Who</u> is <u>directing</u> the film?

Subjects in Imperative Sentences

Imperative sentences give commands or state requests. In an imperative sentence the subject is usually not stated. Since a command is always given to the person spoken to, the subjects is *you*. When the subject *you* is not stated, it is said to be understood.

Although the first word in an imperative sentence is often a verb, a word like *Please* sometimes precedes the verb.

> Leave the package here. (*You* is the understood subject of *Leave*.)
> Please revise this draft. (*You* is the understood subject of *revise*.)

What are the imperative sentences used by the characters in this cartoon?

Sentence Diagraming For information on diagraming interrogative and imperative sentences, see page 755.

THE FAR SIDE   By GARY LARSON

© 1985 Universal Press Syndicate

"Hold still, Omar. ... Now look up. Yep. You've got something in your eye, all right—could be sand."

Exercises

A On your paper, write the simple subject and the verb or verb phrase in each of the following sentences. For imperative sentences write *(You)* to indicate the subject.

1. Under the flap of the envelope was a hidden message.
2. Does *anemone* have three or four syllables?
3. Here is the missing piece of my puzzle!
4. Tell us about your experience at the computer camp.
5. Across the room stretched a welcoming banner.
6. There are more than a half million words in the English language.
7. Can anyone tell me the meaning of the Latin phrase *ex libris?*
8. Through the cave echoed the squeals of the bats.
9. When does the cactus usually bloom?
10. Visit Mammoth Cave on your trip to Kentucky.

B On your paper, rewrite each sentence so that the verb comes before the subject. Follow the directions given in parentheses.

Example   The Thames River flows through the heart of London. (Begin the sentence with *through the heart of London*.)
Through the heart of London flows the Thames River.

1. A rusted weather vane stood on the top of the barn. (Begin the sentence with *on the top of the barn*.)
2. The spices are for the lamb. (Begin the sentence with *here*.)
3. Everyone has a flashlight and a compass for the camping trip. (Change into a question.)
4. The cavalry arrived in the nick of time. (Begin the sentence with *in the nick of time*.)
5. You should exercise for at least ten minutes three times a week. (Change to an imperative sentence.)
6. The winners of the contest danced into the spotlight. (Begin the sentence with *into the spotlight*.)
7. Some species of snakes are poisonous. (Change into a question.)
8. A solitary blue heron stood in the marsh. (Begin the sentence with *in the marsh*.)
9. Serena can say the tongue twister full of *s*'s without a slip. (Change into a question.)
10. You might sample the local lobster and shark on your trip to Boston. (Change into an imperative sentence.)

Checkpoint Parts 3, 4, and 5

A Draw a vertical line between the complete subject and the complete predicate. Then underline the simple subject once and the verb twice.

1. Two debaters from the team won district trophies.
2. Bright banners in the Willowbrook Tech school colors decorated the floats.
3. The nervous actors prepared for the first act.
4. Cranberries grow best in peat bogs.
5. The downhill skiers zipped through the course.

B On your paper, write the verb or verb phrase in each sentence. Then write the subject. Watch for unusual kinds of sentences.

1. There will be a special about penguins on TV tonight.
2. Have you ever ridden in a hydrofoil?
3. By the San Diego Padres's dugout was standing a person in a chicken costume!
4. Did Edgar Allan Poe write ''The Cask of Amontillado''?
5. Out of the lion's cage ran the frightened trainer.
6. Jot down the title of that book for me.
7. Here are the posters for your science project.
8. Why will the banks be closing early tomorrow?
9. There is a secret compartment in that antique desk.
10. Throw out the old newspapers and magazines.

Part 6
Objects of Verbs

The two main kinds of verbs are **action verbs** and **linking verbs**.

An action verb describes an action. It tells that something is happening, has happened, or will happen.

We *skated* on Duck Lake.   I *slept* well afterward.

A linking verb, sometimes called a state-of-being verb, links the subject with another word or words in the predicate.

Ramon *is* an expert swimmer.   The frog *became* a prince.

Complements

Some action verbs do not need other words to complete their meaning in a sentence. The action they describe is complete.

> The players *rested*.   The rain finally *stopped*.
> Nathan *was worrying*.   The T-shirt *will fade*.

However, other action verbs—and all linking verbs—are incomplete by themselves. They need additional words to complete their meaning. These other words are called **complements.**

A complement is a word that completes the meaning of a predicate.

The italicized verbs below are followed by complements.

Action Verbs
Tony *reserved* a space.
Lila *remembered* the formula.

Linking Verbs
The sunset *was* beautiful.
The music *sounded* familiar.

The two kinds of complements that complete the meaning of action verbs are **direct objects** and **indirect objects.** The complements that complete the meaning of linking verbs are **predicate nominatives** and **predicate adjectives.**

Direct Objects

A direct object receives the action of an action verb. It answers the question *what?* or *whom?*

> The snowball startled Kim. (Startled whom? Startled *Kim. Kim* is the direct object.)

To find the direct object, first find the verb. Then form a question by placing *whom?* or *what?* after the verb. The direct object answers this question.

A verb that takes a direct object is called a **transitive verb.** You will learn more about transitive and intransitive verbs in Chapter 25.

Indirect Objects

If a sentence has a direct object, it may also have another kind of complement called an **indirect object.**

An indirect object tells *to whom?* or *for whom?* or *to what?* or *for what?* about an action verb. The words *to* and *for* are not used in the actual sentences, however.

A sentence can have an indirect object only if it has a direct object. The indirect object always comes before the direct object. To find the indirect object in a sentence, first find the direct object. Then ask *to whom?* or *to what?* or *for whom?* or *for what?* The indirect object answers these questions.

> The store sent the customer the wrong carpet. (Sent what? *Carpet* is the direct object. Sent it to whom? *Customer* is the indirect object.)
>
> Andrea handed the teller her deposit. (Handed what? *Deposit* is the direct object. Handed it to whom? *Teller* is the indirect object.)

When the word *to* or *for* appears in the sentence, the word that follows it is not an indirect object, even though it tells *to whom* or *for whom* about the action of the verb. Look at these two sentences.

> My uncle sent us a beautiful painting.
> My uncle sent a beautiful painting to us.

In the first sentence, *us* is the indirect object of *sent.* It comes before the direct object, *painting.*

In the second sentence, *us* follows the word *to.* It comes after the direct object. Therefore, *us* is not an indirect object. It is the object of the prepositional phrase "to us." (For more about prepositional phrases, see pages 584–585.) Verbs that often take indirect objects include *bring, give, hand, lend, make, offer, send, show, teach,* and *write.*

Sentence Diagraming For information on diagraming sentences with direct and indirect objects, see pages 755–756.

Exercises

A Make three columns on your paper. Label them *Verb*, *Indirect Object*, and *Direct Object*. For each sentence, write those parts in the proper columns. If a sentence has no indirect object, write *None*.

Example   We bought Wendy a planter.

Verb	Indirect Object	Direct Object
bought	Wendy	planter

1. Patrick left the friendly waiter a generous tip.
2. The Motion Picture Academy awarded Katharine Hepburn four Oscars.
3. The store sold me a backpack at half price.
4. My Aunt Miranda made a warm sweater for my sister.
5. Several columnists give readers advice on personal matters.
6. Linda wrote her solution on the blackboard.
7. An Indian maharajah sent Queen Victoria a throne of ivory.
8. An eyewitness told reporters the details of the train robbery.
9. Mr. Leonardi showed us slides of his trip to Italy.
10. The rain brought relief to the farmers.

B Rewrite each sentence. Add a direct object to any sentence that does not have one. If a sentence has a direct object, add an indirect object. Underline direct objects once and indirect objects twice.

Example   The director gave detailed directions.
The director gave the <u>actors</u> detailed <u>directions</u>. (Indirect object added.)

1. Jeffrey wrote a thirty-page letter.
2. Frederica always packs long in advance of a trip.
3. Afterward the audience applauded for more than five minutes.
4. At the fair Ernest bought a huge poster.
5. The choral society sang at the assembly.
6. After the football game my friends and I ate at Cynthia's house.
7. That department store gives a ten percent discount.
8. Bernardo exhibited at the science fair.
9. Farmers plant in the spring and fall.
10. On your trip will you send a postcard?

C *Write Now* You are moving to another state and want to leave your friends some mementos. Write a paragraph about what you would give each friend and why. Include indirect objects in some sentences.

Part 7
Subject Complements

You learned earlier that a linking verb does not describe an action. It links the subject with another word in the sentence. This word, which identifies or describes the subject, is a **subject complement.**

A linking verb always needs a subject complement to complete its meaning in a sentence. Otherwise the meaning of the predicate is incomplete.

> The whooping crane is _____. (is what? a rare *bird*)
> The math problem seemed _____. (seemed what? *hard*)
> Matt was _____. (was what? *late*)

In the sentences above, *bird, hard,* and *late* are subject complements.

The verb *be* is the most common linking verb. It has various forms, such as *am, is, are, was, were, will be, has been.*

Other Common Linking Verbs

appear	feel	look	smell	taste
become	grow	seem	sound	

Two kinds of subject complements complete the meaning of linking verbs. These subject complements are called **predicate nominatives** and **predicate adjectives.**

A predicate nominative is a noun or pronoun that follows a linking verb and that identifies, renames, or explains the subject.

In each of the following sentences a noun or a pronoun follows a linking verb and names or identifies the subject.

> Squirrels are rodents.   The winner is he.

A predicate adjective is an adjective that follows a linking verb and that modifies or describes the subject.

In each of the following sentences the word that follows the linking verb describes or modifies the subject.

> Thomas must be angry.   The lake looks choppy.

Some verbs can be completed either by direct objects or subject complements. To determine what kind of complement follows the verb, ask: Is the complement receiving the action of the verb? Is the complement identifying the subject? describing the subject?

> Luisa tasted the *strawberries*. (direct object)
> The strawberries tasted *tart*. (predicate adjective)
> Strawberries are a delicious *treat*. (predicate noun)

Sentence Diagraming For information on diagraming sentences with subject complements, see page 756.

Exercises

A For each sentence write the subject complement if there is one, and identify it as *Predicate Nominative* or *Predicate Adjective*. If there is no subject complement, write *None*.

1. Today, the Siberian tiger is an endangered species.
2. Halley's comet was visible most recently in 1986.
3. After her long trip, my sister appeared tired.
4. A pomegranate is a fruit with tart, reddish seeds.
5. In the 1930's the Marx brothers' films were very popular.
6. English has become the official language of air travel.
7. Can you taste the sulphur in the well water?
8. The Anasazi were prehistoric settlers of the Southwest.
9. All the vending machines in the cafeteria were empty.
10. New video stores are appearing every day.

B On your paper, write all the complements in the following sentences. Identify each by writing *Direct Object, Indirect Object, Predicate Nominative,* or *Predicate Adjective*.

(1) A few years ago I read the labels of cereal and cracker boxes regularly at breakfast. (2) The labels looked surprisingly entertaining. (3) Even better, six boxtops from Coconut Cuties cereal might win me a glow-in-the-dark pen. (4) Then my home economics class spoiled the game because I learned the scientific facts about labels. (5) "The first item under the word ingredients on any label is the main ingredient in the product." (6) I shared this new-found knowledge with Mom. (7) That was my first mistake. (8) The main ingredient in Coconut Cuties is sugar. (9) My mom didn't appreciate that. (10) Now she won't allow Coconut Cuties in the house anymore.

c *WriteNow* Choose a fictional villain, such as Dally Winston in *The Outsiders*, General Zaroff in "The Most Dangerous Game," Darth Vader in *Star Wars*, or another figure you have heard of or can imagine. Write a description of the villain, focusing on his or her personal qualities and actions. In your description, try to determine what qualities make the villain so mean. In doing so, use predicate nominatives and predicate adjectives.

Part 8
Compound Sentence Parts

The word *compound* means "having two or more parts." Each of the sentence parts described so far in this section—subjects, verbs, and complements—can be compound.

The parts of a compound construction are usually joined by one of these conjunctions: *and*, *or*, or *but*. Here are some examples of compound constructions.

Subjects	*Bats* and *sloths* like to hang upside down.
Verbs	The archaeologist carefully *scraped* and *sorted* the shards of pottery.
Direct Objects	The children will play *charades* or *darts* after supper.
Indirect Objects	Carlos made *Roz* and *me* a Mexican dinner.
Predicate Nominatives	Carl Sandburg was a *poet*, *historian*, and *biographer*.
Predicate Adjectives	Often the weather was *clear* but *cold*.

Sentence Diagraming For information on diagraming sentences with compound parts, see pages 756–758.

Exercises

A Write the compound parts in the following sentences. Identify each compound part by writing *Subject*, *Verb*, *Direct Object*, *Indirect Object*, *Predicate Nominative*, or *Predicate Adjective*.

1. Charlie Chaplin wrote and directed many of his films.
2. Manticores, unicorns, and griffins are all mythical creatures.
3. After the audition, Caroline felt cautious but confident.
4. The friar gave Romeo and Juliet advice about marriage.
5. To most people, green persimmons are sour and unappetizing.
6. Is Juneau or Fairbanks the capital of Alaska?
7. Leonardo da Vinci could draw and write at the same time.
8. Modern architecture uses much steel and glass.
9. With the roast we should serve our guest broccoli or asparagus.
10. The first marbles were pebbles or pits.
11. Mrs. Gonzalez gave Hector and me money for the movie.
12. Jaguars and leopards are members of the cat family.
13. Josh plays both the violin and the trumpet.
14. We were excited but worried about moving.
15. Alma carefully washed, dried, and brushed her dog, Snooky.

B Rewrite each of the following sentences, adding compound sentence parts. After each sentence, write *Subject*, *Verb*, *Direct Object*, *Indirect Object*, *Predicate Nominative*, or *Predicate Adjective* to indicate the part you have added. You may also add modifiers.

1. At the picnic my friends devoured _____.
2. Some games that are popular with students are _____.
3. Heroes in adventure movies _____.
4. According to some students, the assigned short story was _____.
5. The amazing new machine produced _____.
6. By noon _____ filled the parade route.
7. On Saturday afternoons in fall, many people _____.
8. You usually find _____ in fairy tales.
9. At the thought of another weekend indoors, Alicia felt _____.
10. Mrs. Ruiz gave _____ the task of washing the lab equipment.

C *Write Now* Think of a famous combination, such as bread and butter or a pencil and an eraser, or of a famous couple, such as Laurel and Hardy or Tarzan and Jane. Write a humorous paragraph explaining how someone might have discovered the combination or how the famous pair might have met.

Checkpoint *Parts 6, 7, and 8*

A On your paper, identify the word in italics as a *Direct Object*, an *Indirect Object*, a *Predicate Nominative*, or a *Predicate Adjective*.

1. The ancient Babylonians established the first organized *schools*.
2. The site of the largest work of art in the world is *Mount Rushmore* in South Dakota.
3. Each rower uses two *oars* in the sport of sculling.
4. On high-speed Japanese trains, servers bring *passengers* hot meals at their seats.
5. Many of the cold sandwiches from the cafeteria in the art museum seem *stale*.
6. Snoopy told *Woodstock* the story of his exciting adventures as a flying ace.
7. As she started to climb the stairs, Edwina heard *howls* coming from the attic.
8. Surprisingly, the week-old carnations still appear *fresh*.
9. John F. Kennedy became *President* in 1961.
10. Maya Angelou has written three autobiographical *books* as well as several books of poetry.

B On your paper write the compound parts in the following sentences. Then tell whether they are compound *Subjects*, *Verbs*, *Direct Objects*, *Indirect Objects*, *Predicate Nominatives*, or *Predicate Adjectives*.

1. Roald Dahl, a contemporary American author, has written many novels, plays, and stories.
2. This gum is sweet but sugarless.
3. What main product do Argentina and Uruguay export?
4. The rowboat bounced and splashed through the waves.
5. Jessie sent Ann and Dana humorous birthday cards.
6. The thrilling acts of traveling circuses entertain many children and adults.
7. The exhibit of fossils at the natural history museum was small but fascinating.
8. The neighbors lent Don and Mary their power lawn mower.
9. Besides being an actor, Woody Allen is a talented writer and director.
10. The king cobra spread its hood and hissed.

Linking
Grammar & Writing

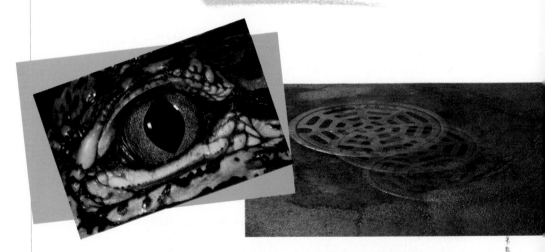

"Urban belief tales" are a popular form of modern folklore. One well-known urban tale concerns alligators that are lurking in city sewers. Another tells about a hitchhiker who eerily appears on the road every twenty miles. Write the complete version of one of these tales, as you have heard it, or relate or invent some other similar story. In your narrative use all four kinds of sentences.

Prewriting and Drafting After you decide on your topic, write answers to the following questions: Who are the characters? Where did the story take place? What was the order of events? You will probably use chronological, or time, order.

Revising and Proofreading As you revise, ask yourself the following questions:

1. Have I answered *who*? *what*? *where*? *when*? and *why*?
2. Can the reader easily follow the order of events?
3. Have I tried to interest the reader in the story?

Additional Writing Topic Some people say that a dog is a person's best friend. Do you agree, or do you think that dogs are appealing only when they are attached to strong chains? Write a paragraph defending your opinion. Use a variety of sentence structures. Include in your sentences at least one direct object, indirect object, predicate nominative, and predicate adjective.

LANGUAGE LORE
Speaking Cajun

Perhaps you have tasted gumbo, or jambalaya, or creole, or other Cajun dishes. These complex recipes are reflections of the culture of the Cajuns, who have lived for more than two hundred years in the bayous of southern Louisiana. During this time, however, the Cajuns have contributed more than food; they have also created a rich and hearty language called the Cajun dialect. Like their food, the Cajun language is a spicy mixture. It is basically a form of French, but it also includes seasonings from English, Native American languages, African languages, and the French spoken in Canada.

The story of the Cajun language begins in 1604, when French settlers founded the colony of Acadia in Canada. When the British captured the colony, they forced out everyone who would not swear allegiance to the British colony. Many of the Acadians moved to Louisiana. There they established their own communities and maintained a separate culture. Their French language did not have the words to describe some of things they encountered in this frontier land, so they borrowed words from the English settlers, Native Americans, and slaves they encountered in this new homeland. Over time, they even changed their own name to 'Cadian, and finally to Cajun.

Today Cajuns still live in southern Louisiana. Their language, like their food, remains a zesty part of American culture.

Chapter 21
Application and Review

A Recognizing Sentences and Sentence Types Some of the following groups of words are fragments. On your paper, write *Fragment* if the item is a fragment, and rewrite it as a sentence. If the item is a sentence, identify it as *Declarative*, *Interrogative*, *Imperative*, or *Exclamatory* and add the correct end marks. Then rewrite it as a different kind of sentence, adding the appropriate end punctuation.

1. Can you remember the winner of last year's Super Bowl
2. Look out for falling rocks
3. The top album on the tallest stack in the living room
4. Why was the universal product code put into use
5. How vicious that piranha looks
6. Sent postcards to ten of her friends every single day
7. People must close their eyes when sneezing
8. Write the Egyptian tourist office for facts about the pyramids
9. Native Americans introduced popcorn to the Pilgrims
10. Playing soccer for the New York Cosmos since 1985
11. Who could have predicted that avalanche
12. The house is on fire
13. Playing jazz at all hours of the day and night
14. Your idea for a research paper on skyscrapers and their influence on the growth of American cities
15. Come and play *Trivial Pursuit* with us

B Finding Subjects and Verbs On your paper, write each of the following sentences. Underline the simple subject once and the verb or verb phrase twice. Watch for unusual kinds of sentences. If the subject is not directly stated, write *You* in parentheses.

1. Tell me the name of one President from Virginia.
2. There were at least fifteen pinball machines at the auction.
3. A roller coaster at King's Island travels at a top speed of sixty-four miles per hour.
4. Some plants can grow without soil.
5. Down the river bobbed the empty canoe.
6. What does this code mean?
7. The pilot has already radioed the tower for his instructions.

8. Layer the noodles for the lasagna with tomato sauce, ground beef, and ricotta cheese.
9. Does Raúl write for the school newspaper?
10. The tickets for the play next Saturday are on the kitchen table.
11. Some streets have not been plowed yet.
12. Around the curve sped the trailer.
13. This bus is seldom late in the morning.
14. The photographs may have arrived in yesterday's mail.
15. In the moonlight Elliot saw a strange, gray little creature coming toward him.

C Understanding Sentence Parts On your paper, write the following sentences. Underline the subject once and the verb twice. Above each direct object (*DO*), indirect object (*IO*), predicate nominative (*PN*), and predicate adjective (*PA*), write the appropriate abbreviation. Some parts may be compound.

1. Anita and her brother served their family tacos and enchiladas at the picnic.
2. The Bermuda Triangle is a mysterious area in the Atlantic Ocean near Florida.
3. The coach and the owner had different strategies for winning the championship.
4. Several critics gave the film on the great balloon race a good review.
5. How long can you hold your breath underwater?
6. Saki and O. Henry are pseudonyms of two famous American short-story writers.
7. The winning pitcher flashed a smile and waved to the cheering crowd.
8. Jill is a jazz musician of great talent.
9. We sent Mom and Dad a bouquet of flowers for their fifteenth anniversary.
10. My father replaced the turntable and the speakers on our old stereo system.
11. Trumpets and cornets sound similar.
12. The tomatoes in my cousin's garden should be ready to pick next week.
13. In New Orleans, street bands play wonderful music at all hours of the day.
14. The salmon from the seafood store was not fresh.
15. Greta lends me *National Geographic* each month.

22
Writing Complete Sentences

A single piece of the photo above reveals little of the completed picture. Only when all the pieces are assembled in their correct positions does the image emerge.

In the same way a sentence fragment is confusing because it does not express a complete thought. Clear writing depends on putting pieces—words—in their proper places. In this chapter you will learn to improve the coherence of your writing by identifying and correcting sentence fragments and run-ons.

Part 1
What Is a Sentence Fragment?

A group of words that is only part of a sentence is called a sentence fragment.

A sentence fragment is confusing because it does not express a complete thought. Sometimes the subject is left out, and the reader wonders *whom* or *what* the sentence is about. At other times the verb is omitted. Then the reader wonders *what happened?* or *what about it?*

Fragment	Shifted into lower gear. (Who shifted? The subject is missing.)
Sentence	The trucker shifted into a lower gear.
Fragment	The quarterback near the ten-yard line. (What happened? The verb is missing.)
Sentence	The quarterback fumbled near the ten-yard line.

Sometimes both the subject and verb are missing.

Fragment	In the middle of the lake. (Who or what is in the middle of the lake? What is happening there?)
Sentence	A canoe tipped over in the middle of the lake.

Fragments Due to Incomplete Thoughts

When you are in a hurry, you sometimes jot down only bits of ideas. As a writer, you understand these fragments of ideas. However, they will probably seem unclear to your reader because at least part of the subject or predicate is missing.

Look at this note left by a student. What does this series of fragments mean?

> Up late listening to birthday albums. Forgot alarm.
> Borrowed money from jar. Working late—more tonight.

These complete sentences show what the writer meant:

> I was up late listening to the albums you gave me for my birthday. I forgot to set the alarm and was late this morning. I borrowed lunch money from the emergency jar. I'm working late today—I'll explain more when I get home tonight.

Fragments Due to Incorrect Punctuation

All sentences end with one of three punctuation marks: a period, a question mark, or an exclamation point. Sometimes a writer uses one of these punctuation marks too soon. The result is an incomplete idea, or sentence fragment.

Fragment   Cars with brake problems. Were recalled.
Sentence   Cars with brake problems were recalled.

Fragment   Are you going? To the state fair?
Sentence   Are you going to the state fair?

Usage Note Some professional writers use fragments deliberately for special purposes. These writers have had long practice in using complete sentences and are aware of what they are doing. In most writing, complete sentences best communicate the writer's message.

Exercises

A Write *S* for each group of words that is a sentence or *F* for each fragment. Add words to change the fragments into sentences.

1. The subway train to downtown.
2. Long shadows from the skyscrapers.
3. The brakes of the bus hissed loudly.
4. The hot-dog stand in the middle of the sidewalk.
5. Large numbers of pigeons in the park.
6. The police cars around the corner.
7. The Don't Walk sign flashed.
8. At five o'clock a flood of people from the office buildings.
9. Someone called to me from the bleachers.
10. Two hours in bumper-to-bumper traffic.

B Rewrite this paragraph, changing five fragments to sentences.

We usually think of mazes as no more than amusing puzzles. Found in magazines or amusement parks. In the past, however, mazes were considered an art form. Also a means of protection or imprisonment. Palaces in Greece and Egypt were designed as mazes. Protected the royal families. In Greek legend, a maze was built to house a horrible monster. The Minotaur. This maze was called the Labyrinth. In the 1700's, formal gardens were designed to include very intricate hedge mazes. The walls of these mazes were tall. Thick bushes.

C Application in Literature As you have learned, professional writers sometimes use fragments for special purposes. Find the fragments in the following passage. Write them on your paper and then add words to make them complete sentences. Compare the two versions and explain why you think Saroyan used the fragments in his writing.

(1) [Homer McCauley] got out of bed and brought out his body-building course from New York and began reading the instructions for the day. (2) His brother Ulysses watched, as he always did. . . . (3) After some ordinary preliminary exercises, including deep breathing, Homer lay flat on his back and lifted his legs stiffly from the floor.

(4) "What's that?" Ulysses said.

(5) "Exercises."

(6) "What for?"

(7) "Muscle."

(8) "Going to be the strongest man in the world?"

(9) "Naah."

(10) "What then?"

(11) "You go back to sleep," Homer said.

(12) Ulysses got back in bed but sat up, watching.

(13) At last Homer began to get dressed.

(14) "Where you going?"

(15) "School."

From *The Human Comedy* by William Saroyan

What Is a Run-on Sentence?

A run-on sentence is two or more sentences written incorrectly as one.

A run-on sentence is confusing because it does not show where one idea ends and another one begins. There are two types of run-on sentences. In the first, two or more sentences are strung together without any punctuation marks to separate them.

Run-on   Tina works as a radio announcer her sister Ann frames pictures at the Big Frame-Up.

Correct   Tina works as a radio announcer. Her sister Ann frames pictures at the Big Frame-Up.

Run-on   Does Tom like country music Carla likes New Wave.

Correct   Does Tom like country music? Carla likes New Wave.

A second type of run-on error is called a **comma splice** or a **comma fault.** In this case, a writer makes the mistake of using a comma instead of a period. Look at the examples below.

Comma Splice   The end caught the pass, he scored a touchdown.

Correct   The end caught the pass. He scored a touchdown.

Comma Splice   Ray began as a back-up singer, now he sings lead.

Correct   Ray began as a back-up singer. Now he sings lead.

Punctuation Note Using semicolons and conjunctions can also correct run-on sentences. See Chapter 31 for a discussion of compound and complex sentences. For now, use only periods to correct run-ons.

Exercises

A On your paper, correct the following run-on sentences.

1. Some radio stations have powerful signals, they can be heard in nearby states.
2. We were going to stop at the next station, the gauge was on *Empty*.
3. In its early days, many people didn't like rock 'n' roll, now public television offers a course in it.
4. February is Black History Month, America formally honors the countless achievements of Black Americans.

5. Pollsters in the Eastern states declared the winner, people in the West were still voting.
6. A few people have arrived, many more are coming later.
7. Eleanor just left, she will be able to make her plane.
8. Tony has a set of barbells he lifts weights every day.
9. We saw an old Hitchcock film, it was a classic thriller.
10. A raccoon visits our back porch every evening we call him the Lone Ranger.

B Find the run-on sentences in the following paragraph. On your paper, rewrite the paragraph correctly.

Today glass is a common, inexpensive material, it is something that we take for granted. Yet long ago it was rare and costly it was even used with gold and semi-precious stones in jewelry. Only the wealthiest women of ancient Egypt could afford to store cosmetics and ointments in glass bottles then some merchants discovered that wine, honey, and oils could be carried and preserved far better in glass than in wood or clay containers. Until the twelfth or thirteenth century, however, glass was used chiefly for ornaments, vases, mosaics, and tableware, some glass was used to make stained-glass church windows a few wealthy families had clear glass windows in their houses. When people moved, they took their valuable glass windows with them, they even handed them down to their children as heirlooms.

Untitled glass platter, Karen Sepanski, 1986.

c *Write Now* Think about a person, time, or event that you remember clearly. Do some freewriting about that memory. Without worrying about capitalization or punctuation, try to put down as many details as you can remember, as well as your feelings about the memory. When you are finished, you should have a series of impressions that will probably be in the form of sentence fragments or run-ons. Develop your notes into one or more paragraphs, making sure that you turn all fragments and run-ons into complete sentences.

Checkpoint *Parts 1 and 2*

A Write *S* for each group of words that is a sentence. For each sentence fragment write *F*. Then add words to change the fragments into sentences.

1. In our neighborhood.
2. A nationally known cartoonist.
3. Scampered quickly up the oak tree in the front yard of the huge mansion.
4. The weather report in the daily paper.
5. The taxi sped around the corner.
6. The overturned truck blocked traffic.
7. The inventor of the telephone.
8. The totem pole was painted in bright colors.
9. Experience is a hard teacher.
10. Draws with charcoal or ink.

B Write *S* for each group of words that is a sentence. For each run-on sentence write *R*. Then rewrite each run-on sentence correctly.

1. First Judy called Nina then she called me about the lost concert tickets.
2. Ben tried to skate backwards, he ended up with a badly sprained arm and several bruises.
3. Barbara noticed the leaves of the unusual bush, they looked like velvet.
4. The peacock's tail feathers were iridescent shades of blue, green, and purple.
5. A pipe burst water flooded the basement and ruined the camping equipment we had stored there.
6. Larry was trained as a carpenter he learned different aspects of the trade quickly.
7. The German neighborhood celebrated Oktoberfest with music, folk dancing, and traditional foods.
8. Eskimos prefer to be called *Inuit*, in their language it means ''native people.''
9. The school sponsors adult classes, many people attend in the evening.
10. Many of our impressions of the Civil War come from photographs by Mathew Brady.

Linking
Grammar & Writing

You are learning to be a court reporter. Since an important part of your job will be to record accurately and quickly everything that happens and everything that is said in the courtroom, you are practicing writing with time limits.

Prewriting and Drafting Choose a scene, event, or conversation, preferably one that is fast paced. Give yourself a time limit of three minutes and write everything you see and hear as rapidly as you can. Do not worry too much about capitalization or punctuation at this point. Then read through your account and write a paragraph from it, changing fragments and run-ons into correct sentences.

The following is an example of what you might write.

> walking past playground large group of children wanting to use swings and slide—1 slightly older child pushes some others—someone gets hit with a swing—a toddler climbs up slide while everyone is watching other kids—gets to top of slide and starts screaming with fright

Revising and Proofreading Ask yourself the following questions when you are revising your final paragraph.

> Have you included all the important details that you wrote in your notes?
>
> Does your paragraph have a written or implied topic sentence that states the main idea?
>
> Are there clear transitions between the events?
>
> Have you corrected all fragments and run-on sentences?
>
> Have you used correct capitalization and punctuation for each sentence?

Additional Writing Topic Advertisers often use fragments and run-ons in their writing. Find at least two examples of such ads in magazines or newspapers. Rewrite the example, changing each fragment or run-on into a complete sentence. Compare your versions with the advertisers'. Decide which pieces are more effective as advertisements. Then explain what effect fragments and run-ons have on the reader and why you think advertising copywriters use them.

Tree-bender or Mud-sender?

Who hasn't made a belly flop? The answer is many people in Rhode Island, who commit belly bumpers. There are also Ohioans who sometimes do belly slappers. In Kansas, people have been known to make belly landings.

What is another word for a heavy rain? It is a dam-buster in Alabama, a hay-rotter in Virginia, a tree-bender in Massachusetts, a mud-sender in California, and a stump-washer in South Carolina.

American English is rich in variations from one part of the country to another. The words that make up these colorful regional dialects are being collected in an ambitious new dictionary, *The Dictionary of American Regional English*. This five-volume work is the result of interviews with 2,777 people from every part of the country. More than 2.5 million responses were collected, and the words are being organized to show where in the country they are used, who uses them, and the history behind the words. The entire dictionary will not be completed until the mid-1990's.

As time passes, regional differences in America are fading. Through this ambitious project, however, the distinctive qualities of America's many dialects are being recorded. "We're doing a job of historical preservation," said Frederic G. Cassidy, the dictionary's editor-in-chief. "We want to represent accurately the way people talk in the United States."

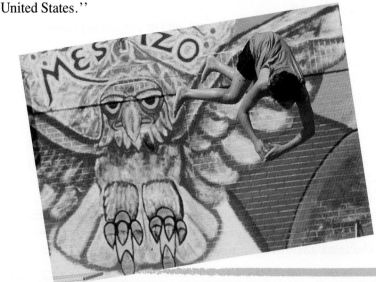

Chapter 22
Application and Review

A Identifying Sentences, Run-ons, and Fragments Write *S* for sentence, *F* for fragment, or *R* for run-on. Then rewrite all fragments and run-ons as complete sentences.

1. Claudia plays the guitar she also plays the flute.
2. Like to sing along with her and practice harmonizing.
3. Sometimes plays for assemblies.
4. Also likes to help others.
5. She has offered to teach some of us.
6. I would love to play the guitar, I wonder if I could learn.
7. Dad's old guitar probably somewhere in the attic.
8. We'll meet on Friday I'm supposed to practice each day.
9. I learned my first chord, but are my fingers sore!
10. Think I'll keep practicing.

B Correcting Fragments and Run-ons The following paragraphs contain fragments and run-on sentences. On your paper, rewrite the paragraphs and correct these errors. Check your capitalization and punctuation.

> You may be familiar with Scotland Yard. From watching British mystery movies. However, it isn't in Scotland and it isn't a yard, it is a nickname. For the Metropolitan Police Force of London.
>
> Scotland Yard got its name from a short street in London. This street was the site of a palace. Where visiting Scottish kings stayed. In 1829 the palace became London's police center. In 1890 the police moved into offices on the Thames Embankment, these offices were named New Scotland Yard.

C Writing Complete Sentences Use the following phrases to write a paragraph. Avoid fragments or run-on sentences.

1. Pluto, planet ninth in distance from the sun
2. Discovered in 1930 by Clyde W. Tombaugh
3. Revolves around the sun once in about 248 years
4. Rotates every 6.4 earth days
5. Thought by astronomers to have been a satellite of Neptune

Cumulative Review

Chapters 21 and 22

A Recognizing the Parts of a Sentence In the following sentences, underline the subject once and the verb twice. Write *DO* for each direct object, *IO* for indirect object, *PN* for predicate nominative, and *PA* for predicate adjective. Some parts may be compound.

1. Ms. Osaka teaches the children karate on Saturdays.
2. Here are the directions to the video recorder.
3. William Hunt invented the safety pin in 1825.
4. Diane Keaton is an actress and a photographer.
5. After the long hike, the cold water tasted delicious.
6. John Sayles writes novels and directs movies.
7. When was the Panama Canal completed?
8. At the tip of Lake Superior is the city of Duluth.
9. The pen name of Hector Hugo Munro was Saki.
10. Asparagus and soybeans are important crops in Michigan.
11. The city awarded the contract to the lowest bidder.
12. The audience gave the cast and director a standing ovation.
13. The senator stepped to the podium and addressed the crowd.
14. In August the weather here is often hot and humid.
15. By the end of the week, the carpenters might be finished.
16. Soon the birds will be flying south for the winter.
17. Several celebrities attended the ceremonies at Stonehenge.
18. The skydiver's performance gave the onlookers a thrill.
19. The old engine pulled slowly into the station.
20. The athletes promised their coaches complete cooperation.

B Recognizing Complete Sentences On your paper, identify each group of words by writing *S* for sentence, *F* for fragment, or *R* for run-on. Then rewrite all fragments and run-ons to make them complete sentences. Add appropriate end punctuation to sentences.

1. The camp at the base of the mountain trail
2. Why did the stock market fall in 1929
3. The building once contained offices, now it is a museum
4. Please fasten your seat belt
5. Broken by the force of the wind
6. Along the banks of the Mississippi River

7. After World War II, U.S. population increased dramatically
8. Dr. Mary McCleod Bethune was a Presidential advisor she also founded Bethune-Cookman College
9. What a spectacular fireworks display this is
10. Barbra Streisand, the singer, actress, and director
11. Julius Erving was a basketball star he retired in 1987
12. Angela is a soprano Louise is an alto
13. Turn right at Oak Street
14. The house with the front porch and brick steps
15. Jack Kemp played football, then he became a congressman
16. The runner finally crossed the finish line, she was exhausted
17. In the middle of the performance, suddenly from outside the auditorium a shattering noise
18. Several new buildings have dramatically changed the silhouette of the city skyline
19. When the entire process has been completed
20. The freshly baked bread was delicious, the family finished every crumb in one meal

C Correcting Fragments and Run-ons The following paragraphs contain both fragments and run-on sentences. Rewrite the paragraphs correctly. Use proper capitalization and punctuation.

Every day articles appear in newspapers, in magazines, and on television. About the advantages and disadvantages of different types of energy. There are many energy choices, it is hard to decide on the best course of action.

What are the options? The fuel most used in the United States is oil this is the same fuel that many experts believe will be exhausted. Within thirty years. Other sources of fossil fuels are natural gas and coal. These are more abundant than oil. Eventually will be exhausted too. In addition, coal produces harmful particles, these particles increase pollution of air and water.

Nuclear reactors currently produce about one-tenth of our energy. Could easily supply more. However, the dangers of radioactivity may be too high a price to pay. For this form of energy.

Solar and wind power are renewable energy sources, they are used very little at present. Some experts say these sources could provide about one-fourth of the country's energy by the year 2000. Until problems with energy sources are solved. Conservation seems to be the best policy.

23

Using Nouns

*N*ouns name all sorts of things—persons, places, things, and ideas. Make a quick list of all the nouns you see in the photos above. Which nouns convey the clearest images?

By choosing nouns carefully you can add interest and precision to your writing. In this chapter you will learn to identify and use common nouns, proper nouns, and their singular, plural, and possessive forms.

What Is a Noun?

A noun is a word that names a person, place, thing, or idea.

The idea named by a noun may be a quality, belief, or feeling.

Persons	aunt, doctor, Gregory, Anita Cruz
Places	kitchen, hotel, Savannah, West Virginia
Things	blanket, mirror, lightning, Statue of Liberty
Ideas	freedom, intelligence, sincerity, democracy

Exercise

Application in Literature Make four columns labeled *Persons, Places, Things,* and *Ideas.* Find at least fifteen nouns in the following paragraph and list each in the proper column.

(1) At that time, Shozo Shimada was Seattle's most successful Japanese businessman. (2) He owned a chain of stores which extended not only from Vancouver to Portland, but to cities in Japan as well. (3) He had come to America in 1880, penniless but enterprising, and sought work as a laborer. (4) It wasn't long, however, before he saw the futility of trying to compete with American laborers whose bodies were twice his in muscle and bulk. (5) He knew he would never go far as a laborer, but he did possess another skill that could give him a start toward better things. (6) He knew how to sew. (7) He set aside his shovel, bought a second-hand sewing machine, and hung a dressmaker's sign in his window. (8) He was in business.

(9) In those days there were some Japanese women in Seattle who had neither homes nor families nor sewing machines and [who] were delighted to find a friendly Japanese person to do some sewing for them. (10) They flocked to Mr. Shimada with bolts of cloth, elated to discover a dressmaker who could speak their native tongue and sew western-styled dresses for them.

From "Of Dry Goods and Black Bow Ties"
by Yoshiko Uchida

Part 2
Kinds of Nouns

Nouns may be classified in several ways.

Common and Proper Nouns

A common noun is a general name for a person, place, thing, or idea. A proper noun is the name of a particular person, place, thing, or idea.

Look at the following examples. As you can see, proper nouns begin with capital letters, and they may consist of more than one word.

Common Nouns	Proper Nouns
city	Burlington
mayor	Mayor Ortiz
game	Super Bowl

Concrete and Abstract Nouns

A concrete noun names an object that can be seen, heard, smelled, touched, or tasted. An abstract noun names something that cannot be perceived through the senses.

Concrete Nouns	Abstract Nouns
Marcia	kindness
thunder	skill
banana	truth

Collective and Compound Nouns

A collective noun names a group of people or things.

committee	club	team	herd
crowd	class	flock	family

A compound noun contains two or more words. It may be written as one word, as two words, or with a hyphen.

sunlamp	ice hockey	Main Street	great-aunt
earthworm	light bulb	one-half	runner-up

Spelling Note A dictionary can tell you whether a compound noun is written as one or two words or as a hyphenated word.

Exercises

A Write the italicized nouns in each sentence. Identify each noun as *Common, Proper, Concrete, Abstract, Collective,* or *Compound.* All nouns will fit at least two categories, and some will fit three.

> *Example* The *team* from Jefferson High won the *debate*.
> team—Common, Concrete, Collective
> debate—Common, Concrete

1. A boy named *Chester Greenwood* had the original *idea* for earmuffs.
2. Our *fox terrier* took two *blue ribbons* at yesterday's dog show.
3. Many *people* are interested in learning about their *ancestors*.
4. The *crowd* at *Cape Canaveral* was awaiting *liftoff*.
5. The *audience* cheered the *E Street Band*.
6. The *truth* of the witness's *testimony* will be challenged in the *cross-examination*.
7. *Bonita* used her mechanical *skill* to repair the doorbell.
8. Small *lap dogs* were popular in *England* in the eighteenth century.
9. Our *hope* is that we will be able to see the *eclipse*.
10. The members of the *class* had great respect for Mr. Wellington's *creativity*.

B Write the fifteen italicized nouns in the following paragraph. Identify the categories to which each noun belongs: *Common, Proper, Concrete, Abstract, Collective, Compound.*

(1) An Eskimo *family* may own as many as twenty dogs. (2) These are usually *malamutes* or Siberian huskies, breeds that are well equipped for *survival* in a harsh climate such as that of *Alaska*. (3) In summer the dogs carry *backpacks* that weigh up to twenty *pounds*, and in *winter* they work in teams to pull heavy *sleds* over ice and snow. (4) A typical *team* consists of six to twelve dogs harnessed in pairs, plus a leader tied to the front. (5) The *driver* usually walks or runs alongside.

(6) Many *Eskimos* own cars and snowmobiles, but dogs are more dependable for travel over rough, snow-covered *terrain*. (7) Dogs are also excellent *protectors* and companions. (8) Eskimo children develop an *attachment* to their dogs that lasts their *lifetime*.

C *Write Now* Find a description that you have written this year. Improve it by replacing some vague nouns with precise ones.

Part 3

The Uses of Nouns

A noun may act as a subject, a direct object, an indirect object, or a predicate nominative. Study the following examples:

Subject	*Meteorologists* study the weather. (*Meteorologists* is the subject of the verb *study*.)
Direct Object	The magician amazed the *audience*. (*Audience* receives the action of the verb *amazed*.)
Indirect Object	The coach showed the *quarterback* a new play. (*Quarterback* tells *to whom* the play was shown.)
Predicate Nominative	Lyn Walker is a carpenter's *assistant*. (*Assistant* follows the linking verb *is*.)

Exercise

Write each italicized noun and tell how each is being used.

1. Nearly a thousand years ago, a *civilization* flourished in an area of New Mexico called Chaco Canyon.
2. The Navajo have given the *people* the name of Anasazi.
3. "Anasazi" is their *word* for "ancient ones."
4. The Anasazi built impressive *villages* about A.D. 1000.
5. They developed a sophisticated *culture*.
6. Then their *culture* vanished mysteriously about A.D. 1300.
7. Today the *land* is the Chaco Culture National Historic Park.
8. Archaeologists search the *ruins* for clues about the Anasazi.
9. Research gives *archaeologists* insights into Anasazi culture.
10. The disappearance of the Anasazi is still a *mystery*.

Anasazi ruins, Chaco Canyon, New Mexico.

Checkpoint *Parts 1, 2, and 3*

A Label six columns *Common, Proper, Concrete, Abstract, Collective,* and *Compound.* Write each noun from the sentences in the correct columns. All nouns will belong to at least two categories.

1. Steamed clams are a popular dish in New England.
2. The owner called the plumber to connect the washing machine.
3. The class is planning a trip to Washington, D.C.
4. Several volunteers showed great courage.
5. Geraldo and his family visited New York City.
6. The new council paid tribute to the former mayor.
7. Did the Vice-President remain silent on the issue?
8. The choir proceeded into the auditorium by candlelight.
9. Sheila and Ted put considerable energy into their winning dance routine.
10. Many communities experienced extreme poverty during the Depression.

B Write each italicized noun below. Tell whether the noun is functioning as a subject, direct object, indirect object, or predicate nominative. Then tell whether the noun is abstract or concrete.

1. A chemical *factory* will be built on this site.
2. Honesty is the *quality* that I admire most.
3. The Prime Minister solemnly addressed *Parliament* about the country's unemployment problem.
4. Our catcher flashed the *pitcher* a secret signal.
5. The first contestant in the rodeo competition roped the *steer* in under thirty seconds.
6. Laurel and Hardy were *actors* in silent films.
7. The *legend* of Big Foot has been told for centuries.
8. Into the hollow log slipped the frightened *fox.*
9. Dad and I made the *best* of the situation.
10. The waiter handed each *diner* a menu.
11. The *mayor* calmly announced his resignation.
12. Did you give the *dog* fresh water?
13. Charity is a *virtue* that Marco practices.
14. Mom organized her *thoughts* before speaking.
15. On the table lay three old *books.*

The Wars of the Words

This section from a book called Have a Word on Me *refers to a series of wars involving the parts of speech that took place many years ago. The writer claims that he found this account in an old manuscript that had been lost for years in a dusty desk drawer. As you read it, remember that nouns have many uses and that the words* subject *and* object *have more than one meaning.*

A royal incident in the year 1213 precipitated the Wars of the Words. King John was in the Nominative case then, with many Subjects to do him honor. One of these Subjects—Matilda, the daughter of Robert Fitzwalter the Valiant, Lord of the Manor of Diss in the County of Norfolk— discovered that she had also become the King's Object; and she Objected.

There ensued a wrangle among the Nouns. Could a Subject also be an Object? And how could one tell which was which? Some hearty old Nouns declared themselves loyal Subjects, and proud of it; others admitted they were Objects. They said any Subject that acted upon them would do so at his own risk. Words led to blows, blows to a pitched battle, and the battle to a carnage among Nouns more bloody than our own Civil War.

Records of the first Wars of the Words are fragmentary, partly because it was difficult to separate who was fighting whom from whom was fighting who.

In the opening war, sometimes the Subjects were ahead, and sometimes the Objects. When the Objects triumphed, they became the Subjects, and the Subjects became the Objects. But this simply meant that they exchanged armor and went on fighting. To make the scoring still more difficult, a Subject that became an Object remained, or became, the Subject of its Subject.

The outcome was the Dark Ages. Armies degenerated into marauding bands. Father turned on son, and brother on brother. Split personalities were the norm. No one is sure how many centuries this chaos lasted. We do know, however, that finally an ancient Noun—his name has long been forgotten—climbed to the top of a barrel in the marketplace of Diss and cried in a quavering voice, "This madness must cease. Whether Subjects or Objects, we are all Nouns together. We are the lords of creation—the First of the Parts of Speech. Who else can turn from Subject to Object and back again at will?"

From then on the Nouns were so busy and happy switching from Subject to Object and back again that they had no time or stomach left for fighting.

Willard R. Espy

Part 4
The Plurals of Nouns

Nouns that name one person, place, thing, or idea are called **singular nouns**. Nouns that name more than one are called **plural nouns**. The following rules tell how to form the plurals of nouns.

1. **To form the plural of most nouns, just add -*s*:**

   prizes   dreams   circles   stations

2. **For most singular nouns ending in *o*, add -*s*:**

   solos   halos   studios   photos   pianos

   For a few nouns ending in *o*, add -*es*:

   heroes   tomatoes   potatoes   echoes   cargoes

3. **When the singular noun ends in *s*, *sh*, *ch*, *x*, or *z*, add -*es*:**

   waitresses   brushes   ditches   axes   buzzes

4. **When a singular noun ends in *y* with a consonant before it, change the *y* to *i* and add -*es*:**

   army—armies   candy—candies   baby—babies

   When a vowel (*a*, *e*, *i*, *o*, *u*) comes before the *y*, just add -*s*:

   boy—boys   way—ways   jockey—jockeys

5. **For most nouns ending in *f* or *fe*, change the *f* to *v* and add -*es* or -*s*. Since there is no rule, you must memorize such words.**

   life—lives   calf—calves   knife—knives
   thief—thieves   shelf—shelves   loaf—loaves

   For some nouns ending in *f*, add -*s* to make the plural:

   roofs   chiefs   reefs   beliefs

6. **Some nouns have the same form for both singular and plural.**

   deer   sheep   moose   salmon   trout

7. **For some nouns, the plural is formed in a special way.**

   man—men   goose—geese   ox—oxen
   woman—women   mouse—mice   child—children

8. **For a compound noun written as one word, form the plural by changing the last word in the compound to its plural form:**

    stepchild—stepchildren   firefly—fireflies

    If the compound noun is written as separate or as hyphenated words, change the most important word to the plural form:

    brother-in-law—brothers-in-law
    life jacket—life jackets

Spelling Note If you are not sure how a particular plural is formed, check the dictionary. Dictionaries show the plural of a word if it is formed in an unusual way.

Exercises

A Write the plural form of each of these nouns. Then use your dictionary to see if you have formed the plurals correctly.

1. chief	6. sky	11. echo	16. spy
2. year	7. knife	12. tomato	17. goose
3. deer	8. tooth	13. bunch	18. calf
4. holiday	9. rodeo	14. window	19. wish
5. coach	10. fox	15. moose	20. copy

B On your paper, rewrite the sentences below, changing the italicized singular nouns to their correct plural forms.

1. *Elf* appear in many of my grandfather's *story*.
2. My *sister-in-law* talk to each other over their two-way *radio*.
3. A series of *analysis* showed that *virus* spread the disease.
4. The steady *wave* in the *bay* make them ideal places to bodysurf.
5. We identified *tree* by the shapes of their *leaf*.
6. *Salmon* live in salt water but spawn in freshwater *river*.
7. Many *species* of *mammal* are found only in Australia.
8. Of all *structure* made by humans, the Great Wall of China is the only one that can be seen by *astronaut* from outer space.
9. My favorite fruits are *pear* and *cherry*.
10. Underwater *reef* threaten all *ship* passing through the strait.

c *Write Now* You are grocery shopping. Carts and shoppers fill the aisles. As you enter the produce section, a fire alarm triggers the sprinkler system, and water sprays everywhere. In one or two paragraphs, describe the scene. Then check the spelling of each plural.

Part 5

The Possessives of Nouns

Possessive nouns show ownership or belonging.

> the child's coat (The child owns the coat.)
> the cat's paw (The paw belongs to, or is part of, the cat.)

Possessive nouns are formed by adding an apostrophe (') and an -*s* or only an apostrophe to the noun. Possessive nouns may also be singular or plural. Look at these three examples of possessive nouns:

> My *mother's* car is in the garage.
> My *parents'* car is in the garage.
> The *children's* bicycles are in the garage.

There are three rules for forming the possessives of singular and plural nouns:

1. **If a noun is singular, add '*s*.**

> mother—my *mother's* car
> Ross—*Ross's* desk

Exception: The *s* after the apostrophe is dropped after *Jesus'*, *Moses'*, and names in classical mythology (*Zeus'*).

2. **If a noun is plural and ends with *s*, just add an apostrophe.**

> parents—my *parents'* car
> the Santinis—the *Santinis'* home

3. **If a noun is plural but does not end in *s*, add '*s*.**

> women—the *women's* coats
> people—the *people's* choice

Exercises

A Write *Singular* or *Plural* to tell the number of each noun below. Then write the possessive form of the noun.

1. believer	6. Hercules	11. Mendozas	16. mice
2. people	7. torch	12. players	17. Charles
3. wolves	8. Randy	13. grass	18. thieves
4. city	9. state	14. ox	19. earth
5. fruits	10. cactus	15. bodies	20. Odysseus

B Each sentence below contains one noun that must be made possessive. Some of these nouns are singular and some are plural. Rewrite the sentences, inserting the correct possessive nouns.

1. The boys mother taught them how to fish.
2. The winners essays focused on the rights of nonsmokers.
3. Many people consider Italy the leader in men fashion.
4. An animal tracks disappeared at the river's edge.
5. Eleanor Roosevelt was one of this century great humanitarians.
6. Several players disagreed with the coach plan.
7. Clyde Tombaugh discovery of Pluto in 1930 was a major event.
8. The string bass low tones echoed throughout the auditorium.
9. Vacationers go to Alaska to explore the state wilderness.
10. If all the existing glaciers were to melt tomorrow, the resulting rise in sea level would submerge most of the world coastal cities.

c *Proofreading* Rewrite the following paragraph, correcting all errors. Pay special attention to the use of possessive nouns.

(1) Our familys' pet mouse, Gizmo, is not as easy to care for as we expected. (2) Their is no avoiding the fact that Gizmo is nocturnal; he is active at night and sleeps allmost all day. (3) Disturbing Gizmos rest will cause him to nip. (4) Like all rodents teeth, Gizmo's are long and very sharp. (5) They must be trimed at the vets office. (6) We try not to disturb Gizmo during the day, but he often disturbs us at night by running on his running wheel. (7) If the wheels' parts are not waxed, the squeaking is horrible! (8) Eventually, we'll decide if our pets' habit's make him more fun than annoying.

Checkpoint *Parts 4 and 5*

A On your paper, write the plural form of each of these words.

1. trout	6. stereo	11. foot	16. grief
2. tax	7. moss	12. embryo	17. passer-by
3. laborer	8. woman	13. berry	18. potato
4. child	9. path	14. wharf	19. doorway
5. cry	10. splash	15. lunch	20. loaf

B On your paper, write the possessive form of each italicized noun in the following sentences.

1. This *morning* assembly is scheduled for 9:00 A.M.
2. My *mother boss* house has solar heating.
3. Emilio lost the *shelves* support brackets.
4. *Mr. Ortiz* porch has a large wooden swing.
5. The newborn *calves* legs were wobbly but strong.
6. The *children* muddy boots are on a mat in the hallway.
7. The *deer* antlers are shed every season.
8. Do *Terry* parents know she lost her library card?
9. According to the census, our *towns* populations are nearly the same.
10. The *needles* points were thin and sharp.
11. We used the *Jacksons* camper for our trip.
12. Please hang the *men* jackets in the hall closet.
13. The *mice* tails were long and curly.
14. The *class* reactions to the exam were mixed.
15. The *sheep* heavy coats will be sheared soon.

C On your paper, complete each sentence by writing a noun of the type called for in parentheses.

1. The _____ eerie calls could be heard all over the island. (plural possessive)
2. Everyone laughed as we tried to catch the _____. (plural)
3. A slimy _____ claw emerged. (singular possessive)
4. Large balloons were launched to honor the _____ feat. (plural possessive)
5. The _____ on the computer screen confirmed that the UFO was approaching. (singular)

Linking
Grammar & Writing

Study the excerpt from an old mail-order catalog below. Then write two descriptions of other items that could be included in this catalog. You might write about a new miracle cure, an article of clothing, a household gadget, or any other product you choose.

Prewriting and Drafting After you select your products, consider these questions: (1) What are your products' distinguishing details—shape, size, etc.? (2) To whom will your products appeal? What is the age group and spending capacity of your audience? (3) How will your products provide convenience, pleasure, or status to the buyer?

Decide on your products' most important features. Then organize your material into clear, convincing sentences. Include several plural nouns and at least two possessive nouns.

Revising and Proofreading Think about these questions as you revise: (1) Does each description present a complete image of your product? (2) Have you convinced the buyer of the products' benefits? (3) Have you used enough precise nouns to identify your products' features clearly?

Additional Writing Topic You won the prize! For two minutes you get to run through a record store and collect all the albums, cassettes, and accessories you can carry. After two minutes, everything you've grabbed is yours. Describe these two minutes.

Surnames

W hat's in a name? Family names, or *surnames*, contain clues about ancestry, family relationships, occupations, and more.

Until the twelfth century, many people got along with just their first names. But as society became more sophisticated, more information was needed. Some people came to be identified with where they lived, giving us such general surnames as Brooks, Hill, and Green (for village green), and such specific ones as Washington and Cleveland.

Others were identified by family relationships. Johnson was obviously the son of John, and Williams was a shortening of William's son. The Scots contributed *Mc* or *Mac*, which means "son of," so McPherson was the son of the parson. In Scandinavia the surname changed from generation to generation. A Carl Svenssen would be Sven's son, but Carl's daughter (dóttir) Helga would be Helga Carlsdóttir, not Helga Svenssen.

Many names can be traced to occupations. Butcher, Carpenter, and Weaver are obvious examples. One of the most common is the metalworker tending the forge—the Smith. The equivalent in Germany was the Schmidt, in Poland the Kowalczyk, in Hungary the Kovács, in Syria the Haddad, and in Spain the Herrera. The person who ran the mill became the English Miller, the German Müller, the Italian Molinari, and the Greek Mylonas. The *-ster* in Brewster and Webster showed that the brewer and the weaver were women.

Names, which may seem to be our most personal possessions, in fact have rich histories of their own.

Chapter 23
Application and Review

A Identifying Types of Nouns On your paper, write each noun in the following sentences. Identify each noun according to kind: *Common, Proper, Concrete, Abstract, Collective, Compound*. Remember, all nouns fit at least two categories.

1. ''Tornado Alley'' cuts directly through Kansas and Missouri.
2. Their culture has changed little since prehistoric times.
3. It took great strength to move that piano.
4. The Hawaiian Islands were formed by volcanic eruptions.
5. The burglars placed the diamonds in a matchbox.
6. Stephanie visited the Lincoln Memorial and the Washington Monument.
7. A herd of dairy cattle grazed in the pasture.
8. The detectives were unable to solve the mystery.
9. The club will release its annual report next week.
10. The flock of ducks skimmed across Clear Lake.
11. That nail polish comes in assorted colors.
12. American pioneers rode in covered wagons.
13. The child was rewarded for her honesty.
14. Our team practiced in the new gymnasium.
15. The concertmaster of the Philadelphia Orchestra will be the first soloist.

B Understanding the Uses of Nouns On your paper, complete each sentence by adding nouns. Make the sentences as interesting as possible. Then tell whether you have used your noun as a subject, direct object, indirect object, or predicate nominative.

1. _____ emerged slowly from the spacecraft.
2. King Kong knocked the _____ and _____ from the sky.
3. _____ tape-recorded the _____.
4. _____ and _____ are fascinating _____.
5. That house has a _____ in the basement.
6. Many dancers are also excellent _____.
7. The animal trainer gave her _____ a _____.
8. The wealthy woman left her _____ only an old _____.
9. Joe gave _____ and _____ an _____ yesterday.
10. _____ is the _____ I admire most.

C Forming the Plurals and Possessives of Nouns Make four columns on your paper and label them *Singular, Singular Possessive, Plural*, and *Plural Possessive*. Next write each of the fifteen nouns below in the correct column. Then write the three other forms of each noun in their proper columns.

	Singular	*Sing. Poss.*	*Plural*	*Pl. Poss.*
Example cat	cat	cat's	cats	cats'

1. moose
2. tax
3. typists'
4. fly's
5. lasso
6. records'
7. roof's
8. clutch's
9. violinist
10. sash
11. symphony
12. lioness
13. councils
14. wives'
15. chimney

D Using Plural and Possessive Forms Correctly On your paper, rewrite the sentences below, changing each italicized singular noun to either its plural or its possessive form. Some nouns need to be both plural and possessive.

1. We heard the *gull* cries as they whirled high above the barren, rocky *cliff*.
2. The *artist* materials were scattered across their *studio*.
3. The *child* come from all around to climb the willow tree in *Mr. Haines* yard.
4. *Louisiana bayou* are home to a variety of snakes.
5. Over twenty *knife* were neatly stored in the *chef* cabinet.
6. No one knows why, but *Willis* cousin Fred always carries three *comb* in his jacket.
7. The *panelist* answers were sealed in *envelope*.
8. After all the *ballot* were counted, the *voter* choice was Ms. Antoinette Tonelli.
9. Our cat caught six *mouse* in one day on our *uncle* farm.
10. The *people* homes in Springville were damaged by two dust *storm* in the same year.
11. The *family* proudest possession is a herd of *ox*.
12. The *player wife* were too nervous to watch the entire championship football game.
13. The assistant *state's attorney* each work hours per day.
14. The *government embargo* on automobiles and electronics were met with criticism from the business group.
15. The *engine* roar scattered the flock of *goose* and sent them into flight.

24

Using Pronouns

*I*n today's complex world, robots accomplish an increasing number of
activities once performed by humans. Perhaps someday
a robot will even be able to take the family dog for a walk.

Just as the robot takes the place of a human being in
the photo above, a pronoun can perform some of the
functions of a noun. In this chapter you will learn about
the various types of pronouns and their uses. By using
pronouns wisely, you can avoid the unnecessary repetition of nouns and add continuity to your writing.

Part 1
What Is a Pronoun?

A pronoun is a word that is used in place of a noun or another pronoun.

Pronouns help present ideas clearly and efficiently. First of all, they help prevent unnecessary repetition. They are also used as transitional devices to tie sentences or paragraphs together.

The noun or pronoun that a pronoun stands for is called the **antecedent** of the pronoun. Find the antecedent of the italicized pronoun in each of the following sentences.

> Lin was late because *she* missed the bus. (*She* refers to the noun *Lin*. *Lin* is the antecedent of the pronoun *she*.)
>
> Raúl read the book and returned *it* to the shelf. (*It* refers to the noun *book*. *Book* is the antecedent of the pronoun *it*.)

The antecedent may be made up of two or more nouns.

> The coaches, players, and fans were happy when *they* heard that the game would not be postponed. (The antecedent of *they* is *coaches, players,* and *fans*.)

Pronouns may also be the antecedents of other pronouns. What are the antecedents of the italicized pronouns in the sentences below?

> You missed *your* bus.   They knew *their* way.

The antecedent and the pronoun may appear in the same sentence, or the antecedent may appear in the preceding sentence.

> The tractor pushed the stones and bricks. *It* cleared a path. (*It* refers to the antecedent *tractor*.)

Occasionally the antecedent appears after the pronoun.

> After *he* had read several articles, Richard took a break. (*Richard* is the antecedent of *he*.)

Exercises

A Write the antecedent of the italicized pronoun in each sentence.

1. The boat was stored in a shed especially made for *it*.
2. Did Ron know the message was for *him*?

3. Although *it* took many hours, the operation was a success.
4. She practiced *her* solo for the band concert.
5. Tony and Jenny taught *themselves* how to type.
6. Mark Twain, who began life as Samuel Langhorne Clemens, borrowed *his* pen name from Isaiah Sellers.
7. Inéz and Teresa had *their* job interviews this morning.
8. Before *he* entered politics, Bill Bradley played basketball.
9. While Ernesto was attempting a somersault, he lost *his* balance.
10. The violinists searched frantically for *their* missing music.

B Sometimes a pronoun refers to a noun in a preceding sentence:

> Antoine Becquerel discovered radioactivity. For *this, he* received a Nobel Prize.

This and *he* tie the two sentences together. Words such as these are called **transitional devices.** Write the sentences below in paragraph form. Substitute pronouns for some of the nouns to provide transitions.

1. The miller was America's first industrial inventor.
2. People of today might consider the miller just another merchant.
3. People don't realize that the miller was banker, businessman, and host to the countryside.
4. The miller also had a strenuous and dangerous job.
5. Early mills were massive and powerful.
6. Mills had huge wheels and gears that could crush a person.

Part 2
Personal Pronouns

Personal pronouns change form to refer to (1) the person speaking, (2) the person spoken to, or (3) the person or thing spoken about.

1. First-person pronouns refer to the person speaking:

> *I* pole-vault.   *We* collect old magazines.

2. Second-person pronouns refer to the person spoken to:

> Did *you* bring *your* calculator?   *You* should go too.

3. Third-person pronouns refer to the person or thing spoken about:

> *She* asked *him* a question.   *They* opened *it* immediately.

The chart below shows the forms of the personal pronouns.

	First Person	Second Person	Third Person
Singular	I, me (my, mine)	you (your, yours)	he, she, it him, her, it (his, her, hers, its)
Plural	we, us (our, ours)	you (your, yours)	they, them (their, theirs)

First- and third-person pronouns change form to show singular and plural. Third-person singular pronouns also change to show gender.

Masculine	he, him, his (refer to males)
Feminine	she, her, hers (refer to females)
Neuter	it, its (refer to things and often to animals)

Possessive Pronouns

Possessive pronouns are personal pronouns that show owner-ship. In the chart above, possessive pronouns are in parentheses. For further discussion of possessive pronouns, see page 508.

Exercises

A On your paper, write the personal pronouns in the sentences below. Label each pronoun first-person, second-person, or third-person.

> *Example* Toby loaded his camera and focused it carefully.
> his, third-person; it, third-person

1. Is her report as complete as yours?
2. My uncle knows every family on his block.
3. The Millers' collie recognizes us when we visit them.
4. Martin Luther King, Jr., said, ''I have a dream.''
5. Nellie Taylor Ross was elected governor of Wyoming in 1924. She was the first American woman so honored.
6. How long have you and she been studying Spanish?
7. They helped us rehearse our lines for the play.
8. We need agile players like you and him to help win the championship.

B Application in Literature On your paper, write the italicized pronouns in the following paragraphs. Identify each pronoun as a first-person or third-person pronoun. Then tell whether the pronoun is singular or plural. Notice how the pronouns add a feeling of warmth and closeness to the passage.

(1) *He* had become blood of *my* blood; he the strong swimmer and *I* the boy clinging to *him* in the darkness. (2) *We* swam in silence, and in silence we dressed in *our* wet clothes, and went home.

(3) There was a lamp lighted in the kitchen, and when we came in, the water dripping from *us,* there was my mother. (4) *She* smiled at us. (5) *I* remember that she called us "boys." (6) "What have you boys been up to?" *she* asked, but my father did not answer. (7) As he had begun the evening's experience with *me* in silence, so he ended *it.* (8) *He* turned and looked at me. (9) Then he went, *I* thought, with a new and strange dignity, out of the room.

From *Discovery of a Father* by Sherwood Anderson

Portrait of Alexander Cassatt and his Son Robert Kelso, Mary Cassatt, 1885.

C *Write Now* Imagine that you have shown a child the sights of your city. Write a paragraph describing what you saw and what your small friend's reactions were. Use a variety of pronouns to refer to your guest and yourself.

The Cases of Personal Pronouns

A personal pronoun, like a noun, can function as a subject, an object, a predicate nominative, or a possessive. Unlike a noun, however, a personal pronoun changes its form, or case, depending on its use in a sentence. The three cases of a pronoun are the **nominative case,** sometimes called the subject form; the **objective case,** sometimes called the object form; and the **possessive case.**

Nominative Case	*He* pitched. (*He* is the subject.)
Objective Case	Riley tagged *him*. (*Him* is the direct object.)
Possessive Case	*His* pitch was wild. (*His* shows possession.)

The Nominative Case Use the nominative case when a pronoun is a subject or a predicate nominative.

Nominative Case

Singular	I, you, he, she, it
Plural	we, you, they

Subject	*I* drew a map.
	You need to leave for school now.
	She plotted our route.
Predicate Nominative	That must be *he*. (*He* follows the linking verb *must be*.)
	The caller was *he*. (*He* follows the linking verb *was*.)

The subject forms of pronouns are also used for predicate pronouns. If that form does not sound natural, try reversing the subject and the predicate pronoun. The sentence should still sound correct.

The singer was *she*.   *She* was the singer.

For a more complete discussion of predicate nominatives, see Chapter 21, pages 447–448.

Usage Note The expression *It's me* is frequently heard in informal conversation, even though it is not grammatically correct. The linking verb *is* calls for a complement in the nominative case: *It is I, This is she*. Most people consider *It's me* acceptable. However, avoid this phrase in formal writing or speaking.

The Objective Case Use the objective case when a pronoun is a direct object, an indirect object, or the object of a preposition.

Objective Case

Singular   me, you, him, her, it
Plural   us, you, them

Direct Object	The answer surprised *her*.
	Are you following *us*?
	Dennis introduced *them* to his neighbor.
Indirect Object	Carole sent *them* a souvenir of her trip.
	The principal gave *him* some good advice.
	Please lend *me* a pen.

The third use of the objective case is the object of a preposition. Prepositions are connecting words like *to, for, into,* and *with.* A pronoun that follows such a word is the object of the preposition.

Object of	They gave a surprise party for *me*.
Preposition	Give this book to *her*.

For further discussion of prepositions, see pages 579–589.

The Possessive Case Use the possessive case to show ownership.

Possessive Case

Singular   my, mine, your, yours, his, her, hers, its
Plural   our, ours, your, yours, their, theirs

Possessive pronouns are often used by themselves. The possessive pronouns *mine, yours, his, hers, its, ours,* and *theirs* replace nouns that function as subjects, predicate nominatives, and objects.

Subject	*Yours* are the best lines in the play.
Predicate Nominative	The leading role is *hers*.
Direct Object	I've heard your lines, but I haven't heard *his*.
Object of	Your part sounds interesting; now I'll tell you
Preposition	about *mine*.

At other times, possessive pronouns are used with the nouns they refer to. In this case the possessive pronouns *my, your, his, her, its, our,* and *their* function as adjectives.

> Read *your* lines slowly and clearly. (*Your* functions as an adjective modifying the noun *lines.*)

In this textbook, however, a possessive pronoun that functions as an adjective is considered a pronoun, not an adjective.

Exercises

A On your paper, write each pronoun in italics and tell whether it is in the *Nominative Case, Objective Case,* or *Possessive Case.*

1. As a teen-ager, Woody Allen wrote jokes and sold *them* to comedians and newspaper columnists.
2. Soprano Marjorie Lawrence sang *her* parts from a wheelchair.
3. The swimmers invited *us* to *their* meet.
4. Did *he* turn down the thermostat again?
5. Mother Teresa's work earned *her* the Nobel Peace Prize.
6. Those pictures are *ours.*
7. Mrs. Lopez and *she* will present *their* petition today.
8. *We* had to wait five minutes for the elevator.
9. The principal gave *him* a hall pass.
10. Janie bought *me* a flannel shirt, but *it* didn't fit.

B Write the correct pronoun. Then read the sentence to yourself.

1. The news shocked (he, him).
2. The waiter spilled spaghetti on (I, me).
3. (They, Them) moved to our neighborhood.
4. The artist sold (her, hers) work at a fair.
5. Was that (he, him) or his twin?
6. All of (we, us) are taller than our parents.
7. The idea was (my, mine).
8. The cashier gave (she, her) incorrect change.
9. The announcer is (she, her).
10. All of those novels were written by (he, him).
11. Garbage surrounded (they, them).
12. Is (he, him) going to the game?
13. The center forward is (she, her).
14. (He, Him) cuts lawns in the summer.
15. Next year, (we, us) will be able to drive.

Marie Curie in her laboratory.

C On your paper, write the correct form of the personal pronoun that fits the context of each of the following sentences. Identify the case, *Nominative, Objective,* or *Possessive,* of each pronoun you provide.

> *Example*   Pierre Curie was also noted for _____ work with magnets. his, Possessive

1. Pierre Curie was born in Paris, and _____ became a professor of physics at the Sorbonne.
2. His wife Marie was born in Warsaw, Poland, and later _____ emigrated to France.
3. _____ were pioneers in research on radioactivity.
4. _____ have _____ to thank for their painstaking efforts in the field of nuclear energy.
5. Pierre and Marie Curie won the 1903 Nobel Prize in physics for _____ work.
6. When Pierre died in 1906, Madame Curie succeeded _____ as professor of physics at the Sorbonne.
7. In 1911 the Nobel Prize in chemistry was awarded to _____ for the discovery of radium.
8. _____ was the first person to win two Nobel Prizes.
9. The Curies' daughter Irène and _____ husband Frédéric Joliot were also noted scientists.
10. The 1935 Nobel Prize in chemistry was awarded to the Joliots for _____ continuing research in radioactivity.

Part 3

Reflexive Pronouns and Intensive Pronouns

Reflexive pronouns and intensive pronouns are formed by adding -*self* or -*selves* to certain personal pronouns.

Singular	Plural
myself	ourselves
yourself	yourselves
himself, herself, itself	themselves

Reflexive pronouns reflect an action back upon the subject.
These pronouns add necessary information to a sentence.

Kim bought *herself* a digital watch.

Doug and Steve made *themselves* a snack.

Intensive pronouns are used to emphasize a noun or pronoun.
They do not add information to a sentence. If intensive pronouns are removed, the meaning of the sentence does not change.

Maggie *herself* opened the vault.
The neighbors *themselves* cleaned the alley.

A reflexive or an intensive pronoun must be used with an antecedent.

Incorrect	*Myself* knitted this sweater.
Correct	*I* knitted this sweater *myself*.

Incorrect	You can come with Ann and *myself*.
Correct	You can come with Ann and *me*.

Exercises

A Write the reflexive pronoun or intensive pronoun in each of the following sentences. Identify each pronoun as reflexive or intensive.

1. We were proud of the song that Ed and I had written ourselves.
2. Agatha Christie earned herself a worldwide reputation.
3. The squid defends itself by emitting an inky cloud.
4. You yourself should take charge of the project.
5. During the epidemic, the doctors themselves became ill.
6. The movie itself was surprisingly dull.

7. The explorers had faith in themselves.
8. The chameleon protects itself by changing color.
9. The governor himself made the request for emergency aid.
10. Grandma Moses taught herself to paint in her seventies.

B Write the reflexive or intensive pronoun that correctly completes each sentence. Identify each as intensive or reflexive.

1. I _____ will speak to the authorities.
2. Ask _____ what you would like to do.
3. James settled _____ into a comfortable chair.
4. By not wearing seatbelts, people endanger _____.
5. We _____ may be to blame.
6. The hikers freed _____ from the quicksand.
7. You _____ should solve the problem.
8. The only thing we have to fear is fear _____.
9. I would like to hear the story from Anita _____.
10. Let's do the dishes _____.

C *Write Now* You are to make lunch for your young cousins. However, you find that they have made their own sandwiches and most of the food is on them. Write a paragraph in which you use reflexive and intensive pronouns to describe their actions.

Checkpoint *Parts 1, 2, and 3*

A Write the pronoun and antecedent in each sentence. Tell whether the pronoun is in the nominative, objective, or possessive case.

1. Gayle is getting her ears pierced today.
2. By the time he was thirteen, Mozart had composed several symphonies.
3. The Coast Guard rescued Matt and gave him food.
4. Not only is Detroit large, it is surrounded by many sizable suburbs.
5. The club selected its officers by secret ballot.
6. The players huddled before the game started, and the coach gave them a pep talk.
7. Neither Marla nor Harriet finished her lunch.
8. Dan, your essay has won first prize!

B Write the italicized pronouns and tell whether they are personal, intensive, or reflexive. Then write the antecedent for each pronoun.

1. The actors *themselves* were distracted by the special effects.
2. Betsy, do *you* have your thesaurus handy?
3. Is the tape *itself* strong enough to hold the package?
4. Tony hurt *himself* on the balance beam.
5. Yolanda and I weren't ready, so Coach Hart skipped *us*.
6. Was Alonso moving the heavy boxes by *himself*?
7. Ina said *she* had read about a new discovery in cancer research.
8. Ernest taught *himself* to speak Spanish.
9. Thomas Jefferson *himself* designed Monticello, his home.
10. The story *itself* wasn't strong enough to inspire the film maker.

Part 4
Demonstrative Pronouns

The **demonstrative pronouns** are *this, that, these,* and *those.*
This and *these* point out people or things that are near in space or time. *That* and *those* point out people or things that are farther away.

> *This* is my book.   *These* are leather boots.
> *That* is yours.   *Those* are plastic.

Usage Note *This, that, these,* or *those* may be used as adjectives.

> *That* is an antique clock. (Pronoun)
> *That* clock is an antique. (Adjective)

Notice how the snakes in the cartoon use demonstrative pronouns.

"Gee, is that you? I thought all this was me !"

Exercise

Write the demonstrative pronoun that correctly completes each of the following sentences.

1. (These, Those) are rose gardens along the far wall.
2. (This, That) is a better record than the one Al was listening to.
3. (This, That) is the old mission, just beyond those olive trees.
4. (These, Those) seem riper than the plums Mom bought last week.
5. That is the faster route home, but (this, that) is more scenic.
6. (This, That) must be the monument in the distance.
7. (These, Those) are my friends, over there.
8. (This, That) is a more humid day than yesterday.
9. (This, That) is the meadow, just beyond those cabins.
10. The apples in this bin are riper, but (these, those) are cheaper.

Part 5
Indefinite Pronouns

Indefinite pronouns do not refer to a definite person or thing. An indefinite pronoun usually does not have an antecedent.

> *Several* of the cars were over ten years old.
> *Each* of the participants was given a prize.

Occasionally an indefinite pronoun has an antecedent.

The chess players began the game. *Both* were concentrating.

Some indefinite pronouns are singular, and some are plural. Others can be singular or plural, depending on their meaning in a sentence.

Indefinite Pronouns				
Singular	another	each	everything	one
	anybody	either	neither	somebody
	anyone	everybody	nobody	someone
	anything	everyone	no one	
Plural	both	few	many	several
Singular	all	any	most	none
or Plural	some	much		

| Singular | *Someone* is whistling off key. |
| Plural | *Both* are examples of Inca pottery. |

| Singular | *Most* of the snow has melted. |
| Plural | *Most* of the children have left. |

Usage Note Some indefinite pronouns function as adjectives when they come before a noun and modify it.

> *Both* answers are correct. (*Both* modifies *answer*.)
> David needed *some* new running shoes. (*Some* modifies *shoes*.)

Exercises

A Write the indefinite pronoun in each of the following sentences.

1. Did someone reserve a picnic table in the shade?
2. All of that jewelry is made of gold.
3. San Francisco Bay is one of the most beautiful harbors in the world.
4. Everyone in the courtroom listened attentively to the judge.
5. The ice storm severely damaged several of the trees.
6. Two roads go over the mountains, but both are closed.
7. None of us caught the early bus.
8. Many of the leaves have already fallen.
9. We found everything intact.
10. Some of these poems are written in blank verse.

B On your paper, write the indefinite pronouns in each of the following sentences. Tell whether each pronoun is singular or plural.

1. Anyone can run for freshman class officer.
2. You might consider one of the other possibilities.
3. Everything was swept away in the flood.
4. Neither of my sisters resembles my mother.
5. Today few remember the Lindy Hop.
6. Many of the jurors were excused.
7. No one could have foretold the terrible fate of the *Titanic*.
8. Mother earns most of her income from her writing.
9. Each of my brothers has a dirt bike.
10. Most of my classmates agreed with me.

C *Write Now* At a football game, your team scores the winning touchdown. Write a paragraph telling how the fans react. Use a variety of indefinite pronouns in your paragraph.

Part 6
Interrogative Pronouns

Certain pronouns, called **interrogative pronouns,** are used to ask questions. The interrogative pronouns are *who, whom, whose, which,* and *what*. An interrogative pronoun does not have an antecedent.

Who won an Emmy award?   *Which* is your favorite?
Whom did Gloria call?   *What* was that noise?
Whose is this parka?

Usage Note Two interrogative pronouns, *what* and *which,* can also be used as adjectives.

Which bike is yours?   *What* grade did you get?

Exercises

A On your paper, write the interrogative pronoun that correctly completes each of the following sentences.

1. _____ knows the age of this tree?
2. _____ was admitted to the Union first—California or Texas?
3. _____ is the difference between a democracy and a republic?
4. _____ will sign for this package?
5. _____ of your classes do you like the most?
6. _____ of the planets has the most moons?
7. _____ is your recipe for beef stew?
8. The top bunk is mine, but _____ is the bottom one?

B Each sentence below is the answer to a question. Write the question, substituting an interrogative pronoun for the underlined word or phrase. You may change or drop other words in the sentence.

Example   Alicia is the student who quilted the banner.
Which student quilted the colorful banner?

1. *A peanut butter sandwich* is my favorite after-school snack.
2. *Mrs. Cuenco* performed a Chopin waltz for our music class.
3. *The sterling silver bracelet* was given to Vanessa for her birthday.
4. *Malcolm* met Tom at the movie theater last night.
5. This antique pocket watch belongs to *Todd*.

Who's on First?

The antics of Abbott and Costello kept audiences laughing for almost thirty years. From 1929 until 1957 the team performed on the vaudeville stage, for radio and TV, and in a series of successful movies. The following sketch is their most famous routine. Every time they did it, they changed it slightly.

Bud: You know, strange as it may seem, they give ballplayers peculiar names nowadays. On the St. Louis team Who's on first, What's on second, I Don't Know is on third.

Lou: That's what I want to find out, the names of the fellows on the St. Louis team.

Bud: I'm telling you. Who's on first, What's on second, I Don't Know is on third.

Lou: You know the fellows' names?

Bud: Yes.

Lou: Well, then, who's playing first?

Bud: Yes.

Lou: I mean, the fellow's name on first base.

Bud: Who.

Lou: I'm askin' you, who is on first.

Bud: That's the man's name.

Lou: That's whose name?

Bud: Yes.

Bud: Well, go ahead, tell me.

Bud: Who is on first base.

Lou: That's what I'm tryin to find out. Wait a minute. Tell me the pitcher's name.

Bud: Tomorrow.

Lou: You don't want to tell me today?

Bud: I'm telling you, man.

Lou: Then go ahead.

Bud: Tomorrow.

Lou: You gotta catcher?

Bud: Yes.

Lou: The catcher's name?

Bud: Today.

Lou: Today. And Tomorrow's pitching.

Bud: Now you've got it.

Lou: Now, I throw the ball to first base.

Bud: Then who gets it?

Lou: He'd better get it! (frenzied) Now I throw the ball to first base.

Bud: Uh-huh.

Lou: Who picks up the ball and throws it to What. What throws it to I Don't Know. I Don't Know throws it back to Tomorrow. A triple play!

Bud: Yeah, it could be.

Lou: Another guy gets up and it's a long fly ball to center. Why? I don't know. And I don't care.

Bud: What was that?

Lou: I said, I don't care.

Bud: Oh, that's our shortstop.

**Bud Abbott
and Lou Costello**

Part 7
Relative Pronouns

A **relative pronoun** is used to relate, or connect, an adjective clause to the word or words it modifies. An adjective clause is a group of words that modifies a noun or pronoun. The clause has a subject and verb, but it cannot stand alone as a complete sentence. (See Chapter 31 for a complete discussion of adjective clauses). The noun or pronoun that the adjective clause modifies is the antecedent of the relative pronoun. The relative pronouns are *who, whom, whose, which,* and *that.*

The author, *whose book we discussed,* is not well known.
(*Whose* is a relative pronoun. Its antecedent is *author.*)

The play *that we saw* is a musical about cats. (*That* is a relative pronoun. The antecedent of *that* is play.)

Depending upon their use in a sentence, *who, whom, whose,* and *which* may be either relative or interrogative pronouns.

Interrogative Pronoun	*Who* is your favorite player?
Relative Pronoun	Keith Hernandez, *who* plays for the Mets, is my favorite player.

Usage Note Use the relative pronoun *who* to refer to people. Use *which* to refer to animals or things. *That* may be used to refer to all three categories: people, animals, or things.

Exercise

On your paper, write each relative pronoun and its antecedent.

1. In the store was a pleasant clerk who helped me.
2. A person whose eyesight is perfect has 20-20 vision.
3. Mrs. Wong sold her brooch, which was an heirloom.
4. Rachel Carson, whose books first alerted the public to environmental pollution, was a marine biologist.
5. Bill Cosby is an entertainer whom I enjoy and admire.
6. The money that I left on the table has disappeared.
7. The landau which was an early auto had a fold-down top.
8. Louis Braille, who was blind, played the organ.
9. The damage, which was overestimated, has been repaired.
10. A nocturne is a composition that suggests evening.

Checkpoint *Parts 4–7*

A Write the italicized pronouns in each sentence. Identify each pronoun as demonstrative, indefinite, interrogative, or relative.

1. With *whom* did you speak about *that*?
2. *Some* of the players asked that *each* of us attend the game.
3. *Those* are the tools *that* you will need for the project.
4. *That* was the science movie *that* lasted over an hour.
5. *All* of the winners *who* attended enjoyed the ceremony.

B Write the italicized word from each sentence. Tell whether it is an adjective or a pronoun. Then, identify each pronoun by telling its kind.

1. *Many* people played a role in the development of the automobile.
2. *One* of the pioneers was Frenchman Nicolas Cugnot.
3. He built a three-wheeled vehicle *that* was powered by steam.
4. *This* is generally considered the first automobile.
5. Cugnot, *who* was an engineer, designed it to haul cannon.
6. *Nobody* had ever seen anything like it before.
7. *That* vehicle had a giant boiler hanging over the front.
8. Cugnot's invention, *which* could travel only three miles per hour, was destroyed during its trial run.
9. In 1908, Ford built a car *that* could travel forty miles per hour.
10. *That* was the Model T, a great development in automotive history.

Model T Ford.

Part 8

Agreement with Antecedents

Pronouns must agree with their antecedents in number, gender, and person.

Use a singular pronoun to refer to a singular antecedent. Use a plural pronoun to refer to a plural antecedent.

> The artist set up *her* easel by the river. (The singular pronoun *her* refers to the singular antecedent *artist*.)

> The artists displayed *their* paintings in the park. (The plural pronoun *their* refers to the plural antecedent *artists*.)

Pronouns in the third person singular must also agree with their antecedents in gender.

> Shelly took *her* last exam this morning, but Jason will take *his* tomorrow. (*Her* refers to the feminine antecedent *Shelly; his* refers to the masculine antecedent *Jason*.)

Notice in the sentences above that the pronouns and antecedents also have another form of agreement. They are all in the third person.

Exercise

On your paper, write the pronoun that correctly completes each sentence. Identify the antecedent of each pronoun you write.

1. Marta organized _____ desk for greater efficiency.
2. The students emptied _____ lockers yesterday.
3. After Yvette finished the dress, she tried _____ on.
4. At dawn, Marco folded _____ sleeping bag and left the tent.
5. Mike, have _____ mailed that letter yet?
6. Dad and I finished breakfast; then _____ walked uptown to the museum.
7. David played _____ new albums for us.
8. Charlotte Brontë and _____ sisters were nineteenth-century English novelists.
9. The team members took the team mascot with _____ to the basketball tournament.
10. In Chester, England, the streets are noted for _____ medieval buildings.

Indefinite Pronouns as Antecedents

When the antecedent is an indefinite pronoun, determine whether it is singular or plural. A pronoun must agree in number with its antecedent. Therefore, use the singular possessive pronouns *his, her,* and *its* and the singular reflexive pronouns *himself, herself,* and *itself* with the singular indefinite pronouns.

> Each of the stores sets *its* own hours.
> Each of the women introduced *herself.*
> Neither of the men gave *himself* enough time for the trip.
> Someone forgot *his* ski cap.
> Someone forgot *her* ski cap.
> Someone forgot *his or her* ski cap.

The phrase *his or her* is sometimes used to show that the indefinite pronoun may refer to a male or a female.

The plural pronouns *their* and *themselves* are used with the plural indefinite pronouns.

> Both of the swimmers timed *their* sprints.
> Few of the passengers left *their* seats.
> All of the tourists found *themselves* lost without guidebooks.

For indefinite pronouns that may be either singular or plural, determine the number from the meaning of the sentence.

Singular	All of the water has chemicals in *it.*
Plural	All of the streams have chemicals in *them.*

Singular	Most of the fire burned *itself* out.
Plural	Most of those fires burn *themselves* out.

Do not be confused by a phrase that appears between an indefinite pronoun and a possessive pronoun.

Incorrect	One of the girls left *their* umbrella. (The possessive pronoun should agree with *one,* not with *girls.*)
Correct	One of the girls left *her* umbrella.

Exercises

A Write the indefinite pronoun that is the antecedent of each italicized pronoun. Then tell whether the indefinite pronoun is singular or plural.

1. Neither of the runners slowed *her* pace at the end.
2. All of the teams brought *their* mascots to the state meet.

3. Has either of your brothers earned *his* black belt?
4. All of the boats in the marina have *their* own name.
5. Everyone should take *his or her* camera on the trip.

B Write the indefinite pronoun in each sentence. Then write the correct pronoun of those given in parentheses.

1. Many of the early twentieth century photographers found (his or her, their) work treated merely as a fad.
2. Of these photographers, one, by the name of Alfred Stieglitz, eventually saw (his, their) work accepted as art.
3. Each of Stieglitz's photographs is remarkable for (its, their) technical innovations.
4. Few of the first modern artists, including Azanno and Picasso, had (his or her, their) work exhibited in the United States until Stieglitz opened a gallery in 1905.
5. Everyone, according to Stieglitz, should always do the best work (he or she, they) can.
6. Several of his most famous photographs used as (its, their) subject Georgia O'Keeffe, the artist who became his wife.
7. Much of O'Keeffe's work used the Southwest as (its, their) theme.
8. Most of Georgia O'Keeffe's paintings have an abstract quality about (it, them).
9. Both of these artists earned (themselves, himself or herself) lasting recognition.
10. Anyone who studies modern art should devote some of (his or her, their) time to the work of Stieglitz and O'Keeffe.

c *Proofreading* Rewrite the following paragraph, correcting all errors. Pay particular attention to agreement of pronouns and antecedents.

Everyone can enjoy their vacation in the Wisconsin Dells. This resort area has attractions for young and old. Most of the teens and children look forward to his or her water fun in the Dells: waterslides, bumper boats, and wave pools are favorites. Their are also amusement parks and minature golf. Each adult will probably spend some of their time in the many museums, and nature parks. The hole family can enjoy it's time fishing, boatting, or watching the many special water shows. There are so many attractions. In the Dells you'll need several days to enjoy it. While each of these activities are open during the summer, season many is closed in the winter.

Untitled monochrome, Barbara Ess.

Part 9
Vague Pronoun Reference

When you write or speak, be sure that each pronoun refers clearly to its antecedent. If a pronoun appears to have more than one antecedent or if there is no apparent antecedent, the pronoun reference is vague. Study the examples of vague pronoun reference in the following sentences. Can you think of other ways to correct the sentences?

Incorrect   We saw the cat's shadow, and then it ran away. (*It* obviously refers to the cat, not to the shadow. However, the pronoun has no antecedent in the sentence.)

Correct   We saw the shadow, and then the cat ran away.

Incorrect   Jean called Harriet when she arrived in town. (Does *she* refer to Jean or Harriet?)

Correct   When Harriet arrived in town, Jean called her.

Incorrect   In this article *it* tells about the new subway tunnel.
Correct   This article tells about the new subway tunnel.

Incorrect   Outside the concert hall, *they* put up barricades.
Correct   Outside the concert hall, the police put up barricades.

Incorrect   On most airlines, *you* need a carrier for *your* dog.
Correct   Most airlines require carriers for dogs.

Exercise

Rewrite each sentence to correct the vague pronoun reference.

1. When the manager spoke to the employee, he was nervous.
2. In this book it describes the valleys of North America.
3. My father is a doctor, and I hope to make it my career.
4. In Pennsylvania they have a dialect called Pennsylvania Dutch.
5. Dad talked to Mr. Greene about his car insurance.
6. When you wear a tie, you look better than with an open collar.
7. I removed the corn from the bag and put it in boiling water.
8. They have not built enough schools in the area.
9. When I tried to put the saddle on the horse, it ran away.
10. Put the flowerpots on those papers and then sort them by size.

Part 10
Problems with Pronouns

When you use pronouns, watch for these problems.

Pronouns in Compound Constructions

Pronouns in compound constructions often cause difficulty. In the sentences below, which form in parentheses is correct?

> *Laura* and (I, me) learned judo. (*Laura and I* is the compound subject. The nominative form, *I*, is correct.)
> She practices with Juan and (I, me). (*Juan and me* is the compound object of the preposition *with*. The objective form, *me*, is correct.

In a compound construction, you can tell which pronoun form is correct by thinking of each part separately. For instance, in the example above, think: *With Juan. With me.*

Exercise

Write the correct pronoun of the two given in parentheses.

1. My cousin and (she, her) own a bicycle shop.
2. Algebra has been a challenge for Lori and (I, me).
3. Leaders for the fund raising will probably be Hank and (she, her).
4. The supervisor gave Anna and (she, her) the keys.

5. Voters had to choose between the mayor and (he, him).
6. Last night the Lees invited David and (me, I) for dinner.
7. Are the new delegates Hiro and (he, him)?
8. The storm made the other campers and (we, us) nervous.
9. My dog always runs on the beach with (she, her) and (I, me).
10. Either you or (they, them) will win the first prize.

Compound Antecedents Using *Or* or *Nor*

When two or more singular antecedents are joined by *or* or *nor*, use a singular pronoun. The singular pronoun refers to each part of the antecedent individually.

Neither *Jeff* nor *Alonso* got *his* test results.

When two or more plural antecedents are joined by *or* or *nor*, use a plural pronoun to refer to them.

Neither the *dancers* nor the *actors* brought *their* costumes.

When one singular antecedent and one plural antecedent are joined by *or* or *nor*, use a plural pronoun to refer to them.

Neither *Alex* nor the other *guests* brought *their* swimsuits.

Pronouns in Comparisons

When a pronoun is part of a comparison using *than* or *as*, use the nominative form. If words are omitted from the comparison, supply the missing words. Then you will be able to choose the correct form.

Kevin is two years older than *I*. (Think: older than *I* am.)

Exercise

Write the pronoun that correctly completes each sentence.

1. Either Wayne or Bill has left (his, their) watch here.
2. My twin sister Jackie is two inches taller than (I, me).
3. No one in our class can type as quickly as (she, her).
4. Neither the players nor the fans can park (his, their) cars here.
5. As a musician, John is more talented than (he, him).
6. Did either Alison or Marie lend you (her, their) notes?
7. We were better qualified than (they, them).
8. Either Monica or Rita will bring (her, their) guitar.
9. Neither the students nor the teachers have (his, their) books.
10. You are a better photographer than (he, him).

Possessive Pronouns and Contractions

Do not confuse the possessive pronouns *its, your, their,* and *whose* with the contractions *it's, you're, they're,* and *who's.* In a contraction, the apostrophe shows where letters have been left out.

Contractions   *It's* time to leave. (*It's* = *It is*)
     You're playing shortstop, aren't you?
     (*You're* = *You are*)
     They're leaving tomorrow. (*They're* = *They are*)
     Who's coming to the lecture? (*Who's* = *Who is*)

The possessive form of a personal pronoun has no apostrophe.

Possessive   Put the kitten in *its* basket.
Pronouns   Here are *your* report covers.
     We gave them *their* tickets.
     Whose book is this?

To decide which word is correct in a sentence, substitute the words the contraction stands for. If the sentence sounds right, then the contraction is correct. If it doesn't, a possessive pronoun is required.

Exercise

Write the word that correctly completes each sentence.

1. The Beatles gave (they're, their) last public performance on August 29, 1966, in San Francisco.
2. (You're, Your) expecting a call, aren't you?
3. You didn't replace the telephone receiver on (it's, its) hook.
4. (It's, Its) a beautiful day.
5. Did (you're, your) ancestors come from Spain?
6. When (they're, their) finished, the electricians will leave.
7. (Who's, Whose) signature is on the hall pass?
8. When (it's, its) ten o'clock in Albuquerque, people are eating (they're, their) lunch in New York.
9. (Who's, Whose) the new manager of the store?
10. Will you meet (you're, your) friends at the bus stop?

Who *and* Whom

Many people have trouble knowing when to use *who* and *whom.* *Who* is in the nominative case. It is used as a subject.

     Who tuned the piano?   *Who* is there?

Whom is in the objective case. Although it may not always sound natural to you, it must be used when the sentence requires an object.

> *Whom* did the Steiners see? (*Whom* is the direct object of the verb *did see.* The Steiners did see *whom.*)
> About *whom* will you write your biography? (*Whom* is the object of the preposition *about.* You will write about *whom.*)

Be especially alert to sentences that begin with the interrogative pronoun and end with a preposition. Such sentences also use *whom.*

> *Whom* was the message directed to? (*Whom* is the object of the preposition *to.* The message was directed to *whom.*)
> *Whom* did the pianist play for? (*Whom* is the object of the preposition *for.* The pianist did play for *whom.*)

We *and* Us *with Nouns*

The pronouns *we* and *us* are often used with nouns: *we students, us students.* Use *we*—in the nominative case—if the noun is the subject of the sentence.

> We hikers hacked our way through the woods. (*Hikers* is the subject of the sentence.)

Use *us*—in the objective case—if the noun is an object.

> Nothing can stop *us* hikers. (*Hikers* is the direct object.)

To decide whether to use *we* or *us,* think of the sentence without the noun. For instance, in the first example above think: *We hacked our way.* In the second example, think: *Nothing can stop us.*

Them *and* Those

Them is a pronoun and is used only as an object. It is not used as a subject or as any other part of speech. *Those,* on the other hand, is a demonstrative pronoun that can also be used as an adjective (see Chapter 26 for discussion of adjectives). Do not use *them* in place of *those.*

Incorrect	*Them* are my favorite snacks. (*Them* is used incorrectly as the subject of the sentence.)
Correct	*Those* are my favorite snacks.
Incorrect	A search party found *them* explorers. (*Them* is used incorrectly as an adjective.)
Correct	A search party found *those* explorers.

Exercises

A On your paper, write the word that correctly completes each of the following sentences.

1. (Them, Those) exhibits of commercial and scientific progress are called World's Fairs.
2. (We, Us) three saw Seattle from the Space Needle at Century 21.
3. (Who, Whom) did the Centennial Exposition honor for inventing the telephone?
4. (Whom, Who) organized Expo '70 in Osaka, Japan?
5. (Those, Them) people were awed by London's Crystal Palace.
6. (Us, We) Americans have had World's Fairs in many major cities.
7. By (whom, who) was the Unisphere at the New York Fair designed?
8. (Those, Them) exhibits explain the process of nuclear fission.
9. Please take (us, we) students to eat at the Atomium.
10. The Columbian Exposition featured (them, those) new electric lights.

Space Needle, Seattle, Washington.

B Rewrite those of the following sentences that have errors in pronoun usage, correcting the errors. If a sentence has no error, write *Correct*.

1. To whom shall I address the thank-you note?
2. Will them shoes be sturdy enough?
3. Who did NASA choose as the first woman astronaut?
4. Them young men are England's most popular singers.
5. Julieta and us will make the float for the parade.
6. Whom received this year's Nobel Peace Prize?
7. The president thanked we committee members for our assistance.
8. To who are you talking?
9. Help Jim and her with those packages.
10. Yesterday us campers hiked up Mount Washington.

c *Write Now* Imagine that you are interviewing people at the scene of an automobile accident. Write a list of at least six questions such as those below. Replace the words in parentheses with *who* or *whom*, and add any other questions you think of.

> (Which driver) hit (which driver)?
> (What person) was injured in the accident?
> With (which company) does each driver have insurance?

Checkpoint *Parts 8, 9, and 10*

A Correct all agreement errors and vague pronoun references.

1. Everyone must bring their own sleeping bag on the bicycle tour.
2. When I opened the door it frightened me.
3. Jed took the shoes from the boxes and tossed them away.
4. Elise gave Dana her newest record album.
5. Neither of the horses ran their best in yesterday's race.
6. Remove the cover from the pan and stir it frequently.
7. They require a high school diploma to join the Marines.
8. One of the runners recorded their personal best time.
9. In the book it says that too much exposure to the sun is harmful.
10. Both of the divers carried his or her own first aid kit.

B *Proofreading* Rewrite the following paragraphs correcting all errors. Pay special attention to pronoun usage.

> Jim Thorpe whom was a Native American was named "Greatest Athlete of the Century" in 1950. Thorpe, who's athletic ability was amazing, was riding a horse by the age of three. In high school he was the star football player on their team.
>
> Us sports fans know of thorpe's performance at the 1912 Olympics. He won two gold medals but was forced to give it back. They discovered that Thorpe had played Baseball for money. According to Olympic rules, this fact made Thorpe a professional. He was disqualified by the same people whom had awarded the metals.
>
> In 1982 the Olympic Committee restored Thorpes medals. His name joins the others who's talent placed them on the list of 1912 champions.

Linking
Grammar & Writing

You are part of a drama group that is putting on a play. Your job is to write stage directions. Use a scene from an actual play or make up a scene. In your directions, tell the actors what to wear, where to stand, when and how to move, what gestures and tone of voice to use, and so on. You should also describe the scenery.

Prewriting and Drafting Make lists of details about the setting, each actor, and the interaction of all the actors with one another in the setting. Decide how to organize the directions so that they are clear and helpful. Use pronouns to simplify your references to people and objects and to make the directions easy to follow. Make sure your pronoun references are clear.

Revising and Proofreading Consider these questions as you revise your work.

> Are your directions accurate and precise?
> Have you included enough details for the actors to understand each set of directions?
> Are your pronoun references clear?
> Do all pronouns agree with their antecedents?

Additional Writing Topic Imagine that you are a millionaire writing your will. There are friends, relatives, and a favorite pet that you would like to remember. Tell what you intend to give to each individual. Explain why each is receiving a reward. Use as many types of pronouns as possible. Be ready to tell what type of pronoun each one is.

He'er *and* Thon

I n 1912 Ella Flagg Young, the superintendent of schools in Chicago, made this surprising statement to a group of principals:

> "A principal should conduct his'er school so that each pupil is engaged in something that is profitable to him'er and where the pupil is required to use knowledge in school in accomplishing his'er task. . . ."

Young was bothered by a common problem with English—no singular pronouns exist that can be used to refer to a mixed group of males and females. When a pronoun is needed to refer to both males and females, writers must either use "his or her", or randomly choose either the male or female pronoun ("A principal should conduct his school . . .").

"The problem has bothered me frequently and the solution of it occurred to me on my way to this meeting," Young said. "Most pronouns of the feminine gender end in 'er, so all you have to do to make the common pronoun is to take the masculine form and add 'er."

Young created the following words: *his'er*, which joins *his* and *her; him'er*, for *him* and *her*; and *he'er*, for *he* and *she*. The principals at the meeting enthusiastically agreed to implement Young's suggestions, but she had little success when she tried to gain national support.

Other people have also tried to fill the gap. In 1884 Charles Crozat Converse, a lawyer and hymn writer, made up *thon*. "By cutting off the last two letters of the English word *that* and the last letter of the word *one*, and uniting their remaining letters in their original sequence in these two words, I produced that word now proposed for the needed pronoun," Converse said. He gave the following example: "If Mr. or Mrs. A. comes to the courthouse on Monday, I will meet thon."

Over the years many other blends have been proposed, including *hizer, shis, hom, shim, heesh, sheehy*, and *shey*. Author June Arnold replaced all third-person pronouns with *na* and *nan* in her 1973 novel *The Cook and the Carpenter*, and other writers have penned their own personal solutions.

Although Converse's and Young's coinages have been included in some dictionaries, they have not become widely accepted. A writer still has no easy solution to his'er problem with pronouns.

Chapter 24
Application and Review

A Identifying Types of Pronouns On your paper, write each pronoun and identify it as *Personal, Intensive, Reflexive, Demonstrative, Indefinite, Interrogative,* or *Relative*.

1. Many of the streets were crowded with traffic.
2. Which of the movies is still playing?
3. While Dave was chopping onions, he cut himself with the knife.
4. This looks best with your blue suit.
5. We painted and decorated the room ourselves.
6. The record that Deanna bought was warped.
7. The pilot asked the passengers to return to their seats.
8. Only one of the answers was correct.
9. The girl who won the award was my neighbor.
10. What do you want for lunch?

B Application in Literature List and label each italicized pronoun below as *Nominative, Objective,* or *Possessive*.

> (1) "No," said the woman. (2) *She* stood up from *her* chair, and now that she put her hand on the little girl's shoulder, Felicia was taken into the sphere of love and intimacy again. (3) "Shall *we* go into the other room, and *you* will do your pirouette for *me*?" the woman said, and *they* went from the kitchen and down the strip of carpet on which the clear light fell. (4) In the front room, they paused, hand in hand . . . and the woman looked about *her*, at the books, the low tables with the magazines and ashtrays on *them*, . . . and then she said quickly, "What time does *your* mother put *you* to bed?"
>
> From *Winter Night* by Kay Boyle

C Correcting Pronoun Errors Rewrite the sentences correcting all pronoun errors.

1. Each of the skaters lost their balance on the ice.
2. All of the children brought his or her own lunches on the trip.

3. At the library they have many old books on display.
4. Neither of the girls could forgive themselves for the mistake.
5. Nancy called Ellen, but she didn't tell her about the exam.
6. Several of the books were missing its covers.
7. One of the men left their newspaper.
8. In the last chapter it implied that the maid was the murderer.
9. Everyone should read the report themselves.
10. Some of these comedians wrote his own material.

D Using Pronouns Correctly Write the correct pronoun from those given in parentheses.

1. Mrs. Roberts told us and (they, them) to work at home.
2. The winner of the photography contest was (she, her).
3. Either you or (they, them) will be chosen for the committee.
4. On the table were letters for Tina and (he, him).
5. They play tennis better than (we, us).
6. Either Roger or Joel lost (his, their) notebook.
7. Neither they nor (we, us) remembered our cameras.
8. I recognized you and (they, them) immediately.
9. Arturo is better equipped for the trip than (he, him).
10. Just between you and (I, me), Lydia is likely to win.
11. (Her, She) and I were encouraged by our drama teacher to audition for the play.
12. My sister acts on impulse more often than (I, me).
13. Neither the elms nor the oaks have shed (its, their) leaves yet.
14. Candice and (she, her) worked until nine o'clock.
15. Neither the dealer nor the manufacturer has given (his or her, their) consent to the proposal.

E Solving Pronoun Problems Write the correct pronoun of the two given in parentheses.

1. Delia was the girl (who's, whose) performance earned a medal.
2. (We, Us) girls have been shopping downtown since noon.
3. (They're, Their) route took them along the ocean.
4. Chicago is known for (its, it's) variety of people.
5. No one knows (who, whom) planned the surprise.
6. Have you tried one of (them, those) delicious egg rolls?
7. A few of (we, us) boys decided to fish at the lake.
8. Did the messenger tell you to (who, whom) the package was sent?
9. (You're, Your) the only one of our friends who can't come.
10. Please make a list of (them, those) suggestions for me.

25
Using Verbs

Poised between going on and back, pulled
Both ways taut like a tightrope-walker,
Fingertips pointing the opposites,
Now bouncing tiptoe like a dropped ball
Or a kid skipping rope, come on, come on,
Running a scattering of steps sidewise,
How he teeters, skitters, tingles, teases,
Taunts them, hovers like an ecstatic bird,
He's only flirting, crowd him, crowd him,
Delicate, delicate, delicate, delicate—now!

"The Base Stealer" by Robert Francis

Colorful, carefully chosen verbs such as *teeters, tingles,* and *hovers* bring life and action to the poem above. They can do the same for your writing and speaking. In this chapter, you will learn how to recognize the different kinds of verbs and how to avoid problems with verb usage.

Part 1

What Is a Verb?

A verb is a word that expresses action, condition, or state of being.

The two main kinds of verbs are action verbs and linking verbs. Helping, or auxiliary, verbs are sometimes used with them.

Action Verbs

An action verb tells that something is happening, has happened, or will happen. It may describe physical or mental action.

> The storm *raged* for several hours. (physical action)
> I *wrote* the question on the board. (physical action)
> I *thought* about the answer. (mental action)

Linking Verbs

A linking verb, sometimes called a state-of-being verb, links the subject with another word or other words in the predicate.

> Claude Monet *was* a painter. (The linking verb *was* links the subject *Claude Monet* to *painter*.)

Common Linking Verbs

be (am, are, is, was,	look	smell	seem
were, been, being)	appear	taste	sound
become	feel	grow	remain

Some verbs can be used as either linking verbs or action verbs.

Linking Verb	Action Verb
The stew *smelled* delicious.	The chef *smelled* the stew.
The bread *tasted* fresh.	Hannah *tasted* the fresh bread.
Jamie *felt* tired.	Rudy *felt* the soft velvet.

To decide whether a word is an action verb or a linking verb, see how it is used in the sentence. Does it express or describe an action, or does it link the subject with a word in the predicate?

Exercises

A On your paper, write the verb in each of the following sentences. Tell whether the verb is an action verb or a linking verb.

1. At times another phone seems a necessity in our house.
2. Our science teacher programmed the computer.
3. Nuanda was a Celtic god.
4. The dog appears restless tonight.
5. Pedestrians struggled with their umbrellas.
6. The clerk seemed anxious for a sale.
7. Judge Suchanek studied Braille at a special school.
8. A traffic helicopter hovered overhead during the rush hour.
9. Margaret Chase Smith first became a congresswoman in 1940.
10. The flight attendant apologized twice for the long delay.

B Application in Literature On your paper, write the italicized verbs from the excerpt below. Tell whether each verb is an action verb or a linking verb. Notice the variety of verbs the author used.

(1) We *were* very poor, and I wore striped overalls and homemade shirts of flannel. (2) In the winter I *wore* a mackinaw coat and high-top brown work shoes that had funny round hard toes. (3) But in the summer I *ran* around in my dusty, and as Mom would say, "rusty" feet. (4) We also *ate* the same things for dinner as for supper. (5) We *had* pinto beans and fried potatoes with gravy and flat bread. (6) Breakfast *was* dried milk and bread which *tasted* much better with sugar. (7) I didn't have toys, so whenever Edmund *bought* Linda Beth some new ones, I usually *played* with the old ones when he was not at home. (8) When he was at home, I often just *went* away by myself and *was* quiet. (9) But if he was asleep, I sat at the kitchen table and *talked* with Mom while she *cooked* or sewed. (10) I *liked* to do that more than most other things.

From "A Short Return" by Durango Mendoza

C *Write Now* Imagine you and your friends are eating supper by a campfire after a long day's hike. Write a paragraph describing the scene. Use a variety of linking verbs and vivid action verbs.

Helping Verbs

A main verb—either action or linking—sometimes has one or more helping verbs, also called **auxiliary verbs.** In these examples, the helping verbs are in italic type. The main verbs are in boldface.

> That tree *will* **grow** fuller every year.
> Their dog *has been* **barking** all night.

The most common helping verbs are forms of *be, have,* and *do.* Several other verbs can also be used as helping verbs.

Common Helping Verbs

Be	is, am, are, was, were, be, been, being
Have	has, have, had
Do	does, do, did

can	will	shall	may	must
could	would	should	might	

The main verb and one or more helping verbs make up a **verb phrase.**

Helping Verb(s) +	Main Verb	= Verb Phrase
am	laughing	am laughing
had	thought	had thought
did	consider	did consider
will be	applauding	will be applauding
must have been	watching	must have been watching

Sometimes the helping verb and the main verb are separated. The words that come between them are not part of the verb phrase. In the following examples, the verb phrase is italicized. Remember that the contraction *n't* is not part of the verb.

> The team *wasn't paying* attention.
> *Did* the press secretary *speak*?

The helping verbs *be, have,* and *do* can also be used as main verbs.

Main Verb	Helping Verb
Samantha *was* busy.	Samantha *was preparing* lunch.
Jill *has* a project.	Jill *has finished* her sculpture.
We *did* the puzzle.	*Did* you *complete* the puzzle?

Exercises

A On your paper, make two columns labeled *Helping Verb* and *Main Verb*. Find the verb phrase in each of the following sentences and write each part in the proper column.

1. The boys were playing Hacky Sack.
2. Cyclists must wear their helmets in the race.
3. I can do most of the problems without help.
4. Someone must have left the lobby door open.
5. Has anyone ever climbed that mountain?
6. A hawk was hovering over the edge of the canyon.
7. A smoke alarm would have alerted the sleeping tenants to the fire.
8. You shouldn't waste your money on junk food.
9. You will probably enjoy this article about whales.
10. Our geraniums have always thrived in that window.

B The helping verbs have been omitted from the following sentences. Write each sentence, adding one or more helping verbs that fit the meaning of the sentence. Underline each verb phrase.

      Example   I _____ already read that book.
                    I *have* already *read* that book.

1. Commercial pilots _____ pass a rigorous physical exam.
2. The concert hall _____ _____ closed indefinitely for repairs to its structure.
3. Michael _____ _____ running every day to strengthen his legs for hockey.
4. _____ Jenny catch in Thursday's game?
5. The temperature _____ _____ reached 98 degrees.
6. _____ the plows cleared the expressway?
7. Someone _____ _____ done the dishes.
8. _____ you expecting a long-distance call tonight?
9. The final game of the season _____ _____ played at Shea Stadium.
10. The lifeguards _____ _____ warned us sooner about the dangerous undertow.

c *Write Now* Choose a movie or television show you have seen recently and write a short review of it. Point out what was good about your choice and what could have been improved. Pay special attention to using helping verbs such as *could*, *should*, *would*, and *might* to strengthen the main verbs in your sentences.

Part 2
Transitive and Intransitive Verbs

In many sentences, an action verb expresses an idea by itself. In other sentences, a direct object is needed to complete the action of the verb. The **direct object,** as you have learned, tells who or what receives the action of the verb.

Verbs that have direct objects are called transitive verbs.

> They *extended* the ladder to the second floor. (The direct object *ladder* completes the action of the verb *extended*.)
> He carefully *stored* the rope. (The direct object *rope* completes the action of the verb *stored*.)

Verbs that do not have direct objects are called intransitive verbs.

> We *met* in the park.
> Everyone *rested* for a while.
> Hal *slept* in the chair.

In the examples above, the words after the verb do not complete the action of the verb.

Some action verbs are always transitive, some always intransitive. Others may be transitive in one sentence and intransitive in another. Compare the sentences below. The direct objects are in boldface type.

Transitive Verb	Intransitive Verb
We *played* the **tape** over and over.	We *played* all afternoon.
The winners *celebrated* their **victory.**	Their fans *celebrated* too.
Irma *practiced* her **speech.**	Irma *practiced* this morning.

Linking verbs are always intransitive because they never take direct objects.

> Those flowers *are* lilies. (*Lilies* is a predicate nominative that renames the subject. It is not a direct object and does not complete the action of the verb.)
> They *seem* healthy. (*Healthy* is a predicate adjective that describes the subject. It is not a direct object.)

Exercises

A On your paper, write the verb in each of the following sentences. Identify each verb as transitive or intransitive. If a verb is transitive, write its direct object.

1. The herd of elephants suddenly charged the hyena.
2. Neon lights flashed rhythmically in the dark.
3. Mrs. LaPorte videotaped the final performance of our play.
4. During the ice storm, LaGuardia Airport canceled all flights.
5. Christopher often swims fifty laps before school.
6. Boll weevils destroyed the entire cotton crop.
7. An eerie cloud rose from the warm, moist bog.
8. The pasta tasted delicious.
9. Through the tangle of branches, we saw luminous eyes.
10. Round and round spun the skaters.

B Follow the directions for Exercise A.

1. One of the greatest jazz musicians was Louis Armstrong.
2. Armstrong grew up in New Orleans.
3. He played the bugle as a teen-ager.
4. In 1922, Armstrong moved to Chicago.
5. Soon orchestras featured him as a trumpet soloist.
6. He also sang in a unique style.
7. In the following decades he led many ensembles.
8. Armstrong developed a classic jazz style.
9. He traveled frequently to foreign countries as the ''goodwill ambassador'' of American jazz.
10. His recordings influenced musicians throughout the world.

Part 3

Active and Passive Voice

The **voice** of a verb tells whether the subject performs the action of the verb or receives the action. There are two verb voices in English: active and passive. Only action verbs have voice. Linking verbs do not.

A verb is in the active voice when the subject of a sentence performs the action.

Shakespeare *wrote* that play in the sixteenth century.

In the sentence above, the subject *Shakespeare* performs the action of the verb *wrote*. Therefore, *wrote* is said to be in the active voice.

A verb is in the passive voice when the subject of a sentence receives the action.

That play *was written* by Shakespeare in the sixteenth century.

In this sentence, the subject *play* receives the action of the verb *was written*. When the subject is the receiver or the result of the action, the verb is said to be in the passive voice.

The passive voice is made by using some form of the helping verb *be* with the past participle. The receiver of the action comes before the verb; it is the subject of the sentence.

Active Voice	Passive Voice
Maria *tutors* the boys.	The boys *are tutored* by Maria.
Lee *finished* the job.	The job *was finished* by Lee.
Ann *hammered* the nail.	The nail *was hammered* by Ann.

To change a particular sentence from active voice to passive, the verb in the original sentence must be transitive (have a direct object). Only verbs that have direct objects can be changed from active to passive. In the sentences above, notice that the direct objects become subjects and subjects become objects of prepositions.

It is not always necessary that the performer of the action be named in a sentence with a verb in the passive voice. In the example below, the person who wrote the play is not mentioned.

The play was written in the sixteenth century.

Be careful not to confuse the terms *action* and *active*. They are not the same. Most action verbs can be in either the active or passive voice.

Using Voice in Writing

In general, use the active voice when you write. It is stronger, more lively, and more direct. The active voice uses fewer words than the passive and highlights the person who is performing the action. Compare these two sentences.

Active   Carla fixed the lamp.
Passive   The lamp was fixed by Carla.

Occasionally, however, the passive voice is appropriate. Use the passive when you want to highlight the receiver of an action or when the performer of the action is unknown or unimportant.

The entire block was demolished by the tornado.
Our town hall was built at the turn of the century.

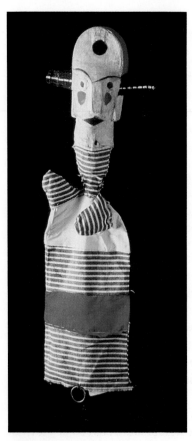

Hand puppet, Paul Klee.

Exercise

Write the verbs in the following sentences. Tell whether each verb is in the active voice or the passive voice.

1. Puppets have always enjoyed widespread popularity in Europe.
2. In Germany and Austria, puppet theater is known as Kasperltheater.
3. The most prominent puppet character in Germany was called Kasperle.
4. The character developed in the seventeenth century.
5. Kasperle was brought to Germany by traveling puppeteers.
6. He was featured in marionette productions of *Faust*.
7. Later, he was established as a hand puppet.
8. Like the English Punch, he adapts jokes to local audiences.

Checkpoint *Parts 1, 2, and 3*

A On your paper, write the verb or verb phrase in each of the following sentences. Tell whether it is an action or a linking verb. Underline helping verbs.

1. Marlee Matlin, a deaf actress, won the Oscar for best actress in *Children of a Lesser God.*
2. The runners looked exhausted after the marathon.
3. The Dallas Mavericks will compete in the playoffs.
4. John Singer Sargent was a great portrait painter.
5. The chile might taste spicy to you.
6. The name of the beginning typing class has been changed to Keyboarding I.
7. Everyone in the family helped with sanding and painting Aunt Mary's house.
8. Kim remained calm during the auditions.
9. To most people, the unusual kiwi fruit tastes something like strawberries.
10. A new sport, arena football, is becoming popular in some areas of the country.

B On your paper, write the verbs or verb phrases in the following sentences. Tell whether each is active or passive. If the verb is in the active voice, tell whether it is transitive or intransitive.

1. The Republican Party was formed in 1854.
2. In the thirteenth century, Kublai Khan ruled China.
3. Typewriters have been replaced by computers in many newspaper offices.
4. The judge will decide the verdict in the controversial case tomorrow.
5. As a young man, Ronald Reagan announced baseball games on the radio.
6. The author James Baldwin was raised in Harlem.
7. The drama class meets three days a week.
8. Meryl Streep performed in *Out of Africa.*
9. The Japanese call their country Nippon, not Japan.
10. Beaded necklaces, bracelets, and earrings were sold at the craft fair.

Part 4

Principal Parts of Regular Verbs

Every verb has four basic forms, called principal parts. The principal parts are the present, the present participle, the past, and the past participle.

Present	Present Participle	Past	Past Participle
learn	(is) learning	learned	(have) learned
open	(is) opening	opened	(have) opened

All verbs add -*ing* to the present form to make the present participle. The present participle is used as a main verb with a form of the helping verb *be*.

No one *is listening* to my explanation.

Verbs that add -*ed* or -*d* to the present to form the past and the past participle are **regular verbs.** The past participle is used with a form of the helping verb *have*. Verbs that form the past and past participle in different ways are called **irregular verbs.** You will learn more about these verbs in Part 5.

Some regular verbs change their spelling when -*ing* or -*ed* is added to the present.

Present	Present Participle	Past	Past Participle
try	(is) trying	tried	(have) tried
slip	(is) slipping	slipped	(have) slipped
notice	(is) noticing	noticed	(have) noticed
knit	(is) knitting	knitted	(have) knitted

Exercise

On your paper, make four columns labeled *Present, Present Participle, Past,* and *Past Participle.* List the principal parts of the following regular verbs in the proper columns.

1. trust
2. want
3. move
4. trot
5. marry
6. follow
7. plan
8. trip
9. cry
10. toss
11. happen
12. copy
13. close
14. act
15. belong

Word Torture

Irregular verbs often cause problems. In this column, Nathaniel Benchley considers one of these problems. Could you come up with a satisfactory answer to Mr. McIntyre's question?

In his column a short time ago Mr. O. O. McIntyre asked who could tell, without looking it up, the present tense of the verb of which "wrought" is the past participle. That was, let us say, of a Thursday. Today my last fingernail went.

At first I thought that it was so easy that I passed it by. But, somewhere in the back of that shaggy-maned head of mine, a mischievous little voice said, "All right—what is it?"

"What is what?" I asked, stalling.

"You know very well what the question was. What is the present tense of the verb from which the word 'wrought' comes?"

I started out with a rush. "I *wright*," I fairly screamed. Then, a little lower, "I wrught." Then, very low, "I wrouft." Then silence.

From that day until now I have been muttering to myself, "I wright—I wraft—I wronjst. You wruft—he wragst—we wrinjsen."

I'll be darned if I'll look it up, and it looks now as if I'll be incarcerated before I get it.

People hear me murmuring and ask me what I am saying.

"I wrujhst," is all that I can say in reply.

"I know," they say, "but what were you *saying* just now?"

"I wringst."

This gets me nowhere.

While I am working on it, however, and just before the boys come to get me to take me to the laughing academy, I will ask Mr. McIntyre if he can help me out on something that has almost the same possibilities for brain seepage. And no fair looking *this* up, either.

What is a man who lives in Flanders and speaks Flemish? A Flem? A Flan? A Floom? (This is a lot easier than "wrought," but it may take attention away from me while I am writhing on the floor.) And, when you think you have got it the easy way, remember there is another name for him, too, one that rhymes with "balloon." I finally looked that one up.

At present I'm working on "wrought."

Nathaniel Benchley

Part 5

Principal Parts of Irregular Verbs

Verbs that do not add *-ed* or *-d* to the present to form the past and the past participle are **irregular verbs.**

Present	Present Participle	Past	Past Participle
cost	(is) costing	cost	(have) cost
lose	(is) losing	lost	(have) lost
wear	(is) wearing	wore	(have) worn
sing	(is) singing	sang	(have) sung
take	(is) taking	took	(have) taken

Because the principal parts of irregular verbs are formed in a variety of ways, you must either memorize these parts or refer to a dictionary. If the dictionary does not list principal parts for a verb, then the verb is regular. For irregular verbs, the dictionary will give two forms if both the past and past participle are the same, as in *catch, caught*. It will give three forms if all principal parts are different, as in *ring, rang, rung*.

Irregular verbs can be broken down into the five main groups that follow.

Group 1 The irregular verbs in this group have the same form for the present, the past, and the past participle. *Hit, let, put,* and *set* are also in this group.

Present	Present Participle	Past	Past Participle
burst	(is) bursting	burst	(have) burst
cost	(is) costing	cost	(have) cost
cut	(is) cutting	cut	(have) cut

Group 2 The irregular verbs in this group have the same form for the past and the past participle.

Present	Present Participle	Past	Past Participle
bring	(is) bringing	brought	(have) brought
lead	(is) leading	led	(have) led
lose	(is) losing	lost	(have) lost
sit	(is) sitting	sat	(have) sat
teach	(is) teaching	taught	(have) taught

Here are some sentences with verbs from Group 2.

> I always *lose* my best tapes. (present)
> The path *led* into the field. (past)
> I have *sat* here for almost an hour. (past participle)

Exercise

Write the past or past participle of each verb in parentheses.

1. Someone had already (lead) the horses into the arena.
2. These skates (cost) twice as much as my old ones.
3. Mr. Lofton has (teach) for over twenty years.
4. A pipe in the basement had (burst) while we were in Tennessee on vacation.
5. I (cut) myself with the can opener.
6. Somehow I had (lose) track of the time.
7. Duncan has (sit) on the bench all season.
8. Tom (lead) by only a few votes in the student election.
9. I had (hit) the target on the first try.
10. The convention (bring) welcome business to the merchants in the town.
11. Once gasoline (cost) less than fifty cents a gallon.
12. Suddenly the cats (burst) into the dining room.
13. Dad (teach) me how to put up wallpaper.
14. The coach has (lead) the team to victory in the playoffs for three years.
15. I (lose) my favorite pair of socks.

Group 3 The irregular verbs in this group form the past participle by adding *-n* or *-en* to the past form.

Present	Present Participle	Past	Past Participle
break	(is) breaking	broke	(have) broken
choose	(is) choosing	chose	(have) chosen
freeze	(is) freezing	froze	(have) frozen
speak	(is) speaking	spoke	(have) spoken
steal	(is) stealing	stole	(have) stolen
wear	(is) wearing	wore	(have) worn

Here are some sentences with the verbs from Group 3.

> I *wear* those heavy socks with these boots. (present)
> He *chose* a red bicycle this time. (past)
> She *has spoken* at assembly before. (past participle)

Exercises

A Write the past or past participle of each verb in parentheses.

1. For centuries people have (choose) bowling or similar sports.
2. Ancient Egyptians (steal) away from work to play such a game.
3. Early sources have (speak) of games called *kegles* or *ninepins*.
4. Washington Irving (speak) of ninepins in his stories.
5. Many Americans (choose) bowling as their favorite sport.
6. Modern bowlers often have (choose) to compete in leagues.
7. League bowlers used their own shoes and (wear) special shirts.
8. No one has (break) Earl Anthony's record of 1981 to 1983.
9. Aleta Sill had (wear) the women's international crown in 1985.
10. Earl Anthony has (steal) honors for lifetime earnings.

B Most of the following sentences have errors in verb forms. On your paper, rewrite those sentences, correcting the errors. If a sentence has no error, write *Correct.*

1. The bickering lawyers have finally choosed a jury.
2. My hands and feet have froze in the icy wind.
3. Carol has broke mom's antique vase.
4. The sign reads, ''Spanish is spoke here.''
5. A pickpocket must have stole my wallet during the rally.
6. Have you spoke to your parents about the class trip?
7. Kay accidentally teared up her bus pass.
8. Pablo spoke clearly into the microphone.
9. Matt's new shoes have already wore down at the heels.
10. Michael has broke his new pair of prescription sunglasses.

Group 4 The irregular verbs in this group change a vowel to form the past and the past participle. The vowel changes from *i* in the present form to *a* in the past form and to *u* in the past participle.

Present	Present Participle	Past	Past Participle
begin	(is) beginning	began	(have) begun
drink	(is) drinking	drank	(have) drunk
ring	(is) ringing	rang	(have) rung
shrink	(is) shrinking	shrank	(have) shrunk
sing	(is) singing	sang	(have) sung
sink	(is) sinking	sank	(have) sunk
swim	(is) swimming	swam	(have) swum

Here are some sentences with verbs from Group 4.

We *sing* in that choir. (present)
Someone *drank* the last of the juice. (past)
The boats in the harbor *have sunk*. (past participle)

Exercises

A On your paper, write the past or the past participle form of each verb given in parentheses in the following sentences.

1. Emilia (begin) baby-sitting last year and now has many clients.
2. Someone must have (drink) all the skim milk.
3. We (ring) the bell several times, but no one answered.
4. I wonder how many times the Beach Boys have (sing) "California Girls."
5. Those curtains (shrink) in the wash.
6. A Japanese freighter (sink) during the hurricane.
7. Have you (swim) out to the raft yet or is the water too cold?
8. It seemed as if we (drink) a gallon of cold water that day.
9. Has the warning bell (ring) yet?
10. They (swim) their laps in record time.

B Most of the following sentences have errors in verb forms. On your paper, rewrite those sentences, correcting the errors. If a sentence has no error, write *Correct*.

1. Have you swam in the ocean before?
2. After the victory, the bells rung wildly.
3. Most of the candidates have already began their campaigns.
4. My new sweater shrank to half its size.
5. The cast sung the opera in English, not Italian.

6. A piranha swum alone in the huge tank.
7. The *Monitor* sunk to the ocean floor off Cape Hatteras.
8. The telephone has rung twice in the last five minutes.
9. We drunk grape juice with our tuna sandwiches.
10. My grandparents and I begun the jigsaw puzzle last night.

Group 5 The irregular verbs in this group form the past participle from the present form, often by adding *-n* or *-en*. In the following list, notice the similarity between the present and past participle forms.

Present	Present Participle	Past	Past Participle
come	(is) coming	came	(have) come
do	(is) doing	did	(have) done
drive	(is) driving	drove	(have) driven
eat	(is) eating	ate	(have) eaten
fall	(is) falling	fell	(have) fallen
give	(is) giving	gave	(have) given
go	(is) going	went	(have) gone
grow	(is) growing	grew	(have) grown
know	(is) knowing	knew	(have) known
ride	(is) riding	rode	(have) ridden
rise	(is) rising	rose	(have) risen
run	(is) running	ran	(have) run
see	(is) seeing	saw	(have) seen
take	(is) taking	took	(have) taken
throw	(is) throwing	threw	(have) thrown
write	(is) writing	wrote	(have) written

Here are some sentences with verbs from Group 5.

Every summer they *grow* corn in their garden. (present)
Yesterday they *went* to a museum and to a play. (past)
I *have ridden* my last horse. (past participle)

Exercises

A Write the past or past participle of each verb in parentheses.

1. The sun has (rise) before six every day this week.
2. Have you (do) your English assignment?
3. We have (give) our old car to my cousin.
4. Mr. Torres has (run) in marathons before.
5. Cary (throw) the ball to the shortstop for an easy out.
6. Have you ever (eat) raw fish?

7. My, how you have (grow)!
8. He (know) the answer to every question in the trivia quiz.
9. We have (take) pictures of everyone except the principal.
10. Have you ever (ride) a bike on a long trip?

B Most of the following sentences have errors in verb forms. Rewrite the sentences correctly. If there is no error, write *Correct*.

1. The dictator had finally fell from power.
2. The job come along just in time.
3. A gymnast done back flips across the mat.
4. I have taken a poll of the entire school.
5. Dennis seen a strange object in the night sky.
6. Has everyone given up on the project?
7. Anna has went to City Hall with her grandparents.
8. The candidate run her campaign honestly.
9. S. E. Hinton has also wrote *The Outsiders* and *Rumble Fish*.
10. Dad has never drove a car with a stick shift.

c *Proofreading* Proofread the following paragraph. Then rewrite it correctly. Pay attention to the use of irregular verbs.

Have you ever heared about the Grate Molasses Flood of 1919 It happened on a brite january day in Boston most people had just ate lunch when a giant molasses tank bursted. Fourteen thousand tons of thick, sticky syrup come pouring out in a brown fifteen-foot wave. The wave was not "as slow as molasses in January." It moved at 35 miles per hour and destroyed everything in it's path. Twenty one people losed there lives; one hundred and fifty were injured.

Checkpoint *Parts 4 and 5*

On your paper, write the correct past or past participle form of each verb given in parentheses.

1. Have you (try) sushi?
2. The federal deficit has (hit) an all-time high.
3. Last winter the pipes (burst) because of the cold.
4. The centerfielder (catch) the ball on the warning track.
5. The old straw hat slowly (sink) to the bottom of the pond.
6. The Thirty Years War (begin) in 1618.
7. The lake has (freeze) solid.
8. Norman Mailer has (write) both fiction and nonfiction.
9. Anita (see) a shooting star last night.
10. U.S. corporations have (lend) millions of dollars to Brazil.
11. It has (take) the construction crew six months to finish the road.
12. It looks as if that T-shirt (shrink) when you washed it.
13. Ellen has (wear) braces for two years.
14. By mistake, I (throw) away the instructions for the machine.
15. Ethan (grow) four inches during the summer, and now all his pants are too short.
16. Beth has (go) back to the gym to look for her sweater.
17. My mother has never (drive) on the freeway.
18. None of the hikers had (bring) any insect repellent.
19. I have (know) about that shortcut for a long time.
20. I finally (choose) the black kitten with the white paws.

Part 6
Verb Tense

By changing the form of a verb, you can indicate whether something is happening now, has happened in the past, or will happen in the future. These changes in form are called **tenses.**

English verbs have three simple tenses (present, past, and future) and three perfect tenses (present perfect, past perfect, and future perfect). The tenses are formed by using the principal parts and the helping verbs *have, has, had, will,* and *shall.*

Simple Tenses

Use the **present tense** to show an action that occurs in the present. To form the present tense, use the first principal part (the present form) or add -s or -es to the present form.

> I *know* the answer.
> Cathy *knows* the answer.

Use the **past tense** to show an action that was completed in the past. To form the past tense, add -ed or -d to the present form or—if the verb is irregular—use the past form listed as one of the principal parts.

> I *asked* for information.
> They *knew* the solution.

Use the **future tense** to show an action that will occur in the future. To form the future tense, use the helping verb *will* or *shall* with the present form.

> Cristo *will help* us.
> I *shall* not *go*.

Perfect Tenses

Use the **present perfect tense** to show an action that was completed either in the recent past or at an indefinite time in the past. To form the present perfect tense, use the helping verb *has* or *have* with the past participle.

> She *has* gone home.
> They *have* finally arrived.

Use the **past perfect tense** to show an action that preceded another past action. To form the past perfect tense, use the helping verb *had* with the past participle.

> They *had left* before we came.
> The plane *had* just *taken* off when we arrived at the terminal.

Use the **future perfect tense** to show an action that will occur before another future action or time. You can form the future perfect tense by using the helping verbs *will have* or *shall have* with the past participle.

> By Sunday, the team *will have played* twelve schools.
> By noon tomorrow, I *shall have completed* my four final exams.

Verb Conjugation

A **verb conjugation** is a list of all the forms of a verb. The following conjugation shows the six tenses of the regular verb *watch*.

Simple Tenses

	Singular	Plural
Present Tense		
First Person	I watch	we watch
Second Person	you watch	you watch
Third Person	he, she, it watches	they watch
Past Tense		
First Person	I watched	we watched
Second Person	you watched	you watched
Third Person	he, she, it watched	they watched
Future Tense		
First Person	I will (shall) watch	we will (shall) watch
Second Person	you will watch	you will watch
Third Person	he, she, it will watch	they will watch

Perfect Tenses

Present Perfect Tense		
First Person	I have watched	we have watched
Second Person	you have watched	you have watched
Third Person	he, she, it has watched	they have watched
Past Perfect Tense		
First Person	I had watched	we had watched
Second Person	you had watched	you had watched
Third Person	he, she, it had watched	they had watched
Future Perfect Tense		
First Person	I will (shall) have watched	we will (shall) have watched
Second Person	you will have watched	you will have watched
Third Person	he, she, it will have watched	they will have watched

Swans, M. C. Escher, 1956.

Exercises

A Write the verb in each sentence and identify its tense.

1. In the Escher print, observers have seen different images.
2. The hikers had already walked ten miles that day.
3. Each guard will take a lie detector test.
4. By midnight they will have begun the final countdown.
5. The other team had already accepted the penalty.
6. Tami won a trophy in her very first relay race.
7. Someone has already set the table for dinner.
8. The custodian raises the flag every morning.
9. The bronco burst out of the chute like a bolt of lightning.
10. Dad sometimes misses the turnpike exit.

B Write each verb in parentheses in the tense given after the sentence.

1. Police (search) the abandoned building. Past
2. Number 7 (kick) most of the field goals. Present
3. They (live) in Hawaii for three years. Present Perfect
4. They (bring) the volleyball net. Future
5. By noon the hikers (reach) the meadows. Future Perfect
6. The burglars (break) through a hole in the roof. Past Perfect
7. We (sing) that song at every concert. Present Perfect
8. Last night I (see) a falling star. Past
9. The teachers (come) to the dress rehearsal. Future
10. Inez (call) ahead for reservations. Past Perfect

c *Write Now* Write a paragraph about your plans for your next holiday. Then rewrite the paragraph in the past tense.

Part 7

Progressive Verb Forms

Each of the simple and perfect tenses has a **progressive form** that shows continuing action. The progressive form is made by using a tense of the helping verb *be* with the present participle.

Present Progressive	We are reading.
Past Progressive	We were reading.
Future Progressive	We will be reading.
Present Perfect Progressive	We have been reading.
Past Perfect Progressive	We had been reading.
Future Perfect Progressive	We will have been reading.

Exercise

On your paper, write the progressive verb forms used in the following sentences. Identify the tense of each progressive form.

1. At sunrise the fog was already rolling in.
2. Will we be going on the same bus as you and Jeremy?
3. The snow is piling up in drifts along the major roads.
4. By noon, we will have been fishing for six hours.
5. Shh! Michael is telling us about his haunted garage.
6. At four, Mozart was playing the piano for the nobility.
7. The band has been practicing for weeks.
8. The clouds were drifting slowly across the clear blue sky.
9. The team is definitely marching in the parade.
10. Before your call, I had been taking a nap.

Part 8
Avoiding Shifts in Tense

When two actions occur at the same time, use the same tense for both actions.

> Galileo *was* a professor at Pisa University, and there he *conducted* his experiments. (Both actions occurred in the past.)
> Tara *is mowing* the lawn, and we *are weeding* the flower beds. (Both actions occur in the continuing present.)

Avoid shifts in tense between sentences or within paragraphs.

Incorrect   The settlers *built* homes when they *arrive*.
Correct   The settlers *built* homes when they *arrived*.

Exercises

A Write the verb needed to avoid a shift in tense.

1. The queen boarded the ship and (knights, knighted) the explorer.
2. The bus (rattles, rattled) into town and stopped at the inn.
3. The batter (hit, hits) a home run and ties the score.
4. Sandra directs the ensemble and (plays, played) piano in it.
5. When the alarm sounds, it (is, was) time to get up.
6. Patrick Henry stood and (delivers, delivered) his speech.
7. Luis (speaks, spoke) Spanish and understands French.
8. When the sun sets, the temperature (drops, dropped).
9. Sondheim composed the music, and Lapine (writes, wrote) the lyrics.
10. Please mail the letters when you (leave, left).

B Rewrite the paragraph below. Correct any improper shifts in tense.

(1) One hundred years ago, the ghost towns of the West flourished and thrived. (2) In Nevada alone, almost 1,300 towns prosper and then die. (3) Most are founded when gold, silver, and copper were discovered. (4) People came seeking to strike it rich. (5) Many are young, earnest, and honest. (6) Others, however, were outlaws who prey on the innocent miners. (7) The towns lasted as long as the mines continued to be productive. (8) When the mines closed, the towns become deserted. (9) Today, some ghost towns are reviving and had been attracting tourists.

Checkpoint *Parts 6, 7, and 8*

A Write each verb or verb phrase and identify its tense.

1. Juan Ponce de León explored the Florida coast in 1513.
2. The workers will complete the foundation next week.
3. Los Angeles has become larger than Chicago.
4. Mozart had composed a symphony by the time he was eight.
5. Japan's economy has been growing rapidly.
6. In 1984 Walter Mondale was running for President.
7. Who will be directing the orchestra?
8. A fireworks display follows the game.
9. The governor is leading in the polls.
10. In 1992, Uganda will have been independent for thirty years.

B On your paper, write the verb or verb phrase that avoids a shift in tense. After each verb, write what tense it is.

1. A lunar eclipse (occurred, occurs) when the earth blocks the sun's light from the moon.
2. I (am going, was going) down the escalator, when I suddenly saw my sister going up the other side.
3. The pillow (had been torn, is being torn) open and hundreds of tiny feathers covered the rug.
4. I will do the dishes if you (had cleared, will clear) the table.
5. The corn plants have withered because we (have had, will have) no rain.

Part 9
Using the Right Verb

The following pairs of verbs are sometimes confused.

Bring and Take

Present	Present Participle	Past	Past Participle
bring	(is) bringing	brought	(have) brought
take	(is) taking	took	(have) taken

Bring refers to movement toward the speaker. *Take* refers to movement away from the speaker.

> *Bring* that hammer to me, please.
> When you go home, *take* your tools with you.

Learn and Teach

Present	Present Participle	Past	Past Participle
learn	(is) learning	learned	(have) learned
teach	(is) teaching	taught	(have) taught

Learn means "to gain knowledge or skill." *Teach* means "to help someone learn."

> We *are learning* the metric system.
> Ms. Rivera *taught* us the metric system.

Let and Leave

Present	Present Participle	Past	Past Participle
let	(is) letting	let	(have) let
leave	(is) leaving	left	(have) left

Let means "to allow or to permit." *Leave* means "to go away from."

> The landlord *will let* us stay until the end of the month.
> They *have left* without their books.

Exercises

A Many of the following sentences have errors in the use of *bring, take, learn, teach, let,* and *leave.* Rewrite those sentences, correcting the error. If a sentence has no error, write *Correct.*

1. The *Mayflower* took some of our ancestors here.
2. Professor Higgins learned Eliza Doolittle to speak correctly.
3. If you go to Alaska in the summer, bring mosquito repellent.
4. Did the director leave anyone attend the dress rehearsal?
5. Many slaves left the South on the Underground Railway.
6. Take a notebook when you come to class.
7. The students learned to speak Spanish.
8. Do you think Ms. Bonilla will leave the class out early?
9. Who learned you to play the guitar?
10. Bring your dad's shirts to the cleaners on your way home.

B *Write Now* Imagine that you have been asked to teach a class about one of your favorite hobbies. Write a notice announcing the class. Include information about what will be taught and what materials students will need. Use the correct forms of *learn, teach, bring, take,* and other verbs you think would be appropriate.

Lie and Lay

Present	Present Participle	Past	Past Participle
lie	(is) lying	lay	(have) lain
lay	(is) laying	laid	(have) laid

Lie is an intransitive verb that means "to rest in a flat position" or "to be in a certain place." It does not take a direct object. *Lay* is a transitive verb that means "to place." It takes a direct object. Don't misuse *lay* as the character in the cartoon does.

Lie on the sofa until you feel better.
The papers *lay* in a heap on the floor.
Lay your jackets there. (*Jackets* is the direct object.)
The President *laid* a wreath on the memorial to Anwar el-Sadat.
  (*Wreath* is the direct object.)

Rise and Raise

Present	Present Participle	Past	Past Participle
rise	(is) rising	rose	(have) risen
raise	(is) raising	raised	(have) raised

Rise is an intransitive verb that means "to go upward." It does not take a direct object. *Raise* is a transitive verb that means "to lift" or "to make something go up." It takes a direct object.

> Steam *rises* and disappears.
> The tax *has risen* to 8 percent.

Raise the curtain slowly. (*Curtain* is the direct object.)
The City Council *has raised* the tax to 8 percent. (*Tax* is the direct object.)

Sit and Set

Present	Present Participle	Past	Past Participle
sit	(is) sitting	sat	(have) sat
set	(is) setting	set	(have) set

Sit is an intransitive verb that means "to occupy a seat." It does not take a direct object. *Set* is a transitive verb that means "to place." It usually takes a direct object.

> She usually *sits* next to me in class.
> Finally, all the passengers *had sat* down.
> *Set* those boxes on the table. (*Boxes* is the direct object.)
> Someone *has set* one cup on top of the other. (*Cup* is the direct object.)

Exercises

A Write the verb from the parentheses that correctly completes each of the following sentences.

1. Litter (lay, lie) all over the sidewalk.
2. Stranded passengers (sat, set) all night in the roadside shelter.
3. The sun has finally (risen, raised).
4. The prospector carefully (laid, lay) the map on the table.
5. Someone must have (sat, set) on my lunch.
6. The colorful hot air balloons (raised, rose) gently over the peaceful valley.
7. Someone's laundry is (laying, lying) all over the floor.
8. The construction crew has (laid, lain) the foundation for the new gym.
9. On a hot day, the chess players usually (set, sit) on a bench in the shade.
10. The factory has (raised, risen) its monthly quota.

B The following sentences have errors in the use of verbs. Rewrite those sentences, correcting the errors.

1. The cat was laying on a rug near the stove.
2. The curtain has raised and the play has begun.
3. On a long trip, I usually set in the seat behind the bus driver.
4. My parents and I layed a new floor in the kitchen.
5. The price of milk has raised this week.
6. The drawbridge was raising, and traffic came to a halt.
7. We sat the pudding in a pan of water to cool.
8. My old sneakers have laid in the bottom of my closet all year.
9. Lie the baby in the crib for a nap.
10. Yesterday we set in the waiting room for two hours.

c *Proofreading* Correct all errors in the passage below.

William Garwood of Evanston, Illinois, invented one of america's favorite treets—the ice-cream sundae. In the 1880's an Evanston law was passed that prohibited the sail of soda-water drinks on Sunday. Garwoods temper rised at this news. He was certain to loose some of his Sunday ice-cream soda business. I'll learn them! he shouted. He quickley sat a soda glass on the counter and filled it with ice-cream and syrup with the soda leaved out. Garwood called his creation a ''Sunday'' later the spelling was changed to ''sundae''.

Checkpoint Part 9

Write the verbs that complete each sentence.

1. The clerk will (learn, teach) you how to fill out the form.
2. A cold mist (raised, rose) from the swamp.
3. Don't (lie, lay) out in the sun too long, or you'll get burned.
4. (Raise, Rise) the shade and (let, leave) the sunshine in.
5. (Lay, Lie) down your tools and come (sit, set) with us.
6. (Let, Leave) those sandwiches alone; they're for the picnic!
7. Kristen asked George to (bring, take) her some iced tea.
8. If I (learn, teach) you how to swim, will you help me study?
9. Amy (lay, laid) on her bed and watched the sun (raise, rise).
10. The nurse (sat, set) the child on her mother's lap.

Linking
Grammar & Writing

Imagine that you are a character in a silent movie. You are dangling from a flagpole that projects from the twentieth story of a building. How did you get into this situation? How are you feeling now? How will you get down safely? Write a humorous narrative about your predicament.

Prewriting and Drafting As you prepare to write, arrange your ideas in three separate lists: (1) details about how you wound up on the flagpole; (2) details about your feelings while you are dangling in the air; and (3) details about how you will get down from the flagpole. Study your lists and then organize the details in the order in which they occur.

Revising and Proofreading Read your draft carefully. Are the ideas in chronological order? Have you used precise verbs? Do your verbs change form as you switch from the past tense to present and future tenses? Do they create a vivid image for the reader?

Additional Writing Topic Think about a humorous situation like the one pictured. Write a narrative about that humorous situation in the past tense. Then write it again in the present tense. Decide which version is funnier.

Chapter 25
Application and Review

A Identifying Types of Verbs Write the verb in each sentence and tell whether it is *Action* or *Linking*. Then tell whether each action verb is *Transitive* or *Intransitive*.

1. Light travels at the speed of 186,282 miles per second.
2. *The Hound of the Baskervilles* may be the best of the Sherlock Holmes stories.
3. The reporter searched frantically for a phone booth.
4. Maria adjusted the squeaky brakes on her bike.
5. The evil little troll gloated at the hero's dismay.
6. The term *doozy* originated with the Duesenberg auto.
7. Before the storm, the sky appeared yellow-green.
8. Michelangelo painted the ceiling of the Sistine Chapel.
9. No one could have been more surprised than I.
10. The timekeeper reset the clock for the next race.

B Using Principal Parts and Tenses of Verbs Draw four columns on your paper. Label them *Present, Present Participle, Past,* and *Past Participle*. Write the principal parts of the following verbs in the proper columns. Then choose three of the verbs and write them in each of the six main tenses.

1. sing	4. play	7. allow	10. worship	13. ride
2. jog	5. act	8. describe	11. start	14. live
3. camp	6. cheat	9. write	12. dress	15. catch

C Using Verb Tense and Voice For each sentence write the verb or verb phrase. Identify the tense of the verb (one of the six main tenses or one of the six progressive forms). Rewrite the sentence, changing the verb to the tense or voice indicated in parentheses.

1. After an introduction, Leontyne Price sang several famous arias. (Future)
2. The injured gull had climbed over the rocks and driftwood along the shore. (Present Perfect Progressive)
3. The monsoon rains have arrived in full force. (Future)
4. The pilot of the small plane peered anxiously into the dense fog. (Present Progressive)

5. Poisonous gases from a chemical factory have killed hundreds of people in India. (Passive)
6. Aaron and Eva study modern dance. (Past Perfect Progressive)
7. Mahavira founded Jainism, an Indian religion. (Passive)
8. I will never read a scarier book. (Past Perfect)
9. Tony has studied Russian. (Future Progressive)
10. Aren't you forgetting the mustard? (Present Perfect)

D Using Verbs Correctly The paragraph below is weak because some verbs are in the passive voice and some sentences contain improper shifts in tense. Replace the italicized passive verbs with active ones, and make any other necessary corrections.

(1) During the Middle Ages (A.D. 400–1500), many folk tales *were composed* by European peasants. (2) Some stories told about real people, and some are fantasies. (3) No one wrote down these stories; instead, traveling mistrels and common people tell them to one another. (4) In the mid-1800's, many of these folk tales *were* still *being told*. (5) To the delight of children everywhere, most of the stories, including ''Cinderella'' and the legends of Robin Hood and Friar Tuck, *have been collected* and *published*.

E Choosing the Correct Verb Write the correct verb in each of the following sentences.

1. Two young girls have (swam, swum) the English Channel.
2. Medical care has never (costed, cost) more.
3. The raft (brang, brought) us safely to the island.
4. The Celtics (lost, losed) by one point.
5. Someone has (tore, torn) down all of the notices about the benefit auction.
6. Has anyone (spoke, spoken) to the career counselor?
7. Agatha Christie has (wrote, written) eighty-seven novels.
8. The hikers (drank, drunk) thirstily from the cool brook.
9. Eliza (saw, seen) the filming of a movie during her trip.
10. Can you (learn, teach) me how to windsurf this summer?
11. (Let, Leave) me take the controls now.
12. Please (bring, take) me the Bunsen burner.
13. The potter (set, sat) his vases in the kiln.
14. Meredith (lay, laid) awake all night with a fever.
15. Large quantities of spilled oil have (raised, risen) to the surface of the ocean.

Cumulative Review

Chapters 23, 24, and 25

A Identifying Nouns, Pronouns, and Verbs On your paper, write the word in each sentence that is of the type that is indicated in parentheses.

1. Several of the candidates announced their platforms. (Indefinite Pronoun)
2. Members of the football team traveled to London last winter. (Proper Noun)
3. The soup Marla made tastes wonderful. (Linking Verb)
4. The judge is seeking the truth. (Abstract Noun)
5. Although the plane left late, it will arrive on time. (Future Tense Verb)
6. That was the best album she recorded. (Demonstrative Pronoun)
7. She left her keys at home on the kitchen counter. (Possessive Pronoun)
8. Mr. Lewis is an accountant, but he plays drums in a jazz band on weekends. (Transitive Verb)
9. What is your favorite movie of last year? (Interrogative Pronoun)
10. As they entered the stadium, the players waved to the crowd. (Collective Noun)
11. I am studying for a test, but I will finish before dinner. (Progressive Verb)
12. Is this your first painting? (Demonstrative Pronoun)
13. Yolanda's mother is one of nine children. (Plural Noun)
14. Jerry writes the songs, but they are performed by others. (Active Voice Verb)
15. This belongs to one of you. (Personal Pronoun)

B Using Nouns, Pronouns, and Verbs On your paper, write the word that correctly completes each of the following sentences.

1. Each of the participating teams brought (its, their) own equipment to the game.
2. The (gooses, geese) have begun to fly south.
3. The winners of the dance contest were Tina and (he, him).
4. The great and powerful wizard has (spoke, spoken).
5. Workers are (laying, lying) pipe for the new sewer.

6. The (women's, womens') organization meets every Tuesday.
7. Did (your, you're) ancestors come from Poland?
8. The forty-niners traveled to California and (search, searched) for gold.
9. (Who, Whom) did Harry Truman defeat for the Presidency of the U.S. in 1948?
10. Idaho license plates say "Famous (Potatoes, Potatos)."
11. In 1941 a German submarine (sank, sunk) the *Reuben James*.
12. The (roofs, rooves) of the houses were covered with sod.
13. Did the waitress give the check to (they, them)?
14. The dignitaries (sat, set) on the reviewing stand.
15. Many (salmon, salmons) are caught in Lake Michigan.
16. Charles Lindbergh received a (heroes', hero's) welcome after his solo flight across the Atlantic.
17. At the end of the day, Claudette divided the profits from the garage sale between (she and I, her and me).
18. After comparing our answers to the algebra quiz, Cindy and (I, me) wondered (who, whose) were correct.
19. How many miles per day have you (swam, swum) in preparation for the regional swim meet?
20. She (lended, lent) me her sweater when she noticed my teeth chattering and my nose turning blue.

C Proofreading for Errors in Usage and Mechanics The following paragraphs contain errors in the use of concepts you have studied in Chapters 23–25 as well as errors in punctuation and spelling. On your paper, rewrite the paragraphs and correct the errors.

One of the worlds greatest mystery writers was Agatha Christie. She was an English women born in 1890. Her father died when she was young, she was rised by her mother. Her mother did not send Christie to school she hired a tutor who learned Christie at home.

The heros of many of Christies' novels are Hercule Poirot and Miss Jane Marple. Each uses a different style to solve their mystery.

By the time she died in 1976, Christie had wrote many novels, short stories, and plays. Including *Witness for the Prosecution* and *Murder on the Orient Express*. Critics praise her books and reader's loved them. Her and Shakespeare are the two English writers who's works are translated most often into other languages.

26
Using Modifiers

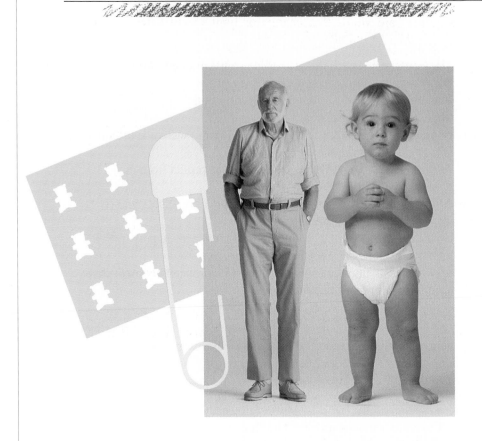

I magine how difficult it would be to describe the picture above without using any adjectives or adverbs.

Adjectives and adverbs are modifiers—words that describe or clarify nouns, pronouns, and verbs. They add precision and color to your writing. In this chapter you will learn to recognize and use adjectives and adverbs to create striking verbal images.

Part 1
Adjectives

Modifiers are words that change or limit the meaning of other words. One kind of modifier is an adjective.

An adjective is a word that modifies a noun or a pronoun.

An adjective can change or limit the meaning of a noun or a pronoun by answering one of these questions:

What Kind?	*purple* paint, *shiny* floor, *hilarious* story, *windy* day
Which One or Ones?	*that* girl, *next* time, *those* cars, *last* exit
How Many? or *How Much?*	*three* months, *several* boxes, *less* pain, *more* snow

More than one adjective may modify the same noun or pronoun.

> *Two black* cars pulled into the driveway. (*How many* cars? *Two* cars. *What kind* of cars? *Black* cars.)

Adjectives are usually placed immediately before the noun or pronoun they modify. Occasionally, however, a writer may decide to add variety to a sentence by putting adjectives in other positions.

> The runners, *confident* and *eager*, started the race.
>
> *Confident* and *eager*, the runners started the race.

Punctuation Note Adjectives that appear in these positions are set off from the rest of the sentence by commas or a comma.

Articles

The most common adjectives are the **articles** *a, an,* and *the. The* is the **definite article.** It points out a specific person, place, thing, or idea.

> Keep *the* ball in play. (a particular ball)

A and *an* are **indefinite articles.** They do not point out a specific person, place, thing, or idea.

> Did you bring *a* ball? (not a specific ball)
> He made *an* error on the play. (not a specific error)

Use the indefinite article *a* before a word beginning with a consonant sound: *a* ball, *a* game. Use the indefinite article *an* before a word beginning with a vowel sound: *an* error, *an* honor.

Proper Adjectives

One special kind of adjective is the **proper adjective.**

A proper adjective is formed from a proper noun. Proper adjectives are always capitalized.

Proper Noun	Proper Adjective
Japan	*Japanese* car
Mexico	*Mexican* culture
Britain	*British* accent
China	*Chinese* checkers
Bach	*Bach* aria

Predicate Adjectives

Another kind of adjective is the **predicate adjective.** Unlike most adjectives, predicate adjectives follow the words they modify.

A predicate adjective comes after a linking verb and modifies the subject of the sentence.

Nothing seemed *clear* anymore.
(*Clear* modifies the subject, *nothing.*)

Her hair is *auburn.*
(*Auburn* modifies the subject, *hair.*)

Clear and *auburn* are predicate adjectives. They follow the linking verbs *seemed* and *is,* and each modifies the subject of the sentence.

A predicate adjective can be compound, as can modifiers in any other part of the sentence. In the following examples, two predicate adjectives follow each linking verb.

The car was *rusty* and *dilapidated.*

Angelo looked *tired* but *happy.*

For a review of linking verbs, see Chapter 25, pages 517–518.

Sentence Diagraming For information on diagraming sentences with adjectives, see page 758.

Exercises

A On your paper, write the adjectives in the following sentences. After each adjective, write the word it modifies. Do not include articles.

> *Example* The young clerk seems very efficient.
> young, clerk
> efficient, clerk

1. The kookaburra is an aggressive Australian bird with a loud, boisterous cry.
2. The new stereo sounds loud and full.
3. Ellie spilled blue paint on the white rug.
4. The massive stalagmites in the cave felt cool and moist.
5. Several foreign leaders had a private meeting in Geneva.
6. Many hikers were hot and hungry after the long march home.
7. A voice, harsh and tinny, sounded over the microphone.
8. We drank several glasses of water with the salty fish and chips.
9. A newborn giraffe has long, gangly legs.
10. The large ears of the African elephant distinguish it from the Indian elephant.

B Application in Literature Write the italicized adjectives in the following paragraph. After each adjective, write the word it modifies. Which adjectives help create the lonely mood in this passage?

> (1) The snow began quietly *this* time, like an afterthought to the *gray Sunday* night. (2) The moon almost broke through once, but toward daylight a *little* wind came up and started *white* curls, *thin* and *lonesome*, running over the *old* drifts left from the New Year storm. (3) Gradually the snow thickened, until around eight-thirty the *two* ruts of the winding trails were covered and undisturbed except down in the Lone Tree district where an old *yellow* bus crawled heavily along, feeling out the ruts between the *choppy sand* hills.
>
> From *Winter Thunder* by Mari Sandoz

c *Write Now* Imagine that you are browsing through items at a rummage sale when you discover a unique and very valuable item. In one or two paragraphs, describe your "find." Use specific adjectives that will help your reader picture the item.

Part 2

Nouns and Pronouns as Adjectives

Both nouns and pronouns can sometimes function as adjectives in sentences.

Nouns as Adjectives

Possessive nouns function as adjectives in sentences. Nouns show possession by adding -'s or -s' to the singular form: *girl's, girls'*.

> My *sister's* goal is to become an auto mechanic.
> The coach collected the *players'* uniforms.

Other nouns function as adjectives without a change in form.

> *Fruit* trees flourish in the *California* sun.

Pronouns as Adjectives

The following kinds of pronouns can function as adjectives.

Possessive	my, your, his, her, its, our, their
Indefinite	some, any, many, few, several, one
Demonstrative	this, that, these, those
Interrogative	what, which, whose

> The candidates filed *their* petitions.
> I received only *one* package.
> *That* evidence should be disregarded.
> *Which* book belongs to you?

Exercise

Write the nouns and pronouns used as adjectives in the following sentences. Write the word that each adjective modifies.

1. Which flower arrangement do you prefer?
2. Some cats won't eat cat food.
3. This room seems suitable for our club meeting.
4. Their brother is a professional soccer player.
5. Has your dog graduated from obedience school?
6. What kind of air transportation services that city?

7. Mother's friend painted a mural for the city's centennial.
8. Because of a sudden April shower, the street parade was canceled.
9. Few players agreed with the commentator's account of the game.
10. On Monday's hike we saw some woodpeckers and an oriole nest.

Checkpoint *Parts 1 and 2*

On your paper, write the adjectives in the following sentences. Tell which word each adjective modifies. Include nouns and pronouns used as adjectives but do not include articles.

1. The life story of our country is told in the faces of its people.
2. American Indians were the earliest inhabitants of the land.
3. Other American citizens originally came from many different African nations.
4. Some came from distant Asiatic countries.
5. In the nineteenth century, European immigrants flocked here.
6. Their reasons for coming were various.
7. Many people migrated because of food shortages at home.
8. Some came in search of political freedom.
9. They settled in areas with familiar climates.
10. Numerous Scandinavian immigrants settled in Wisconsin and Minnesota.
11. People from southern Italy chose sunny California.
12. Chinese and Japanese people found homes on the west coast.

13. Some newcomers were serious and thrifty.
14. Others were jovial and energetic.
15. In recent years newcomers have arrived from our neighbor countries.
16. America is like a colorful tile mosaic.
17. Each different cultural group contributes a new beauty.
18. New peoples introduce new and delicious foods.
19. They share lively music and expressive dances.
20. This variety gives our country its unique character.

Part 3
Adverbs

An adverb is another kind of modifier.

An adverb is a word that modifies a verb, an adjective, or another adverb.

An adverb answers one of the following questions about the word it modifies:

How?	works *accurately*, studies *hard*, plays *well*, *quietly* walked
When?	opens *soon*, visited *yesterday*, exercises *daily*, was paved *recently*
Where?	stood *there*, sat *here*, sleeps *upstairs*, ran *everywhere*
To What Extent?	*almost* missed, *never* stops, *completely* finished

The adverbs *not* and *never* tell to what extent and when.

We did *not* plant tulips this year. (*Not* modifies *did plant* and tells to what extent.)
Those trees will *never* bloom. (*Never* modifies *will bloom* and tells when.)

Forming Adverbs

Many adverbs are formed by adding *-ly* to an adjective. Notice that the addition of *-ly* may cause a change in spelling.

weak + -ly = weakly	formal + -ly = formally
possible + -ly = possibly	happy + -ly = happily

Some adverbs, however, do not end in *-ly*:

Commonly Used Adverbs				
afterwards	fast	low	often	there
almost	forth	more	seldom	today
already	hard	near	slow	tomorrow
also	here	never	soon	too
back	instead	next	still	well
even	late	not	straight	yesterday
far	long	now	then	yet

Adverbs and the Words They Modify

Adverbs frequently modify verbs. An adverb may appear before or after the verb it modifies.

> We *proudly* displayed our posters.
> The line moved *quickly*.
> *Where* are you going? (*Where* modifies the verb *are going*.)

Adverbs sometimes modify adjectives and adverbs. Such adverbs usually tell to what extent something is true.

> My cousin is *partially* blind. (*Partially* tells to what extent. It is an adverb modifying the predicate adjective *blind*.)
> I did *very* well on the test. (*Very* tells to what extent. It is an adverb modifying the adverb *well*.)

Here is a list of adverbs that often modify adjectives or adverbs. These words are sometimes called **intensifiers.**

> too   quite   rather   most   more   extremely
> just   nearly   so   really   truly   somewhat

Some words can be either adverbs or adjectives. *Late* is one of these words. Some others are *still, north,* and *straight.*

> The doctor arrived too *late*. (adverb)

> Marta took the *late* train. (adjective)

Sentence Diagraming For information on diagraming sentences with adverbs, see page 759.

Exercises

A Find the words used as adverbs in these sentences. Write the word each modifies, as well as that word's part of speech.

1. The skydiver very skillfully controlled the fall.
2. Have we left too early for the concert?
3. Many of the spectators have suddenly become rather restless.
4. The bus stopped quite unexpectedly.
5. Cautiously the search party advanced through the tangled vines.
6. Some folk legends about health are surprisingly accurate.
7. At sundown a chill wind arose, and we soon started homeward.
8. When will the game be scheduled more definitely?
9. Patrick has never played the flute so beautifully.
10. Next, the guide described the rock specimens on display.

B Write the adverbs in this paragraph and the word each modifies. Also tell that word's part of speech.

(1) At dawn the wind fell away, and the ship cruised slowly in the deceptively calm sea. (2) The crew had just finished its morning chores. (3) Suddenly the rain came down in torrents. (4) It soon filled the empty water drums. (5) Then the clouds lifted and the sun broke through. (6) Steam rose from the soaked decks and gradually drifted away. (7) By dark, however, the boat was pitching wildly. (8) Finally, the captain headed the ship south, and it eventually sailed beyond the squall.

Diamond Shoal, Winslow Homer, 1905.

Part 4
Using the Correct Modifier

It is sometimes difficult to decide whether to use an adjective or an adverb. The explanations and examples in Part 4 will help you choose the correct kind of modifier.

Adjective or Adverb?

In the following sentence, which modifier correctly completes the sentence—the adjective *sudden* or the adverb *suddenly*?

The blast happened _____.

To decide, ask yourself the following questions:

1. What kind of word does the modifier describe?

If the modified word is an action verb, an adjective, or an adverb, use the adverb *suddenly*. If the modified word is a noun or a pronoun, use the adjective *sudden*.

2. What does the modifier tell about the word it describes?

If the modifier tells *how, when, where,* or *to what extent,* use the adverb *suddenly*. If the modifier tells *which one, what kind,* or *how many,* use the adjective *sudden*.

If you apply both tests to the sentence "The blast happened _____ ," you will be able to determine that the adverb *suddenly* is the correct choice to modify the verb *happened*.

Adverb or Predicate Adjective?

You have learned that a predicate adjective follows a linking verb and modifies the subject. Besides forms of *be,* other linking verbs are *become, seem, appear, look, sound, feel, taste, smell,* and *grow*.

> This melon smells sweet. (*Sweet* modifies *melon.*)
> The parking lot looks full. (*Full* modifies *lot.*)
> The thunder grew louder. (*Louder* modifies *thunder.*)

In the sentences above, the words *smells, looks,* and *grew* are linking verbs. Therefore, the words that follow them are adjectives. However, these same verbs can also be action verbs, as can *sound, appear, feel,* and *taste*. When these verbs are action verbs, they are followed by adverbs.

Here are sentences using the same words as linking verbs and as action verbs.

Linking Verbs with Adjectives	Action Verbs with Adverbs
The water *looked* clear.	Dave *looked* quickly.
The team *appeared* eager.	Clouds *appeared* suddenly.
This music *sounds* peaceful.	The alarm *sounds* often.
Tanya *felt* bad.	Al carefully *felt* the fabric.

If you have trouble deciding whether a sentence needs an adverb or a predicate adjective, ask yourself the following questions:

1. Can you substitute *is* or *was* for the verb? If so, use an adjective.
2. Does the modifier tell *how, when, where,* or *to what extent*? If so, use an adverb.

Exercise

Write the correct modifier of the two in parentheses. Then tell whether the modifier is an adjective or an adverb.

> *Example*   Julio spoke (patient, patiently) to the children.
> patiently, adverb

1. Singing the marching songs, the hikers walked (quick, quickly) along the path.
2. An (extreme, extremely) upset man burst into the office.
3. In a bright light, stained glass looks (brilliant, brilliantly).
4. The teller sounded the alarm (immediate, immediately).
5. My older sister looks particularly (nice, nicely) in that bright shade of red.
6. A figure in a cape appeared (sudden, suddenly) out of the darkness.
7. It was (terrible, terribly) hot during our drive.
8. After losing the game in overtime, they felt (bad, badly).
9. The two animals battled (fierce, fiercely) for the food.
10. The new grandparents looked (proud, proudly) at their red-haired grandchild.
11. The mayor's new plan worked (beautiful, beautifully).
12. The maple leaves are (colorful, colorfully) in October.
13. Herb spoke (quiet, quietly) as he answered the police officer's questions.
14. These scissors aren't (sharp, sharply) enough to cut cloth.
15. Alfred juggled (amazing, amazingly) in the talent show.

Checkpoint *Parts 3 and 4*

A On your paper, write the adverbs in the following sentences. Tell which word each adverb modifies. Then rewrite each sentence using different adverbs.

> *Example*   I nearly missed the bus yesterday.
> nearly, missed; yesterday, missed
> I almost missed the bus today.

1. The hikers were slightly injured by the tremor.
2. Yesterday the weather was terribly humid.
3. Luckily the letter was delivered quite early.
4. The designer hastily sketched an unbelievably wild outfit.
5. The children filed into the hospital somewhat apprehensively.
6. Taste this and tell me if it is still too peppery.
7. The pioneers willingly followed the trail.
8. Mr. Kelly is usually quite understanding, and he always grades fairly.
9. Penny slowly packed her bags and tearfully said goodbye.
10. I thought the movie was very funny, but some critics found it extremely offensive.

B On your paper, write the correct modifier of the two given in parentheses. Tell whether the modifier is an adjective or an adverb.

1. The rolling black storm clouds approached (sudden, suddenly), and everyone ran for cover.
2. The acoustics in the tiny theater were (excellent, excellently).
3. In the corner the children whispered (quiet, quietly).
4. The orange juice tastes too (sweet, sweetly).
5. Nora missed rehearsal because of a (terrible, terribly) cold.
6. The stunt pilot appeared (confident, confidently) as he climbed into the cockpit.
7. The pocketknife didn't feel (sharp, sharply) enough to cut the twine on the package.
8. From her lifeguard's perch, Nicole looked (watchful, watchfully) at the rolling surf.
9. Would you feel (angry, angrily) if I lost your picture?
10. Tovah's parents were (awful, awfully) proud of the medal she won in the Special Olympics.

Pony express used for mail delivery, 1860–61.

Part 5
Using Modifiers in Comparisons

Adjectives and adverbs can be used to compare two or more things. You might describe air mail as being *faster* than the pony express. Or you might describe one member of a team as having played *better* than another. Modifiers use special forms to make comparisons.

Degrees of Comparison

There are three degrees of comparison: the positive degree, the comparative degree, and the superlative degree.

A modifier in the **positive degree** describes one person, place, thing, idea, or action. The positive degree is the basic form of the modifier—the one you will find in the dictionary.

A modifier in the **comparative degree** compares two persons, places, things, ideas, or actions.

A modifier in the **superlative degree** compares three or more persons, places, things, ideas, or actions.

Positive	Seikan is a *long* railroad tunnel in Japan.
Comparative	Seikan is *longer* than Burlington's Cascade Tunnel.
Superlative	Seikan is the *longest* railroad tunnel in the world.

Regular Comparisons

Most modifiers change in regular ways to show comparison.

1. A one-syllable modifier forms the comparative and superlative by adding *-er* and *-est*.

Positive	Comparative	Superlative
big	bigger	biggest
wide	wider	widest
kind	kinder	kindest

2. Most two-syllable modifiers form the comparative and superlative by adding *-er* and *-est*: *clumsy, clumsier, clumsiest*. Sometimes, a two-syllable modifier sounds awkward when *-er* and *-est* are added. If so, use *more* and *most* to form the comparative and superlative.

Positive	Comparative	Superlative
hopeful	more hopeful	most hopeful
cautious	more cautious	most cautious

   Two-syllable adverbs that end in *-ly* form comparisons by using *more* and *most*: *quickly, more quickly, most quickly*.

3. Modifiers of three or more syllables use *more* and *most* to form the comparative and superlative.

Positive	Comparative	Superlative
beautiful	more beautiful	most beautiful
anxiously	more anxiously	most anxiously

Irregular Comparisons

Some modifiers form the comparative and superlative in ways that are different from the regular comparisons. Study the following list.

Positive	Comparative	Superlative
good	better	best
well	better	best
bad	worse	worst
much	more	most
many	more	most
far	farther	farthest
little	less or lesser	least

To make a negative comparison, use *less* and *least* before the positive form of the modifier: *helpful, less helpful, least helpful*.

Ask Mr. Language Person

Once again it is time for "Ask Mr. Language Person," the popular feature wherein we discuss the kinds of common grammatical concerns with which common people tend to encounter problems with.

We'll begin with the first question:

Q What is the purpose of the apostrophe?

A The apostrophe is used mainly in hand-lettered small-business signs to alert the reader that an "S" is coming up at the end of a word, as in: WE DO NOT EXCEPT PERSONAL CHECK'S, or: NOT RESPONSIBLE FOR ANY ITEM'S.

Another important grammar concept to bear in mind when creating hand-lettered small-business signs is that you should put quotation marks around random words for decoration, as in "TRY" OUR HOT DOG'S, or even TRY "OUR" HOT DOG'S.

Q When do you say "Who," and when do you say "Whom"?

A You say "who" when you want to find out something like, for example, if a friend of yours comes up and says, "You will never guess which of your immediate family members just lost a key limb in a freak Skee-Ball accident." You would then reply: "Who?" You say "whom" when you are in Great Britain or you are angry, as in: "And just WHOM do you think is going to clean up after these otters?"

Q Like many writers, I often get confused about when to use the word "affect," and when to use "infect." Can you help me out?

A Here is a simple pneumatic device for telling these two similar-sounding words (or gramophones) apart: Just remember that "infect" begins with "in," which is also how "insect" begins, while "affect" begins with "af," which is an abbreviation for "Air Force."

Q Some business associates and I are trying to compose a very important business letter, and we disagree about the wording of a key sentence. My associates argue that it should be, "Youse better be there alone with the ransom money, on account of we don't want to have to whack nobody's limbs off." I say this is incorrect. Can you settle this argument?

A Tell your associates they'd better bone up on their grammar! The sentence they're suggesting ends with the preposition "off," and should be corrected as follows: ". . . don't want to have to whack nobody's limbs off with a big knife." ***Dave Barry***

Exercises

A Find the errors in comparison in the following sentences and write the sentences correctly. If a sentence has no errors, write *Correct*.

> *Example*   Denise spells best than anyone else in our school.
> Denise spells better than anyone else in our school.

1. According to a recent study, the teen-ager today is physically more strong than the teen-ager of the past.
2. The sun shines more brightly at this time of year.
3. Of the three Brontë sisters, Anne was the less popular.
4. Our kitchen is now most spacious than before.
5. In Greek mythology Hades was the most deep region of the underworld.
6. The senator spoke more sensibly than his opponent.
7. Of all the starters on the team, Cindy pitches the better.
8. That is the tamest horse in the stable.
9. This year, we bowled more better than last year.
10. He is the less temperamental of the four singers.

B On your paper, write the form of the modifier given in parentheses.

> *Example*   The construction of the ancient pyramids required (much—comparative) workers than such a project would today. more

1. Egypt's pyramids are considered one of the (great—superlative) wonders of the world.
2. The (early—superlative) pyramids were built about 2700 B.C.
3. The three (famous—superlative) pyramids are in Giza.
4. The first pyramid at Giza was built by King Khufu and is (massive—comparative) than the other two.
5. It is (large—comparative) than any other ancient structure except the Great Wall of China.
6. Some people say that this pyramid is the (impressive—superlative) structure ever built.
7. The second pyramid was built by Khufu's son Khafre and is much (small—comparative) than the first.
8. Today, however, Khafre's pyramid is in (good—comparative) condition than his father's.
9. Structures similar to the pyramids were built much (late—comparative) than those in Egypt.
10. These later pyramids were built (quickly—comparative) than those at Giza.

c *Write Now* People who write advertising copy often use the comparative and superlative forms of modifiers. For example, a copywriter might describe one brand of facial tissue as being *softer* than another or one kind of cereal as being the *crispiest* on the market. Write an advertisement in which you use comparisons.

Part 6
Using Correct Comparisons

The explanations in Part 6 will help you use comparisons correctly.

Avoiding Double Comparisons

A double comparison occurs when *-er* or *-est* is used with *more* or *most*.

Incorrect	She can type more faster than I.
Correct	She can type faster than I.

Incorrect	Tokyo is the most largest of the three cities.
Correct	Tokyo is the largest of the three cities.

Avoiding Illogical Comparisons

An illogical comparison is one that does not make sense because of missing or illogical words.

Unclear	A queen termite lives longer than any insect.
Clear	A queen termite lives longer than any *other* insect. (Since a queen termite is itself an insect, it can only live longer than *other* insects.) Always use the word *other* when you compare one thing with all other things of the same kind)

Unclear	Adrienne likes that movie better than Hernando.
Clear	Adrienne likes that movie better than Hernando *does*. (Adrienne does not like the movie better than she likes Hernando. Hernando does not like the movie as much as Adrienne does.)

Unclear	Mark's bicycle is newer than Fred.
Clear	Mark's bicycle is newer than Fred's. (The comparison is between Mark's bicycle and Fred's bicycle, not between Mark's bicycle and Fred.)

Exercises

A Write each incorrect sentence below, correcting the error in comparison. If a sentence is correct, write *Correct*.

1. Of all my friends, you are certainly the most stubbornest.
2. Chicago is colder than any city I've lived in.
3. The thick red sauce is certainly the more milder of the two sauces.
4. The picture of your vegetable garden is clearer than your flower garden.
5. I'm feeling more better today.
6. The new shortstop is a better hitter than anyone else on the team.
7. A bull terrier is the most ugliest dog I've ever seen.
8. This small maple chair is more solid than any piece of furniture in the house.
9. Of the two expensive-looking tapes on sale at the music store, this is certainly less expensive.
10. Those stereos in the window are cheaper than our local store.

B *Proofreading* The following paragraphs contain errors in the use of comparisons. Rewrite the paragraphs, correcting all errors.

Throughout history soldiers have used special coverings for protection. These special coverings, or armor, made them more safer by guarding them against enemy weapons'.

In the Stone Age warriors used several layers of skin to protect themselves from club and ax attacks? Many years later, people made themselves sheilds and body armor from metal, a more stronger material.

The metal suits from the Middle Ages were heavier than any armor. These suits of armor, made from thin sheets of metal or metal links, covered knights from hed to foot. Each knight hoped his armor would be stronger than anyone.

Renaissance armor and coat of arms.

Checkpoint *Parts 5 and 6*

A Write the correct modifier from the two in parentheses.

1. Which is the (longer, longest) bridge in the country?
2. Carl Lewis ran (faster, fastest) than his competitor.
3. FORTRAN is a (difficulter, more difficult) language than BASIC.
4. Of all the actors Van spoke the (most clearly, clearliest).
5. Lisa has (less, least) experience than Jean.
6. The tennis team played (worse, worst) today than yesterday.
7. Bob Beamon leaped (farer, farthest) of all the jumpers.
8. Carrie feels (weller, better) today than yesterday.
9. Some injuries heal (less rapidly, least rapidly) than others.
10. Of the three southern cities, Atlanta is the (larger, largest).

B Find the errors in comparison in the following sentences and rewrite the sentences correctly on your paper. If a sentence has no errors, write *Correct*.

1. The gymnast performed easier in the second event.
2. Snow blowers are more expensive here than at our local store.
3. Knowledge about business computers is importanter than ever before.
4. Food cooks more faster over an open fire.
5. Of all my friends, Helena speaks more openly.
6. Some cars run better on unleaded gas.
7. That yacht is bigger than any boat in the harbor.
8. Of the three tapes, this one is the cheaper.
9. We ate fish more often when we lived in Maine.
10. Epoxy glue holds bestest of all.
11. Tomatoes from our Uncle Theodore's garden are better than the store.
12. Minnesota is more farther from here than Michigan is.
13. Swimming in the ocean is more fun than a pool.
14. Jordan competes more vigorously than Adam.
15. Of the four pitchers, Kelly throws more accurately.
16. Bananas seem to ripen faster than any fruit.
17. Anna has the most highest voice of anyone in chorus.
18. Who scored the most baskets during the game, Sam or Nick?
19. Which of the six poisonous snakes is more deadlier?
20. All of the performers were good, but Karla was better.

Part 7
Problems with Modifiers

Certain modifiers are frequently used incorrectly. By studying the following pages carefully, you can avoid these errors.

The Double Negative

A **double negative** occurs when two negative words are used and only one is necessary. Avoid using double negatives.

Incorrect	We didn't take no time-outs.
Correct	We didn't take *any* time-outs.
Incorrect	My sister never eats no dessert.
Correct	My sister never eats *any* dessert.
Incorrect	John couldn't eat nothing all day.
Correct	John couldn't eat *anything* all day.

Contractions like *couldn't* contain a shortened form of the negative *not*. Do not use other negative words after them.

Some common negative words are *no, none, not, nothing,* and *never*. Instead of these words, use *any, anything,* or *ever* after negative contractions.

Incorrect	Amy hasn't never seen the Tigers play.
Correct	Amy hasn't *ever* seen the Tigers play.
Incorrect	Michelle couldn't find no leeks at the market.
Correct	Michelle couldn't find *any* leeks at the market.
Incorrect	The new council didn't change nothing.
Correct	The new council didn't change *anything*.

Other negative words are *hardly, scarcely,* and *barely*. Do not use them with negative contractions like *hasn't* and *didn't*.

Incorrect	Rick couldn't barely control the machine.
Correct	Rick could *barely* control the machine.
Incorrect	The movers hadn't scarcely begun.
Correct	The movers had *scarcely* begun.
Incorrect	Lightning hardly never strikes houses.
Correct	Lightning *hardly ever* strikes houses.

Exercise

Correct each of the sentences that contains a double negative. If a sentence is correct, write *Correct*.

1. I don't care for no dressing on my salad.
2. For some reason there isn't nobody working at the computer terminal this morning.
3. Haven't you never seen a soccer match?
4. We know hardly nobody from that school.
5. Amy doesn't want any reward for returning the keys she found.
6. I can't find nothing wrong with your camera.
7. I haven't scarcely begun my report on the Old West.
8. The bite of the black widow is hardly ever fatal.
9. We couldn't find no marigold seeds at Garden World.
10. At the concert I couldn't barely see the stage.

Those *and* Them

Those can be used as an adjective or a pronoun.

> Where are the controls for *those* power saws? (adjective)
> *Those* are the Jackson twins. (pronoun)

Them is never an adjective and cannot be used in place of *those*.

Incorrect We framed *them* photos.
Correct We framed *those* photos.

Unnecessary Here *and* There

"This here" and "that there" are repetitious phrases. The word *this* includes the idea of *here*. The word *that* includes the idea of *there*. Avoid "this here" and "that there."

Incorrect This here sandwich is stale.
Correct *This* sandwich is stale.

This Kind *and* These Kinds

This and *that* modify the singular nouns *kind* and *sort*. *These* and *those* modify the plural nouns *kinds* and *sorts*. *Kind* and *sort* are usually singular when the noun in the prepositional phrase following these words is singular.

> *This kind* of project is exciting. (*This kind* and *project* are singular.)

Kind and *sort* are usually plural when the noun in the prepositional phrase is plural.

> *These sorts* of projects are fun. (*These sorts* and *projects* are plural.)

Good *and* Well

Although *good* and *well* have similar meanings, you cannot always substitute one word for the other. Look at these sentences:

> That is a *good* photo of you. (The adjective *good* modifies the noun *photo*.)
> You sing *well*. (The adverb *well* modifies the verb *sing*.)

Good is always an adjective, modifying a noun or a pronoun. *Good* is never used to modify a verb; the adverb *well* is used instead.

Incorrect   Jeff planned the party good.
Correct   Jeff planned the party well.

Well generally functions as an adverb. In the sentence above, for example, *well* is used as an adverb modifying an action verb. *Well* can also be used as a predicate adjective after a linking verb. When *well* is used as an adjective, it always means ''in good health.''

> Nina doesn't feel *well*. (The adjective *well* modifies *Nina*.)

Usage Note Since *good* and *well* can both be adjectives, they can both be used as predicate adjectives following the linking verb *feel*. Remember that *feel well* refers only to health. *Feel good* refers to happiness, comfort, or pleasure.

> Sylvia stayed home because she didn't feel well.
> I felt good when I saw that *A* on my paper.

Exercises

A Write the correct choice of the two in parentheses.

1. (Them, Those) cheerleaders sound hoarse.
2. (This, This here) video recorder has remote control.
3. You did very (good, well) at the track meet.
4. (This sort, These sorts) of shoes are recommended for aerobics.
5. I don't care for (that kind, those kinds) of fruit.
6. The movie we saw last night was very (good, well).
7. Are you feeling (good, well) enough to play?
8. (That, That there) car has electronic fuel injection.
9. Are (them, those) compact discs on sale?
10. (That kind, Those kinds) of palm tree grows in Florida.

B Rewrite each incorrect sentence, correcting errors in the use of modifiers. If a sentence is correct, write *Correct*.

1. You ski good for a beginner.
2. Them are the best oranges I've ever tasted.
3. Is that there restaurant open on Mondays?
4. She looks well despite her cold.
5. Although he speaks good, Ed doesn't like to make speeches to large groups.
6. Have you ever gone through them caves in Kentucky?
7. You must wear those sort of kneepads when skateboarding.
8. These kinds of boats are called catamarans.
9. This here antibiotic is as effective as penicillin.
10. Ella has taught them parrots to talk.

c *Proofreading* Proofread the following paragraphs. Then rewrite them, correcting all of the errors. Pay special attention to the use of adjectives and adverbs.

Scientists divide whales into two main groups according to there method of feeding. The largest group is called toothed whales. These kind of whales do not feed on nothing smaller than fish. Among these toothed whales are dolphins porpoises, and killer whales.

The second group, called baleen whales, are more larger in size than toothed whales, baleen whales feed on tiny shrimp-like animales known as plankton. The blue whale, part of this second group, is larger than any animal. Oddly, the group of larger whales eats the more smaller sized food.

Checkpoint Part 7

A The following sentences contain errors in the use of modifiers. On your paper, write each sentence, correcting the error.

1. Are temperatures in the nineties common in that there area?
2. These kinds of skirt is fashionable today.
3. My brothers scarcely never fight.
4. The cellist Yo-Yo Ma played so good that he got a standing ovation.
5. These kinds of motorbikes use hardly no gasoline.
6. That there baseball player is in the Hall of Fame at Cooperstown.
7. Take this here claim check to the cashier for your refund.
8. The site of the fort is marked by them monuments.
9. It rained so hard we couldn't hardly see the road.
10. The newspaper reporter covered the story good.
11. The team's effort made the coach feel well.
12. Before he learned word processing, Sean didn't turn nothing in without dozens of mistakes.
13. I find them wool argyle socks too itchy.
14. Evan didn't get no more strikes after the first game.
15. Haven't you never stayed up to see the sun rise?
16. If you push that there button the machine will self-destruct.
17. This kind of riding boots give your ankles the best support.
18. The music sounded quite well, even without amplification.
19. Them telephone-answering machines always make me nervous.
20. Roger Ebert and Gene Siskel always give ''thumbs down'' to those kinds of movies.

B Complete the following sentences with the correct word or words from those in parentheses.

1. I would not trim (them, those) rose bushes if I were you.
2. (This kind, These kinds) of dogs are easy to train.
3. Hal may look fine, but he doesn't feel (good, well).
4. (This, This here) egg salad has a bit of curry powder in it.
5. Please be careful with (those, them) open paint cans.
6. Teresa sketches animals (more better, better) than Larry does.
7. I haven't seen (any, no) mosquitos in this neighborhood lately.
8. Whoever washed (them, those) pans forgot to put them away.
9. (This kind, these kinds) of thunderstorm makes me nervous.
10. Haven't you made (any, no) plans for the summer?

Linking
Grammar & Writing

Think about a real or an imaginary visit to an unusual building, a cave, or an exotic setting like the one shown below. Write a paragraph in which you describe the place.

Prewriting and Drafting For each of the five senses, list as many appropriate details as you can to help describe your subject. Refer to this prewriting list as you draft.

Revising and Proofreading Read through your first draft and eliminate any unnecessary modifiers. Replace vague modifiers with modifiers that are more precise and colorful. Proofread your paragraph for errors.

Additional Writing Topic Rewrite the following movie review. Replace overused or weak modifiers with colorful, precise ones.

> The best movie of this season is *Gold Fever,* director I.M. Specshul's smash hit. Based on a good book by Vera Bose, the movie re-creates the great atmosphere of the Klondike gold rush in the 1890's. Against this background an interesting story unfolds. The story tells of a couple torn between their love for each other and their love for that shiny metal. The really nice thing about this movie is Hope Foran Oscar's portrayal of Yukon Jim's unusual sidekick. This movie is great entertainment for both children and adults.

For Your Amusement

When you listen to music or visit a museum, nine Greek goddesses are looking after you. These nine goddesses, the Muses, cared for artists in Greek mythology. They dwelt in the springs and fountains at the base of sacred Mount Parnassas, and each Muse was a source of inspiration for a form of music, poetry, art, or the sciences.

Their inspiration continues in the words that have been made from their name. *Music* can be traced to the Greek word *mousikos*, meaning "belonging to the Muses." *Museum* is from *mouseion*, the "Temple of the Muses." *Muse* itself means a spirit or power watching over artists, poets, and musicians; in a more general sense, it simply means the power of inspiration. *Amuse* and *bemuse* are also closely associated with the Muses.

Greek mythology has been a rich source of words that have unusual stories behind them. *Siren*, for example, can be traced to the mythic creatures of the same name who were half woman and half bird. They sat on the rocks by the shore and used their sweet singing to lure ships to destruction. *Echo* comes from the Greek nymph Echo, who talked too much. As punishment, she was allowed only to repeat what others said. She wasted away in sadness until nothing was left of her but her voice. *Titan*, *fury*, *volcano*, *herculean*, and many other words commonly used today can also be traced to the stories of the supernatural heroes of ancient civilization.

Three female figures,
eastern pediment,
Parthenon, Athens, 447–432 B.C.

Chapter 26
Application and Review

A Identifying Modifiers On your paper, write the modifiers in the following sentences. Identify them as adjectives or adverbs and tell which word each one modifies. Include nouns and pronouns used as adjectives but do not include articles.

1. That melody sounds vaguely familiar.
2. Yesterday Dee practiced steadily for two hours.
3. Max answered my sincere question in a somewhat sarcastic tone.
4. A bowl of hot chicken soup would taste delicious now.
5. Several lilac bushes are already blooming.
6. A Shakespearean comedy often involves unbelievable situations.
7. As they flew from the marsh, the migrating Canada geese squawked loudly.
8. The use of smallpox vaccine has drastically reduced outbreaks of the disease.
9. An experienced photographer can focus this complicated camera quite quickly.
10. They laughed hysterically at the child's antics.
11. Which cadet disobeyed the captain's order?
12. Congress is seriously studying the other energy sources.
13. Proud and majestic, the peacock displayed its colors.
14. The tuna fleet always returns here in the evening.
15. The defense attorney spoke quietly and eloquently to the jury.

B Making Correct Comparisons Write each incorrect sentence, fixing errors in comparisons. If a sentence is correct, write *Correct*.

1. The Amazing Adams Brothers juggle more better than any other act I have seen.
2. Ada is more dependable than anyone in her family.
3. Which river is longest, the Amazon or the Volga?
4. Maine is farer from here than North Dakota.
5. Who is the most popular Peanuts character, Lucy or Snoopy?
6. Of the three finalists Katarina Witt skated more gracefully.
7. His part in the play was shorter than the movie.
8. The fire was the worse disaster in the city's history.
9. Bobby Rahal drove most quickly of all the qualifiers.
10. That pitcher works harder than any other player on the team.

11. The actress was more short than she looked on television.
12. The budget for welfare was smaller than the art programs.
13. Who was the youngest of all the U.S. Presidents?
14. The children clapped most loudliest of all.
15. Hanna sees good with her new glasses.

C Using Modifiers Correctly Many of the following sentences contain errors in the use of modifiers. Write each incorrect sentence, correcting the error. If a sentence is correct, write *Correct*.

1. The apples from this tree taste sweetly.
2. We didn't scarcely have time to complete the quiz.
3. Please don't play the stereo so loudly.
4. Her voice sounded calmly over the phone.
5. These sort of flowers grows well in sandy soil.
6. Hardly no good seats are available at the playhouse no more.
7. This kind of scarf matches your complexion.
8. Them are unusual photographs.
9. That there Victorian house is more than one hundred years old.
10. After eating the wild berries, we didn't feel good.
11. The wind shifted sudden and the temperature dropped.
12. The White Sox look good in their new uniforms.
13. Take off them wet clothes before you catch cold.
14. This here record is scratched.
15. The fog was so thick we couldn't see nothing.

D Using Modifiers Correctly Rewrite the following paragraph, correcting the errors in the use of modifiers.

(1) The yacht *Stars and Stripes* won the America's Cup in 1987 when it sailed faster of all the yachts. (2) The yacht's skipper, Dennis Conner, felt jubilantly because he had lost the cup four years earlier to an Australian boat. (3) For the 1983 competition, the Australians developed a boat that was more quicker than Conner's. (4) Conner couldn't do nothing to overcome the disadvantage in speed. (5) In preparing for the 1987 competition, Conner decided to employ high technology boat designers to develop a sailboat that would be the more highly advanced of all the competitors. (6) His designers did good. (7) The boat they developed didn't lose no races in the final round. (8) In the first three races, Conner's sailboat beat its Australian competitor bad. (9) In the final race the Australian boat was beaten worse of all. (10) Conner had regained the America's Cup easy.

27

Using Prepositions, Conjunctions, and Interjections

S ubway lines and bus routes link the neighborhoods of metropolitan areas. A map such as the one above shows the locations of these routes and transfer points between them. The map helps clarify spatial relationships and allows people to use the system efficiently.

In a similar way, prepositions and conjunctions create verbal maps by indicating the relationships between words in a sentence. In this chapter you will learn how to recognize and use prepositions and conjunctions. You will also learn how to use interjections to add emotion and emphasis to your writing and speaking.

Part 1
What Is a Preposition?

A preposition is a word used to show the relationship between a noun or pronoun and some other word in the sentence.

In the following examples, notice how changing the preposition can affect the meaning of the sentence as a whole.

> Sara skated *off* the ice.
> Sara skated *onto* the ice.
> Sara skated *over* the ice.

The prepositions *off, onto,* and *over* show the relationship between the noun *ice* and the verb *skated.* In each of the sentences above, *ice* is the **object of the preposition.**

The following list presents words often used as prepositions.

Commonly Used Prepositions

about	at	down	near	to
above	before	during	of	toward
across	behind	except	off	under
after	below	for	on	underneath
against	beneath	from	onto	until
along	beside	in	out	up
among	between	inside	over	upon
around	but (except)	into	since	with
as	by	like	through	without

Some prepositions consist of two or three words. These are called **compound prepositions.**

Compound Prepositions

according to	because of	in place of	on account of
ahead of	due to	in spite of	on top of
along with	in addition to	instead of	out of
as of	in front of	next to	prior to

The Object of the Preposition

The object of a preposition is always a noun, a pronoun, or a group of words used as a noun.

> *With poise,* Meryl Streep walked to the stage and accepted her Academy Award. (The noun *poise* is the object of the preposition *with*.)
>
> The city welcomed the British Prime Minister and scheduled a sightseeing tour *for her*. (The pronoun *her* is the object of the preposition *for*.)
>
> Give the Springsteen concert tickets *to whoever asks for them first*. (*Whoever asks for them first* is a group of words functioning as a noun. It is the object of the preposition *to*.)

Like the other sentence parts, the object of a preposition may be compound.

> *Between January and July,* Franklin gained twenty pounds. (*January* and *July* are the compound objects of the preposition *between*.)

The Prepositional Phrase

A prepositional phrase consists of a preposition, its object, and any modifiers of the object.

A preposition does not show relationships by itself. It always begins a phrase, a group of words without a subject or verb. The prepositional phrases in the following sentences are italicized.

> Martha indicated her approval *by nodding*.
> The figures *on a totem pole* have special significance.

Punctuation Note There are three situations in which a prepositional phrase that comes at the beginning of a sentence should be followed by a comma.

1. If the phrase is followed by a natural pause when read:
   According to the fire marshal, smoke detectors can save many lives.
2. After a series of prepositional phrases:
   After three weeks of heavy rain in April, the fields were wet and muddy.
3. To avoid confusion:
   Next to the school, houses were being built.

Preposition or Adverb?

Many words used as prepositions may also be used as adverbs. How can you tell if a word is a preposition or an adverb?

A preposition is never used alone. It is always followed by a noun or pronoun used as the object of the preposition. If the word does not have an object, it is probably an adverb.

> The visitors walked *around the courtyard*. (preposition)
> The visitors walked *around*. (adverb)

> The giant sequoias towered *above the trail*. (preposition)
> The giant sequoias towered *above*. (adverb)

> Can you jump *over that hurdle?* (preposition)
> Can you come *over* later? (adverb)

Exercises

A Write the prepositional phrases in the following sentences. Some sentences may have more than one prepositional phrase. With each phrase, underline the preposition once and its object twice.

> *Example*   Caroline works at the mall.
> at the <u>mall</u>

1. The raccoons in our neighborhood are bold.
2. During the season Zachariah pitched three no-hitters.
3. Did you know that dogs perspire through their paws?
4. The video store was crowded on Friday and Saturday.
5. Renaldo does five hundred sit-ups every evening before dinner.
6. By all means, talk to another doctor.
7. A pit of quicksand stretched between my dog and me.
8. My mother and father met for the first time at a sock hop.
9. According to the legend, the old prospector found a rich vein of silver in the once-abandoned mine.
10. At the end of the season the coach gave an award to whoever had worked the hardest.
11. Leaping high for the ball, the left fielder made the catch right in front of the fence.
12. These sandwiches are called ''subs'' in New York, ''hoagies'' in Kansas, and ''poor boys'' in New Orleans.
13. For months Katja talked about the dance.
14. With fear, the expedition approached the top of the mountain.
15. The proof of the pudding is in the eating.

B Application in Literature Write ten of the prepositional phrases you find in the following passage. With each phrase, underline the preposition once and the object of the preposition twice. Notice how the author uses prepositional phrases to add detail to this description of nature in winter.

> Other interesting things are going on wherever there is shelter. Slugs, of all creatures, hibernate inside a waterproof sac. All the bumblebees and paper wasps are dead except the queens, who sleep a fat, numbed sleep, unless a mouse finds one and eats her alive. Honeybees have their own honey for fuel, so they can overwinter as adults, according to Edwin Way Teale, by buzzing together in a tightly packed, living sphere. Their shimmying activity heats the hive; they switch positions from time to time so that each bee gets its chance in the cozy middle and its turn on the cold outside. . . . Ladybugs hibernate under shelter in huge orange clusters sometimes the size of basketballs.

From *Pilgrim at Tinker Creek* by Annie Dillard

c *Write Now* Describe what you see in the picture below. In your description use prepositional phrases.

Checkpoint *Part 1*

A On your paper, state whether the italicized words are prepositions or adverbs. Identify the compound prepositions by writing *Compound*.

1. The golf ball ricocheted *off* a tree trunk.
2. The Grand Ole Opry is *in* Nashville, Tennessee.
3. I have not seen Juanita *around* the locker room.
4. Many of the birds have migrated, but these ducks have remained *behind*.
5. *Prior to* graduation, Peter visited several colleges.
6. Turn the lights *off* to conserve energy.
7. There was a long line *outside* the theater.
8. The cafeteria now serves the students salads *in addition to* hot lunches.
9. *Outside,* a heavy rain was falling.
10. We pitched our tent *on top of* the hill.
11. Have you mowed the lawn and taken the garbage *out* yet?
12. One year ago I received a letter from my friend, but I have not heard from her *since*.
13. *Along with* two of his friends, Sam delivered the documents to the mayor.
14. If you are going to play miniature golf, may we go *along* too?
15. Do you see my glasses *around* here?

B Write the prepositional phrase or phrases from each sentence on your paper. Then underline the object of each preposition. Finally, re-write the sentences changing one of the prepositional phrases.

1. My aunt Florence lives in a bungalow on San Juan Island.
2. Seagulls waited on the pier for handouts from tourists.
3. Protons and neutrons are in the nucleus of an atom.
4. That rusty old car has been parked in the street next to my house for a month.
5. Don't stand in front of the speakers when the band begins.
6. The point of the story was lost by everybody.
7. In amazement, I watched my friend put peanut butter on his pizza.
8. We passed several abandoned farms during our bike trip.
9. Weight lifting without proper guidance can lead to injury.
10. Electricity passes through superconductors with no loss of energy.

Part 2
Prepositional Phrases as Modifiers

Modifiers are often single words. However, groups of words may also function as modifiers. Prepositional phrases, for example, work like adjectives or adverbs to modify various parts of a sentence.

An adjective phrase is a prepositional phrase that modifies a noun or pronoun.

Like adjectives, adjective phrases tell *which one* or *what kind*. Here are three examples.

> The last room *on the right* is haunted.
> > (*On the right* is an adjective phrase, modifying the noun *room*. The phrase tells *which one*.)
> All *of the restaurant workers* wear weird purple hats.
> > (*Of the restaurant workers* is an adjective phrase that modifies the pronoun *all*. The phrase tells *what kind*.)
> No one could explain the reason *for his sudden departure*.
> > (*For his sudden departure* is an adjective phrase, modifying the noun *reason*. The phrase tells *which one*.)

An adverb phrase is a prepositional phrase that modifies a verb, an adjective, or an adverb.

Like adverbs. an adverb phrase tells *how, when, where,* or *to what extent* something occurred.

> The bottles are sealed *by a huge machine*.
> > (*By a huge machine* is an adverb phrase telling *how*. It modifies the verb *are sealed*.)
> Hendricks sulked *on the bench*.
> > (*On the bench* is an adverb phrase. It tells *where* about the verb *sulked*.)
> She was courageous *during the crisis*.
> > (*During the crisis* is an adverb phrase. It tells *when* about the adjective *courageous*.)
> The sun shone hot *as fire*.
> > (*As fire* is an adverb phrase. It tells *to what extent* about the adverb *hot*.)

Sometimes one prepositional phrase follows another. Sometimes both phrases modify the same word.

> We fished *with minnows during the evening*.
> (The adverb phrase *with minnows* tells *how* about the verb *fished*. The adverb phrase *during the evening* tells *when* about the verb *fished*.)

Frequently, however, the second phrase is an adjective phrase that modifies the object in the first phrase.

> Okawa topped the salad *with bits of cheese*.
> (The adverb phrase *with bits* tells *how* about the verb *topped*. *Of cheese* is an adjective phrase describing the noun *bits*.)

Sentence Diagraming For information on diagraming prepositional phrases, see pages 759–760.

Exercises

A Write the prepositional phrases in the following sentences. Some sentences may have more than one phrase. After each phrase, write the word the phrase modifies and tell whether the phrase functions as an adjective or adverb.

> *Example*   Birds of a feather flock together.
> of a feather, Birds, adjective

1. Little Red bought a riding jacket with a deep hood.
2. The Greek epic *The Iliad* relates the events at the end of the Trojan War.
3. The word *dandelion* comes from the French language and literally means "tooth of the lion."
4. Sacramento was full of activity during the gold rush.
5. The home of Abe Lincoln is open to the public.
6. In 1519 Ferdinand Magellan began his voyage around the world.
7. During our vacation we toured Mark Twain's home in Hartford.
8. The Navajos and the Apaches were foes for many years.
9. We spent most of the day at the zoo.
10. During the storm everyone except Dee stayed inside the bus.
11. Ted walked to school with a cast on his leg.
12. The Akita is a breed of dog that originated in Japan.
13. At low tide we saw the hull of the ancient ship.
14. In 1429, Joan of Arc led the French army to victory.
15. Out of nowhere rode a man with a black cape.

B Application in Literature Write the italicized prepositional phrases from the passage below. For each phrase, tell what word it modifies and whether it functions as an adjective or adverb.

> (1) The baying *of the hounds* grew nearer, then still nearer, nearer, ever nearer. (2) *On a ridge* Rainsford climbed a tree. (3) *Down a watercourse,* not a quarter *of a mile* away, he could see the bush moving. (4) Straining his eyes, he saw the lean figure *of General Zaroff.* (5) Just ahead *of him* Rainsford made out another figure whose wide shoulders surged *through the tall jungle weeds.* (6) It was the giant Ivan, and he seemed pulled forward *by some unseen force.* (7) Rainsford knew that Ivan must be holding the pack *in leash.* (8) They would be *on him* any minute now.
>
> From "The Most Dangerous Game" by Richard Connell

c *Write Now* Write a description similar to the one in Exercise B. Use prepositional phrases to give your reader a clear picture.

Part 3
Using Prepositions Correctly

Often, prepositions are used incorrectly and unnecessarily.

Prepositions Often Misused

among, between *Between* refers to two people or things. *Among* refers to a group of three or more. Use *between* when you are thinking of two objects at a time, regardless of how many are in the group.

> There is a peace treaty *between* the two countries.
> We divided the work *among* the four of us.
> The differences *between* the three stereos were apparent.

beside, besides *Beside* means "at the side of." *Besides* means "in addition to."

> Secret Service agents stand *beside* the President.
> There are other motives *besides* greed.

in, into *In* means "inside something." *Into* suggests motion from the outside to the inside.

> Sis stayed *in* the car.
> I went *into* the house.

off, from Do not use the word *off* when you mean *from*.

Incorrect   Tony borrowed a
            coat *off* me today.
Correct   Tony borrowed a
            coat *from* me today.

Misusing prepositions can lead to problems like the one above.

on, onto *On* means "upon something." *Onto* suggests motion to the top of something.

> The tag teams were *on* the beach.
> The beach ball sailed out *onto* the water.

"Goldberg, you idiot! Don't play tricks on those things—they can't distinguish between 'laughing with' and 'laughing at'!"

Prepositions Used Unnecessarily

Prepositions like *at, of,* and *to* may be used unnecessarily. Often these prepositions come at the end of a sentence.

Incorrect   Where are my gym clothes *at?*
Correct   Where are my gym clothes?

Incorrect   Nicole could not feel her toes inside *of* her ski boots.
Correct   Nicole could not feel her toes inside her ski boots.

Incorrect   Where did the Brooklyn Dodgers move *to?*
Correct   Where did the Brooklyn Dodgers move?

Misplaced Prepositional Phrases

A prepositional phrase should be placed near the word it modifies. Otherwise, the meaning of your sentence may not be clear.

Incorrect   Pablo told many stories of his fascinating childhood *in our class.* (Did Pablo spend his childhood in our class?)
Correct   *In our class,* Pablo told many stories of his fascinating childhood.

Exercises

A Write the correct word from the pair in parentheses.

1. The average temperature (on, onto) Venus is over 800°F.
2. In 1455, the Wars of the Roses broke out (among, between) the House of York and the House of Lancaster.
3. In a joint session of Congress, the Speaker of the House sits (beside, besides) the Vice-President.
4. Someone was (in, into) our car while we were away.
5. Japan gets much of its food (off, from) other countries.
6. When you walk (in, into) a home in Japan, take off your shoes.
7. The Pirates acquired Roberto Clemente (off, from) the Dodgers.
8. What other explorers ventured to the New World in the sixteenth century (beside, besides) Hernando de Soto?
9. The Middle East is the largest producer of oil (among, between) the oil regions of the world.
10. The hockey players skated (on, onto) the ice.

B The following sentences contain some unnecessary prepositions and some misplaced phrases. Rewrite the sentences, correcting the errors.

1. Don't go inside of that grizzly bear's cage.
2. Sergeant Lewis sent a package to the officer with secret documents.
3. Where is the country of Belize at?
4. Elsie examined the car engine she had tuned with her hands in her pockets.
5. Where is that group of teachers going to?

C *Proofreading* Rewrite the following passage, correcting all of the errors. Pay particular attention to the use of prepositions and prepositional phrases.

At the age of 32, Thomas Edison completed his most famous invention, the electric light. He had spent two years searching for the right filament with great determination. Finally he tryed carbonized thread inside of his bulb, the bulb glowed brightly for a day and a half.

Beside the electric light, edison also invented the storage battary, the mimeograph, and the dictaphone in addition, he improved many other inventions, such as the telephone and the typewriter. Where did he get all his ideas at. Between his many inventions and improvements, the phonograf was Edison's personal favorite.

Checkpoint *Parts 2 and 3*

A On your paper, write the italicized prepositional phrases in the following sentences. Then identify the phrases as adjective or adverb.

1. Ancient Greek commanders communicated their battle plans *through coded messages*.
2. *In 1930*, miniature golf was the latest fad in America.
3. There is something *about Princess Diana* that fascinates Americans.
4. Exhausted but happy, the marathon runner rested *against a tree* near the finish line.
5. My bedroom is *above the kitchen*.
6. Marianas Trench, located in the Western Pacific Ocean, is the lowest point *below sea level*.
7. I never drink tea *without lemon*.
8. Fortunately, we reached the park's shelter just *before the rainstorm*.
9. Leslie found a dance club *about three blocks* from her home.
10. *Within minutes* Jean had checkmated her chess opponent.

B Some of the following sentences contain misused prepositions or misplaced prepositional phrases. If a sentence has such an error, rewrite the sentence correcting the error. If there is no error in a sentence, write *Correct*.

1. Maria is taking other classes beside lifesaving and tennis.
2. In the summer Mike makes money off tourists by offering a taxi service.
3. Our school orchestra will present works composed by Handel on Saturday night.
4. Lana worried about going to the dentist for two weeks.
5. One of the world's earliest civilizations began between two rivers, the Tigris and the Euphrates.
6. Besides Mount Everest there are three other mountains over 27,000 feet in the Himalaya range.
7. Important decisions are made inside of the Oval Office.
8. Where did that video store relocate to?
9. The mountain climbers moved onto the ledge with nerves of steel.
10. Among all the Allied generals, Dwight D. Eisenhower was chosen to lead the invasion.

Part 4

Conjunctions

A conjunction connects words or groups of words.

Lee wrote *and* narrated the skits.
Dr. No smiled *as* he entered the laboratory.
My typing is fast; *however*, I usually make a few errors.

There are three kinds of conjunctions: coordinating, correlative, and subordinating conjunctions. Conjunctive adverbs also function as conjunctions.

Coordinating Conjunctions

Coordinating conjunctions connect ideas of equal importance.

Coordinating Conjunctions

and	but	for	nor	or	so	yet

Words connected by coordinating conjunctions are compound subjects, compound objects, compound verbs, and compound sentences.

Compound Subject	Did the Italians *or* the Chinese invent pasta?
Compound Object	We will visit *New York* or *Miami* in June.
Compound Verb	Simon overslept *and* missed soccer practice.
Compound Sentence	The deadline is next week, *so* you still have time.

Correlative Conjunctions

Like coordinating conjunctions, **correlative conjunctions** join similar words or groups of words. However, these conjunctions are always used in pairs.

Correlative Conjunctions

both . . . and	neither . . . nor	whether . . . or
either . . . or	not only . . . but also	

Notice the pairs of conjunctions in each of the following sentences.

Both oak *and* walnut are used for furniture.
Not only did Rosa win, *but* she *also* broke her record.
The coach debated *whether* to kick *or* to run.

Exercises

A Make three columns on a piece of paper. In the first column write the conjunction in each of the following sentences. In the second column write the words connected by the conjunction. In the third column tell whether the conjunction is coordinating or correlative.

> *Example*   The car skidded and swerved.
>   and   skidded, swerved   coordinating

1. Which has the larger population—Mexico City or Tokyo?
2. The storm intensified, so the ski slopes were closed.
3. Is Mom cooking dinner or ordering pizza?
4. An octopus has eight tentacles and three hearts.
5. Not only does our team lack relief pitchers, but it also lacks experienced coaches.
6. The brontosaurus weighed thirty tons, but it had a tiny brain.
7. Neither Kim nor Chris got the lead role in the play.
8. That restaurant specializes in salads and falafel sandwiches.
9. The yo-yo originated in the Philippines, and it was used there as a hunting weapon.
10. Neither Sasha nor her sister could locate the car.

B Find the conjunctions in the following paragraph and write them on your paper. Then tell whether they are coordinating or correlative.

(1) The careers of Dorothea Lange and Margaret Bourke-White, two famous American photographers, show some interesting similarities. (2) Both of them grew up in the East in the early 1900's and both attended Columbia University, where they studied under the renowned photographer Clarence H. White. (3) By 1934 both Lange and Bourke-White were focusing on the Great Depression and the toll it was taking in rural America. (4) Their stark photos revealed with simple honesty how people lived, forcing the viewer to understand the reality of hardship. (5) Not only did the photos set the standards for the photo documentary, but they also called attention to the desperate needs of rural America.

c *Write Now* Write a paragraph of comparison about the two photos on this page. Identify any similarities and differences that you see. Use the paragraph in Exercise B as a model.

Part 5
Subordinating Conjunctions

A **subordinating conjunction** begins a clause that cannot stand alone and joins it to a clause that can stand alone. A **clause** is a group of words with a subject and verb. For more information on clauses see Chapter 31.

Commonly Used Subordinating Conjunctions				
after	as though	in order that	than	when
although	because	provided	till	where
as	before	since	unless	whereas
as if	if	so that	until	while

The following two sentences contain subordinating conjunctions.

The fans were quiet *while* the golfer putted.
Although I prefer peaches, I also like strawberries.

Punctuation Note When a subordinating conjunction begins a sentence, a comma follows the subordinate group of words.

Conjunctive Adverbs

Certain adverbs, called **conjunctive adverbs,** can join sentences.

Commonly Used Conjunctive Adverbs				
accordingly	consequently	hence	nevertheless	still
also	finally	however	otherwise	therefore
besides	furthermore	instead	similarly	thus

A conjunctive adverb is usually preceded by a semicolon and followed by a comma. Notice how conjunctive adverbs clarify the relationship between the two parts of these sentences.

> The chemical leak polluted the town's water; *consequently*, the town needed a new water supply.
> The evidence sounded convincing; *still*, the jury believed the defendant's story.

Exercises

A Write the subordinating conjunction or conjunctive adverb in each of the following sentences.

1. Exploring the sea had been Mel Fisher's passion since he was a boy.
2. Fisher searched for the ship *Nuestra Senora de Atocha* in the waters south of Florida where it had sunk in 1622.
3. Because the *Atocha* was returning from conquests in the New World, the ship was full of silver.
4. The *Atocha* treasure had remained hidden while Fisher struggled with false leads and near-bankruptcy.
5. Fisher told his crew every day, ''Today's the day,'' but that day never came; still, Fisher kept his dream.
6. On July 20, 1985, Fisher's son was searching in a new area, when he spotted a reef of silver bars.
7. Wherever the divers looked after that, they found treasure.
8. The divers hauled up silver ingots weighing seventy pounds each; also, they found chests filled with jewels.
9. The treasure was valued at $400 million; accordingly, it was declared the largest find ever recorded.
10. While Fisher celebrated, he planned his next adventure.

B Write each pair of sentences as one sentence by using the key word in parentheses. Use the sense of the sentence to determine whether the conjunction belongs at the beginning or the middle of the combined sentence. Remember to use appropriate punctuation.

1. The team uniforms faded in the wash. The school colors were now pink and powder blue. (because)
2. The speed limit was changed to fifty-five miles per hour. The number of traffic accidents dropped. (after)
3. We must leave for the game right now. We will miss the kickoff. (otherwise)
4. A tropical cyclone forms in the South China Sea. It is called a typhoon. (when)
5. Our plane left an hour late and flew through a blinding snowstorm. We arrived two hours late. (consequently)
6. He was six years old. Mozart had composed minuets and other musical pieces. (before)
7. The alien creatures decided not to take Alice. She had schoolwork due the next day. (since)
8. Santiago had not caught a fish in eighty-four days. He continued to sail out into the Gulf each day. (still)
9. You may think you hear the ocean in a seashell. It is actually the reflected sound of blood moving through your ear. (while)
10. Our new school is clean and well equipped. The courses are interesting and relevant. (furthermore)

Part 6
Interjections

An interjection is a word or phrase used to express feeling or emotion.

Interjections may be either phrases or words. They express feelings such as joy, anger, terror, pain, fear, surprise, disgust, or sadness. Because interjections are not part of the main structure of the sentence, they are set off by an exclamation mark or a comma.

> *Unbelievable!* Look at those giant submarine sandwiches.
> *Oh,* I thought you were meeting me in the cafeteria.
> We went to the shore, and, *oh,* it was fun.
> *Never!* I couldn't think of going without my sister.

Exercise

Write each italicized word and its part of speech.

1. Picture yourself bounding along *on* the lunar surface.
2. Scientists discover over 7,000 new kinds of insects annually. *Incredible!*
3. I can't go shopping *because* I don't have enough time.
4. Our basketball team advanced *to* the state tournament.
5. *Well*, how much of the earth's surface is covered by ocean?
6. Is Portland *or* Salem the capital of Oregon?
7. *Oh no!* I spilled some sulfuric acid.
8. Country music has influenced *both* rock *and* soul.
9. *Amazing!* Queen Victoria ruled Great Britain for sixty-four years.
10. Evelyn Ashford won the gold medal *in* the 100-meter dash.

Checkpoint *Parts 4, 5, and 6*

A Write the conjunctions and interjections you find in the following sentences. Then identify each word. Use the labels *Coordinating Conjunction, Correlative Conjunction, Subordinating Conjunction, Conjunctive Adverb*, or *Interjection*.

1. Cindy won two hundred dollars in the contest; however, she lost it on her way home.
2. Ugh! I can't stand getting up early in the morning.
3. I learned that warm-blooded animals include both mammals and birds.
4. Roxanne can't decide whether to call Ron or Rocky for help with her project.
5. It's Saturday night, and I have to stay home to clean the house. Boring!
6. All right, do you know what the rings stand for?
7. On this algebra test you scored twenty points higher than on your last test. Congratulations!
8. Although Father Hildago of Mexico was a priest, he was also a political leader.
9. The divers had no luck searching for the ship near Bermuda; therefore, they decided to search elsewhere.
10. Although the boy lost three homework assignments in a row, he kept his sunny disposition.

B Write the following sentences on your paper. Complete the meaning by using subordinating conjunctions, conjunctive adverbs, and interjections to fill in the blanks.

> *Example*   It's beautiful outside, *but* I have to stay in to watch my baby brother. *Unfair!*

1. Nina was unable to play handball this season; _____, she attended every match.
2. Karl's broken leg is almost healed; _____, he still needs crutches to walk. _____!
3. The trains were too crowded; _____, we rode the bus.
4. Takeo was excited _____ he was chosen for the team.
5. Lupe had to scale the mackerel _____ frying it. _____!
6. While he was ill, Lorenzo had missed several chemistry classes; _____ , he was excused from the exam.
7. The rain is delaying play; _____, we will finish the game.
8. _____ Chiang wins his match, he will be our tennis champ.
9. Without success I looked for my keys; _____, I found them under my dresser.
10. Though I have only a learner's permit, _____ a licensed driver sits beside me, I can drive legally.

C Write the following sentences, filling in the type of conjunction called for in parentheses. Some sentences may have more than one right answer.

1. _____ carrots _____ celery are vegetables often used in salads. (correlative)
2. _____ a scorpion's wound is painful, it does not usually cause death. (subordinating)
3. The outfielders wear glasses; _____, the sun won't blind them. (conjunctive adverb)
4. _____ Charles _____ José saw the mayor. (correlative)
5. Karen designs _____ fires her own pottery and clay sculpture. (coordinating)
6. During World War II, the Academy Award Oscars were made of plaster _____ metals were rationed. (subordinating)
7. _____ the cat's away, the mice will play. (subordinating)
8. Larry saw the tree _____ could not avoid skiing directly into it. (coordinating)
9. My new stereo will be ready for pickup by Friday _____ Saturday. (coordinating)
10. Jana enjoys _____ rock _____ jazz. (correlative)

Linking
Grammar & Writing

You are the restaurant critic for a major newspaper. Your most recent project is to visit the two best-known pizza parlors in your town and then write a comparison of the two pizzas you had. In your comparison, make use of a variety of conjunctions.

Prewriting and Drafting Make a list of the characteristics a good pizza should have, and another list of the things that make a pizza bad. Add other factors, such as service, atmosphere, and price. Keep in mind the questions the readers of your column might have.

Revising and Proofreading Have at least one other person read your article. Ask for suggestions and corrections. As you write your second draft, be aggressive about changing your wording to make your points clearer. Consider these questions:

1. Have you made the differences (and similarities) between the pizzas clear?
2. Have you used conjunctions to help make these comparisons?

Additional Writing Topic Describe in detail how to perform the activity pictured below or some other athletic activity. Circle all of the prepositions that you use in your description.

Peking or Beijing

I n the past decade Peking, the capital of China, has disappeared. So have Canton, Tibet, and Inner Mongolia. In their places are Beijing, Guangzhou, Xizang, and Nei Mongol.

China has not changed, but the system for translating the Chinese language has. Since Chinese does not use the same alphabet as English, translation is a complex process. Unlike English, which is written using the 26-character Roman alphabet, Chinese is written in pictorial symbols called ideograms. The Chinese people must learn about 6,000 ideograms to be able to communicate effectively, and there are a total of about 45,000. Translating Chinese involves spelling words so that they sound like their Chinese pronunciation.

Chinese Palace, Beijing.

For more than a century a process called the Wade-Giles system was the most widely used means of transcribing Chinese. Peking, Mao Tse-Tung, and Chou En-Lai are the products of the Wade-Giles system. In 1979, however, the Chinese government adopted a new system. It is called Pinyin, which is Chinese for ''phonetic spelling,'' and it uses Roman letters in a different manner. So Peking has become Beijing, Mao Tse-Tung is Mao Zedong, and Chou En-Lai is Zhou Enlai.

The Pinyin system is simpler than Wade-Giles, but its adoption has caused many adjustments in the West. Mapmakers in particular have been confronted with a country in which all the familiar places have been wiped off the face of the map.

Chapter 27
Application and Review

A Identifying Prepositional Phrases Write the prepositional phrase or phrases in each sentence. Label each phrase *Adjective* or *Adverb* and tell what word it modifies.

1. The archaeologist wouldn't wait inside the tomb alone.
2. The wig on the dancer's head was a bright blue.
3. *Nova*, a show on PBS, deals with unusual subjects of interest.
4. At the edge of the forest, we saw a deer.
5. With little trouble, Perez sprayed the outfield with singles.
6. I have changed my mind about the party.
7. Between Spain and France lies the tiny mountainous country of Andorra.
8. The annual Pendleton Round-Up draws huge crowds of spectators.
9. The angelfish wove through the coral of the huge reef.
10. The woman with the briefcase is Dr. Sanchez.

B Recognizing Parts of Speech Number your paper from 1 to 15 and list the italicized words in this passage. Then label each word *Preposition, Conjunction*, or *Interjection*. Identify conjunctions as *Coordinating, Correlative, Subordinating*, or *Conjunctive Adverbs*.

(1) San Francisco began as a missionary post *in* 1776. (2) It was founded *by* Spanish priests who named it Misión San Francisco de Asís.

(3) California became a Mexican territory in 1821 *when* Mexico won independence *from* Spain. (4) Twenty-five years later English-speaking Californians rebelled *against* Mexican rule. (5) This revolt was called the Bear Flag Rebellion *because* the Californians' flag had a grizzly bear *on* it.

(6) *Gold*! In 1848, *at* Sutter's Mill in the foothills of the Sierras, gold was discovered. (7) *As* the gold rush began in 1849, San Francisco had 800 inhabitants; *however*, two years later it had 25,000.

(8) In 1906, a tremendous earthquake *and* the resulting fire destroyed most *of* the city. (9) Seven hundred people died, *and* 300,000 were left homeless. (10) The people of San Francisco quickly rebuilt their city, and it has emerged *as* a key center of culture and industry.

28

Reviewing
Parts of Speech

W hat do the images above have in common? If you were to classify them, what category would you choose? You might group them according to their visible features—*things that are black and white* or *things that have legs*—or perhaps you can determine another category.

Words can also be classified in categories, called *parts of speech*. Each part of speech has different features and functions. In this chapter you will learn to classify words as nouns, pronouns, verbs, adjectives, adverbs, prepositions, conjunctions, and interjections. This system of classification provides a vocabulary for discussing word usage that can help you improve your writing and speaking.

Part 1
The Parts of Speech

The following chart will help you review the eight parts of speech.

Part of Speech	Definition	Examples
Noun	names a person, place, thing, or idea	child, Montana, song, happiness
Pronoun	used in place of a noun or other pronoun	I, you, my, these, herself, who, all
Verb	expresses action or state of being	is, does, have, catch, tastes
Adjective	modifies a noun or a pronoun	purple, ten, tiny, old, lovely, good
Adverb	modifies a verb, an adjective, or another adverb	very, too, well, here, not, yester-day, quickly
Preposition	shows a relationship between a noun or pronoun and another word	after, of, in, on, with, from, under, below, according to
Conjunction	connects words or word groups	and, but, or, if, neither . . . nor
Interjection	word showing emotion	Ouch! Terrific! Oh!

Part 2
Using Words as Different Parts of Speech

The same word can be used as different parts of speech. For example, a word might be used as a noun in one sentence and as a verb in another.

The only way to identify the part of speech of any word is to determine how that word functions in a specific sentence.

Noun or
Verb?
    The one hundred dollar *bill* has a picture of Benjamin Franklin. (*Bill* is a noun used as a subject.)
    The plumbers will *bill* us for their work. (*Bill* is used as the main verb.)

Noun or Adjective?	The artist folded *paper* into unusual shapes. (*Paper* is used as a noun, the direct object of *folded*.) At the picnic, we ate on *paper* plates. (*Paper* is used as an adjective, modifying *plates*.)
Pronoun or Adjective?	*What* is your favorite rock song? (*What* is used as a pronoun, the subject of the sentence.) *What* new shows are on TV now? (*What* is used as an adjective, modifying the noun *shows*.)
Adjective or Adverb?	A *low* wall surrounded the giant estate. (*Low* is used as an adjective, modifying the noun *wall*.) A seaplane cruised *low* over Myrtle Beach. (*Low* is used as an adverb, modifying the verb *cruised*.)
Adverb or Preposition?	After her persuasive speech, Sally sat *down*. (*Down* is used as an adverb, modifying the verb *sat*.) We sailed our raft *down* the Mississippi. (*Down* is used as a preposition.)
Preposition or Conjunction?	*After* the season, the debate team had an awards banquet. (*After* is used as a preposition.) *After* the moon came up, Tom and Huck sneaked out. (*After* is used as a subordinating conjunction, beginning a group of words that contains a subject and a verb.)
Interjection or Adverb?	*Never*! I won't try sky-diving again. (*Never* is used as an interjection.) Mr. Bailey *never* raises his voice in class. (*Never* is used as an adverb, modifying the verb *raises*.)

Exercises

A Write the italicized word. Next to it, write the part of speech it functions as in the sentence.

1. *Really*! Do you expect me to believe that story?
2. Mom *really* wants to see Paris.
3. *That* shop specializes in exotic pets.
4. *That* was Katharine Hepburn's best role.
5. *Name* a famous player who was with the New York Yankees.
6. One *name* for the Conestoga wagon was "camel of the desert."
7. The student made a speech to the *school* board.

8. The students discussed a new bus service for the *school*.
9. The ocean liner sighted the iceberg *before* the crash.
10. *Before* the ship crashed, few people worried about the insufficient number of lifeboats.

B Write two sentences for each of the following words. Use the words as the parts of speech indicated in parentheses.

1. comedy (noun, adjective)
2. toboggan (noun, verb)
3. those (pronoun, adjective)
4. along (preposition, adverb)
5. fantastic (interjection, adjective)
6. as (preposition, conjunction)
7. open (adverb, adjective)
8. signs (noun, verb)
9. this (pronoun, adjective)
10. picture (noun, adjective)

c *Write Now* A word's part of speech can often be determined by the ending of the word and its position in a sentence. Here is the first line of a nonsense poem. ''The *vapy koobs besaked* the *citar lently*.'' Try to identify the parts of speech of the italicized words. Write each word and its part of speech on your paper. Now create the next three lines of this poem, using a similar word order.

Checkpoint *Parts 1 and 2*

A Write the italicized word in each sentence and its part of speech.

1. That *picture* sold *for* half a million dollars.
2. *This* is the third time I've run *that* program.
3. *Ouch*! That antiseptic *really* stings.
4. *Canadians* celebrate their national independence *on* July first.
5. The emergency room at the hospital *is always* crowded.
6. The leaves of the *ancient* ginkgo tree look like small *fans*.
7. There was a ''No Swimming'' sign, *but* no one *saw* it.
8. The *Navajo* woman *wove* blue yarn into the blanket's design.
9. Are *you* studying vertebrates in biology *now*?
10. Ms. Diaz showed us her Mexican *and African* masks.

B Application in Literature On your paper, list the italicized words and tell what part of speech each word is.

(1) [Theseus] had not gone *far* when he met a huge man in a bearskin carrying an *enormous* brass club. (2) *This* was *Corynetes*, the cudgeler, terror of travelers. (3) He reached out a hairy hand, seized Theseus by the throat and lifted his club, which glittered *in* the hot *sunlight*.

(4) "Pardon me," said Theseus. (5) "*What* are you planning to do?"

(6) "Bash in *your* head."

(7) "Why?"

(8) "That's what *I* do."

(9) "A beautiful club you have *there*, sir," said Theseus.

(10) "So bright *and* shiny. (11) You know, it's a *positive* honor to have my head bashed in *with* a weapon like this."

(12) "Pure brass," growled the bandit.

(13) "Mmm . . . but is it *really* brass? . . . (14) A brass club *would be* too heavy to lift."

(15) "Not too heavy for me," said the bandit, "and it's pure brass. (16) Look . . ."

(17) He held out his club, which Theseus accepted, smiling. (18) Swinging it in a *mighty* arc he *cracked* the bandit's head as if it were an egg.

(19) "Nice *balance* to this," said Theseus. (20) "I think I'll keep it."

From *Heroes & Monsters of Greek Myths* by Bernard Evslin

Photo transformation,
Lucas Samaras, 1973.

Linking
Grammar & Writing

Imagine that you work for an advertising agency and that your supervisor has assigned you the task of writing an ad for a new means of transportation. The manufacturers of the product claim that it will make cars obsolete. Your boss says to you, "Make every word count! Give me powerful verbs! Dynamic nouns! Dazzling modifiers! Perfect pronouns and punchy interjections!" You have been given a limit of one hundred words to "Sell that product!"

Prewriting and Drafting First, brainstorm about this "new means of transportation." What can you visualize that would "make cars obsolete"? How would it get from one place to another? In what ways could this new machine improve on cars as a form of transportation? Make a sketch to help you picture your product.

Once you have a clear idea of your new product, then start thinking about the things you can say to sell it. Make five lists with these headings: *Powerful Verbs, Dynamic Nouns, Dazzling Modifiers, Perfect Pronouns,* and *Punchy Interjections.* Come up with at least five good word choices for each list.

Now, draft your ad, keeping in mind the following elements:

1. Be certain to use details that will give your reader a clear picture of the product you are selling.
2. Emphasize each of the qualities that make your product a wonderful improvement over cars.
3. Try to use at least two words from each of your lists of verbs, nouns, modifiers, pronouns, and interjections.

Revising and Proofreading As you revise, consider these points:

1. Will your ad capture your reader's attention?
2. Will the ad persuade the reader to buy the product?
3. Have you effectively used words from your lists?
4. Have you proofread for errors in grammar, punctuation, and spelling?

Additional Writing Topic Write a brief story, using one of the following words: *out, finish, down, cut.* In your story, use the word several times, each time as a different part of speech. See how many grammatical uses you can think of for each word.

Wilderness Words

The seventeenth-century settlers who carved out a homeland in the New World not only had to tame a wilderness. They also had to find new words to describe the unfamiliar creatures, plants, and landscape they found. In doing so, they drew on the English terms they brought with them. They also borrowed from Native Americans and from settlers from other European nations. Some of their most descriptive words, however, were ones they invented. Using their senses, they created vivid words that gave a clear picture of their new environment.

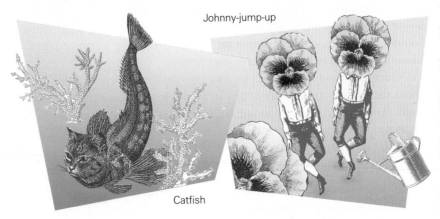

Johnny-jump-up

Catfish

Just one look makes it clear how the lightning bug got its name. Similarly, the razorback hog, catfish, and garter snake can be identified easily by using the sense of sight. Listen, and it's easy to understand how the chickadee, katydid, bobwhite, and whippoorwill got their names. The taste of the sweet potato and the look and feel of eelgrass are obvious.

Some of the plants the settlers encountered looked familiar, but the names needed fine tuning. Thus, there is the black walnut tree, since its wood is darker than the European variety, and the live oak, which seems to be green all year. The settlers even made up new names, such as the Johnny-jump-up and the basswood, for existing European plants. As they explored their new home, features of the land came to have simple and clear new words too, such as foothills, divide, and backwoods. Although the words created by the early settlers were simple, their appeal to the senses made them clear and descriptive.

Chapter 28
Application and Review

A Recognizing the Parts of Speech List the italicized words in this passage and tell what part of speech each is.

(1) *At* 2 A.M. on October 12, 1492, Christopher Columbus landed on a *small* island in the New World. (2) *Many* of the facts of this voyage are known, *but* one simple question remains—*where* did *Columbus* first land?

(3) Experts have argued their cases *for* nine different islands in the Bahamas. (4) Until recently, the choice of many scholars *had been* Watling Island, *which* was renamed San Salvador. (5) In 1986, a team led by Joseph Judge of the National Geographic Society *produced* what appears to be *conclusive* evidence that Columbus's first landing was at an island 60 miles southeast of Watling. (6) Using a sophisticated computer, Judge's team *electronically* re-created the suggested routes the fleet took *across* the Atlantic. (7) Computer analysis *indicated* that on October 12, Columbus's fleet would have arrived at the tiny island of Samana Cay.

B Understanding the Parts of Speech Write two sentences for each word below. Use the word as a different part of speech in each sentence.

that   inside   whistle   around   rose   end   run

C Using Parts of Speech Complete this short story.

(1) It (verb) a dark (conjunction) (adjective) night. (2) The (adjective) detectives, (proper noun) and (proper noun), were investigating a (noun) which took place (prepositional phrase). (3) "There definitely (verb) some kind (prepositional phrase) here," said (proper noun) to (proper noun). (4) (Pronoun) crept (adverb) around the (noun) only to find (noun). (5) Then the two detectives (verb) (prepositional phrase) and realized that (pronoun) was missing!

29

Using Verbals and Appositives

S ome people add excitement and variety to their lives by skydiving. Some wrestle alligators. Others might take up race-car driving.

Writers who want to add excitement and variety to their writing don't have to do anything that extreme. One way, however, that good writers can make their writing more lively and interesting is by using verbals and appositives.

In this chapter you will learn how to use verbals and appositives to make your writing livelier and more fun to read.

Part 1

Gerunds

A **verbal** is a word formed from a verb that does not function as a verb. There are three types of verbals: **gerunds, participles,** and **infinitives.** Verbals and the phrases made from them can make your writing more fluid and efficient.

The first verbals you will study are gerunds.

A gerund is a verb form that functions as a noun.

A gerund ends in *-ing*. It may be used in any way that a noun is used—as a subject, a direct object, an object of a preposition, or as a predicate nominative.

Subject	*Drawing* is Alissa's hobby.
Direct Object	Betsy tried *surfing*.
Object of a Preposition	The best place for *jogging* is the cinder trail around the Harvest Reservoir.
Predicate Nominative	One of the major industries of northern Minnesota is *mining*.

The Gerund Phrase

A gerund phrase consists of a gerund plus its modifiers and complements. The entire phrase functions as a noun.

Because a gerund is formed from a verb, it can have an object.

> We won by *scoring a touchdown* in the last minute. (*Touchdown* is the object of *scoring*.)

Like a verb, a gerund can be modified by adverbs.

> Elliott started *laughing again*. (The adverb *again* modifies *laughing*.)

Since a gerund functions as a noun, it can also be modified by adjectives.

> *Quick acting* saved us. (The adjective *quick* modifies *acting*.)

Gerunds can also be modified by prepositional phrases.

> *Sitting on these benches* is uncomfortable. (*On these benches* modifies *sitting*.)

The entire gerund phrase, like a single-word gerund, functions as if it were a noun.

Subject	*Eating pizza* was Joe's favorite pastime.
Direct Object	We enjoyed *seeing the movie the second time*.
Object of a Preposition	Kari got the concert tickets by *waiting in line overnight*.
Predicate Nominative	Nancy's favorite summer job was *working at the zoo*.

Usage Note When a gerund is preceded by a noun or pronoun, the possessive form of that noun or pronoun must be used.

Patty's coming late to music class distracted the students. (The possessive form, *Patty's*, must be used when it precedes a gerund in this way.)

The improvement in my math grade was due to *my completing the extra-credit assignment*. (The possessive form, *my*, must be used when it precedes the gerund.)

Sentence Diagraming For information on diagraming gerunds and gerund phrases, see pages 760–761.

Exercises

A Find the gerunds or gerund phrases in each sentence and write them on your paper.

1. Yelling at the umpire caused Joanne's laryngitis.
2. Mark tried losing fifteen pounds before the tryouts for the basketball team.
3. Windsurfing is one sport I'd like to try when my family visits Florida next winter.
4. Faulty wiring started the fire in the modern apartment complex.
5. We were tired from running so far.
6. Our vacation plans include a day of deep-sea fishing on the Pacific Ocean.
7. The citizens' main concern this year was flooding along the Des Plaines River.
8. Some people hate ironing, but I don't.
9. Marshall took a course in logical thinking at the University of Wisconsin in Madison.
10. One worthwhile way to spend free time is volunteering at a health clinic.

B Write the gerund or gerund phrase in each sentence. Then tell how each one functions in the sentence: *Subject*, *Direct Object*, *Object of the Preposition*, or *Predicate Nominative*.

1. Moving to Boston stirred Ken's interest in history.
2. Jean's current goal is sharpening her tennis game.
3. Will writing to the editor have any effect?
4. My grandmother enjoys scuba diving.
5. Sonya tried painting a dragon on the van.
6. Mending nets took much of the old fisherman's time.
7. How many calories does an hour of walking burn?
8. John remembered putting his key down.
9. One of the Olympic events is throwing the discus.
10. The fire chief warns against keeping the oven on for warmth.

C *Write Now* Gerund phrases are helpful when you write instructions about how to do something. For example, if you were explaining how to change a bicycle tire, you might begin like this:

> *Assembling your materials* is the first step in *changing a tire*.

Choose something you know how to do well, perhaps making a pizza or hitting a ball. Pretend you are preparing to teach the procedure to a class. Write clear, step-by-step instructions that explain the process. Use some gerund phrases.

Part 2
Participles

A participle is a verb form that functions as an adjective.

You have learned that the **past participle** is one of the principal parts of a verb. The past participle of a regular verb is formed by adding *-d* or *-ed* to the present tense, as in *walk—walked*, *dance—danced*. The past participles of irregular verbs are formed differently and must be learned separately: *tear—torn*, *sing—sung*. For a review of irregular verbs and principal parts, see Chapter 25, "Using Verbs."

You have also learned that there is another kind of participle called the **present participle.** The present participle is always formed by adding *-ing* to the present tense: *dance—dancing*, *dress—dressing*, *tear—tearing*, *sing—singing*.

Verb	Past Participle	Present Participle
look	looked	looking
bring	brought	bringing
cry	cried	crying

Participles are often used as parts of verb phrases: *had danced*, *am going*. When they are used as verbals, however, participles always function as adjectives. A participle modifies a noun or a pronoun.

> *Exhausted*, Lauren sat down with a sigh. (*Exhausted* is a past participle modifying the noun *Lauren*.)
> *Whistling*, he made his way home through the dark night.
>   (*Whistling* is a present participle modifying the pronoun *he*.)
> A *fallen* tree blocked my driveway. (*Fallen* is a past participle modifying the noun *tree*.)

The Participial Phrase

A participial phrase consists of a participle plus its modifiers and complements. The entire phrase functions as an adjective.

Because a participle is formed from a verb, it can have an object.

> The goat *chewing the shoe* belongs to Carla. (*Shoe* is the object of the participle *chewing*.)

Also, the participle can be modified by adverbs or adverb phrases.

> We heard the foghorn *moaning in the distance*. (*In the distance* is a prepositional phrase modifying the participle *moaning*.)

The participial phrase, like the single-word participle, always functions as an adjective.

> *Sprinting wildly*, Carlos beat the throw to home plate.
> (*Sprinting wildly* modifies *Carlos*.)

Punctuation Note A participial phrase at the beginning of a sentence is followed by a comma, as in the example sentence above.

Sentence Diagraming For information on diagraming participles and participial phrases, see pages 761–762.

Participle, Gerund, or Verb?

All present participles, all gerunds, and some verbs in verb phrases end in *-ing*. To distinguish among them, ask these questions:

1. Is the word or phrase used as an adjective? If so, it is a participle or part of a participial phrase.

   Tuning the piano, Hank listened carefully to each note. (*Tuning the piano* is an adjective modifying *Hank*.)

2. Is the word or phrase used as a noun? If so, it is a gerund or part of a gerund phrase.

   Tuning the piano will improve its sound. (*Tuning the piano* is a noun and the subject of the sentence.)

3. Is the word preceded by an auxiliary verb? If so, it is a verb in a verb phrase.

   Hank *had been tuning* the piano for two hours. (*Had been tuning* is a verb phrase.)

Exercises

A Write the participle or participial phrase in each of the following sentences. After each participle or phrase write the word it modifies.

1. Stars have varying degrees of brightness, or magnitude.
2. One measuring device for brightness is a photoelectric cell.
3. This cell, attached to a telescope in place of an eyepiece, can determine the brightness of a distant star.

The Pleiades in Taurus,
Hansen Planetarium,
Salt Lake City, Utah.

4. Early astronomers, classifying stars on the basis of brightness, developed an odd numerical system.
5. A dim star has a larger assigned number than a bright one.
6. Color is another attribute of stars studied by astronomers.
7. To the casual observer, most sparkling stars seem white.
8. Trained astronomers filter starlight through various colors.
9. The filtered light can be identified as red, yellow, white, or blue.
10. This color, observed scientifically, indicates a star's temperature.

B Write two sentences for each of the following verbal phrases. One sentence should use the phrase as a gerund, and one should use the phrase as a participle. Label your sentences *Gerund* and *Participle*.

> *Example*   peering into a telescope
> Peering into a telescope was a nightly ritual for Willie. (Gerund)
> Peering into a telescope one evening, Willie saw a luminous disk approaching. (Participle)

1. playing video games
2. frying bacon
3. delivering telegrams
4. reading science fiction
5. singing to large audiences

Part 3
Infinitives

An infinitive is a verb form that usually begins with the word *to* and functions as a noun, adjective, or adverb.

You have learned that the word *to* is a preposition when it is followed by a noun or a pronoun as its object. However, when *to* is followed by a verb, it forms an infinitive. The *to* is called the *sign of the infinitive*. Compare these examples:

Prepositional Phrases	Infinitives
We went *to the juice bar*.	We went *to swim*.
Josephine came home *to an empty house*.	Josephine came home *to study*.
I shouted *to him*.	I shouted *to warn him*.

The Infinitive Phrase

An infinitive phrase consists of the infinitive plus its modifiers and complements. The entire phrase functions as a noun, adjective, or adverb.

Because an infinitive is formed from a verb, it can have an object.

> Megan planned *to have a party*. (*Party* is the object of the infinitive *to have*.)

An infinitive may also be modified by adverbs or adverb phrases.

> The choir tried *to sing together*. (*Together* is an adverb modifying the infinitive *to sing*.)
> One customer demanded *to talk to my manager*. (*To my manager* is an adverb phrase modifying the infinitive *to talk*.)

Unlike gerunds and participles, infinitives can be used as more than one part of speech. An infinitive or infinitive phrase can be used as a noun, an adjective, or an adverb.

Infinitives and infinitive phrases can function in many of the ways a noun functions. They are often used as subjects or direct objects.

Subject	*To learn a new language* takes time. (*To learn a new language* is the subject.)
Direct Object	Diane forgot *to send the entry fee*. (*To send the entry fee* is the direct object.)

The infinitive or infinitive phrase is used as an adjective if it modifies a noun or a pronoun. It is used as an adverb if it modifies a verb, adjective, or adverb.

Adjective	Shelly needs someone *to advise her*. (*To advise her* modifies the pronoun *someone*.)
Adverb	Reginald is afraid *to talk to Jessica*. (*To talk to Jessica* modifies the predicate adjective *afraid*.)

Usage Note A modifier placed between the word *to* and the verb of an infinitive is said to *split* the infinitive. Usually, a split infinitive sounds awkward and should be avoided.

Awkward	Marietta tried to *patiently* wait.
Better	Marietta tried to wait *patiently*.

Sentence Diagraming For information on diagraming infinitives and infinitive phrases, see pages 762–763.

The Word Wizard

Comedians Bob and Ray have been performing in comic radio interviews since 1946.

Bob: And now it's time for another informative session with Doctor Elmer Stapley, the Word Wizard. Doctor Stapley is one of the nation's leading authorities on the meaning and derivation of English words. And he's here to answer the questions that you listeners send in about our language and its correct use. Doctor, our first letter to the Word Wizard comes from a woman in Ohio. She writes: "I am very upset about the grammar my nine-year-old son uses. Every day, he comes home and says, 'I ain't gotten no money.' How can I explain this complicated mistake so he'll stop saying it?"

Stapley: Well, I don't see what's complicated. Just tell him to get a job and earn some money. Then he'll stop saying he doesn't have any.

Bob: Well, I don't think that quite answers the woman's question, Doctor. Her son is only nine, so he can't very well get a job. I think she just wants to explain to him why it's wrong to say, "I ain't gotten no money."

Stapley: Well, problematically, the thing that's bothering her is that word "gotten." You see, her son is using the past icicle instead of the present tension. But that's hard to explain to a child. So I'd suggest having the kid use a completely different verbal and say, "I ain't in possession of no money."

Bob: And that's the only grammatical change . . . you'd recommend?!

Stapley: Of course. And please don't try to change my mind—because once I've solved a problem, I remain abominable.

Bob: This last letter comes from a lady in North Carolina. And she writes: "I work on the switchboard for a firm called Fleckny, Ignass, Wateford, and Swope. Frequently, I get calls from people who want to talk to Mr. Fleckny, Mr. Ignass, Mr. Wateford, or Mr. Swope. If they're all out to lunch, should I say, "None of them is here" or "None of them are here'?"

Stapley: The correct thing to say is: "All of them are not around."

Bob: Yes. I'm sure that would get the message across. Thank you for being with us today.

Stapley: Not at all. I was petrified to come.

Bob: Well, we always get a little nervous about having you here, too, but we seem to keep inviting you back anyway.

Bob Elliott and Ray Goulding

The *Voyager.*

Jeana Yeager and
Dick Rutan.

Exercises

A Write the infinitive or infinitive phrase in each of the following sentences.

1. The dream of pilots Dick Rutan and Jeana Yeager was to fly around the world without refueling.
2. Scientific advances enabled them to make a very fuel-efficient and lightweight plane.
3. The *Voyager* was designed to be a flying fuel tank.
4. The weight of the fuel made it difficult for the plane to take off.
5. In their tiny cockpit Rutan and Yeager had to endure the constant buffeting of the plane.
6. When storms bashed the plane, the goal was just to survive.
7. Mechanical problems, such as a faulty fuel gauge and a stalled engine, continued to cause worry.
8. With fuel to spare, the *Voyager* returned home after 25,000 miles.
9. Thousands of people at Edwards Air Force Base cheered the pilots' courageous refusal to give in.
10. The success of the *Voyager* may make it possible for planes to fly farther and more economically.

B Find the infinitives or infinitive phrases in the following sentences. Write them on your paper. Then tell whether each infinitive is used as a *Subject, Direct Object, Adjective,* or *Adverb.*

1. Don neglected to mention a few important facts.
2. The coat was too expensive to buy.
3. Ruth is too intelligent to believe entirely in luck.

4. Luis had hoped to play in the New York Philharmonic.
5. To own a horse is Sheila's dream.
6. I studied to learn more about the Mayan civilization.
7. Jeff needs something to do during his free time.
8. Our group's plans to hike the Appalachian Trail were changed.
9. The forty-niners hoped to make their fortunes in California.
10. To become a West Point cadet is Brian's goal.

Checkpoint *Parts 1, 2, and 3*

A Make two columns on your paper. In the first column, write the gerunds, gerund phrases, participles, and participial phrases from each of the following sentences. In the second column, tell whether a gerund is used as a *Subject, Direct Object, Object of a Preposition,* or *Predicate Nominative* and which word the participle modifies.

1. Jonas tried pitching with his left hand after he walked three players in the sixth inning.
2. The wildflowers growing in the park are goldenrod, bee balm, and goatsbeard.
3. Sue found the toddler painting on the wall.
4. Rabbits survive by running away from danger.
5. Gluing the pottery fragments together took several hours of tedious work.
6. Leaping out of the water, the dolphin aimed for the hoop.
7. Nora insisted on returning the carton of sour milk.
8. My friend suggested viewing the city from the skyscraper's observation deck.
9. Life is like playing a violin solo in public and learning the instrument as one goes on. Butler
10. Hidden rocks endangered boats that entered the channel.
11. Show me a thoroughly satisfied man, and I will show you a failure. Edison
12. We watched the glowing embers of the campfire.
13. Kayaking looks like fun.
14. Fame is a fickle food/Upon a shifting plate. Dickinson
15. Deserting the other hikers, the leader left to find a trail.
16. A rolling stone gathers no moss.
17. Washing clothes in hot water might shrink them.

18. A source of income for teen-agers is baby-sitting.
19. Ten sound tracks were used in making this record.
20. The hikers found a deserted cabin.

B Write the verbal or verbal phrases in each sentence. Tell whether the verbal is a gerund, a participle, or an infinitive. When you identify an infinitive, tell whether it is used as a *Subject, Direct Object, Adjective,* or *Adverb.*

1. The government tries to warn us of health hazards.
2. The burglar entered through an unlocked window in the basement.
3. To admit mistakes takes courage.
4. Jeans made in America are popular all over the world.
5. The passenger wanted to take the night flight.
6. Each carrier has a certain amount of mail to deliver.
7. Our mayor campaigned to become governor.
8. To live your life, you must discipline it.   Florence Nightingale
9. Theresa tried juggling five oranges and failed.
10. Martin woke to the smell of frying bacon.
11. The wagon master was responsible for leading the wagon train.
12. The defeated candidate accused the winner of vote fraud.
13. Talking before a group is difficult for many people.
14. My mother bought a suit to wear on the first day of her job.
15. Diving for the ball, the fullback brought the fans to their feet.
16. Steven Spielberg's movies are wonderful to watch.
17. To hike in this heat would be foolish.
18. The wastebasket was filled with crumpled papers.
19. I hope to see Waylon Jennings in Nashville.
20. Turning on the siren, the police officer drove her squad car through the busy intersection.

C Combine each of the following pairs of sentences. Follow the instructions given in parentheses. Eliminate the italicized word or words. You may need to make other changes in the sentence.

> *Example*   A radio can distract a driver.
> *It* blares. (Use a participle.)
> A blaring radio can distract a driver.

1. Over 40 million Americans enjoy *an interesting sport.*
   They sail pleasure craft. (Use a gerund.)
2. *Some* boats require an experienced hand.
   Some boats are driven only by the wind. (Use a participle.)

3. Boaters must learn *various skills*.
   They must hoist sails and handle lines. (Use an infinitive.)
4. Every trip on a sailboat is an experience.
   People on the boat are learning. (Use a participle.)
5. *This activity* provides an exciting challenge.
   This activity is sailing. (Use a gerund.)

Part 4
Misplaced and Dangling Modifiers

Place a verbal or verbal phrase as close as possible to the word it modifies.

If a verbal or verbal phrase is misplaced, it may appear to modify the wrong word and can confuse the reader. A word that modifies the wrong word or group of words is called a **misplaced modifier.**

Unclear   The Simpson children attempted to wash the family dog, *giggling wildly*. (Is the dog *giggling wildly*?)

You can easily correct this sentence by bringing the participial phrase and the word it modifies closer together.

Clear   *Giggling wildly,* the Simpson children attempted to wash the family dog. (The participial phrase, *Giggling wildly,* now clearly modifies *children*.)

Another kind of error is the **dangling modifier.** This error occurs when the word that the verbal phrase should logically modify is not in the sentence.

Unclear   *To mow the lawn,* the grass must be dry. (Who will mow the lawn? The grass?)

One way to correct a dangling modifier is to add the word that the phrase logically modifies. Sometimes additional rewording is necessary to make the sentence clear.

Clear   *To mow the lawn,* you should make sure the grass is dry. (Notice how the wording of this sentence has been changed. The phrase *To mow the lawn* now modifies *you*.)

Exercises

A Each of the following sentences contains a misplaced modifier or a dangling modifier. Revise the sentences to make the intended meaning clear.

1. To teach about computers, the camp hired an instructor.
2. Elliott saw several kinds of sheep motoring across England.
3. Slashing across the town, the people tried to escape the tornado.
4. By working at two part-time jobs, the trip to Europe was financed.
5. To change a diaper, the baby must be lying on its back.
6. Based on a novel by Alice Walker, we recently saw the film *The Color Purple*.
7. Diving for the fumble, the football bounced toward the goal line.
8. To learn the dance routine, the practices were long.
9. Walking home late, the cool night air felt refreshing.
10. Driving along the road, the skunk darted in front of our car.

B *Proofreading* Rewrite the paragraph. Correct all errors in spelling, punctuation, capitalization, and usage. Revise any sentence that contains a misplaced or dangling modifier.

Fireworks, safe only in the hands of an expert, is also called *pyrotechnics*. Combining gunpowder and other ingredents, most states prohibit the use of fireworks by individuals. The federal government limits the explosive power of fireworks. That can be used by individuals. Hollow tubes of paper are packed with gunpowder to create fireworks, coarse gunpowder propels rockets through the air. By adding special chemicals, beautiful colors are created in fireworks.

Part 5
Appositives

An appositive is a noun or pronoun that usually follows another noun or pronoun and identifies or explains it.

The appositive adds detail to your writing. Unlike gerunds, participles, and infinitives, appositives are not based on verbs.

> Tim O'Brien, the novelist, is a Vietnam War veteran. (The appositive *the novelist* identifies *Tim O'Brien*.)
>
> Old Faithful, a geyser, erupts nearly every 67 minutes. (*A geyser* identifies *Old Faithful*.)

The Appositive Phrase

An appositive phrase consists of the appositive and modifiers.

> Jean Nicolet, *the French explorer,* landed on the shore of Green Bay in 1634. (The adjective *French* modifies the appositive *explorer*. The entire phrase identifies *Jean Nicolet*.)
>
> The giant panda, *a black and white bearlike animal of China and Tibet,* seldom eats anything but bamboo. (The adjectives *black, white,* and *bearlike* and the prepositional phrase *of China and Tibet* all modify the appositive *animal*.)

Sometimes the appositive phrase precedes the word it modifies.

> *An epic tale of adventure and heroism,* the story of King Arthur is beloved by people of all ages.

There are two kinds of appositives—nonessential and essential. A **nonessential** appositive adds extra meaning to a sentence that is already clear and complete. In other words, the sentence could be read without the appositive, and the main idea would still be clear. Set off nonessential appositives from the rest of the sentence with commas.

> Grover Cleveland, *a bachelor,* was married in the White House.

Essential appositives make the main idea of a sentence complete. If the sentence were read without the essential appositive, meaning would be lost. Commas are not used with essential appositives.

> The cartoon cat *Garfield* is overweight, out of shape, and grumpy.

Sentence Diagraming For information on diagraming appositives and appositive phrases, see page 763.

Exercises

A Write the appositive or appositive phrase in each sentence.

1. Chief Crazy Horse, a Sioux leader, helped defeat General Custer.
2. On his fourth voyage to the New World, Christopher Columbus took his son Ferdinand.
3. Susan Gendrich, 1985's Tennessee Teacher of the Year, helped the Asian students of Murfreesboro, Tennessee.
4. The Florida Everglades, the largest marshland wilderness in America, is a birdwatcher's paradise.
5. Mary Shelley wrote the classic horror tale *Frankenstein*.
6. Venus, one of the most brilliant natural objects in the night sky, is sometimes mistaken for a UFO.
7. The first English child born in America, Virginia Dare, was a member of the lost colony of Roanoke.
8. A popular President, Dwight D. Eisenhower served two terms.
9. The poinsettia plant was named after the first U.S. Ambassador to Mexico, Dr. Joel Poinsett.
10. The *Nautilus,* a nuclear submarine, can stay under water for two to three years without refueling.

B Combine each pair of sentences by using an appositive phrase. Eliminate the italicized words and use commas as necessary.

> *Example*   Dr. Maas lived in Berlin. *Dr. Maas is* my math teacher.
> Dr. Maas, my math teacher, lived in Berlin.

1. Pearl S. Buck won the Nobel Prize for Literature in 1938. *Pearl S. Buck was* a popular author.
2. Last year my family visited Death Valley. *Death Valley is* the lowest elevation in the Western Hemisphere.
3. John Glenn became a U.S. Senator. *John Glenn was* the first American astronaut to orbit the earth.
4. On the starting line we stood next to Joan Benoit-Samuelson. *Joan Benoit-Samuelson was* the gold medalist in the marathon.
5. One English zoologist is famous for her study of primates in their natural habitats. *Her name is* Jane Goodall.
6. Angel hit a ball out of the park. *Angel is* the team's best player.
7. Boggs calmed Sheba by singing to her. *Sheba was* his panther.

8. Chief Joseph hoped to bring his people to Canada. *Chief Joseph was* the leader of the Nez Percé Indians.
9. When Bob opened the door, he bumped into his math teacher. *Bob's math teacher was* Mrs. Billings.
10. Andrew Young became mayor of Atlanta, Georgia. *Andrew Young was* a former United Nations Ambassador.

Checkpoint *Parts 4 and 5*

A Revise the following sentences, placing the modifiers close to the words being modified. You may need to rearrange or add words.

1. Flying through the air, we watched the trapeze artist.
2. The fans cheered the team standing by the sidelines.
3. To forgive a friend, a big heart and a sense of humor are helpful.
4. Scampering into the burrow, Susan saw the rabbit.
5. I finally caught my first pike trying my new lure.
6. Shaking in her boots, Alice tried to comfort the terrified girl.
7. I painted Eric's picture using my new brushes.
8. To save money for a bike, budgeting and patience must be used.
9. Misha identified the robber from a photograph, focusing intently.
10. Having sewn on the button, a large rip came to my attention.

B Write the appositive or appositive phrase in each sentence.

1. The slugger Don Mattingly was in a batting slump.
2. Marie Curie, a pioneer in the study of radioactivity, received Nobel prizes in physics and chemistry.
3. They saw the top of our highest mountain, Mount McKinley.
4. The villagers were used to the hot Saharan wind, the sirocco.
5. Seeing Eye, the first guide-dog school, was founded in 1929 in Nashville, Tennessee.
6. Mardi Gras, a holiday in New Orleans, means "fat Tuesday."
7. After many years, I told my family secret to my friend Markovich.
8. An African tribe, the Tuareg, delayed their migration so they could watch the last episode of *Dallas*.
9. Elena's grandfather once met Roald Amundsen, the first explorer to reach the South Pole.
10. Nadia Nogueira, a Brazilian medical researcher, has spent years studying parasite-transmitted diseases.

Linking
Grammar *&* Writing

Imagine that, at age seventy, you have been asked to summarize the outstanding achievements of your career for a magazine's "Person of the Year" cover story. The magazine editor requests that you first list seven events, beginning each statement with a gerund, such as: "*Graduating* from high school" or "*Starting* my own business."

Then, the editor wants you to choose the item that you consider the most important and write a paragraph explaining it in detail.

Prewriting and Drafting To think of possible events, consider the various areas of your life: school, work, family and friends, personal achievements, and pastimes. Use techniques such as brainstorming or clustering to help you create imaginary events.

As you focus on one of the events for your paragraph, remember to tell all the details that made the event your greatest achievement.

Revising and Proofreading Ask at least one other person to read your list and paragraph and make suggestions for changes. As you revise your draft, be certain to check for the following items:

1. Is the event told in detail so that it is clear to the reader?
2. Did you explain the reasons why the event is important to you?

Additional Writing Topic You are the host of a talk show called "Off the Wall." You have invited several unique people, such as those pictured below, to be on your show tonight. Write some facts about each of your guests. Use gerunds and participles in your sentences.

Chapter 29
Application and Review

A Application in Literature Write the italicized words or phrases in the following passage. Tell whether each verbal is a *Gerund, Participle,* or *Infinitive.* As you read, notice how much descriptive power the verbals add to the story.

(1) The dragon Smaug approached the village. . . . *Roaring,* he swept back over the town. (2) A hail of dark arrows leaped up and snapped and rattled on his scales and jewels; and their shafts fell back, *kindled by his breath* burning and hissing into the lake. (3) No fireworks you ever imagined equalled the sights that night. (4) At the *twanging of the bows* and the *shrilling of the trumpets,* the dragon's wrath blazed to its height, till he was blind and mad with it. (5) No one had dared *to give battle* to him for many an age; nor would they have dared now, if it had not been for the grim-voiced man (Bard was his name), who ran to and fro *cheering on the archers* and urging the Master *to order them* to fight to the last arrow.

(6) Fire leaped from the dragon's jaws. (7) He circled for a while high in the air above them, *lighting all the lake;* the trees by the shores shone like copper and like blood, with *leaping* shadows of dense black at their feet. (8) Then down he swooped, straight through the arrow-storm, reckless in his rage, taking no heed *to turn his scaly sides towards his foes,* seeking only to set their town ablaze.

From *The Hobbit* by J.R.R. Tolkien

B Using Verbals and Appositives to Combine Sentences Combine each of the following pairs of sentences. Follow the instructions given in parentheses. Eliminate the italicized word or words. You may need to make other changes in the sentences.

1. Our committee sorts programs for the Software Swap.
   We work all weekend. (Use a participle.)
2. The baby cannot be comforted.
   She screams uncontrollably. (Use a participle.)

3. The South American tourists drove through the Loop and the Near North Side.
They are neighborhoods of Chicago. (Use an appositive.)
4. Where did Ted learn *that?*
Ted can speak fluent Spanish. (Use an infinitive.)
5. Theresa will try *something*.
She will juggle five oranges and two bananas. (Use a gerund.)
6. In 1954, Roger Bannister became the first man to run a mile in under four minutes.
Roger Bannister was a medical student from England. (Use an appositive.)
7. Joan Chen is idolized by a billion fans.
Joan Chen is the most well-known actress in China. (Use an appositive.)
8. Donna returned the record album.
It had a scratch. (Use a participle.)
9. President John F. Kennedy had hoped *something*.
He would resolve the issue of civil rights. (Use an infinitive.)
10. *Something* is expensive.
Barrie trains in gymnastics. (Use a possessive and a gerund.)

C Using Phrases Correctly Each of the following sentences contains a misplaced modifier or a dangling modifier. Revise the sentences to make the meaning clear.

1. Swimming on the glass microscope slide, I carefully observed the paramecia.
2. Rumpled in a corner, Pat finally found the shirt he wanted.
3. Callie spoke on the phone to Barb while washing grandfather's breakfast dishes.
4. Reading the want ads, several job possibilities arose.
5. The dolphins put on a great show for the spectators, leaping through rings and doing somersaults.
6. To study effectively, sufficient lighting and a quiet place are needed.
7. Dropped on my street like a heavy, white blanket, I trudged through the new-fallen snow.
8. To compete in the state track meet, a qualifying time must be run.
9. Pretending to have a tea party, the teddy bears and teacups surrounded the toddler.
10. After examining the results of the experiments, a new hypothesis was formulated.

Cumulative Review

Chapters 26–29

A Identifying Modifiers, Prepositions, Conjunctions, Interjections, Verbals, and Appositives On your paper, identify the word or phrase that is of the type indicated in the parentheses following each sentence.

1. The United States of America imports many Korean products. (proper adjective)
2. Whenever it rains, the backyard and basement flood. (subordinating conjunction)
3. Please turn the lights in the kitchen off right now. (preposition)
4. Appearing in concert is Joni Mitchell, the popular singer. (appositive phrase)
5. Silver is heavy, but gold is heavier. (comparative adjective)
6. Wow! That play was great! (interjection)
7. Gene, exhausted after jogging six miles, took a break. (participle)
8. The mountain trail was extremely steep for the horses to climb. (adverb)
9. To earn a scholarship is important to many high school students. (infinitive phrase)
10. The national parks in Colorado are crowded during the summer. (prepositional phrase used as an adverb)

B Using Modifiers, Prepositions, and Verbals On your paper, rewrite the following sentences, correcting the errors in the use of modifiers, prepositions, and verbals. If there are no errors in a sentence, write *Correct*.

1. Trade problems between the three nations were discussed at a special conference.
2. Kareem Abdul Jabbar scored more points than any player who has played the game.
3. Looking for bargains, the bankrupt department store was full of eager shoppers.
4. After investigating the cause of the fire, the fire marshal blamed it on faulty wiring.

5. The ducks delighted the nursery school children eating the bread crumbs.
6. The mechanics couldn't find nothing wrong with the motor in the antique car.
7. I borrowed the history notes off Hank so I could study for the test.
8. Where will the 1992 World's Fair be held at?
9. The players felt bad about losing the basketball championship in overtime.
10. We saw the Great Smoky Mountains driving through Tennessee on our way to Florida.

C Recognizing the Parts of Speech, Verbals, and Appositives On your paper, identify each italicized word or phrase as being a *Noun, Pronoun, Verb, Adverb, Adjective, Conjunction, Preposition, Interjection, Gerund, Infinitive, Participle*, or *Appositive*.

(1) *Volcanoes* are openings in the earth's crust. (2) From these openings, gases *and* lava are expelled under great pressure. (3) Lava, hot liquid *rock*, comes from far beneath the earth's surface. (4) When the opening of a volcano *is blocked* by solid material, the various gases beneath the earth's surface force *themselves* up in a series of explosions. (5) The gas and lava then *erupt* from the new opening.

(6) *One* of the most famous volcanic eruptions in *history* took place in Italy in A.D. 79, when Mount Vesuvius, thought to be extinct, erupted. (7) The explosion destroyed the towns of *Pompeii* and Herculaneum, among others. (8) *Roman* observers wrote that there was a strong earth tremor *on* the first morning, followed by an explosion that sent a tower of ash and rock twelve miles into the sky. (9) *Incredible!* After this catastrophe, there was a fall of lava ash and cinders about three feet deep. (10) *Fleeing* saved some people; others tried *to take* shelter inside, *thinking* that the grim catastrophe would *soon* be over. (11) However, the next day there was *another* eruption that caused a rain of molten lava, pumice rock, and cinders that buried Pompeii and killed more than *two* thousand citizens.

(12) *Since* that time Mount Vesuvius has *never* been completely inactive. (13) An *eruption* in 1631 killed eighteen thousand people. (14) The last major eruption *occurred* in March 1944. (15) Mount Vesuvius has been quiet since then, *emitting* only puffs of gas; *but* scientists do not expect *it to remain* quiet for long.

30
Making Subjects and Verbs Agree

B allet requires the careful coordination of many different movements. A ballerina would find it awkward to perform in high top gym shoes. Ballet shoes, on the other hand, allow the ballerina to move with ease and grace.

In a similar way the subject and verb of a sentence must work together. A singular subject takes a singular verb; a plural subject requires a plural verb. In this chapter you will learn to make your writing graceful and unambiguous by identifying and correcting errors in subject-verb agreement.

Part 1
Agreement in Number

The **number** of a word indicates whether the word is singular or plural. A word is **singular** when it refers to one thing and **plural** when it refers to more than one thing. If a subject and verb are the same in number, they agree.

A verb must agree in number with its subject.

If a subject is singular, its verb must be singular. If a subject is plural, then its verb must be plural. The singular form of a verb ends in -*s*. A plural verb does not usually end in -*s*.

Singular	The gymnast dismounts gracefully.
	The cat stalks its prey.
	The reporter rushes to the scene.
Plural	The gymnasts dismount gracefully.
	The cats stalk their prey.
	The reporters rush to the scene.

In a sentence with a verb phrase, the first helping verb must agree with the subject.

The corn crop has withered in the blazing August heat.
The peaches have been ripening for a month.

Agreement of subjects and verbs usually occurs naturally. However, problems may arise when the subject of the sentence is not clear.

The subject of the verb is never found in a prepositional phrase.

When you make subjects and verbs agree, disregard any prepositional phrase that separates the subject from the verb.

The tapes on this shelf are mine.
The sound of the Bow Bells is familiar to Londoners.
Many constellations in the sky have names from Greek myths.

Phrases beginning with words such as *with, together with, including, as well as,* and *in addition to* are not part of the subject.

Honesty, as well as courage, is a virtue.
Broccoli soup, in addition to veal, was prepared by the chef.
Alice, as well as her sister, will perform in the talent show.

Exercises

A Write the form of the verb that agrees with each subject.

1. Even the best tennis players (try, tries) to improve their technique.
2. The mission of the Air Force pilots (was, were) accomplished with the help of ground control personnel.
3. The radio, as well as the flashlights, (was, were) ruined by leaking battery fluid.
4. The bottom row of the bleachers (is, are) almost empty.
5. Two of the bones in her foot (is, are) broken.
6. The oil from the damaged tanker (was, were) harmful to sea birds.
7. Homes near the river, including the mayor's, (has, have) to be evacuated before the dam breaks.
8. The woman in the white toe shoes (dances, dance) the lead.
9. Jane's earrings, as well as her bracelet, (jingle, jingles) when she walks.
10. Those photographs, including the one of Jake, (is, are) too dark to use in the school newspaper.

B On your paper, write the correct present-tense form of the verb in parentheses for each of these sentences.

1. An accident victim with third-degree burns (require) immediate medical help.
2. Leslie, as well as many other students in my class, (take) the subway to school.
3. The mongrel with the lame hind leg (lead) that pack.
4. The crews of the boats in the bay (have) races every Labor Day.
5. Some members of the committee, along with their friends, (be) planning the class Spring Fling dance.
6. The keys on the old player piano (be) worn and chipped from frequent use by my great-grandmother.
7. Only two theaters in Bedrock (show) first-run movies.
8. Snow (fall) until May in these mountains.
9. The pumpkins in this patch (be) ready for the Harvest Festival.
10. A doe, with her twin fawns, (be) grazing in the meadow.
11. Carbohydrates in food (supply) the body with needed energy.
12. Those denim jackets in the store (have) rhinestone trim on them.
13. Ted's guidebook, along with your maps, (describe) the best route to Starved Rock.
14. The music on that station (appeal) to listeners of all ages.
15. All the soccer players, as well as the coach, (wear) team jackets.

c *Proofreading* Proofread the following paragraphs. Rewrite them on your paper, correcting all errors. Pay particular attention to subject–verb agreement.

Among the most popular of American illustraters are Norman Rockwell (1894–1978). His paintings of familiar situations and common people tells accurate storys about american life. Best known is his cover illustrations for *The Saturday Evening Post* and other magazines. These covers are fine examples of Rockwells detailed, realistic stile.

Scenes from the cirkus appears frequentley in Rockwell's work. He has also used the theater, parks, and homes as settings for his famous illustrations a boxing ring, a blacksmith shop, and the White House is some of his more unusual settings. However, Rockwell is essentially an artist of the poeple. His most memerable paintings is simple, sentamental scenes of middle-class American life.

Part 2

Compound Subjects

A compound subject whose parts are joined by *and* is plural. Therefore, it requires a plural verb.

Jute and other natural fibers are woven together in the wall
hanging.
Steve and Marcella write for the student newspaper.

When the parts of a compound subject are joined by *or* or *nor*, the verb should agree with the subject nearer to the verb.

Neither Jan nor his friends eat sushi.
Either the jugglers or the tightrope walker performs next.

Usage Note Sometimes a subject appears to be compound when it is actually a single unit. In this case the subject takes a single verb.

Peas and carrots is a popular Danish dish.
Rock and roll was influenced by American jazz.

Exercises

A On your paper, write the form of the verb that agrees with the subject of each sentence.

1. Huck and Tom (was, were) creeping through the cold, clammy cave when they suddenly heard footsteps behind them.
2. Bacon and eggs (is, are) a typical English breakfast meal.
3. Either the cinch or the stirrups (has, have) to be adjusted before it is safe to jump.
4. A horse and buggy (is, are) still a common sight in communities of the Amish.
5. Neither the potholes nor the curb (has, have) been repaired.
6. Neither the curb nor the potholes (have, has) been repaired.
7. Either the Smoky Mountains or Yellowstone National Park (is, are) my choice for camping and climbing.
8. Ecuador and Colombia (exports, export) coffee beans.
9. Both Liz and Marilyn (bowls, bowl) on teams even though their scores are never very good.
10. Most people don't realize that neither the tomato nor the cucumber (is, are) truly a vegetable.

B Some of these sentences contain errors in subject–verb agreement. On your paper, rewrite the sentences correctly. If a sentence contains no error, write *Correct*.

1. Neither the drugstore nor the grocery open until 8 A.M.
2. Either Ms. McGee or Mr. Baez wear the gorilla outfit at the costume party every year.
3. Hail and windstorms damage many acres of crops annually.
4. On a hike cheese and crackers are a good snack.
5. Neither the mother panda nor her cub are on view yet at the zoo.
6. Because of torrential rains, neither the parade nor the fireworks were as spectacular as usual this year.
7. Cancer and tuberculosis attacks people of all ages and all occupations.
8. Either the soprano or the tenors is off-key.
9. Neither the cabinet members nor the President are available for a press conference.
10. Rockets and missions to outer space were once only science fiction.

C *Write Now* Think of two things that can be compared, and write a paragraph about their similarities and differences. You might choose two sports or hobbies, two classes, or two friends. Include sentences with compound subjects. Begin at least one sentence with *Both* and one with *Either*. Check for subject–verb agreement.

Checkpoint *Parts 1 and 2*

On·your paper, write the form of the verb that agrees with the subject of each sentence.

1. My recipe for corn muffins (is, are) unbeatable.
2. Both the lemur and the tree-shrew (is, are) among the primates.
3. The monkeys in that cage (seems, seem) livelier than most.
4. Three of my ties, including the green one, (needs, need) cleaning.
5. Bushes or a hedge (provides, provide) shelter.
6. Neither the flock of chickens nor the cow (has, have) been sold.
7. Victor, as well as his sisters, (plays, play) in a band.
8. The list of grievances (grows, grow) each month.
9. Two pieces of the puzzle (is, are) missing.

10. Either grits or a biscuit (comes, come) with breakfast.
11. Both the moon and the sun (has, have) an effect on tides.
12. The President, with his advisors, (is, are) visiting Canada.
13. I understand that French, as well as English, (is, are) spoken in that department store.
14. Neither the dictionary nor the thesaurus (is, are) mine.
15. The reasons for the confusion (was, were) quite clear.
16. The beginnings of human language (is, are) still a mystery.
17. Neither flour nor pecans (is, are) in the recipe.
18. A bag of nuts and raisins (is, are) my favorite movie snack.
19. Latitude and longitude (form, forms) a grid on the earth's surface.
20. Many students, including Marion, (has, have) never tried skiing.

Part 3
Indefinite Pronouns

To make a verb agree with an indefinite pronoun that is used as the subject, you must determine whether the pronoun is singular or plural.

Singular Indefinite Pronouns

another	each	everything	one
anybody	either	neither	somebody
anyone	everybody	nobody	someone
anything	everyone	no one	

Singular indefinite pronouns take singular verbs.

Nobody here knows the answer.

Plural Indefinite Pronouns

both   few   many   several

Plural indefinite pronouns take plural verbs.

Several of the candidates agree on the issues.

The pronouns in the box above take singular verbs when they refer to one thing. They take plural verbs when they refer to several things.

> <u>All</u> of the casserole <u>is burned</u>.
> <u>All</u> of the representatives <u>were</u> present.

> <u>Most</u> of the lake <u>has</u> a mud base.
> <u>Most</u> of the beaches <u>have</u> lifeguards.

> <u>Some</u> of the treasure <u>has</u> never <u>been recovered</u>.
> <u>Some</u> of the coal barges <u>are docked</u> at a pier in Duluth.

Exercises

A Write the present-tense form of each verb given in parentheses.

1. Most of my friends (enjoy) going to the zoo.
2. One of the world's largest zoos (be) The San Diego Zoo.
3. Most of the world's zoos (resemble) miniature cities.
4. Some of the zoo animals (come) directly from the wild.
5. Barriers between viewer and animals (be) minimized in zoos.
6. Some of the bird population (consist) of very rare species.
7. Either of Chicago's zoos (offer) a pleasant recreational afternoon.
8. Everything in a zoo (be) carefully selected for public appeal.
9. The zoos we have visited (provide) valuable educational services.
10. No one I know (have) ever been bored at the zoo.

B Write the verb form that agrees with the subject of each sentence.

1. Few of the rumors (seems, seem) likely to be true.
2. Not all of the Pacific islands (is, are) inhabited.
3. Some of the wranglers (was, were) heading to Omaha.
4. Nobody in town (has, have) spoken to the stranger.
5. Some of the spaghetti sauce inevitably (splatters, splatter).
6. Neither of the pens (has, have) a fine enough point.
7. The Alaskan people (is, are) gathering for the ceremony.
8. Most of the raffle tickets (has, have) been sold.
9. Many of us (wants, want) to take archery next year.
10. No one here (know, knows) how to jump start a car.

c *Write Now* Write a brief science fiction story involving time travel. You are the main character, and you are able to go backward or forward to any point in the past or future that you wish. Some of the scenes you see on your trip might be like the one pictured above.

Describe what you see and how people behave. Your story should include several indefinite pronouns as subjects of sentences. Check your work to make sure you have eliminated all errors in agreement.

Part 4
Other Agreement Problems

There are several other situations that can cause problems in subject-verb agreement.

Doesn't *and* Don't *with Pronouns*

Doesn't is singular. Use *doesn't* with the subjects *she, he,* and *it*. *Don't* is plural. Use *don't* with all other personal pronouns.

It doesn't matter to me.	I don't like jogging.
He doesn't live near Seattle.	We don't watch much TV.
She doesn't enjoy sports.	You don't come to the games.

Inverted Sentences

Sometimes the verb comes before the subject rather than after it. Such a sentence is called an **inverted sentence.** Inverted sentences often occur as questions, as sentences beginning with *there, here,* or *where,* and as sentences beginning with phrases. To find the subject in an inverted sentence, turn the sentence around to its natural order, placing the subject first. Then make sure subject and verb agree.

> <u>Did</u> the commuter <u>train</u> <u>arrive</u> on time? (The commuter train did arrive on time.)
> Here <u>is</u> your beach <u>towel</u>. (Your beach towel is here.)
> Into the sunset <u>rode</u> the <u>cavalry</u>. (The cavalry rode into the sunset.)

Nouns Plural in Form

Some words appear to be plural. That is, they end in *-s* as most plural nouns do. However, these words are singular in meaning: *mumps, news, molasses.* Use a singular verb with such words.

> Dark <u>molasses</u> <u>is</u> especially thick and gooey.
> <u>Mumps</u> sometimes <u>causes</u> eye or ear problems.

Many words ending in *-ics* refer to a science or branch of study and are considered singular: *physics, mathematics, genetics.* Occasionally such a word is used with a plural verb, usually when the word refers to qualities. When you are unsure about a particular word, consult a dictionary.

> <u>Physics</u> <u>is</u> taught at this school.
> <u>Acoustics</u> <u>is</u> a useful science.
> The <u>acoustics</u> here <u>are</u> good.
> His <u>politics</u> <u>are</u> strange.

Collective Nouns

A **collective noun** names an entire group of people or things: *class, team, flock, crowd.* A collective noun may be either singular or plural. When the noun refers to the group as a single unit, it is singular. Use a singular verb. When the collective noun refers to the individual members of the group, it is plural. Use a plural verb.

> The <u>majority</u> of the recruits <u>complete</u> basic training in six weeks. (Individual recruits complete training)
> The <u>majority</u> <u>rules</u>. (*Majority* is a single unit.)

Words of Amount and Time

Words or phrases that identify periods of time, weights, measures, and numbers, including fractions, are usually considered to be single units. Use singular verbs with these words and phrases.

> Two hours is a very long time to stand at attention.
> Just four teaspoons of hot sauce seasons this chili to my taste.
> About two-thirds of the fruit salad has disappeared already.

Titles

A title of any work of art, literature, or music is considered singular even though it may contain plural words.

> *Dubliners,* by James Joyce, is a book of short stories.
> Vincent van Gogh's *The Potato Eaters* was on display at the gallery.
> *Babes in Toyland,* with Laurel and Hardy, was filmed in 1934.

Exercises

A Write the correct form of the verb for each sentence.

1. Ten pounds of clay (is, are) enough to start your sculpture.
2. There (doesn't, don't) seem to be a possible road up the mountain.
3. The freshman class (is, are) sponsoring a float in the parade.
4. Heading for the warehouse (was, were) several fire trucks.
5. (Doesn't, Don't) the bus run late on week nights?
6. *Great Expectations* (is, are) on my reading list.
7. There (is, are) submerged rocks along this pier.
8. The news from the flood zone (is, are) that damage is severe.
9. Two cups of milk (is, are) all you need to add.
10. Statistics (is, are) an important field of study.

B Some of the following sentences contain errors in subject–verb agreement. On your paper, rewrite these sentences correctly. If a sentence has no error, write *Correct.*

1. There is special box seats for famous visitors.
2. It don't take me long to write a basic computer program.
3. Measles are a viral disease, not a bacterial disease.
4. Is five days enough time to get the job done?
5. Ethics are the study of conduct and values.
6. A swarm of bees attack any invader to the hive.

7. Three hours is excellent time for running a marathon.
8. Do junipers grow in rocky terrain, or do they prefer wetlands?
9. Our volleyball team play five-game matches.
10. Were *The Cardplayers* painted by Cézanne?

Checkpoint *Parts 3 and 4*

On your paper, write the form of the verb that agrees with the subject of each sentence.

1. Everyone in the stands (cheers, cheer) when the teams enter for the state playoffs.
2. There (is, are) a number of beautiful sights in New Mexico.
3. It (doesn't, don't) take long to learn this dance if you pay attention to the instructors.
4. Either of these paths (leads, lead) to the clearing but this one is prettier.
5. Mathematics (is, are) not difficult for my sister although it certainly is for me!
6. (Has, Have) any of those children played together before?
7. All of the water in those underground tanks (has, have) been contaminated.
8. Many of King Arthur's knights (was, were) looking for the grail.
9. Fifty feet (is, are) the width of a regulation basketball court.
10. *The Magnificent Ambersons* (was, were) a motion picture directed by Orson Welles.
11. There (is, are) a swinging bridge across the canyon, but no one in our group would cross it.
12. Neither of the routes across the mountains (is, are) passable during the winter months.
13. Some of the words in the English language (comes, come) from Arabic.
14. Some of the heavy traffic (has, have) been diverted.
15. (Is, Are) ten dollars too much to pay for this meal?
16. (Does, Do) either of these books explain falconry?
17. A few of the things in our flooded basement (is, are) ruined.
18. Here (is, are) a wood-burning stove and some fuel.
19. The exhausted jury (is, are) going to their hotel rooms for a rest.
20. The jury (has, have) finally reached a verdict.

Linking
Grammar & Writing

Imagine that you are responsible for selecting a musical group for the school's Fall Festival. To determine musical tastes, you survey students and teachers. Here are the results. Write a report on the results.

	Students	Teachers
Do you enjoy music?	100%	100%
Do you enjoy loud music?	70%	25%
Do you prefer rock?	60%	40%
Do you prefer country?	30%	20%
Do you prefer jazz?	10%	40%

Prewriting and Drafting Make a list of statements summarizing the results of your survey. Consult this list as you write your draft. Keep your audience in mind and remember that your purpose is to help the student council make a selection. Decide whether you will only summarize the results of your survey or whether you will add your own opinions. Use indefinite pronouns in your writing.

Revising and Proofreading Make sure that you have stated your main point clearly and in such a way that your readers can refer to it easily. You may wish to place this main point in your final paragraph, with a heading such as "Recommendations" or "Survey Results."

Additional Writing Topic Zyxxt and Qlut are extraterrestrials who have just landed on earth. Qlut has prepared a speech in English, but she has made some mistakes in subject–verb agreement. Rewrite the speech for her, correcting all errors. Note, however, that in some circumstances incorrect usage can add humor to writing.

> Greetings Earth People:
> We, Zyxxt and Qlut, come in peace from the planet Thorax. We doesn't want to frighten you. Zyxxt don't mean harm, and I doesn't either. Where are your leader? We want to explain our mission. Here is some gifts of fruits from our planet. There is glimps, blyds, and flizzers for you to eat. Doesn't they look delicious? We doesn't plan to stay on earth very long, but we hope you will visit our home in the future. There is many things to see and do on Thorax.

LANGUAGE LORE

O.K.

A merican Presidents are remembered for many contributions to world history, but President Martin Van Buren was responsible for what is surely one of the most unusual contributions—he popularized the expression *OK*.

Van Buren and Ruin, political cartoon.

No one is exactly sure when *OK* was used for the first time. Some scholars claim it can be traced to a West African expression in use before the American Revolution. Others think it came from a port in Haiti called "Aux Cayes." Still others link it to an expression in the early nineteenth century, "Orl Kerrect." In any case, it came to prominence during President Van Buren's reelection campaign in 1840.

Van Buren, who was elected President in 1836, was a native of Kinderhook, New York. He was known by the nickname "Old Kinderhook," or "O.K." His supporters formed the O.K. Democratic Club, and "O.K." became a familiar cry of approval for the candidate. People chanted "O.K." at rallies, and the letters appeared frequently on placards and in political cartoons. Foreign coverage of the campaign even carried the expression to Europe and Latin America. Since then, *OK* has traveled all around the world. It has become a term of approval that is understood and used in almost every language.

Unfortunately for President Van Buren, its popularity did not mean Old Kinderhook was OK with the voters. Van Buren was defeated in his reelection bid by William Henry Harrison.

Chapter 30
Application and Review

A Understanding Subject–Verb Agreement For each of the following sentences, write the correct present-tense form of the verb given in parentheses. Then identify each subject and verb as *Singular* or *Plural*.

1. The lane for bicycles (be) on the west side of the road.
2. A truckload of bananas (have) spilled on the highway five miles from the downtown area.
3. Warm gloves and a down jacket (be) critical for winter sports in Minnesota.
4. Fog and rain (have) inspired both painters and poets.
5. My recipe for corn fritters (be) simple.
6. Tolerance and honesty (be) easier to teach than to practice.
7. Neither cardinals nor chickadees (fly) south in winter.
8. The sounds of a foghorn (echo) across the harbor every morning at 6:00 A.M.
9. In *The Odyssey,* a bag of winds (cause) problems for Odysseus.
10. Neither the North Pole nor the South Pole (be) suitable for human inhabitants.
11. Neither white rice nor white bread (provide) as much nutrition as brown rice.
12. All roads leading from town (be) flooded.
13. The purpose of the rugged camping trips (be) to develop survival skills.
14. Both salt water and chlorine (aggravate) an infection.
15. Farming and ranching (have) replaced buffalo hunting for many Native Americans on the Plains.

B Correcting Agreement Errors Some of the following sentences contain errors in subject–verb agreement. On your paper, re-write the sentences correctly. If there are no errors in a sentence, write *Correct.*

1. Genetics are the branch of biology that includes the study of heredity.
2. All of the snow in front of the house has blown into drifts.
3. Almost three-fourths of the soybean crop in Arkansas have been harvested.

4. Do each of the gondolas carry ten passengers?
5. The litter of kittens are in a wicker basket near the warm stove.
6. Another of those old westerns, *High Noon,* are on TV tonight at 8:00 P.M.
7. The *Confessions* of Rousseau are still read today.
8. Don't Kerry and Tim have the lead roles?
9. Here is several abandoned miners' huts.
10. A flock of blackbirds create a deafening noise.

C Recognizing Agreement Errors On your paper, rewrite the following sentences, correcting errors in subject–verb agreement. If a sentence has no error, write *Correct.*

1. About 15 million Americans runs more than a mile several times a week.
2. The popularity of the sport has led to a wealth of scientific research.
3. Many advantages of running has been well documented.
4. This vigorous exercise strengthen the heart muscle.
5. It also releases a stress-reducing hormone in the brain.
6. There is, however, some disadvantages to running.
7. Shin splints, runner's knee, Achilles' tendonitis, and heel spurs is short-term runners' ailments.
8. More long-term damage result from running with minor injuries and over-racing.
9. Most runners does not need to worry about serious injury.
10. A reasonable training program of up to thirty miles a week are considered safe.

D Making Subjects and Verbs Agree Complete each sentence. Make sure that your subjects and verbs agree. Write your sentences in the present tense.

1. Both Washington and Hawaii
2. Few in the crowded hall
3. Neither exercises nor diet
4. Each of the band members
5. The ringmaster, as well as several performers,
6. Some of the caves in the Smoky Mountains
7. Lee, Ann, and Sara all
8. Swimming and jogging
9. Either my grandparents or my great-uncle
10. Several of the stray dogs

31

Clauses and Sentence Structure

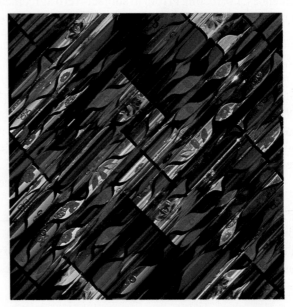

Diagonal, stained glass,
Fredrica H. Fields.

*R*ich colors and diverse shapes add to the beauty of this stained-glass window. As light passes through the window, it seems to glow warmly.

Diversity can add richness and beauty to language as well. You can make your writing more interesting by using a variety of sentence structures. In this chapter you will learn how to use independent and subordinate clauses to form compound, complex, and compound-complex sentences.

Part 1
What Is a Clause?

A clause is a group of words that contains both a subject and a predicate. There are two kinds of clauses: independent clauses and subordinate clauses.

Independent Clauses

A clause that can stand alone as a sentence is an independent, or main, clause.

Each sentence below has two independent clauses.

> The World Series ended, and the football season began.
> The instructions were vague, but the nurse nodded.

In both sentences, the subject of each clause has been underlined once. The verb has been underlined twice. The clauses in both examples can stand alone as sentences.

> The World Series ended.
> The football season began.
> The instructions were vague.
> The nurse nodded.

In the sentence below, which clause can stand alone as a sentence?

> If the treaty is signed, the President will return tomorrow.

Both clauses have a subject and a verb. However, only the independent clause can stand alone as a sentence.

Not a Sentence   If the treaty is signed.
Sentence   The President will return tomorrow.

Subordinate Clauses

A clause that cannot stand alone as a sentence is a subordinate clause. A subordinate clause is sometimes called a dependent clause.

Here are two examples of subordinate clauses. In each clause the subject is underlined once and the verb twice.

> when the fog lifted   that I like best

To form a sentence with a subordinate clause, add an independent clause.

$\overset{\displaystyle\text{Subordinate}}{\underset{\displaystyle\text{When the fog lifted,}}{}}$ $\overset{\displaystyle\text{Independent}}{\underset{\displaystyle\text{we could see the mountains.}}{}}$

Subordinate ⌐⌐¬ ⌐⌐—Independent ⌐¬
When the fog lifted, we could see the mountains.

Independent⌐¬ ⌐ Subordinate⌐
This is the view that I like best.

If a clause can stand alone as a sentence, it is independent. If it cannot stand alone as a sentence, it is subordinate.

The holiday was over before we knew it.
The holiday was over. (The clause can stand alone as a sentence. It is an independent clause.)
Before we knew it. (The clause cannot stand alone as a sentence. It is a subordinate clause.)

Certain words are frequently used to introduce subordinate clauses. You will learn more about these introductory words on pages 651, 655, and 659. Some of these introductory words are listed below.

after	if	when	which
because	that	where	who

Do not confuse a clause with a phrase. A phrase does not have a subject and a verb. For discussion of phrases, see Chapters 27 and 29.

Clause   The character <u>who wore</u> *the sly grin* seemed the most likely suspect. (The clause *who wore the sly grin* has a subject, *who,* and a verb, *wore*.)

Phrase   The character *with the sly grin* seemed the most likely suspect. (The prepositional phrase *with the sly grin* does not have a subject and a verb.)

The character *wearing a sly grin* seemed the most likely suspect. (The participial phrase *wearing a sly grin* does not have a subject and a verb.)

Exercises

A On your paper, write the following sentences. Draw one line under each subordinate clause and two lines under each independent clause. Two sentences do not have subordinate clauses.

1. We arrived after the mayor had made her acceptance speech.
2. Do you know where the Isle of Skye is located?
3. Reading that book in ten days will be difficult.

4. The tree that my grandparents planted is over twenty feet high.
5. If the storm becomes worse, will the game be postponed?
6. We followed a trail that gave us a good view of the mountains.
7. The Council scheduled the meeting for two weeks from today.
8. The fans objected when the referee penalized the forward.
9. Penguins are social animals that nest in huge colonies.
10. Alana, who played superbly, won the piano competition.

B On your paper, write the italicized words from each sentence. Then tell if the words are a phrase or a clause.

1. *With a sigh of relief,* Shannon wrote the last word of her report.
2. *If you measure carefully,* you can adjust the pattern to fit.
3. Please don't slam the door *when the baby is sleeping.*
4. *As the bus pulled away,* I remembered my umbrella.
5. Jim finally found the missing shoe *under his bed.*
6. She did better as a yearbook photographer *than I did.*
7. *With a frown,* Ms. Rollins turned and faced the class.
8. Jan, *humming softly,* spread her towel on the sand and sat down.
9. *If you don't call before noon,* I'll assume you have a ride.
10. Our friend, *who is from Japan,* performed a tea ceremony for us.

c *White Now* Write an account of walking home at night on a dark, shadowy street. Use some sentences with dependent clauses.

Checkpoint Part 1

A Identify the two clauses in each sentence: *Independent + Independent, Subordinate + Independent,* or *Independent + Subordinate.*

1. Although the factory has closed, it will reopen soon.
2. The map is old, but it will serve as a general guide.
3. The courtroom artists sketched as the witnesses talked.
4. The radio doesn't play well unless it is facing south.
5. Debra applied for a job at the riding stable, and she was hired.
6. When we awoke at four o'clock, the sky was already light.
7. Chief Joseph fought hard to keep the country that he loved.
8. When we visited Yellowstone Park, we saw Old Faithful erupt.
9. The ship's cat was ten years old, and it lived a life of action.
10. They scaled Kings Peak, which is the tallest peak in Utah.

B Application in Literature On your paper, write the italicized groups of words. Tell whether the word group is a phrase or a clause. Identify clauses as subordinate or independent. Notice how the use of clauses adds detail to the paragraph and variety to the sentences.

(1) She was a large woman *with a large purse* that had everything in it but a hammer and nails. (2) *It had a long strap,* and she carried it slung across her shoulder. (3) It was about eleven o'clock at night, dark, and she was walking alone, *when a boy ran up behind her and tried to snatch her purse.* (4) The strap broke *with the sudden single tug* the boy gave it from behind. (5) But the boy's weight and the weight of the purse combined caused him to lose his balance. (6) Instead of taking off full blast *as he had hoped,* the boy fell on his back on the sidewalk and *his legs flew up.* (7) *The large woman simply turned around and kicked him right square in his blue-jeaned sitter.* (8) Then she reached down, picked the boy up by his shirt front, and shook him *until his teeth rattled.*

(9) *After that* the woman said, "Pick up my pocketbook, boy and give it here."

From "Thank You, M'am" by Langston Hughes

Part 2
Adjective Clauses

An adjective clause is a subordinate clause that is used as an adjective to modify a noun or a pronoun.

Like adjectives, adjective clauses tell *what kind* or *which one*. However, an adjective clause usually follows the word it modifies.

Adjective   *Part-time* students are excused early.

Adjective Clause   Students *who work part time* are excused early.

Words That Introduce Adjective Clauses

Most adjective clauses are introduced by a relative pronoun:

Relative Pronouns				
who	whom	whose	that	which

A relative pronoun links or relates the clause to the word it modifies. The relative pronoun also functions within the clause as a subject, an object, or a modifier.

Subject   There is the artist *who painted the mural.* (The relative pronoun *who* is the subject of the verb *painted* in the adjective clause.)

Direct Object   The person *whom we asked* was helpful. (The relative pronoun *whom* is the object of the verb *asked* in the adjective clause.)

Object of   The girl *with whom I spoke* is a cousin.
Preposition   (The relative pronoun *whom* is the object of the preposition *with* in the adjective clause.)

Modifier   Children *whose parents work here* go to the day-care center. (The relative pronoun *whose* modifies the subject of the adjective clause.)

Where, when, why, before, and *since* may also introduce adjective clauses. Such words are sometimes called **relative adverbs.**

We visited a studio *where recordings are made.*

Sometimes the introductory word in an adjective clause is omitted. However, the clause still contains a subject and verb and functions as an adjective.

Lincoln is the President *most historians admire*. (The relative pronoun *whom* has been omitted.)

Sentence Diagraming For information on diagraming sentences with adjective clauses, see page 764.

Exercise

Write the adjective clause in each of the following sentences. Then underline the relative pronoun or the relative adverb that introduces the clause. After each clause, write the word that it modifies.

> *Example*   The dentist whose office is upstairs is an
> orthodontist.
> <u>whose</u> office is upstairs, dentist

1. The architect designed a house that is made of steel and glass.
2. This is the friend whom we met in New York.
3. Early spring is the time of year when flash floods often occur.
4. The directions she gives are always clear.
5. Dave is a manager whose word is law.
6. The mayor gave several reasons why the beach should be closed.
7. E.E. Cummings is the poet who seldom uses capital letters.
8. Degas is the artist whose work is on display now.
9. That is the carpenter of whom I spoke.
10. Staph germs head for body tissue that is damaged.

Essential and Nonessential Adjective Clauses

An essential adjective clause is a clause that is essential to the meaning of the sentence.

If an essential clause is omitted, the meaning of the sentence changes or is incomplete. Because essential clauses are necessary to complete the meaning of the sentence, they are not set off with commas. Essential clauses are sometimes called restrictive clauses.

In the city, I need a bike *that can bounce out of potholes*. (Without the clause, the reader would not know what kind of bike is needed in the city.)

A nonessential adjective clause merely adds extra information to the sentence.

The meaning of the sentence would be complete and clear without the clause. Nonessential clauses, sometimes called nonrestrictive clauses, are set off with commas.

> This touring bike, *which I borrowed from my aunt,* is perfect for the open road. (The clause simply adds more information to the sentence.)

In Chapter 33 you will learn more about identifying and punctuating essential and nonessential clauses.

Sentence Diagraming For information on diagraming sentences with adjective clauses, see page 764.

Exercises

A On your paper, write the adjective clause in each of the following sentences. Underline the subject of the clause once and the verb twice. After the clause, write the word that it modifies.

> *Example*   The bracelet that I like is silver.
> that I like, bracelet

1. The girl to whom I spoke is a Congressional page at the capitol for our senator.
2. My sister made a pet of a lizard that has found a home in our garden.
3. The table, which they bought at a garage sale, has a marble top and wrought iron legs.
4. In books I usually prefer characters who have a highly developed sense of humor.
5. Alice Walker is a writer whom I admire.
6. Harry Houdini, whose escapes astounded audiences, was from Wisconsin.
7. Is Grant Wood the artist who painted the picture titled ''American Gothic?''
8. We found a restaurant where we could enjoy Angeline's birthday dinner.
9. The tiger lily, which is a popular garden flower, originally came from Asia.
10. Spring is the season when almost all the trees in the park are in blossom.

B Combine each of the following pairs into a sentence with an adjective clause. Use the introductory word given in parentheses.

> *Example*   The weaver is Peruvian.
> He made this cloth. (who)
> The weaver who made this cloth is Peruvian.

1. Here is a list of players.
   Their contracts have been renewed. (whose)
2. The window was repaired yesterday.
   It was broken. (that)
3. This is the lake.
   I caught my first fish. (where)
4. The guide was courteous.
   We asked for directions. (whom)
5. We found the check in a letter.
   The letter had been put aside. (that)

C *Write Now* You are a junior editor for a nature magazine and must improve the following paragraph about lichens. Rewrite the paragraph, changing italicized sentences into adjective clauses.

> Lichens can survive after being frozen most of the year. *They are among nature's toughest plants.* These survivors are found in strange places. *You would never expect to discover plants there.* They anchor themselves onto bare rocks. They etch the rocks with acid. Then they grow into pits. *The acid has created the pits.*

Part 3
Adverb Clauses

An adverb clause is a subordinate clause that is used as an adverb to modify a verb, an adjective, or another adverb.

Adverb   We arrived *late*.
Adverb Clause   We arrived *after the <u>bus had left</u>*.
                  (The adverb clause modifies the verb *arrived*.)
                  We were sorry *that <u>we had missed</u> the bus*.
                  (The adverb clause modifies the adjective *sorry*.)
                  The bus left earlier *than <u>we had expected</u>*.
                  (The adverb clause modifies the adverb *earlier*.)

Like adverbs, adverb clauses tell *how, when, where,* or *to what extent.* They can also tell *why, how much,* and *under what condition.*

How	They spoke *as though <u>they had solved</u>* the crime.
When	*Before <u>it rained,</u>* we planted the seeds.
Where	Many plants thrive *where the <u>winter is cold.</u>*
To What Extent	He does not play the flute as well *as <u>Dermot does</u>.*
Why	*Because a <u>storm was coming,</u>* school closed early.

In the following examples, the subject or the verb or both are omitted from an adverb clause. Clauses from which words have been left out are called **elliptical clauses.**

> They are more experienced *than I*. (The verb has been omitted: *than I am.*)
>
> Complete the test *as soon as possible*. (The subject and the verb have been omitted: *as soon as it is possible.*)

Words Used to Introduce Adverb Clauses

All adverb clauses start with subordinating conjunctions. A **subordinating conjunction** relates the subordinate clause to the independent clause. Look at the following list.

Commonly Used Subordinating Conjunctions

after	as though	provided that	until
although	because	since	when
as	before	so that	whenever
as if	even though	than	where
as long as	if	though	wherever
as soon as	in order that	unless	while

Exercise

Write the adverb clause in each sentence. Put parentheses around the subordinating conjunction. Underline the subject once and the verb twice. Then write the word or words that the clause modifies.

> *Example*   We watched as the artist painted.
> (as) the <u>artist</u> <u>painted</u>, watched

1. Maurice Prendergast enjoyed drawing when he was still a child.

Umbrellas in the Rain, Venice, Maurice Prendergast, 1899.

2. He studied art in Paris, although he was born in Canada.
3. When he was in France Prendergast admired the work of Whistler.
4. Since he carved picture frames for a living, his interest in art grew.
5. Prendergast is considered a Postimpressionist because he used broad areas of color.
6. Watercolor was his preferred medium when he was young.
7. *Umbrellas in the Rain* was painted while Prendergast lived in Europe.
8. Although Prendergast used oils for his later works, these had the same mosaic-like effect as his watercolors.
9. While this talented painter's early works were gay and luminous, his later paintings had a wistful look.
10. Because the artist exhibited in unpopular shows, his following was never great during his lifetime.

Punctuating Adverb Clauses

An adverb clause at the beginning or in the middle of a sentence is set off by commas. No comma is needed if the clause comes at the end of the sentence.

> Although she was tired, Hannah did her exercises.
> Hannah, although she was tired, did her exercises.
> Hannah did her exercises although she was tired.

Sentence Diagraming For information on diagraming sentences with adverb clauses, see page 764.

Exercises

A On your paper, write the adverb clause in each of the following sentences. Put parentheses around the subordinating conjunction, and underline the subject once and the verb twice. After the clause, write the word or words that it modifies.

> *Example*   Unless it rains tomorrow, we are going to Tiger Stadium.
>
> (Unless) it <u>rains</u> tomorrow, are going

1. As he made his way across the stage, the actor appeared nervous.
2. When the bugle blows, the campers will gather for a ceremony.
3. This year's election winners were announced sooner than we had expected.
4. Since Gail had taken CPR training, she offered her help.
5. You hold the dog while I put its collar on.
6. Does sugar dissolve faster than salt?
7. The general will not return until the treaty is signed.
8. Our cat sometimes acts as though it were in charge of us!
9. Although there were storm warnings, several fishermen took their boats out anyway.
10. As the President spoke, his speech was translated into many languages and broadcasted around the world.

B On your paper, combine each of the following pairs of sentences into one sentence with an adverb clause. Use the subordinating conjunction given in parentheses. Be sure that your combined sentence is punctuated correctly.

> *Example*   The storm came up. (when)
>
> Everyone ran for the bus.
>
> When the storm came up, everyone ran for the bus.

1. The buses kept running. (even though)
   The roads were icy.
2. Down jackets are both lightweight and warm. (because)
   They are popular among winter hikers.
3. Neil Armstrong made history in 1969. (when)
   He became the first person to walk on the moon.
4. You have tears. (if)
   Prepare to shed them now.
5. The results will not be published. (until)
   The data has been verified.

c *Write Now* You have just had a day that was made up of one disaster after another. Write a paragraph in which you describe what happened. Use a variety of adverb clauses as shown in the following example. The clauses are in italics.

> *Because the dog had run off with one of my socks,* I went down to the basement for another pair. *While I was in the laundry room,* the toast burned. There was no more bread, so I ate cereal. *Since we were also out of milk,* I ate the cereal dry. *As I ran for the bus,* it suddenly pulled away from the curb. My days usually do get worse *before they get better!*

Part 4
Noun Clauses

A noun clause is a subordinate clause that is used in a sentence as a noun.

Noun clauses may be used in any way a noun is used. However, they most frequently function as subjects, direct objects, indirect objects, predicate nominatives, and objects of prepositions. Study the examples below. The sentences show the various ways that noun clauses may be used.

Subject	Our greatest *concern* is inflation. (Noun)
	What concerns us most is inflation. (Noun Clause)
Direct Object	Can scientists predict *earthquakes?* (Noun)
	Can scientists predict *when earthquakes will occur?* (Noun Clause)
Indirect Object	We will give the first *caller* a free trip. (Noun)
	We will give *whoever calls first* a free trip. (Noun Clause)
Predicate Nominative	His problem was *survival.* (Noun)
	His problem was *how he might best survive the shipwreck.* (Noun Clause)
Object of Preposition	She was worried about the *results.* (Noun)
	She was worried about *whether she had placed first in the meet.* (Noun Clause)

Words Used to Introduce Noun Clauses

Noun clauses are introduced by pronouns and by subordinating conjunctions.

Pronouns	who, whom, whose, which, what, that, whoever, whomever, whatever
Subordinating	how, that, when, where, whether, why, if, since
Conjunctions	(For a complete list of subordinating conjunctions, see page 592.)

Sentence Diagraming For information on diagraming sentences with noun clauses, see pages 764–765.

Exercises

A Write the noun clause in each of the following sentences. Tell whether the clause is used as a subject, a direct object, an indirect object, a predicate nominative, or an object of a preposition.

> *Example*   Where the ship has gone remains a mystery.
> Where the ship has gone, subject

1. Whoever wrote these directions never put a tricycle together.
2. No one could understand what the child was saying.
3. The principal gave a certificate to whoever had a perfect attendance record.
4. Most sportswriters believe that Hank Aaron's home-run record will stand for a long time.
5. The painful truth is that we have been outplayed by a far better team.
6. Send whoever is on this list an invitation.
7. The planning committee disagreed about where the fair should be held.
8. The brilliant Inspector Clouseau concluded that a cat left the catprints on the wall.
9. The speaker gave a graphic account of what happened when the volcano erupted.
10. My problem is how I can write two reports in a week.

B *Write Now* Write a paragraph about the origin of a popular food such as the hamburger, the sandwich, or french fries. Your report may be humorous or serious, factual or fictional. Be sure, however, to use a variety of clauses in your paragraph.

Checkpoint *Parts 2, 3, and 4*

A Write the subordinate clause in each of the following sentences. Tell whether the clause is an adjective clause, an adverb clause, or a noun clause. If the clause is an adjective or an adverb clause, write the word or words that it modifies. If the clause is a noun clause, write its use in the sentence.

1. Trees that follow day-night cycles may be damaged by bright street lights.
2. Who will pitch the opening game is the coach's decision.
3. I sketched the view I saw from our cabin window.
4. During the periods when the glaciers melted, rivers deposited sand and gravel on the continental shelf.
5. If your jaw swells after a tooth extraction, apply an ice pack.
6. The guide gave information to whoever asked for it.
7. What the audience wanted was another curtain call.
8. While he is in training, Julio will not drink soda.
9. The fact is that our car is too small for our family.
10. The trip went more smoothly than we had expected.

B On your paper, write the subordinate clauses in the following paragraphs. Tell whether each clause is an adjective clause, an adverb clause, or a noun clause.

(1) If you ask Americans to name their favorite dish, they might say hamburger or apple pie. (2) There are some people, however, who consider pizza the most popular American food. (3) The year 1984 marked the first time when pizzerias outnumbered hamburger restaurants in the United States. (4) Pizza is inexpensive. (5) This is no doubt one reason why it is so popular. (6) Also, it contains most of the basic nutrients that are usually listed on food labels.

(7) Pizza was invented in 1889, when a baker from Naples prepared a special pie for the Queen of Italy. (8) Using tomato, basil, and mozzarella cheese, he produced a pie that incorporated the red, green, and white of the Italian flag. (9) If the baker saw some modern pizzas, he would discover that they are stuffed or topped with everything from artichokes to zucchini, and in the Pacific Northwest even pineapple.

Part 5
Sentence Structure

In Chapter 21 you learned that sentences may be grouped into categories according to purpose:

Declarative	We are raking leaves. (makes a statement)
Interrogative	Will you help? (asks a question)
Imperative	Join the group. (gives a command)
Exclamatory	How fast we'll finish! (expresses strong emotion)

Now you will learn how sentences may be grouped into categories according to structure. The two basic types of clauses—independent and subordinate—can be combined to form four sentence structures: simple, compound, complex, and compound-complex.

Simple Sentences

A simple sentence contains one independent clause only.

The parts of a simple sentence may be compound. Each of the following sentences is a simple sentence with compound parts.

Compound Subject	*Freshmen* and *sophomores* faced one another on Field Day in a tug of war.
Compound Verb	Both teams *struggled* and *strained* in the mud.
Compound Direct Object	The winning team got *medals* and a *trophy*.
Compound Predicate Adjective	The losing team was *muddy* and *unhappy*.

Compound Sentences

A compound sentence contains two or more independent clauses that are joined together.

The clauses in a compound sentence may be joined with a comma and a coordinating conjunction: *and, but, nor, or, for,* or *yet.*

The <u>pitcher</u> <u><u>threw</u></u> a fast ball, *and* the <u>batter</u> <u><u>swung</u></u>.
The subway <u>car</u> <u><u>was crowded</u></u>, *but* <u>we</u> <u><u>piled</u></u> in anyway.
Either <u>we</u> <u><u>are</u></u> late *or* <u>you</u> <u><u>are</u></u> early. (Note that a comma is not necessary in a short compound sentence.)

The clauses in a compound sentence may be joined by a semicolon.

<u>Sharon</u> <u><u>writes</u></u> the newsletter; <u>we</u> <u><u>distribute</u></u> it.

The clauses in a compound sentence may also be joined by a semicolon and a conjunctive adverb: *therefore, however, moreover, nevertheless, consequently.* (For a complete list of conjunctive adverbs, see page 593.)

<u>Alligators</u> <u><u>appear</u></u> slow; *nevertheless,* <u>they</u> <u><u>can move</u></u> quickly.
(Note that a conjunctive adverb is usually followed by a comma.)

Sentence Diagraming For information on diagraming compound sentences, see page 765.

Exercise

On your paper, write the following sentences. Underline the subject of each independent clause once and the verb twice. Label each sentence *Simple* or *Compound*. Remember that a simple sentence may have one or more compound parts.

Example   <u>Hamilton</u> and <u>Madison</u> <u><u>defended</u></u> the Constitution and <u><u>secured</u></u> its ratification. Simple

1. The Native Americans of the Southwest have unique crafts.
2. Theodore Roosevelt and Franklin D. Roosevelt were Presidents with strong personalities.
3. The movie was dull, but the book was exciting.
4. Fog and drizzle have closed the runways at Edinburgh Airport, and all flights have been canceled.
5. The judge heard the evidence and then dismissed the case.
6. Dr. Jekyll was the kind doctor; Mr. Hyde was evil.

7. The filter should be replaced regularly, or the furnace will not operate at top efficiency.
8. Vanilla and unsweetened chocolate smell good but taste bitter.
9. The state suffered a serious drought last year, and farm production dropped.
10. The railroad is on strike; consequently, my parents drove to work this morning.

Complex Sentences

A complex sentence is one that contains an independent clause and one or more subordinate clauses.

┌── Independent Clause──┐ ┌─Subordinate Clause ──┐
<u>Clara</u> <u>purchased</u> a weed-eater although <u>she</u> <u>wanted</u> a tape recorder. (complex sentence with one subordinate clause)

┌── Subordinate Clause──┐ ┌─ Independent Clause ─┐
After <u>she</u> <u>cashed</u> her paycheck, my <u>mother</u> <u>bought</u> a VCR

┌──── Subordinate Clause ────┐
on which <u>she</u> <u>had left</u> a small deposit. (complex sentence with two subordinate clauses)

In the first example, the subordinate clause is an adjective clause. In the second example, the first subordinate clause is an adverb clause; the second subordinate clause is a noun clause.

Sentence Diagraming For information on diagraming complex sentences, see page 766.

Exercise

On your paper, write the following sentences. Underline the subject of each independent and subordinate clause once. Underline the verb twice. Label each sentence *Simple, Compound,* or *Complex.*

1. An article in this month's *Discover* magazine discusses dinosaurs.
2. My highest grade was 98; my lowest was 80.
3. My father gave me the cameo that had belonged to his grandmother.
4. I sometimes wonder what you will say next.
5. My cousin Delia was born in Puerto Rico but moved to New York.
6. Does anyone know why the governor vetoed the bill?

7. Pluto, which is a small planet, was not discovered until 1930.
8. When Hernando Cortez landed in Mexico, the Aztecs thought that he was a god.
9. The members of the Drama Club read and perform plays.
10. The Liberty Bell cracked as it tolled John Marshall's death.

Compound-Complex Sentences

A compound-complex sentence is a sentence that contains two or more independent clauses and one or more subordinate clauses.

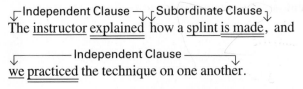

It may help you to think of a compound-complex sentence as a compound sentence with a subordinate clause.

> When we heard the news, we ran home, but the fire was out.
> (The compound sentence is *We ran home, but the fire was out.*
> The subordinate clause is the adverb clause *When we heard the news.* The adverb clause modifies *ran.*)

Sentence Diagraming For information on diagraming compound-complex sentences, see page 766.

Exercises

A On your paper, write the following sentences. Underline the subject in each independent and subordinate clause once, the verb twice. Label each sentence *Compound, Complex,* or *Compound-Complex.*

1. Colonists settled Roanoke Island, but then they disappeared.
2. After I wrote my report, I proofread it and made a clean copy.
3. The airlines know that some passengers will never appear; therefore, extra seats are booked for most flights.
4. Astronomers have identified a cloud of comets that is made of dust, rock fragments, and frozen gases.
5. Foreign leaders who visit Washington, D.C., stay at Blair House.
6. Meteorites blaze only a few seconds; nevertheless, their trails can be seen for miles.
7. We tried the exercises that the gym teacher demonstrated, but we couldn't quite master them.

8. After the polls close, the election judges count the ballots.
9. A bola is a weighted rope; it is used to catch cattle.
10. Hiawatha was the hero of a poem by Longfellow; moreover, he was the chief who founded the Iroquois League.

B Rewrite and combine the sentence sets below. Follow the directions given in parentheses. Use correct punctuation.

1. The audition began. Rachel was nervous. She played extremely well. (Use *before* and *but* to form a compound-complex sentence.)
2. Tourists expect the coast of Peru to be a jungle. The coastline is actually arid. (Use *however* to form a compound sentence.)
3. An airplane trip from Chicago to Orlando takes less than three hours. An auto trip takes about twenty-four hours. A train trip takes three days. (Use semicolons to make a compound sentence.)
4. We were sailing near the cove. The wind died. (Use *when* to make a complex sentence.)
5. The sun set. The wind started up. The temperature dropped to 65°. (Use *when* and *and* to form a compound-complex sentence.)
6. Sara sprained her ankle. She completed the marathon. (Use *although* to make a complex sentence.)
7. Connie read the novel. She did not see the movie. (Use *but* to form a compound sentence.)
8. I preferred ball point pens. I tried a fine-line marker. (Use *until* to make a complex sentence.)
9. Karen doodles on the phone book. Jason twists the phone cord. They talk on the telephone. (Use *and* and *while* to make a compound-complex sentence.)
10. The hurricane hit Galveston, Texas. Many people were left homeless. (Use *after* to make a complex sentence.)
11. Irma will have forty dollars in her savings account. She doesn't make a withdrawal. (Use *provided* to form a complex sentence.)
12. Field bees return to the hive. They transfer the nectar to worker bees. They convert it to honey. (Use *and* and *which* to form a compound-complex sentence.)
13. Many investigative reporters faithfully follow one rule. Never reveal a source. (Use a semicolon to form a compound sentence.)
14. You are not sure about the store's hours. Phone first. (Use *if* to form a complex sentence.)
15. Keep your brush moving. You apply watercolor. You will create harsh edges in your painting. (Use *as* and *or* to form a complex-compound sentence.)

Edible-nest swiftlet, Gomanton Caves, Borneo.

c *Proofreading* Revise the following paragraph by breaking up the strings of short, choppy sentences. Change some of the simple sentences into compound, complex, or compound-complex sentences. You may add or delete words as necessary. Also proofread and correct any errors in spelling or mechanics that you find. Make a clean copy of your revised paragraph.

One of the worlds greatest delicacies is bird's nest soup. This Oreintal soup is made with the white nests of a tiny bird. The birds are called swiftlets. The swiftlets build there nests on the high walls of sea caves. The caves are located along the coasts of Southeast Asia. The nests are very hard to find. They are even harder to collect. The nests are very fragile. Nest collectors use bamboo ladders to clime up the walls of the caves. Some ladders are 200 to 300 feet tall. Collectors carry candles for light. It can take as long as an hour to climb back down. The nests are extremely valuable. In fact, they are actually worth their wieght in gold. Becauze of the nests' value, the caves are guarded night and day to prevent outsiders from stealing them.

Part 6

Using Clauses Correctly

As you begin to add clauses to your sentences, watch for the problems of sentence fragments and misplaced clauses.

Avoiding Sentence Fragments

Although a subordinate clause has a subject and a verb, it cannot stand alone as a sentence because it does not express a complete thought. Notice the difference between the following word groups.

> The TV is on.   While the TV is on.

The first word group is a sentence. It expresses a complete thought. The subordinate clause *While the TV is on* leaves the reader wondering what happens while the TV is on. Treating a subordinate clause as if it were a sentence is one of the most common causes of fragments in writing. You can correct this kind of sentence fragment by making the clause part of a sentence.

> While the TV is on, we can't hear the doorbell.

See Chapters 21 and 22 for more about sentence fragments.

Exercise

Decide whether each word group below is a sentence or a fragment. If the word group is a sentence, write *Sentence* on your paper. If the word group is a fragment, make it a complete sentence.

> *Example*   When it was enlarged.
> When it was enlarged, the picture became grainy.

1. What did the announcer say?
2. What the announcer said.
3. After the rain stops.
4. After a while everyone went for a swim.
5. That showroom is filled with new cars.
6. Why the dogs are barking.
7. The books that you need.
8. Why is the flag at half-mast?
9. Before the test began.
10. When the players left the dugout and ran onto the field.

Avoiding Misplaced Clauses

Place adjective clauses and adverb clauses as close as possible to the words they modify. Otherwise the sentence may be absurd, inaccurate, or unintentionally humorous.

Unclear	They carelessly set the plant on a table that was dripping wet. (Since the clause seems to modify *table,* the sentence is not accurate.)
Clear	They carelessly set the plant that was dripping wet on a table.

Sometimes a misplaced clause makes the meaning of a sentence unclear. In the two revisions below, notice how the meaning changes.

Unclear	Mother told me as soon as I got home to start dinner. (The meaning is unclear.)
Clear	As soon as I got home, Mother told me to start dinner. (I was told as soon as I got home.)
Clear	Mother told me to start dinner as soon as I got home. (I was to start dinner as soon as I got home.)

Remember to place clauses so that the intended meaning is clear.

Exercise

On your paper, rewrite the following sentences, correcting each misplaced clause. Some words may require repositioning.

1. The trellis is in the rose garden which was built by my three brothers.
2. At the flea market I bought a horn for my bike that cost only a dollar.
3. There is a picture in the museum that the famous artist, Andy Warhol, painted.
4. The TV set is out on the lawn that suddenly exploded.
5. Jerome asked us as soon as the ball game started to wake him up.
6. We saw a baby in the nursery that had red, curly hair.
7. There was a nest in the tree that was made of mud and pieces of metal.
8. Consuelo found a box under the bed that was full of old sheet music and letters.
9. When my plane landed, my grandfather asked me to call.
10. We discovered a quilt in the attic that must have been my great-grandmother's.

Using **Who** and **Whom**

Who is a subject form. *Whom* is an object form. The use of *who* or *whom* in a subordinate clause depends on whether the pronoun is used in the clause as a subject, a predicate nominative, or an object.

Subject	The outfielder *who made that catch* is a rookie.
Predicate Nominative	Do you know *who that player is*? (That player is who.)
Direct Object	The outfielder *whom we cheered* tipped his cap. (We cheered whom.)
Object of Preposition	The rookie *to whom he hit the ball* made a spectacular catch. (Hit the ball to whom.)

Exercise

On your paper, write the pronoun that correctly completes each of the following sentences.

1. Give the envelope to the person (who, whom) answers the door.
2. Was it Prometheus (who, whom) gave fire to us mortals?
3. The cousins (who, whom) we are visiting live in Maine.
4. The senator to (who, whom) we wrote answered our letter.
5. The player (who, whom) caught the pass made a first down.
6. Teri is the aide (who, whom) everyone at the nursing home likes.
7. Lee is the delegate (who, whom) we have selected.
8. The student of (who, whom) I spoke does calligraphy.
9. Jo photographed two scientists (who, whom) tracked the meteor.
10. The biker (who, whom) I interviewed is winning.

Checkpoint *Parts 5 and 6*

A On your paper, identify each sentence as *Simple, Compound, Complex,* or *Compound-Complex.*

1. A useful tool for a writer is a thesaurus, which lists synonyms.
2. In reaching for the brush, Ricardo spilled the paint.
3. I like your sculpture of the elephant, but only the judges' opinions count.
4. Biltmore, which is in North Carolina, is the largest private home in the United States; it has 250 rooms.
5. Jambalaya and shrimp are specialties in New Orleans cooking.

6. With her arms full of pompons, Mrs. Perez announced that the tryouts for cheerleaders were about to begin.
7. One bird that can live over fifty years is the raven.
8. The hubcap fell off and clattered down the road.
9. Jason was the youngest child in his family, and he had often worn hand-me-downs.
10. Jana knew the movie was interesting, but she was so tired that she soon fell asleep.

B Each group of words below is either a sentence fragment or a sentence with a misplaced clause or incorrect use of *who* or *whom*. Rewrite each sentence correctly. If the word group is a sentence fragment, add words to make it a complete sentence.

1. While we waited for the train.
2. I found the key in my tennis shoe that I thought was lost.
3. The dog lay sleeping on the steps of the back porch that had puppies last week.
4. When the miners finally reach a vein of ore.
5. That the bald eagle has been identified by environmentalists as an endangered species.
6. I called the reporter whom had written about the basketball game.
7. I wrote to one of the friends who I met last summer at camp.
8. We knew after she was married that she would move to Iowa.
9. Before the tow truck arrived but after everyone had left the scene of the accident.
10. Everyone wondered who the class would elect for president of the student council.

c *Proofreading* Proofread the following paragraph for sentence fragments, misplaced clauses, errors in the use of *who* and *whom*, and spelling errors. Then make a clean copy, correcting each error.

Our next-door nieghbor, with who I am friendly, has a fence around her property that is made of thick wood. Every month or so, I climb up the fence for a quick survay. Of what she has in the backyard. An old rocker sits in a corner that belonged to her grandmother. A henhouse stands next to the rocker that is always empty. Since it is ilegal to keep chickens within the city limits. A steamer trunk leans against the fence which intrigues me. What my neighbor keeps in it. That will probably remain a mistery. At the far end of the yard is a kennel for my neighbor's German shepherd which was custom-bilt.

Linking
Grammar & Writing

Americans often set aside special times to honor someone or something. For example, the first week in April is National Laugh Week and August 2 is Friendship Day. Choose a person or an idea that you think should have a holiday. Write three paragraphs that explain why and how the person or idea should be honored.

Prewriting and Drafting First decide whether you want your composition to be serious or humorous. For a serious tone, list people you admire, ideas you value, and appropriate celebrations. For a humorous tone, consider exaggerating the importance of your subject.

Revising and Proofreading As you revise your composition, ask yourself these questions:

1. Are your reasons for honoring the subject clear?
2. Are the details of the celebration specific?
3. Have you used a variety of clauses to show relationships?

Proofread your composition carefully for sentence fragments, misplaced clauses, and other errors.

Additional Writing Topic Imagine that you are a reporter at a memorable fictitious event, such as the discovery of the lost continent of Atlantis by deep-sea divers. Use only simple sentences to write an account of the event. Then revise the account, using a mixture of sentence structures. Which is more interesting?

Chapter 31
Application and Review

A Recognizing Types of Sentences Identify each sentence below as *Simple, Compound, Complex,* or *Compound-Complex.*

(1) Today, photography is a national hobby and we owe it all to George Eastman, a shy man who rarely allowed his picture to be taken. (2) The work of Eastman and others led to greatly improved cameras. (3) Now, if you can push a button, you can take a picture. (4) Cameras have also become much smaller and they are inexpensive. (5) In fact, you can even buy a camera that you use once and then discard!

B Application in Literature Write *Adjective, Adverb,* or *Noun* to identify each italicized clause.

(1) *When I think of the home town of my youth,* all that I seem to remember is dust—the brown, crumbly dust of late summer—arid, sterile dust (2) *that gets into the eyes and makes them water, gets into the throat and between the toes of bare brown feet.* I don't know (3) *why I should remember only the dust.* Surely there must have been lush green lawns and paved streets under leafy shade trees somewhere in town; but memory is an abstract painting—it does not present things as they are, but rather as they feel. And so, (4) *when I think of that time and that place,* I remember only the dry September of the dirt roads and grassless yards of the shanty-town (5) *where I lived.*

From "Marigolds" by Eugenia Collier

C Using Different Kinds of Clauses On your paper, write each sentence. Add a subordinate clause, following the instructions in parentheses.

1. _____, we canceled our trip. (an adverb clause beginning with *Because*)
2. The umpire's ruling was _____. (a noun clause used as the predicate nominative)

3. A person _____ is my grandmother. (an adjective clause beginning with *whom*)
4. My younger brother asked me _____. (a noun clause used as the direct object)
5. _____, the bases were loaded, and there were two outs. (an adverb clause beginning with *When*)

D Understanding Sentence Structure On your paper, rewrite each example below, changing it to the kind of sentence named in parentheses. Add, change, or delete words as necessary.

1. The UN has tripled in size since its founding in 1948. (complex)
2. The beanbag chair that you have in your living room is extremely comfortable. (simple)
3. Although Rachel seems shy, she has a wonderful sense of humor. (compound)
4. Read the directions that appear on each section of the math test carefully! (simple)
5. English grammar, which seems hard to some, is really simple if you compare it with Chippewa grammar. (compound-complex)

E Writing Sentences Correctly Each example below contains an error: a sentence fragment, a misplaced clause, or an incorrect use of *who* or *whom*. On your paper, write each sentence correctly.

1. We sent the pictures to a newspaper that we had taken of the flood.
2. There is a very good radio in that car that gets both AM and FM stations.
3. Ernie ordered spaghetti and meatballs. Although he was not hungry enough to eat.
4. Pavarotti is the opera singer who I enjoy the most.
5. Rafaella had never seen a skyscraper or an elevated train. Until she came to Chicago.
6. I found the bathing suit in Aunt Jennifer's old trunk that doesn't fit anymore.
7. I liked the movie version of *Gone With the Wind*. I wondered whom the producer was.
8. The recipe called for butter. Which Juan did not have. He used margarine instead.
9. Be sure to send all Ralph's trousers and sports jackets to the cleaners that are dirty.
10. Mara's family was not rich. Although they were wealthy in many important ways.

Cumulative Review

Chapters 30 and 31

A Kinds of Sentences and Subject-Verb Agreement On your paper, identify each of the following sentences as *Simple, Compound, Complex,* or *Compound-Complex.* Some contain errors in subject-verb agreement. Rewrite those sentences correctly.

(1) You have probably heard of the seven wonders of the ancient world. (2) Did you know, though, that only one of these seven wonders are still standing? (3) That wonder is the Egyptian Pyramids; they was originally built as big tombs for kings. (4) The largest pyramids are found near Cairo. (5) The second wonder were the Hanging Gardens of Babylon. (6) These gardens hung about seventy-five feet above the ground, and they were irrigated by slaves who hauled up water from the Euphrates River. (7) The third wonder was the statue of the god Zeus at Olympia. (8) The forty-feet-high gold and ivory statue were made by the Greek sculptor Phidias. (9) The fourth wonder was the temple of the goddess Artemis at Ephesus, and it was once famous for its decoration. (10) Archaeologists in Turkey recently found a few fragments. (11) How excited they must have been when these was unearthed!

(12) No traces of the other three wonders remains. (13) One were a giant tomb built for Mausolus, who was an official of the Persian empire. (14) Its size and beauty was so famous that now large tombs built above the ground are called "mausoleums." (15) There were a colossal statue of Apollo in the harbor of Rhodes, Greece; this was said to be over one hundred feet tall, so large that ships could pass between its legs. (16) Finally, there was a huge lighthouse of white marble, which stood on the island of Pharos in the harbor of Alexandria, Egypt. (17) After guiding boats for a thousand years, the lighthouse were finally toppled by an earthquake.

(18) Ancient builders contributed many marvels of sculpture and engineering to the civilized world. (19) How much more awesome, though, is the events of nature that destroyed even these magnificent structures! (20) Which of our own modern wonders of art and architecture will survive these powerful natural forces and which will most impress future generations?

B Using the Parts of Speech and Sentences The following paragraphs contain errors in the use of concepts you have studied in Chapters 21–31. Rewrite the paragraphs and correct the errors.

(1) One hundred million years ago were the heyday of the dinosaurs. (2) The world was ruled by them gigantic reptiles. (3) Until they disappeared about 65 million years ago.

(4) Why did the dinosaurs become extinct. (5) No one can be sure, because different scientists blame it on different things. (6) Here is some of the theories.

(7) One of the theories suggest that comets bombarded the earth and spewed enough debris into the atmosphere to block the sun for months. (8) As a result, temperatures dropped, plant life died, and hardly no species living at the period survived. (9) A related theory is that a giant asteroid crashed into the earth, disrupted the atmosphere, and causes mass extinction of plant and animal life.

(10) Another theory suggests the dinosaurs could of died because mammals ate their eggs. (11) Still another states that over several centuries poisons built up in the food they ate, and it killed them.

(12) Even though they have became extinct, dinosaurs have not been forgotten. (13) Starring in numerous monster movies, comic books, and popular stories, many people are still fascinated by them.

C Writing Good Sentences Rewrite each sentence on your own paper. Follow the directions given in parentheses. The directions cover concepts you have studied in Chapters 21–31.

1. A volcanic eruption at Mount St. Helens took place in 1980. About two thousand people were evacuated from its path. (Change these simple sentences to one complex sentence.)
2. Repairs are needed on this highway. Accidents could occur. (Change these simple sentences to one compound sentence by adding the word ''otherwise'' and the proper punctuation.)
3. The slime monster was subdued by the furious chemist. (Change this passive verb to an active verb.)
4. Stephen made linguine for dinner, and Sarah made marinara sauce. (Change this compound sentence to a simple sentence with a compound subject and a compound direct object.)
5. To become an oceanographer. (Add words to change this fragment into a sentence.)

32

Capitalization

A dramatic difference exists between the residence of the American President and any old white house. That's why writers must make absolutely sure that readers know to which white house they are referring. They do this by capitalizing the proper noun, *White House,* and writing the common noun and its modifier in lower-case letters, as *white house.*

In this chapter you will learn to use capitalization to distinguish proper nouns—names of specific people, places, things, and ideas—from common nouns. Making this distinction in your writing will help you convey your meaning more precisely.

Part 1

Proper Nouns and Proper Adjectives

Capitalize proper nouns and proper adjectives.

A **proper noun** is the name of a particular person, place, thing, or idea. A common noun, on the other hand, names a general class. Proper nouns are capitalized. Common nouns are not.

Proper Noun	Common Noun
Shakespeare	writer
India	country

A **proper adjective** is an adjective formed from a proper noun.

Proper Noun	Proper Adjective
Shakespeare	Shakespearean
India	Indian

There are many different kinds of proper nouns. The following rules will help you to identify them and capitalize them correctly.

Names of People and Personal Titles

Capitalize people's names. Also capitalize the initials that stand for people's names.

> John Lennon   **H. G.** Wells   Susan **B. A**nthony

Capitalize titles used before people's names. Also capitalize abbreviations for those titles.

> Justice Sandra Day O'Connor   Dr. Elizabeth Blackwell
> Senator Daniel Webster   Gen. Bradley

The titles *Miss, Ms., Mrs.,* and *Mr.* are always capitalized. The abbreviations *Jr.* and *Sr.,* which follow names, are also capitalized.

> Mrs. Bennett   Mr. Ralph Bouquard, Jr.

In general, do not capitalize a title when it follows a person's name or when it is used without a proper name.

> Barb Sloan, president of Lake Bank, is on the school board.
> The judge has given the jury instructions.

Capitalize a title used without a person's name if it refers to a head of state or anyone in a uniquely important position.

the **P**resident of the United States
the **V**ice-**P**resident of the United States
the **S**ecretary of **S**tate (and other Cabinet members)
the **C**hief **J**ustice of the Supreme Court
the **P**ope

Family Relationships

Capitalize the titles indicating family relationships when such titles are used as names or as parts of names.

What was **D**ad like when he was sixteen, **G**randma?
The person who just called was **A**unt Allison.

If the title is preceded by a possessive adjective or by *a, an,* or *the,* it is not capitalized.

Our uncle works as a scientist overseas.
My mom's car needs a new battery.

The Supreme Being and Sacred Writings

Capitalize all words referring to God, to the Holy Family, and to religious scriptures.

the **A**lmighty	the **B**ible	**A**llah
the **L**ord	the **T**almud	the **N**ew **T**estament

Capitalize personal pronouns referring to God.

They asked the Lord for **H**is blessing.

Exercises

A On your paper, write the following sentences, using capital letters where necessary.

1. The real name of ann landers is eppie lederer.
2. My aunt was the person who introduced mom to dad.
3. State senator j. m. stansky will oppose the bill.
4. The story of moses is recorded in the bible.
5. The term of office of the U.S. president is four years.
6. My cousin nels and I spent spring break in florida.
7. "In god we trust" is stamped on American coins.

8. Miss havisham, mr. micawber, and mr. skimpole are characters in the novels of charles dickens.
9. My favorite food is aunt marta's chili.
10. The first adhesive postage stamp, which was issued in 1841, had a portrait of queen victoria on it.

B The following paragraph contains errors in capitalization. On your paper, write the words correctly after the number of the sentence in which they appear. One sentence is correctly capitalized.

(1) The hot-air balloon *children's moon* is a flying sculpture created by an artist from vienna. (2) the artist, andré heller, considers the sky an "incredible stage" that most other artists have overlooked. (3) As a child, Heller dreamed about a moon with six eyes. (4) The viennese artist used this dream as the inspiration for *children's moon*. (5) This and two other flying sculptures, *kiki* and *the dream lab*, were given to America by the people of vienna, austria. (6) Flying high over large american cities like philadelphia, they have often been reported to the police as UFO's. (7) The flying Sculptures, which range in height from 69 to 123 feet, are flown by licensed pilots with the help of computers.

(8) The art of mr. heller has also extended in other directions. (9) In the summer of 1987, he created a show that included a carousel by keith haring, a glass labyrinth by roy lichtenstein, an "enchanted" tree by david hockney, and works by twenty other artists. (10) This show was planned to extend heller's reputation throughout europe and north america.

Children's Moon, André Heller, 1987.

Part 2

Geographical Names

In a geographical name, capitalize the first letter of each word except articles and prepositions.

If the article *the* appears before a place name, it is not part of the name and is therefore not capitalized.

Continents	Africa, North America, Europe, Asia
Bodies of Water	the Indian Ocean, the Ohio River, the Gulf of Mexico, the South China Sea, Hudson Bay, the Panama Canal, Lake Michigan, Yosemite Falls
Land Forms	Mount Cook, the Aleutian Islands, Death Valley, the Allegheny Mountains, the Black Hills, Cape Horn, the Atacama Desert
World Regions	the Orient, the Far East, the Middle East
Special Terms	the Southern Hemisphere, the Equator, the Tropic of Capricorn, the South Pole
Political Units	Florida, Denver, the Province of Ontario, the Republic of Kenya, the State of Israel, the Thirteenth Congressional District
Public Areas	Glacier National Park, Fort Lee, Badlands National Monument, Central Park,
Roads and Highways	Route 66, Interstate Highway 610, the Santa Fe Trail, Hampton Road, Fifth Avenue,

When a word that names a geographical feature is not used as part of a proper noun, it is not capitalized.

The highest falls in the world are in Venezuela.
We visited the historic town of Marshall, Michigan.

Directions and Sections

Capitalize names of sections of the country or the world.

The West has many old ghost towns.
The Sorensons moved from New England to the West Coast.
Japan has close economic connections with the West.

Capitalize proper adjectives that come from names of sections of the country or the world.

a **M**idwestern town   the **S**outhern states
an **E**ast **C**oast company   **E**astern religions

Do not capitalize directions of the compass.

Fairbanks, Alaska, is north of Anchorage.
Drive east on Interstate 80 to New York.

Do not capitalize adjectives that merely indicate direction or a general location.

The parking lot is on the north side of the main building.
The hurricane hit the southern coast of Florida.

Bodies of the Universe

Capitalize the names of planets and other objects in the universe. Do not capitalize the words *sun* and *moon*.

Pluto   the **M**ilky **W**ay   an eclipse of the sun
Mars   Halley's **C**omet   rocks from the moon

Capitalize the word *earth* only when it is used with the names of other planets. Do not capitalize *earth* after the article *the*.

On Mercury the average daytime temperature is 625 degrees
    Farenheit; on Earth it is only 60 degrees Farenheit.
Many communication satellites circle the earth.

Exercises

A On your paper, write the following sentences, using capital letters when necessary.

1. The sahara in africa is moving south at five miles a year.
2. Some southern foods, such as cornbread, are now found on many restaurant menus in the north.
3. Many Japanese cities, such as tokyo, osaka, and yokohama, are densely populated.
4. The most famous address in the nation is 1600 pennsylvania avenue in the district of columbia.
5. The largest of south america's lakes is lake titicaca, which lies in a high basin in the andes mountains.
6. Jefferson national forest is north of route 58 in virginia.

7. The cascade range in the northwest is named for the ferocious rapids in the columbia river.
8. All of central america lies in the northern hemisphere.
9. The two moons of mars are named phobos and deimos.
10. Did you know that yellowstone national park covers parts of idaho, montana, and wyoming?

B *Proofreading* On your paper rewrite the following paragraph. Correct all errors in spelling, punctuation, and capitalization.

Australia is a land of oddities. In addition to the Continent's unusual animals, such as koalas and kangaroos, there are several geographical features that make it unique. One of the strangest lakes in the world is lake George, which is near Australias capitol city of Canberra. The Lake keeps appearing and disappearing, its disappearances apparently due to a combination of evaporation and low rainfall. The largest coral structure in the world extends for 1,250 miles along the northwestern coast of Austrailia and is called the great barrier reef it is home to at least 350 species of coral and teams with marine life. Another feature that looks almost as if it came straight from the Moon is Ayers rock, which towers 1,000 feet over the flat desert floor of northern Australia. Australia's Landscape has vast stretches of dry, open spaces. A visitor can fly 1,900 miles Northeast across Australia and see only a few signs of human habitation.

C *Write Now* You have just discovered gold. Write a paragraph describing the location of the find. Make up geographical names if you want, but be sure to capitalize them correctly.

Ayers Rock, Australia.

Part 3

Organizations, Events, and Other Subjects

Capital letters are needed to distinguish names of organizations, nationalities, and events.

Organizations and Institutions

Capitalize the names of organizations and institutions.

Use capital letters in the names of political parties, governmental bodies or agencies, schools, colleges, churches, hospitals, clubs, and businesses. Also capitalize abbreviations of these names.

Republican Party	Federal Aviation Administration
Federal Trade Commission	Children's Memorial Hospital
Stevenson High School	Universal Motor Corporation
St. Joseph's Church	AFL–CIO

Do not capitalize such words as *school, company, church,* and *hospital* when they are not used as parts of names.

Several people from our church do volunteer work at the hospital.

Races, Languages, Nationalities, and Religions

Capitalize the names of all races, languages, nationalities, and religions.

Greek	Polish	English	Hinduism
Oriental	German	Catholicism	Judaism

Also capitalize any adjectives that come from these names.

the Italian heritage	Native American cultures
a Thai restaurant	Polish sausage

Events, Documents, and Periods of Time

Capitalize the names of historical events, documents, and periods of time.

Battle of Concord	Panama Canal Treaty
the Hundred Years' War	the Middle Ages

Months, Days, and Holidays

Capitalize months, days, and holidays, but not seasons.

July   Thursday   Thanksgiving Day   winter

Abbreviation for Time

Capitalize the abbreviations *B.C., A.D., A.M.* and *P.M.*

The Pyramids of Egypt were begun about 3000 B.C.
Mohammed was born in A.D. 570.
The flight takes off at 10:25 A.M.
The practice ended at 2:15 P.M.

School Subjects

Do not capitalize the general names of school subjects. Do capitalize titles of specific courses that are followed by a number. Always capitalize the title of language courses.

history   Math 300   Woodworking I   Spanish

Ships, Trains, Airplanes, and Spacecraft

Capitalize the names of specific ships, trains, airplanes, and spacecraft.

U.S.S. *Constellation*   *Spirit of St. Louis*
Orient Express   *Voyager II*

Monuments, Bridges, and Buildings

Capitalize the names of monuments, bridges, and buildings.

Vietnam Memorial   Gateway Arch   Sears Tower

Awards and Special Events

Capitalize the names of awards and special events.

Pulitzer Prize   World Series   Mardi Gras

Brand Names

Capitalize the brand names of products. Do not capitalize a common noun that follows a brand name.

Dazzle detergent   White Teeth toothpaste

Exercises

A On your paper, write the following sentences, using capital letters where necessary.

1. Labor day is both an american and a canadian holiday; the american holiday is observed on the first monday in september.
2. My father will travel on the *southwest limited* this summer to attend a convention of the american dental association.
3. The thirteenth amendment to the constitution officially brought slavery to an end throughout the United States.
4. Both spanish I and my math class meet at 8:30 a.m.
5. King Tutankhamen, the egyptian ruler whose tomb was discovered almost intact, was buried about 1352 b.c.
6. Banana computer company, which makes the bananarama personal computer, has its offices in the world trade center.
7. The metropolitan museum of art in New York is the largest art museum in the United States.
8. From a.d. 1450 to 1532, the empire of the incas stretched for 2,500 miles.
9. The winner of the national hockey league championship receives the stanley cup.
10. The exodus of the hebrews from Egypt about 1250 b.c. is a major event in the history of judaism.
11. World War I led to the collapse of three ancient monarchies: the austro-hungarian, the german, and the russian.
12. On May 20, 1927, Charles Lindbergh landed at Le Bourget field near paris.
13. The United States senate and the house of representatives together make up congress.
14. One of the most beautiful buildings in the world is the palace of versailles in france.
15. Despite President Wilson's strong support for the league of nations, a peace-keeping organization, the U.S. did not join.

B On your paper, write the following sentences, using capital letters where necessary and correcting improperly capitalized words.

1. In a.d. 1542, Juan Rodriguez Cabrillo became the first european to sail into what is now San Diego Bay.
2. Cabrillo was a portuguese navigator exploring for spain.
3. Cabrillo national monument commemorates his exploration.
4. His landing is re-created during the september cabrillo festival.

5. Junipero Serra, a franciscan missionary, established the first mission in San Diego in 1769.
6. The serra museum in Presidio Park is named after him.
7. On july 29, 1846, the U.S. sloop *cyane* landed in San Diego with troops to fight in the mexican war.
8. The city is known for its warm Winters and mild Summers.
9. It is the home of tourist attractions, such as the san diego zoo, and research centers, such as the salk institute.
10. The university of california at San Diego is known for its challenging Science courses.

c *Proofreading* Rewrite the following paragraph on your paper. Correct all errors in spelling, punctuation, and capitalization.

The Bermuda triangle has mystified navigators for at least 500 years. As far back as 1492, Christopher Columbuss crew on the *santa maria* were terrified by their experiences in the sargasso sea. (This sea is part of the Atlantic ocean located within the Bermuda Triangle.) There the water and air were so calm that the sailors could hardly breathe. The ocean floor was so covered with seaweed that it resembeled an underwater jungel. Columbus's crew were even more nervous because in that Area their compass no longer pointed to the north star; it pointed six degrees Northwest. On october 12, 1492, Columbus's log reported an eerily glowing patch of white water. Centurys later, this strange phenomenon was reported by other explorers—the astronauts of *apollo 12!*

Checkpoint Parts 1, 2, and 3

On your paper, write the following sentences, adding capital letters where necessary.

1. In 1909 admiral robert e. peary reached the north pole.
2. Whitney young, jr., headed the national urban league.
3. The prime minister of israel was ms. golda meir.
4. The missouri river flows into the mississippi river near st. louis, missouri.
5. A delegation of presbyterian ministers met with the republican candidate for mayor.
6. The election will be held on the first tuesday in november.
7. After ten years of work, the panama canal opened august 15, 1914.
8. Lech Walesa, a union leader in poland, won the nobel peace prize in october 1983.
9. My mother works at the elm street antique shop.
10. The U.S.S. *constitution,* also known as *old ironsides,* was launched from Boston in 1797.
11. The largest U.S. monument is death valley national monument.
12. The academy awards are presented at the dorothy chandler pavilion.
13. Is scandinavia considered a part of europe?
14. The gulf of california borders mexico.
15. The highest peak in the continental U.S. is mount whitney in california.
16. The sixteenth amendment to the U.S. constitution allowed Congress to levy an income tax.
17. Susan b. anthony day is celebrated on february 15.
18. If the groundhog sees its shadow on groundhog day, winter continues six weeks longer.
19. The trojan war ended in 1200 b.c.
20. Drive west on sunset boulevard to the sea.
21. Is the sun shining on the west coast?
22. Is saturn closer to earth than jupiter is?
23. A respected western school is stanford university in california.
24. The magna carta was signed in a.d. 1215.
25. You can register for a general computer course or word processing 101.

Part 4

First Words and the Pronoun I

Capitalize the first word of every sentence.

The system of writing called Braille was devised for the blind.

Poetry

Capitalize the first word of every line of poetry.

By the rude bridge that arched the flood,
    Their flag to April's breeze unfurled,
Here once the embattled farmers stood,
    And fired the shot heard round the world.

From "Concord Hymn" by Ralph Waldo Emerson

Usage Note Sometimes, especially in modern poetry, the lines of a poem do not begin with capital letters.

Quotations

Capitalize the first word of a direct quotation.

A **direct quotation** tells the exact words of a speaker or writer.

Emerson said, "The only way to have a friend is to be one."

A **divided quotation** occurs when a direct quotation is broken into two parts by words such as *he said*. Do not capitalize the first word of the second part unless it starts a new sentence.

"I believe," Tina said, "that a good friend is rare. Don't you?"

Letter Parts

Capitalize the first word in the greeting of a letter. Also capitalize the name or title of the person addressed.

Dear Ms. Valdez: Dear Mr. Nash: Dear Sir or Madam:

In the complimentary close, capitalize only the first word.

Very truly yours,   Sincerely yours,

Outlines

Capitalize the first word of each item in an outline. Also capitalize letters that introduce major subsections of the outline.

    I. **H**olidays
        A. **C**hief legal holidays
            1. **N**ational
            2. **S**tate or local
        B. **R**eligious holidays

Titles

Capitalize the first word, the last word, and all other important words in titles. Do not capitalize conjunctions, articles, or prepositions with fewer than five letters.

Book Title	*The **O**ther **S**ide of the **M**ountain*
Newspaper	*Los **A**ngeles **T**imes*
Magazine	*Ebony*
Play	*You **C**an't **T**ake **I**t with **Y**ou*
Movie	*The **S**ound of **M**usic*
Television Series	*Wide **W**orld of **S**ports*
Work of Art	*The **S**unflowers*
Musical Composition	*Carmen*
Short Story	"**T**o **B**uild a **F**ire"
Poem	"**A** **W**ord **I**s **D**ead"
Song	"**I** **W**ant to **H**old **Y**our **H**and"
Chapter	**C**hapter 3, "**T**he **M**editerranean **W**orld"
Magazine Article	"**T**oday's **C**hanging **F**amily"

The word *the* at the beginning of a title is capitalized only when it is part of the formal name. Similarly, the word *magazine* is capitalized only when it is part of the formal name.

*The **T**imes*	the *Chicago **T**ribune*
*Audubon **M**agazine*	*Newsweek* magazine

When you write titles, underline them or put them in quotation marks. Rules for punctuating titles are given in Chapter 33, page 729.

The Pronoun I

Capitalize the pronoun *I*.

Stanley and **I** rented *2001: A Space Odyssey*.

Exercises

A On your paper, rewrite each of the following items, capitalizing words where necessary. In writing, underline any words that are italicized in the exercise.

1. einstein wrote, ''imagination is more important than knowledge.''
2. *the guinness book of world records* set its own record by being the fastest-selling book in the world.
3. Toni Cade Bambara tells the story of a spunky girl named Squeaky and her handicapped brother in a story titled ''Raymond's run.''
4. it was many and many a year ago,
      in a kingdom by the sea,
   that a maiden there lived whom you may know
      by the name of annabel lee.
       From ''annabel lee ''by Edgar Allan Poe
5. ''dave,'' Joyce called, ''watch while i try a half-gainer.''
6. The history assignment for Thursday is to read all of chapter 9, ''the civilization of ancient India.''
7. ''It is hard enough to write books and stories,'' said Ernest Hemingway, ''without being asked to explain them as well.''
8. The song ''why can't the english?'' in the musical *my fair lady* is a humorous treatment of proper pronunciation.
9. I. geography of the philippines
      a. climate
      b. natural features
   II. natural environment
10. ''i won't forget my locker combination anymore,'' said Dale. ''it's now written inside my locker door.''
11. dear sir or madam:
      i would like to order two tickets to the performance of *a christmas carol* on Monday, December 4. enclosed is the payment of $20 (twenty dollars).
                              very truly yours,
                              Clair Flanagan
12. last Sunday's *washington post* had a feature article titled ''the new music: what's new with it?''
13. alice walker's poem ''women'' celebrates the strength of hardworking women like her mother.
14. For her birthday, we gave Anna a handmade card and a year's subscription to *seventeen* magazine.
15. The legend of the boy who saved Holland from flooding is told in Mary Elizabeth Dodge's book, *Hans Brinker, or, the silver skates.*

Yogi Berra, New York Yankees, 1958.

B Find the words that should be capitalized in the following paragraph. On your paper, write the words correctly after the number of the sentence in which they appear.

(1) i am one of the few people i know who hate sports. (2) i can confess to never having watched the super bowl. (3) further, it baffles me how anyone can remember which baseball teams are in the national league and which are in the american league. (4) i do, however, enjoy humorous stories and anecdotes about sports, particularly ones about baseball, and most particularly those about yogi berra, the former baseball player. (5) once a reporter asked yogi, ''how did you like school when you were growing up, yogi?'' (6) yogi replied, ''closed.'' (7) another time yogi commented, ''you can't think and hit at the same time.'' (8) i also like humorous books about baseball, especially joe garagiola's *baseball is a funny game*. (9) nothing, however, has made me want to go to see a baseball game in person, and i can only agree with yogi once again. (10) ''if the people don't want to come to the park,'' yogi once observed, ''nobody's going to stop 'em.''

C *Write Now* Every week your school paper includes a feature article on ten students. This week you are one of the ten. To complete the article, the paper needs to know the titles of your favorite song, book, and movie. Write the information in a letter to Alice Evans, the paper's editor. You should also include a quotation from a poem that you enjoy. Use correct capitalization throughout.

Checkpoint *Parts 1–4*

A On your paper, write the following sentences, adding capital letters where necessary.

1. great wits and valors, like great estates,
    do sometimes sink with their own weights.
    From *Hudibras* by Samuel Butler
2. the announcer said, ''ladies and gentlemen, start your engines.''
3. *to kill a mockingbird* by Harper Lee has a great impact on readers.
4. dear personnel director:
    i would like to apply for the job advertised in the *houston chronicle*. please send me an application form.

    yours truly,

5. I. publications
    a. books
    1. fiction
    2. nonfiction
    b. periodicals
6. ''the recipe was in *good housekeeping*,'' Anne said.
7. ''when i am in california,'' said Theodore Roosevelt, ''i am not in the west. i am west of the west.''

8. did Madeleine L'Engle write *a wind in the door*?
9. have you read Longfellow's poem ''hymn to the night''?
10. Marlee Matlin performed in the movie *children of a lesser god*.

B Application in Literature In the following paragraph, some capitalization mistakes have been made. Return the paragraph to its original state by correcting all capitalization errors.

> (1) One Summer, along about 1904, my father rented a camp on a Lake in maine and took us all there for the Month of august. (2) We all got ringworm from some Kittens and had to rub pond's extract on our arms and legs night and morning, and my Father rolled over in a canoe with all his clothes on; but outside of that the Vacation was a success, and from then on none of us ever thought there was any place in the World like that Lake in Maine.
>
> From ''Once More to the Lake'' by E. B. White

Linking
Mechanics & Writing

The year is 2010. You are on a space mission and have discovered a new planet. As your reward, the government has given you the honor of naming the planet, its land forms and bodies of water, the various creatures it contains, and so on. Tell about this strange new world in a few paragraphs.

Prewriting and Drafting Begin by making a list of some of the various features—such as mountains, lakes, rivers, valleys, deserts—of the planet you have discovered. After you have chosen at least five different features, give them names and arrange them in the order you would like to describe them. Use spatial order for your description, perhaps going from east to west or north to south across the region. Describe the features in as much detail as you can.

Revising and Proofreading As you revise, consider the following questions:

1. Have you included a variety of features?
2. Have you given names to each place? Is each described in clear and convincing detail?
3. Have you capitalized the names of the planet and its features?

Additional Writing Topic If you could travel across the United States, what states, historical places, or natural wonders would you want to visit? What unusual or odd sights would you plan to see? Write out a route that would take you to at least five of the places you would most like to visit in the United States.

◄ Corn Palace, Mitchell, South Dakota.

Dinosaur Park, ► Rapid City, South Dakota.

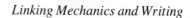

Chapter 32
Application and Review

A Using Capital Letters Correctly On your paper, rewrite the following sentences, capitalizing words as necessary.

1. my brother and my parents are visiting the university of alabama this weekend.
2. gazelles are found in africa, the near east, and asia.
3. Willa Cather's novel *death comes for the archbishop* is set in the west and southwest.
4. we drove south on highway 1 all the way from san francisco to the baja peninsula.
5. the book of psalms in the bible contains prayers and hymns.
6. the lydians produced the first coin about 640 b.c.
7. the office of revell industries will close at 3 p.m. on december 31.
8. "my birthday is next week, dad," helen reminded her father.
9.   I. national historic sites
         a. tuskegee institute
         b. hopewell village
     II. national parks
10. the eiffel tower is the most famous french landmark.
11. the soviet union's *venera 9* was the first spacecraft to photograph the surface of venus.
12. freshmen at isabel sand high school must take general science I and an english course.
13.   in the deserted moon-blanch'd street,
        how lonely rings the echo of my feet!
    From "A Summer Night" by Matthew Arnold
14. memorial day originated in the south after the civil war.
15. "sir, i look upon every day to be lost," said samuel johnson, "in which i do not make a new acquaintance."
16. the special olympics becomes a bigger and more exciting event every year.
17. we vacationed in new hampshire near lake winnipesaukee, south of the white mountains.
18. who was vice-president during president ford's term?
19. i bought a new suntan lotion called bronze beauty.
20. my sister sang the song "tomorrow" when she auditioned for a part in *annie*.

B Using Capital Letters Correctly On your paper rewrite the following sentences, capitalizing words where necessary.

1. prince charles and princess diana are often in the news.
2. has the pope made more than one trip to poland?
3. "dad, can you and mom pick me up on sunday?" asked diane.
4. france celebrates its independence on bastille day.
5. our band trip took us through the ohio valley, over the blue ridge mountains, and into maryland.
6. uncle sid plays tight end for the cincinnati bengals.
7. central high school has a garden on the south side of the campus.
8. susan works at the a.s.p.c.a. office on lincoln avenue.
9. the normans conquered britain in the battle of hastings.
10. the united nations was founded on october 24, 1945.

C Correcting Errors in Capitalization Proofread the following letter for incorrect capitalization. Then rewrite the letter correctly.

624 Washtenaw avenue
Ypsilanti, michigan 48109
july 4, 19—

dear Lynn,

    I received your letter this afternoon, and i'll be happy to accept your invitation! I've always wanted to see the southwest, and traveling with you and aunt Pat sounds like the perfect way to do it. When I asked mom if I could go, she said, "only if I can go too!" She was just teasing, of course!

    My summer school classes, chemistry 2 and the math class I told you about, will be over thursday.

    Please send me the details of our trip. I have a reservation on east airlines leaving detroit on saturday, july 30, at 10:00 a.m. and arriving in tulsa at 3:10 p.m.

your cousin,

Anita

33

Punctuation

A musical score tells a player not only what notes to play but when to start, stop, and pause. Musical notation uses certain symbols to indicate the pitch and duration of each tone. For example, the symbol ⌐ tells a musician to pause, and the symbol :‖ tells a musician to repeat a passage. Other symbols tell the musician how to play the piece, whether *p* for very soft or *f* for loud.

Written language uses symbols too. Punctuation marks such as periods, question marks, and exclamation points tell a reader where one sentence stops and another begins. They also indicate the tone of the sentence—whether it is a statement, a query, or an expression of strong feeling. In this chapter you will learn to use these and other marks of punctuation to lend clarity to your writing.

Part 1

End Marks

End marks are the punctuation marks that indicate the end of a sentence. The three kinds of end marks are the **period,** the **question mark,** and the **exclamation point.**

The Period

Use a period at the end of a declarative sentence.

A **declarative sentence** is a sentence that makes a statement.

The American artist Grandma Moses began painting full time in her seventies.

Use a period at the end of most imperative sentences.

An **imperative sentence** is a sentence that gives a command or makes a request.

Please clean your brushes before the end of class.

When an imperative sentence expresses strong emotion, an exclamation point, not a period, is used at the end of the sentence.

Get away!   Hurry up!   Help!

Use a period at the end of an indirect question.

An **indirect question** indicates that someone has asked a question. However, it does not give the reader the exact words of the question.

Captain Ahab asked whether the ship was on course.

Notice how a **direct question** differs:

Captain Ahab asked, ''Is the ship on course?''

A direct question shows the exact words of the person asking the question. A direct question ends with a question mark.

Use a period at the end of an abbreviation or an initial.

An **abbreviation** is a shortened form of a word. An **initial** is a first letter that stands for a word.

Gov. James R. Thomas	4:00 P.M. on Aug. 4
Lt. Margaret B. Hill	5 lb. 12 oz.

For certain abbreviations, periods are optional. Use your dictionary to check whether periods are required.

CIA, C•I•A• (Central Intelligence Agency)
USA, U•S•A• (United States of America)
UN, U•N• (United Nations)

For more about abbreviations, see Chapter 34, pages 746–748. Be careful not to let abbreviations and initials cause confusion for you as they do for the character in the cartoon below.

Use a period after each number or letter in an outline or a list.

Outline	List
I• Sports	1• nails
A• Team	2• hammer
1• Football	3• putty
2• Baseball	
B• Individual	
II• Hobbies	

Use a period between dollars and cents and also to indicate a decimal.

$13•64 $2•98   3•14   •007

The Question Mark

Use a question mark at the end of an interrogative sentence.

An **interrogative sentence** is a sentence that asks a question.

Why does the tail of a comet point away from the sun ?

The Exclamation Point

Use an exclamation point to end an exclamatory sentence.

An **exclamatory sentence** shows strong emotion.

That's terrific! You look great!

Use an exclamation point after a strong interjection.

An **interjection** is one or more words that show strong feeling. Sometimes the interjection is a sound, as in the first example below.

Whoops! Not again! Super! Hurray!

When an interjection is followed by a sentence, the sentence end mark may be a period, a question mark, or an exclamation point.

Oh, oh! I forgot to call her. Great! When do we leave?

Exercises

A Write the following, adding the correct punctuation. In punctuating abbreviations, consult a dictionary if necessary.

1. Where is Lieut Moseley stationed
2. Aaron asked whether the USSR bordered China
3. Fantastic Those shirts have been marked down to $999
4. Is 8:15 AM or PM the time she wants us to call
5. Oh, no Why did you do that
6. I Foods containing calcium
   A Dairy products
     1 Milk
     2 Cheese
7. The initials DC stand for the District of Columbia
8. Dr Sam Shaw, Jr, and Dr Sam Shaw, Sr, have new offices
9. Gena's new address is PO Box 12, Altoona, Pennsylvania
10. Does the winter sun really set by 3:00 P M in Alaska

B Write the following sentences, adding the correct punctuation.

(1) Imagine that you are on a hiking trip in the mountains and you become separated from your party (2) You are alone in the wilderness (3) It is already 6:00 PM, and the temperature is too cold for your thin jacket (4) Uppermost in your mind is how to survive until morning (5) How can you overcome fear and win your struggle with nature

Part 2
The Comma

Commas can help you express your ideas clearly when you write. They can slow down the rhythm of a sentence, show a shift in thought, or add clarity. The following rules will help you understand when commas should be used.

Commas in a Series

Use a comma after every item in a series except the last one.

A series consists of three or more items of the same kind. Your writing may contain a series of words, phrases, or clauses.

Words	Woody Allen is a writer, an actor, and a director.
Phrases	We searched under beds, inside drawers, and in closets.
Clauses	The doctor explained how the blood test is made, what it reveals, and why it is necessary.

Use commas after words like *first, second,* and *third* when they introduce a series. Note also the use of semicolons (;) in the following example. For more about semicolons, see pages 713–716.

There are four steps to any painting job: first, scraping; second, sanding; third, priming; and fourth, painting.

and **Use commas between two or more adjectives of equal rank that modify the same noun.**

Kristen applied a blue, shiny glaze to the vase.

To determine whether the adjectives are of equal rank, try placing *and* between them. If *and* sounds natural and if you can reverse the order of the adjectives without changing the meaning, use a comma.

Dr. McFadden treated the cold *and* wet *and* sick dog. (The *and*'s sound natural. Changing the order of the adjectives does not change the meaning. Commas are needed.)
Dr. McFadden treated the cold, wet, sick dog.

Mom bought Dad a brown *and* easy chair for Father's Day. (The *and* sounds awkward, and the order of the adjectives cannot be reversed. No comma is necessary.)
Mom bought Dad a brown easy chair for Father's Day.

Exercises

A Write the following sentences, adding necessary commas.

1. January February and March are cold bitter months in Minnesota.
2. Jeff plays baseball in the spring tennis in the summer and basketball in the winter.
3. My brother asked three things about the car: first its age; second its condition; and third its price.
4. Tired crews of workers picked grapes in the hot dusty fields.
5. Ron groped for the alarm shut it off and went back to sleep.
6. The battered old radio squawked out news of a fire an airplane crash and a bus strike.
7. Kerry lifted the tone arm of the turntable removed the dust from the needle and set the tone arm back down.
8. Seth has had three jobs: first as a newspaper carrier; second as a cook; and third as an usher.
9. As the children were lifted onto the ponies, their eyes widened brightened and seemed to smile.
10. A pleasant courteous guide told the tourists when Greece was founded how it was governed and what its major exports were.

B Application in Literature Some commas have been omitted from the following sentences. Write the word before each missing comma. Then add the comma.

1. His startled sisters looked, and before the servant girl could get there, the bread plate wobbled slid flew to the floor and broke into slivers. Katherine Mansfield
2. Having no radios few newspapers and no magazines we were somewhat unaware of the world outside our community.
   Eugenia Collier
3. On the walls were pictures of animals a relief map of Australia and a map of Burgenland, the province of Austria that adjoins Hungary. John Hersey
4. I can call back the solemn twilight and mystery of the deep woods: the earthy smells the faint odors of the wild flowers the sheen of rain-washed foliage. . . . I can call it all back. Mark Twain
5. The man at Burkesville was a major in the army. He is the manager there. He is a cold rather severe rather formal man.
   Sherwood Anderson
6. The kitchen, like the rest of the house, had a rich bold musty smell.
   Elizabeth Enright

7. At the left, as you entered, was a tobacco-magazine counter behind which, as a rule, sat Mr. Marshall: a squat square-faced pink-fleshed man with looping manly white mustaches. Truman Capote
8. It suddenly came to me that each day we had been staying a little longer at Mrs. Dubose's that the alarm clock went off a few minutes later every day, and that she was well into one of her fits by the time it sounded. Harper Lee
9. The concrete highway was edged with a mat of tangled broken dry grass. . . . John Steinbeck
10. The hired carnival workers settled into the rhythm of their work, punching tickets locking bars into place fastening chain gates easing gears into action. Sue Ellen Bridgers

c *Write Now* You have just returned from a shopping mall where you visited the following stores:

> an exotic pet store
> a record shop
> a sporting goods store
> a health-food store

Write a sentence about each store that includes a list of three or more items you saw inside. Then write a sentence about each item. Use at least two adjectives to describe each item. Use commas correctly.

Commas with Introductory Elements

Use a comma after introductory words or mild interjections such as *oh, yes, no,* and *well.*

> No , we didn't see any rattlesnakes while we were hiking.
> Oh , I thought you were getting a haircut tomorrow.

Use a comma after two or more prepositional phrases at the beginning of a sentence.

> After four rounds with the champ , Diaz was ready to call it a day.

A single prepositional phrase that begins a sentence may be set off by a comma if it is followed by a natural pause when read.

> Because of a sore throat , Janna was unable to sing her solo.

When there would be almost no pause in speaking, or the phrase is very short, a comma is not necessary.

> At noon the farm auction will begin.

Use a comma after verbal phrases and adverb clauses that begin a sentence.

> Spinning wildly , the folk dancers left the stage. (verbal phrase)
> When the party ended , we started to clean up. (adverb clause)

Commas with Interrupters

Use commas to set off one or more words that interrupt the flow of thought in a sentence.

> The judge , after long deliberation , sentenced the prisoners.
> William , moreover , made the all-state hockey team.
> The prices of some foods , especially fish , have risen.
> The tire has a slow leak , by the way .

The following words and phrases are commonly used as interrupters. Set them off with commas when you write.

Words or Phrases Often Used as Interrupters

however	moreover	after all
therefore	I believe	of course
for example	by the way	furthermore
I suppose	in fact	nevertheless

Use commas to set off nouns of direct address.

The name of someone who is spoken to directly is the **noun of direct address**. Nouns of direct address may also be common nouns, as shown in the last example.

> Marsha , call a timeout!
> In the hallway , Mark , is a package for you.
> Will you assemble the telescope for me , Cindy?
> When you leave , girls , lock the garage.

Use commas to set off most appositives.

As you know, an appositive is a word or phrase that explains or identifies another word. Usually the appositive comes directly after the word it explains. There are two types of appositives—nonessential and essential. In order to punctuate them correctly, you must understand the differences between them.

Most appositives are **nonessential**. These appositives merely add extra information to an already clear and complete sentence. Nonessential appositives must be set off by commas. Abbreviations such as *Jr.* and *Sr.* are nonessential appositives.

> Timmy, the smallest of the boys, was teasing my sister.
> The Super Bowl, the biggest game of the year, is held late in January.

Essential appositives, however, are needed to make the meaning of the sentence clear. Without them, the writer's message is incomplete. Do not use commas with essential appositives.

> The author Ernest Hemingway is known for his simple, unadorned writing style.
> The musical *Les Misérables* is based on a novel written by Victor Hugo in 1862.

For more information about appositives, see pages 622–624.

Exercises

A Commas have been left out of the following sentences. Write the word that comes before each missing comma, and add the comma.

1. The reporter a prize-winning journalist overheard a startling conversation.
2. To tell the truth Henry venison with turnips and boiled mustard greens is not my favorite meal.
3. The British however usually do not like iced tea.
4. Trembling from cold and fatigue the swimmer a refugee from the mainland finally reached the beach.
5. After she talked with the coach Susan felt better about the loss.
6. Moreover other nations share our pollution problems.
7. Thrilled at the prospect of a summer in Maine Mark took the job.
8. I'm afraid Uncle Bob the rust has eaten completely through the doors of your car.
9. No you will not be disgraced if you miss the Sadie Hawkins Dance.
10. Kara's performance the highlight of the evening was videotaped.
11. Raphael please add the pepper and parsley to the stew now.
12. Yes I remembered to bring the napkins and cups for the picnic.
13. Which do you prefer Mrs. Ruiz the blue skirt or the yellow one?
14. When the test was over Mia felt relieved.
15. Where is the stapler Curt in your room or in the kitchen?

B Ten commas have been left out of the following paragraph. Number your paper 1–10. Write the word that comes before each missing comma. Then place the comma correctly.

(1) Almost unknown in her own time Emily Dickinson has become one of America's most widely read poets. (2) Emily born in 1830 lived a very quiet life in Amherst, Massachusetts. (3) Her father Edward Dickinson was a prominent local attorney. (4) Although she was encouraged as a poet by important writers and editors only seven of Dickinson's poems were published during her life. (5) Nevertheless her poetry is considered among the best in American literature. (6) Common themes in Dickinson's poems are love death and eternity. (7) For many of her poems Dickinson does not provide a title.

c *Write Now* Imagine that you have reached a point in your life when you must make an important decision. You have discovered that a good way to make an intelligent decision is to carry on a conversation with yourself, carefully weighing your choices. Write out such a conversation. See page 727 for help in punctuating conversation. Include explanatory words. For example, ''Instead of going to college, I might be able to work full-time right after graduation,'' I say. ''But if I don't go to college, I might miss a lot of opportunities for a successful future,'' I reply.

Michael Jordan, professional basketball player.

Commas with Quotations

Use commas to set off the explanatory words that precede or follow a direct quotation.

Explanatory words are statements such as *he said, Greg replied,* and *Sheila asked.* They are not part of the quotation. Use a comma after explanatory words when they precede the quotation.

> Rich said , ''Take the expressway to the third exit.''

Now look at this quotation:

> ''Take the expressway to the third exit ,'' Rich said.

In the sentence above, the explanatory words come after the quotation. Notice that the comma belongs at the end of the quotation inside the quotation marks.

Sometimes a quotation is broken into two parts. The explanatory words separate the two parts. Here is a divided quotation:

> ''Take the expressway ,'' Rich said , ''to the third exit.''

In a divided quotation, use a comma within the quotation marks at the end of the first part of the quotation. Also use a comma after the explanatory words.

An **indirect quotation** does not include the speaker's exact words. Do not use a comma before an indirect quotation.

> Rich said that we should take the expressway to the third exit.

Commas in Compound Sentences

Use a comma before the conjunction that joins the two main clauses of a compound sentence.

> The Dodgers won the pennant , but they lost in the seventh game of the World Series.

The comma is not necessary when the main clauses joined by *and* are very short.

> We made popcorn and then we watched the movie.

Do not confuse compound sentences with sentences that have compound predicates. There is no comma before the *and* that joins the parts of a compound predicate.

> Elizabeth jumped into the pool *and* rescued the struggling child.

Exercises

A Commas have been left out of the following sentences. Write the word that comes before each missing comma. Then place the comma correctly. If no commas are needed in a sentence, write *Correct*.

1. "You have to watch the ball and keep your elbow straight" explained Travis.
2. I went home and I called my friend Maria.
3. Don's sketch won the prize for the best in its class and was displayed at the Art in the Park show.
4. "Please submit your application to Dr. Juanita Vasquez" the director of the project said. "Then you may leave."
5. Shawn said "The breakfast will be held in the banquet hall."
6. "The sun" whined the pitcher "was in my eyes."
7. Coleman repaired the stereo and then he left.
8. Captain Kidd supposedly buried treasure but no one has found it.
9. "I need a volunteer for my experiment" said Dr. Jekyll.
10. "Your engine" said the mechanic "needs a lot of work."

B Application in Literature Number your paper 1–15. For every sentence write the word that comes before each missing comma. Then add the comma. If no commas are needed, write *Correct*. Notice how commas clarify and separate ideas.

(1) "Ivan is an incredibly strong fellow" remarked the general "but he has the misfortune to be deaf and dumb. (2) A simple fellow but I'm afraid like all his race, a bit of a savage."

(3) "Is he Russian?"

(4) "He is Cossack" said the general and his smile showed red lips and pointed teeth. (5) "So am I."

(6) "Come" he said "we should not be chatting here. (7) We can talk later. (8) Now you want clothes food rest. (9) You shall have them. (10) This is a most restful spot."

(11) Ivan had reappeared and the general spoke to him with lips that moved but gave forth no sound.

(12) "Follow Ivan, if you please, Mr. Rainsford" said the general. (13) "I was about to have my dinner when you came. (14) I'll wait for you. (15) You'll find that my clothes will fit you I think."

From "The Most Dangerous Game" by Richard Connell

c *Write Now* Three people want to share in buying a birthday present for a friend, but they cannot agree on what to buy. All have different hobbies or interests that affect their choices. Write out a conversation that these three people might have. Each speaker should suggest a different gift. Speakers should address each other by name and should be identified by means of an appositive. Place commas correctly, and include at least one divided quotation.

Example Laura, an enthusiast of weightlifting, suggested, ''I think she'd probably like a set of barbells.''
''No,'' objected Joe, the gardener, ''she'd prefer a rosebush for her flower garden.''
''Why not give her a basket that she could attach to her bicycle?'' questioned Bianca, the cycling expert.

Commas with Nonessential Clauses

Use commas to set off nonessential clauses.

Clauses, like appositives or appositive phrases, may be either nonessential or essential. A **nonessential clause** is a clause that merely adds extra information to a sentence. The sentence would be complete without the clause.

An **essential clause** is a clause that is necessary for the meaning of a sentence. If an essential clause is dropped from a sentence, the meaning changes.

To see if a clause is essential or nonessential, read the sentence without it. If the meaning doesn't change, the clause is nonessential. Use commas before and after it.

Nonessential *Clause*	Babe Ruth, *who had a lifetime total of 714 home runs,* began his career in the major leagues as a pitcher. Babe Ruth began his career in the major leagues as a pitcher. (The adjective clause is nonessential; it can be dropped.)
Essential *Clause*	Babe Ruth was the famous home run hitter *who began his career in the major leagues as a pitcher.* Babe Ruth was the famous home run hitter. (The adjective clause is essential; it cannot be dropped.)

For more information on essential and nonessential clauses, see Chapter 31, pages 651–653.

The New Punctuation

As section chief with the Department of Words and Letters, I have . . . develop[ed] a new punctuation more in keeping with today's usage.

The purpose of punctuation, as I understand it, is to make meanings of sentences unmistakably clear, something which I believe the new punctuation accomplishes.

⊙ **The Halt**—Stronger than a period. The halt signals an abrupt and serious stop.
1. . . . that's it, folks ⊙
2. The next one who speaks is middle class ⊙

The Crescendo—Used to show something is building, as anger.
1. If I have to tell you to sit down one more time, Sitzfleish, I'll explode.₀₀₀°
2. Here's Johnnny₀₀₀°

△ **The Delta-Sarc**—indicates spoken sarcasm.
1. I'll just bet you do △
2. Brilliant, Harold, now what do we do △

The Sigh—Used to emphasize resignation.
1. Oh well, I guess so ⁊
2. Isn't she magnificent ⁊

The Diddledy Dot—The diddledy dot is used to indicate frivolity.
1. Oh ho, he makes $400,000 a year, does he ₀°₀

2. Sorry, didn't mean to walk in on you like that ₀°₀

A Word About Pausals

Pausals are used in place of knowledge to fill the gaps and ellipses in our speech. Because of their frequency . . . they require symbols.

Ӿ This is the symbol for "you know," by far the most popular crop of pausals.
1. I'd like to go Ӿ, but I can't. Ӿ how it is, Ӿ, if I could, I would, Ӿ

Ɩ This is the symbol for "uh," somewhat old-fashioned but still very much with us.
1. Ladies and gentlemen, I'd, Ɩ , like to tell you, a, Ɩ , few things about, Ɩ , the company.

⋈ The symbol for "agh," the lesser of the pausal weeds but the choice of some.

The Segue—The segue is used to make elegant transitions, as from the middle of a sentence or paragraph . . . to the end. Usually it is made with subtle prose; however, when the writer has nothing to say, he may substitute the segue.

● **The Fin**—The end. Finality. That's it baby.

Lewis Burke Frumkes

Exercise

Write each of the following sentences, adding the necessary commas. If a sentence does not need commas, write *Correct*.

1. The first American automobile which some called a ''gasoline buggy'' was completed on April 19, 1892.
2. The gentleman who left his wallet here yesterday should come to the lost-and-found department.
3. Hal Smith who left his wallet here yesterday should come to the lost-and-found department.
4. The prize will go to the actor who gave the best performance.
5. The French chemist who produced poison chloride gas in World War I also developed neon lights.
6. Seth Nicholson who is an astronomer at the Mount Wilson Observatory in Pasadena discovered four of the moons of Jupiter.
7. The Brazilian city that is best known is Rio de Janeiro.
8. Brasilia which is 400 miles inland is now the capital.
9. Sarah Bernhardt whom many consider France's greatest actress lived from 1844 to 1923.
10. The story concerned a toad that loved rock but detested ragtime.

Commas in Dates, Place Names, and Letters

In dates, use a comma between the day of the month and the year. When only the month and the year are given, the comma is not necessary.

> February 22, 1989   May 8, 1945   October 1966

When a date is part of a sentence, a comma also follows the year.

> The first talking picture was shown to the public on July 6, 1928, in New York.

Use a comma between the name of a city or town and the name of its state or country.

> Detroit, Michigan   Santiago, Chile
> Athens, Greece   Houston, Texas

When an address is part of a sentence, use a comma after each item. Do not put a comma between the state name and the ZIP code.

> Jackson lived in Yuma, Arizona, until his death in 1951.
> For more information, write to the American Library Association, 50 East Huron Street, Chicago, IL 60611.

Use a comma after the salutation of a friendly letter. Use a comma after the complimentary close of a friendly letter or a business letter.

Dear Gretchen,   Yours truly,

Commas to Avoid Confusion

Use a comma whenever the reader might otherwise be confused. Without commas, these sentences could be misunderstood:

On the river boats drifted lazily with the current.
Inside everything was a mess.
Whoever called called twice.

With commas, the sentences are clearer.

On the river, boats drifted lazily with the current.
Inside, everything was a mess.
Whoever called, called twice.

Exercises

A On your paper, write each of the following sentences, adding the necessary commas.

1. The walking catfish was first reported near Clearwater Florida on May 25 1968.
2. Dear Nicole
   My summer address will be 205 Linden Street Ladysmith Wisconsin 54848. Please write.

                                    Sincerely
                                    Katie
3. On May 24 1844 the first telegraph message was transmitted.
4. Taconite Minnesota is one city on the Iron Range that produces much iron ore.
5. Country and gospel music are both produced in Nashville a city with many recording studios.
6. On November 1 1835 Texas became independent.
7. Coins are made at mints in Denver Colorado and Philadelphia Pennsylvania.
8. John Brown's raid on Harper's Ferry West Virginia began on October 16 1859 and was crushed on October 18.
9. Our store is at 655 Nevada Avenue Ames Iowa 50010.
10. In our school teachers and students work well together.

Sites of Tunguska Event, 1908.

B Commas have been left out of the following items. Number your paper 1–15. For each item, copy the word or number that comes before each missing comma. Then place the comma correctly. If no commas are needed, write *Correct*.

1. Dear Alonzo
2. In the letter you wrote last week you asked what I had been studying in science.
3. I can't imagine why you want to know but here goes.
4. On second thought however I think you might find it interesting.
5. On June 30 1908 a ball of fire blazed across the sky of Siberia.
6. It touched the earth causing a tremendous explosion.
7. In fact it destroyed about 2,000 square kilometers of forest.
8. Yet the interesting part of the story is that there was no impact crater left on the site where the fireball hit.
9. Scientists have suggested many theories for this phenomenon which is called the Tunguska Event.
10. It might have been caused by a black hole a meteor or even the crash of an extraterrestrial vessel.
11. However most scientists believe that a comet was involved.
12. That is in 1908 a piece of a comet struck the earth in Central Siberia Russia.
13. What's your theory?
14. Your friend
15. Amy

Checkpoint *Parts 1 and 2*

On your paper, write the following sentences, adding periods, question marks, exclamation points, and commas where they are needed. If the punctuation is correct, write *Correct*.

1. Who was the first woman named to the US Supreme Court
2. San Francisco Oakland and Palo Alto are located near San Francisco Bay
3. At the tent sale on Saturday Julio bought a red pickup truck
4. Gen Robert E Lee surrendered at Appomattox
5. Your Honor may I approach the bench
6. Shirley MacLaine the noted actress is also a best-selling author
7. The *Titanic* was supposed to be unsinkable but it sank on its first voyage after striking an iceberg
8. Robin Williams was born in Chicago Illinois on July 21 1952
9. Wow Did you see that incredible catch by the right fielder
10. Henry David Thoreau the nineteenth-century American author and philosopher lived in seclusion at Walden Pond for two years
11. Watch out for that truck
12. The President decided therefore to veto the bill
13. Mark Twain wrote *The Adventures of Tom Sawyer*
14. Mothers Against Drunk Driving or MADD is a growing group
15. If the amount is $991 or more round it off to ten dollars
16. Abe Cohn a specialist in intensive-care nursing was consulted
17. No Dallas is not the capital of Texas
18. Please meet me at 8:00 AM at the station and we will talk further
19. When there is a new mail carrier, we get our neighbor's letters.
20. After dialing Tony's number Rita had second thoughts and hung up

Part 3
The Semicolon and Colon

Like commas, semicolons separate elements in a sentence. The semicolon, however, signals a more emphatic break than a comma. Colons are generally used to point out what comes next. A colon causes an abrupt break in the rhythm of the sentence.

Use a semicolon to join the parts of a compound sentence if no coordinating conjunction is used.

The overseas operator interrupted the call; our time was up.

When there are several commas in the parts of a compound sentence, separate the clauses with a semicolon.

On this plan I can eat whole-grain bread, fruits, and vegetables; but candy, soft drinks, and desserts are forbidden.

When commas occur within parts of a series, use semicolons to separate the parts.

In the Olympics the first place winner gets a gold medal; second place, a silver medal; and third place, a bronze medal.

Use a semicolon before a conjunctive adverb that joins the clauses of a compound sentence.

You know that the parts of a compound sentence are sometimes joined by such words as *therefore, however, otherwise, consequently, besides, nevertheless,* and *moreover.* These words, called **conjunctive adverbs,** are preceded by a semicolon and followed by a comma.

Tamika is good at batting; however, her pitching is weak.

Usage Note Many of the words listed above can also be used as interrupters. In this case, use commas to set off the word.

Tony turned in his paper a day late; however, he got a high grade. (conjunctive adverb)
Mr. Becker, however, gave Tony a high grade. (interrupter)

The Colon

Use a colon to introduce a list of items.

Use a colon when it might have the meaning ''and here it is'' or ''and here they are.'' A colon often follows a word or phrase such as *these* or *the following items*.

The FBI investigates the following federal crimes: spying, treason, kidnapping, and counterfeiting.

Never use a colon after a verb or a preposition.

The term *mass media* refers to television, radio, newspapers, magazines, and books.

Use a colon after the greeting of a business letter.

Dear Ms. Nolan: Dear Sir or Madam:

Use a colon between numerals indicating hours and minutes.

4:30 P.M.   8:15 A.M.

Use a colon between two sentences when the second explains or summarizes the first.

It's obvious why you're tired: you've stayed up late three nights in a row.

Use a colon to introduce a long or formal quotation.

George Bernard Shaw once said: The reasonable man adapts himself to the world. The unreasonable one persists in trying to adapt the world to himself. Therefore, all progress depends on the unreasonable man.

Exercises

A On your paper, write the following sentences, adding the necessary semicolons, colons, and commas.

1. The fullback outran the ball the fans went wild.
2. Some people object to the following clothes made from animal skins leopard furs, sealskin coats, and alligator shoes.
3. Dear Madam
    The item that you ordered is out of stock therefore we are unable to fill your order at this time.
4. Skaters, cyclists, and joggers crowded the path it was not a good place to stroll.
5. From the road the ocean looked blue however it was dull brown at the shore.
6. The Community Center requests the following foods dry milk canned meat canned soup coffee flour sugar and cereals.
7. The flight to Honolulu was scheduled to depart from Los Angeles at 730 however we did not even board the airplane until 815.
8. Chris explained his lateness he missed the bus and had to walk to practice.
9. These three cities are growing quickly Calcutta India San Juan Puerto Rico and São Paulo Brazil.
10. In 1792 Mary Wollstonecraft declared "I do not wish them [women] to have power over men but over themselves."

B Write the following sentences on your paper. Wherever necessary, add colons and replace commas with semicolons.

1. The two could not agree, therefore, a third party was called in.
2. The picnic tables held bowls of barbecue sauce, platters of fried chicken, and loaves of crispy, freshly baked bread.
3. Karen built a large, roaring fire, gathered the chilled, tired campers around it, and told a tale that made everyone laugh.
4. Barb told us why she could not come she works after school.
5. Some popular home remedies for colds include the following fruit juices, chicken soup, garlic cloves, and aspirin.
6. Dear Resident
   Would you like to win $500 a week for life?
7. Ernesto is perfect for the part, besides, he volunteered.
8. At 730 P.M. on Labor Day, the lifeguard closes the pool.
9. In Cajun cooking, spices are used for the following reasons they preserve food, they add variety to meals, and they are flavorful.
10. This year flu is widespread, the shots are being given at the clinic.

c *Proofreading* On your paper, copy the following letter. Add each missing punctuation mark.

Dear Ms Evans
    Thank you for your interest in Cloudhopper Airlines. Here are the scheduled departure times for flights to Indianapolis, Indiana 804 A.M., 1232 P.M. and 956 P.M.
    Regarding your question about bringing your guitar aboard, I've checked you usually can. The rule is this you may bring the instrument as carry-on baggage if you have a first-class ticket. There are three qualifications you must be at the gate thirty minutes before flight time the guitar must be in a case and you must have no other carry-ons.
    It is generally advisable to make reservations well in advance. Fares will increase on June 1.

        Sincerely

        Marvin T Jet

Part 4

The Dash and Parentheses

Like commas, dashes and parentheses are used to set off words that break into the main idea of a sentence. Use commas for material closely connected to the main idea. Use dashes to show a looser connection, and parentheses to set off material with only a slight connection.

Dashes with Interrupters

Commas set off words and short phrases, such as *however* and *by the way,* that interrupt a sentence. With an abrupt change of thought, or an idea that breaks into the flow of a sentence, use dashes.

> People grew impatient—the parade was already thirty minutes behind schedule—and began to leave.

The Dash Before a Summary

Use a dash after a series to indicate that a summary statement will follow.

> Edsels, Packards, and Hudsons—these cars are no longer made.

Do not use dashes to replace semicolons or periods.

Parentheses

Except for enclosing source documentation in reports, parentheses are rarely needed by student writers. Since parentheses are used to separate material that is only vaguely connected to the main idea of a sentence, it is usually better to put this material in a separate sentence. Use commas or dashes for more closely related ideas.

The following examples of the use of parentheses are adapted from work by professional writers.

> It was a black suit with a formal Mao jacket (what the Chinese call a Sun Yat-sen suit), and black cloth shoes to match.
> If anything is not "quite right" with your order (fit, style, or even color), please return it for a full refund or exchange.
> Even the old shell game (which shell covers the pea?) goes back to the beginnings of recorded history.
> After a semicolon pause, which my appearance seemed to produce (for he eyed me closely as I approached), he gave a whoop, and swore that he could out-swap any man that ever walked the hills.

Exercise

On your paper, write the following sentences, inserting dashes as needed.

1. Layoffs one nearby factory cut one hundred workers are one way to lower costs.
2. Taxi fares, school busing, and a new shopping district all this was discussed by the city council.
3. The Marshfield track team what a great season they're having will be here next week.
4. That magazine the new one I told you about is in the library on the third floor.
5. The coach talked about teamwork, timing, concentration the keys to any victory.
6. Trains, cars, buses, planes all were halted by the snowstorm in Colorado.
7. The summer of 1987 one I won't forget set records for heat throughout the United States.
8. We can take the elevator unless it is broken again to the tenth floor.
9. Parks, beaches, shops, festivals Toronto has them all.
10. The speaker talked about condors, whales, and mountain lions all of them endangered.

Part 5

The Hyphen

Use a hyphen if part of a word must be carried over from one line to the next.

> The FBI has about 169,000,000 fin-
> gerprints on file.

Only words having two or more syllables can be broken by a hyphen. Never divide one-syllable words like *growl* or *weight*. A single letter should not be written or typed at the end of a line. For instance, these divisions would be wrong: *e-lection, cloud-y*.

Use hyphens in compound numbers from twenty-one to ninety-nine.

> seventy-six trombones   fifty-five glass marbles

Use hyphens in fractions.

> a two-thirds majority   one-fourth of the votes

Use hyphens in certain compound nouns.

Words like *brother-in-law, drive-in, great-grandmother,* and *self-control* are hyphenated.

> The *editor in chief* of the local paper is my *sister-in-law*.

Use a hyphen or hyphens between words that make up a compound adjective used before a noun.

> Stephen King's latest thriller is a well-written book.

Compound adjectives after a noun are not usually hyphenated. Use a dictionary to determine whether a word needs a hyphen.

> Stephen King's latest thriller is well written.

Exercise

Copy the word or words that should be hyphenated in each sentence. Then add the necessary hyphens. Use a dictionary if necessary.

1. Historically, honey has always been a much valued product.
2. Ancient Greeks considered it an all purpose remedy.

3. They even used it as a hair restoring preparation!
4. Athletes depended on it as a long lasting energy source.
5. It was also an easy to obtain antiseptic.
6. Actually, honey contains hydrogen peroxide, a well known, dependable germ killer.
7. Besides, honey is used in many tried and true recipes.
8. An old recipe for Roman dates calls for one half cup of honey.
9. A soft orange flavored rice dish from North Africa also contains some honey.
10. Your great grandmother probably knew ninety nine different ways of using honey herself!

Three decorative honey pots.

Checkpoint *Parts 3, 4, and 5*

On your paper, write the following sentences, adding those semi-colons, colons, dashes, and hyphens that have been left out.

1. The bus was due at 825 P.M. however, it was late.
2. There are thirty one states in Mexico.
3. Racquetball, tennis, and badminton Mark can play them all well.

4. Oscar Wilde, a British playwright of the early 1900's, once said "There is only one thing in the world worse than being talked about, and that is not being talked about."
5. The Confederates surrendered the four-year Civil War had ended.
6. This weekend I can hardly wait we'll be leaving for the lake.
7. The superintendent, the principal, and the assistant principal these people will address the assembly.
8. Wendy can remember everything she reads furthermore, she understands the material and can apply it to other subject areas.
9. At eighty six, my great uncle still has an optimistic view of life.
10. The quartet will be played by the following instruments violin, flute, cello, and bass violin.
11. Corn and soybeans these are important crops in Iowa.
12. The solution is obvious a new library must be built.
13. Lori had only a four week course in self defense however, she has already acquired basic skills and self confidence.
14. The three largest U.S. cities are New York, New York Los Angeles, California and Chicago, Illinois.
15. Three fourths of the students listed these long term goals an interesting, well paying job, education, and a happy family life.

Part 6
The Apostrophe

Use the apostrophe to form the possessive of nouns.

To use the apostrophe correctly, you must know whether a noun is singular or plural. To form the possessive of a singular noun, add an apostrophe and *s* even if the singular noun ends in *s: student's, Les's.* To form the possessive of a plural noun ending in *s,* add only the apostrophe: *racers', Smiths', boys'.* Plural nouns that do not end in *s* take an apostrophe and *s: women's, children's.* For a complete discussion of forming possessive nouns, see Chapter 23, pages 477–479.

To form the possessive of an indefinite pronoun, use an apostrophe and *s*.

everybody + 's = everybody's   someone + 's = someone's

Do not use an apostrophe with a possessive personal pronoun.

hers   ours   yours   its   theirs

Use an apostrophe in a contraction.

In contractions, words are joined and letters are left out. An apostrophe replaces the letter or letters that are missing.

she's = she is *or* has	hasn't = has not
we'll = we will	won't = will not
they're = they are	I'm = I am
it's = it is	shouldn't = should not

Use an apostrophe to show the omission of numbers in a date.

the spring of '89 (the spring of 1989)

Use an apostrophe and *s* to form the plurals of letters, figures, and words used as words.

ABC's   two *n*'s   three *4*'s   *yes*'s and *no*'s

Exercises

A Find the words in which the apostrophe is used incorrectly. Write each word correctly on your paper.

1. An orangutans weight can be up to 200 kilo's.
2. Many orangutans skeletons' reveal broken bones, suggesting that they were too heavy for the trees they lived in.
3. Acrobatic skill is among some species notable traits.
4. Gibbon apes abilities include leaping great distances in trees.
5. A chimpanzee is curious and it's temperament is lively.
6. Chimpanzees diet's include termites and ants.
7. Its clear that grooming is important in chimps' lives.
8. Combing each others hair is a sign of friendship.
9. That some chimps learn human sign language cant be denied.
10. In comparison with humans, their's is an interesting story.

B There are nine errors in apostrophe use in the following passage. Find the words with errors and write them correctly on your paper.

(1) The guenons' are a genus of monkey found throughout sub-Saharan Africa. (2) They've all got long tails. (3) The smallest of all guenon monkey's is the Allen swamp monkey. (4) Its the size of a large squirrel. (5) It's face is black with pale gray circles around the eyes. (6) It has dark whisker's and a yellow throat, chest, inner arms, and inner legs. (7) A swamp monkeys home is the damp, often flooded, African jungle.

(8) Another guenon monkey is the talapoin, a native of the Congo River region. (9) One of the talapoins favorite foods is green nuts that are so bitter humans cant eat them. (10) The talapoin can be recognized by its yellow mustache and whiskers' and orange-ringed eyes.

c *Write Now* Rewrite the following paragraph in a smoother style. Replace the italicized phrases with possessive forms or contractions as required. Be sure to use apostrophes correctly.

Example   This is the coat *of Nan,* but the gloves *are not of her.*
This is Nan's coat, but the gloves aren't hers.

(1) Chris Jones went to the office *of her boss* and asked whether she could receive the wages *of this week* a day early. (2) She explained that it was almost time to go to the annual family reunion *of the Joneses.* (3) She said that *she would* need the money because her car engine needed to be tuned. (4) The request *of Chris* was fairly well received. (5) The comment *of the boss* was, ''I *would not* like to disappoint you. (6) However, *I would* like the work *of a day* for the pay *of a day.''*

Part 7
Quotation Marks

Use quotation marks at the beginning and at the end of a direct quotation.

Quotation marks are used to show that a speaker's exact words are being stated.

Linda said, ''Someone is following me.''

Quotation marks are not used with indirect quotations. The word *that* often signals an indirect quotation.

Linda said *that* someone was following her.

When explanatory words come at the beginning of a sentence, use a comma directly after them. Begin the quotation with quotation marks. Place the period at the end of a sentence inside the quotation marks.

> The flight attendant announced, "Fasten your seat belts."

Sometimes explanatory words end the sentence. In such cases, the quoted statement at the beginning of the sentence is followed by a comma. The comma belongs inside the quotation marks.

> "Fasten your seat belts," the pilot directed the passengers.

To write a quote within a quote, use single quotation marks to enclose the inside quotation. In these instances a double quotation mark follows the single quotation mark.

> "It was Captain James Mugford who originally said, 'Don't give up the ship,' " Mr. Gomez told us.

Divided Quotations

Sometimes a quotation is divided by explanatory words. Then each part of the quotation is enclosed by quotation marks.

> "One healthful snack," Pamela said, "is granola with yogurt."

When the divided quotation is a single sentence, begin the second part with a small letter, as in the example above. When the second part begins a new sentence, use a capital letter.

> "There is entertainment at half time," Toby noted. "The marching band will perform."

The first part of a divided quotation is followed by a comma. Commas always appear inside closing quotation marks.

> "By the way," Mario said, "there is an inchworm on your shoulder."

The explanatory words in the middle of a divided quotation are followed by either a period or a comma. Use a period if the first part completes a sentence. Use a comma if the sentence continues.

> "Before you set up camp," Eric cautioned, "check for rattlesnakes."
>
> "First, we spread paste on the wallpaper," Ginger said. "Then we hang the paper and trim the excess."

Exercise

Write each of the following sentences as a direct quotation in three different ways. Use explanatory words other than *said* in some of your sentences.

1. Don't talk to me while I'm working.
2. Yes, Bob Dylan writes many of his own songs.
3. I'm sorry that I forgot to call you.
4. In the last two minutes, the Wildkits took the lead.
5. Finally, a wrecking crew attacked the vacant building.

Other Punctuation with Quotation Marks

Place question marks and exclamation points inside the quotation marks if they belong to the quotation itself.

> Jacob asked, "Have you met my dog Brutus?"
> Reuben exclaimed, "What a beautiful animal!"

Place question marks and exclamation points outside the quotation marks if they do not belong to the quotation.

> Did Ray say, "I can't come to class next week"?
> What a surprise it was to hear Mr. Adams say, "I'll give you the notes later"!

Commas and periods, as you have seen, always appear within closing quotation marks.

Exercises

A On your paper, rewrite the following sentences. Punctuate them correctly with quotation marks, end marks, and commas. (There are three indirect quotations that need only end punctuation.)

1. Watch out for the hornet's nest yelled Pat as her friend climbed the stepladder
2. Mindy asked Do you like that yellow sports car
3. Oh said Ann a little glue will fix that broken statue in a minute
4. Ms. Pappas explained why copper wiring is used
5. I have finally had my ice skates sharpened Tisha said to her skating instructor
6. Terry announced proudly I knocked down all ten pins
7. Adam said that he was going to a summer sports camp for additional training
8. We locked this door when we left said Harris nervously Why is it open now
9. Did Dr. Korshak say that you should tape your ankle
10. Was it the principal who canceled the pep rally Glenn asked

B On your paper, write each of the following sentences as a direct quotation. Add explanatory words such as "Maria said." In some examples, put the quotation first. In others, put the quotation last. Also, divide some quotations. In the divided quotations, explanatory words interrupt the quotation.

1. Is Costa Rica part of Central America?
2. Don't say that!
3. I called the fire department from a neighbor's house.
4. There's a restaurant by the bowling alley.
5. I never know what Merle will say next.
6. By next June I will have finished repairing the roof.
7. We swam in the quarry.
8. Stand back!
9. Was that dog a bull terrier?
10. This weekend I have to help my cousin.

c *Write Now* Imagine that you have just taken a job as a server in a restaurant. Today is your first day, and you are a bit nervous. Your first table is a party of twelve children for a ten-year-old's birthday party. Write the conversation that develops as you attempt to take the order.

Using Long Quotations

When two or more sentences are spoken by the same person, do not use an end quotation mark until after the final sentence.

> "I'll be up early to get your breakfast, boys. Your father says you can go to the show." As she handed the money to the eldest, she felt a sudden throb of allegiance to her husband and said sharply, "And you be careful of that, an' don't waste it. Your father worked hard for his money."
>
> From "The Sentimentality of William Tavener" by Willa Cather

Punctuating Dialogue

Dialogue is conversation between two or more people. Begin a new paragraph each time the speaker changes.

> The boy was probably twelve years old, but under-sized. He wore overalls and a torn shirt . . . .
>
> He said, "I can chop some wood today."
>
> I said, "But I have a boy coming from the orphanage."
>
> "I'm the boy."
>
> "You? But you're small."
>
> "Size don't matter, chopping wood," he said. "Some of the big boys don't chop good. I've been chopping wood at the orphanage a long time."
>
> . . . . I was well into my work and not inclined to conversation. I was a little blunt. "Very well. Go ahead and see what you can do."
>
> From "A Mother in Mannville" by Marjorie Kinnan Rawlings

If one speaker's words continue for more than a paragraph, each paragraph begins with a quotation mark. However, the closing quotation mark is not used until the end of the entire quotation.

> Tony said, "Katherine Hepburn was nominated twelve times for an Academy Award and won four times.
>
> "Bette Davis was the next most-nominated star. She was nominated ten times and won two Oscars."

Stevie Wonder.

Exercises

A On your paper, rewrite the following dialogue, adding the correct punctuation and paragraph divisions.

> The interviewer, Mr. Brown, asked Stevie Wonder How did you learn to cope with your handicap? The singer-composer replied I've never seen my blindness as the handicap others do. Why is that? pursued Mr. Brown. Being blind, said Stevie Wonder, you don't judge books by their covers. . . . The people I feel sorry for are those who have sight but still don't see.

B Rewrite the following dialogue. Punctuate it with quotation marks, end marks, and commas. Begin new paragraphs when necessary. There are three indirect quotations that need only end punctuation.

> (1) I have to do a report on Isak Dinesen Cleo told her friend Pat (2) Isak who Pat asked Isn't he a famous singer (3) Cleo shook her head Isak Dinesen was an author—and a woman (4) Cleo then explained that the author's true name was Baroness Karen Blixen (5) A baroness exclaimed Pat What did she write about—castle gossip (6) Cleo explained Karen Blixen owned and managed a coffee plantation in Kenya from 1914 to 1931 (7) She wrote about her experiences in Africa (8) Pat asked about the titles of the baroness's books (9) Her most famous book is called *Out of Africa* stated Cleo but she wrote many other stories, too (10) *Out of Africa* Pat shrieked That's not a book That's a movie starring Robert Redford (11) Cleo sighed and asked Pat when she would realize that popular movies are often based on literary works

Punctuating Titles

Use quotation marks to enclose the titles of magazine articles, chapters, short stories, TV episodes, essays, poems, and songs.

Magazine Article	"Fads of the Eighties"
Chapter Title	Chapter 2, "The New World"
Short Story	"Clothes Make the Man"
TV Episode	"Lucy and Desi in London"
Essay	"The Dog That Bit People"
Poem	"The Raven"
Song	"The Star-Spangled Banner"

Underline the titles of books, newspapers, magazines, plays, movies, TV series, works of art, and long musical compositions.

In writing or typing, such titles are underlined, like this: <u>Old Yeller</u>. In print, these titles appear in italics. Note that the word <u>the</u> is not underlined unless it is actually part of the title: <u>The Columbus Dispatch</u>, but the <u>Chicago Tribune</u>.

Book Title	<u>All Creatures Great and Small</u>
Newspaper	<u>New Haven Register</u>
Magazine	<u>Field and Stream</u>
Play	<u>The Miracle Worker</u>
Movie	<u>The Pink Panther Strikes Again</u>
TV Series	<u>I Love Lucy</u>
Work of Art	<u>Mona Lisa</u>
Long Musical Composition	<u>The Pirates of Penzance</u>

Exercises

A Copy the following sentences, adding quotation marks around titles or underlining titles where necessary.

1. The story Saving the Pieces was published in Audubon magazine.
2. Yankee Doodle was a popular song during the Revolutionary War.
3. I read Althea Gibson's article I Always Wanted to Be Someone.
4. Monet's painting Waterlilies has been reproduced on bedsheets.
5. Our city was featured on the TV show 60 Minutes.
6. Marta is singing Happy Talk from the musical South Pacific.
7. A well-known St. Louis newspaper is the Post-Dispatch.
8. West Side Story is a modern version of Romeo and Juliet.
9. The article appeared in the book Out of the Bleachers.
10. Many people enjoy the music of Stravinsky's ballet The Firebird.

B Find ten titles in the following paragraph. Rewrite them on your paper, using correct punctuation.

(1) In her autobiographical book I Know Why the Caged Bird Sings, Maya Angelou tells about the problems she experienced growing up as a black girl in America. (2) There were many obstacles to overcome—racism, sexism, poverty, family crises—but Angelou overcame them all. (3) She was named ''Woman of the Year'' in communications in 1976 by the Ladies Home Journal, a popular magazine. (4) Maya Angelou has enjoyed great success as a writer, an actor, a director, a singer, a dancer, a teacher, and an activist for civil rights. (5) She has written numerous short stories, magazine articles, songs, and poetry, including such poems as Still I Rise and My Arkansas.

(6) During the 1960's she lived in Africa, where she wrote for two newspapers, the Arab Observer and the Ghanian Times. (7) She has written several screenplays, and she directed the film All Day Long. (8) For the television series Black African Heritage, she narrated the episode entitled The Slave Coast. (9) In addition, she toured twenty-two countries in a production of the opera Porgy and Bess.

(10) She has taught at several universities and has often given lectures at institutes of higher learning. (11) She once worked for Dr. Martin Luther King, Jr., as a coordinator for his civil-rights work.

Maya Angelou

c *Write Now* Imagine that you are a famous writer who has published books, magazine articles, and song lyrics. You are on tour promoting your latest novel. A talk-show host who is interviewing you asks you about the new book as well as your earlier work. Write the conversation. Use quotation marks and underlining correctly.

Checkpoint *Parts 6 and 7*

Write the following sentences. Punctuate each of the sentences correctly, adding apostrophes, quotation marks, commas, and underlining where necessary.

1. Why asked Kim dont we ask representatives from each class to help us decide?
2. Lisas interest in painting portraits changed to a fascination with drawing cartoons.
3. I read the article Crisis in Medicine in Newsweek magazine.
4. There is a Texas newspaper David said called the Taco Times.
5. Mystery writer Agatha Christie once said The best time for planning a book is while you're doing the dishes.
6. Freeze! the police officer shouted. Put your hands in the air!
7. The musical My Fair Lady was derived from the play Pygmalion.
8. Before 1791, the Gazette of the United States was the only newspaper that specialized in national politics.
9. In the fall of 89 my dad took me aside and said Its time to get serious about school, or you'll have regrets later.
10. Ordinary People, by Judith Guest, was both a novel and a movie.
11. Julia Ward Howe wrote The Battle Hymn of the Republic.
12. John Tenniel, who illustrated the book Alice in Wonderland, also drew cartoons for the magazine Punch.
13. Ms. Lopez said Your assignment is to read Shakespeares Hamlet.
14. Surely you can think of a better title and topic for your essay than What I Did During My Summer Vacation.
15. Please read Chapter 10, Reformers Worked for Social Change.
16. Are you familiar with Langston Hughes poem Dreams?
17. Harold said that his favorite movie was Casablanca.
18. I can't believe I received two As, four Bs, and no Cs this quarter.
19. Our teacher asked Who said Give me liberty or give me death?
20. The drama department is holding tryouts for A Raisin in the Sun.

Linking
Mechanics & Writing

You are an agent for Dan D. Tripps travel agency. A client wants you to put together an itinerary for an exciting five-day vacation. For each day, include the following information: the date; the starting place and destination; the times of departure and arrival; the method of transportation; places of interest; the activities planned, including admission or ticket fees; the arrangements for meals; and the names and addresses of hotels.

Include in the itinerary at least one series of items; several introductory words, such as *first* and *next;* one or more compound sentences; a possessive noun; and a compound word. Your itinerary may be realistic, or it may be highly imaginative. The following entry is a sample:

> Monday, July 1: Leave Des Moines, Iowa, at 8:40 A.M.
> Travel by Budget Airlines to Los Angeles, arriving 11:18 A.M.
> Take shuttle bus to Vacation Manor Hotel in Anaheim. Arrive
> at Wonderland theme park at 1:00 P.M. Admission to Wonder-
> land is $15.00.

Prewriting and Drafting Think of a place to go that has many points of interest, such as a large city. In this way it will be easy to imagine a parallel series of items (such as stops along a tour or things to see at a museum). Organize the ideas for your tour chronologically.

Revising and Proofreading If you have more material than you need, edit it to a reasonable five-day vacation. In proofreading, pay particular attention to details that include numbers, dates, and times.

Additional Writing Topic Following is a fragment of a conversation between two boys. Extend the conversation, revealing the place the boys went and why Stanley is reluctant to return. Use quotation marks and commas correctly.

> "No, I won't go back. If you want to go, find somebody else who doesn't know what it's like," protested Stanley.
> "But you must've forgotten," replied Bill, "how much fun we had the last time. Why don't you want to go?"
> "Well, maybe you think being scared out of your wits is fun, but everybody doesn't feel the same way," said Stanley, trying to quicken his steps so that he'd leave Bill behind.

Chapter 33
Application and Review

A Using Punctuation Correctly On your paper, write the following sentences, adding the missing punctuation.

1. Skateboards are becoming more popular but bicycles certainly have not been forgotten.
2. Are you finished Ron Mike asked We want to leave for the soccer game early
3. Should Carol bring her own pliers wrench and wire to the class tomorrow
4. Joan of Arc the French heroine was declared a saint in 1920
5. Ms Doyle Dr Antonelli and Mr McCoy are meeting at 800 PM on Saturday September 3
6. On March 13 1852 the first cartoon of Uncle Sam appeared in the Lantern, a weekly comic in New York
7. Oh no Did you really lose the tickets for the fourth game of the World Series
8. Robin bought the hockey tickets but then she lost them
9. Yes Mel I remembered to bring my new album
10. Georgia looked in her address book rummaged through a stack of old mail and finally found this address 215 Main Street Carrolton Georgia 30177

B Using Semicolons, Colons, Dashes, and Hyphens Write the following sentences on your paper, adding semicolons, colons, dashes, and hyphens where they are needed.

1. Arriving at 715 P.M. are the following guests the Prime Minister, the general, and my brother in law.
2. Dear Sir
   Your order for twenty five half baked pizzas will be delivered on Friday afternoon.
3. In just two and one half weeks I can hardly wait we'll be leaving for Ontario.
4. The results of the survey were surprising eighty five people said they would be willing to pay higher taxes for improvement of our public parks.
5. Margie took a ten week class in public speaking however, she still feels nervous in front of a crowd.

C Using Apostrophes, Quotation Marks, and Underlining Write the following sentences on your paper, putting in necessary apostrophes, quotation marks, and underlining.

1. Rachel said, I read about DC-6s and 747s in Rons book, Famous Airplanes.
2. The students homecoming theme is based on the musical Grease.
3. Did the teacher say, Please read Tillie Olsens story I Stand Here Ironing?
4. I don't see Meryl Streeps picture in this copy of People, said Beth. Maybe its in last weeks issue.
5. John Ciardis poem Beagles is one of my favorites.

D *Proofreading* Proofread the following letter for incorrect or missing punctuation and other errors. Rewrite the letter correctly.

> 3006 Merton Road
> Palo Alto California, 94306
> May 23 19—
>
> Sales Manager
> Rockinwell Corporation
> 680 broadway
> New York New York 10006
>
> Dear Sir or Madam,
>
> On april 26 I ordered twenty three songbooks listed in your catalog entitled Tunes from the 1940s. For some reason the books I recieved contained the following Music; songs by Billy Joel the Rolling Stones and Phil Collins, tunes from Cats, Oklahoma, and Annie, and blues by Muddy Waters.
> Despite your Companys error, my mother in laws choral group likes these books alot. As she stated too me last week Son these tunes are real lively.
>
> Sincerely,
>
> Martin E. Hudnut

E Adding the Correct Punctuation On your paper, write the following passage. Add the missing punctuation, and break the passage into paragraphs.

Whats up said the father putting his cap on the rack. I have a friend the boy said forcing the panic out of his voice. You mean Bob Spanner, Malcolm Price? his father said. No its another friend the boy said He might be going to die. Well I suppose his mother and father have called a doctor in? No said the boy He comes from Pennsylvania He hasnt anyone in Germany. You mean hes over here alone? the father said and now he walked toward the library with his arm around his sons thin shoulders. Well he got to be alone the boy said He didn't want to He didnt start out that way.

From "The Soldier Ran Away" by Kay Boyle

F Using Apostrophes, Quotation Marks, and Underlining Write each sentence, putting in necessary apostrophes, quotation marks, and underlining.

1. Walt Disneys feature cartoon films, like Cinderella and Bambi, are shown every seven years.
2. Most American families have two or more TVs, Mr. Lloyd said to the audience.
3. The freshmens lockers are on the first floor of the red-brick building.
4. Juan said, I definitely like the TR-7s that were designed in the early 1970s.
5. Is it true, asked Glorias brother, that the injured basketball player is my sister?
6. Jodys grandfather described the events of the stock-market crash of 29 to our business club.
7. Ken shouted, Somebodys car is rolling down the hill toward the iron gate!
8. Its somebodys problem, but its certainly not yours, said Ms. Kane emphatically.
9. Eubie, Bonnie explained, is a musical about ragtime musician Eubie Blake.
10. Do most students parents help them with homework? Ms. Richardson asked.

34

Spelling, Numbers, and Abbreviations

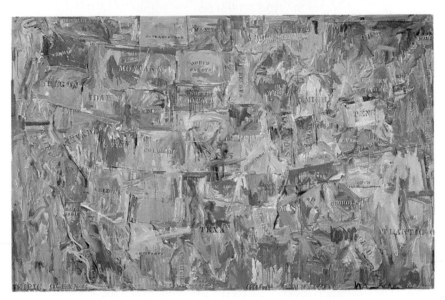

Map, Jasper Johns, 1961.
Oil on canvas, 6'6" × 10'3⅛". Collection, The Museum of Modern Art, New York. Gift of Mr. and Mrs. Robert C. Scull.

*D*oes the abbreviation MA refer to Massachusetts or Maine? Is Alaska abbreviated AL or AK? How many letter *s*'s are there in Mississippi?

Accuracy in spelling and the proper use of numbers and abbreviations will help make your writing easy for others to read. In this chapter you will learn rules and strategies for improving spelling and for using numbers and abbreviations correctly.

Part 1

Improving Your Spelling

Good spelling is important in all writing, from personal messages and letters to school tests and essays, job applications, and the reports, memos, and letters you may someday write in the business world. To improve your spelling, study the following rules and methods.

1. **Locate and conquer your own specific spelling problems.** What spelling errors do you make over and over? Study your past writing assignments and make a list of the misspelled words.

2. **Pronounce words carefully.** People can misspell words if they don't pronounce them correctly. If you are writing *nucular* for *nuclear*, for instance, you are probably mispronouncing the word.

3. **Use memory helps, called mnemonic devices, for words that give you trouble.** *Stationery* has *er* as in *letter;* there is ''a rat'' in *separate; Wednesday* contains *wed*.

4. **Always proofread your writing.** Many misspellings are actually careless mistakes. By examining your writing, you may catch such errors. Some students find that reading backward from the end of a sentence to the beginning helps them see spelling errors.

5. **Look up difficult words in a dictionary.**

6. **Learn the important spelling rules explained in this chapter.**

The suggestions in the following chart will help you master the spelling of a particular word.

Mastering the Spelling of a Word

1. **Look at the word and say it to yourself.** Make sure you pronounce it correctly.
2. **Close your eyes and try to visualize the word.** Look at it again, noticing any prefixes, suffixes, or double letters.
3. **Write the word from memory.** Then look at it again to check your spelling.
4. **Repeat the process.** Repeat it once if you spelled the word correctly. If you made an error, repeat the process until you have spelled the word correctly three times.

Part 2
Using Spelling Rules

Adding prefixes and suffixes can affect the spelling of a word.

The Addition of Prefixes

When a prefix is added to a word, the spelling of the word remains the same. When a prefix creates a double letter, keep both letters.

mis- + use = misuse   dis- + agree = disagree
mis- + spell = misspell   dis- + solve = dissolve

The Suffixes -ly and -ness

When the suffix *-ly* is added to a word ending in *l*, keep both *l*'s. When *-ness* is added to a word ending in *n*, keep both *n*'s.

cruel + -ly = cruelly   even + -ness = evenness
general + -ly = generally   lean + -ness = leanness

Exercise

Write the words in each pair, adding prefixes and suffixes.

1. skillful + -ly
   cautious + -ly
2. dis- + appoint
   dis- + satisfy
3. accidental + -ly
   strenuous + -ly

4. mis- + stated
   mis- + understood
5. un- + important
   un- + necessary
6. re- + read
   re- + entry

7. individual + -ly
   conscious + -ly
8. un- + noticed
   un- + opposed
9. mis- + spelling
   mis- + fortune

Suffixes with Silent e

When a suffix beginning with a vowel or y is added to a word ending in silent *e*, the *e* is usually dropped.

save + -ing = saving   value + -able = valuable
style + -ish = stylish   shine + -y = shiny

When a suffix beginning with a consonant is added to a word ending with a silent *e*, the *e* is usually retained.

hope + -ful = hopeful   like + -ly = likely

Exceptions: *truly, argument, ninth, wholly, judgment.*

Suffixes with Final y

When a suffix is added to a word ending in y preceded by a consonant, the y is changed to i except with the suffix -ing.

carry + -ed = carried   silly + -ness = silliness
study + -ous = studious   thirty + -eth = thirtieth

When -*ing* is added, the *y* does not change.

carry + -ing = carrying   study + -ing = studying

When a suffix is added to a word ending in y preceded by a vowel, the y usually does not change.

play + -ed = played   enjoy + -able = enjoyable
play + -er = player   enjoy + -ing = enjoying
play + -ful = playful   enjoy + -ment = enjoyment

Exercise

On your paper, copy each sentence. Add the prefixes and suffixes as shown. Some words will have both a prefix and a suffix added.

1. I made (absolute + -ly) sure that the campfire was out.
2. The havoc a tornado can cause is (un- + believe + -able).
3. Carlos wrote a short story about the (mystery + -ous) disappearance of the statue in the park.
4. The governor was present to help dedicate the new Vietnam War (Memory + -al).
5. The police officers were commended for (rescue + -ing) two children from an ice floe.
6. Kay, a veterinarian, says that her job is (satisfy + -ing).
7. June and Jed had a friendly (argue + -ment).
8. The restaurant posted a ''Help Wanted'' (advertise + -ment) in the front window.
9. It snowed (steady + -ly) for a night and a day.
10. Later, it rained and the highways turned (ice + -y).
11. The results of the survey were (dis- + appoint + -ing) to the mayor and his staff.
12. My dad always has a (worry + -ed) look on his face when he pays the monthly bills.
13. Sportswriters claimed that the team's losses were due to (mis- + manage + -ment).
14. I am (true + -ly) sorry for the trouble I caused you.
15. ''Don't leave without me!'' (cry + -ed) Arlene.

Doubling the Final Consonant

In one-syllable words that end with a single consonant preceded by a single vowel, double the final consonant before adding a suffix beginning with a vowel.

beg + -ing = begging   slip + -ery = slippery

Words of two syllables or more are more complicated. Before adding a suffix beginning with a vowel, double the final consonant in two-syllable words only if both of the following conditions exist:

1. The word ends with a single consonant preceded by a single vowel.
2. The word is accented on the second syllable.

ad·mit′ + -ed = admitted   re·gret′ + -able = regrettable

Words of two syllables that do not fit both of the conditions above do not have the final consonant doubled.

gar′·den + -er = gardener (The word ends with a single consonant preceded by a single vowel but is accented on the first syllable.)
re·load′ + -ing = reloading (The word is accented on the second syllable but ends with a single consonant preceded by *two* vowels.)

Note A few words do not follow these rules.

cancel + -ed = canceled *or* cancelled
equip + -ed = equipped

Check a dictionary if you are unsure whether to double the consonant.

Exercise

On your paper, write the following word pairs, adding the suffixes shown. Underline the word in each pair in which you had to double the final consonant.

1. bat + -ed
   cheat + -ed
2. bang + -ed
   shrug + -ed
3. swap + -ing
   keep + -ing
4. chain + -ed
   pin + -ed
5. patrol + -ed
   detail + -ed

6. prefer + -ed
   murmur + -ed
7. confer + -ed
   gather + -ed
8. spoil + -ing
   control + -ing
9. steer + -ed
   scar + -ed
10. regret + -able
    detest + -able

11. conquer + -or
    begin + -er
12. rerun + -ing
    listen + -ed
13. occur + -ence
    humor + -ous
14. dial + -ed
    propel + -er
15. repel + -ent
    recoil + -ed

Words with the "Seed" Sound

English contains twelve words that end with the "seed" sound. Eight of the words end with *-cede,* three end with *-ceed,* and only one ends with *-sede.*

-cede   accede, antecede, cede, concede, intercede, precede, recede, secede

-ceed   exceed, proceed, succeed

-sede   supersede

Words with ie and ei

Deciding between *ie* and *ei* in words like *niece, receive,* and *weigh* is easy if you remember these rules:

1. When the sound is long *e* (ē), the spelling is *ie,* except after *c.*

niece	fierce	receive	conceit
piece	field	deceive	ceiling
believe	chief	shield	receipt

2. When the sound is long *a* (ā), the word is spelled *ei.*

   | sleigh | weight | neighbor | surveillance |
   | neigh | freight | reign | beige |

The following words are exceptions: *either, friend, handkerchief, leisure, mischief, neither, seize, species,* and *weird.*

Plurals of Nouns

The plurals of nouns are formed in several ways. To learn how to spell the plurals of nouns, see pages 475–476 in Chapter 23.

Exercise

On your paper, write each incomplete word in the sentences below, supplying the missing letters.

1. Whales have r___gned supreme over the oceans of the world for more than sixty-five million years.
2. All whales are ___ther toothed whales or baleen whales.
3. The toothed whales feed ch___fly on fish and squid.
4. The narwhal, a sixteen-foot whale, has an ___ght-foot tusk.
5. The killer whale is generally conc___ded to be the f___rcest predator of the polar seas.
6. The killer whale becomes manageable in captivity, willingly carrying and retr___ving objects for its trainer.
7. The sperm whale can dive to depths exc___ding two miles.
8. A baleen whale has large bony plates that act as s___ves to filter plankton, krill, and other tiny sea creatures.
9. The finbacks can w___gh more than fifty tons.
10. Today many whales are on the endangered spec___s list.

Checkpoint *Parts 1 and 2*

A Combine the word parts in parentheses to make words that fit each sentence. Then correct any misspelled words in the sentence.

1. Naturaly the unopposed candidate will be (re- + elected).
2. Lydia was (dis- + satisfy + -ed) with the hastyly prepared meal.
3. The floor's (un- + even + -ness) made the cieling appear slanted.
4. An injection will (im- + mobilize) the animal for a brief time.
5. Jim's performance in the diveing contest was (electrify + -ing).
6. José refered to the dictionary to spell (murmur + -ing).
7. My aunt (can + -ed) vegatables and peaches in September.
8. Martin finally succeded in (make + -ing) the old radio work.
9. Neither child would admit (responsible + -ity) for the mischeif.
10. As the water receded, the farmers were (hope + -ful) that their crops could be saved.

11. The director (mis- + stated) the time of the rehearsal, causing confuseion among the actors.
12. The sky became (un- + natural + -ly) dark as the clouds sliped in.
13. Jared's arguement was (il- + logical) and totally confusing.
14. The despot's riegn was peaceful, (whole + -ly) unlike what had been expected.
15. Elena's (grace + -ful) routine had the audience claping.

B *Proofreading* Rewrite the following journal entry, correcting all spelling, punctuation, and mechanical errors that you find. The entry is from a novel about Charlie Gordon, a mentally handicapped man who undergoes an operation to raise his intelligence level.

progris riport 4–Mar 8

Their going to use me! Im so excited I can hardly write. Dr. Nemur and Dr. Strauss had an argament about it first. Dr. Nemur was in the office when Dr. Strauss brot me in. Dr. Nemur was worryed about using me but Dr. Strauss told him Miss Kinnian rekemmended me the best from all the people who she was teaching. I like Miss Kinnian because shes a very smart teacher. She said Charlie your going to have a second chance. If you volenteer for this experament you mite get smart. They don't know if it will be perminint but theirs a chance.

From *Flowers for Algernon* by Daniel Keyes

A List of Commonly Misspelled Words

abbreviate	description	intelligence	realize
accidentally	desirable	knowledge	recognize
achievement	despair	laboratory	recommend
all right	desperate	lightning	reference
altogether	dictionary	literature	referred
amateur	different	loneliness	rehearse
analyze	disappear	marriage	repetition
anonymous	disappoint	mathematics	representative
answer	discipline	medicine	restaurant
apologize	dissatisfied	minimum	rhythm
appearance	efficient	mischievous	ridiculous
appreciate	eighth	missile	sandwich
appropriate	eligible	misspell	schedule
argument	eliminate	mortgage	scissors
arrangement	embarrass	municipal	separate
associate	emphasize	necessary	sergeant
awkward	enthusiastic	nickel	similar
bargain	environment	ninety	sincerely
beginning	especially	noticeable	sophomore
believe	exaggerate	nuclear	souvenir
bicycle	exhaust	nuisance	specifically
bookkeeper	experience	obstacle	success
bulletin	familiar	occasionally	syllable
bureau	fascinating	occur	sympathy
business	February	opinion	symptom
calendar	financial	opportunity	temperature
campaign	foreign	outrageous	thorough
candidate	fourth	parallel	throughout
certain	fragile	particularly	together
changeable	generally	permanent	tomorrow
characteristic	government	permissible	traffic
column	grammar	persuade	tragedy
committee	guarantee	pleasant	transferred
courageous	guard	pneumonia	truly
courteous	gymnasium	politics	Tuesday
criticize	handkerchief	possess	twelfth
curiosity	height	possibility	undoubtedly
cylinder	humorous	prejudice	unnecessary
dealt	imaginary	privilege	vacuum
decision	immediately	probably	vicinity
definitely	incredible	pronunciation	village
dependent	influence	psychology	weird

Part 3
Writing Numbers

The form for writing numbers should be consistent. Numbers that can be expressed in fewer than three words are usually spelled out. Longer numbers are usually written in figures.

> There are *seven* days in a week, and *twenty-four* hours in a day.
> Ticket sales amounted to *$2,125*.

Spell out round numbers in hundreds, thousands, or millions when no more than two words are needed to express the amount. (*Thousand* is used only in even thousands; *1,500* is written as *fifteen hundred*.)

> The benefit concert raised more than *ten thousand* dollars.
> The town has a population of *eighteen hundred*.

Very large numbers may be expressed in figures with the words *million* or *billion*.

> The cost of the satellite will exceed *150 million* dollars.

Numbers at the beginning of a sentence are always spelled out.

> *Three hundred sixty-five* days make a year.

Dates, street and room numbers, telephone numbers, temperatures, decimals, percentages, and page numbers, are written in figures.

> The Battle of Concord took place on April *19, 1775*.
> The clinic is at *66* West Schiller in Room *35*.
> Matthew's phone number is *328-6610*.
> Last night the temperature went down to *10* degrees.
> Ann ran the hurdles in *15.8* seconds.
> The new *6* percent sales tax is discussed on page *16*.

Write out numbers used as modifiers.

> She took *third* place in the contest.

Punctuation Note Commas are used to separate the figures in large sums of money and in large numbers. Hyphens are used with all compound modifiers from twenty-one to ninety-nine.

> The attendance at the football game was *59,472*.
> My grandmother will be *seventy-five* next month.

Exercise

On your paper, copy the sentences, correcting errors in the use of numbers. If a sentence has no errors, write *Correct*.

1. 1 barrel of oil is equal to 31 gallons.
2. 1000 grams equal little more than 2 pounds.
3. A movie projects 1435 frames of film per minute.
4. The typical adult has over 60000 miles of blood vessels.
5. The answer to the 4th problem is on page twenty.
6. The Milky Way contains over 2000000000 stars.
7. Sheila lives at 80 West Second Street.
8. The distance from the sun to the earth is ninety-two million and seven hundred and fifty thousand miles.
9. Only thirteen percent voted for the referendum.
10. It takes light over 9 minutes to travel from the sun to the earth.
11. The serial number of the typewriter is 20,002.
12. 1st prize is one thousand two hundred and fifty dollars.
13. On March eighteenth, 1,959, Hawaii became the 50th state to join the Union.
14. 3 weeks ago the Chandlers moved to 1,682 Garfield Street.
15. This year's profit is fourteen percent higher than last year's.

Part 4
Using Abbreviations

Abbreviations are shortened forms of words. In ordinary writing, only three kinds of abbreviations are acceptable.

1. You can use the abbreviations *Mr., Mrs., Ms., Dr., Jr.,* and *Sr.* when they are part of a name.

   Mr. Sanchez is our school principal.
   Dr. Laura Sherwood is the superintendent of schools.

2. You can use abbreviations such as A.M., P.M., A.D., and B.C. in expressions of time and in dates.

   Rome was founded in the eighth century B.C.

3. You can use abbreviations for governmental agencies like the *FBI* (Federal Bureau of Investigation). Such abbreviations are usually written without periods. (If you are not sure whether an abbreviation has periods, look it up in your dictionary.)

Abbreviations are not acceptable in formal writing for names of countries and states, months and days, or words that are part of addresses or firm names. Exceptions are the two-letter state abbreviations when used on envelopes and abbreviations that are part of a company's official name.

> *Canada* has vast areas of wilderness.
> Farmers from *Illinois* helped farmers in the Southeast.
> The inauguration was on *Monday, January* 12, 1987.
> My father works for the Carson Computer *Company* on *Third Avenue.*
> McGregor and Saxe, *Inc.*
> 3 Maple Street
> Lindenwold, *NJ* 08021

Exercise

Copy the following sentences on your paper. Use abbreviations and punctuation correctly.

1. Mr. Frank Jiminez, Jr., is our new hist. teacher.
2. Dr. Val Evans gave the commencement address at Truman H.S.
3. Mister Nelson organized the U.N.I.C.E.F. fund-raiser.
4. Mrs. Sweeney is applying for a govt. grant to start a center for sr. citizens.
5. Cleopatra, the queen of Egypt, lived in the first cent. BC.
6. Pres. Franklin Delano Roosevelt closed all the banks in the U.S. on Mar. 6, 1933.
7. The Lakeside Bottling Co. has a plant on Oak Ave.

8. Last Fri. our home ec. class visited Mercy Hosp.
9. Detroit, Mich., is called "Motor City."
10. Next Tues., Nov. 2, is Election Day.

Checkpoint *Parts 3 and 4*

A On your paper, copy the sentences, correcting all errors in the use of numbers and abbreviations. If the use of an abbreviation is not correct, write the word for which the abbreviation stands. If an abbreviation is acceptable, make sure that it is punctuated correctly.

1. There were one hundred forty-nine people on the *Mayflower*.
2. The voyage of the *Mayflower* lasted for 65 days.
3. The 12 jurors assembled in Rm. 35 of the courthouse.
4. In nineteen fifty-four the population of France was about 55,000,000.
5. Maria's fever went down to ninety-nine degrees at 3:00 PM.
6. Next Mon. our school will welcome its 9th exchange student from London, Eng.
7. Mount Everest is 29,028 ft. high.
8. Sylvia Nash, who is an agent for the F.B.I., lives and works in Wash., D.C.
9. The polls opened at 5:00 AM and closed at 6:00 PM.
10. Ms. Maureen Edgar lived in Atlanta, Ga., for the 1st twenty years of her life.

B *Proofreading* Rewrite the following paragraphs, correcting all errors in spelling and the use of numbers and abbreviations.

The history of roller coasters is fascinateing. The 1st American coaster was built in 1884 at N.Y.'s Coney Island. Riders rolled and dipped over a 450-ft. track at six m.p.h. The coaster was not terribley fast, but it was very popular!

Over 1000 coasters were built during the 20's, considered the golden age of coasters. Amusment parks declined during the Depression, and many coasters were abandoned.

In the late 1950's, the first steel roller coaster was built in Calif. at Disneyland. The competition to build biger, faster, scaryer coasters swelled. America now seems to be in its 2nd golden age of roller coasters.

Linking
Mechanics & Writing

W. M. CURRIER & CO.,
Nos. 167, 169 & 171 UNION ST.,
LYNN, MASS.

According to *The Book of Firsts,* the first roller skates were worn to a costume party in 1760 by a man named Joseph Martin. Martin skated into the ballroom—playing a violin, no less—and promptly crashed into a mirror. Turn this incident into a short story told from the point of view of someone else at the party. Check and correct your spelling as you write and revise.

Prewriting and Drafting Begin by considering questions like these:

1. Who will the narrator be? A friend of Joseph Martin? An enemy? A fly on the ceiling, perhaps, or a mouse in a corner?
2. What did the narrator think when Martin appeared on roller skates? What details can you add to bring the incident to life?
3. What tone will the story have? Will it be humorous or serious?

Revising and Proofreading As you revise and proofread your story, ask yourself the following questions:

1. Do you have an interesting beginning?
2. Have you used conversation to add a touch of realism to the story?
3. Have you spelled all words correctly?

Additional Writing Topic Write a story in which a mad professor is working on one of his horrifying projects. Use at least fifteen words from the "List of Commonly Misspelled Words" on page 744.

Chapter 34
Application and Review

A Adding Prefixes and Suffixes On your paper, write the words in parentheses, adding prefixes and suffixes as shown.

1. Susan said that none of her answers were (in- + correct).
2. Who was the (win + -er) of the masquerade contest?
3. The campers rationed their (limit + -ed) water supply.
4. We found an insect (embed + -ed) in a piece of amber.
5. The explorers (final + -ly) reached their destination.
6. Most of the old letters were completely (il- + legible).
7. A lighthouse operator has to combat (lonely + -ness).
8. A (fury + -ous) storm ravaged the tiny island.
9. The report was based (entire + -ly) on scientific research done during the past five years.
10. At the age of ten, she began (write + -ing) her memoirs.
11. The heavy rains were (destroy + -ing) the crops.
12. That dog will have to stop (bury + -ing) its bones in my petunias.
13. No life relieves the (barren + -ness) of the moon's surface.
14. Those thunderclouds definitely aren't (line + -ed) with silver.
15. The demands of his new job may be causing his uncharacteristic (mean + -ness).

B Finding Misspelled Words Find one misspelled word in each sentence. On your paper, write the word correctly.

1. The fierce cougar dissappeared into the cave.
2. Marcy's horse gracefully steped and trotted around the ring.
3. Annie is planning to send the inviteations today.
4. The wide receiver was completly unaware of the coach's new game plan.
5. David shouted angryly at his friends but immediately was sorry.
6. Some taxpayers worried that the money was mispent.
7. The uneveness of the slope makes skiing unusually hard.
8. Police cars generally preceed the President's car in a parade.
9. In all of the excitment, we accidentally misplaced our concert tickets.
10. The weight of the ship's cargo excedes ten tons.
11. Feirce winds knocked the pier into the lake.
12. The doctor conceded that only time would relieve the pain.

13. In the preceding weeks we enjoyed our liesure time.
14. Neither of the advertisments is meant to deceive us.
15. We recieved directions to the new baseball field.

C Correcting Spelling Errors Find at least one misspelled word in each sentence. On your paper, write each misspelled word correctly. There are twenty misspellings.

1. It was the sillyest arguement we had ever had.
2. Mary Chase's play *Harvey* is truely entertainning.
3. The merryment continued even after people started leaveing the party.
4. Bill was cooking dinner, and Monica was bakeing dessert.
5. The losing candidate eventualy decided to consede the election to her opponent.
6. Which occurence are you refering to?
7. To his amazment, the fierce winds uprootted a tree.
8. To ensure the eveness of each coat of paint, we used an expensive paint thiner.
9. Coach Marowitz spoke forcefuly about the need for modifiing our defenseive strategy.
10. The dog proceded to retreive the stick and break it.

D Using Numbers and Abbreviations Correctly On your paper, copy the following sentences, writing all the numbers and abbreviations correctly.

1. The Pres. flew to Peking from Washington, D C, a trip of six thousand nine hundred and sixty-five miles.
2. The Yangtze River in China is three thousand four hundred and thirty-four miles long.
3. 3 billion people live on the continent of Asia.
4. The Pacific Ocean is a little over 36,000 feet deep.
5. The sun is 1 of 100 billion stars that are a part of the earth's galaxy.
6. Ms Beth Henley won the Pulitzer Prize for her play *Crimes of the Heart* in nineteen hundred and eighty-one.
7. Mister McKay organized the 1st Fourth of July parade in Ames.
8. Does the Green Lawn Co. have an office in Houston, Tex or in Indianapolis, IN?
9. Last Wed. our Eng. class read the 1st chapter of *Stories of the Amer. Civil War*.
10. The dr. told me to drink 8 oz. of water with every meal as well as every morning and evening.

Cumulative Review

Chapters 32, 33, and 34

A Correcting Mechanics and Spelling On your paper, rewrite the following paragraphs, correcting the errors in capitalization, punctuation, and spelling.

(1) Last Saturday my mothers youngest brother, uncle jack, went with me to the museum of science and industry. (2) On display was a collection of artistic scientific and Technological inventions of the chinese. (3) This exhibit had been recommended by my Industrial Arts I teacher my Sceince teacher and also by my principle.

(4) We saw a waterclock made in Ad 1,068 that stood 2 stories high. (5) Because I am especially interested in astronomy I enjoyed the planetarium, in which a chinese astronomer could sit and be surrounded by a view of the stars. (6) I was amazed to find out that this device was built (more then 1000 years ago.) (7) We saw many other inventions, including irrigation machines compasses and looms, to.

(8) There were also demonstrations of ancient Arts and Crafts. (9) Most of the visual arts developed during four dynasties; the han, the T'ang, the sung, and the ming. (10) I asked a man who was demonstrateing chinese ink painting to write my name in chinese characters on a peice of stationery. (11) He asked, ''how do you pronounce your name''? (12) When he had finished writing my name he stamped it, with a red seal that showed his own name.

(13) Then My Uncle and I proceded to the silkworm exhibit. (14) According to Chinese Legend, silk was discovered in 2700 b.c. in the garden of the emperor. (15) 1 five-year-old girl really enjoyed observing the silkworms produce silk fibers. (16) She asked if ''she could take a worm home to play with.'' (17) The guard explained that the worms were needed to make silk. The girl recieved a sample of silk thread.

(18) After viewing the exhibit we browsed through a special shop. (19) This shop carryed alot of products made in china. (20) After looking at everything, I finally bougt a silk handkerchief for my mother to remember this exhibit.

B *Proofreading* The following paragraphs contain errors in the use of the concepts you have studied throughout this book. On your paper, rewrite the paragraphs and correct the errors.

On july 4 1862 Charles lutwidge dodgson and a friend took 3 little girls on a picnic. What an important day it would be for the young englushman. The girl's asked to here a story so Dodgson invented one. Since one of the girls was named Alice Liddell, Dodgson told a story about a girl named Alice whom fell down a rabbit hole. She saw many unbeleivable things as she explored inside the hole.

When Dodgson finished telling the story the real-life Alice asked him to write it down, he returned to his room at Oxford university and begun writing. Finishing at 6 a.m. he didn't get much sleep that night. When Alice recieved the story, she could not have been more pleased. A novelist who Alice's family knew read Dodgson's story, and he said ''he thought it should be published.''

Dodgson taked the advice however first he asked a famous illustrator to make drawings to go with the story. In 1865, they're book, ''Alice's Adventures in Wonderland,'' were published. Dodgson published the book under the pseudonym or pen name Lewis Carroll because he did not want to use his real name for a ''nonsense'' book. Nevertheless the book sold real good, and Dodgson went on to write another book about Alices unbelievable adventures.

Which was called Through the Looking-Glass and What Alice Found There. Appealing to both adults and childrens, Dodgsons book's have had long-lasting success.

Sentence Diagraming

A sentence diagram is a drawing that shows how all the parts of a sentence fit together. The base for a sentence diagram is made up of a horizontal main line that is crossed by a short vertical line:

In most diagrams, other lines are added to the base shown above.

Subjects and Verbs

Place the simple subject on the horizontal main line to the left of the vertical line. Place the simple predicate, or verb, to the right of the vertical line.

Adam spoke.

| Adam | spoke |

Dogs were barking.

| Dogs | were barking |

In diagraming, capitalize only those words that are capitalized in the sentence. Do not use punctuation except for abbreviations. Single-word modifiers are written on slanted lines below the words they modify. (See pages 758 and 759.)

Sentences Beginning with There or Here

To diagram a sentence beginning with *There,* first decide whether *There* tells *where* or is an introductory word. If *There* tells *where,* place it on a slanted line below the verb.

There stood the mayor.

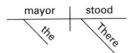

If *There* is an introductory word, place it on a horizontal line above the subject.

There has been a mistake.

There

| mistake | has been |

Unlike *There,* the word *Here* always tells *where.* In a sentence diagram, therefore, place *Here* on a slanted line below the verb.

Here comes the winner.

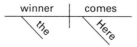

In both sentences, the subject comes *after* the verb. Notice, however, that in the diagram the subject is placed *before* the verb, to the left of the vertical line.

Interrogative Sentences

In an interrogative sentence, the subject often comes after the verb or after part of the verb phrase. In diagraming, remember to place the subject before the verb to the left of the vertical line.

Is your watch running?   Are the geese migrating?

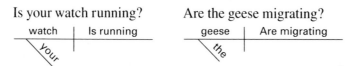

Imperative Sentences

In an imperative sentence, the subject is usually not stated. Since commands are given to the person spoken to, the subject is understood to be *you.* To diagram an imperative sentence, place the understood subject *you* to the left of the vertical line. Enclose *you* in parentheses.

Listen!

Direct Objects

In a diagram, place the direct object on the main line after the verb. Separate the direct object from the verb with a vertical line that does not extend below the main line.

Lana bought a poster.

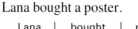
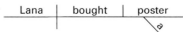

Indirect Objects

To diagram an indirect object, draw a slanted line below the verb. From the bottom of the slanted line, draw a line parallel to the main line. Place the indirect object on the parallel line.

Lana bought her brother a poster.

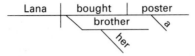

Subject Complements

In a diagram, place a predicate nominative or a predicate adjective on the main line after the verb. Separate the subject complement from the verb with a slanted line that extends in the direction of the subject.

Ms. Freed is our advisor. (*Advisor* is a predicate nominative.)

That tire looks flat. (*Flat* is a predicate adjective.)

Sentences with Compound Parts

Compound Subjects To diagram a compound subject, place the parts on parallel horizontal lines. Then connect the parallel lines with a broken line, and write the conjunction that connects the parts of the compound subject. Attach the compound subject to the main line with diagonal lines.

Sheep, goats, and wild horses roam the foothills.

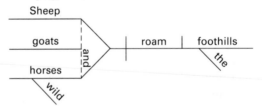

Compound Verbs To diagram a compound verb, place the parts on parallel horizontal lines. Write the conjunction that connects the parts on the broken line. Attach the compound verb to the main line.

The freighter tossed, pitched, and rolled.

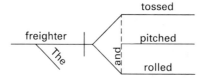

If a compound verb has an object or a subject complement, place the object or subject complement on the parallel line after the verb.

The guests ate the fish and became ill.

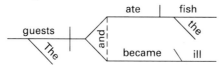

Compound Direct Objects and Indirect Objects To diagram a compound direct or indirect object, place the objects on parallel horizontal lines. Connect those lines with a broken line. Write the conjunction on the broken line. Attach the compound object to the main line.

Gonzales hit a homer and two singles. (*compound direct object*)

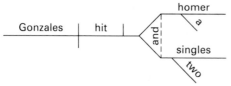

The director gave Brendan and Sandra lead roles.
   (*compound indirect object*)

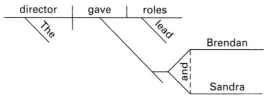

Compound Subject Complements To diagram a compound predicate nominative or predicate adjective, place the parts on parallel horizontal lines. Connect the parts with a broken line and write the conjunction on that line. Attach the compound predicate nominative or predicate adjective to the main line.

The new coaches are Brock and Rudolph.
(*compound predicate nominative*)

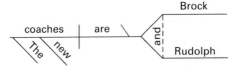

The stereo sounds rich and full. (*compound predicate adjective*)

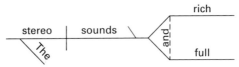

Adjectives

To diagram an adjective, place it on a slanted line below the word it modifies. Keep in mind that *a, an,* and *the* are adjectives and that more than one adjective can modify the same word.

Our new cat has a sunny disposition.

When two or more adjectives are connected by a conjunction, place the adjectives on slanted lines below words they modify. Connect the slanted lines with a broken line, and write the conjunction on it.

A tired but happy team boarded the chartered bus.

If an adjective modifies a word that is part of a compound subject, object, or subject complement, place the adjective on a slanted line under the word it modifies.

A small child and her anxious parents joined the line.

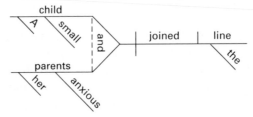

Adverbs

To diagram an adverb that modifies a verb, place the adverb on a slanted line under the verb. Keep in mind that words like *not* and *never* are adverbs.

The fire did not spread rapidly.

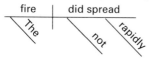

To diagram an adverb that modifies an adjective or an adverb, place the adverb on a line connected to the modified adjective or adverb as shown below.

Too many jobs pay very poorly.

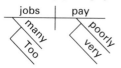

If an adverb modifies a compound verb, place the adverb under the word it modifies.

They studied very hard and passed the test easily.

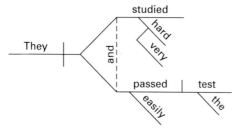

Prepositional Phrases

To diagram a prepositional phrase, draw a slanted line below the word that the phrase modifies. From the slanted line, draw a line parallel to the main line. Place the preposition on the slanted line and the object of the preposition on the parallel line. Words that modify the object of the preposition are placed on slanted lines below the object.

The guests on the show talked about their new movies.

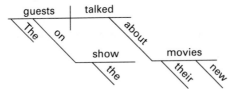

If a preposition has a compound object, place the objects on parallel lines as shown below.

We fished for trout and bass.

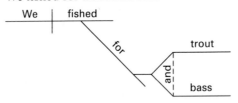

Gerunds and Gerund Phrases

To diagram a gerund, place it on a line drawn as a step (   ). Put the step on a forked line (   ) that stands on the main line. The placement of the forked line shows how the gerund or gerund phrase is used in the sentence.

Skydiving is a rigorous sport. (*gerund used as subject*)

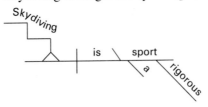

This job requires fast, accurate typing.
(*gerund phrase used as direct object*)

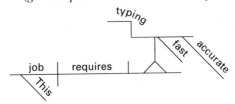

To diagram a gerund phrase that includes a direct object, place the direct object after the gerund.

Telling jokes will cheer us up. (*gerund phrase used as subject*)

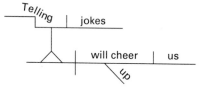

His hobby is painting miniatures.
(*gerund phrase used as predicate nominative*)

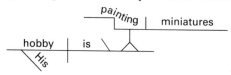

To diagram a gerund or a gerund phrase that is the object of a preposition, place the preposition on a slanted line that extends from the modified word. Place the step and the forked line below the main line.

We thanked Valerie for helping us.
(*gerund phrase as object of preposition*)

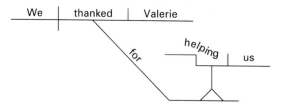

Participles and Participial Phrases

To diagram a participle, place the participle on an angled line below the word it modifies.

The outfielder made a diving catch.

To diagram a participial phrase that includes a direct object and modifiers, place the object on a straight line extending from the base of the angled line. Place any modifiers on slanted lines below the words they modify.

Reading the fine print carefully, Erin studied the contract.

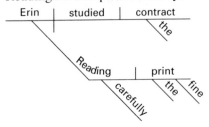

Infinitives and Infinitive Phrases

To diagram an infinitive used as a noun, place the infinitive on an angled line. Write the word *to* on the slanted part of the angled line and write the verb on the horizontal part of the angled line. Put the angled line on a forked line that stands on the main line. The placement of the forked line shows how the infinitive or infinitive phrase is used in the sentence.

I like to swim. (*infinitive used as direct object*)

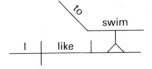

To diagram an infinitive used as a modifier, place the angled line on a horizontal line below the modified word. Attach the horizontal line to the main line as shown below.

This stroke is easy to learn. (*infinitive used as adverb*)

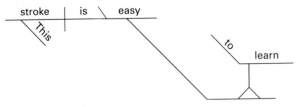

To diagram an infinitive phrase that includes an object and modifiers, place the object after the infinitive. Separate the object from the infinitive with a vertical line. Place modifiers on slanted lines below the words they modify.

Dale tried to answer the questions correctly.
(*infinitive phrase used as direct object*)

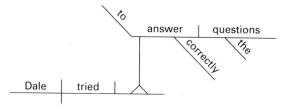

Sandpaper is used to smooth the wood.
(*infinitive phrase used as adverb*)

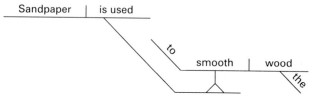

Appositives and Appositive Phrases

To diagram an appositive, place the appositive in parentheses after the word it identifies or explains.

Our neighbor, Mr. Frazer, writes historical novels.

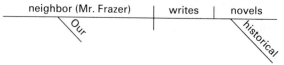

To diagram an appositive phrase, place the modifiers on slanted lines below the appositive.

The kiwi, a flightless bird of New Zealand, is very shy.

Adjective Clauses

To diagram an adjective clause, place it on a horizontal line below the main line, diagraming the clause as a sentence. Use a broken line to connect the relative pronoun in the adjective clause to the word in the independent clause that the adjective clause modifies.

The people who run the space program are in Houston.

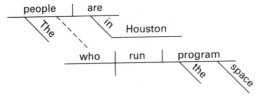

One of the players on whom we depend was injured.

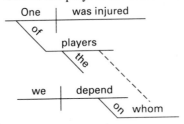

Adverb Clauses

To diagram an adverb clause, place the clause on a horizontal line below the main line, diagraming the clause as a sentence. Use a broken line to connect the adverb clause to the word it modifies in the clause. Write the subordinating conjunction on the broken line.

When Carlos was twelve, he moved to New York.

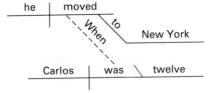

Noun Clauses

To diagram a noun clause, place it on a separate line that is attached to the main line with a forked line. The placement of the forked line shows how the noun clause is used in the sentence.

What you need is a sense of humor.
(*noun clause used as subject*)

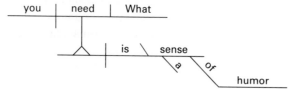

Many people say that good times are coming.
(*noun clause used as object of verb*)

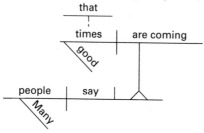

The candidate talked to whoever would listen.
(*noun clause used as object of preposition*)

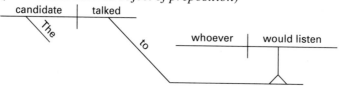

Compound Sentences

To diagram a compound sentence, place the independent clauses on parallel lines. Use a broken line with a step to connect the verb in one clause to the verb in the other. Write the conjunction on the step. If clauses are joined by a semicolon, leave the step blank.

The press secretary spoke first, and then the President held a press conference.

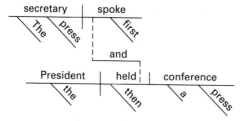

Complex Sentences

To diagram a complex sentence, decide whether the subordinate clause is an adjective clause, an adverb clause, or a noun clause. Then use the information on page 764 to diagram the sentence.

Compound-Complex Sentences

To diagram a compound-complex sentence with an adjective or an adverb clause, diagram the independent clauses first. (See page 764.) Then attach the subordinate clause or clauses to the words they modify. Leave room to attach a subordinate clause where it belongs.

I would have bought the book that you recommended, but the clerk could not find it.

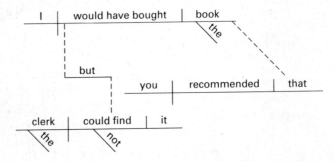

To diagram a compound-complex sentence with a noun clause, decide how the noun clause is used in the independent clause. Then diagram the noun clause in the position that shows how it is used.

Galileo taught that the earth moves, but few people accepted his theory. (The noun clause *that the earth moves* is the direct object in the first independent clause.)

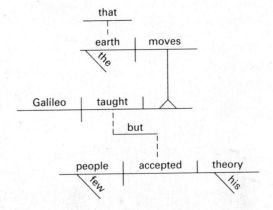

Writer's Handbook

Ideas for Writing

Ideas for writing are everywhere. You need only to recognize them and build upon them. To help get your mental wheels rolling, read the following sections and use your thinking skills to generate topics. The first sections list ideas according to types of writing and subject areas. The next part lists trigger words. The fourth section presents guidelines for using the fine art and photographs in this book.

Ideas for Writing

Descriptive
a new creature,
   place, or planet
a secret hideaway
a person throwing
   a tantrum
a soggy newspaper
an abandoned
   building
an airport or train
   station
a hidden treasure

Narrative
stage fright
breaking loose
the awful truth
learning to adapt
incident unex-
   plained
the last laugh
rained out
prehistoric hunt
the crystal ball
note found in the
   trash
ghost story
broken promises

Expository
(Process)
how to use a 35mm
   camera
how the human
   embryo develops
how a neon sign
   glows
how a heat-seeking
   missile finds its
   target
how to mop up oil
   spills

(Cause-Effect)
What causes food to
   spoil?
How does hand-
   writing reflect
   personality?
Why does laughter
   help mental
   health?
What are the effects
   of advertising?
What are the causes
   and effects of
   shoplifting?

(Compare/Contrast)
Compare/contrast...
music to language
football to war
a blind date to a
   surprise package
a book to a movie
the same person
   poor and rich
our country at two
   different times

Persuasive
Should schools run
   year round?
Should athletes be
   so highly paid?
Should all citizens
   serve on juries?
Should single
   parents adopt
   children?
Does vitamin C
   prevent colds?
Should medical
   experiments on
   animals be pro-
   hibited?

Ideas for Writing in Subject Areas

Art
how to make a
   clay sculpture
how to engrave
   folk art
lithographs
ceramics
Why visit the art
   museum?
Compare/contrast
   contemporary
   and classical art.

Consumerism
how to budget
   your money
what to look for
   when buying an
   automobile
how banks work
fads and crazes
Why read labels?

Health
How does diet
   affect health?
the causes of heart
   attacks
how to test for
   allergies
aerobic exercises
How do vaccines
   prevent disease?
Compare/contrast
   jogging and
   walking.
relationship of
   body weight
   to heredity

Math
why calculators
   are popular
how geometry is
   useful in
   everyday life
mathematics and
   video games
how to measure
   the speed of a
   train
how to show
   percentages with
   a circle graph
careers for
   mathematicians
Why make bar
   graphs?

Music
Compare/contrast
   two popular
   singers.
how to read music
how to play an
   instrument
the life of a fam-
   ous musician
how music alters
   your moods
Compare/contrast
   60's music
   and 80's music.
how to break into
   the music
   business
the effect of back-
   ground music on
   living patterns

Science
What causes acid
   rain?
how an organ is
   transplanted
What causes earth-
   quakes?
Why explore space?
How is aluminum
   recycled?
the effect of
   nuclear waste on
   cities and towns
astronomy
accidental discov-
   eries
how a tornado
   forms
the advantages of
   solar heating

Social Studies
events that changed
   history
Should illegal
   aliens be given
   amnesty?
Compare/contrast
   the city and the
   suburbs.
Agree/disagree:
   "All of the
   nations suffer
   when one person
   suffers the loss
   of civil rights."
Should a president
   serve more than
   two terms?

Trigger Words

The words listed below should trigger many different writing ideas. Use them along with the Thinking Skills on pages 24–53 to generate new writing ideas.

Trigger Words

bottleneck	network	target
chord	puzzle	telescope
computer	radar	ticket
fountain	robot	treasure
junk	satellite	triangle
magnet	shadow	vacation
maze	spectrum	violin
menu	spotlight	vulture
mirror	star	weirdness

Fine Art and Photographs

You have learned to generate writing ideas from a wide range of subjects and experiences. You can apply those same skills to the photographs and fine art that appear throughout this text. Turn to an image at random and ask yourself questions such as the following:

1. What do I see in this picture? How could I describe it?
2. How does this picture make me feel? What memories or personal associations spring from this feeling?
3. What might have occurred just prior to the scene shown in this picture? What might occur just after it?
4. Who are the people in this picture? Could they make good characters in a story?
5. How might I analyze this image? What could I say about the subject, colors, composition?
6. What do I know about the artist or photographer? What could I say about his or her technique? Did this person have an interesting life or career that might be worth investigating?
7. What writing possibilities might be suggested by the setting or the time period that is represented here?
8. What aspects of our history or culture are demonstrated here? Might these be worth exploring?

Outlining and Other Graphic Organizers

Graphic aids are excellent devices for organizing ideas. They are also useful for taking notes as well as for planning a composition or speech. Basically there are two kinds of organizers you can use: outlines and graphic organizers. Both will help you record and organize information in a concise and logical manner.

Types of Outlines

A **formal outline** gives detailed information and indicates relationships between ideas. Use a formal outline to organize a formal composition or speech or a chapter for study purposes.

Formal outlines can be either **sentence outlines** or **topic outlines.** In a sentence outline, each main topic and subtopic is written in complete sentences. Here is a portion of a sentence outline.

Walt Disney and the Animated Film

Thesis Statement: Walter Elias Disney was an important pioneer in the field of animated film.

I. Walt Disney was interested in cartooning as a youth.
   A. He was born in Chicago in 1901.
   B. At the age of 16, he studied art in Chicago.
   C. At age 19, he worked for the Kansas City Film Company, creating crude cartoon advertisements.

II. Disney started his own film business.
   A. In 1923, he moved to Los Angeles to draw cartoons for movies.
   B. He started a film studio in his garage.
   C. His first successful character was Mickey Mouse.
   D. Disney achieved several movie-making firsts.
      1. His cartoon *Flowers and Trees* was the first film made in full technicolor.
      2. *Steamboat Willie* was the first to use sound.

The **topic outline** uses words or phrases for each main topic and subtopic. It is not as detailed or complete as a sentence outline. The following shows a portion of a topic outline.

The Arctic

I. Arctic lands
   A. The true arctic
   B. The subarctic
      1. Not part of true arctic
      2. Warmer summers than true arctic

II. Natural resources
   A. Minerals
      1. Coal
      2. Radioactive minerals
         a. Thorium
         b. Uranium
      3. Petroleum
   B. Animals

Decide whether a sentence or topic outline better suits your purpose and personal style. Once you begin your outline, do not mix forms within a given outline.

Correct Outline Form

In general, the same form applies to topic and sentence outlines.

1. Write the title at the top of the outline. The title, introduction, and conclusion are not considered parts of the outline.
2. Use the following arrangement of numerals and letters for main points and subpoints.

   I. (Main point)
      A. (First subpoint)
      B. (Second subpoint)
         1.
         2.

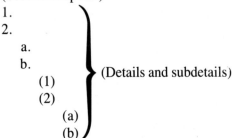

            a.
            b.
              (1)
              (2)   (Details and subdetails)
                  (a)
                  (b)

3. Indent each division of the outline. Place the letter or numeral directly underneath the first letter in the first word of the larger heading above.

4. Do not use a single subheading. A heading should not be broken down if it cannot be divided into at least two points. If there is a *1* under *A*, there must be at least a *2*.
5. In a topic outline, keep items of the same rank in parallel form. For instance, if *A* is a noun, then *B* and *C* should also be nouns. Subtopics need not be parallel with main topics.
6. Begin each item with a capital letter. Do not use end punctuation in a topic outline.

Writing an Informal Outline

An **informal outline** is used to organize information quickly and in as few words as possible. Main ideas are listed as separate headings. Supporting details are written beneath each heading. You may use numbers, letters, dashes, or indentations for informal outlines. Parallel structure is not necessary.

Informal outlines are useful for taking notes during a lecture, for preparing to answer exam questions, and for making prewriting notes during an essay test. The following is an example of an informal outline on archaeology.

I. How archaeologists gather information
—surveying sites
—excavation
—record and preserve material

II. Famous archaeological finds
—discovery of Troy, 1870
—King Tut's tomb, 1922
—found treasure ship off coast of England, 1939

Other Graphic Organizers

A **graphic organizer** is still another way of organizing information you have collected for your composition or report. Graphic aids include charts, cause-effect schemes, tree diagrams, clusters, and any other "sketch" of ideas.

Charts are useful when analyzing or comparing information. When you fill out a chart, you can easily see where there are gaps in your information. Charts present information about one or more subjects called **variables.** These subjects are called variables because the information associated with them varies. The variables in the following chart include *condition or illness, appearance, area affected,* and *duration.*

Common Skin Problems

Condition/ Illness	Appearance	Area Affected	Duration
chicken pox	flat red spots, then tiny blisters that break and crust	back, chest, and abdomen first, then rest of body	about seven days
hives	raised red bumps	any area	a few minutes to a day
poison ivy	red, swollen skin, rash, and blistering	exposed areas	one to two weeks

A **cause-effect scheme** states that something happened because of something else. The following is an example of a cause-effect scheme that could be used to analyze the effect of the setting on a character in a short story. You can develop a similar chart whenever you need to understand a cause-effect relationship.

Cause-Effect Chart

"The Most Dangerous Game"

Setting (cause)	Effect on the Character
1. treacherous water surrounding island	1. causes Rainsforth to fall off boat, sends him to island
2. island setting	2. cuts Rainsforth off from any outside help or possibility of escape
3. Zaroff's mansion	3. creates a misleading impression of Zaroff, so Rainsforth is unprepared for what is to come
4. jungle	4. provides new dangers and the opportunities for possible escape

A **cluster** is a type of personal brainstorming that can help you explore and organize related ideas. Begin by writing a word or phrase on a piece of paper. Circle it. Now, outside that circle, write down any word or idea that you associate with the "nucleus" word. Put each in its own circle and connect it with a line to the nucleus word. Branch out from the new ideas in the same way.

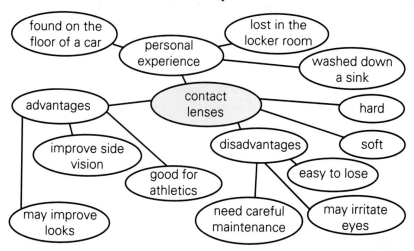

A **tree diagram** is another type of brainstorming that is useful for showing relationships among ideas. Begin by drawing a straight line down the center of your paper. Next, write a word or phrase at the base of this line. It will become your main idea. Write down any words or phrases that you associate with the main idea. Put each new idea on a line that stems from the main idea. Branch out from the new stems in a similar manner.

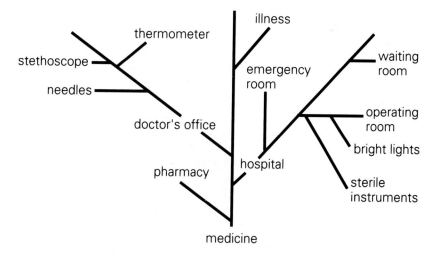

Good Manuscript Form

Good manuscript form increases the impact of what a writer says. Your papers should be typed double-space or written neatly in dark blue or black ink.

Preparing the Manuscript

Leave a one-inch margin at the top, bottom, and right side of the page; leave a slightly larger margin on the left side. Follow the instructions of your teacher for the heading. Here are some other guidelines for manuscript preparation.

Placement of Title

Place the title only on the first page. Allow two lines between the title and the first line of your copy. Do not underline the title; do not place it in quotation marks unless it is a quotation from another source.

Numbers in Writing

Spell out numbers that can be written in two words or less; write longer numbers in figures. Always spell out a number at the beginning of a sentence.

> They gathered *thirty-one* bushels of apples.
> The loss amounted to *$4,280*.
> *Eight hundred* people were suddenly left homeless by the flood.

Use figures for dates, street numbers, telephone numbers, page numbers, decimals, and percentages.

> Shakespeare's birth date was April 23, 1564.
> Yesterday the temperature reached 101 degrees.

Italics for Titles

When a writer wants to indicate that a word would be printed in italics, he or she underlines it in the manuscript.

Titles of books, plays, newspapers, magazines, motion pictures, works of art, and long musical compositions are printed in italics. Names of ships, trains, and airplanes are printed in italics.

Manuscript Form The <u>Santa Maria</u> was a famous sailing ship.
Printed Form The *Santa Maria* was a famous sailing ship.

Common Usage Problems

The following are problems most commonly mentioned by teachers of writing. Review them periodically to improve your writing. Also use these as a guide when proofreading. For help with commonly misused words see pages 788–793.

Abbreviations

In general, abbreviations should not be used in formal papers with the exception of titles (Mr., Mrs., Ms., Dr.), dates, and times (A.M., P.M., B.C., A.D.). For more information on the use of abbreviations, see pages 746–747.

Clauses

See Essential and Nonessential Clauses.

Clichés

A **cliché** is a trite or overused expression. Good writers avoid clichés because they make writing dull. Avoid the trite expressions listed below and any others that come to mind. Instead, look for fresh ways to express your ideas.

> beyond a shadow of a doubt
> cool as a cucumber
> tried and true

Comparisons, Illogical

The word *other* or the word *else* is required for a comparison of an individual member with the rest of the group.

Incorrect	Julie swims faster than any member of the team. (This implies Julie is not a member of the team.)
Correct	Julie swims faster than any other member of the team.

Both parts of a comparison must be stated completely if there is any chance of its being misunderstood.

Confusing	I like spaghetti better than you. (Do you like spaghetti better than you like me?)
Clear	I like spaghetti better than you do.

See also page 566.

Dangling Modifiers

See Modifiers.

Double Negatives

Negatives are words such as *no, not, never, nothing,* and *none.* A **double negative** occurs when two negative words are used where only one is needed. Double negatives are nonstandard usage. *Hardly* or *barely,* used with a negative word, is also nonstandard.

Incorrect	The suspect did*n't* know *nothing* about the missing gold ring.
Correct	The suspect did*n't* know *anything* about the missing gold ring.
Incorrect	I *never* had *no* allergic reactions to strawberries before this summer.
Correct	I *never* had *any* allergic reactions to strawberries before this summer.
Incorrect	Maria had*n't hardly* eaten her dinner.
Correct	Maria *had hardly* eaten her dinner.

See also page 569.

Essential and Nonessential Clauses

An **essential clause** identifies or points out the person or thing that it modifies. It cannot be dropped without confusing the meaning of a sentence or making the meaning incomplete. Essential clauses are not set off from the rest of the sentence by commas. Most essential clauses are introduced by *that* or *who* and not by *which.*

> The candidate *who withdrew from the governor's race* plans to return to business at the end of January. (The clause tells which candidate.)
> The books *that you left on the bus* belong to the library. (The clause tells which books.)

A **nonessential clause** merely adds extra information to a sentence. It can be dropped without changing the meaning of the sentence. Nonessential clauses are set off by commas from the rest of the sentence. They may be introduced by *which* or *who* but not *that.*

> The ticket, *which he threw in the trash,* was outdated.
> Charles Dickens, *who was a British author,* wrote *Oliver Twist* and *A Tale of Two Cities.*

Exercise

Identify the error in each of the following sentences. Then rewrite each sentence correctly.

1. I couldn't barely read your scribbled handwriting.
2. We decided to bury the hatchet after three days of fighting.
3. We were amazed that José didn't leave no message for his mother and father.
4. Playing basketball is something I enjoy more than you.
5. Jerry is a better hockey player than anyone on the team.
6. The prize which Susan won was a gold trophy.
7. All through the scorching summer, she was as busy as a bee.
8. Add a tsp. of food coloring to make green eggs and ham.
9. David hasn't never missed a day of practice.
10. *Watership Down* which concerns a society of rabbits is an interesting book.

Gerunds Preceded by Pronouns

A **gerund** is a verb form that functions as a noun and ends in *-ing*. A gerund may be the *subject, object, object of a preposition,* or *predicate nominative* in a sentence.

When a pronoun precedes a gerund, it should be in the **possessive case.** Do not use objective case pronouns before a gerund.

Incorrect   Mr. Henderson doesn't like *us* being late for woodworking class.

Correct   Mr. Henderson doesn't like *our* being late for woodworking class.

Incorrect   Mother doesn't approve of *me* talking on the phone for hours.

Correct   Mother doesn't approve of *my* talking on the phone for hours.

See also pages 609–610.

Infinitives

An **infinitive** is a verb form that usually begins with *to: to relax, to dance.* An adverb placed between *to* and the rest of the infinitive causes a **split infinitive.** Most writers try to avoid split infinitives because they often lead to awkward writing. To avoid splitting an infinitive, place the adverb before or after the infinitive or infinitive phrase.

Incorrect	Jason hopes *to* occasionally *drive* his brother's car.
Correct	Jason hopes *to drive* his brother's car occasionally.

Incorrect	Marla plans *to* eventually *finish* reading the novel.
Correct	Marla plans eventually *to finish* reading the novel.

See also pages 614–615.

Italics

See Good Manuscript Form, page 776.

Jargon

Jargon is the special vocabulary of people who belong to the same profession. For example, the medical profession uses words such as *coronary, peritonitis,* and *toxin.* Word processors use words such as *mainframe, access, printouts, hardware,* and *software.* Such words provide a shortcut to meaning for people within the profession, but those outside the profession often find them confusing. Always remember your audience. Do not use a special vocabulary if your audience will not understand it. Study the following example.

Jargon	Consult a lexicon when researching the statements of the meanings, etymologies, and the representations in phonetic symbols of unfamiliar words.
Simplified	Use a dictionary to find the meaning, origin, and pronunciation of unfamiliar words.

Modifiers

Adjective-Adverb Confusion Sometimes you may have trouble deciding whether to use an adjective or an adverb. Use an adjective to modify a noun or pronoun. Adjectives tell *which one, what kind, how many,* or *how much.* Adverbs modify verbs, adjectives, or other adverbs. Adverbs tell *where, when, how,* or *to what extent.*

Incorrect	Walk *careful* on the slippery pavement.
Correct	Walk *carefully* on the slippery pavement.

Good-Well *See* page 571.

Hopefully Writers sometimes use the adverb *hopefully* when they mean to use *I hope.* Study the example below.

Incorrect	*Hopefully,* that will solve my problem.
Correct	*I hope* that will solve my problem.

See also pages 559–560.

Comparative and Superlative Forms Use the **comparative form** to compare two things and the **superlative form** to compare more than two things. Do not use the superlative form to compare two things.

Incorrect	Of the two novels, that one was the *most* interesting.
Correct	Of the two novels, that one was the *more* interesting.

Do not use *-er* and *more* or *-est* and *most* together.

Incorrect	Harold is the *most strongest* linebacker on the team.
Correct	Harold is the *strongest* linebacker on the team.

See also pages 562–563.

Dangling and Misplaced Modifiers When a modifier is placed so that it appears to modify the wrong word, it is called a **misplaced modifier.** To correct this error, move the modifier as close as possible to the word that it modifies.

Misplaced Modifier	Carlos wrote his speech while traveling from New York City to Hartford on the back of an envelope.
Correct	While traveling from New York City to Hartford, Carlos wrote his speech on the back of an envelope.

When a modifier refers to a word that is missing from the sentence, the modifier is said to be a dangling modifier.

Dangling Modifier	Looking upward, clouds began to form overhead. (Were the clouds looking upward?)
Correct	Looking upward, *I* noticed that clouds began to form overhead.

See also pages 620–621.

Exercise

Gerunds, Infinitives, Jargon, Comparisons, Modifiers Identify the error in each of the following sentences. Then rewrite each sentence correctly.

1. Mayor Hernandez promised to quickly settle the city transportation strike.
2. This is the most softest pillow I have ever felt.
3. Of the two astronauts, she is most likely to be selected for the moon mission.

4. Hopefully that bottle of upholstery cleaner will not harm your favorite chair.
5. Driving down the highway, a deer raced across the road and hit Dad's car.
6. He was determined to completely ignore any distraction from the street below.
7. Mrs. Rosenberg didn't approve of us chewing gum in the new auditorium.
8. To maximize disposable income, invest wisely.
9. Filling the glass with juice, one slipped out of my hand and crashed to the floor.
10. Julio and his friends could not understand why their parents would object to them driving low-rider cars.

Parallelism

When *and* is used to join sentence parts of equal value, such as noun and noun, verb and verb, or phrase and phrase, the constructions are said to be parallel. An error in parallel structure occurs when *and* is used to join unequal constructions.

Not Parallel	The new student in French class was noisy, disruptive, and came to class unprepared. (two adjectives and a predicate)
Parallel	The new student in French class was *noisy, disruptive,* and *unprepared.* (three predicate adjectives)
Not Parallel	In photography club, we learned about composition and how to control lighting. (a noun and a phrase)
Parallel	In photography club, we learned about *composition* and *lighting.* (two nouns)

Person, Shifts in

Person refers to the point of view that a writer uses. A writer may use first-, second-, or third-person point of view, but the point of view should always remain consistent. If a writer changes or shifts point of view in the middle of a composition, the reader will be confused.

Shift in Person	To get the most from a lecture, *students* should listen carefully and take notes. *You* should not, however, try to record every word.
Consistent	To get the most from a lecture, *students* should listen carefully and take notes. *They* should not, however, try to record every word.

Pronouns

Agreement A pronoun must agree with its antecedent in number. If the antecedent is singular, the pronoun must be singular. If the antecedent is plural, then the pronoun must be plural.

Incorrect	A *teen-ager* often feels pressure put on *them* by *their* friends.
Correct	*Teen-agers* often feel pressure put on *them* by *their* friends.

Indefinite pronouns sometimes cause problems in agreement. The following indefinite pronouns are always singular: *anyone, anybody, anything, each, either, everybody, everyone, everything, neither, nobody, no one, one, somebody*, and *someone*.

Incorrect	*Everyone* must bring *their* own mitt to the game.
Correct	*Everyone* must bring *his* or *her* own mitt to the game.

Use a singular pronoun when two singular antecedents are joined by *or* and *nor*.

> Either *Ann* or *Jennifer* will bring *her* recorder to class.
> Neither *Bob* nor *Jeff* rode *his* bike to the zoo.

Ambiguous Reference The reference of a pronoun is ambiguous if the pronoun may refer to more than one word.

Ambiguous	After Bob removed the greasy pan from the oven, he cleaned *it*. (cleaned the oven or the pan?)
Clear	Bob cleaned the greasy pan after he removed it from the oven.

Lack of Antecedents Do not use a pronoun without an antecedent. The meaning of the sentence will be unclear.

Unclear	When a child is very sensitive and lacks the maturity to deal with *it*, he or she is easily hurt. (deal with what?)
Clear	When a child is very sensitive and lacks the maturity to deal with a parent's *anger*, he or she is easily hurt. (*it* is identified as a parent's anger)

Nominative and Objective Cases Pronouns change forms, depending on their use in sentences. The **nominative case** is used when pronouns take the place of subjects or follow a form of the verb *be*.

> Charlotte made the suggestion. *She* influenced the whole group. (takes the place of the person's name)
> It was *I* who followed your directions. (follows a form of *be*)

The **objective case** is used when pronouns take the place of objects.

> Susan invited *us* to her graduation ceremony. (direct object)
> The store manager gave *them* a raise. (indirect object)
> Will you read the story to *her?* (object of preposition)

When the objects are compound, be sure to use the objective case for pronouns. To decide which pronoun form to use in a compound object, try each part of the object by itself.

> Ron sent Gabriel and (I, *me*) two tickets for the ballet.
>   (Compound indirect objects; think, Ron sent *me* two tickets)
> Enrico divided the profits between (he, *him*) and (I, *me*).
>   (Compound objects of the preposition; think, divided between *him,* divided between *me*)

See also pages 485–511.

Exercise

Parallelism and Pronoun Problems Identify the error in each of the following sentences. Then rewrite each sentence correctly.

1. Neither the department store nor the jewelry store opened their doors before 10:00 A.M.
2. We went bicycle riding and for a swim in the lake.
3. Everybody who attended the movie received their own poster.
4. Between you and I, I wouldn't do that.
5. She unpacked the radio from the carton and then took it upstairs to her room.
6. When training for a race, an athlete should run every other day to allow your muscles time to rest.
7. In heavy rain, go down into the basement and close it.
8. Either Leticia or Danielle left their books in the library.
9. Was it him who ate the dessert before dinner?
10. Though she was unprepared for it, she answered quickly.

Redundancy

A statement is **redundant** if it contains repetitious words. Remove redundant words to make your writing more concise.

Redundant	*Every day* he practiced his *daily* violin lesson.
Better	*Every day* he practiced his violin lesson.

Redundant	You need to do the assignment *over again*.
Better	You need to do the assignment *over*.

Sentence Errors

Fragments A group of words that does not express a complete thought is a **sentence fragment**. It is missing a subject, a predicate, or both. To correct a sentence fragment, add the missing part or parts.

Fragment   Traveled around the West last July. (missing subject)
Sentence   *Dianna* traveled around the West last July.

Fragment   That raced through the tunnel. (missing both subject and predicate)
Sentence   *The train* that raced through the tunnel suddenly *stopped*.

See also pages 457–458.

Run-on Sentences A **run-on sentence** is two or more sentences written as though they were one sentence. The most common run-on is the joining of two sentences by a comma. This error is called a **comma fault**. To correct, add the proper punctuation.

Comma Fault   The instructor showed us how to use the computer, she then gave us our first assignment.
Correct   The instructor showed us how to use the computer. She then gave us our first assignment.

Other ways to correct run-on sentences are to join them with a comma and a coordinating conjunction or with a semicolon.

The child spilled the blocks all over the floor, then he built a tower with them. (run-on sentence)
The child spilled the blocks all over the floor, *and* then he built a tower with them. (comma and coordinating conjunction)
The child spilled the blocks all over the floor; then he built a tower with them. (semicolon)

See also page 460.

Slang

Colorful words and phrases associated with a particular time or group are called **slang**. Slang is common in everyday speech, but should never be used in formal writing. It may be used with caution in informal writing. The following are examples of slang.

laid back   easygoing
scalp   to sell tickets for more than their face value
take a bath   to lose badly, as in business or gambling

Exercise

Redundancy, Fragments, Run-ons, Slang   Identify the errors in the following sentences. Then rewrite each sentence correctly.

1. Clouds drifted above, they formed interesting patterns against the blue sky.
2. A row of marble statues lining the garden walkway.
3. Took the groceries out of the bag and put them away.
4. The light of early morning dawn offers spectacular possibilities for outdoor photography.
5. Many of Edgar Allen Poe's stories are weird and off the wall.
6. For a brief quick moment, lightning danced in the evening sky.
7. The majestic cathedrals of France and England.
8. The mist rolled in from the sea, it obscured our view of the lighthouse.
9. Authorities agree that the employment prospects for high school dropouts are not so hot.
10. Waiting impatiently for the light to turn green.

Verb Tense

Tense means "time." Most verbs change their forms to show present, past, and future time. Each verb has three **simple tenses** and three **perfect tenses.**

Sometimes a writer confuses the reader by changing the verb tense in the middle of a sentence. Avoid this type of error.

Incorrect	She *watered* the plants, and then she *pulls* weeds.
Correct	She *watered* the plants, and then she *pulled* weeds.

See also pages 534–536.

Voice

Verbs are said to have two voices, active and passive. When the subject performs the action, the verb is in the **active voice.** When the subject receives the action, the verb is in the **passive voice.** Good writers prefer active voice because it is more lively than passive voice.

Passive Voice	Cement was spilled on the ground by the bricklayer.
Active Voice	The bricklayer spilled cement on the ground.
Passive Voice	The papers were stacked by Julio and his friends.
Active Voice	Julio and his friends stacked the papers.

See also pages 523–524.

Who and Whom

Who is the subject form of the pronoun. It is used as the subject of a sentence. *Who* can also act as the subject or the predicate nominative of a clause.

> *Who* was Medusa in Greek mythology? (subject of the verb *was*)
>
> She was the Gorgon *who* tried to turn Perseus to stone. (subject of the verb *tried*)

Whom is the object form of the pronoun. It is used as the direct object or as the object of the preposition in a sentence or clause.

> *Whom* did Toni Morrison choose as the central character of her novel *Beloved?* (direct object of the verb *did choose*)
>
> Give it to the girl with *whom* you are working on your science project. (object of the preposition *with*)

You, Use of

Do not use "you" in your writing unless you mean the reader.

Incorrect   In many high schools, you are not allowed to leave for lunch. (The writer does not mean *you,* personally.)

Correct   In many high schools, students are not allowed to leave for lunch.

Exercise

Verb Tense, Voice, *Who* and *Whom*, Use of *You*. Identify the error in each sentence. Then rewrite the sentence correctly. If there is no error, write *Correct.*

1. Harry entered the art contest at the school of design and waits impatiently for the judges' decision.
2. People who have asthma realize that you should not ignore the signs of trouble.
3. Several alternatives were explored by the group.
4. To who have you written?
5. In San Francisco you are always driving up and down hilly streets.
6. Soccer players need to stay in top physical condition because you cannot stop to rest in a game.
7. Ask the person whom is in charge of the auditions.
8. The car was driven by a boy who had no license.
9. When asked a question, she paused, reflects, and then responds.
10. When you went to South Dakota, who did you stay with?

Word Usage

The words in this section are often used incorrectly. Study them so that you can learn to use the right word at the right time.

accept means ''to agree to something'' or ''to receive something willingly or with approval.''
except means ''to leave out.'' *Except* also means ''not including.''

> ''I *accept* the blame,'' Todd said.
> ''We'll *except* you from this rule,'' the counselor said.
> We bought all the supplies *except* glue.

affect means ''to influence.''
effect means ''the result of an action.''

> The fine reputation of the history teacher *affected* Amanda's decision.
> Lack of rainfall had a devastating *effect* on the crops.

agree on means ''to come to an understanding about.'' You and others *agree on* a plan.
agree to means ''to consent to.'' You *agree to* something, such as a change someone wants to make.
agree with means ''to have the same opinion as another.'' You agree *with* somebody. *Agree with* may also be used colloquially to refer to something being suitable, as when foods don't *agree with* you.

all ready means ''all are ready.''
already means ''by or before the given time'' or ''even now.''

> Tell us when they are *all ready* to leave.
> She had *already* left when we arrived.
> He had *already* been accepted by three colleges by the end of the summer.

all right is the correct spelling. The spelling *alright* is nonstandard English and should not be used.

> *All right*, I'll turn off the TV.
> Ariel felt *all right* after she got off the boat.

a lot means ''a great number or amount.'' It is used only in informal writing or speaking. The spelling *alot* is incorrect and should not be used.

> I have *a lot* of clothes that no longer fit me.
> We picked *a lot* of apples in the orchard today.

among, between See "Using Prepositions, Conjunctions, and Interjections," page 586.

anywhere, nowhere, somewhere, and **anyway** are standard usage. *Anywheres, nowheres, somewheres,* and *anyways* are nonstandard.

Incorrect	She wasn't *anywheres* in sight.
Correct	She wasn't *anywhere* in sight.

Incorrect	I know that clip is here *somewheres*.
Correct	I know that clip is here *somewhere*.

beside, besides See "Using Prepositions, Conjunctions, and Interjections," page 586.

between each, followed by a singular noun, is incorrect. *Between* should not be used with a singular noun.

Incorrect	*Between each game* the Bears practice hard.
Correct	*Between games* the Bears practice hard.

Incorrect	The elevator stopped *between every floor*.
Correct	The elevator stopped *between floors*.

borrow means "to receive something on loan." Don't confuse it with *lend,* meaning "to give out temporarily."

Incorrect	Will you *borrow* me your pen?
Correct	Will you *lend* me your pen?
Correct	May I *borrow* your pen?

bring, take See "Using Verbs," pages 540–541.

Exercise

On your paper, write the correct answers.

1. The President (accepted, excepted) the resignation of his aide.
2. Raoul couldn't find his calculator (anywhere, anywheres).
3. I earned (alot, a lot) of money from my summer job.
4. Every block (except, accept) ours has sidewalks.
5. Will you (lend, borrow) me your bicycle?
6. Mr. Scott (agreed on, agreed to) our plan to leave early.
7. The entire city was (affected, effected) by the power failure.
8. Michelle (already, all ready) finished wallpapering the room.
9. (Anyway, Anyways), I'm heading for home.
10. (Between, Among) classes we had a five-minute break.

capital means "most important." It is used to refer to an upper-case letter. It also names the city or town that is the official center of government for a state or country.

capitol refers to the building where a state legislature meets.

The **Capitol** is the building in Washington, D.C., where the United States Congress meets. Notice that the *c* is capitalized.

> The *capital* of New York is Albany.
> The state *capitol* dome can be seen for miles.
> Farmers protested outside the *Capitol* in Washington.

des'ert means "a dry, barren region."
de sert' means "to abandon."
des sert' is a sweet food at the end of a meal.

> The explorers were stranded in the *desert*.
> A true friend will never *desert* you.
> Our *dessert* tonight is kiwi fruit.

different from is used to compare things that are unlike. *Different than* is nonstandard.

Incorrect   My outline was *different than* yours.
Correct   My outline was *different from* yours.

farther means "more distant."
further means "additional."

> Denver is *farther* from Los Angeles than San Jose is.
> This matter requires *further* attention.

fewer refers to numbers of things that can be counted.
less refers to amount or quantity.

> Did Nicklaus win *fewer* tournaments than Snead?
> We hear *less* noise in the country.

from, off See "Using Prepositions, Conjunctions, and Interjections," page 587.

hear means "to listen to" or "to receive sound by the ear."
here refers to *this place*.

> Did you *hear* the screeching brakes?
> A new record store will open *here*.

in, into See "Using Prepositions, Conjunctions, and Interjections," page 587.

its, it's See "Using Pronouns," page 508.

kind of a and **sort of a** are nonstandard. The *a* following the preposition *of* is not necessary.

Incorrect	What *kind of a* radio do you have?
Correct	What *kind of* radio do you have?

Incorrect	There is some *sort of a* problem here.
Correct	There is some *sort of* problem here.

lay, lie See "Using Verbs," page 542.

learn, teach See "Using Verbs," page 541.

leave, let See "Using Verbs," page 541.

like can be a preposition. Using *like* as a conjunction before a clause is unacceptable in formal English. It is better to use *as* or *as if*.

Incorrect	*Like* I said, you can depend on Sara.
Correct	*As* I said, you can depend on Sara.

Incorrect	Ramon talked *like* he had a cold.
Correct	Ramon talked *as if* he had a cold.

loose means either "not tight" or "free and untied."
lose means "to be unable to find or keep." It is also the opposite of *win*.

> My shoelaces are always too *loose*.
> Several snakes from the zoo are *loose*.
> *I lose* my balance when I spin on skates.
> Did the wrestlers *lose* the meet?

may be means "to be possible or likely to."
maybe means "perhaps." It is used only in informal writing and speaking.

> You *may be* the winner of the contest.
> *Maybe* it will snow today.

Exercise

On your paper, write the correct answers.

1. We ate (desert, dessert) out on the porch.
2. Jim looks (like, as if) he needs more time.
3. Kate has (fewer, less) lines to memorize in this play.
4. What (kind of a, kind of) penalty did the referee call?

5. From the top of the Washington Monument, we looked down at the skyline of the nation's (capital, capitol, Capitol).
6. Ballet slippers should be tight, not (loose, lose).
7. Michael and I could (hear, here) the fire engine's siren four blocks away.
8. Sand dunes in the (desert, dessert) are always shifting because of the wind.
9. (May be, Maybe) she will be a pediatrician when she completes medical school.
10. After we move, I will live (farther, further) from school than my friend Terry does.

of is sometimes incorrectly used in phrases like *could of, shouldn't of,* and *must of.* The correct wording is *could have* or *should have.*

Incorrect	Darryl *should of* locked his bike.
Correct	Darryl *should have* locked his bike.

on, onto See "Using Prepositions, Conjunctions, and Interjections," page 587.

passed means "went forward, through, or out."
past means "of a former time" or "gone by."

> She *passed* through Austria on her way to Italy.
> The book has pictures of fashions from *past* centuries.

principal means "leading," "chief," or "highest in importance."
principle refers to a basic truth, rule, or law.

> The *principal* industry here is steel-making.
> The *principle* of freedom is essential to a democratic society.

raise, rise See "Using Verbs," page 542.

real means "actual; true."
really means "in reality; in fact."

> Marcia never explained her *real* reasons.
> Does she *really* have her own car?

set, sit See "Using Verbs," page 543.

stationary means "not moving; fixed."
stationery refers to writing paper and envelopes.

> The trailer can move, but right now it's *stationary.*
> The drugstore sells boxes of *stationery.*

than is a word used to introduce the second part of a comparison.
then means "next in order."

> Miguel is taller *than* Henry.
> Wash the car and *then* wax it.

their, there, they're See "Using Pronouns," page 508.

to means "toward" or "as far as."
too means "also" or "extremely."

> Tracy slid *to* home plate.
> I read the book and saw the movie *too*.
> Your speech was *too* long.

way refers to distance; **ways** is nonstandard.

Incorrect	We drove a short *ways* down the road.
Correct	We drove a short *way* down the road.

weather refers to the condition of the atmosphere, such as its heat or cold, wetness or dryness.
whether indicates a choice between two things.

> The *weather* in Hawaii is usually pleasant.
> Ask Stacy *whether* she is going or staying.

who's, whose See "Using Pronouns," page 508.
your, you're See "Using Pronouns," page 508.

Exercise

On your paper, write the correct answers.

1. The (principals, principles) stated in the Hippocratic Oath are still important to doctors.
2. The bowling ball veered (to, too) far to the left.
3. I wonder (weather, whether) I should call or write her.
4. Elliot (passed, past) his driving test and got his license.
5. Smoking is one of the (principal, principle) causes of lung cancer.
6. The council must (have, of) held an emergency meeting.
7. Denver is a long (way, ways) from Baltimore.
8. The photography class presented a (real, really) fine exhibit on the use of color.
9. Jennifer's sister plans to open her own (stationary, stationery) store next year.
10. Those boxes are much heavier (than, then) these.

Index

descriptive writing, 168–72
in essay tests, 397
expository writing, 216–20, 223, 228, 234, 235
literature, 276–95
narrative writing, 192–95
paragraphs, 100–102
persuasive writing, 252–57, 260
in prewriting, 69
in reports, 304
and, 590
in sentence combining, 142–44
Anecdotes
for introductions, 125
in persuasive writing, 259
Announcements, making, 422
Antecedents, 485, 782, 783
for indefinite pronouns, 496
Antonym questions, 399
any, verb agreement with, 637
anyway, 789
anywhere, 789
Apostrophes, 721–23
in contractions, 722
in plurals of letters or numbers, 722
in possessives, 477, 721
Applications, filling out, 414
Appositives, 608, 622–23
adding, to sentences, 147
appositive phrases, 622–23
commas with, 703–704
defined, 622
diagraming, 763
essential, 622
nonessential, 622
Argument, in literary analysis, 288
Art
capitalization of titles, 689
underlining or italics for titles, 729
Articles, 551–52
as, as if, 791
Associating, 33–37, 41
at, used incorrectly, 587
Atlases, 308, 376
Audience
and expository writing, 223
identifying, 67
and level of language, 353
for narrative writing, 198
and persuasive writing, 260, 261
for reports, 303, 306
Audio-visual reference materials, 378
Author cards, 372–73, 374
Authoritative opinions, in persuasive

writing, 259
Autobiography, in libraries, 371
Auxiliary verbs, 438. *See also* Helping verbs
Awards, capitalization of names of, 684
Awareness, improving, 6–9

B

B.C., 684, 746
Back matter, in dictionaries, 367
Bandwagon appeal, 264
Base words, 336
because
sentences combined with, 152
beside, besides, 586–87
between, among, 586
between each, 789
Bibliographies
checking, for reports, 321
working, 309
Bibliography cards, guidelines for, 309
Biographical references, 308, 375
Biography
classification of, in libraries, 371
as narrative writing, 208–209
Blends, 350, 351
Block form, for business letters, 405
Bodies of water, capitalization of, 680
Body
of business letters, 405, 407
of literary analysis, 285–86
in persuasive writing, 266
of reports, 316
Books
bibliography cards for, 309
capitalization of titles of, 689
classification of, 370–72
underlining or italics for, 729
borrow, 789
Borrowed words, 349
both . . . and, 590
Brainstorming, 35–37, 62, 228, 243, 258
Brand names, capitalization of, 684
Bridge building, 74
Bridges, capitalization of, 684
bring, take, 540
Buildings, capitalization of, 684
Business letters, 404–13
appreciation letters, 412–13
complaint letters, 412–13
envelopes for, 409
forms for, 405–406
order letters, 411
parts of, 405, 406–408
request letters, 410

but, 590
   in sentence combining, 142–43

C

Cajun, 453
Call numbers, 372
capital, capitol, 790
Capitalization, 676–95
   first words, 688–89
   geographical names, 680–82
   I, 689
   in letters, 688
   organizations, events, and other subjects, 683–86
   in outlines, 689
   proper nouns and adjectives, 677–79
   in quotations, 688
   in titles, 689
Card catalogs, 372–74
Case
   nominative, 489, 783
   objective, 489, 490, 783
   possessive, 489, 490–91
   see also Direct objects; Indirect objects; Object of the preposition
Catalogs, 369
Causal ordering, 46
Cause-to-effect pattern, 230
Cause and effect
   charts of, 773
   in compositions, 130
   as context clue, 331–32
   in expository writing, 227–33
   ideas for, 768
   in paragraphs, 112
   in reports, 304
   see also Causal ordering
Cause-and-effect fallacy, 264
Chairperson, 417, 418
Chapters
   capitalization of titles of, 689
   punctuation of titles of, 729
Character, 193, 283
Charting, 38–39, 62, 289
Charts, 62, 772
Checklists
   for revising a cause-and-effect composition, 232
   for revising comparison and contrast compositions, 239
   for revising compositions, 137
   for revising descriptive writing, 183
   for revising narrative writing, 202
   for revising persuasive writing, 268

   for revising a process composition, 226
Cherokee language, 346
Chinese language, 598
Chronological order, 45, 71–72
   in a cause-and-effect essay, 230
   in compositions, 129
   in paragraphs, 109
Circular reasoning, 264
Classifying, 43–44
Classroom tests, 393
Clauses, 592, 646–60, 667–70
   adjective, 651–54, 668
   adverb, 654–58, 668
   in complex sentences, 663
   in compound-complex sentences, 664
   in compound sentences, 662
   defined, 592, 647
   dependent. *See* Subordinate clauses
   elliptical, 655
   essential, 652, 708, 778
   as fragments, 667
   independent, 647
   misplaced, avoiding, 668
   nonessential, 652, 708, 778
   nonrestrictive. *See* Nonessential clauses
   noun, 658–60
   reduced to phrases, 161
   relative, 651
   restrictive. *See* Essential clauses
   in simple sentences, 661
   subordinate, 647–48
   vs. phrases, 648
   with *who* and *whom*, 669
   see also Sentence structure
Clichés, 777
Climax, 283
Clipped words, 350, 351
Closing, for business letters, 405, 408
Clustering, 34–35, 37, 199, 774
Coherence
   in compositions, 129
   in descriptive writing, 179
   in paragraphs, 115–17
Collective biography, 371
Collective nouns, 470
   subject-verb agreement and, 639
Colloquial English, 352–54
Colons, 714–16
   in business letters, 715
   to introduce a list, 714
   in notations of time, 715
   between sentences, 715
Combining sentences. *See* Sentences, combining

indirect objects, 444, 445
interrogative, 433, 440–41
inverted, and agreement, 639
objects in, 443–46
overloaded, 157–59
padded, 160–62
predicates, 435–39
predicates, simple, 437–39
run-on, 460–61, 786
subject complements, 447–49
subjects, 435–39
subjects, in unusual positions, 440–43
subjects, simple, 437–39
verb phrase in, 438
writing complete, 456–67
see also Punctuation; Sentence structure
Sentence structure, 646, 661–66
complex sentences, 663
compound-complex sentences, 664
compound sentences, 662
simple sentences, 661
Series
commas in, 700
semicolons in, 714
set, sit, 543
Setting, 193, 283
Sharing. *See* Presenting
Ships, capitalization of, 684
Short-answer questions, 397
Short stories
capitalization of titles of, 689
punctuation of titles of, 729
Sight, using sense of in writing, 10–12
Sight words, 12
Signature, for letters, 405, 408
Silent *e,* spelling rules and, 738
Similarities and differences, 44, 234
see also Comparison and contrast
Similes, 181
Simple sentences, 661
Simple tenses, 535, 536, 786
Single quotation marks, 724
sit, set, 543
Skimming, 381
Slang, 354, 785
Slow drafts, 75
Smell, using sense of in writing, 17–18
Smell words, 18
Snob appeal, 264
Songs
capitalization of titles of, 689
punctuation of titles of, 729
sort of a, kind of a, 792
Spacecraft, capitalization of, 684

Spatial order, 72
in descriptive writing, 175–76
in paragraphs, 110
Speaking, informal, 422–24
guidelines for, 424
Specialized dictionaries, 363
Spelling, 736, 737–44
commonly misspelled words, 744
doubling the final consonant, 740
improving, 737
and plurals of nouns, 742
and prefixes, 738
and suffixes, 738–39, 740
words with *ie* and *ei,* 741
words with the ''seed'' sound, 741
Split infinitive, 615, 779
SQ3R study method, 383
Stacks, in libraries, 369
Standard English, 352–54
Standardized tests, 393, 398–401
Starting from Literature, 8–9
State-of-being verbs. *See* Linking verbs
States, abbreviations for, 747
stationary, stationery, 792
Statistical tables, 388–89
Statistics, as supporting details, 106
Study skills, 380–91
adjusting reading speed, 381–82
graphic aids, 388–90
memorizing, 387
note-taking, 384–86
SQ3R method, 383
see also Reading skills
Style, in writing sentences, 140–65
Subject-by-subject comparison, 236
Subject cards, 373, 374
Subject complements, 447–49
Subjects, 435–39
agreement with verb, 630–45
complete, 435–36
compound, 449, 661
compound, and subject-verb agreement, 634
diagraming, 754
in imperative sentences, 441
noun clauses as, 658
nouns as, 472
simple, 437–39
in unusual positions, 440–43
you, understood, 441
see also Agreement, subject-verb
Subordinate clauses, 152–53, 647–48
in complex sentences, 663
in compound-complex sentences, 664

Time
  capitalization of abbreviations for, 684
  capitalization of periods of, 683
  colons in notations of, 715
Time lines, 62
  for chronological order, 71
Time words, subject-verb agreement and,
    640
Title cards, 373, 374
Titles (of papers), 776
Titles (personal), capitalization of, 677, 678
Titles (of works)
  capitalization of words in, 689
  italics for, 729, 776
  punctuation of, 729
  subject-verb agreement and, 640
to, as sign of the infinitive, 614
to, too, 793
Topic outlines, 770
Topics
  choosing for expository writing, 223
  choosing for narrative writing, 198
  choosing for reports, 302–303
  finding, 63–65
  ideas for writing, 768–69
  limiting, for reports, 304
  for persuasive writing, 261
  selecting, for persuasive writing, 258
  see also Ideas, exploring; Ideas, generat-
    ing
Topic sentences, 107–108
  position of, 108
  and unity in paragraphs, 113–14
Touch, using sense of in writing, 15–16
Touch words, 16
Trains, capitalization of, 684
Transitional devices, 486
Transitions
  and coherence in paragraphs, 116, 117
  in comparison and contrast compositions,
    237
  in compositions, 131
  in expository writing, 225, 231
  in narrative writing, 204
Transitive verbs, 445, 521
Tree diagram. *See* Idea trees
Trigger words, 769
True-false questions, 394, 395

U

Unabridged dictionaries, 362
Underlining, for titles, 729, 776
Unity
  in compositions, 129

in descriptive writing, 179
in paragraphs, 113–15
Usage questions, on standardized tests, 400

V

Variables, in tables, 389, 772
Verbal phrases, commas after, 702
Verbals, 608–21
  dangling modifiers, 620–21
  distinguishing between, 612–13
  gerunds, 609–10
  infinitives, 609, 614–15
  misplaced modifiers, 620–21
  participles, 609, 611–13
Verb phrases, 438, 519
  placement of, 440–41
Verbs, 516–49
  action, 443–44, 517
  active voice, 523–24, 787
  agreement with subject, 630–45
  auxiliary, 438
  compound, 661
  conjugation of, 536
  defined, 517
  diagraming, 754
  helping, 438, 519
  intransitive, 521
  irregular, 526, 528–32
  linking, 443–44, 517
  main, 438
  passive voice, 523–24, 787
  perfect tenses, 535, 536
  principal parts of irregular, 528–32
  principal parts of regular, 526
  progressive forms, 538
  regular, 526
  simple tenses, 535, 536
  tenses, 534–36
  tenses, avoiding shifts in, 538–39
  transitive, 521
  see also Agreement, subject-verb
Verb suffixes, 341
Vertical files, 308, 376
Vocabulary. *See* Language, learning about;
    Language Lore; Vocabulary, building
Vocabulary, building, 329–35
  analyzing word parts, 336–41
  exercises in, 342–45
  inferring word meaning from context,
    329–35
Vocabulary questions, on standardized tests,
    398–400
Voice, 523–24, 786

W

way, ways, 793
we, us, 509
weather, whether, 794
well, good, 571
what, 498
"What If?" questions, 34
whether . . . or, 590
who, 498, 500, 669
who, whom, 508–509, 787
who's, whose, 508
whom, 498, 500
    using properly, 669
whose, 498, 500
Word order, in sentences, 440–41
Word parts
    defined, 336
    and determining word meaning, 336–41
Word processing, 94–97
Words
    denotation and connotation, 358
    hearing, 14
    hyphens between syllables of, 719
    sight, 12
    smell, 18
    taste, 17
    touch, 16
    used as words, 722
    see also Language, learning about; Language Lore; Vocabulary, building
Words of amount, subject–verb agreement and, 640
Working bibliography, 309
Writer's Handbook, 768–93

Writing
    description in, 166–89
    ideas for, 768–69
    purposes for, 66
    using the senses in, 4–23
    see also Compositions; Creative writing; Descriptive writing; Expository writing; Literature, writing about; Narrative writing; Persuasive writing; Reports; Writer's Handbook; Writing process
Writing Inside Out, 64–65, 126–27, 180–81, 206–207, 262–63
Writing process, 58–77, 78–93
    defined, 60
    drafting, 60, 74–75
    flexibility of, 62–63
    peer editing, 87–90
    presenting, 60, 91
    prewriting, 60, 61–73
    revising, 60, 80–83
    self-editing, 84–86
    see also Drafting; Guidelines; Presenting; Prewriting; Proofreading; Revising; Thinking skills; Word processing

Y

Yearbooks, 308, 375
yet, 590
you
    understood as subject, 441
    use of, 787
your, you're, 508

Z

ZIP codes, 409

Editorial Credits

Executive Editor, Language Arts: Bonnie L. Dobkin
Senior Editor: Julie A. Schumacher
Editors: Diane E. Carlson, Marcia Crawford Mann
Associate Editor: Richard Elliott
Assistant Editor: Peter P. Kaye
Project Assistance: Ligature, Inc.

Sources of Quoted Materials *(continued)*

Death to Morning by Thomas Wolfe; copyright 1932, 1933, 1934, 1935 by Charles Scribner's Sons. **15:** Don Congdon Associates, Inc.: For an excerpt from *A Sound of Thunder* by Ray Bradbury; copyright 1952 by Crowell Collier Publishing Co., renewed 1980 by Ray Bradbury. **56:** Atheneum Publishers, a Division of Macmillan, Inc.: For excerpts from Jan. 11, Feb. 9, & Feb. 10 in *Be True to Your School: A Diary of 1964;* copyright © 1987 John Deadline Enterprises, Inc. **132:** Henry Holt & Company: For an excerpt from *There's Nothing That I Wouldn't Do if You Would Be My Posslq* by Charles Osgood; copyright © 1981 by CBS, Inc. **140:** Macmillan Publishing Company: Chapter 7 and 14 contain, in revised form, some materials that appeared originally in *English Arts and Skills*, Grade 9, by Ronald J. Wilkins et al., copyright © 1965, 1961 by The Macmillan Company. Used by arrangement. **166:** Robert Bly: For an excerpt from "Driving Toward the Lac Qui Parle River" by Robert Bly. **170:** Atheneum Publishers, an Imprint of Macmillan Publishing Co.: For excerpts from *Dragondrums* by Anne McCaffrey; copyright © 1979 Anne McCaffrey. **186:** Houghton Mifflin Company: For an excerpt from "The Porcupine" in *Body Rags* by Galway Kinnell; copyright © 1967 by Galway Kinnell. **194:** Grove Press, Inc.: For "Silent Song," from *A Pinecone, A Toy Sheep* by Pablo Neruda; published in *Evergreen Review*, Jan./ Feb. 1962. **218:** The New York Times: For "Slice of Life" by Russell Baker, 11/24/74; © 1974 by The New York Times Company, reprinted by permission. **253:** *Sierra* Magazine: For an excerpt from "Two-Wheeling in the Urban Jungle" by Reed McManus, which appeared in the November-December 1987 issue of *Sierra* Magazine. **254:** Houghton Mifflin Company: For "Fable for Tomorrow" and pages 5–6 from *Silent Spring* by Rachel Carson; copyright © 1962 by Rachel L. Carson. **272:** Triangle Communications, Inc.: For an excerpt from "Word Up," which appeared in the November 1987 issue of *Seventeen* Magazine. **278:** The Organization of American States, *Americas* Magazine: for "Lather and Nothing Else" by Hernando Téllez, originally appeared in *Americas*, bimonthly magazine published by the General Secretariat of the Organization of American States in English and Spanish. **357:** Simon & Schuster, Inc.: For an entry "court," from *Webster's New World Dictionary*—student edition; copyright © 1976, 1981 by Simon & Schuster, Inc. **359:** The Putnam Publishing Group: For an excerpt from *New Rogets Thesaurus in Dictionary Form;* copyright © 1978 by G. P. Putnam's Sons. **365:** Simon & Schuster, Inc.: For page 689 from *Webster's New World Dictionary*—student edition; copyright © 1976, 1981 by Simon & Schuster, Inc. **377:** H. W. Wilson Company: For entries from *Readers' Guide to Periodical Literature,* page 64, November 1986 issue; copyright © 1986 by The H. W. Wilson Company. **382:** World Book, Inc.: For the entry on "Mammal" (Volume 13, page 92e) from *The World Book Encyclopedia;* copyright © 1987 World Book, Inc. **388:** Nielsen Media Research: For "Average Television Viewing Time" chart. **391:** World Book Inc.: For the entry on "Mars" (Volume 13, page 180) from *The World Book Encyclopedia;* copyright © 1987 World Book Inc. **399:** College Board ATP, Princeton, N.J.: For two excerpts from *Taking the SAT 1987–88.* **474:** Simon & Schuster, Inc: For excerpts from "The Wars of the Words," from *Have A Word On Me* by Willard R. Espy; copyright © 1981 by Willard R. Espy. **499:** Viking Penguin, Inc.: For excerpts from "Who's on First," from *The Big Broadcast* by Frank Buxton and Bill Owen. **514:** Watkins/Loomis Agency, Inc. for Kay Boyle: For an excerpt from "Winter Night" by Kay Boyle, as appeared in *The New Yorker,* Jan. 19, 1946. **516:** Wesleyan University Press: For "The Base Stealer," from *The Orb Weaver* by Robert Francis; copyright 1948 by Robert Francis. **527:** Harper & Row, Publisher, Inc.: For "Word Torture," from *The Benchley Roundup* by Nathaniel Benchley; copyright 1938 by Robert C. Benchley. **564:** Miami Herald: For excerpts from Dave Barry's "Notes on Western Civilization" 2/14/88 and 11/17/85 columns. **616:** The Putnam Publishing Group: For excerpts from "The Word Wizard," from *The New! Improved! Bob and Ray Book* by Bob Eliott and Ray Goulding; copyright © 1985 by Goulding-Elliott-Greybar Productions, Inc. **626:** Houghton Mifflin Company: For pp. 259–260 "Roaring, he swept . . . their town ablaze," from *The Hobbitt* by J. R. R. Tolkien; copyright © 1966 by J. R. R. Tolkien. **709:** McGraw-Hill Book Company: For excerpts from "The New Punctuation," from *How to Raise Your I.Q. by Eating Gifted Children* by Lewis Burke Frumkes; copyright © 1979, 1980, 1982, and 1983 by Lewis Burke Frumkes. The authors and editors have made every effort to trace the ownership of all copyrighted selections found in this book and to make full acknowledgment for their use.

Photographs:

Assignment photography: Ralph Brunke *r* **21,** *l* **21, 45, 48, 55, 59, 91, 94, 95, 108, 109,** *t* **119,** *l* **135,** *b* **139, 190, 200,** *l* **201,** *in* **197,** *all* **368, 385, 409, 415, 420, 421, 432, 459,** *l* **516, 522, 527, 531, 539, 571, 578,** *r* **613, 616, 633, 657,** *r* **666, 676,** *r* **691, 700, 705;** Gregg Eisman *r* **630,** *l* **631;** Eric Futran *t* **201, 251,** *b* **281, 362, 380, 399;** Greg Gillis **402;** Richard Hellyer **5, 140, 219, 392; 4:** Collection of the Modern Art Museum of Fort Worth; Gift of the William E. Scott Foundation; **9:** Fred Leavitt, Click/Chicago; **11:** David Heald, Solomon R. Guggenheim Museum; **15:** Collection, Walker Art Center; Minneapolis, Art Center Acquisition Fund, 1966; **19:** M. Thonig, H. Armstrong Roberts; **23:** *c* Bill Tucker; *l* Balthazar Kurab, Uniphoto; **25:** Albright-Knox Art Gallery, Buffalo, New York; **29:** Marcia Keegan; **32:** Katsuhiro Mizuno, Image Bank; **39:** G & J Images, Image Bank; **50:** Georg Gerster, Photo Researchers; **53:** *b* Hokin/Kaufman Gallery, Timothy Curtis; *t* Cary Bernstein, Eastman Kodak Company; *l* Ernst Haas Studio; **56:** Steve Arazmus; **58:** James Tallon, Outdoor Exposures; **64:** Todd Kendall; **68:** Lou Jones; **71:** *all* E. Gebhardt, FPG; **77:** *t* Rick Doyle, Photophile; *b* Ed Malles, Photo Options; **79:** Jay Laurie, FPG; **85:** Culver Pictures; **89:** Bill Ross, West Light; **96:** David Jacobson; **97:** Courtesy Dover Publications; "How to Marbleize Paper," Gabrielle Grunebaum, Dover Publications, Inc. NY, 1984. Used by permission of publisher; **98:** Lou Jones; **99:** Martha Swope; **102:** Larry Kolvoord; **105:** Tom Nelson, Frozen Images; **112:** The Studio Museum in Harlem, NYC, Collection Stephanie E. Pogue, Hyattsville, M.D. Photographed by Chris Eden; **119:** *b* Steve Krongard, Image Bank; *cb* John Welzenbach, Joni Tuke; *ct* John Welzenbach, Joni Tuke; **120:** Cavan Butler, Tradhart Ltd.; **121:** ESM/Art Resource; **124:** *b* Camerique, H. Armstrong Roberts; *c* C. D. Geissler, Image Bank; *t* Hubert Schriebel, Burton Snowboards; **130:** *r* Thomas Kitchin, Tom Stack and Assoc.; *l* Jerry Ferrara, Photo Researchers; **135:** *r* David

Madison; **139:** *t* The Cleveland Museum of Art, Purchased with a grant from the National Endowment for the Arts and matched by gifts from members of the Cleveland Society for Contemporary Art; *c* Art Wolfe; **141:** Eric Hausman; **146:** Francois Robert; **151:** *all* Lucas Film LTD.; **154:** Ronald Seymour; **159:** *r* Click/Chicago; Robert Frerck; *l* Lee Boltin; **162:** Peter B. Kaplan Photography; **163:** Historical Pictures Service, Chicago; **166:** Tom Nelson, Frozen Images; **167:** Craig Aurness, West Light; **173:** James Meiuto, FPG; **177:** Melissa Grimes, Courtesy TGI Fridays; **180:** Ruben Guzman; **182:** Allen Philiba; **189:** *t* Walter Wick; *b* Malcolm Kirk, Peter Arnold; **190:** *r* Galen Rowell, Mountain Light Photography; **191:** Galen Rowell, Mountain Light Photography; **195:** Four by Five; **198:** Joe Barrera, Jr., San Antonio Express and News; **206:** Todd Kendall; **211:** Frances Cox, Stock, Boston; **213:** *l* Joe Abell, San Angelo Standard Times; *r* Terry Vitacco; **214:** Joseph Jacobson, Journalism Services; **215:** R. Hamilton Smith, Frozen Images; **222:** The Geffen Film Company; **229:** *c.* Arthur Gloor, Animals, Animals; *l* and *r* Breck Kent; **233:** *l* E. Gebhardt, FPG; *r* Charles Gupton, Stock, Boston; **238:** Francois Robert; **242:** Tom Bean; **245:** *b* Amon Carter Museum, Fort Worth; *t* R. J. Muna; **248:** *t* Art Brown Collection, Hillstrom Stock Photography; **250:** Courtesy Laurie ShoulterKarall; **251:** Eric Futran; **255:** Oil on canvas. 34 x 44 inches. Collection of Whitney Museum of American Art. Gift of Gertrude Vanderbilt Whitney; **260:** Frank Jensen, Royce Bair & Associates; **262:** Tribune Media Services; **264:** Grant Heilman; **265:** John Colwell, Grant Heilman; **269:** Jeffrey Rotman; **275:** *l* Selective Service System; Gary Milburn, *c* Tom Stack and Assoc.; *r* 1986 © Chicago Tribune Company. All rights reserved. Used with permission; **276:** Bradley Smith; **277:** Bradley Smith; **284:** *all* Nancy Holt, U.S. General Services Administration Art-in-Architecture Program; **290:** Victor Englebert, Photo Researchers; **298:** United Feature Syndicate Inc.; **300:** G & J Images, Image Bank; **301:** Georg Gerster, Photo Researchers; **305:** *all* NASA; **311:** 1987 ©, Reebok International; **314:** *c.* David Cavagnaro; *l* David Cavagnaro; *r* Shorty Wilcox, DPI; **319:** Mike Mitchell, After Image; **322:** Gay Bumgarner, Click/Chicago; **325:** *l* Barry Winiker; *r* Dennis Hamilton, Jr., Florida Times Union; **328:** Philadelphia Museum of Art: A. E. Gallatin Collection.; **332:** 1987 United Feature Syndicate, Inc.; **335:** *r* Jeff Miller, West Stock; *l* Chuck O'Rear, Click/Chicago; **343:** Craig Wayne Matthews, New Jersey State Teen Arts Program; **346:** *l* Benn Mitchell, Image Bank; *r* Hermann Zapf, Courtesy Society of Typographic Artists; **348:** *l* Melchor Di Giacomo, Image Bank; *r* Francois Robert; **352:** Art Wolfe; **355:** The Bettmann Archive; **358:** Siede Preis Photography; **360:** Pete Saloutos, Stock Market; **364:** By Permission of Johnny Hart and North America Syndicate, Inc.; **366:** Kenneth Rapalse, Root Resources; **378:** Movie Still Archives; **382:** Superstock/Three Lions; **396:** 1985 Universal Press Syndicate; **413:** Dan McCoy, Rainbow; **416:** Rene Sheret, Journalism Services; **423:** Paul Robert Perry, Uniphoto; **430:** David Holman, West Stock; **432:** Gregg Eisman; **436:** Berlitz, Click/Chicago; **441:** Universal Press Syndicate © 1985; **444:** Debbie Dlott; **449:** Aaron Rapoport, Wheeler Pictures; **452:** *l* Raymond Mendez, Animals, Animals; *r* Steve Arazmus; **453:** *l* Bob Daemmrich Photos; **456:** Bob Daemmrich, Stock, Boston; **459:** Bob Daemmrich, Stock, Boston; **460:** *r* Geoff Manasse, Aperture; **461:** Dennis Chobot; **462:** Grant Faint, Image Bank; **464:** Larry Kolvoord; **468:** *l* Norma Morrison; *r* Geoff Manasse, Aperture; **472:** Tom Algire, Tom Stack and Assoc.; **478:** Siede Preis Photography; **480:** Courtesy of McDougal, Littel & Company; **481:** Terry Vitacco; **484:** G. Heisler, Image Bank; **488:** W.P. Wilstach Collection, Philadelphia Museum of Art and gift of Mrs. William Coxe Wright; **492:** *l* The Bettmann Archive; *r* Todd Kendall; **495:** Ed Nofziger/Saturday Evening Post, 1940; **499:** The Bettmann Archive; **501:** Glenn Knudsen, Click/Chicago; **505:** Curt Marcus Gallery; **510:** D. R. Frazier Photo; **512:** *l* Jim Shea, Paper Moon Graphics; *r* Four by Five; **516:** *r* Diane Johnson, Focus West; **522:** *l* The Bettmann Archive; **524:** Adriano Heitmann, Archive Pictures; **530:** Brunswick Co.; **533:** Leslie Jones, Boston Society; **537:** Art Resource; **539:** *l* Superstock; **542:** © Curtis Publishing. Reprinted with permission from the Saturday Evening Post; **545:** Peter Langone, Uniphoto; **550:** Carl Fischer; **555:** *c* Brian Vikander, West Light; *r* Owen Franken, Stock, Boston; *l* Owen Franken, Stock, Boston; **558:** Collection IBM Corporation, Armonk, New York; **562:** Historical Pictures Service, Chicago; **564:** Tribune Media Services; **567:** *all* The Bettmann Archive; **574:** © Mark Segal, Panoramic Stock Images; **575:** Trustees of The British Museum; **578:** *r* Paul Myatt, Courtesy Washington Metropolitan Area Transit Authority; *l* David Doody, Tom Stack and Assoc.; **582:** David Peters, Paper Moon Graphics; **587:** © Universal Press Syndicate; **592:** *l* John Cavanagh, Archive Pictures; *r* Mark Godfrey, Archive Pictures; **597:** Focus West; **598:** Paul Harper, West Stock; **600:** *c* Donald Specker, Animals, Animals; *r* Chun Y. Lai, Esto Photographics; *l* V. Compagnone, Focus West; **604:** Collection, Walker Art Center; Minneapolis, Art Center Acquisition Fund, 1980; **608:** Pat Rogers, Sportschrome; **613:** California Institute of Technology; **617:** *l* James Sugar, Black Star; *r* J.P. Laffont, Sygma; **620:** *l* Mark Miller, Southern Light; **625:** *l* Diana Rasche; *r* Francois Robert; **638:** Geoffrey Gove, Image Bank; **643:** Historical Pictures Service, Chicago; **646:** Fredrica Fields; **650:** Gilles Peress, Magnum Photos; **656:** Prendergast. American. Watercolor. 20½ x 13⅝ in. Charles Henry Hayden Fund. Museum of Fine Arts, Boston; **661:** Gene Stiver, The Gas Company; **663:** Art Wolfe; **666:** *l* Michael Freeman; **671:** G. Rossi, Image Bank; **676:** *l* George Schwartz, FPG; *r* Jon Feingersh, Tom Stack and Assoc.; **679:** Courtesy The Fontayne Group, © U.S. Press; **682:** *r* D. Hallinan, FPG; *l* Ken Stepnell, Bruce Coleman; **691:** *l* The Bettmann Archive; **693:** *r* James Rowan, Click/Chicago; *l* Raymond Barnes, Click/Chicago; **696:** Charles Gupton, Southern Light; **698:** Reprinted by permission: Tribune Media Services; **705:** Charles Gupton, Uniphoto; **712:** *all* Tass from Sovfoto; **717:** Robert Schaap, Third Coast Stock Source; **720:** *all* The Grand Beehive, Hal Cannon (Salt Lake City; University of Utah Press), 1980; permission granted by publisher.; **723:** Tom McHugh. Photo Researchers; **725:** Peter Fronk, Click/Chicago; **728:** Motown Record Corp.; **736:** The Museum of Modern Art, New York; **740:** Superstock, John Silverberg, Photo Source; **743:** G. Gscheidle, Image Bank; **747:** 1977 United Feature Syndicate Inc.; **749:** National Museum of Roller Skating, Lincoln, Nebraska.

Illustrations:
Lynn Fischer: *c* opener, **198, 368;** David Honeysmith: *t* **32, 54–55, 64–65, 126–127, 180–181, 206–207, 262-263, 441, 492, 604, 608–609;** Precision Graphics: **24, 171, 389, 608–609;** Laura Tarrish: **606.**

Proofreading Symbols

∧	Add letters or words.	⌢	Close up.
⊙	Add a period.	¶	Begin a new paragraph.
≡	Capitalize a letter.	∨	Add a comma.
/	Make a capital letter lower-case.	∩	Trade the position of letters or words.
		—— or ⸤	Take out letters or words.

Proofreading Checklist

1. Have I ended each sentence with the proper punctuation mark? — Pages 697-699

2. Have I used commas, semicolons, apostrophes, hyphens, and quotation marks correctly? — Pages 700-730

3. Have I capitalized where necessary, especially sentence beginnings and proper nouns and adjectives? — Pages 677-679

4. Have I used a dictionary to check the spelling of all unfamiliar words? — Pages 362-367

5. Have I spelled all plural and possessive forms correctly? — Pages 738-741

6. Have I corrected all run-ons and fragments? — Pages 457-461

7. Have I made all verbs agree with their subjects? — Pages 631-640

8. Have I used correct pronoun forms? — Pages 502-510

9. Have I used all adjectives and adverbs correctly? — Pages 566-572